Fractal Design Painter® 3.1 Unleashed

Denise Tyler

PUBLISHING

201 West 103rd Street
Indianapolis, Indiana 46290

This book is dedicated to those who are physically challenged, and to the people who help them realize their dreams.

Copyright © 1995 by Sams Publishing

Trademarks

Overview

Contents

Contents

Contents

Contents

Contents

Contents

Acknowledgments

There are many people who worked behind the scenes during the development of this book, and I want to take the time to thank all of them for their wonderful assistance and guidance.

The hard-working folks at Sams Publishing became old buddies during the making of this book. To Chris Denny, thanks for giving me this wonderful opportunity—you know how much it's appreciated. To Angelique Brittingham, thanks for your keen insights on how to pull everything together to make this a *real* book. To Mary Inderstrodt, thanks for your dedication while correcting all my boo-boos, and for some really great discussions. To Steve Flatt for your wonderful enthusiasm and for putting together a great CD! Thanks also to Anne Barrett, Fran Blauw, Chuck Hutchinson, Kathy Ewing, Deborah Frisby, Sean Medlock, Ryan Rader, Johnna Van Hoose and Joe Williams.

To Laurie Hemnes and Priscilla Shih of Fractal Design Corporation for wading through endless numbers of pages of material and adding some wonderful tips! Thanks also to Shawn in Tech Support for very thorough answers to tech support questions.

To Martha Harrah of Microsoft Corporation, for your generous assistance with Microsoft Multimedia Viewer. Your contribution helped the interactive CD reference jump from inside my mind onto the screen.

To the folks at Autodesk, Calcomp, Caligari, Corel Corporation, Elastic Reality, HSC Corporation, and Kurta for their assistance in providing material for this book. Also thanks to Stefan Van Der Bijl for porting the Command and Palette Reference to the Mac.

Last, but not least, to Ed Erickson, my partner and best friend, for your assistance during development of the Painter Unleashed CD Reference. It wouldn't have become a reality without your help. Thanks for all the great suppers, too!

In closing, I want to thank *you* for purchasing this book. I enjoy sharing my enthusiasm for computer art and animation with others. If there is even only one technique contained in this book that helps you grow, then I have accomplished my goal. Enjoy your journey with Painter 3!

Denise

About the Author

Denise Tyler is a computer graphics artist and animator who resides in Madison, Wisconsin. After a 15-year career as an engineer, she started her own computer graphics and animation business, Brick Wall Productions. She specializes in creating computer graphics and animation for games and multimedia. Denise is a co-author of *Tricks of the Game Programming Gurus* (Sams Publishing, 1994). You can contact Denise on CompuServe at 72134,2617, where she frequents several forums including AMMEDIA, GUGRPA, ULTIATOOLS, and GAMEDEV.

Introduction

I imagine that many of you are just like me. I'm just a regular person who likes to draw pictures. After working with several different types of art media, I investigated computer graphics as another way to express my creativity. With the first release of Painter, I found a program that took me back to the old tools with remarkable realism. I was hooked right away. The robust features of Painter 3 impress me daily with what can be accomplished. When given the opportunity to write a book about Painter, I accepted it eagerly, because I knew it would be a lot of fun!

Painter is one of those programs that reveals more and more as you delve deeper into its capabilities and features. It's also the type of program that will be different for everyone who uses it, because there are many ways to achieve results. There is no doubt that you will discover tricks and techniques of your own as you explore the program further.

Fractal Design Painter 3.1 Unleashed is designed to teach you the features of Painter while you work on several different projects. When forming the projects, I kept those that have smaller amounts of memory (under 16 MB) in mind. This was a tricky task when the animation features of Painter were discussed, due to the hefty memory requirements of multiple true-color frames. Nevertheless, you can easily take the principals of these small projects and apply them to larger ones if your system's resources allow.

You can complete the projects in this book whether you are using Painter 3.0 or Painter 3.1. The term *Painter 3* used in the text refers to features or commands that are used Painter 3.0 and Painter 3.1. If the version number is specifically mentioned, the feature is typical to that version only.

As Mac users might notice, the book utilizes screen shots from the Windows version of Painter. Don't let this deter you from following the projects, because the Windows and Mac versions are virtually identical, except for minor differences in system architecture. I have made every attempt I can to note where there are such differences.

In general, the differences lie in the quick-key commands. The following table is a quick reference to the shortcuts between the two versions.

Group	Function	Windows Shortcut	Mac Shortcut
Palettes	Tools	Ctrl-1	Cmd-1
	Brushes	Ctrl-2	Cmd-2
	Art Materials	Ctrl-3	Cmd 3
	Brush Controls	Ctrl-4	Cmd-4
	Objects	Ctrl-5	Cmd-5
	Controls	Ctrl-6	Cmd-6
	Advanced Controls	Ctrl-7	Cmd-7
	Color Sets	Ctrl-8	Cmd-8
File Menu	New	Ctrl-N	Cmd-N
	Open	Ctrl-O	Cmd-O
	Close	Ctrl-W	Cmd-W
	Save	Ctrl-S	Cmd-S
	Get Info	Ctrl-I	Cmd-I
	Print	Ctrl-P	Cmd-P
	Quit	Ctrl-Q	Cmd-Q
Edit Menu	Undo/Redo	Ctrl-Z	Cmd-Z
	Cut	Ctrl-X	Cmd-X
	Copy	Ctrl-C	Cmd-C
	Paste	Ctrl-V	Cmd-V
	Drop Current Floater	Shift-Ctrl-D	Shift-Cmd-D
	Select All	Ctrl-A	Cmd-A
	Deselect	Ctrl-D	Cmd-D
	Reselect	Ctrl-R	Cmd-R
	Clear Mask	Ctrl-U	Cmd-U
	Auto Mask	Shift-Ctrl-M	Shift-Cmd-M
Effects Menu	Last Effect	Ctrl-/	Cmd-/
	Second to Last Effect	Ctrl-;	Cmd-;
	Fill	Ctrl-F	Cmd-F
	Equalize	Ctrl-E	Cmd-E
	Adjust Colors	Shift-Ctrl-A	Shift-Cmd-A
	Super Soften	Shift-Ctrl-S	Shift-Cmd-S

Group	Function	Windows Shortcut	Mac Shortcut
Canvas Menu	Tracing Paper	Ctrl-T	Cmd-T
	Dry (Wet Layer)	Ctrl-Y	Cmd-Y
	Resize Image	Shift-Ctrl-R	Shift-Cmd-R
	Grid	Ctrl-G	Cmd-G
Tools Menu	Build Brush	Ctrl-B	Cmd-B
	Edit Rectangular Selection	Shift-Ctrl-E	Cmd-Shift-E
	Load Nozzle	Ctrl-L	Cmd-L
Window Menu	Hide/Display Palettes	Ctrl-H	Cmd-H
	Zoom In	Ctrl-+	Cmd-+
	Zoom Out	Ctrl--	Cmd--
	Full Screen/ Window	Ctrl-M	Cmd-M
Screen Navigation	Scroll Image with Grabber	Spacebar	Spacebar
	Center Image Zoom In	Spacebar-Click Spacebar-Ctrl-Click	Spacebar-Click Spacebar-Cmd
	Zoom Out	Spacebar - Ctrl-Alt-Click	Spacebar-Cmd-Option
	Define magnification area	Click and drag	Click and drag
	Rotate Image	Spacebar-Alt	Spacebar-Option
	Un-rotate Image	Spacebar-Alt-Click	Spacebar-Option-Click
	Constrain rotate 90 degrees	Shift-Alt-Spacebar	Shift-Option-to Spacebar
Frame Stacks Navigation	First Frame of Stack	Home	Home
	Last Frame of Stack	End	End
	Next Frame	Page Up	Page Up
	Previous Frame	Page Down	Page Down
	Stop at Current Frame	Stop Button-Alt	Stop Button-Option

Group	Function	Windows Shortcut	Mac Shortcut
	Stop and Return to Starting Frame	Ctrl-.	Cmd-.
Rectangular Selection Tool	Constrain to Square	Control	Shift-Ctrl
	Adjust current selection rectangle	Shift	Shift
	Edit Rectangular Selection	Shift-Ctrl-E	Shift-Cmd-E
Oval Selection Tool	Constrain to Circle	Shift-Ctrl	Control
Painting	Resize Brush	Ctrl-Alt	Cmd-Option
	Build Brush	Ctrl-B	Cmd-B
	Constrain to 45 degrees in straight line mode	Shift	Shift
	Adjust Opacity in 10% increments	1 - 0 keys	1 - 0 keys
Wet Layer	Post-diffuse	Shift-D	Shift-D
Cloning	Set Clone Source	Cloner Brush-Shift	Brush-Option
	Re-link Clone Source	Ctrl-Clone Command	Option-Clone Command
Outline Selection Tool-Freehand	Edit Path	Shift	Shift
	Add area	Ctrl	Cmd
	Subtract Area	Ctrl-Alt	Cmd-Option
	Close Path	(automatic)	Enter
	Stroke width change with pressure	Alt	Control
Outline Selection Tool-Straight Lines	Constrain to 45-degree angles	Shift	Shift
	Close Path	Enter	Enter
Outline Selection Tool Bézier Curves	Corner/Curve -Toggle	Alt-drag on handle	Control-drag on handle
	Equal Length Curves	Shift-drag on handle	Shift-drag on handle

Group	Function	Windows Shortcut	Mac Shortcut
	Make last point corner	Alt-drag on point	Option-drag on point
	Delete Last Point	Backspace	Delete
Path Adjuster Tool	Duplicate Move path by 1 screen pixel	Alt-click Arrow Keys	Option-click Arrow Keys
	Delete selected paths	Backspace	Delete
	Render/un-render path	Enter	Enter
	Resize path	Drag corner handles	Corner handles
	Resize/preserve aspect	Shift-drag corner handles	Shift-corner handles
	Resize/one direction	Drag side handles	Side handles
	Skew	Ctrl-drag side handles	Cmd-side handles
	Rotate	Ctrl-drag corner handles	Cmd-corner handles
Path List	Item layer order	Click and drag item in list	Click and drag item in list
	Select/Deselect multiple list items	Shift-Click	Shift
	Attribute dialog for selected path	Double-click	Double-click
	Render/un-render path	Enter	Enter
Floating Selection Tool	Duplicate Move floater by 1 screen pixel	Alt-click Arrow Keys	Option-click Arrow keys
	Hide/Display Marquee	Shift-Ctrl-H	Shift-Cmd-H
	Attribute dialog for current floater	Enter	Enter
	Delete selected floater	Backspace	Delete

Group	Function	Windows Shortcut	Mac Shortcut
Floater List	Item layer order	Click and drag item in list	Click and drag item in list
	Select/deselect multiple list items	Shift-Click	Shift
	Attribute dialog for current floater	Enter	Enter
	Adjust opacity in 10% increments	1 - 0 keys	1 - 0 keys
Paint Bucket	Limit fill extents	Click and drag Paint Bucket	Click and drag Paint Bucket
	Magic Wand fill	Alt-Click and drag Paint Bucket	Cmd-Click and drag Paint Bucket
Dropper	Measure mask density	Shift	Shift
	Dropper access	Ctrl-Paint Bucket Tool	Cmd-Paint Bucket Tool
		Ctrl-Floating Selection Tool	Cmd-Floating Selection Tool
		Ctrl-Oval Selection Tool	Cmd-Oval Selection Tool
		Ctrl-Rectangular Selection Tool	Cmd-Rectangular Selection Tool
		Ctrl-Brush	Cmd-Brush
Color Sets	Add current color to set	Shift-Ctrl-K	Shift-Cmd-K
	Replace current color in set	Alt-Click color	Option-Click color
Magic Wand	Add Color to Selection	Shift-Wand	Shift-Wand
	Find all instances in area	Selection-Wand	Selection-Wand
Spiral Gradations	Adjust spirality	Ctrl-Angle Adjustment	Cmd-Angle Adjustment

Chapters 20 through 27 discuss integrating with third-party applications. Though some of these programs are PC-based, there are some commands and procedures discussed in these chapters that don't appear elsewhere in the book. Mac users may not be directly familiar with the software discussed in the forementioned chapters, but the techniques and procedures will be applicable to similar software applications available on the Mac platform.

The CD-ROM furnished with this book contains an interactive command reference for both platforms. There are also all sorts of other goodies contained on the CD—software demos, plug-in filters, photos and textures, and lots more. Use the material on the CD to expand your horizons, especially if you are new to animation!

Painter Basics

An Infinite Paintbox

Imagine the following scenario:

You've got an inspiration for a painting. The idea is vivid in your mind, and you want to sketch it out before it flies away. You go to your basement but can't find any canvases. "Oh well," you think, "maybe I'll stretch and gesso a piece of fabric."

You open your paintbox, and the charcoals are all crushed. You discover you're nearly out of your favorite colors, so you scrounge through and find a couple of really old tubes, with just enough color in them to get by. But the caps are stuck on so tight that even applying heat won't remove them. The kids forgot to place the caps on your markers, rendering them dry and useless. You sink with disappointment.

Then, from the corner of your eye, you see your trusty computer sitting in the corner of the room, its LEDs winking at you.

"Wait! There's Painter!"

What Painter Is

Fractal Design Painter is an artist's dream come true. It's an endless supply of drawing and painting tools in digital form, with realistic representations of traditional art media. Watercolors act like watercolors. Airbrushes act like airbrushes. You can even produce realistic 3-D brush strokes such as those painted with palette knives. All this and more—without smelly brush cleaners, oily rags, dirty hands, and destroyed garments. In other words, you can get into your art without it getting into you. Figure 1.1 gives you a glimpse of some of the tools available for you to use.

Figure 1.1.
This screen shows just a glimpse of the tools available in Painter 3.

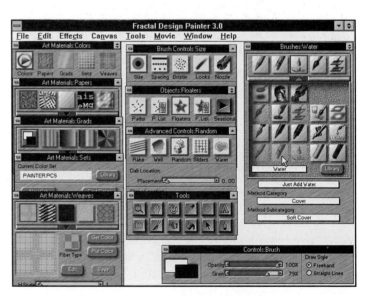

Imagine having over 100 different types of brushes, pens, pencils, and other tools in your collection. Painter gives you over 130 different variants of tools. This includes representations of natural media such as the following:

- Airbrushes (five variants), shown in Figure 1.2.
- Brushes (twenty variants)
- Chalk (five variants)
- Charcoals (three variants)
- Crayons (two variants)

- Erasers (fourteen variants)
- Felt pens (five variants)
- Liquid tools (nine variants)
- Pens (ten variants)
- Pencils (six variants)
- Watercolors (nine variants)
- Water tools (eight variants)
- Dodge and burn (lightening and darkening tools)

Figure 1.2.
There are 18 types of
brushes in Painter,
each having several
variants. For example,
Airbrushes, shown
here, have five variants
to choose from.

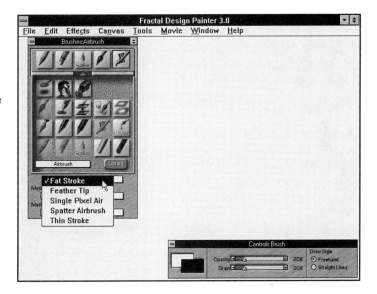

In addition, there are other tools that go beyond traditional art media—tools that will let you mimic the style of classic artists such as Van Gogh, Seurat, and the Impressionists. There are others that will let you take a photograph and repro-duce, or *clone* it, using any of Painter's tools. There is also a new type of tool called the Image Hose, which will let you spray a series of images into a docu-ment or a movie to create special effects. Figure 1.3 shows an example of what an Image Hose can do. The tools that go a bit beyond the traditional are as follows:

- Artists (five variants)
- Cloners (twelve variants)
- Image Hose (fourteen variants)
- Masking (six variants)

Figure 1.3.
Some of Painter's
brushes go beyond
traditional media.
Image Hoses, shown
here, spray images into
your document instead
of paint.

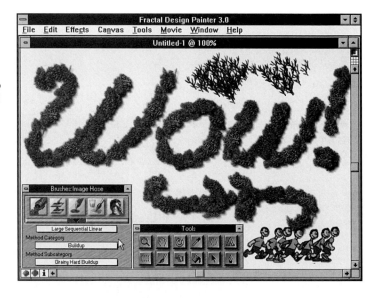

That's not all. There are also art materials such as papers, patterns, textures, gradations, and weavings. Figure 1.4 shows you some of the art materials that are pre-made for you in Painter 3. And if all this isn't enough for you, you can create your own brushes and art materials, and keep them organized in libraries for easy retrieval. That's why I call Painter an infinite paintbox.

Figure 1.4.
Painter's Art Materials
are plentiful, and you
can create your own
materials and organize
them into libraries.

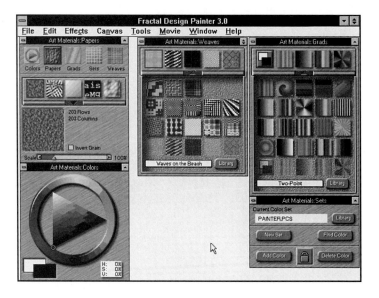

Painter is also a composition tool. You can make selections of areas and float them around, maneuvering and repositioning them until you achieve just the right appearance. You can save a Painter document with these floaters still floating around, ready and waiting for the next Painter session. You can group and ungroup floaters, and rearrange which layer they appear on in the composition. After you've decided things are just where you want them, you can set them into your drawing permanently.

Figure 1.5.
Portions of images can
be selected, floated,
and repositioned in
layers in documents,
making Painter an
excellent composition
tool.

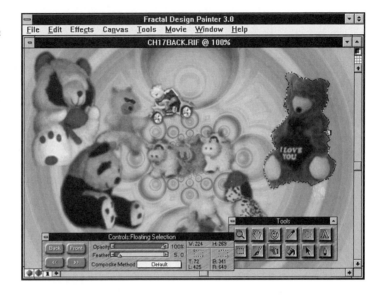

Finally, with Painter's new movie capabilities, you can use Painter to create animation frames, or for post-production of images created in traditional animation software. You can apply effects to one or several frames, if you like, adding Painter's special flair to your animations.

Figure 1.6.
Painter's new anima-
tion capabilities enable
you to create movies
and apply Painter's
effects to several
frames.

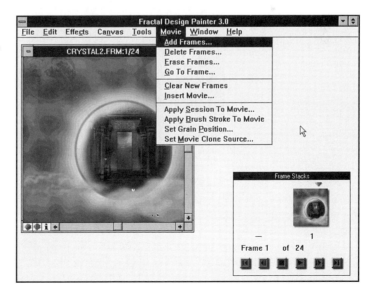

What Painter Is Not

Painter is not like other drawing or paint packages that automatically draw filled circles and squares in the "traditional" sense. You can, however, create a rectangular or elliptical selection (which can also be used to produce squares and circles) and paint inside it or fill it in with a solid color, a gradient, a weaving, or a clone image.

Painter doesn't work with text in the same way as most other paint programs either. In Painter, text is a *selection tool;* if you want solid text, you can type in your text over a solid area. The typed text acts as a floating selection, an example of which is shown in Figure 1.7. After it's selected, you can move or paste it into the location where you want it to appear. The beauty of this approach is that your text no longer has to be solid; you can cut out any type of image and use it for impressive effects.

Figure 1.7.
Text can be cut out of an image and used as a floating selection during composition.

Painter is a *raster-based* graphics program—one based on coloring individual pixels rather than creating vectored or rescalable objects. It is best to create your document in the appropriate resolution and scale for your destination. Reducing raster-based images can cause deterioration in quality, and enlarging them creates an overly granular look. Painter offers solutions that make size calculations simple. If your final image will be 4 inches by 6 inches and will be printed at 150 dpi, that's exactly what you tell Painter. When creating a new document, you enter those very figures in the New Picture dialog box, shown in Figure 1.8. Painter will create a document that's just the right size for you. The resulting file size for this example would be a whopping 3 MB for a true-color image. You can see why a large amount of memory is recommended for *any* graphics software.

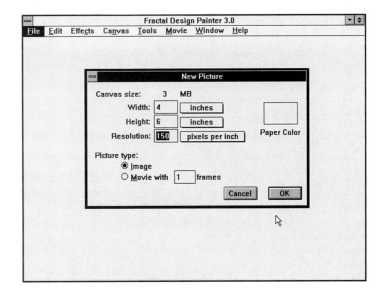

Figure 1.8.
Painter easily lets you
create the right-size
document for your
desired output.

New Features of Painter 3.0 and 3.1

Several new brushes, commands, and art materials have been added to Painter
3. Unless specifically mentioned as a new Painter 3.1 feature, the items described in this chapter are also new to Painter 3.0. New animation features
allow you to create Painter documents that move. For those of you who are
familiar with older versions of Painter, the X2 extensions are now included in
Painter 3.

New Commands

In Painter 3.0 and 3.1, you can now open three new and different types of
documents—Painter Movies, Video for Windows .AVI files (Windows version),
QuickTime movie files (Mac version), and sequentially numbered files. You can
also create a new movie and specify how many frames it will contain. Once
frames are created, you can add, delete, or erase frames. You can apply Painter
sessions to a movie, apply brush strokes or cloning techniques to a movie, and
even insert other movies within movies. Painter's new animation features are
covered in Chapter 18, "Working with Painter Movies", and Chapter 19, "Creating a Cartoon Animation."

In addition to the file formats already mentioned, Painter 3.1 adds compatibility
with 256-color GIF format as well as JPEG (.JPG) format. When you save your
Painter document in GIF format, it can be displayed on an Internet World Wide
Web page! Users of Adobe Photoshop 3.0 will find that Painter 3.1 now reads
and writes files using that format, including the conversion of Painter floaters
into Photoshop layers and vice versa.

9

Selection commands have been incorporated into Painter's new Tool menu, as shown in Figure 1.9. The selection tools enable you to edit selections, convert them to curves (such as converting text to objects that can be reshaped), convert the curves back into selections again, use .EPS files as selections, and more. There is also the addition of a Path Mover, which enables you to create libraries of selections and move selections between them. Similarly, the Floater Mover creates a library of floating selections and lets you move floaters between libraries. Other new movers allow you to create libraries of lighting arrangements, weavings, and custom gradients. Figure 1.10 shows where you can find the new movers.

Figure 1.9.
New Selection
commands appear in
the Painter 3 Tools
menu.

The new Image Hose tools can be found in the Brushes Palette, as shown in Figure 1.11. You can load a group of specially prepared floaters (floating objects) as an Image Hose nozzle file. Then you can paint them into any image with the Image Hose; or, you can spray a series of movie frames into another image or movie file. Now that Painter can open and create movies from Video for Windows (Windows version) or QuickTime (Mac version) files, numbered files, or other Painter movies, the possibilities in creating your own Image Hose nozzle files are enormous. Chapter 15, "Image Hose Project," tells you how to create and paint with your own Image Hose nozzle files.

Figure 1.10.
Painter 3 has some
new movers—
the Path Mover,
the Floater Mover, the
Lighting Mover, the
Weaving Mover, and
the Gradation Mover.

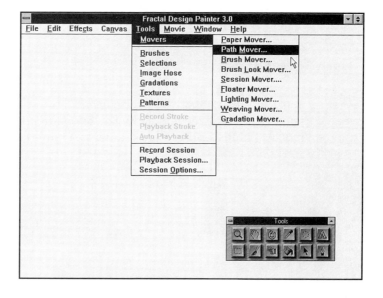

Figure 1.11.
The new Image Hose
tools let you paint with
pictures instead of
paint.

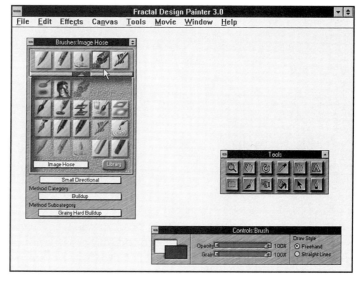

The Edit menu now contains several new masking commands, which are shown in Figure 1.12. Combined with the new masking tools found in the Brushes palette, you can now paint in Painter's masking layer, protecting areas from being painted or altering how floating objects interact with the background image. Masks can be automatically applied to protect the currently selected color, or you can apply a mask that varies in opacity based on the light and dark areas in your image.

In Painter 3.1, Multiple Undo and Redo features have been added to the Edit menu. The Multiple Undo command enables you to undo and redo up to 32 levels of changes. The number of levels is set with the Edit | Preferences | Undo command, shown in Figure 1.13.

Figure 1.12.
New masking com-
mands, as well as the
addition of masking
tools, allow you to
paint in your image's
masking layer.

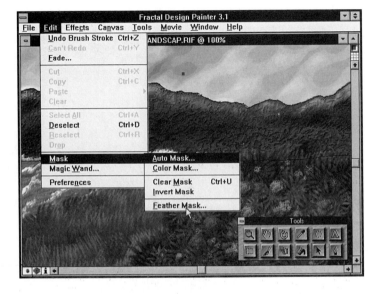

Figure 1.13.
Painter 3.1 has a
multiple undo feature.
You can set up to 32
levels of Undo with the
Edit | Preferences |
Undo command.

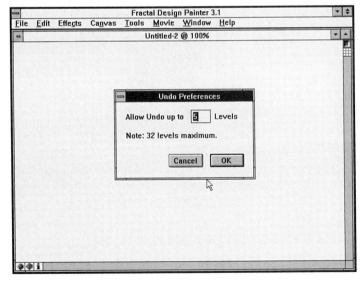

Version 3 of Painter now allows you to create and capture gradations and apply them to your images. You can also create a library of gradations and save them for use in other projects. You can find the Gradation commands in Painter's

Tools menu, and the gradation libraries are maintained in the Art Materials | Grads Palette. Both of these are illustrated in Figure 1.14.

In Painter 3.1, you can also design algorithmic gradients. The Tools | Gradation |Edit Gradation command provides complete control over color placement and blending between colors.

Figure 1.14.
Gradations are created
and maintained in art
material libraries in
Painter 3.

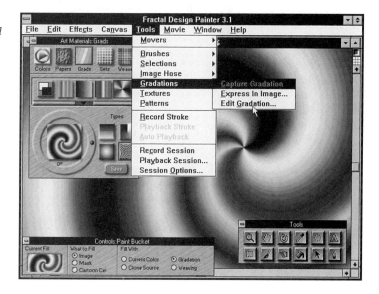

Do you need even more brushes than the ones provided with Painter? Now you have the ability to create your own. With the Capture Brush command, shown in the Tools menu in Figure 1.15, you can create a brush shape in black and white, and use grays to define partially transparent areas of the brush. Using a selection tool, you then capture this shape and use it to create an entirely new brush. In Chapter 14, "Working With the Brush Tools," you will learn how to capture your own brush dab, assign properties to it, and save it as a custom Painter brush.

Four new commands, located in the Canvas menu, perform functions relating to the size of the canvas, its color, and the colors used in your image. The new Canvas Size command enables you to change the size of your canvas by adding pixels to the top, bottom, or sides without altering the remainder of the drawing. The Set Paper Color command allows you to change the paper color at any time while creating or editing an image. You can now label colors in your images with the Annotate command and selectively view or hide the color annotations on your drawing with View Annotations. These four commands are shown in Figure 1.16.

Figure 1.15.
Using the Capture Brush command, you can create your own brushes from scratch.

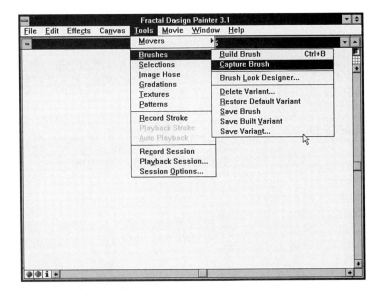

Figure 1.16.
Canvas Size, Set Paper Color, Annotate, and View Annotations are four new commands in the Edit menu.

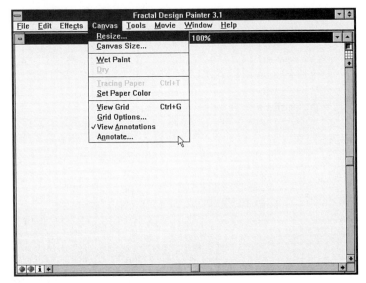

Painter 3.1's New and Enhanced Effects and Tools

Enhancements to some effects have been provided with Painter 3.1. In addition, a few new effects have been added to Painter's repertoire.

The new Effects | Esoterica | Growth command in Painter 3.1 enables you to create branch-like designs in your Painter documents. These designs resemble overhead views of trees, similar to how they are rendered in drafting. Several control adjustments can be made to vary the number of branches and forks, as well as their thickness or thinness. Figure 1.17 shows an example of this command in use.

Figure 1.17.
The Effects | Esoterica
| Growth command
enables you to generate
tree-like patterns in
your documents.

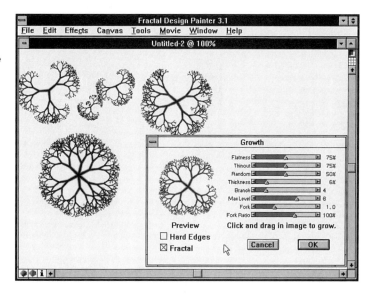

Another new effect in Painter 3.1 is available with Effects | Surface Control | Express Texture command, shown in Figure 1.18. Using this command, you can generate a light contrast grayscale version of an image. It can also be used to achieve results similar to printing on high contrast paper.

Figure 1.18.
The Effects | Surface
Control | Express
Texture command
creates light contrast
grayscale versions of an
image.

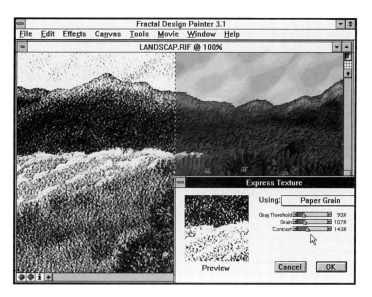

Fractal patterns and designs can be generated in Painter 3.1 with the Tools | Patterns | Make Fractal Pattern command. These patterns can be used for background textures, or converted to paper textures with the Tools | Textures | Capture Texture command. Figure 1.19 shows an example of the types of textures this command produces.

Figure 1.19.
You can generate
fractal patterns and
designs with the
Effects | Tonal Control
| Express Texture
command.

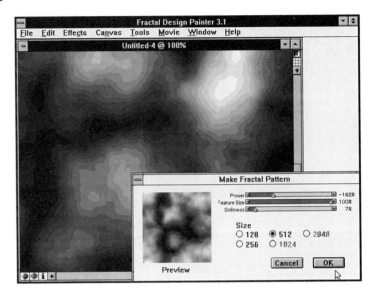

The Effects | Fill command has been enhanced in Painter 3.1. You can now specify the amount of opacity of the fill, whether filling with current color, a clone source, a gradation, or a weaving. Figure 1.20 shows the enhanced dialog box provided in Painter 3.1.

Figure 1.20.
Enhancements to
the Fill command in
Painter 3.1 allow you
to adjust the opacity
of the fill.

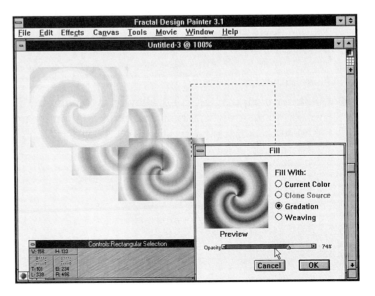

The Effects | Surface Control | Apply Surface Texture command has also been enhanced in Painter 3.1, as shown in Figure 1.21. Now, you can add fine lighting adjustments as well as colored lighting effects while applying surface texture to your image.

Figure 1.21.
You can now make fine lighting adjustments in the Apply Surface Texture command in Painter 3.1.

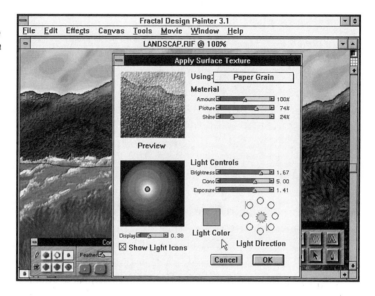

New Brushes

Painter has two new categories of brushes—Image Hoses and Masking brushes—to add to its collection of tools. There are also several new brushes that use the new captured brush-dab capability, as well as some that use the new Bristle brush controls. The new brushes are as follows:

- **Image Hose variants:** Fourteen in all, paint pictures with pictures. You can use a group of selections or even a Painter movie as the paint source. These brushes are discussed and demonstrated in Chapter 15, "Image Hose Project."

- **Masking variants:** Six in all, allow you to paint in the masking layer, protecting an area from being painted or altering how a floater interacts with the background. Painting with black produces opaque areas in the masking layer, and painting with white creates transparent areas. In-between shades of gray produce varying levels of transparency.

- **Brushy:** A Brush variant that produces smooth, antialiased strokes that cover those beneath them. Created with a captured brush dab, this brush has many fine bristles that dry out quickly and then pick up colors that it's dragged through. The brush also randomly reacts to paper grain. Its size varies with the pressure of the stylus. (This brush is one of my new favorites.)

- **Coarse Hair Brush:** A Brush variant, it produces smooth, antialiased strokes that cover those beneath them. Stroke size, opacity, and grain vary with the pressure of the stylus. Also created with a captured brush dab, this brush has coarse hairs that change scale quickly.

- **Fine brush:** A Brush variant created with a captured brush dab. It produces smooth, antialiased strokes that cover those beneath them and change scale quickly. Stroke size, opacity, and grain vary with stylus pressure. The brush hairs are very fine.

- **Smaller Wash Brush:** A Brush variant—a new bristle brush, produces semi-antialiased brush strokes that react to paper grain. It smears the currently selected color in with the colors in an image. Stroke size, opacity, and grain vary with stylus pressure.

- **Sable Chisel Tip Water Brush:** A Brush variant created with a captured brush dab. It produces smooth, antialiased strokes that cover those beneath them. Stroke size and grain vary with stylus pressure, and the brush uses a water effect to smear colors in an image.

- **Ultrafine Wash Brush:** A Brush variant—a new bristle brush that produces semi-antialiased brush strokes that react to paper grain. This brush is similar to the Wash brush, but it has a greater number of fine bristles. Stroke size, opacity, and grain vary with stylus pressure.

- **Medium Tip Felt Pens:** A Felt Pen variant—a wider version of the Fine Tip Felt Pen found in this and previous versions of Painter. It produces soft, anti-aliased strokes that build up the colors beneath them, just as a real felt-tip pen would.

New Methods

For those of you who like to create your own brushes, there are seven new brush methods with which to experiment. They are described in detail in the reference documents on the accompanying CD, but they will be listed here for reference purposes. The new methods are

- Soft Grain Colorize
- Flat Mask Cover
- Grainy Edge Flat Mask Cover
- Grainy Hard Mask Cover
- Grainy Soft Mask Cover
- Linoleum Scribe
- Soft Mask Cover

New Brush Controls

Painter now lets you control brush bristles with as much accuracy as you desire. With the new Bristle controls, you can adjust the thickness of the bristles, their clumpiness (how they stick together), and the hair scale and size. The Smaller Wash Brush is one that uses Bristle settings to define its appearance and behavior. Brush Controls and Advanced Controls are discussed in Chapter 14, "Working with the Brush Tools."

Interface Changes

Now that you've learned what's new, the next logical thing to ask is "What's changed?" The new menus and palettes are revamped, and some things have moved around a little. To help you become acquainted with the changes, I'll tell you where the old commands could be found and where they are now.

Options Menu Relocations

One of the most obvious changes is that the Options menu has been deleted. Its commands have been placed into several more appropriate areas, which are illustrated in Table 1.1. Most of the commands have been relocated to the new Tools menu, but others are in the new Canvas menu.

Table 1.1. Relocation of the Options Menu commands.

Old Options Menu Command Name	New Location of Command
Set Clone Source	File | Clone Source
Wet Paint	Canvas Menu
Dry	Canvas Menu
Tracing Paper	Canvas Menu
Grid Overlay	Now View Grid in the Canvas Menu
Grid Options	Canvas Menu
Paper Mover	Tools | Movers menu
Brush Mover	Tools | Movers menu
Brush Look Mover	Tools | Movers menu
Session Mover	Tools | Movers menu
Frisket Mover	Now Path Mover in the Tools | Movers menu
All Options | Brushes commands	Tools | Brushes menu
Options | Capture Texture	Tools | Textures | Capture Texture
Options | Make Repeating Texture	Tools | Patterns

Brush Stroke Menu Relocations

The Brush Stroke menu has also been deleted. Some of its commands have been split between the Tools | Stroke Recorder and the Tools | Session Recorder headings. In addition, the commands relating to recording and playback of sessions have been placed within the new Objects Palette. The Brush Stroke Designer and the Build Brush command have also been moved to the new Tools menu. Table 1.2 shows the relocation of the Brush Stroke commands.

Table 1.2. Relocation of the Brush Stroke Menu commands.

Old Brush Stroke Menu Command Name	New Location of Command
Record Stroke	Tools	Record Stroke
Playback Stroke	Tools	Playback Mode (toggle on)
Stop Playback	Tools	Playback Mode (toggle off)
Auto Playback	Tools	Auto Playback
Record Options	Tools	Session Options
Record Session	Tools	Record Session
Stop Recording Session	Tools	Stop Recording Session
Playback Session	Tools	Playback Session
Draw Freehand	Now selectable on Controls	Brush Palette
Draw Straight Lines	Now selectable on Controls	Brush Palette

Other Menu Changes

The Edit | Paste and Edit | Paste Into New Picture commands of previous Painter versions have been changed slightly. The Edit Menu now shows the Paste Command only, with a right arrow that brings up the two options: Paste | Normal, and Paste Into New Image.

The Edit | Set Preferences command is now divided into five categories: General preferences deal with default libraries and cursor preferences. Brush Tracking preferences deal with customizing the stroke of your stylus or mouse, which should be done with each Painter session. The Interface preferences customize the interface appearance. The Plug-Ins preferences allow you to choose which directory your third-party, plug-in filters are stored in. The Windows preferences customize Windows memory-usage options and bitmap-display options.

The new Canvas menu also contains the former File | Resize command.

Palette Changes

The palettes that were formerly selectable in the Window menu have been changed somewhat. The changes are shown in Table 1.3 below.

Table 1.3. Relocation of palettes in the Window menu.

Palette Command in Version 2.0	New Location of Palette or Command
Toolbox	Now called Tools Palette
Brush Palette	Now called Brushes Palette
Color Palette	Contained in Art Materials Palette
Paper Palette	Contained in Art Materials Palette
Fill Palette	Various Fill types in Art Materials Palette
Brush Size	Contained in Brush Controls Palette
Brush Behavior	Contained in Advanced Controls Palette
Expression Palette	Contained in Advanced Controls	Sliders Palette
Brush Stroke Designer	Tools	Brushes	Brush Look Designer
Brush Looks	Contained in Brush Controls Palette
Frisket Palette	Now called Paths in Objects Palette
Color Palette	Colors, in Art Materials Palette
Zoom Factor	Now selectable with Magnifier in Tools Palette

Summary

You now have a general idea of what Painter is, the tools and materials you have to work with, what's new in version 3, and what's changed from earlier versions. Before the tutorials, which begin in Chapter 5, the next three chapters will help you learn more about the basics of Painter—installing it in your system, browsing through the new menus and interface, and customizing Painter to suit your own personal preferences.

Getting Up and Running

Now that you have an idea of what Painter can accomplish, you're probably very anxious to get the program up and running so you can be creative. In this chapter, I'll show you how to install and launch Painter. I'll also discuss Painter's system requirements, as well as other hardware that can enhance your use and appreciation of the software.

System Requirements

Like many graphics programs, the performance of Painter is affected by your computer's processor speed and how much memory your system has. Painter has some minimum requirements for system architecture.

For PC-based systems, the system recommendations are as follows:

- 386, 486, Pentium IBM PC, or compatible (Pentium recommended).
- A hard-disk drive (15 MB required for full installation).
- A color monitor.
- A Super VGA video board (256 colors).
- 8 MB of Random Access Memory (RAM); 16 MB or more is preferable.
- Microsoft Windows 3 or later.
- Some features of Painter 3 require that you have a Floating Point Unit (FPU), otherwise known as a math coprocessor. This is true for some of the effects filters, which are highly calculation-intensive. These types of routines can bog down your computer's Central Processing Unit (CPU) and slow things to a crawl. The FPU is directed to handle the intensive calcula- tions while the CPU does its basic program-execution thing. To experience all of Painter's special-effects features, an FPU is highly recommended. You may have the necessary FPU if your computer's processor is identified as a DX rather than an SX model.

For Mac-based systems, the system recommendations are as follows:

- 68020 or faster processors, all Macintosh models, and Power Macs.
- Color monitor.
- Hard-disk drive.
- 6 MB of Random Access Memory (8 MB for Power Macs). More recom- mended.
- Apple system software version 6.0.7 or higher. Painter supports System 7.0 or higher.
- A floating point unit (FPU) is required for some effects.

Other Hardware Recommendations

Though not required to work with the Painter program, there are other hard- ware accessories or additions you can incorporate into your system that will greatly enhance your use and appreciation of Painter.

24-Bit (True-Color) Video Cards

If your system's video display card is capable of displaying only up to 256 colors, you should consider purchasing a true color display card, which would allow a display of up to 16 million colors. There are many on the market, and they range in price from around one hundred to several hundred dollars.

For PC users, some true color boards are Windows accelerators; that is, their design and drivers are optimized for faster performance while running in Windows. Some boards allow you to display only 640×480 pixels in true-color mode. These boards are generally equipped with 1 MB of memory. But, with the addition of more memory, you can display in true-color mode in higher resolutions, such as 1024×768. If you normally like to work in these higher resolutions, ensure that the graphics board you intend to purchase has enough onboard memory to handle it.

Painter is optimized to run with a true-color display board. If you run Painter using 256-color video drivers, the performance of the program is actually slowed down a tad while it dithers (approximates) the true colors it normally displays on the screen. So, the addition of a true-color display board might actually improve the performance of Painter on your system. Another benefit is aesthetic: you'll be able to see every color imaginable with a true-color display, including subtler shadows, more detailed brush strokes, and smooth antialiasing. If you normally see your Painter documents in 256 colors and think they look nice, seeing them in true color will definitely impress you!

When selecting a video board, PC users must take note of the type of slot and bus it is designed to operate with. There are some available for standard 16-bit bus slots, but there are two new standards that are becoming popular: the VESA Local Bus (VLB) and the PCI Bus. These types of boards are not interchangeable. Therefore, if you purchase a VLB card only to discover that you don't have VLB card slots in your computer, you're out of luck.

NOTE Video boards also come with drivers that allow you to run programs in several resolutions, usually 640×480, 800×600, and 1024×768. Several color depth choices are also available, ranging from 16 colors to 16 million colors.

If, when you start up Painter, you get an error message that reads "Painter requires a 256-color display driver," you are probably set up to operate in 16-color mode. Use Windows Setup (Windows), the Monitors control panel (Mac), or any custom software provided with your video card, to choose a 256-color (or higher-color depth) driver.

You should also check to see if updated drivers have become available for your video board since shipping. It's always best to use the most recent drivers for your equipment.

Digitizing Tablets

You might already be aware that drawing and painting with a mouse is unnatural. It's something that takes a lot of getting used to, especially if you are accustomed to drawing and painting with traditional tools. There's not as much response, and you can't move your arm and hand naturally as you would with a pencil or brush. Though Painter does make accommodations for mouse users by providing alternatives in the Advanced Controls | Sliders Palette, the strokes still don't look quite the same as those you can achieve with a pressure-sensitive stylus and tablet.

I can't say enough good things about working with a tablet and stylus. Once you try one, you'll never want to draw with a mouse again. It takes some getting used to at first; for example, until you are acclimated to the tablet, you may keep reaching for your mouse out of habit. You'll forget that the stylus is actually a computer tool and mistakenly put it in your pocket or purse. (It feels just about that natural. I've even found myself doodling with Painter while I talk on the phone—just as I do with "real" pencils and pens!)

The most striking difference, though, is in the quality achieved when you use a pressure-sensitive stylus with software that is designed for it. Painter uses the features of a pressure-sensitive stylus beautifully. Strokes made with a pressure-sensitive stylus are far more natural in their appearance, and they are more quickly accomplished. You can get variances in stroke size, color, opaqueness, and reaction to paper grain just by applying different pressure to your stylus as you make the stroke.

Just as you pay more for higher-quality brushes and paints, the same is true for tablets and styli. If you are serious about the quality of your art, you usually buy the best tools you can afford, because you really do get what you pay for. Some of the options you should consider in tablets and styli are as follows:

- **Stylus features:** Stylus pens come in several different forms. Some have a cord that attaches to the back of the tablet. Others are cordless and operate with batteries. Though cordless stylus pens are easier and more convenient to work with, they tend to be a bit more bulky due to the battery requirement. However, those that I have tried are not uncomfortable to use and feel quite natural. If you get a stylus that operates on batteries, be sure to pick up a few extra, as they can wear out quickly if you do a lot of drawing or you mistakenly store the stylus standing on its tip (which leaves it in the ON mode). Stylus pens can also have varying numbers of buttons, some of them being programmable with the tablet software. Programmable options are a nice addition to a tablet's features.

- **Pressure sensitivity:** Painter supports up to 256 levels of stylus pressure, the current limit of stylus-and-tablet technology. Some tablet manufacturers support fewer levels, and there are other models that are not pressure-sensitive at all. If you want to buy a tablet for Painter, you probably will want a good pressure-sensitive stylus to go along with it. Tablets with this feature are usually more expensive, however.

- **Tablet size:** Tablets come in various sizes. The smallest have drawing areas of 4×5 inches, 6×8 inches, or 6×9 inches. These tablets are ideal for placing on a desktop or even on your lap while you draw. Small tablets are finely suited for use with Painter. Larger tablets, with 12×12 drawing areas and up, are also available, but they are less handy if you want to place them in your lap.

- **Connections:** Do you have a spare serial port on your computer? How about the pinouts? Would you need a 9-pin or a 25-pin connector for your tablet? Do you want to use both the tablet and your mouse? These are all things that need to be addressed when selecting a tablet. If you need a 25-pin connector for your serial port and the tablet comes with a 9-pin connector, you will need an adapter to make it work. Some tablets come with adapters, and some don't. For PC users, if you want to keep your mouse on your COM1 serial port, you should check to make sure that your tablet can be configured to work on COM2. Chances are it can be, but it doesn't hurt to be sure.

- **Tablet Software:** The ability to customize the buttons and menus for your tablet and stylus is a nice plus. A variety of drivers is also a nice feature. For example, for PC-compatible tablets, drivers for DOS and Windows are usually provided with your tablet software. Some tablets come with Autodesk ADI drivers, which would allow the tablet and stylus to be used within AutoCAD and 3D Studio. If you work with these programs, you would want to verify that the tablets have ADI capability. Painter is compatible with tablets that support either the WINTAB or Pen Windows tablet driver standards. Some tablets also include a Windows 3.0-compatible mouse-type pressure driver that works within Painter.

NOTE As with drivers for video boards, you should also verify that you have the most current tablet drivers.

- **Tracing Overlay:** Another nice feature, though not necessary, is the addition of a clear plastic or mylar overlay that will allow you to place a sheet of paper underneath for tracing. This holds the paper still, without the use of masking tape.

There are several manufacturers of digitizing tablets, but the most popular are CalComp, Hitachi, Kurta, Summagraphics, and Wacom. I've had the opportunity to work with two tablets, and I'll share my impressions with you here.

Kurta XGT Serial Digitizing Tablet

The Kurta XGT comes in both PC and Mac-compatible versions. It is a well-thought-out product. In fact, the only thing that I found missing was an adapter so that I could connect the tablet's 9-pin connector to my 25-pin COM port. No problem, though—I had one readily available and I knew I could easily find one nearby.

The Kurta XGT comes with an extra set of batteries (it uses three standard hearing-aid batteries), as well as several replacement stylus tips.

The hardware is solid and well-designed. The cord attaching the tablet to the serial (COM) port is sturdy and enables you to sit up to six or seven feet away from your computer with the tablet on your lap. The overall dimensions of the tablet I use are 11-inches wide, 8-1/2-inches high, and about 3/8-inch deep, making it the size of a small notebook and very suitable for desktop use. The overall drawing area is 8-inches wide and 6-inches high. A menubar across the top of the tablet allows for customization of tablet features, and the mylar tracing overlay contains registration marks to indicate the tablet's drawing area. Different "personalities," or stylus and mouse emulations, can be assigned to the tablet, and the Application Directory appendix suggests settings for over 100 graphics and CAD programs (for both DOS and Windows), including Painter.

The cordless, battery-powered stylus is a bit more bulky than a standard pencil or pen, with a diameter of about a half inch, but I found it to be comfortable and well-balanced. It includes a pen clip for those of you who like to stick pens and pencils in your pocket. Battery replacement is easy and quick; the top of the stylus screws off, and the batteries are simply dropped inside. There are, in effect, three buttons available for use: the tip and two additional buttons at the side of the stylus. The pressure sensitivity, with 256 levels, is a joy to work with and is very responsive.

Installation went smooth as silk. The manual claims that the installation should take about 20-25 minutes, but I think it was even quicker than that. The software automatically and correctly detected the COM port to which I attached the tablet. It asked me if I wanted to modify my AUTOEXEC.BAT, WIN.INI, and SYSTEM.INI files before doing so, and it informed me what changes it made. In short, it's one of those intuitive installation programs that everyone loves to see. The Pensmith drivers and software, in DOS and Windows versions, offer even more customization options.

CalComp Drawing Slate

The CalComp Drawing Slate also comes with a full list of features. The tablet, with a 9×6-inch drawing area, measures 11-inches wide by 10-inches high, with a depth of about 1/4-inch. Its menubar, located along the top edge of the tablet, allows configuration setups for a total of 18 customized configurations and macros. The tablet comes with a 25-pin serial connector, as well as an adapter to connect to a 9-pin serial port. The cord between tablet and computer is not quite as thick as that of the Kurta, but it's nice and long: about 10 feet. A mylar overlay is also furnished with this tablet. Settings for over 60 applications and tablet emulations are featured in the manual. The CalComp Drawing Tablet boasts a lifetime warranty to the originally registered owner.

The pressure-sensitive cordless stylus looks and feels very much like a real pen. In fact, you'd be hard-pressed to tell the difference once it's in your hand. The stylus uses four hearing-aid batteries for operation, and replacement requires a bit of care because of the casing that holds the batteries in place. This stylus also has three buttons: its tip and two additional buttons located near the base of the pen. The stylus has 256 levels of pressure sensitivity, and it is also responsive to stylus *tilt* and *bearing*, which can be used as expression options in Painter. Currently, the CalComp tablets are the only ones that support these expressions. The stylus responds extremely well to subtle variations in pressure.

 TIP To implement the use of the Tilt and Bearing settings for the Calcomp tablets, insert the following line in the [Pen Driver] section of your Windows SYSTEM.INI file:

```
calaft=1
```

Installation is accomplished with a DOS-based installation routine, and it includes options to install DOS, ADI, and Windows drivers. The DOS and Windows applications allow further customization of functions and macros. The tablet is also furnished with WinTab drivers, which are recommended for use with Painter and are installed separately from the standard drivers.

TWAIN-Compliant Scanners

Some people like to scan in original artwork or photographs to be modified and enhanced with Painter. If this is your desire, you will need to work with a scanner that has TWAIN-compliant drivers. TWAIN is a standard developed for the scanning process that is now supported and implemented by several scanner manufacturers and software programs. The scanner you purchase should be furnished with the appropriate drivers for use with TWAIN-compatible programs. If you are using a scanner that was purchased before development of the TWAIN standard, you should contact the scanner manufacturer about obtaining updated drivers and utilities.

Options are several, and scanners come in both handheld and desktop models. You can also get grayscale scanners as well as those that scan in color. Sometimes color scans are done in three passes (one pass each for the red, green, and blue components of the original), but there are also scanners that accomplish the scanning of color originals in one single pass. You should consider purchasing a scanner that allows you to adjust the dots per inch (dpi) of the scan. Some scanners allow the option of scanning at 100, 200, 300, or 400 dpi, but others allow user-specified dpi settings. The higher the resolution, the finer your scan will be—although higher resolutions also increase file size proportionately.

Desktop scanners are similar in appearance to small photocopiers. Some desktop scanners work by feeding the original document into a sheet feeder, which rolls the document through the scanning area and delivers it back to you after it's scanned. Other desktop scanners allow you to place your original document atop a glass plate and cover it while it's being scanned. A nice feature is to have a cover that allows for some height, in the event that your original document is thick or is contained within a book.

Handheld scanners generally have a scan width of about 4 to 4-1/2 inches. Their advantage is that they are usually lower in cost than desktop models. Scanning guides, available as a separate purchase in many software stores, enable you to keep your scanner straight while digitizing. These guides are low-cost (generally under $50.00) and are highly recommended if you use a handheld scanner. If you decide on a handheld scanner, the inclusion of software that enables you to seamlessly stitch multiple scans together into a larger image is highly recommended.

NOTE Painter is not optimized to work with handheld scanners. If you are having problems scanning while using Painter's File | TWAIN Acquire command, you can scan and stitch your scans together using other software and import them easily into Painter as a .TIF file.

Installing Painter 3 for Windows

Installing Painter 3 is straightforward; the basic procedure is common to all Windows programs. Installation is typically done by launching the Windows Program Manager, which is shown in Figure 2.1. The program disks contain compressed versions of the Painter 3 files, which are decompressed by the Painter installation program and placed into the proper directories on your hard drive.

To install Painter 3 for Windows, do as follows:

1. From the Windows Program Manager, choose File | Run. A dialog box appears that will prompt you for a command line.

2. Insert the first Painter disk into your floppy disk drive. In this example, we are using drive A as the installation drive.

3. In the Program Manager Command Line box, shown in Figure 2.2, enter the following command: A:\INSTALL (substitute your drive letter if different than shown).

Figure 2.1.
Painter installation
begins by launching
the Windows Program
Manager.

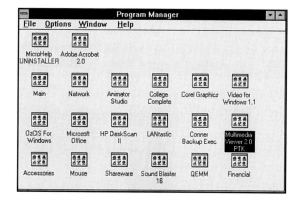

Figure 2.2.
The command to start
installing Painter 3 is
entered in the Program
Manager Command
Line box.

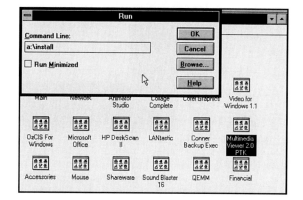

4. After a brief initialization process, you will be welcomed to Fractal Design Painter 3, as shown in Figure 2.3. To proceed with the installation, click Continue. To cancel the installation, click Exit.

5. The next step is to specify the hard drive and directory to which you want to install Painter 3. By default, it will be installed to the C:\PAINTER3 (for Painter 3.0) or C:\PAINT31 (for Painter 3.1) directory. If you want to modify this directory and path, click the Set Location button in the Custom Installation dialog box. The Installation Location dialog box will appear, where

you can highlight the path in the box and type in your desired drive and path, as shown in Figure 2.4. After clicking OK, you will be returned to the Custom Installation dialog box where you can select to install extra files, such as the tutorials and the Video for Windows runtime files.

Figure 2.3.
In the welcome screen,
click Continue to
continue the program
installation.

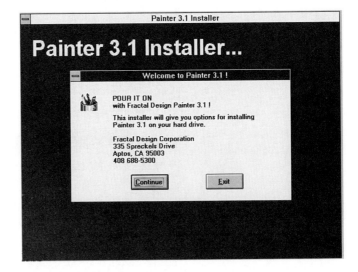

NOTE Painter will install Video for Windows unless you specifically uncheck the option to do so. If you choose to install Video for Windows, you will need to restart Windows after the Painter installation is complete so that the Video for Windows drivers are started correctly.

Video for Windows must be installed on your system for Painter to run. If Painter starts up with the error "Cannot find AVIFILE.DLL," Video for Windows is not active in Windows. Run the Painter installation program again, selecting only the Video for Windows install option to resolve this problem.

6. The Painter installation program will then copy the files from the first disk to your hard drive. After all the files on the first disk are copied, you will be prompted to insert the remaining disks into your floppy drive in sequence. After each additional disk is inserted, click OK to continue. A screen of the typical prompt to insert any of the following disks is shown in Figure 2.5.

Figure 2.4.
Enter the drive and
directory where you
want to install Painter
into the Installation
Location dialog box.

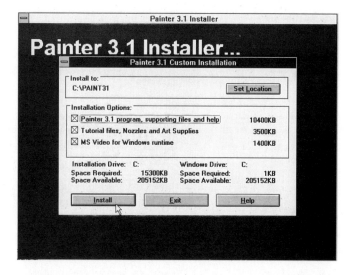

Figure 2.5.
After inserting the
remaining disks as
prompted by the
installation program,
click OK to copy the
files to your hard drive.

7. At this point, if you elected to install Video for Windows, the Microsoft
   Video for Windows Setup screen shown in Figure 2.6 appears. Follow the
   directions on the screen to install the Video for Windows runtime files to
   your hard disk.

Figure 2.6.
If you elected to install
Video for Windows, its
setup screen will
appear next.

8. When the Video for Windows setup completes, you will be asked to restart Windows, as shown in Figure 2.7. If you installed Video for Windows on your system for the first time, you should restart your computer to initialize its drivers before you start Painter. If you don't want to restart your computer at this time, click the Don't Restart Now button, but remember to restart Windows before you enter Painter.

Figure 2.7.
Restart your computer
before entering Painter
if you installed Video
for Windows.

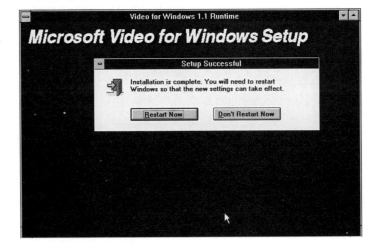

9. You should see the Installation Complete dialog box shown in Figure 2.8, indicating that the installation process was successful. Clicking the View ReadMe button will open a file that informs you of late-breaking release notes and features of Painter. Clicking the Run Painter 3 (in Painter 3.0) or Run Painter 3.1 (in Painter 3.1) button will immediately launch Painter. Clicking the Return to Windows button will exit the installation program and return you to the Windows Program Manager.

Figure 2.8. After successfully installing Painter, clicking Return to Windows will exit the installation program and return you to the Windows Program Manager.

The installation program creates a Fractal Design Painter program group in the Program Manager, as shown in Figure 2.9. Included in this program group is an icon to launch Painter 3. Double-clicking this icon or highlighting the title and pressing Enter will launch the Painter program.

The first time you start Painter, you will be prompted to enter the serial number of your copy of Painter. The serial number can be found on the READ ME FIRST card provided with the full version of Painter 3, as well as on the back of the first installation disk. This number should be placed in safekeeping, and is entered into the screen shown in Figure 2.10.

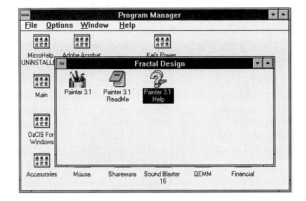

Figure 2.9.
The Painter 3 icon,
located in the new
Fractal Design Painter
program group, will
launch the Painter
program.

NOTE It is important to enter your serial number exactly as shown on the installation disks, including zeroes and hyphens in the serial number. Entering the serial number incorrectly will abort the installation process. If you are upgrading from previous versions, your old serial number will not work with Painter 3.

The serial number is entered in the second text field of the screen. The first is for your name. When entering the serial number, remember the following points:

■ Enter all letters in uppercase.

■ Enter only zeroes and ones; there are no letter Os or Is in the serial numbers.

■ Two hyphens (--) appear in the serial number. They should be included.

The next step that will appear during the first time you launch Painter is to specify the location of your plug-in directory. Painter supports the use of third-party, plug-in filters, such as those provided with Kai's Power Tools. You can select a plug-in directory from the dialog box shown in Figure 2.11 when launching Painter the first time, or by using the Edit | Preferences | Plug-In Filters command at any later Painter session.

To specify a plug-in directory, scroll to the drive and directory where your plug-in filters reside. Then, click the name of one of the filters contained in that directory, and choose OK or press Enter to continue.

Figure 2.10.
Enter the serial number
of your copy of Painter
to personalize your
program. The serial
number is located on
the back of your first
installation disk, or on
the README FIRST
card provided with the
Painter documentation.

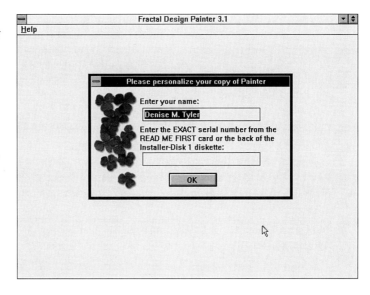

Figure 2.11.
Specify the directory
where your plug-in
filters are located, and
choose OK or press
Enter to continue.

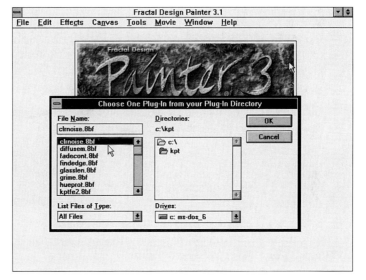

NOTE Painter has to load each plug-in every time you start the program. If you are using a large number of plug-ins, the program will take much longer to launch and may appear to hang momentarily.

Also, plug-ins included with Adobe Photoshop 2.5 and 3 will not work within Painter, due to changes implemented by Adobe.

Installing Painter 3 for the Mac

Mac users will find the Painter installation to be like most other program installations. The following steps are used to install Painter 3 to your system:

1. Insert Painter's Installer Disk 1 into your computer.

2. Double-click the Painter 3 Installer application. The Painter installer opening screen appears. Click Continue to proceed with the installation process.

3. A Painter 3 README file appears. This file contains late-breaking news about the Painter release. You can read or print it before you proceed with the install. The file will also be saved to your hard disk if you want to read it later.

4. Next, choose your installation options from the dialog box that appears after the README file.

    Click Install if you want to choose the Easy Install procedure. This installs everything including Painter 3, all support files, and Apple QuickTime.

    If you want to install some, but not all, of these options, click the Custom button. A list of custom installation options appears. Click an option to highlight it. Use Shift-Click to choose additional options. Then, click Install to continue the installation. If you click the Standard button, you will revert back to the Easy Install option.

5. In the next dialog box, select the version of Painter you want to install.

    Click 680×0 if your Macintosh has a 68000-series processor.

    Click PowerPC if you have a Power Macintosh.

    Click Universal if you want to install a version of Painter that runs on any Macintosh.

6. Next, a dialog box appears where you specify where you want to install Painter on your hard disk. After making your selection, click Install.

7. Enter the remaining Painter installation disks as prompted.

8. The first time you start Painter, you will be prompted for a serial number. Follow the note that follows the Windows installation instructions to enter your serial number.

NOTE If you are having trouble running Painter on your Mac, restart your computer with extensions disabled. To do this, hold down the Shift key while restarting. If the trouble disappears, you may have extensions that are incompatible with Painter. Older versions of some INITs, CDEVs, and drivers might be incompatible with Painter.

Summary

This chapter discussed the system requirements of Painter, as well as optional hardware that will enhance your Painter experience. After following the installation procedure outlined in this chapter, you should now have Painter installed onto your hard drive, ready to go. In the next chapter, "A Look Around Painter," we'll take a brief tour through Painter's menus and palettes in order to acquaint you with the features of the program and its new interface.

A Look Around Painter

The main purpose of this book is to provide you with a complete guide to Painter by using real-world examples to walk you through the commands. This chapter will acquaint you with Painter's menus and palettes while giving you a general sense of their function. Here I will discuss the tasks of opening and closing new and existing documents. You will get a preview of the commands found in each of Painter's menu categories. Finally, you will learn how to use Painter's sleek, new interface.

For a more in-depth look at these topics, I have included a complete reference of Painter's features on the CD accompanying this book. This reference includes command procedures, brush-stroke samples, a complete guide to brush controls, and more. For now, though, let's continue our basic overview of Painter.

Opening New and Existing Documents

If you're continuing from Chapter 2, you have launched Painter by double-clicking the Painter 3 icon. You won't be able to see some of the items we're discussing here without opening a document, so let's start by learning how to open both new and existing documents.

Creating a New Document

New documents are created in Painter in the same manner as other programs: by using the File | New command. This command lets you specify the size, resolution, and paper color of the document. The procedure to create a new document is as follows:

1. Choose File | New from the menu command bar. Figure 3.1 shows the location of this command.

Figure 3.1.
A new document is
created using the File |
New command.

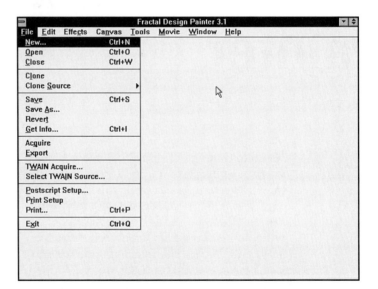

TIP Windows users can also create a new document by simultaneously pressing the Ctrl (Control) key and the letter N (Ctrl-N). Mac users can simultaneously press the Cmd-N key combination.

2. The New Picture dialog box will appear. This dialog box is shown in Figure 3.2. Take note here of the data-entry boxes. These entries allow you to change the width, height, and resolution of the document. The figure that appears to the right of the Canvas size: heading represents the amount of memory or disk space that your image will consume. This number will increase or decrease as you modify the default settings in this dialog box. You are also prompted to enter whether you want to create a single image file or a movie file. There is also a square located in the top right hand corner of the dialog box, marked Paper Color. Clicking inside this square enables you to choose a background color for your image. I'll get into these in more detail in the tutorials; for now, leave all the settings at their default for the purposes of our tour.

Figure 3.2.
The New Picture dialog box prompts you to enter information about your document.

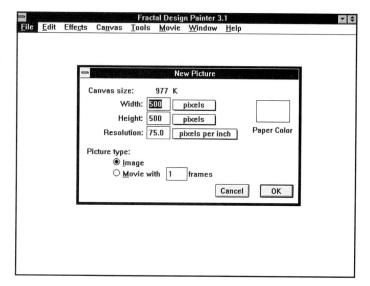

3. Click OK. A new document window will open, with the name Untitled-X in the title bar, with X being a number representing the most recent number of the untitled documents you have opened during your Painter session. The title bar also displays the zoom factor of the document. 100% indicates that the document is being displayed at its normal zoom level. If you don't see your entire image in the document window, you can zoom out using the Window | Zoom Out command (Ctrl-- in Windows, or Cmd-- in Mac).

Figure 3.3.
A new untitled document window appears after all the necessary entries in the New Picture dialog box have been entered.

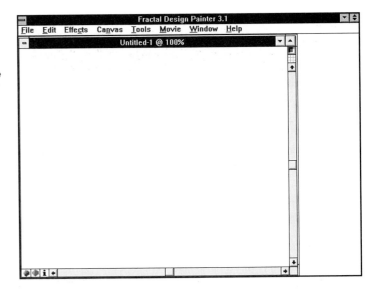

NOTE Try to keep aware of how many untitled documents you have opened, because this is an indication that a document hasn't been saved yet. Consider it smart practice to save documents periodically as you are working on them—especially if you've created something you don't want to lose! You will be prompted to save any unsaved or revised documents when you exit Painter.

The Document Window Scrollbar Symbols

Let's take a moment to look at the new document window in Figure 3.3. You will notice that the scrollbar along the right side of the document has two symbols. The upper symbol, just underneath the document's maximize button, turns Painter's tracing paper on or off. Tracing paper is typically used when cloning an image or tracing frames in movies. The second button in the right scrollbar turns Painter's grid display on or off.

Along the bottom of the document window, you will see some symbols at the left of the scrollbar. The first symbol, the Drawing Visibility icon, appears, allowing you to choose how masking will affect the image. The second symbol, the Mask Visibility icon, allows you to choose how to display the mask while you're working on the image. Finally, clicking the third symbol displays image information, such as dimensions and format.

> **TIP** To view the entire document on the screen, choose the Window | Screen Mode Toggle command (or use Ctrl-M in Windows, or Cmd-M in Mac), which alternates between full-screen and normal viewing modes.

Opening Existing Documents

Existing documents are those that have already been created and saved, either in Painter or other graphic software packages. Painter supports several graphics file formats that can be brought into Painter for editing or effects. Painter also supports opening still images (discussed here), Painter Movies, Video for Windows animation files (Windows version), QuickTime movie files (Mac version), and a series of numbered files for converting into Painter movies.

To open an existing image document, do as follows:

1. Choose File | Open from the menu command bar. Figure 3.4 shows the location of this command.

> **TIP** You can also open an existing document by simultaneously pressing Ctrl-O in Windows or Cmd-O in Mac.

Figure 3.4.
An existing still-image document is opened by selecting the File | Open command.

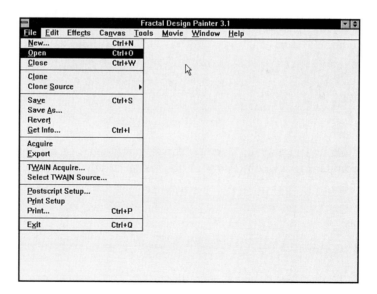

2. The Select Image dialog box will appear in the Windows version. Similarly, the File Open dialog box will appear in the Mac version. This enables you to select the file that you wish to open. If the file you want to locate does not appear in the list, you can choose another directory or folder to display.

   To change the drive in the Windows version, click the down arrow to the right of the Drives drop-down box. To select the directory, you can double-click the root directory that appears in the directory list box, and then double-click again on the desired subdirectory. A list of available files will then appear in the File Name window. Scroll through this list until you locate the file you wish to open. If you click the box beneath the List Files of Type: header in the dialog box, you will see a list of formats that Painter supports. These are shown in Figure 3.5. Table 3.1 shows the available file extensions and their descriptions.

TIP   If you click the Browse button in the Select Image (Windows) or File Open (Mac) dialog box, you can view thumbnails of the images in the current directory or folder. Thumbnails will appear if the files have been created or saved in Painter. When there are no thumbnails available, the image information will appear beneath a blank thumbnail window.

Figure 3.5.
The Select Image
dialog box enables you
to choose an existing
drawing to work on.

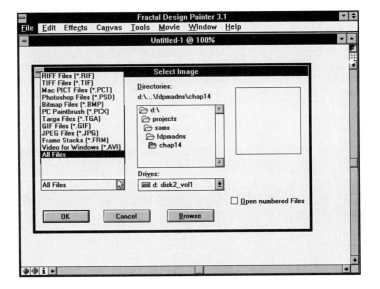

3. Once the desired file is displayed in your directory, you can open it in one of three ways: highlighting the selection with your pointing device and clicking OK (Windows) or Open (Mac); double-clicking the filename; or

highlighting the selection and pressing the Enter (Windows) or Return (Mac) key on your keyboard. A window will appear with the document inside, ready for editing.

NOTE To open a series of numbered files, click inside the box beside Open Numbered Files. This checkbox appears at the lower-right corner of the Select Image dialog box in the Windows version, or beneath the Images file list in the Mac version. You will then be prompted to select the first and last files in the numbered sequence. The numbered files will be opened as a Painter movie frame stack.

Table 3.1. Painter's supported file formats for opening documents.

File Extension	Description
.RIF	Painter's custom format
.TIF	Tagged Interchange File Format
.PCT	Mac Pict Format
.PSD	Adobe Photoshop Format
.BMP	Windows Bitmap
.PCX	Z-Soft "PC Paintbrush" format
.TGA	Targa (true color) file format
.GIF	256-color or less GIF format (Painter 3.1)
.JPG	JPEG file format (Painter 3.1)
.FRM	Painter Frame Stacks
.AVI	Video for Windows files (Windows Version)

QUICK TIME MOVIE FILES (MAC VERSION)NEW PAINTER 3.1 FEATURE!
Painter 3.1 supports reading and writing image data in Photoshop 3 format, including the conversion of Photoshop layers into Painter floaters and vice versa.

An Overview of the Menubars

As is customary with most Windows and Mac programs, the menubar is located along the top of the screen. Menu command options appear when you click the headings. Windows users can also depress the Alt key in conjunction with the underlined letter in the menu title. For example, the File menu's drop-down list can be displayed by entering Alt-F, and the Canvas menu's drop-down list can be displayed by entering Alt-N.

The File Menu

Figure 3.6 shows the available commands in the File menu, which contains functions that will enable you to open and close documents for use in Painter. This menu also contains the commands for scanning documents (hardware input) and printing documents (hardware output). There is also another series of commands that allow for *cloning* documents. Cloning is a process in Painter that allows for modifying or adding special effects to a document without affecting the original.

Figure 3.6.
The File menu con-
tains commands for
file input and output
functions.

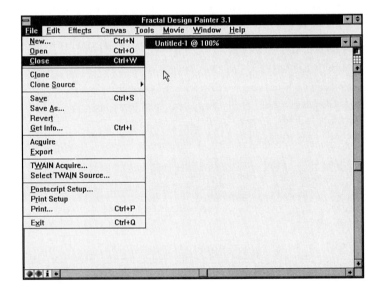

The File Menu commands are as follows:

New (Ctrl-N in Windows, Cmd-N in Mac): Creates a new Painter document.

Open (Ctrl-O in Windows, Cmd-O in Mac): Opens an existing document.

Close (Ctrl-W in Windows, Cmd-W in Mac): Closes the currently active document. If the document has been revised since its last save, you will be prompted to save the changes before closing.

Clone: Creates a clone copy of the currently active document, after which you can re-create it using any of Painter's tools.

Clone Source: Allows you to create a link between two documents, by establishing any other open document as the clone source of your current document.

Save (Ctrl-S in Windows, Cmd-S in Mac): Saves, or updates, the currently active document to disk, using the same filename and file type.

Save As: Renames or saves a document to a different image format or a different filename.

NEW PAINTER 3.1 FEATURE!

In addition to the many file formats supported in Painter 3.0, Painter 3.1 now allows you to save your documents to 8-bit .GIF format and .JPG format.

Revert: Reverts a document to the last saved version of the currently opened file.

Get Info (Ctrl-I in Windows, Cmd-I in Mac): Displays image information (size, resolution, and image format).

Acquire: Brings up your scanner's software interface.

Export: Allows saving of images to foreign file types by accessing third-party plug-in filters.

TWAIN Acquire: Brings up your scanner's software interface.

Select TWAIN Source: Presents a dialog box from which you select any TWAIN-compliant scanner on your system.

Page Setup (Mac version): Brings up a dialog box that enables you to choose and select parameters for printing to QuickDraw or PostScript printers.

PostScript Setup (Windows version): Brings up a dialog box that enables you to choose and select parameters for PostScript printers.

Print Setup (Windows version): For choosing and setting your printer parameters (such as your default printer, print orientation, paper size, and paper source).

Print (Ctrl-P in Windows, Cmd-P in Mac): Used to print a document to your selected printer, and allows you to set print quality, number of copies, the page range, and type of printing.

Exit (Ctrl-Q in Windows, Cmd-Q in Mac): Exits the Painter program and closes all open documents. You are prompted to save any documents that have been edited since the last save.

Edit Menu

The Edit menu is where you will find commands for selecting all or parts of your image for modification. This is also the area that contains commands to place

parts of your image into the clipboard. In addition, the commands for customizing your Painter directories, cursor appearance, and interface preferences are located here. (I'll discuss how to customize Painter in the next chapter.) Figure 3.7 shows where the Edit Menu commands can be found.

Figure 3.7.
The Edit Menu con-
tains commands for
placing areas in the
Clipboard, selecting
all or parts of your
image, and setting
preferences.

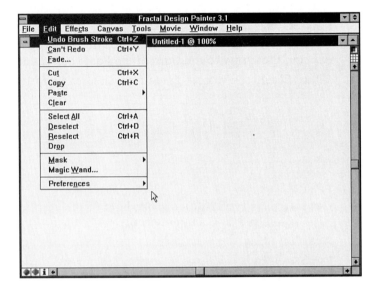

The following is a brief description of the commands in the Edit menu:

Undo/Redo/Can't Undo (Ctrl-Z in Windows, Cmd-Z in Mac): This command appears in Painter 3.0. It toggles between Undo, Redo, and Can't Undo. Undo, as the name implies, undoes the last step that you performed on your document. After Undo is performed, you are given the opportunity to Redo the step again—in other words, Redo undoes the Undo. The command option will show as Can't Undo if there is no action to be undone.

Undo/Can't Undo (Ctrl-Z in Windows, Cmd-Z in Mac): In Painter 3.1, a multiple Undo feature has been added. Multiple Undo allows you to undo and redo up to 32 levels of changes. The number of levels is set with the Edit | Preferences | Undo command.

Redo/Can't Redo (Ctrl-Y in Windows, Cmd-Y in Mac): This command appears in Painter 3.1. As with the Multiple Undo feature, the number of levels that you can undo is determined by the setting chosen with the Edit | Preferences | Undo command. Note also that in Painter 3.0, the Ctrl-Y or Cmd-Y quick-key combinations pertain to the Canvas | Dry command.

Fade: This command partially undoes the previous action applied to a document. If, for example, you have painted an area too dark or too light, Fade will allow you to remove the stroke by removing part of its opacity.

Cut (Ctrl-X in Windows, Cmd-X in Mac): Removes a selected area from the image and places it into the Windows Clipboard.

Copy (Ctrl-C in Windows, Cmd-C in Mac): Copies a selected area from the image and places it into the Windows Clipboard.

Paste: Pastes the contents of the Windows Clipboard into the active image (Paste | Normal, or Ctrl-V in Windows, Cmd-V in Mac), or into a new document (Paste | Into New Image). These two options are selectable by clicking the arrow to the right of the Paste command.

Clear: Clears the selected area from the image without placing it into the Windows Clipboard.

Select All (Ctrl-A in Windows, Cmd-A in Mac): Selects the entire image.

Deselect (Ctrl-D in Windows, Cmd-D in Mac): Deselects the selected area or areas.

Reselect (Ctrl-R in Windows, Cmd-R in Mac): Reselects a selection and turns it back on.

Drop: Drops the currently selected floater into the background layer. The quick-key combinations of Shift-Ctrl-D in Windows or Shift-Cmd-D in Mac accomplish the same function.

Mask | Auto Mask: Used to create floater and background masks. You can also use the quick-key combination of Shift-Ctrl-M in Windows or Shift-Cmd-M in Mac to invoke the Auto Mask command.

Mask | Color Mask: Used to create color masks, which can be feathered based on hue, saturation, and value.

Mask | Clear Mask (Ctrl-U in Windows, Cmd-U in Mac): Removes the mask completely from the background or the currently selected floater.

Mask | Invert Mask: Reverses the state of the mask so that masked areas become unmasked and unmasked areas become masked.

Mask | Feather Mask: Adjusts the feathering of the mask, in pixels.

Magic Wand: Selects areas according to pixel color(s).

Preferences: Brings up dialog boxes that enable you to customize Painter preferences in five areas: General preferences, Brush Tracking preferences, Interface preferences, Windows preferences, and Plug-In preferences.

NEW PAINTER 3.1 FEATURE!

A sixth Preference command has been added to Painter 3.1. The Edit | Preferences | Undo command has been added to specify how many levels of undo and redo that you would like in your Painter documents. Note that memory requirements increase as the number of levels increases. The default number of levels is set to 5, but you can set up to 32 levels of undo and redo.

The Effects Menu

The Effects menu, shown in Figure 3.8, is a doorway to many different types of special effects that can be applied to selections or documents. At first glance, this menu looks pretty short—but notice that there are arrows to the right of most of the commands. These arrows give you access to several different subcategories of effects.

Figure 3.8.
The Effects Menu
contains doorways to
many types of special
effects that can be
applied to selections or
images.

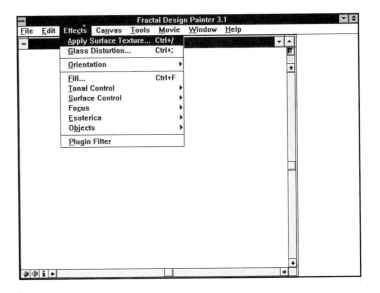

The top two commands shown in Figure 3.8 are Apply Surface Texture, using a quick-key combination of Ctrl-/ in Windows or Cmd-/ in Mac, and Glass Distortion, using the quick-key combination of Ctrl-; in Windows or Cmd-; in Mac. If you have already been working with Painter, your display of the first two commands in this menu might appear differently. The reason for this is that Painter uses these two areas as placeholders for the two most recent effects commands you have used. Then, you can use the quick-key combinations of Ctrl-/ (or Cmd-/) and Ctrl-; (or Cmd-;) to quickly gain access to these effects if you want to use them repetitively.

Effects | Orientation Commands

Clicking the arrow to the right of the Orientation command reveals an additional submenu of commands. These commands are shown in Figure 3.9. With them, you can modify your image by enlarging, reducing, rotating, and scaling images, floaters, or selected areas. The Orientation commands are as follows:

> **Rotate** turns the selection clockwise or counter-clockwise.
>
> **Scale** enlarges or reduces the selected area.
>
> **Distort** warps the selected area.

Flip Horizontal mirrors the image horizontally.

Flip Vertical creates a vertically-mirrored image.

Figure 3.9.
The Effects | Orienta-
tion commands enable
you to change the
orientation of an image
in various ways.

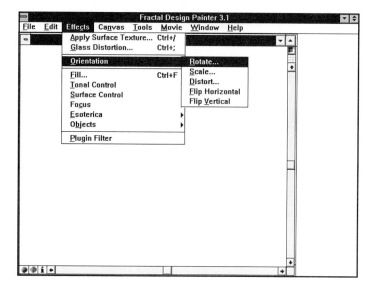

The Fill Command (Ctrl-F in Windows, Cmd-F in Mac)

The Fill command, which can be accessed with the quick-key combination of Ctrl-F in Windows or Cmd-F in Mac, has four options. After choosing the Fill command, you can choose to fill the selected area with the currently selected color, with a gradation, with a clone source, or with a weaving. These options are chosen in the Fill dialog box, shown in Figure 3.10.

Figure 3.10.
The Fill command in
Painter 3.0 offers four
ways to fill an area or
image.

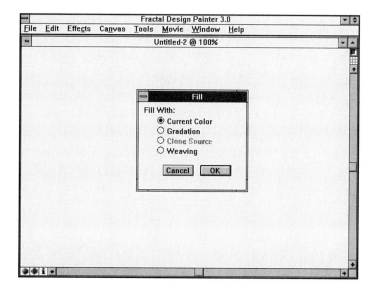

Figure 3.11.
The Fill command in
Painter 3.1 adds the
ability to adjust the
opacity of the fill.

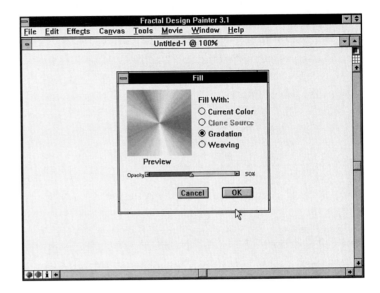

Tonal Control Commands

Clicking the arrow to the right of Tonal Control reveals its submenu of commands, shown in Figure 3.12. Here, you are offered several different ways to adjust the colors in an image. The Tonal Control commands are as follows:

Adjust Colors adjusts the hue, saturation, or value of overall colors in an image. The quick-key combination of Shift-Ctrl-A in Windows or Shift-Cmd-A in Mac will invoke this command.

Adjust Selected Colors enables you to adjust colors in an image based on the adjusted colors' nearness to a selected color.

Brightness/Contrast adjusts the brightness and contrast of an image.

Equalize (Ctrl-E in Windows, Cmd-E in Mac) improves the contrast of an image by redistributing the available brightness levels.

Negative turns your image or selection into a negative.

Posterize sets a limit on the number of colors in your image.

Printable Colors replaces any non-printable colors in your image with printable ones.

Video Legal Colors replaces objectionable video colors (usually bright yellows and cyans) in your image.

Posterize Using Color Set forces the colors in an image to only those colors contained in the currently open color set.

Figure 3.12.
The Tonal Control commands allow you to adjust, redistribute, and reduce the colors in an image or selection.

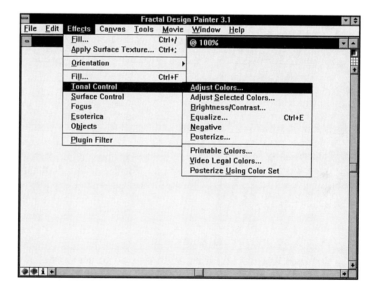

Surface Control Commands

Surface Control commands are accessed by clicking the arrow at the right of the Surface Control option. These commands, shown in Figure 3.13, enable you to add texture to the image or selection in a variety of ways.

Apply Lighting, which requires a computer with a floating point unit (or math coprocessor), lets you add lighting effects to the image or selected area.

Apply Screen adds texture to your image by combining luminance, the chosen paper texture, and three selectable colors to produce the effect.

Apply Surface Texture adds three-dimensional effects to the image by using paper grain, brush strokes, image luminance, and more.

NEW PAINTER 3.1 FEATURE!

The Apply Surface Texture command in Painter 3.1 has additional controls for fine lighting adjustments. You can have colored lights interact with paper grain to produce different effects on the surface!

Color Overlay concurrently adds color and texture to the selected area.

Dye Concentration adjusts the color intensity and adds surface texture to the selection.

Image Warp allows you to stretch and distort areas of an image as though it were pliable.

Figure 3.13.
Surface Control
commands apply
effects that alter the
texture of the image
or selection.

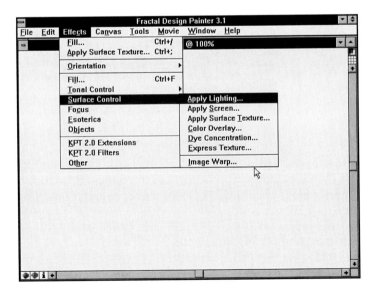

Focus Commands

The Focus commands, shown in Figure 3.14, alter the sharpness or softness of the image.

Glass Distortion gives the appearance that the selection or image is behind a pane of bumpy-textured glass.

Motion Blur gives the appearance that the selection is in motion.

Sharpen intensifies the focus of the selection and makes it more sharp.

Soften defocuses, or softens, the selection.

TIP You can invoke Painter's Super Soften command by using the Shift-Ctrl-S keyboard combination in Windows, or the Shift-Cmd-S keyboard combination in Mac.

Figure 3.14.
The Focus commands
provide ways to alter
the sharpness or
softness of an image.

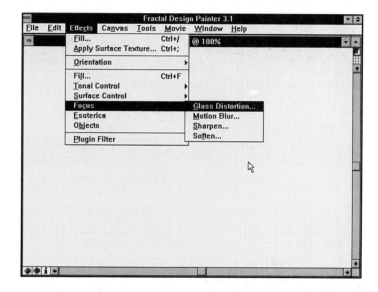

Esoterica Commands

The Esoterica effects commands, accessed by clicking the arrow to the right of the Esoterica menu option, are the fun ones—those that provide stunning effects automatically thanks to Painter's clever calculations. These commands are shown in Figure 3.15.

Apply Marbling creates marbled patterns in your image.

Auto Clone makes a copy of a document using any of Painter's drawing or painting tools, although some work better than others. I will discuss this in Chapter 16, "Visiting Van Gogh: The Cloner and Artist Brushes."

Auto Van Gogh automatically repaints a document in the multicolored, bold-brushstroke style of Van Gogh.

Blobs, typically used in conjunction with the Apply Marbling command, applies a stone pattern to the contents of the Clipboard or your current color.

Grid Paper adds a grid of lines (horizontal, vertical, or both) to your image.

NEW PAINTER 3.1 FEATURE!

Painter 3.1 has a new effect that creates branch-like growth patterns. By using the Effects | Esoterica | Growth command, you can create overhead views of tree branches using your current color.

Highpass creates an effect that suppresses gradual or smooth transitions in brightness levels. This leaves just the edges of an image that contain pronounced shifts between levels of brightness.

Figure 3.15.
The Esoterica sub-
menu contains com-
mands to automatically
clone or marble an
image, as well as
others.

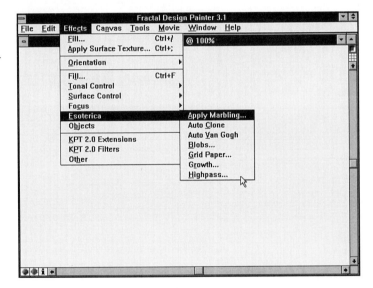

Objects Command

The Objects menu option, shown in Figure 3.16, contains only one command: Create Drop Shadow. Using this command will allow you to create drop-shadowed text in your documents, but you aren't limited to just text. You can apply a drop shadow to any floater, regardless of size or shape.

Figure 3.16.
The Create Drop
Shadow command
enables you to add a
drop shadow to any
floater.

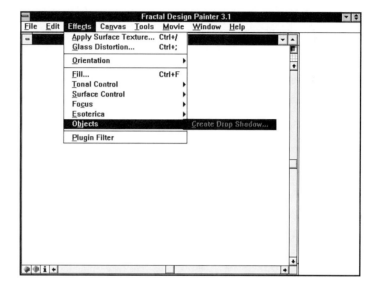

Plugin Filters

The Plugin Filter command section is a placeholder that will provide access to third-party, plug-in filters you identify during Painter installation, or with the Edit | Preferences | Plugins command. It gives you access to third-party plug-in filters, such as those contained in Kai's Power Tools. This modular approach to drawing-program enhancements allows for a wide variety of special effects that can be added to the program.

Canvas Menu

The Canvas menu, shown in Figure 3.17, contains commands that relate to canvas size, type, and color. It also includes commands that allow you to customize the grid. In addition, there are commands that enable you to create and view notes regarding the colors used in your image.

Figure 3.17.
The Canvas menu
includes commands
relating to canvas size,
color, grid setup, and
annotation of colors.

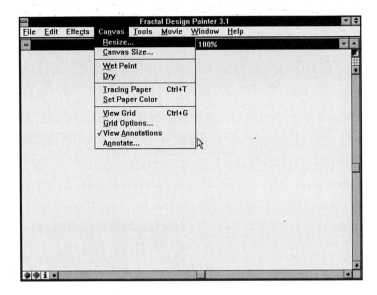

The Canvas menu commands include the following:

Resize changes the resolution or dimensions of the image.

Canvas Size allows you to add pixels to the top, bottom, right, or left side of an image without affecting the rest of the canvas.

Wet Paint, used in conjunction with watercolor paints, turns on the wet layer in Painter to produce realistic watercolor strokes and effects.

Dry (Ctrl-Y in Windows and Cmd-Y in Mac, for Painter 3.0 only) is used to set the colors and strokes painted in the wet layer into the main layer of the image.

Tracing Paper (Ctrl-T in Windows, Cmd-T in Mac) is used to trace images during cloning and allows easier visibility of strokes made during a cloning session by viewing a ghosted image of the document. This command can also be implemented by clicking the tracing paper icon located in the right document window scrollbar.

Set Paper Color changes the color of the canvas, if necessary, after a new document is created.

View Grid (Ctrl-G in Windows, Cmd-G in Mac) toggles display of the grid (as set in Grid Options) on and off.

Grid Options sets up the grid parameters to your preferences.

View Annotations shows or hides the annotations of color names created with the Annotation command.

Annotate allows you to label the colors in your image using color names from a color set.

Tools Menu

The Tools menu contains commands that allow you to customize Painter even further by creating your own brushes, textures, selection lists and other tools, and to maintain them in libraries of your own. Here you will also find commands to record singular strokes or series of strokes, called sessions, for replay and automatic painting.

Tools | Movers Commands

The Movers commands, accessed by clicking the arrow to the right of the Movers section, allow you to create and maintain libraries of your own Painter elements. The Movers commands, shown in Figure 3.18, are as follows:

Paper Mover creates and maintains libraries of papers that you can edit and move papers between.

Path Mover creates and maintains libraries of selections that you can edit and move selections between.

Brush Mover creates and maintains libraries of brushes that you can edit and move brushes between.

Brush Look Mover creates and maintains libraries of brush looks that you can edit and move brush looks between.

Session Mover creates and maintains libraries of sessions that you can edit and move sessions between.

Floater Mover creates and maintains libraries of floaters that you can edit and move floaters between.

Lighting Mover creates and maintains libraries of lighting arrangements created with the Edit | Surface Control | Apply Lighting command.

Weaving Mover creates and maintains libraries of weaves that you can edit and move weaves between.

Gradation Mover creates and maintains libraries of gradations that you can edit and move gradations between.

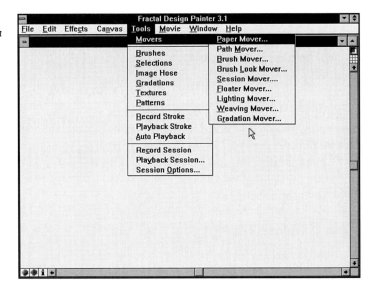

Figure 3.18.
The Movers provide you
with ways to create
your own libraries of
brushes, papers,
effects, and more.

Tools | Brushes Commands

The Brushes submenu, shown in Figure 3.19, contains commands that allow you to create, save, delete, and modify brushes. The commands are shown after the following note.

> **NOTE**   Many of Painter's brushes now build automatically, so you don't have to use the Build command as often as you did in previous versions!

Build Brush (Ctrl-B in Windows, Cmd-B in Mac) builds a brush, or a variant of a brush, after it is created or edited.

Capture Brush captures a shape you have designed so that you can create a custom brush from it.

Brush Look Designer lets you view the changes and what your brush stroke looks like as you design your own brushes.

Delete Variant deletes a brush variant from the brush library.

Restore Default Variant restores a brush that was saved with Save Built Variant to its default settings.

Save Brush saves a new brush that you have created.

Save Built Variant saves a modified version of an existing brush in the brush library.

Save Variant allows you to save up to 32 variants of a particular brush.

Figure 3.19.
The Brushes com-
mands of the Tools
menu allow you to
create your own
brushes as well as
modify existing ones.

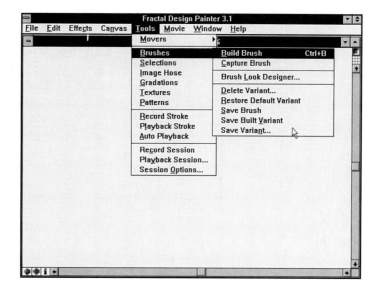

Tools | Selections Commands

The Selections submenu, shown in Figure 3.20, contains commands that enable you to edit and manipulate selections. These commands are as follows:

Convert to Curve converts selections created with the Oval Selection tool, Text Selection tool, and Outline Selection tool into editable curves.

TIP

> Try reshaping some of your text! Convert the text to curves using the Convert to Curve command. Reshape the text by moving the control points and handles, and then convert back to a selection with the Convert to Selection command. It can add some pizzazz to your text!

Convert to Selection converts a Bézier curve path back into a selection.

Edit Rectangular Selection (Shift-Ctrl-E in Windows, Cmd-Shift-E in Mac) enables you to adjust the size and shape of a rectangular selection.

Stroke Selection applies the current brush's stroke and color around active selections, creating an outline effect.

Open EPS as Selection allows you to open an .EPS file and use it as a selection.

Figure 3.20.
The Selections menu contains commands to edit and convert selections.

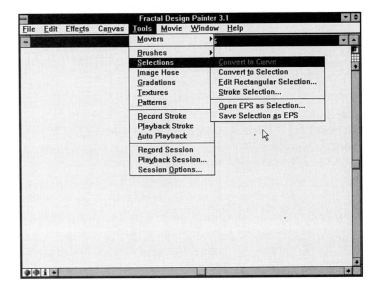

Tools | Image Hose Commands

The Image Hose commands let you identify which nozzle file will be loaded into an Image Hose, and offer two ways of creating Image Hose nozzle files. The Image Hose commands, shown in Figure 3.21, are as follows:

Load Nozzle (Ctrl-L in Windows, Cmd-L in Mac) allows you to choose a specially prepared Painter .RIF document to spray from your Image Hose.

Make Nozzle from Group allows you to create an Image Hose nozzle file that utilizes a group of selections as the paint for an image hose.

Make Nozzle from Movie allows you to create an Image Hose nozzle file from a Painter movie frame stack.

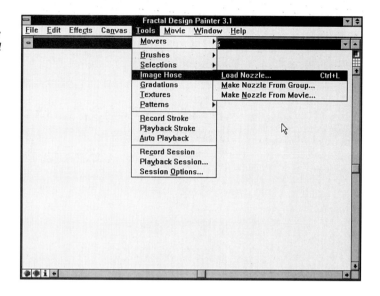

Figure 3.21.
Image Hose commands
allow you to create and
use Image Hose nozzle
files.

Tools | Gradations Commands

The Gradation commands, shown in Figure 3.22, allow you to create and use custom gradations in your image. The Gradation commands are as follows:

Capture Gradation captures a gradation from your image and allows you to retrieve it later from a gradation library.

Express in Image replaces colors in an image with colors in a gradation.

NEW PAINTER 3.1 FEATURE!

Painter 3.1 now allows you to design algorithmic Gradations with a Gradation editor. The Gradation editor can be accessed with the new Tools | Gradations | Edit Gradation command.

TIP The Sepia Tones gradient in the default Grads Palette library is great to use with the Express in Image command. Turn color documents into sepia tone prints!

Figure 3.22.
With the Gradation
commands, you can
create your own
gradations or apply
them to your image.

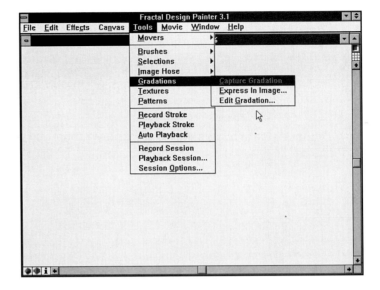

Tools | Textures Commands

The Textures commands, shown in Figure 3.23, allow you to create and use custom textures in your image. The Textures commands are

> **Capture Texture** turns a portion of an image into a paper texture that will become available in the Papers palette.

> **Make Paper Texture** lets you make your own paper textures using patterns from a pop-up menu.

Figure 3.23.
The Textures com-
mands allow you to
create your own
papers, which can be
accessed in the Art
Materials | Papers
palette.

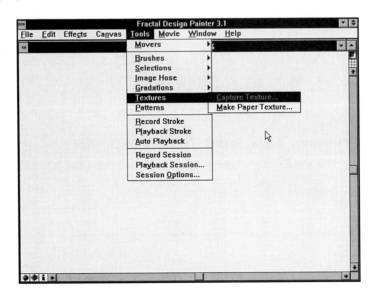

Tools | Patterns Commands

The Tools | Patterns commands, shown in Figure 3.24, provide ways to capture and create repeatable or seamless patterns in your Painter documents.

Capture Pattern captures a selection and places it into an untitled document. This pattern can then be used as a clone source with the Paint Bucket to fill an area repetitively.

Define Pattern allows you to create a wraparound pattern, or seamless image.

NEW PAINTER 3.1 FEATURE!

The Tools | Patterns | Make Fractal Pattern, new to Painter 3.1, allows you to design fractal patterns and apply them to your image.

---

*Figure 3.24.
The Patterns commands offer ways to create repeating patterns and textures with Painter.*

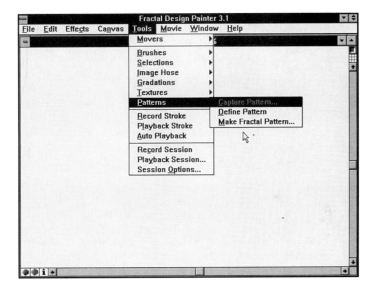

Additional Tools Menu Commands

Three commands, shown in Figure 3.25, allow you to record and playback strokes with each click of your pointing device, or to automatically fill an area. The commands are as follows:

Record Stroke records a brush stroke so that it can be played back repetitively.

Playback Stroke plays back a recorded stroke at the location where the mouse or stylus is clicked.

Auto Playback plays back a stroke automatically in a selected area until canceled by the user.

Figure 3.25.
Record Stroke
commands are used to
record and play back an
individual stroke.

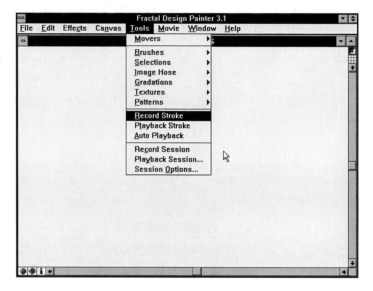

There are also three commands in the Tools menu that relate to recording and playing back Painter Sessions. Sessions are used to record multiple strokes and commands, which can later be played back into another Painter document or applied to a movie. These commands are shown at the bottom of the Tools menu, in Figure 3.26.

Record Session initiates recording of a Painter session, wherein strokes and commands can be recorded and later played back into an image or applied to a Painter movie.

Playback Session allows you to choose a session file that can be played back into a document or applied to a movie.

Session Options offers options to be applied to your sessions during recording.

TIP   You can also select and work with sessions from within the Objects | Sessions
Palette.

Figure 3.26.
Session commands
initiate recording of a
session and allow you
to choose session
recording and playback
options.

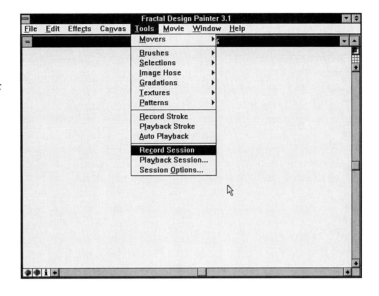

Movie Menu

The commands in the Movie menu are provided to assist you in creating and editing Painter movie frame stacks. These commands are shown in Figure 3.27.

Add Frames adds a specified number of frames to the movie, either before a frame, after a frame, at the beginning of a movie, or at the end of a movie.

Delete Frames deletes a frame or group of frames from a movie.

Erase Frames erases one or more frames and keeps the blank frames in the movie.

Go To Frame jumps to a specific frame in the movie.

Clear New Frames is a toggle that lets you insert either a blank frame or a copy of the last frame at the end of the movie when the fifth button in the Frame Stacks Palette is pressed.

Insert Movie inserts a movie within a movie.

Apply Session to Movie opens a dialog box that allows you to select a session to be played back into each frame of your movie.

Apply Brush Stroke to Movie applies a brush stroke to all frames of the movie, placing a portion of it in each frame.

Set Grain Position allows you to specify whether you want the paper grain to stay still, move randomly or linearly in the movie.

Set Movie Clone Source, with two movies open, allows you to select the currently active movie as the clone source.

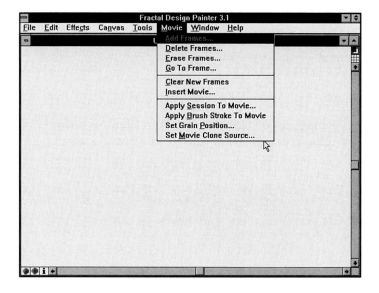

*Figure 3.27.
Movie menu com-
mands enable you
to create and edit
Painter movies and
apply effects to one
or more frames.*

Window Menu

The Window menu commands, shown in Figure 3.28, contain the commands that open and close Painter's palettes. You can also zoom in, zoom out, or view your image full screen with commands in this menu.

Hide Palettes (Ctrl-H in Windows, Cmd-H in Mac) toggles the display of all the active palettes on and off.

Zoom In (Ctrl-+ in Windows, Cmd-+ in Mac) zooms in closer to your image, allowing for fine editing.

Zoom Out (Ctrl-- in Windows, Cmd-- in Mac) zooms away from the image, allowing you to view more of the image while painting or editing.

Tools (Ctrl-1 in Windows, Cmd-1 in Mac) toggles the display of the Tools Palette on and off.

Brushes (Ctrl-2 in Windows, Cmd-2 in Mac) toggles the display of the Brushes Palette on and off.

Art Materials (Ctrl-3 in Windows, Cmd-3 in Mac) toggles the display of the Art Materials Palette on and off.

Brush Controls (Ctrl-4 in Windows, Cmd-4 in Mac) toggles the display of the Brush Controls Palette on and off.

Objects (Ctrl-5 in Windows, Cmd-5 in Mac) toggles the display of the Objects Palette on and off.

Controls (Ctrl-6 in Windows, Cmd-6 in Mac) toggles the display of the Controls Palette on and off.

Advanced Controls (Ctrl-7 in Windows, Cmd-7 in Mac) toggles the display of the Advanced Controls Palette on and off.

Color Set (Ctrl-8 in Windows, Cmd-8 in Mac) toggles the display of the Color Set on and off.

Screen Mode Toggle (Ctrl-M in Windows, Cmd-M in Mac) toggles the full-screen display of the currently active image on and off.

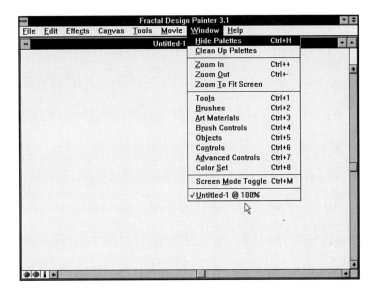

Figure 3.28.
The Windows menu
toggles Painter's
various palettes on
and off.

The Help Menu

The components of the Help menu, shown in Figure 3.29, are as follows:

Index provides a general index of the Help file.

Keyboard shows the keyboard commands available in Painter.

Using Help explains how to use the Help file.

About Painter displays information about Painter, including registration information.

Figure 3.29.
The Help menu
provides online help
to the features and
procedures of Painter.

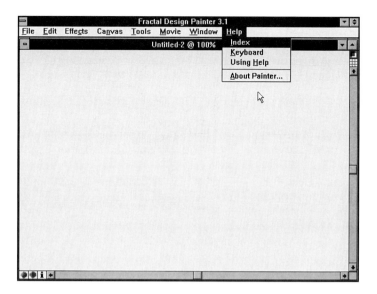

An Overview of Painter's Palettes and Drawers

Painter's brushes, art materials, and brush controls are located in *palettes*.
Simply put, palettes are small organizational areas that contain items and
features which are similar in function. For example, the Brushes Palette contains the various types of brushes available for use. Likewise, the Art Materials
Palette contains items such as paper, gradations, and color-selection methods
(your "paint"). These palettes have some features that may be common to more
than one palette. I'll discuss these common features here.

Opening the Drawers

Figure 3.30 shows an example of one of Painter's palettes: the Brushes Palette.
You can show this palette on your screen by using the quick-key combination
Ctrl-2 in Windows or Cmd-2 in Mac. In this example, the palette is shown in its
smallest size. There are five icons placed in the palette's *drawer front*.

Below the five brush icons is a bar with a down-arrow located in its center. You
can gain access to the additional brushes contained inside the drawer by
clicking anywhere on this bar to open the drawer. Figure 3.31 shows the
Brushes Palette with its drawer open, revealing all 18 brush types.

Figure 3.30.
Palettes contain icons
on their drawer fronts
to gain quick access to
tools.

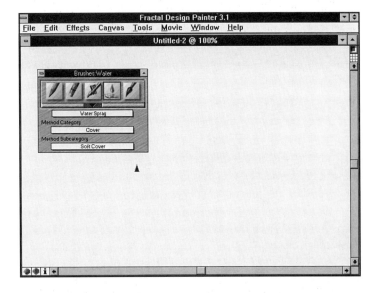

Figure 3.31.
Clicking the bar below
the drawer front opens
the drawer to reveal
additional selections of
tools.

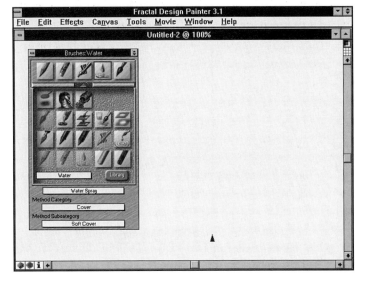

Placing Items in the Drawer Front

Notice in Figure 3.31 that five of the icons inside the drawer (the area below the
bar you just clicked) appear ghosted. The ghosted icons are those tools already
contained in the front of the drawer. To place different icons in the front of the
drawer, simply click the icon for the type of brush you want to use.

When you select an icon inside the drawer, it will trade places with the least-used icon on the drawer front. After moving an icon to the front of the drawer, you will see its image ghosted inside the drawer. The icon that it traded places with will be returned to its home location inside the drawer, and its image will become opaque.

Once you have selected the tools you wish to place in the front of the drawer, close the drawer by clicking again on the bar with the arrow on it.

Showing Setting Options in Palettes

Some palettes provide setting options to achieve different looks or functions of a brush or tool. To illustrate this example, you can bring up the Art Materials Palette using the quick-key combination of Ctrl-3 in Windows or Cmd-3 in Mac. Figure 3.32 shows the Art Materials Palette opened and set to the Colors Palette.

Figure 3.32.
Some palette sections
contain settings that
can be adjusted. This
screen shows the
Colors Palette with the
optional settings
hidden.

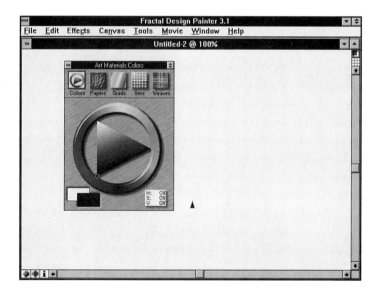

At the upper-right corner of the Colors Palette is a maximize button, shown with an upward and downward arrow. Clicking this button reveals some settings and adjustments that can be made to your current color or brush. For example, in Figure 3.33, the settings to control color variability in a brush stroke are revealed after you click this button. Checkboxes also exist to turn your brush into a cloning brush, or to paint only those colors that are printable. Other palettes similarly have selections that can be made after clicking the maximize button. To revert back to the original state of the palette, click the maximize button again.

*Figure 3.33.
Clicking the maximize
button at the top right
of some palettes
reveals additional
settings that can be
adjusted.*

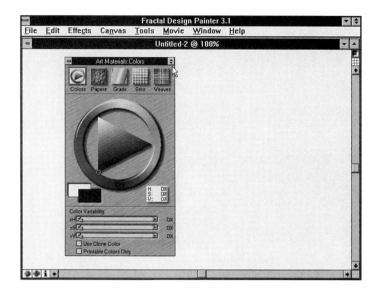

Tear-Off Feature

Sometimes you may need more than one feature of a palette open at the same time. For example, you might want the Color Sets and Colors Palettes, both contained within the Art Materials Palette, to be open at the same time when you're creating a color set. For this purpose, you can use Painter's tear-off feature.

Items can be torn off from the drawer front. To tear off an item from a palette, click and drag any of the unhighlighted items toward the outside of the palette. You will see a ghosted outline of the selected feature until you release the mouse button or stylus outside its home palette. Figure 3.34 shows the Color Sets, Papers, and Colors Palettes opened concurrently—all parts of the Art Materials Palette. You can tear off as many features in a palette as you like, except that one item must remain in the home palette. The tear-offs can be closed by clicking the button in the upper left of their title bars.

Figure 3.34.
Sections can be torn
off when you wish to
work with more than
one section of a palette
at once.

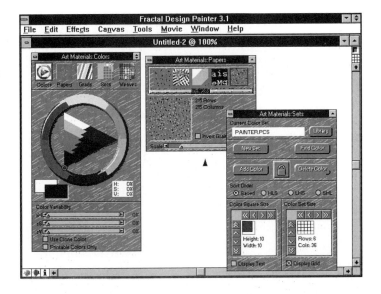

Now that we've discussed some of the items that are common to more than one of Painter's palettes, we'll look at the functions of each palette individually.

The Controls Palette (Ctrl-6 in Windows, Cmd-6 in Mac)

The Controls Palette changes its display to reflect the current tool or palette choice. You can selectively show and hide the Controls Palette by either selecting the Window | Controls command or by the quick-key combination of Ctrl-6 in Windows or Cmd-6 in Mac.

Basically, the Controls Palette gives you quick access to those options and functions most commonly adjusted when working with a particular tool. For example, when you select a brush, the Controls Palette displays the heading Controls | Brush. It displays your currently selected primary and secondary colors, allows you to adjust the opacity and grain of the brush, as well as to select drawing freehand or straight lines. Figure 3.35 shows what the Controls Palette looks like when a brush tool is selected.

Figure 3.35.
The Controls Palette
provides convenient
access to the most
common adjustments
for your currently
selected tool.

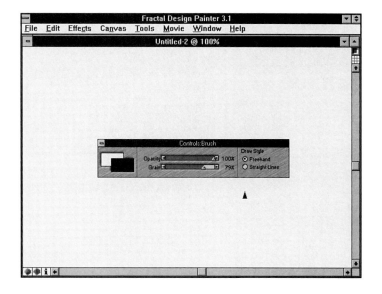

The Tools Palette (Ctrl-1 in Windows or Cmd-1 in Mac)

The Tools Palette, shown in Figure 3.36, allows you to select your current action in Painter. You can view the Tools Palette by selecting the Window | Tools command, or by the quick-key combination of Ctrl-1 in Windows or Cmd-1 in Mac. Here, you can select if you want to paint with a brush, rotate the canvas, create a selection and pick a color from your current image—and other items as outlined on the next page. The function of each tool and the settings available for use in the Controls Palette are identified in the descriptions that follow.

Figure 3.36.
The Tools Palette is
used to select your
current action.

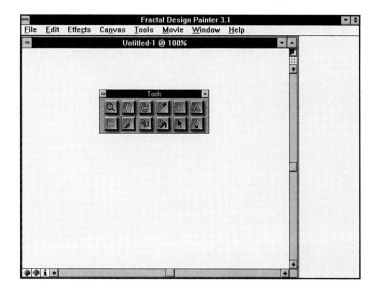

The Magnifier tool zooms in and out of the image at various zoom factors. The Controls | Magnifier Palette allows you to adjust the zoom level by clicking in the box displaying the current zoom level.

 The Grabber tool enables you to move the image within the current active document window. The Controls | Grabber Palette also allows you to change the zoom level by clicking in the box that displays the current zoom level.

 The Rotate Page tool enables you to rotate the canvas at any angle just as you would a regular piece of paper or canvas while painting. The Controls | Rotate Page Palette displays the angle rotation as you are rotating and also allows you to adjust the zoom level of the image.

 The Dropper tool allows you to select a color from the current image by clicking inside the image. The Controls | Dropper Palette displays both HSV and RGB values of the selected color while displaying the selected color in a rectangular window.

 The Oval Selection tool allows you to create a circular or oval path. The Controls | Oval Selection Palette displays the overall width and height of the selection as well as its X and Y coordinates (top left and bottom right) within the current image. Feathering of the selection can also be adjusted.

 The Text Selection tool allows you to create a selection by typing in text, using fonts installed in Windows. The Controls | Text Selection Palette lets you select the font, and adjust its point size and tracking (the space between letters).

 The Rectangular Selection tool allows you to select a square or rectangular area. Unlike the Oval Selection Tool, this does not create a path. The Controls | Rectangular Selection Palette displays the width and height of the selected area, as well as its X and Y coordinates (top left and bottom right).

 The Brush tool allows you to paint with the currently selected brush. The Controls | Brush Palette has two overlapping rectangular windows that show your selected color or colors. You can adjust the opacity and grain of the brush in this palette, and you can also indicate whether you wish to draw straight or freehand lines.

 The Floating Selection tool allows you to work with floaters and how they are applied to the image. With the Controls | Floating Selection Palette, you can send floaters forward or backward in layers, set their opacity and feathering, and select composite methods. The overall dimensions and X and Y coordinates of the floater are also displayed.

The Paint Bucket fills solid areas of an image or selection with the current color, a clone source, a gradation, or a weaving. The Controls | Paint Bucket Palette shows the currently selected fill. With it, you can fill an image, a mask, or a cartoon cel.

 The Path Adjuster tool identifies how you wish to use an active path (or selection). The top three symbols on the Controls | Path Adjuster Palette, the Drawing Visibility buttons, identify how the current selection will affect your image: no effect (selection "shut off"), masked inside the selection, or masked outside the selection. The next three symbols, the Mask Visibility buttons, identify how you view the mask of the selection: not seen but operable, display the masked area in red, or view the selection surrounded by a marquee. The plus and minus keys identify whether the selection's mask will be positive or negative. The feathering of the selection can be adjusted. Also, the overall height and width of the selection, as well as its X and Y coordinates, are displayed.

 The Outline Selection Tool allows you to select an area by freehand drawing, Bézier curves, or straight lines. The Controls | Outline Selection Palette adjusts feathering and allows you to identify selection usage and viewing as in the Path Adjuster Palette, discussed previously.

The Brushes Palette (Ctrl-2 in Windows or Cmd-2 in Mac)

The Brushes Palette contains all of your drawing and painting tools. The Brushes Palette can be shown or hidden by selecting the Window | Brushes command, or by the quick-key combination of Ctrl-2 in Windows or Cmd-2 in Mac. Here, you will find over 130 different variants of brushes. I've already shown, in Figure 3.31, how to open the drawer to find all the brushes available.

Selecting Brushes

As previously mentioned, there are five icons for placement of brushes on the drawer front of the Brushes Palette. You can select a variant from inside the drawer or from the drawer front. Figure 3.37 shows the process of selecting a brush variant for use. In the example, you are in the process of selecting one of the Felt Pens to work with next.

To select a brush variant, do as follows:

1. Click the icon that represents the type of brush you wish to work with. In the example, this would be the Felt Tip icon.

2. To select a variant of the brush, click and hold the variant name that appears beneath the five icons in the drawer front when the drawer is closed. The list will expand to reveal the additional variants contained within that category.

3. Once the listing of variants appears, slide the mouse or cursor to the variant you want to use and release the mouse button or stylus.

Figure 3.37.
You can select a brush
variant from the drop-
down list at the
bottom of the drawer
front.

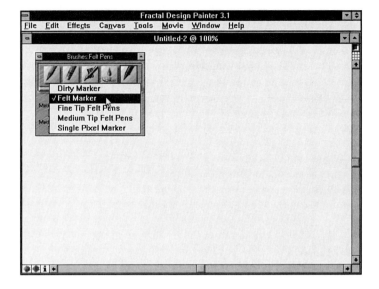

When a brush is selected, its icon in the drawer front will be outlined in red and its variant name will show in the window beneath the icons. The Controls | Brushes Palette will change to reflect the following options and adjustments while using a brush:

- Overlapping rectangles showing your primary (front rectangle) and secondary (back rectangle) colors.

- Sliders to adjust the brush stroke's opacity (cover power) and grain (reaction to paper).

- Radio buttons to select whether you want to draw freehand strokes or straight lines.

Painter's Brush Types

Painter's 18 different brush types contain a combined total of over 130 brushes. The icons located in the Brushes Palette represent the following brush types and variants:

 This icon represents Painter's Masking tools. There are six variants: Big Masking Pen, Grainizer, Masking Airbrush, Masking Chalk, Masking Pen, and Single Pixel Masking.

 This icon represents Painter's Burn tool, which darkens colors beneath areas where its strokes are applied.

This icon represents Painter's Dodge tool, which lightens colors beneath areas where its strokes are applied.

 This icon represents Painter's Liquid tools. There are nine variants: Coarse Distorto, Coarse Smeary Bristles, Coarse Smeary Mover, Distorto, Smeary Bristles, Smeary Mover, Thick Oil, Tiny Smudge, and Total Oil Brush.

 This icon represents Painter's Brush tools. There are 21 variants: Big Loaded Oils, Big Rough Out, Big Wet Oils, Brushy, Camel Hair Brush, Coarse Hairs, Cover Brush, Digital Sumi, Fine Brush, Graduated Brush, Hairy Brush, Huge Rough Out, Loaded Oils, Oil Paint, Penetration Brush, Rough Out, Smaller Wash Brush, Small Loaded Oils, Sable Chisel Tip Water Brush, and Ultrafine Wash Brush.

 This icon represents Painter's Artists tools. There are six variants: Auto Van Gogh, Flemish Rub, Impressionist, Piano Keys, Seurat, and Van Gogh.

 This icon represents Painter's Cloner tools. There are 12 variants: Chalk Cloner, Driving Rain Cloner, Felt Pen Cloner, Hairy Cloner, Hard Oil Cloner, Impressionist Cloner, Melt Cloner, Oil Brush Cloner, Pencil Sketch Cloner, Soft Cloner, Straight Cloner, and Van Gogh Cloner.

 This icon represents Painter's Water Color tools. There are nine variants: Broad Water Brush, Diffuse Water, Large Simple Water, Large Water, Pure Water Brush, Simple Water, Spatter Water, Water Brush Stroke, and Wet Eraser.

 This icon represents Painter's Pen tools. There are 10 variants: Calligraphy, Fine Point, Flat Color, Leaky Pen, Pen and Ink, Pixel Dust, Scratchboard Rake, Scratchboard Tool, Single Pixel, and Smooth Ink Pen.

 This icon represents Painter's Image Hose tools. There are 14 variants: 3 Rank R-P-D, Large Directional, Large Random Linear, Large Random Spray, Large Sequential Linear, Medium Directional, Medium Random Linear, Medium Random Spray, Medium Sequential Linear, Small Directional, Small Luminance Cloner, Small Random Linear, Small Random Spray, and Small Sequential Linear.

 This icon represents Painter's Felt Pen tools. There are five variants: Dirty Marker, Fine Tip Felt Pens, Felt Marker, Medium Tip Felt Pens, and Single Pixel Marker.

 This icon represents Painter's Crayon tools. There are two variants: Default and Waxy Crayons.

 This icon represents Painter's Airbrush tools. There are five variants: Fat Stroke, Feather Tip, Single Pixel Air, Spatter, and Thin Stroke.

 This icon represents Painter's Pencil tools. There are eight variants: 2B Pencil, 500 lb. Pencil, Colored Pencils, Large Colored Pencils, Medium Colored Pencils, Sharp Pencil, Single Pixel Scribbler, and Thick and Thin Pencils.

 This icon represents Painter's Eraser tools. There are 14 variants: Fat Bleach, Fat Darkener, Fat Eraser, Flat Eraser, Medium Bleach, Medium Darkener, Medium Eraser, Single Pixel Bleach, Small Bleach, Small Darkener, Small Eraser, Ultrafine Bleach, Ultrafine Darkener, and Ultrafine Eraser.

 This icon represents Painter's Water tools. There are eight variants: Big Frosty Water, Frosty Water, Grainy Water, Just Add Water, Single Pixel Water, Tiny Frosty Water, Water Rake, and Water Spray.

 This icon represents Painter's Chalk tools. There are five variants: Artist Pastel Chalk, Large Chalk, Oil Pastel, Sharp Chalk, and Square Chalk.

 This icon represents Painter's Charcoal tools. There are three variants: Default Charcoal, Gritty Charcoal, and Soft Charcoal.

The Art Materials Palette (Ctrl-3 in Windows, Cmd-3 in Mac)

Let's now turn our attention to the Art Materials Palette, which can be accessed by the Window | Art Materials command or the quick-key combination of Ctrl-3 in Windows or Cmd-3 in Mac. Here you will find your paints (colors), papers, gradations, and weavings. You can also create your own custom color sets. The icons in the Art Materials Palette represent the following materials:

 Small Colors enables you to choose colors in the same way as in previous Painter versions. This choice will appear in the Art Materials Palette if you have chosen Hue Slider and Triangle as your color palette type with the Edit | Preferences | General command.

 RGB Colors enables you to choose colors by entering an RGB color mixture. This choice will appear in the Art Materials Palette if you have chosen Red-Green-Blue as your color palette type with the Edit | Preferences | General command.

Colors enables you to choose colors by a method similar to a traditional color wheel. The default color palette type, this choice will appear in the Art Materials Palette if you have chosen Color Ring and Triangle as your color palette type with the Edit | Preferences | General command.

 Papers contains several different paper textures, as well as access to a library of your own customized papers.

 Grads contains several pre-made gradations, as well as access to a library of your own customized gradations.

 Sets contains the tools needed to create your own color sets.

 Weaves contains several weaving patterns, as well as the tools needed to create and save your own weavings.

Selecting Colors in Painter

As briefly mentioned in the preceding section, there are three ways you can select colors in Painter 3, each shown in Figure 3.38. You identify which method you want to use by using the Edit | Preferences | General command and choosing your default color palette type in the General Preferences dialog box. In all three methods, two rectangles display your current primary and secondary colors. The topmost rectangle in the color window will change as your primary color is selected. To change the secondary color, click its rectangle to activate it and select a color in the usual manner.

The Colors Palette, shown at the left in Figure 3.38, lets you pick colors by using a form of the traditional color wheel. The general hue of the color is selected on the outer wheel, and the saturation and value of the color is selected in the triangle within the wheel. Hue, Saturation, and Value (HSV) percentages are indicated at the bottom right of the wheel, and the primary and secondary colors selected are shown in overlapping rectangles at the bottom left side of the color wheel. Color variability settings and other options can be shown or hidden with the button at the upper-right side of the palette.

The Small Colors Palette, shown in the center in Figure 3.38, selects colors in a manner similar to previous versions of Painter. The general hue of the color is selected on a color bar beneath the triangle, and the saturation and value of the color are selected in the triangular area. HSV values and color rectangles appear to the right of the color triangle. Color variability settings and other options can be shown or hidden with the button at the upper-right side of the palette.

RGB Colors, shown at the lower right in Figure 3.38, allows you to specify the Red, Green, and Blue mixture of a color in a range of 0 to 255. Overlapping rectangles show the selected primary and secondary colors. Color variability settings and other options can be shown or hidden with the button at the upper-right side of the palette.

Figure 3.38.
The Art Materials
Palette provides
three different
methods for selecting
colors.

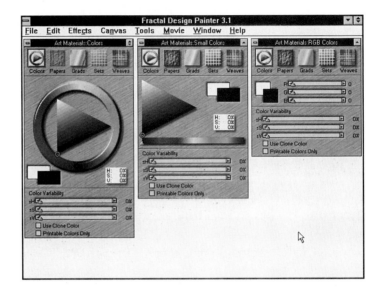

Color Sets

Before you begin painting with traditional media, you place the colors you are going to work with on a palette. In a way, a color set is Painter's palette. Though you can easily pick a color from an image you did long ago by using the Dropper tool, there is one very good reason for creating color sets. You can use them in conjunction with Painter's new Annotate command to identify the colors you used in your image by name; or you can use them to confine your color choices to a selected few that take up a smaller space on your screen. Figure 3.39 shows the Sets Palette.

Figure 3.39.
The Art Materials |
Sets Palette allows you
to create your own
groups of colors to use
or annotate an image.

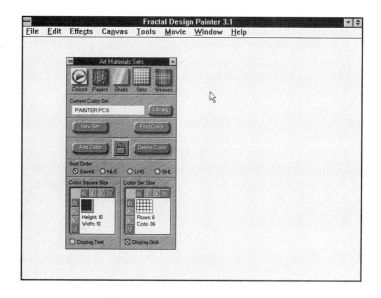

Selecting Papers

Papers can be selected by choosing the Papers icon in the Art Materials Palette. The Paper Palette is shown in Figure 3.40.

Like the Brushes Palette, the Papers Palette offers five places on the drawer front in which to place different paper choices. Opening the drawer front reveals additional paper types, as well as a library button where you can load in your own customized paper libraries. To select a paper, click the icon that represents the type of paper you wish to work with to make it active.

Figure 3.40.
The Papers Palette
contains several types
of papers, as well as a
library to save your
own custom-made
papers.

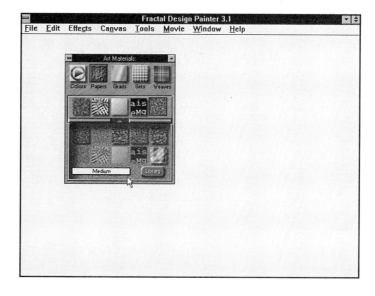

Weavings and Gradations

The Art Materials Palette contains two new types of materials to explore. Weaves, shown on the left side of Figure 3.41 with its drawer open, can now be created in Painter using custom-made color sets and intricate weaving patterns you can create. Warp and weft colors and patterns are entered to create traditional-looking weaving patterns which you can place in a library. You can see in the figure that many patterns have already been created for you.

In Painter 3, you can also create your own gradations. The gradations provided with Painter are shown in the Grads Palette on the right side in Figure 3.41. Gradations can be created by modifying those provided or by drawing a gradation on the screen and capturing it. As with Painter's other tools, gradations can be saved in a library for future use.

TIP There is some undocumented entertainment contained in the Grads Palette. Choose or create a spiral gradient for the best effect. Then close the drawer to go to the front of the Grads Palette. You'll notice a preview of the gradient contained within a circle at the left side of the palette. Click once on this preview. I won't tell you what happens. It will spoil the surprise!

To stop this fun feature, click anywhere on the circle surrounding the gradient.

Figure 3.41.
Weaves and Gradations
are two new art
materials in Painter 3.

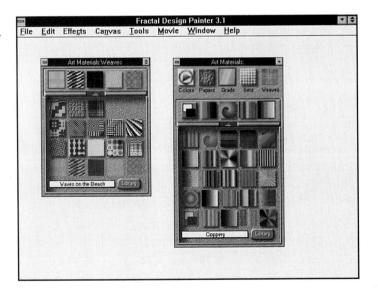

The Brush Controls Palette (Ctrl-4 in Windows, Cmd-4 in Mac)

The Brush Controls Palette contains some of the various settings that make up a brush. Additional controls can be found in the Advanced Controls Palette, described later. It is in these two palettes that you can make modifications to a brush or define the settings to create brushes of your own. Figure 3.42 displays the Brush Controls Palette with its drawer open, revealing the 11 icons contained within.

Figure 3.42.
The Brush Controls
Palette contains five
different areas that
together contain the
properties of a brush.

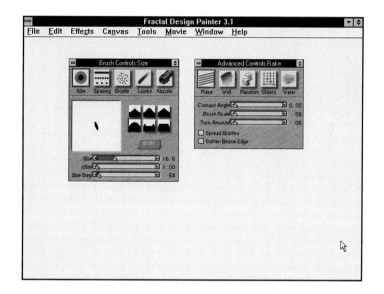

Though it may seem a bit complicated at first, a careful study of the properties of a brush will further your understanding of the results you can expect from a particular brush. With this knowledge, you will soon be customizing and creating your own brushes and brush libraries. I discuss brush customization in Chapter 14, "Working with the Brush Tools." Additionally, the Brush Controls Palette reference included on the CD accompanying this book will help you explore this area in great detail.

The icons in the Brush Controls Palette represent the following areas:

 The *Size Palette* is probably the most commonly used of the controls palettes while painting. Here you can adjust the size of the brush stroke, and you can also adjust the variance between the narrowest and widest portion of the stroke. Additionally, you can set the profile of the brush here to six different types of brush dabs.

Brush Spacing controls the space between the successive dabs that make up a brush stroke. Widening the settings makes a brush appear like a dotted line; narrowing the settings makes the stroke more continuous.

Bristles allows you to create the look of a real brush, complete with hair lines. The diameter of the bristles, random variations in brush marks, the density of the bristles, and their size variation can all be customized in this palette. This is a new Painter 3 feature.

The *Looks palette* allows you to create and save your own *brush looks*—combinations of brush, paper, color variation, and Image Hose nozzle, if applicable. These brush looks can be maintained in libraries for retrieval during a later Painter session.

The *Nozzle Palette* contains settings that are typical for Image Hoses only. These settings allow you to select whether you would like a sequential, random, or directional spray from the hose. The spray can be one or a combination of two or all of these elements. You can elect to spray the images snapped to Painter's grid or paint within the masking layer.

The *Advanced Controls Palette* contains one area that allows you to set how a brush responds to your stroke, as well as settings that are more typical of specialized Painter brushes.

Rakes are strokes that are composed of multiple strokes, side by side, giving a somewhat bristly appearance. Rake Palette settings determine the characteristics of a rake stroke: how much of the brush touches the canvas, the spacing between the bristles, how it reacts when you turn the brush, if the brushes spread farther with pressure, and if the edges of the brush paint softer than the inner bristles.

The *Well Palette* provides settings that tell the brush how to interact with the painting medium, and how it flows from the brush. There are settings for determining how much colors mix together, and how quickly the paint flows from the brush (the brush dryout time).

Random settings cause strokes to appear jittered along their edges in a random manner. They also randomize the colors that are picked up from a clone source, as well as randomizing placement of paper grain in any image.

The *Sliders Palette* identifies how the stroke will react to the way you paint it. Various parameters can be set for the stroke's personality; the stroke size, jitter, opacity, grain, color, angle, resaturation and bleed power can all be user-customizable. Each of these parameters can be elected to vary based on velocity (the speed at which you paint the stroke), the direction the stroke is painted, the pressure of the stylus, the tilt of the stylus (not available on some stylus pens), the bearing of the stroke (also not available on some stylus pens), your clone source, or a random change. You can also elect not to assign one of the personality areas by choosing "none."

 The *Water Palette* contains settings that are applicable to water-color brushes only. These settings determine how the stroke reacts to Painter's wet layer. One setting simulates how water colors absorb into the canvas (diffusion); the other, how a stroke's color builds up around the edges (wet fringe).

The Objects Palette

The five components contained in the Objects Palette are shown in Figure 3.43. Here you will find the tools to create and edit *paths* (formerly called *friskets*) and *floaters* (floating selections). Selections and floaters can each be grouped, ungrouped, put into libraries, and manipulated in many other ways. You will also find the Session Recorder in this palette.

Figure 3.43.
The Objects Palette contains tools to create and edit selections, floaters, and session recordings.

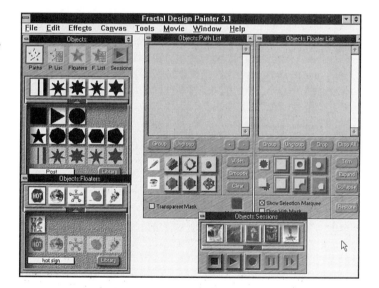

Paths

Basically, a *path* is a portion of your image's background that you want to mask or perform a certain effect on. We've already discussed the various selection tools that are found in the Tools Palette. The Paths Palette, shown on the upper-left side of Figure 3.43, contains several more shapes that can be used as paths: star-shaped polygons and regular polygons. There is also a library button in the Paths Palette to load and save paths of your own making.

Path Lists (P.List)

When you make a path, using the tools in the Tools Palette or converted from masks, a spot is assigned for it in the Path List. (See the center of Figure 3.43 for a picture.) You can rename the path something other than its default name of *Path (number)* so that its identity is more recognizable. Paths can be reordered within the list and grouped so that effects can be applied to multiple selections at once.

The Path List Palette also offers the same options regarding how the path's mask will be viewed and applied to the image. Additionally, you can select if you want the path's mask to be positive (normal selection method) or negative.

Floaters

Basically, a *floater* is a floating selection: an area that you can move around freely without affecting the background or other floaters. A selection is turned into a floater when you click it with the Floating Selection tool, chosen from the Tools Palette.

The Floaters Palette, shown in the upper-right portion of Figure 3.43, contains several pre-built floaters for your use. You can also create and save your own floaters in a library for later retrieval. If you like, you can save a Painter image (in Painter's native format only) with these floating selections still floating. This allows you to create a composition over several Painter sessions, if necessary. Floaters have their own masking layers. Depending on how these layers are arranged, edited, and masked, you can get a wide variety of effects before your final image is complete.

Floaters come with their own special effects: *gel, colorize, reverse-out, shadow map, magic combine,* and *pseudocolor. Gel* tints the area beneath the floater with the colors contained in the floater. *Colorize* replaces the hue and saturation of an area with those of the floater. *Reverse-out* turns the area beneath the floater into a negative. *Shadow map* blocks light beneath the floater, creating shadows. *Magic combine* creates a double-exposure, of sorts, between the background and the floater. *Pseudocolor* transforms luminance values of the floater into hue values.

Floater Lists (F.List)

The Floater List Palette is shown at the bottom right of Figure 3.43. As with the Path Lists, floaters can be rearranged in groups to perform actions on several floaters at once. In addition, floaters can be arranged in layers. Depending on which layer a floater resides on, and the effects or masking applied to it, many different results can be achieved.

Sessions

A session is a recording of several brush strokes recorded in a Painter session. You can apply these brush strokes to the same image, to a different image, or to a movie by saving them to a file for later retrieval. The Sessions Palette, shown at the bottom left of Figure 3.43, has a control panel similar to that of a VCR. There are five locations on the drawer front in which to place sessions for quick retrieval.

Exiting Painter

There are four ways to close the currently active document window:

- Choose File | Close.
- Use the quick-key combination Ctrl-W in Windows or Cmd-W in Mac.
- Double-click the button box at the upper-left corner of the document window.
- Single-click the button box at the upper-left corner of the document window and then click Close.

Any one of the preceding commands will close the document. If you have made any changes to the document since it was last saved, you will be asked if you want to save the changes before closing it.

To exit Painter, choose the File | Exit command. After you select this command, Painter will prompt you to save any files that have been edited since you last saved them. After you close all the opened files, the application will quit.

Summary

This chapter covered the basic commands for opening new and existing documents, as well as for saving them and exiting the program. You've also taken a look at Painter's many tools and palettes. Now you should have a pretty good idea of where you can find things. You may want to customize some areas in the program to suit your needs. The next chapter discusses some items that you can customize in the Painter program, including directory defaults, memory management, and interface.

Customizing Painter

As you use Painter more and more, you may want to customize the software to work with brushes, papers, color sets, selections, and floaters that you have created yourself. Painter offers several different settings that will allow you to tailor the program to suit your needs. In this chapter, I'll discuss four areas that contain settings for customization. Tablet users will learn how to let Painter know how to respond to the way you make a stroke; and mouse users will learn how to add a little more expression to their mouse strokes.

Setting Up a Tablet

Tablets come with their own special drivers and customization software. Typically, tablet software installs the appropriate drivers for you automatically. Often, tablet software

modifies configuration files to replace your standard mouse driver with one that causes the stylus to emulate a mouse. However, this might mean that you would use your stylus to replace a mouse in all your software, not just Painter. If this isn't desired, you may use both a mouse and a stylus at the same time. The documentation provided with your tablet should inform you of the procedure to do this.

NOTE Verify that your tablet is operating with the most current version of your tablet drivers, especially with new releases of software. Check with the manufacturer of your tablet to verify that you have the most current drivers!

Setting Brush Tracking

Different artists have different touches—and one artist can actually have different touches on a daily basis. For example, I draw with a very light touch when drawing freehand, but when doing drafting work I bear down harder on the pencil. After hours of drafting, it affects the way I normally draw in Painter.

To compensate for the differences in the way you press your stylus at any given time, or how rapidly you move the mouse or stylus when creating a stroke, you can let Painter know how to respond. You can find the procedure in the Edit | Preferences | Brush Tracking command, shown in Figure 4.1.

Figure 4.1.
The Brush Tracking command provides a means to tell Painter how to respond to your brush strokes.

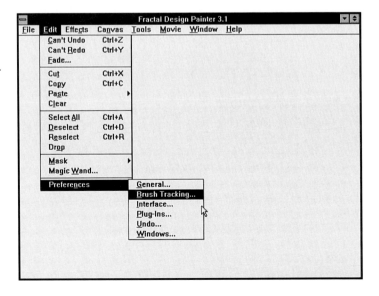

After selecting the Brush Tracking command, the Brush Tracking dialog box appears. This dialog box is shown in Figure 4.2.

Figure 4.2.
The Brush Tracking dialog box contains a window in which to draw some sample strokes for Painter to track.

Inside the Brush Tracking dialog box is a large window. The purpose here is to make a brush stroke, to perform a sort of calibration for how Painter will respond to your stroke action.

Here's how it works. Let's say you draw a quick stroke in the box. Basically, Painter strokes are a series of closely spaced dots (*dabs*, as they are called in the Brush Controls Palette), so if your stroke is too fast, you'll initially see a dotted line in the Brush Tracking window. *But*, Painter looks at those dots in the stroke and calculates an adjustment. You'll see the Velocity Scale and Velocity Power sliders on the bottom of the window move to compensate for the speed in your stroke. If you repeat the stroke exactly the way you did it the first time (or at least close), it will appear more like a continuous stroke.

The same is true for the pressure settings (if you are working with a pressure-sensitive stylus). The Pressure Scale and Pressure Power sliders will adjust to compensate for lighter strokes and heavier strokes. Those working with a mouse will not see any variance in the Pressure sliders.

The Velocity and Pressure sliders can also be adjusted manually if you want.

Once you're done setting up the Brush Tracking, simply click OK to exit the window. Your settings will be used for your entire Painter session, unless you go back and recalibrate again. Painter doesn't save these settings—but this is for a good reason. I think it's pretty much a given that your strokework will be different the next time you enter the program. It's a good idea to invoke the Brush Tracking screen before each Painter session.

Customizing Your General Preferences

Painter's General Preferences window, shown in Figure 4.3, is accessed with the Edit | Preferences | General command. It enables you to customize items such as cursor appearance, libraries, and some items that may enhance the performance of Painter on your system.

Figure 4.3.
The General Prefer-
ences window enables
customization of
cursors, libraries, and
items to enhance
program performance.

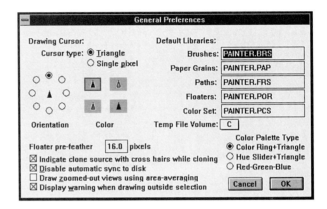

Cursor Settings

In the upper-left quadrant of the General Preferences window, there are a number of settings to customize your cursor appearance. You can elect to show the cursor as an arrow or as a single pixel by clicking one of the radio buttons to the right of the Cursor type: heading.

If you are using the arrow as your cursor symbol, you can change the angle at which it is pointing. Above the Orientation heading, you will notice a circle of eight radio buttons. Clicking any one of these buttons will cause the cursor to point in that direction. For example, it may be preferred by left-handed individuals to have the cursor pointing toward the northeast orientation, and for right-handed individuals to point toward the northwest.

To the right of the Orientation circle are four choices of cursor color. In the Windows version of Painter, you can select a black cursor, black with a white outline, white with a black outline, or a halftone gray cursor. If you are working on a dark image, it may be easier to view the location of the cursor if you change it to white. Conversely, if your image is very light, a darker cursor may be your preference. In the Mac version of Painter, you can choose one of four colors (red, green, blue, or black) for your cursor.

Setting the Default Libraries

In the upper-right quadrant of the General Preferences dialog box, you will find a list of five different libraries that you can elect to use as a default. As you work with Painter, you'll find that you will begin to develop your own papers, brushes, and other items that you use most frequently. Before identifying the custom libraries that you want to use as default, they have to be created using the appropriate Mover.

To select your custom libraries as those to be loaded when Painter starts, do the following:

1. Highlight the existing name in the appropriate area. For example, to specify a new brush library in the Windows version, highlight the PAINTER.BRS name, as shown in Figure 4.3. Mac users highlight the Painter Brushes name in this example.

2. Type in the name of the library you want to use as the custom library, including the appropriate file extension (examples: MYBRUSH.BRS for Windows, or My Brushes for Mac). This file will be used as the default brush library the next time you start Painter.

Setting the Temp File Volume

Just below the area where default libraries are specified is an area to select a new Temp File Volume. Painter does not work with the standard Windows swap file. Instead, it has its own *virtual private scrap* file, which is a large clipboard that will work on an image of any size. Areas that are cut, copied, and pasted are sent and retrieved from this scrap file. Windows users can elect to have Painter use a drive other than its default drive of C by typing a new drive letter in the Temp File Volume box. Mac users can type in the name of their chosen hard drive. The virtual private scrap file, named PAINTER.TMP, is written in the root directory of the selected drive. There must be enough space on the destination drive to accommodate the scrap file.

NOTE For opening or editing an image, Painter requires anywhere from three to five times the working size of the file in a combination of available RAM and hard disk space.

The working size of the file is about twice the size of the file as saved to disk. Therefore, a file that is 2 MB in size when saved to disk will expand to a 4 MB working file. Multiplying this by 3 will give you a figure of at least 12 MB that will be required in memory and hard drive space when editing the document.

Once the PAINTER.TMP file is created, it will not decrease in size or be deleted from your hard drive until you exit Painter.

Other General Preferences

The General Preferences window also has five other settings that can be customized. They are as follows:

Floating selection pre-feather: A bounding box is created for each floater, based on the number of pixels entered in this field. You can feather floaters up to this limit. The default setting is 16 pixels, and it can be set up to 50.

Indicate clone source with cross hairs while cloning: With this box checked, a crosshair will appear within your clone source while you are cloning an image. A crosshair enables you to keep track of which area in the clone source is being reproduced in your clone document.

Disable automatic sync to disk: Checking this box will improve the speed at which Painter runs when files are being accessed to and from the virtual scrap file.

Draw zoomed-out views using area-averaging: When zooming out from an image, to levels less than 100%, area averaging is used to improve the speed of the screen redraw. Checking this box will increase the speed at which the file is displayed, but it will display the image less accurately. Leaving the box unchecked will decrease performance but will display the image more accurately.

Display warning when drawing outside frisket: In the Objects | Floater List Palette, there is a checkbox that enables or disables the display of a selection marquee around a floater when it is active. If you normally like to work on floaters with their outlines hidden, checking this option in the General Preferences dialog box will display a warning when you are painting outside the floater's boundaries.

> **NOTE** Beginning users of Painter may find it best to check the Display warning when drawing outside the frisket option.

Customizing Interface Preferences

If you like, you can change the appearance of the Painter interface by choosing the Edit | Preferences | Interface command. After you select this command, the Interface Preferences dialog box, shown in Figure 4.4, appears on the screen.

Figure 4.4.
You can customize
the appearance of the
Painter interface
by choosing Edit |
Preferences | Interface.

The areas that can be customized are as follows:

Icon Selection Color: Normally when you select a brush or other item from one of the palettes, the currently selected item is surrounded by a red border. If you click the Use Current Color button in this window, the tool will be surrounded by a box of the currently selected color.

Rectangular Shadows: Entering new figures in these three boxes will change the size and softness of the shadows underneath the interface items.

Rectangular Pillowing: Entering new figures in these three boxes will change how much the interface items are pushed in to the interface box. Increasing the numbers makes the interface look softer and more pillowy.

Palette Background Texture: Painter's default background for palettes looks like brushed aluminum. You can change the appearance to look like the current paper texture by clicking the Use Current Texture button. You can also elect to show the background in grayscale or in the current colors. To use a captured pattern for the palette background texture, use the Rectangular Selection Tool to draw a square or rectangle around the area you want to use as a pattern. Then select the Tools | Patterns | Capture Pattern command. After performing the command, enter the Interface Preferences dialog box and click the Use Current Pattern button. This option is disabled if a pattern is not captured first.

Drawer Bottom Texture: Painter's default background for drawer bottoms also looks like brushed aluminum. You can change its appearance to look like the current paper texture by clicking the Use Current Texture button. It can be shown in grayscale or in the current colors.

Window Background Color: Can be shown in the currently selected color by clicking the Use Current Color in this category.

Interface Sets: These are customizable, and can be loaded and saved to your hard disk by clicking the appropriate action button.

TIP   There are a number of very nice interface set files located on the Painter 3 Extras CD, which comes furnished with Painter 3!

To return to the default Painter interface, click the Default button in this dialog box. When you are done customizing your interface, click the OK button to exit the dialog box.

Customizing Undo Preferences

The Multiple Undo and Redo features of Painter 3.1 were mentioned in the previous chapter. To set the number of levels that you would like to undo, choose the Edit | Preferences | Undo command. After choosing this command, the Undo Preferences dialog box appears. In this dialog box, enter the number of levels of Undo/Redo that you would like to apply to all your Painter documents.

NOTE   Note that the Undo/Redo steps are cumulative. For example, let's say you have set the number of Undo steps to ten. If you have three documents open and have already undone two levels in one document, you have eight of the ten remaining undo steps to use in any of the open documents.

Memory requirements increase as the number of Undo/Redo steps increases. If your memory is at a premium, keep the number of Undo steps low.

Customizing Windows Preferences

The Windows Preferences dialog box, shown in Figure 4.5, is displayed after selecting the Edit | Preferences | Windows command. This menu option is not available in the Mac version of Painter.

Figure 4.5.
The Windows
Preferences screen
enables you to set
preferences for memory
usage, printing, and
bitmap display.

The settings available in this dialog box are as follows:

Physical Memory Usage: You can elect to allocate half of your available memory to Painter (the default), or you can allocate the maximum memory you have.

NOTE Selecting Maximum Memory for Painter means that Painter will use nearly all available RAM on your system. This setting is recommended when working on moderate to large images or movies, or have a number of Painter documents open at once. Painter may take longer to start up, and printing difficulties may occur on systems with 8 MB or less of memory using this option.

Selecting Half of Memory for Painter will tell Painter to use only part of your available RAM. If you are working on small images or movies, or if you run other programs concurrently with Painter (not recommended), this choice may be preferable.

The Painter 3 Extras CD, furnished with the Painter program, contains six pages of memory management tips in the \SUPPORT\TIPSHINT\TIP_HINT.EXE file. It is highly recommended that you review these tips to configure Windows for optimum Painter performance.

Printing Options: With Free Memory for Printing checked, your active image will be written to disk. This will increase printing speed and the amount of memory available for the print manager and printer driver.

Checking the No Print Banding option will disable print banding for devices that support it. Disabling print banding (checking this option) will increase performance of some PostScript printers and might also help if you are having problems printing in landscape orientation. However, those that use dot matrix printers or bitmap printers such as the Hewlett-Packard DeskJet printers, may find performance adversely affected if this option is checked.

Display Option: Checking No Device Dependent Bitmaps may resolve color irregularities experienced when 32,000-color video display drivers are used. If you don't use a 32,000-color video display, this option won't have an effect on your system.

Customizing Your Plug-In Preferences

The Edit menu also contains preference settings to specify which plug-in filters you want to use with Painter. This procedure is discussed in Chapter 20, "Integrating with Kai's Power Tools."

Customizing the Grid

Painter has a grid that can be displayed or hidden by clicking the grid square in the upper-right corner of the right scrollbar, or by selecting the Canvas | View Grid command. This grid comes in handy when you want to draw straight lines, as you can have the lines snap to the coordinates of the grid. Figure 4.6 shows a grid displayed, with straight lines drawn in the image.

TIP   You can also constrain straight line angles to 45 or 90 degrees with or without the grid displayed. Press the Shift key while you draw in straight line drawing mode to accomplish this.

Painter's grid can be customized in size and appearance by selecting the Canvas | Grid Options command. After selecting this command, you will see the Grid Options dialog box, shown in Figure 4.7. Here you can customize the horizontal and vertical spacing of the grid, its colors, and the grid type.

Figure 4.6.
Painter's grid comes in
handy if you want to
draw straight lines,
using snap points from
the grid's coordinates.

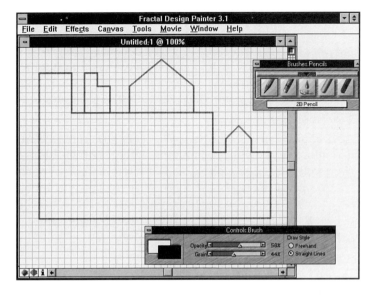

Figure 4.7.
The Grid Options
dialog box provides
settings to customize
the grid display.

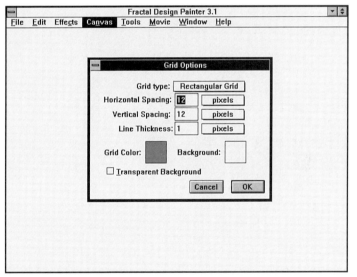

By clicking the square adjacent to the Grid Type heading, you can select one of four types of grid displays. A rectangular grid will display both horizontal and vertical lines in the grid. Vertical Lines and Horizontal Lines display lines in one direction, as their names imply. If you choose to display a dot grid, no lines will be displayed, but there will be a dot placed at each grid-snap point.

Horizontal and Vertical Spacing units can be displayed in pixels (the default), inches, centimeters, points, picas, columns (2"×2" squares), and percentage. In the case of the latter example, if you choose a horizontal and vertical spacing of 25 percent in each, your image will be divided into four equal sections both horizontally and vertically, for a total of 16 segments. You can also change the line thickness in units of pixels as well as in the other units of measure listed herein.

When you click in the color squares adjacent to the Grid Color and Background headings, a color-selection dialog box will appear. The Grid Color signifies the color of the lines in the grid, and the background color signifies the color of the background of the grid. If you want the grid background to be displayed transparently, such that you can view your image more clearly with the grid display on, check the box to the left of Transparent Background.

Once you have selected all the options for your grid display, clicking OK will return you back to normal painting.

TIP Many of Painter's brushes are set up to respond to stylus pressure to vary the size of the stroke, its opacity (or covering power), and its reaction to paper grain. Mouse users can achieve similar results by making manual adjustments on the Controls | Brush Palette, or by changing settings in the Advanced Controls | Sliders Palette.

Changing Brush Size

The brushes listed below are preset to change size based on the pressure applied by the stylus.

Brushes: Big Loaded Oils, Big Wet Oils, Brushy, Coarse Hairs, Cover Brush, Fine Brush, Hairy Brush, Loaded Oils, Oil Paint, Sable Chisel Tip Water, Small Loaded Oils, Ultrafine Wash Brush

Cloners: Hairy Cloner

Masking Brushes: Masking Pen

Pen: Calligraphy, Scratchboard Rake, Scratchboard Tool, Smooth Ink Pen

Water Colors: Diffuse Water, Large Simple Water, Large Water, Pure Water Brush, Simple Water, Water Brush Stroke

TIP
There is a quick way to resize a brush without opening the Brush Control | Size Palette. While using a brush, press the Ctrl-Alt keys in Windows, or the Cmd-Option keys in Mac. A dropper symbol will appear on your document. While pressing the keys and mouse or cursor, drag the dropper symbol and watch the size of the circle that follows the cursor. Release the mouse or stylus and the keys when the size of the circle indicates the width of the brush stroke you want.

There are two other ways that stroke size can be adjusted. The first way to adjust the size of the stroke is to open the Brush Controls | Size Palette. This palette is shown in Figure 4.8.

Figure 4.8.
Brush size can be
changed by using the
Brush Controls | Size
Palette.

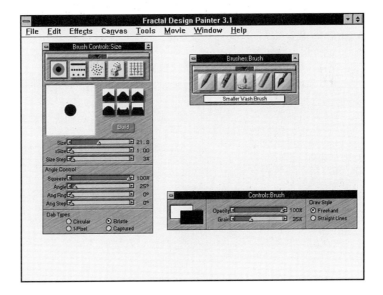

To change the size of a brush, do the following:

1. Select the brush you wish to alter. In the example, I selected the Smaller Wash Brush variant of the Brush tool.

2. Move the size slider in the Brush Controls | Size Palette (located just beneath the sample window) until the brush sample in the window appears to be the desired brush size. Moving the slider toward the left decreases the brush size. Moving the slider to the right increases the brush size.

3. Click the Build button, or use the key combination Ctrl-B in Windows or Cmd-B in Mac. You can now paint with the adjusted brush. Note that this step may not be necessary for some brushes. If it is necessary to build the brush, the Build button will be raised. If the brush does not require building, the button will be disabled.

TIP If you find yourself repeatedly changing the size of the same brush, you can save the adjusted brush to a library by using either the Save Variant or Save Built Variant command in the Tools | Brushes menu. The Save Variant command will save your revised brush as a new brush variant, and the Save Built Variant will write over the previous version of the brush you revised.

Another way for mouse users to vary the size of the brush is to change the setting in the Advanced Controls | Sliders Palette to vary size based on either the direction you drag the mouse or the velocity at which you drag the mouse. Figure 4.9 shows the Advanced Controls | Sliders Palette and the settings for the Smaller Wash Brush that were used in our previous example.

Figure 4.9.
Stroke size can also be
adjusted to respond to
Direction or Velocity in
the Advanced Controls
| Sliders Palette.

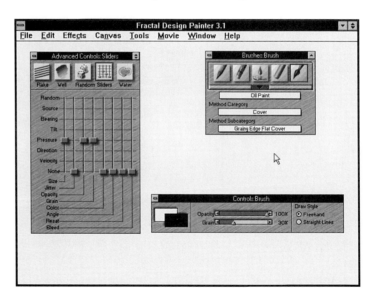

In the Sliders Palette, you will see a number of sliders that correspond to different properties of a brush stroke. For purposes of this example, notice that the slider corresponding to Size is the first of eight sliders. Currently the slider bar is placed in the category of Pressure, which is ineffective when using a mouse. The slider can be moved down one notch, which will base the stroke on the direction you drag the mouse, or down two notches, which will base the stroke on the speed at which you drag the mouse. You'll have to experiment to see which setting works best for you—but you'll soon find that changing the settings will add a little more character to your brush strokes automatically while you paint. Also, as the preceding Painter tip points out, you might want to save the new variation of the brush so you can easily recall it later.

Opacity and Grain

The brush I have chosen also has two more categories set to respond to stylus pressure—opacity, discussed here, and grain, which will follow. Opacity can best be described as the cover power of a brush. The Grain setting represents how the brush will interact with paper grain.

Figure 4.9 also shows the Controls | Brush Palette at the lower-right side of the screen. Notice here that there are sliders to adjust the opacity and grain of the brush. Mouse users can vary these sliders to achieve similar results to those of a stylus. If the values are set high for opacity, the stroke will cover more. Conversely, the lower the opacity setting, the lighter the stroke will be. If desired, the Opacity slider in the Advanced Controls | Sliders can also be set to respond to velocity or direction.

Following is a list of brushes that have their Opacity sliders set to respond to pressure applied with the stylus.

> **Burn**
>
> **Dodge**
>
> **Airbrushes:** All
>
> **Brushes:** Big Loaded Oils, Big Wet Oils, Camel Hair, Coarse Hairs, Cover Brush, Fine Brush, Hairy Brush, Oil Paint, Small Loaded Oils, Smaller Wash Brush, Ultrafine Wash Brush
>
> **Chalks:** All
>
> **Charcoals:** All
>
> **Cloners:** Chalk Cloner, Hairy Cloner, Pencil Sketch Cloner
>
> **Crayons:** All
>
> **Erasers:** Fat Bleach, Fat Darkener, Fat Eraser, Medium Bleach, Medium Darkener, Medium Eraser, Small Bleach, Small Darkener, Small Eraser, Ultrafine Bleach, Ultrafine Darkener, Ultrafine Eraser
>
> **Felt Pens:** All
>
> **Liquid:** Coarse Distorto, Coarse Smeary Bristles, Coarse Smeary Mover, Distorto, Smeary Bristles, Smeary Mover, Thick Oil, Total Oil Brush
>
> **Masking:** Masking Chalk
>
> **Pens:** Scratchboard Rake

Pencils: 2B Pencil, 500 lb. Pencil, Sharp Pencil, Single Pixel Scribbler, Thick and Thin Pencils

Water Color: Broad Water Brush, Diffuse Water, Large Water, Simple Water, Spatter Water, Wet Eraser

Water: All except Single Pixel Water and Water Spray

Following is a list of brushes that have their Grain slider set to respond to stylus pressure. When using the Controls | Brush Palette, a high setting for grain will allow less of the paper grain to show through. A low grain setting will allow more of the paper to show through the stroke. The grain slider in the Advanced Controls | Sliders Palette can also be set to respond to velocity or direction.

Airbrushes: Single Pixel Airbrush, Spatter Airbrush

Brushes: Big Rough Out, Hairy Brush, Huge Rough Out, Oil Paint, Penetration, Rough Out, Smaller Wash Brush, Ultrafine Wash Brush

Chalks: All

Charcoals: All

Cloners: Chalk Cloner, Hairy Cloner, Pencil Sketch Cloner, Soft Cloner

Crayons: All

Erasers: Flat Eraser, Single Pixel Bleach

Liquids: Coarse Distorto, Coarse Smeary Bristles, Coarse Smeary Mover, Smeary Bristles, Smeary Mover, Thick Oil, Total Oil Brush

Masking Pens: Big Masking Pen, Masking Airbrush, Masking Chalk

Pens: Pen and Ink, Scratchboard Rake, Small Pen and Ink, Smooth Ink Pen

Pencils: All

Water Colors: Large Simple Water, Large Water, Simple Water, Spatter Water, Wet Eraser

Water: All except Single Pixel Water and Water Spray

Summary

You now know how to install Painter and get it up and running. You have a good overview of what the commands and palettes do. And now, you know how to customize Painter's performance and interface. Additionally, you know how to change the size, grain, and opacity of brushes.

I think it's about time we started drawing and painting—don't you?

Elementary Art Revisited

5

Crayons Project

One of the first things you probably learned to draw with as a child was a crayon. If you were lucky, you had a set of crayons that included at least 100 different colors. But the problem was that you had favorite colors that you used all the time, and others that went untouched. As a result, you would have to buy another set to get more of the colors you liked—and a growing box filled with the colors you didn't like or use.

If you had a crayon set that included each of the 16.7 million colors that Painter can use, you would need a box about 100 miles long to fit all the crayons side by side. The beauty of Painter's crayons is that they don't break, and they never are used up. Painter's crayons work and look just like their real-life counterparts—only better. The colors build up on each other, allowing for shading. They react to the texture of the paper on which they are applied. And they get lighter or darker depending on how hard you press on your stylus.

Just Like a Coloring Book

Because crayons are typically associated with children's coloring books, I've set up this first project as exactly that. If you've never worked with a paint package before, this project will let you ease in to the world of digital art by just playing. Don't worry about this project looking like a masterpiece. Its main focus is to teach you some of the basic skills needed to work in Painter.

In addition to showing you Painter's two crayon variants, this project goes a bit beyond using the crayons to create a Painter picture. Although you will learn some of the tricks to use while working with crayons, you will also learn some of the basics about using masks, selections, and selection lists. This chapter also discusses filling areas with solid colors and gradients.

The Crayons and Their Variants

Painter's Crayons produce semi-antialiased strokes that react to the grain of the paper. Semi-antialiased strokes are those that have a combination of hard and soft edges, blending partially into the colors beneath the strokes.

The crayons are based on a *buildup method,* which means that a color gets darker as you layer it. Repeating strokes one over another will eventually turn an area black. This can produce some nice shading effects. Of the two crayon variants, the Waxy Crayon produces softer strokes and melts a bit of the underlying color in with it. This makes the Waxy Crayon a nice choice for shading areas.

TIP If you find that the strokes turn black too quickly, you can move the Opacity slider in the Controls | Brush Palette toward the left. This causes the strokes to stay lighter longer. Or, if you find that you've built up your colors too dark and want to apply a lighter color over an area, you can use one of following two procedures.

Select a tool that uses one of the Cover methods. A Chalk or Charcoal variant will serve well for this purpose. You can use a Cover method brush to paint over the dark areas with a lighter color.

Another way to apply a lighter color to an area is to use the Canvas | Set Paper Color command to select the color that you want to lighten to. Then you can use one of the Eraser variants, such as the Ultrafine Eraser, to erase the dark area to the lighter paper color.

Because Painter's crayons are also made using one of the Grainy methods, you can choose different paper textures to produce different effects. Applying light pressure on the stylus will reveal more of the paper grain, and more pressure will increase the coverage of the paper grain. Mouse users can simulate this effect by adjusting the Grain slider in the Controls | Brush Palette. Moving the Grain slider to the left enables more paper grain to show through the strokes; moving the slider toward the right makes the strokes darker and denser. Mouse users also can alter the reaction to paper grain by choosing to vary Grain response with Direction or Velocity in the Advanced Controls | Sliders Palette. For further information on how to make these adjustments, you can refer to the interactive reference included on the CD with this book or to Chapter 14, "Working with the Brush Tools."

Crayons also get lighter or darker depending on stylus pressure. Lighter pressure produces lighter strokes, and heavier pressure creates darker strokes. Mouse users can simulate this effect by adjusting the Opacity slider in the Controls | Brush Palette, or by basing Opacity on Direction or Velocity in the Sliders Palette.

Default Crayon

Painter's Default crayon variant has the appearance of traditional crayons. Crayon strokes are semi-antialiased and react to paper grain. The strokes of crayons get darker as you layer them, just as with real crayons. This enables you to shade by building up strokes of the same color over previous ones. If the strokes turn dark too quickly, you can reduce the Opacity setting on the Controls | Brush Palette.

TIP To get a lighter stroke over an area that has already been darkened with crayons, you can erase the area with an eraser or pick a tool that has a cover method to lighten the area.

Mouse users can adjust the Opacity and Grain sliders on the Controls | Brush Palette. Or, set the Opacity and Grain settings in the Advanced Controls | Sliders Palette to respond to Velocity or Direction.

Waxy Crayons

The Waxy Crayon smears underlying color in with the current color. These crayons are similar in appearance to traditional crayons, but with a more waxy appearance. Its strokes are semi-antialiased and react to paper grain. The strokes get darker as you layer them, just as with real crayons. This lets you shade by building up strokes of the same color over previous ones. If the strokes turn dark too quickly, you can reduce the Opacity setting on the Controls | Brush Palette.

Drawing with the Crayons

Drawing with Painter's crayons is similar to drawing with traditional crayons. To draw with the crayons:

1. Position the mouse or stylus where you want the stroke to begin.

2. Push down on the stylus or click the mouse, and drag to produce short or long strokes.

3. Let up on the stylus or release the mouse when the stroke is complete.

The Crayons Project

As mentioned, the first project is set up like a page from a coloring book. Included on the CD is a file called STRAWBER.PCX (for Windows users) or Strawberry Pict (for Mac users). This file is a line-art drawing that was prepared in another paint program. You're going to color some areas with the crayons and fill other areas with a couple of different gradients.

Preparing for the Project

If you don't want to make changes to your existing brushes, color sets, and art materials, you can tell Painter to use other sets as defaults. You can make copies of Painter's default libraries and rename them for use within this book. Instructions for this follow.

Step 5.1—Changing Painter's Default Libraries

These instructions should be completed if you want to replace your own default libraries with copies of Painter's default libraries.

As discussed in the previous chapter, Painter's General Preferences can be revised by using the Edit | Preferences | General command. After this command is chosen, the General Preferences dialog box, shown in Figure 5.1, appears. This dialog box enables you to customize items such as cursor appearance, libraries, and some items that may enhance the performance of Painter on your system.

On the upper-right quadrant of the General Preferences dialog box is a list of five different libraries that you can elect to use as default. As you work with Painter, you'll find that you will begin to develop your own papers, brushes, and other items that you use most frequently. Before you identify the custom libraries that you want to use as default, the libraries have to be created using the appropriate Mover.

*Figure 5.1.
Painter's General
Preferences dialog
box enables you to
set several options,
including default
libraries.*

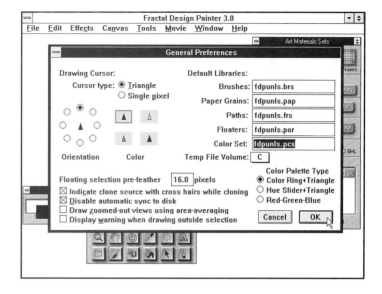

NOTE Note that the files you specify in the General Preferences dialog box
must be resident in the directory that Painter is installed to. If you used the
default settings when installing Painter, these files are found in the
C:\PAINTER3 directory.

To change your default libraries to copies of the default libraries, follow these
steps:

1. Windows users can use the Windows File Manager or another file management program to make copies of Painter's default files, and rename them
   appropriately. Similarly, Mac users can create copies of Painter's default
   libraries and rename them. Table 5.1 shows some examples for each of the
   default libraries that appear in the General Preferences dialog box.

2. Start Painter by clicking the program icon.

3. Choose Edit | Preferences | General. The General Preferences dialog box
   appears.

4. In the Default Libraries section, highlight the existing name in the appropriate area. For example, to specify a new brush library, Windows users
   highlight the PAINTER.BRS name, and Mac users highlight the Painter
   Brushes filename.

5. Type in the name of the library you want to use as the custom library.
   Windows users should include the appropriate file extension. For example,
   FDPUNLS.BRS can be entered in the Windows version, and Painter

Brushes can be entered in the Mac version. This new file will be loaded as the default brush library the next time you start Painter. Use names similar to those outlined in Table 5.1 to replace the default libraries if you want.

6. Click OK or press Enter (Windows) or Return (Mac) when you are done.

Table 5.1. Selecting New Libraries for your Default Libraries.

Library Type	Default	Change To
Default Brush Library (Win)	PAINTER.BRS	FDPUNLS.BRS
Default Brush Library (Mac)	Painter Brushes	Unleashed Brushes
Default Paper Grain Library (Win)	PAINTER.PAP	FDPUNLS.PAP
Default Paper Grain Library (Mac)	Paper Textures	Unleashed Papers
Default Path Library (Win)	PAINTER.FRS	FDPUNLS.FRS
Default Path Library (Mac)	Painter Paths	Unleashed Paths
Default Floaters Library (Win)	PAINTER.POR	FDPUNLS.POR
Default Floaters Library (Mac)	Painter Portfolio	Unleashed Portfolio
Default Color Set (Win)	PAINTER.PCS	FDPUNLS.PCS
Default Color Set (Mac)	Painter Colors	Unleashed Colors

Step 5.2—Opening the Strawberries and Cream Project File

To start the project, open the STRAWBER.PCX or Strawberry Pict file. The image is a black-and-white line art "coloring book" type image of a container of strawberries and a creamer.

To open the file:

1. Choose File | Open. The Select Image dialog box will appear in the Windows version. The Open dialog box will appear in the Mac version.

PAINTER SHORTCUT

You also can open an image by using the quick-key combination of Ctrl-O in Windows (the Control key and the letter O pressed simultaneously) or Cmd-O in Mac (the Command key and the O key pressed simultaneously).

2. From the Select Image dialog box, scroll to the directory on the CD that contains the project file. Look for the filename STRAWBER.PCX (Windows users) or Strawberry Pict (Mac users).

3. To open the file, you can do one of three things. You can highlight the filename and press Enter (Windows) or Return (Mac), double-click the filename, or highlight the filename and click Open. Your screen should now look like the one shown in Figure 5.2.

Figure 5.2.
The STRAWBER.PCX (Windows) or Strawberry Pict (Mac) file will start you off in learning to use Painter's crayons.

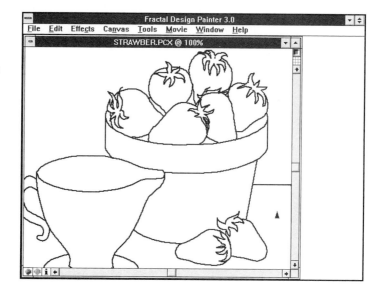

The Magnifier Tool

The Magnifier tool zooms in and out of the image at various zoom levels. Figure 5.3 shows the location of the Magnifier tool on the Tools palette.

You'll use the Magnifier tool to zoom out and reduce the size of the image for the first few step of your project. But before using the tool, take a look at the basic steps of using the Magnifier tool:

1. From the Tools Palette, choose the Magnifier tool. The cursor will change to a magnifier. If the Controls | Magnifier Palette does not appear, choose the Window | Controls command, or use the quick-key combination of Ctrl-6 (Windows) or Cmd-6 (Mac).

2. Set the Zoom Level amount on the Controls | Magnifier Palette. The Zoom Level amount is the amount you would like to zoom in or out of the image with each click of the Magnifier tool.

3. Click the image with the Magnifier tool to zoom in. There will be a plus sign (+) inside the magnifier when a click zooms in.

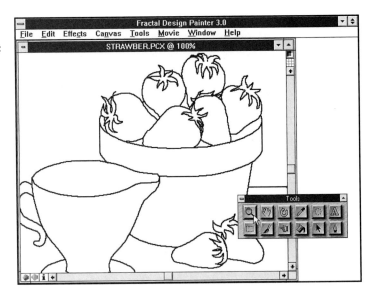

*Figure 5.3.
The Magnifier tool is
used to zoom in and out
of images.*

TIP   Simultaneously pressing the Ctrl and spacebar keys in Windows or the Cmd and spacebar keys in Mac while any other tool is selected enables you to zoom in closer to an image (enlarge its size in the window) with each click of the mouse or stylus.

If you want to zoom out, simultaneously press the Ctrl and Alt keys in the Windows version or the Option key in Mac while clicking the mouse or stylus. A minus sign (-) appears inside the Magnifier tool in this mode.

Simultaneously pressing the Ctrl, Alt, and spacebar keys in Windows or the Option-Cmd-spacebar keys in Mac while any other tool is selected enables you to zoom out farther from an image (reduce its size in the window) with each click of the mouse or stylus.

5. To zoom in on a specific area with the Magnifier tool selected, draw a square or rectangle around the area you want to zoom into. The selected area fills the active document window at the appropriate zoom level.

While you are using the Magnifier, the Controls | Magnifier Palette also enables you to adjust the zoom level by clicking in the box displaying the current zoom level. You can choose to display the image at any one of the percentage levels indicated in the drop-down box. Or you can set a value that the image will be enlarged or reduced by each time the Magnifier tool is clicked. The zoom percent levels are as follows: 8.3, 10, 12.5, 16.7, 20, 25, 33, 50, 100, 200, 300, 400, 500, 600, 800, 1000, and 1200.

NOTE The zoom level also can be adjusted from the Controls | Grabber Palette and the Controls | Rotate Page Palette when you use either the Grabber or the Rotate Page tools.

Step 5.3—Using the Magnifier Tool in Your Project

Now that you know the basics of using the magnifier and the Controls | Magnifier Palette, put it to use in your drawing:

1. Open the Tools Palette by choosing the Window | Tools command. You also can open the Tools Palette by using the quick-key combination of Ctrl-1 (Windows) or Cmd-1 (Mac).

2. Open the Controls Palette by choosing the Window | Controls command, or by using the quick-key combination of Ctrl-6 (Windows) or Cmd-6 (Mac).

3. Select the Magnifier from the Tools Palette (the first symbol on the top row).

4. From the Controls | Magnifier Palette, click the drop-down box that shows the current zoom level, and—keeping the mouse or stylus depressed—drag to the 50% choice and release the mouse or stylus. Your screen should now look similar to that shown in Figure 5.4.

Figure 5.4.
The Magnifier tool is used to reduce the size of your image down to 50%.

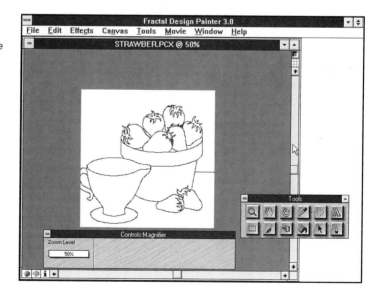

Step 5.4—Moving the Image with the Grabber

The Grabber tool enables you to move the image within the current active document window. You'll move your image to the upper-left corner of the document window to allow space for the brushes and art materials.

To move the image with the Grabber tool, do the following:

1. Click the Grabber icon (the hand) in the Tools palette. The Controls palette turns into the Controls | Grabber Palette.

2. Move the cursor into the image. It will change into the shape of a hand. Click and hold the mouse button or stylus while dragging the image in the window. Move it to the upper-left corner of the window.

3. Release the mouse or stylus to stop moving the image. Your screen should now look like that in Figure 5.5.

PAINTER SHORTCUT

When another tool is active, the cursor will change into a Grabber as long as the spacebar is held down. This is the same in both Windows and Mac versions.

Figure 5.5.
Using the Grabber, move the image to the upper-left corner of the document window.

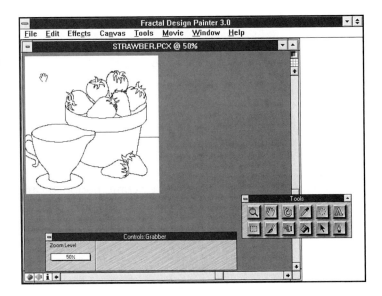

While the Grabber is selected, the Controls | Grabber Palette enables you to change the zoom level by clicking in the box that displays the current zoom level. You can see the Controls | Grabber Palette in Figure 5.5.

Step 5.5—Choosing a Different Color Set

Although you chose a default color set when setting some of the General Preferences earlier in this chapter, a special color set was made to create this image.

Before you begin painting with traditional media, you place the colors you are going to work with on a palette. In a way, a color set is Painter's palette. With color sets, you can organize your colors into smaller groups—or save colors that look good together. Alternate color sets are chosen when you click the Sets icon in the Art Materials Palette. This reveals the Sets Palette, shown in Figure 5.6.

Figure 5.6.
The Sets Palette
enables you to load,
save, and create color
sets of your own.

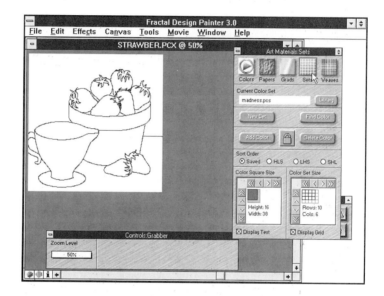

To select the special color set, perform the following steps:

1. Open the Art Materials Palette by choosing the Window | Art Materials command, or with the quick-key combination of Ctrl-3 for Windows or Cmd-3 for Mac.

2. Select the Sets icon from the Art Materials Palette. The Sets Palette appears.

3. Click the Library button (just beneath the five icons on the drawer front). The Select Color Set dialog box appears for Windows users. This dialog box is shown in Figure 5.7. For Mac users, the file directory dialog box appears.

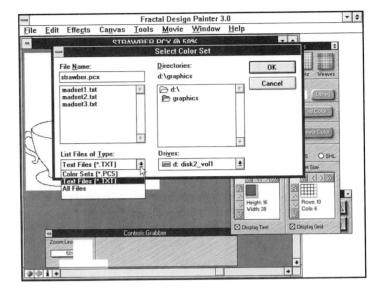

Figure 5.7.
The Select Color Set
dialog box, accessed
from the Art Materials
| Sets Palette, enables
you to load custom
color sets.

4. In the dialog box, choose the color set file you want to load. Windows users choose files with a .TXT extension to find custom color sets. Color sets that you create are saved to an editable text file.

5. Select the drive and directory on the CD that the UNLSET2.TXT file resides in. Highlight the filename and click OK or press Enter. The color set will appear on your screen as shown in Figure 5.8.

Figure 5.8.
The color set chosen
from the Select Color
Set dialog box will
appear on the screen.

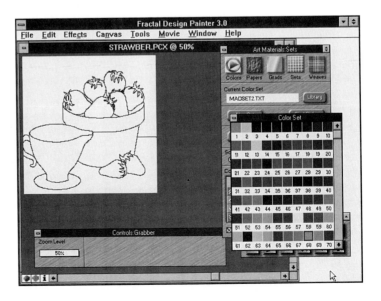

NOTE Though a color set is not always visible on the screen, it lies waiting in the background until you choose to display it. Do notice, though, that the name of the color set you just chose also appears beside the Library button in the Sets Palette. To show or hide the currently active color set, choose the Window | Color Set command or use the quick-key combination of Ctrl-8 (Windows) or Cmd-8 (Mac).

Step 5.6—Choosing a Gradation Library

Gradations, Grads for short, are stored in libraries—either Painter's default library or those that you create yourself with the Gradation Mover. For this project, I've created a couple of custom gradients. Now you will load the library that they are contained in.

To open a gradation library, perform the following steps:

1. From the Art Materials Palette, which should still be open on your screen, click the Grads icon to access the Grads Palette.

2. You will notice slots on the drawer front to place five gradations that you can access quickly while creating a document. Beneath these five icons is a bar with a downward arrow in its center. Click this bar, the handle of the drawer, to open the Grads Palette and reveal its contents. Your screen should look similar to that shown in Figure 5.9.

Figure 5.9.
The inside of the
Grads Palette contains
several gradations to
choose from and a
Library button to select
even more.

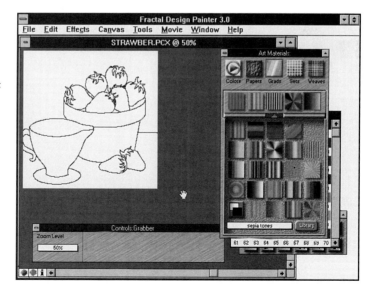

3. At the bottom of the inside of the drawer, a drop-down box shows the name of the currently selected gradient. Next to this box is a Library button. Click the button and the Open Gradation Library File dialog box, shown in Figure 5.10, will appear.

Figure 5.10.
The Open Gradation Library File dialog box enables you to select a different library of gradations.

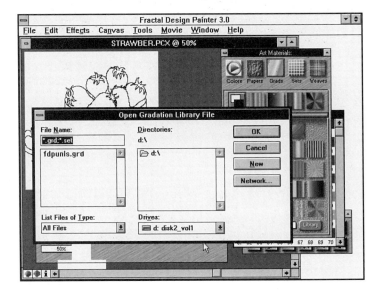

4. Scroll to the directory in which your gradation library is located. In the Windows version, Gradation libraries are saved with a .GRD extension.

5. Double-click or highlight the FDPUNLS.GRD filename (Windows) or Chapter 5 Gradations file (Mac), and click Open (or press the Enter key in Windows or the Return key in Mac). The new selection of gradations will appear inside the drawer.

Step 5.7—Choosing Gradations

You'll want to use a couple of the gradations in this library. The first one, used in a later step, is Cherry Wood. You can select a gradation by clicking one of the icons or by clicking the name of the gradient.

To select a gradation visually, perform the following steps:

1. From the Art Materials Palette, click the Grads icon to access the Grads Palette.

2. If the gradation you want to use is not displayed on the drawer front, click the handle of the Grads Palette to open its drawer. You can place up to five gradations in the drawer front.

3. Click the icon of the gradation you want to use. It will appear on the drawer front and will become the currently active gradation.

To select a gradation by name, perform the following steps:

1. From the Art Materials Palette, click the Grads icon to access the Grads Palette.

2. Click the handle of the Grads Palette to open its drawer.

3. At the bottom of the Grads Palette to the left of the Library button is a box that displays the name of the currently selected gradient. If you click and hold on this box, a drop-down list will appear. Slide your mouse or stylus down until the name you want to choose is highlighted, and then release the mouse or stylus. The selected gradient will appear on the drawer front and in the name box. It will become the currently active gradation.

Using this last method, select the Cherry Wood gradation. Your screen should look similar to Figure 5.11.

Figure 5.11.
Select the Cherry Wood gradation from the new Gradation Library.

Before You Begin...

Before you start coloring, I'd like to make a couple of general comments. These comments involve correcting errors and saving the document periodically so that you don't lose anything you like.

Undoing Mistakes

Painter is a forgiving program. If you draw something you don't like, you can undo it and try again. In Painter 3.0, the Undo command undoes your most recent change or brush stroke. This command entry toggles between three states:

- Undo undoes the last step that you performed on your document.

- Can't Undo shows in the display if there is no action to undo, or if the action cannot be reverted. In general, path moves or edits cannot be undone.

- Redo undoes the undo; that is, if you selected Undo and changed your mind before implementing another command, you can reapply the last action again to the document.

To use the Undo command in Painter 3.0, you must use it directly after the action that you want to undo. Simply choose Edit | Undo, or use the quick-key combination of Ctrl-Z in Windows or Cmd-Z in Mac. Your last action will be removed from the screen.

In Painter 3.1, you can use Edit | Undo (Ctrl-Z in Windows or Cmd-Z in Mac) to undo multiple steps in succession. For example, if you want to undo the last five steps performed on a document, you choose the Undo command five times in a row. The number of levels of Undo is limited by the amount set with the Edit | Preferences | Undo command, and the total number of levels can be divided between multiple opened documents.

Painter 3.1 also includes a multiple redo command. Choose Edit | Redo (Ctrl-Y in Windows or Cmd-Y in Mac) to redo undone steps. Like the multiple Undo command, you can redo multiple steps across one or more opened documents. The Redo command uses the same limit set with the Edit | Preferences | Undo command.

Saving a Document Under a Different Name or Format

Your project document is currently loaded as a .PCX or Pict format document. If you choose the File | Save command, it will save this drawing in the same format. You might want to save it in Painter's .RIF format if you can't complete the tutorial in one session.

What advantages does Painter's .RIF format offer? If the document is saved in any other format, any masking, floaters, or selections are combined with the background layer and aren't available to use and manipulate anymore when you reopen the document. Painter's native format saves the document with all these items intact, so that you can begin your document exactly where you left off. I think it's a good idea to save the document in the .RIF format before beginning.

The File | Save As command saves the current document to your hard disk under a different filename or file format. It also can be used to save your document for the first time. A document can be saved in one of the following formats: Painter's Raster Image File format (.RIF), Aldus Tagged Image File format (.TIF), Mac PICT format (.PCT), Adobe Photoshop format (.PSD), Windows

Bitmap (.BMP), ZSoft PC Paintbrush (.PCX), Encapsulated PostScript (.EPS), and TrueVision Targa (.TGA).

To save the project document into the .RIF format, do the following:

1. Choose File | Save As. In the Windows version, the Save Image As dialog box, shown in Figure 5.12, appears.

Figure 5.12.
The Save Image As
dialog box enables you
to save a document
under a different name
or file format.

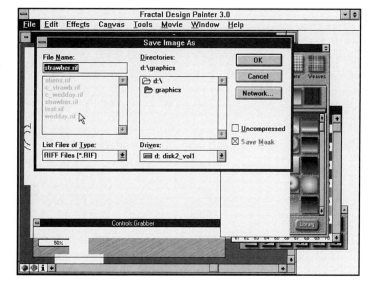

2. In the dialog box, choose the directory into which you want to save your file.
3. Under the List Files of Type heading (Windows) or Type heading (Mac), choose to save the document in the .RIF format.
4. Type the name of the document in the File Name box. In the Windows version, the name defaults to the STRAWBER.RIF if you don't type anything in.
5. Click OK. The document is saved under the name you type, in the RIF format.

Saving Your Document

After you've saved your document in the .RIF format, you can use the File | Save command or the quick-key combination of Ctrl-S (Windows) or Cmd-S (Mac) to periodically update your changes to the hard disk.

> *TIP* It is a wise practice to save documents frequently, especially before attempting effects and procedures for the first time. Before you experiment with a new feature or effect, save the document. This way, you can undo the changes if they don't turn out as you expected.

Let's Start Working!

Now that all of your materials are selected, you can start working on your image. First, you're going to learn how to mask some of the areas to protect or select them to perform certain operations. Then, you'll start coloring with the crayons to finish the project. Ready?

Creating and Filling Mask Selections

If you look at the project drawing, you will see that it is made up of three basic areas—the wall, the table, and the items in the foreground. The wall and the table areas are fairly large, and it would be much easier to fill these areas rather than hand-color them.

In Painter, you can select areas of an image to apply effects or procedures to. These selections, or *paths*, are basically outlines that cut out holes in Painter's *mask layer*, causing portions to become unmasked.

What does Painter's mask layer do? Consider this: When you are painting the walls in your house, you apply masking tape to the areas on the wood trim and windows. Airbrush artists apply masks with paper or tape to accomplish the same task. Other types of masks are made with rubber cement. In all these cases, the purpose of the mask is to protect some areas from receiving the paint.

Painter's masks do exactly the same thing. However, after creating a selection you can mask everything inside the area you select, or mask everything outside the area you select. The mask layer is an area that floats above the background image and is invisible unless you display it using one of the Mask Visibility buttons (discussed later). Masks also can be used to create selections, which will also be discussed.

Step 5.8—Using the Paint Bucket to Fill Areas

There are a number of ways to create selections in Painter: You can draw outlines manually or use some of Painter's selection tools from the Tools Palette. Or you can create a mask selection, which you can try here.

The .PCX or Pict file that you loaded for your project contains only two colors: black and white. You'll add a couple of new colors to fill areas and then mask those areas to create selections.

The Paint Bucket fills solid areas of an image, or a selected area, with the current color, a clone source, a gradation, or a weaving. Areas also can be filled by using the Effects | Fill command, but this command is used when you want to fill either the entire image or an area that has already been selected.

Here's how to fill the wall area with a different color:

1. From the project's color set, scroll to the bottom of the color set, and click Deep Blue (color #220). You can select any color that does not already appear in the image for this step—so this color was chosen at random.

2. Choose the Paint Bucket from the Tools Palette (fourth symbol in the bottom row). The Controls | Paint Bucket Palette will appear.

NOTE Remember that if the color set does not appear, it is because you have it hidden. Use the Ctrl-8 (Windows) or Cmd-8 (Mac) command to redisplay it.

3. In the Controls | Paint Bucket Palette, click the radio button beside Image under the What to Fill category.

4. Select, under Fill With, to fill the item with the Current Color. The preview square in the Controls | Paint Bucket Palette will change to reflect the current color.

5. Click anywhere in the area of the wall with the Paint Bucket, as shown in Figure 5.13.

Figure 5.13.
Click anywhere inside the wall area with the Paint Bucket.

Paint Bucket —

The area will be filled until it meets a color other than the white color you clicked with the Paint Bucket. In this case, the fill will stop when it meets the black lines. Your screen should look similar to that shown in Figure 5.14. Now, you can mask this area.

Figure 5.14.
The wall area will
be filled with the
chosen color.

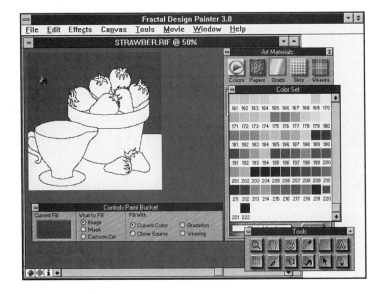

Step 5.9—Masking the Currently Selected Color

You can use the Auto Mask command to mask the color you just applied to the image. The Auto Mask command will mask an area in one of several different manners. Use the Current Color option to generate the mask.

To mask the color in the wall area:

1. Verify that the color used in the wall is still your current color. It should be surrounded by an outline in the active color set.
2. Choose Edit | Mask | Auto Mask. This command is shown in Figure 5.15.
3. The Auto Mask dialog box appears. This dialog box is shown in Figure 5.16. Inside the Auto Mask dialog box is a drop-down menu that contains several options. Choose Current Color, which will create a mask that protects the currently selected color.
4. After selecting the previous options, click OK or press Enter (Windows) or Return (Mac) to generate the mask.

Figure 5.15.
The Auto Mask command lets you generate a mask based on the currently selected color, among other options.

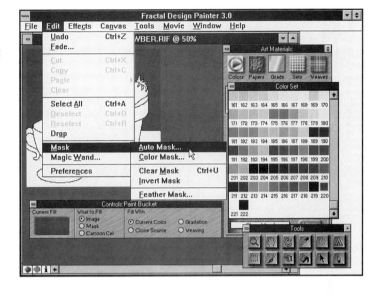

Figure 5.16.
To generate the mask, select the Current Color option.

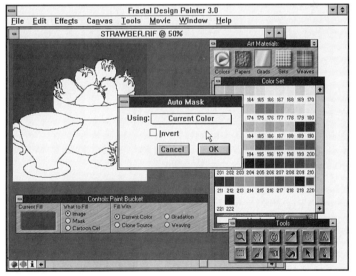

TIP   You can also generate a mask for the wall area if you use the Edit | Mask | Color Mask command. After you choose this command, the Color Mask dialog box appears. A prompt in the dialog box instructs you to click inside your image to specify the center color for the mask. Click the wall area you just filled.

Notice in the preview window of the Color Mask dialog box that the white areas in your document are partially masked. To unmask those areas, move the V Extents slider toward the left (near 0 or 1%). Click OK to generate the mask.

Step 5.10—Viewing the Mask

You might ask, "How do I know that the mask is there?"

The Path Adjuster is used to activate, move, or manipulate selections. Choose the Path Adjuster tool now to prepare for the next step. The Path Adjuster tool is the fifth symbol (the arrow) on the bottom row of the Tools Palette. When you choose the Path Adjuster tool, the area you just masked becomes surrounded with a green-and-white selection marquee.

> **NOTE** A selection marquee, otherwise known as *marching ants*, appears around an area when it is selected for an action. There are three types of selection marquees, each defined by different colors.
>
> - A black-and-white marquee defines an outline selection. These types of selections are typically created using Painter's selection tools.
> - A red-and-white marquee defines a negative outline selection. They are typically created using Painter's selection tools, but are used to "cut out" areas of outline selections.
> - A green-and-white marquee defines a selection that was created from a mask.

When the Path Adjuster tool is selected, the Controls | Path Adjuster Palette appears. This control palette enables you to set options to view and manipulate the mask. At the left side of this palette are six icons placed in two rows. These icons also appear in the Objects | Path List Palette, discussed later, and are also selectable by clicking the icons appearing in the scrollbar at the lower-left corner of the document window.

The top row of buttons adjacent to the pencil symbol in the Path Adjuster Palette are the Drawing Visibility buttons. These buttons control how the mask will be applied to your image.

Mask Off: The first button turns the mask off, and drawing or painting on the image can be done on the entire image in the usual manner.

Masked Inside: The second button masks the inside of the selection. Painting is allowed on the outside of the selection only, with this button enabled.

Masked Outside: The third button masks the outside of the selection, allowing painting on the inside of the selection.

The bottom row of buttons, those adjacent to the eye symbol, are the Mask Visibility buttons. These buttons enable you to show or hide the mask from view.

Hide Mask: With the first button enabled, you will not be able to see the mask, but it will be operable as dictated by the setting of the Drawing Visibility buttons.

Red Mask: Choosing the second button shows the masked areas in red and displays the areas you can paint in their normal colors.

Marqueed Mask: The third button displays the masked areas surrounded by a selection marquee.

You can view the mask you just created if you turn on the middle Mask Visibility button, which displays the masked area in red. To see the mask, perform the following steps:

1. In the top row of icons, click the center Drawing Visibility button to mask the inside of the selected area.

2. In the bottom row of icons, click the center Mask Visibility button to display the mask in red. The masked area of the wall then changes from blue to red on your screen. This is shown in Figure 5.17.

Figure 5.17.
Select the center Drawing Visibility and Mask Visibility buttons to display the masked area in red.

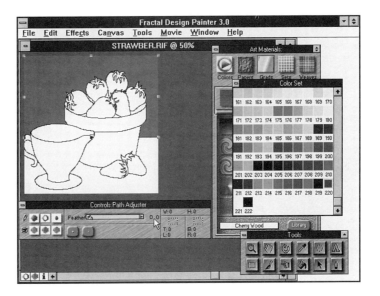

Step 5.11—Converting the Mask to a Selection

The Objects | Path List Palette command enables you to name selections and control which multiple selections are active or inactive. Because you will have two selections in your document (the next one is covered in the following steps), this palette lets you choose which selection you want to operate with.

Though the mask you just generated is currently surrounded by a selection marquee, it will be replaced when you generate the mask for the table area. You have to convert the wall area's mask selection to an outline selection in order to retain the area it defines.

Viewing the masked area first in red, like you already have, confirms that you have the right area chosen for conversion into a selection.

NOTE As you become more accomplished with Painter, you probably won't need to view the mask in red first. The Drawing Visibility and Mask Visibility buttons in the lower-left corner of the document window will become familiar enough to use as indication.

Now, you're going to convert this area to a selection:

1. Open Objects | Path List Palette. To do so, choose the Window | Objects command or use the quick-key combination Ctrl-5 in Windows or Cmd-5 in Mac. Then, click the P.List icon (the second icon in the top section of the Objects Palette).

2. Choose the Tools | Selections | Convert to Selection command. This changes the masked area into an outline selection that can be manipulated using the Path List Palette. Notice now that the marquee selection surrounding the wall is a black-and-white marquee. It is now an outline selection.

TIP If you work with multiple selections in a document, it is rather difficult to remember what areas the Mask Groups or outline selections identify. You can rename them to something more descriptive.

3. Double-click the Mask Group 1 name in the Path List Palette. The Path Attributes dialog box appears. Highlight the current name if it is not highlighted and then retype a name that describes the current Mask Group. In this case, type in the word Wall. Then, click OK or press Enter (Windows) or Return (Mac). The name of the selection will be updated in the Path List. (See Figure 5.18.)

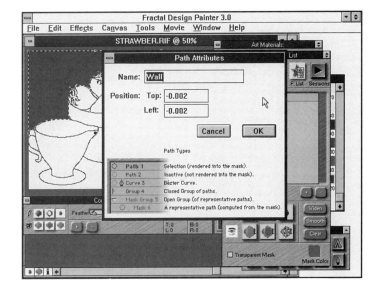

Figure 5.18.
Rename the selection
group Wall to identify
it more easily.

Step 5.12—Masking the Table Area

Next, you'll create a mask for the table. Notice that there are two areas that have to be included in the mask: the table and the inside of the creamer handle. You don't need to create two separate selections. You can fill in both areas with the same color, and the Auto Mask command will do the rest.

1. From the chapter color set, choose Green (color #210). This color is just above the blue that was selected to fill the wall area.

2. Select the Paint Bucket from the Tools Palette.

3. Choose Edit | Deselect or use the quick-key combination of Ctrl-D (Windows) or Cmd-D (Mac) to deselect the wall area.

4. If the Controls | Paint Bucket is not showing on your screen, make it visible by using the Ctrl-6 (Windows) or Cmd-6 (Mac) keyboard combination.

5. Verify that the Paint Bucket will fill the Image with the Current Color.

6. Click inside the table area and click again inside the creamer handle to fill the area with the currently selected green color. The steps performed thus far are shown in Figure 5.19.

Figure 5.19.
The table and inside
the creamer cup
handle are filled with
another color.

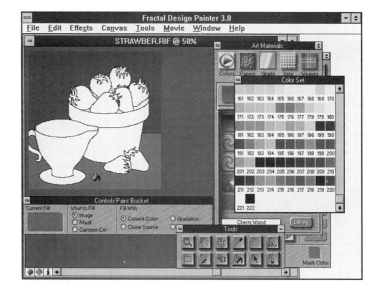

7. To convert this new area to a selection, choose the Edit | Mask | Auto Mask command again. If it is not still selected, choose to apply the mask based on Current Color and click OK.

8. From the Objects | Path List Palette, turn on the second Drawing Visibility button and the second Mask Visibility button. This masks the inside of the selection and displays it in red. Your screen should look similar to the one in Figure 5.20.

Figure 5.20.
Display the new mask
in red to verify that you
have the correct area to
convert to a selection.

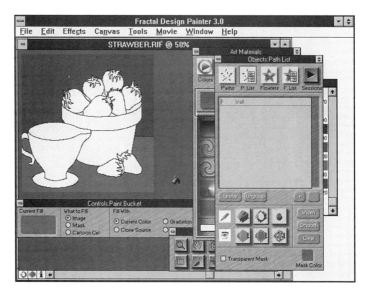

9. Choose the third Mask Visibility button to surround the selection with a marquee. A new selection group will appear in the Path List Palette.

10. To name the new selection, turn off the marquee by clicking the first Mask Visibility button. Then, double-click the name of the selection in the Path List. Name the selection Table. The screen should now look as shown in Figure 5.21.

11. Choose Tools | Selections | Convert to Selection to convert the mask selection to an outline selection. The selection marquee will turn to black and white.

Figure 5.21.
Both the Table and the
Wall selections appear
in the Path List Palette.

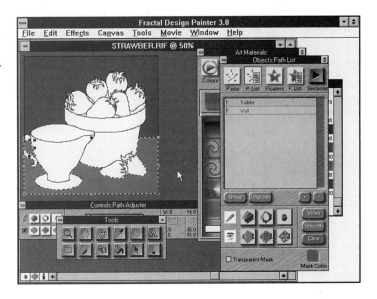

 TIP   This might be a good place to save your drawing—if you haven't already done so. Save it using the File | Save As command and Painter's .RIF format. This keeps the selections you've just made intact in the saved drawing.

If you have already saved it in .RIF format, you can update the file using the File | Save command or the quick-key combination Ctrl-S (Windows) or Cmd-S (Mac).

Step 5.13—Filling the Table with a Gradation

Next, you'll fill the table with a wood-grain gradation. Sound impossible? Not in Painter!

Painter comes with a few gradations that can be used to create wood grain looks. I took one of these gradations and modified the colors a bit using some of the Effects | Tonal Control commands, so that the color scheme would better fit my composition. The FDPUNLS.GRD gradation library contains this gradation, called Cherry Wood.

To fill the table using the Cherry Wood gradation, do the following:

1. From the Path List Palette, which should still be visible on screen, click the arrow beside the Table path in the list. You will see two masks appear beneath the Table path. Beside each of these mask list items is a circle. If this circle is dotted, the path is active; if the circle is a gray solid line, the path is inactive. If they are not active, click the circles beside the table paths to make them active. That is, you want the circles to be displayed with dotted lines.

2. In a similar manner, verify that the path for the wall is not active. To deactivate the path for the wall, click the arrow beside the Wall heading to drop down the list and then click the circle beside the associated path to make the path inactive (a solid-lined gray circle).

3. Click the third Drawing Visibility button and the second Mask Visibility button to mask outside the selection, and to display the masked area in red. You should see everything but the table area in red.

4. Click the third Mask Visibility button to outline the path with a marquee, as shown in Figure 5.22. It is now an active selection.

Figure 5.22.
Everything but the
table area is masked to
prepare to fill the table
with a gradation.

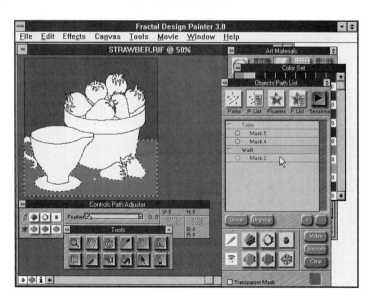

5. If, for some reason, you no longer have the Cherry Wood gradation on screen that was selected earlier, select it at this time from the Art Materials | Grads Palette. It can be selected visually (see Figure 5.23 for its location), or by name (by clicking and holding the drop-down listbox and scrolling to the name with the mouse or stylus).

Figure 5.23.
Select the Cherry Wood gradation from the Art Materials Palette if it is not currently selected.

6. Click the drawer handle to close the drawer. You should now see the gradation tools.

7. Pull the red dot in the outside circle around until the gradation angle shows 270 degrees (6 o'clock position). Notice that when the gradation is in a straight line, it doesn't quite look like wood grain.

8. Move the red dot a slight bit more until the angle reads 271 degrees. Notice the difference? All of a sudden, it does indeed look a bit like wood grain! Refer to Figure 5.24 for the placement of the red dot in the outer circle.

9. To add a little more wood grain effect, select the third Order selection in the bottom row. Refer to Figure 5.25 for its location. If these Order selections are not visible on your screen, maximize the palette by clicking the button in the upper-right portion of the palette. This Order selection cuts the size of the gradation in half and then repeats it.

Figure 5.24.
Adjust the angle of the gradation to 271 degrees, and it looks like wood grain.

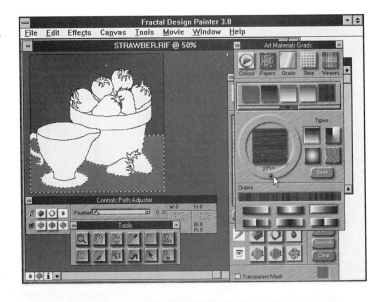

Figure 5.25.
Choose the third Order method in the bottom row to fill the area with two runs of the gradation.

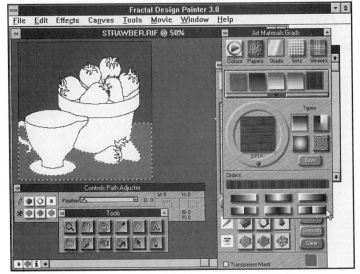

10. Choose the Paint Bucket from the Tools Palette. Verify on the Controls | Paint Bucket Palette that you are filling the Image with a gradation. (The gradation should be automatically selected after you choose a gradation from the Grads Palette).

11. Click anywhere inside the selected area to fill both selections with the gradation. Your image should look like the one shown in Figure 5.26.

Figure 5.26.
After filling with the Paint Bucket, the table looks as though it is made of cherry wood.

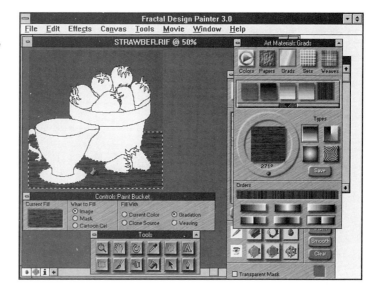

12. Choose Edit | Deselect (Ctrl-D in Windows, Cmd-D in Mac) to turn off the selection marquee.

Step 5.14—Filling the Wall with a Gradation

Now that you've been through filling one area with a gradation, the next one should be a piece of cake!

To fill the wall using the Basic Red gradation, do the following:

1. From the Path List Palette, click the circles beside the table paths to make them inactive. That is, you want the circles to be displayed with solid gray lines.

2. In a similar manner, activate the path for the wall. Click the circle beside the associated path to make the path active (displayed with a dotted line). The wall becomes outlined with a selection marquee.

3. Click the third Drawing Visibility button and the second Mask Visibility button to mask outside the selection, and to display the masked area in red. You should see everything but the wall area in red, as shown in Figure 5.28. After you verify that the correct area is masked, choose the third Mask Visibility button to surround the area with a selection marquee.

4. Choose the Basic Red gradient from the Art Materials | Grads Palette if it is not already selected. It can either be selected visually (second gradation in the bottom row of icons) or by name (by clicking and holding the drop-down listbox and scrolling to the name with the mouse or stylus).

Figure 5.27.
The table area is
deactivated, and
the wall area is acti-
vated from the Path
List Palette.

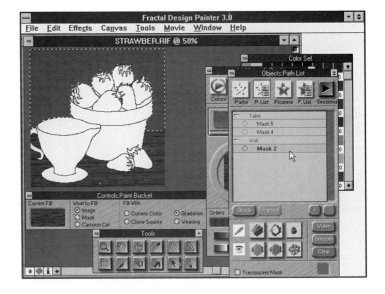

5. Click the drawer handle to close the drawer. You should now see the gradation tools.

6. Pull the red dot in the outside circle around until the gradation angle shows 135 degrees.

7. Select the third Order selection in the top row. Your screen should now look as shown in Figure 5.28.

Figure 5.28.
The Basic Red
gradation is selected
and ready to paint into
the image.

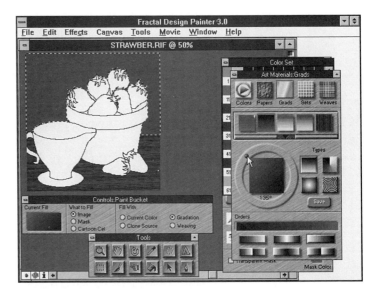

8. Choose the Paint Bucket from the Tools Palette. Verify on the Controls | Paint Bucket Palette that you are filling the Image with a Gradation.

9. Click anywhere inside the selected area to fill the wall with the gradation. Your image should now look like the one shown in Figure 5.29.

Figure 5.29.
The wall is filled
with the Basic
Red gradation.

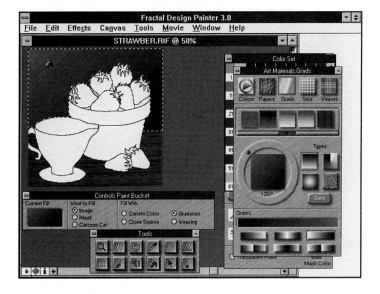

10. Choose Edit | Deselect (Ctrl-D in Windows, Cmd-D in Mac) to turn off the selection marquee.

At this point, you can save your document again. You also can close the Grads Palette or select the Papers Palette from the Art Materials to prepare for a later step.

Prepare to Color!

After all this, you finally get to use the crayons! Actually, this is the easiest part of the entire chapter, because it's all free form and enjoyable. Because you now know how to find most of the tools you'll be using, it will be very straightforward. This will give you a chance to relax your brain a little bit while you're learning!

Step 5.15—Protect What You've Done!

1. In the Objects | Path List Palette, make all the paths active—those of the table and the wall. Click the gray-lined circles to make them dotted.

2. Select the center Drawing Visibility button to mask the inside of the selections.

3. Select the center Mask Visibility button to display the mask in red. Your screen should look similar to Figure 5.30.

Figure 5.30.
The wall and table gradations are protected from the crayon strokes.

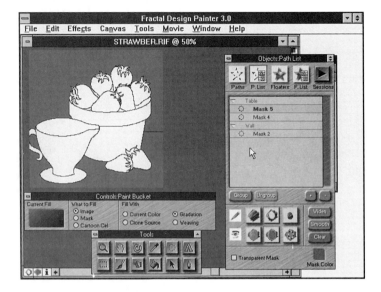

4. Using the Magnifier tool, draw a rectangular area that surrounds the strawberries in the container in order to zoom up on them. You can use the Grabber tool to position the image out of the way of your palettes. Your screen should look similar to Figure 5.31.

Figure 5.31.
Zoom in closer to the strawberries with the Magnifier.

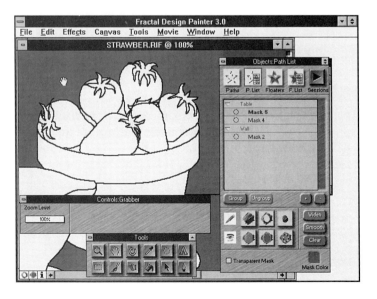

5. If you want to view the background while you color, click the first Mask Visibility button in the Path List Palette. The red areas will disappear, and the gradations will show through the mask, as shown in Figure 5.32. If you leave the Drawing Visibility selected at its current state of Masking Inside the selections, your wall and table will be protected from your crayon strokes.

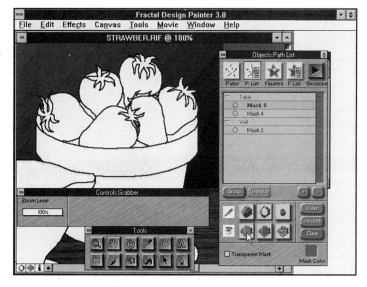

Figure 5.32. Changing only the Mask Visibility button selection enables you to see the areas already painted while still protecting them with their masks.

6. You can now close the Objects | Path List Palette, because you won't need it for a while.

Step 5.16—Choosing Your Brush, Paper, and Color

After you choose a brush (the crayon), paper texture, and color, you're off and running. These steps are pretty simple:

1. Open the Brushes Palette, if it's not already open, by choosing the Windows | Brushes command or by using the quick-key combination Ctrl-2 (Windows) or Cmd-2 (Mac).

2. If the Crayons are not visible on the drawer front, click the drawer handle to open the drawer. Select the Crayons by clicking the icon or choosing the name from the drop-down listbox inside the drawer. Choose the Default crayon, as shown in Figure 5.33.

Figure 5.33.
*Select the Default
crayon from the
Brush Palette.*

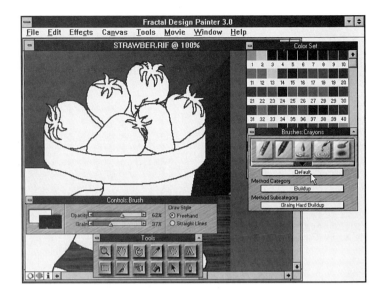

3. Open the Art Materials Palette if you closed it in a previous step. It can be reopened quickly by using the Ctrl-3 (Windows) or Cmd-3 (Mac) keyboard combination.

4. From the Art Materials Palette, select the Papers icon. Open the drawer by clicking the handle and select the Rougher paper from the drop-down listbox. Your screen should look similar to the one in Figure 5.34.

Figure 5.34.
*From the Art Materials
| Papers Palette,
choose the Rougher
paper texture.*

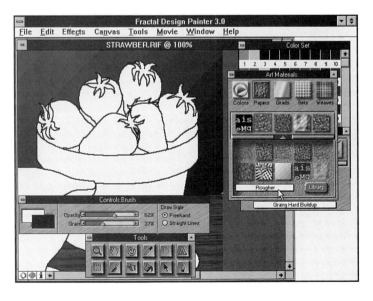

5. From the chapter color set, choose Red (color #11).

Coloring the Strawberries

Begin coloring the strawberries in the container. Notice as you color that the Default crayon reacts to the grain of the paper texture you chose. Notice also that the lighter you press on a pressure-sensitive stylus, the lighter the stroke is and the more paper grain shows through the stroke. Figure 5.35 shows all the strawberries filled in with a layer of red crayon.

Figure 5.35.
Begin coloring the
strawberries with
bright red.

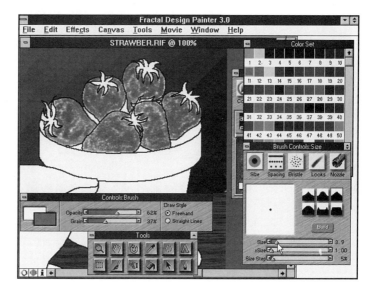

Step 5.17—Adjusting the Brush Size

You can vary the size of the stroke by adjusting the Size Slider in the Brush Controls | Size Palette. This palette can be opened by choosing the Window | Brush Controls command or by using the quick-key combination Ctrl-4 (Windows) or Cmd-4 (Mac).

When you are coloring the strawberries, especially around the leaves, the standard width of the crayon might be too wide. You can reduce the width of the brush by moving the Size slider, located just beneath the Size preview window. Moving the slider toward the left reduces the width of the brush, and moving it toward the right increases its width. A brush size of 7 or 8 works fairly well for getting in between the leaves. Refer to Figure 5.36 for an example of the brush size reduction. You can save your own variations on a brush size. We will discuss how to do this Chapter 6, "Creating a Label with Pencils."

To start the shadowed areas, you can layer more strokes over the previous ones using the same color, or you can choose a deeper shade of red. The former method was used when creating the final version of this project. When you shade, try creating strokes that follow the contour of the strawberries. You may

need to adjust the size of the brush several times while doing this to accommodate the areas around the leaves.

Figure 5.36.
The size of a brush can
be enlarged or reduced
with the Brush
Controls | Size Palette.

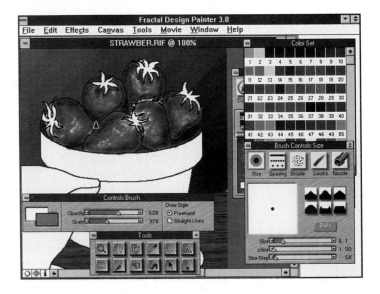

> **NOTE** Waxy crayons can be very nice for applying shadows to crayon drawings,
> but one caution must be taken. Because the Waxy Crayons smear the color of
> underlying strokes along with the color they apply themselves, care must be
> taken when using them. For example, if you applied the stroke of the Waxy
> Crayons over, or close to, the black lines in this picture, the black color would be
> smeared into the area you are shading. Sometimes this enhances the look of the
> document, but other times it muddies things up. The lines could be protected
> with a mask to protect them somewhat, however.

Figure 5.37 shows the strawberries shaded around their edges and around
areas that fall beneath other objects. The shading was done with the Default
crayon, using the same base color.

Step 5.18—Applying Light Colors over Buildup Brushes

One thing that you might notice when coloring, especially if you're experimenting a little bit, is that the color builds up on top of itself until it eventually
gets black. This is true of any of the brushes that use a buildup method.
Unfortunately, this is also true when applying lighter-colored strokes over
darker-colored strokes. If, for instance, you drew a red-and-white barber pole
and colored it all red first, applying a white crayon over the red would only
make the red areas darker—not lighter as you might think.

Figure 5.37.
*Shading is applied to
the strawberries, using
repeated strokes of the
same color.*

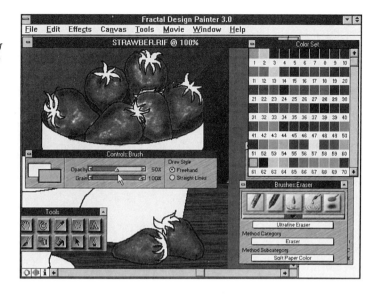

So, how do you get a lighter color over a darker one when using a buildup method brush? There are two ways. One approach is to select a brush that uses a cover method. The methods are shown in the Brushes Palette when you select a brush. Airbrushes, oil brushes, and pens are examples of Cover method brushes. These types of brushes cover underlying strokes rather than build upon them.

There's another method that is very interesting. You can change the color of the paper and erase it using one of the Eraser variants. That's the method discussed when you paint the seeds on the strawberries.

The Canvas | Set Paper Color command changes the color of the paper or background after the image has been created. Changing the paper color will not affect the rest of your document. For example, you won't see the creamer or strawberry container change color when this command is applied. This comes in handy when you are working with buildup brushes that have already built up the color to black and you want to apply a lighter color in the area. Using the Eraser tool will reveal the chosen paper color when you erase an area.

To color the seeds with a different paper color, do the following:

1. Select the Golden Yellow (color #61) from the chapter color set.

2. Choose Canvas | Set Paper Color. Though not apparent, the paper color will be set to the color selected in the first step.

3. From the Brushes Palette, click the Eraser icon to select the Eraser tools. Then, choose the Ultrafine Eraser variant.

4. The Controls | Brush Palette should appear. If it does not, use the quick-key combination Ctrl-6 (Windows) or Cmd-6 (Mac) to display it.

5. Move the Opacity slider in the Controls | Brush Palette to around 50%. This will soften the effect of the eraser.

6. Draw in the seeds in the strawberries. Don't forget the two on the table! Your screen should begin to look like that shown in Figure 5.38.

Figure 5.38.
The strawberry seeds
are colored using an
Eraser and a selected
paper color.

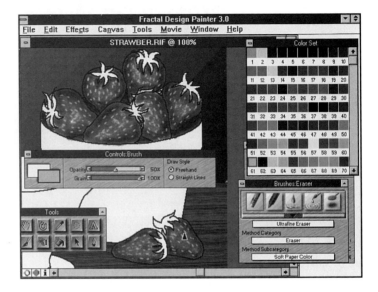

Step 5.19—Coloring the Leaves

The leaves were colored with a shade of green and then highlighted using the same paper color and eraser you just used. To color the strawberry leaves, do the following:

1. Reselect the Default crayon from the Brush Palette.

2. Choose Green (color #201) from the chapter color set.

3. Adjust the brush size to around 4.5 or 5.

4. Set the Opacity on the Controls | Brush Palette to around 50%.

5. Fill in the leaves with the green color. It's beginning to look a lot like Christmas, isn't it?

6. To apply the highlights to the leaves, reselect the Ultrafine Eraser.

7. Since you haven't selected another paper color, the golden yellow color is still active.

8. On the Controls | Brush Palette, reduce the Opacity of the eraser to somewhere between 30 or 40%.

9. Draw in the leaf highlights using a narrow brush width (2 to 4). There you have it; the leaves are done! They should now look something like the ones in Figure 5.39.

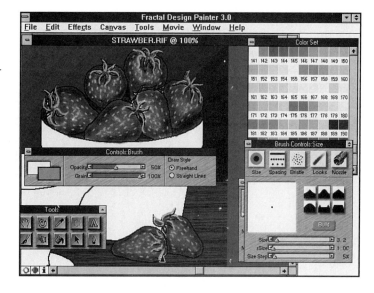

Figure 5.39.
Using both the Default
crayon and the
Ultrafine Eraser, the
leaves on the strawber-
ries are colored.

Step 5.20—Finishing the Strawberries

There's one more extra added touch. Strawberries sometimes have little light-pink, unripe areas scattered here and there. Warning—this is a test! I'm going to see if you know how to select all of this yourself now. The unripe areas were done as follows:

- Paper Color was set to Off-White (color #13) from the color set.
- The Ultrafine Eraser was used at 25% Opacity.
- The brush size was set to around 6 or 7.

After you're done, your strawberries should look as shown in Figure 5.40. By the way, have you saved your drawing lately?

Step 5.21—Coloring the Strawberry Container

We're going to cheat a little on the strawberry container and start by filling the areas with another gradient. If, during the process of coloring the strawberries and leaves, you used one of the erasers to erase strokes that extended into the rim of the container, there may be some areas that aren't filled with the Paint Bucket. If this occurs, you can probably cover over it with shading strokes in subsequent steps, or use the Just Add Water variant of the Water Tools to blend the uncovered areas with the filled areas a bit. If the amount of non-coverage is objectionable, the areas could also be filled using the Cartoon Cel Fill method, discussed in Chapter 7, "Pen Project."

Figure 5.40.
*Some strawberries now
look like they were
picked a little too soon!*

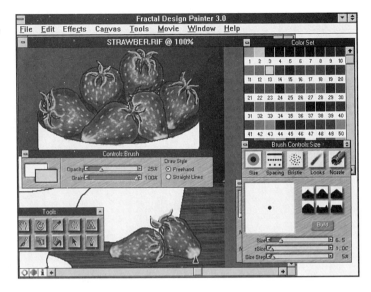

To fill the container with a gradient, do the following:

1. If it isn't still open, open the Art Materials Palette using Ctrl-3 (Windows) or Cmd-3 (Mac) and select the Earthy 1 gradient (third in the bottom row). Adjust the red dot to the 180-degree position and choose the bottom middle Order. Figure 5.41 shows a screen shot of this step.

Figure 5.41.
*Prepare the Earthy 1
gradient to fill the
strawberry container.*

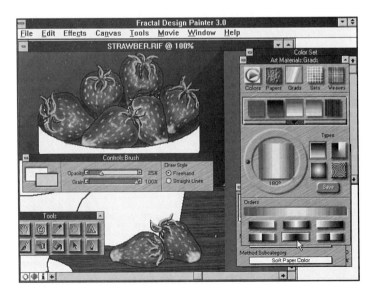

2. Using the Paint Bucket, fill the rim and the bowl of the container with the Earthy 1 gradient. The areas will take on a cylindrical look because of the ping-pong effect of the gradation order, as shown in Figure 5.42.

Figure 5.42.
The container takes
on a cylindrical shape
after it's shaded with
the gradient.

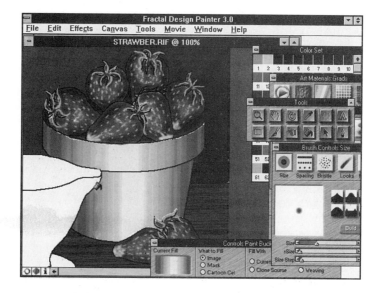

3. While in the Art Materials Palette, select the Eggscape paper grain from the Papers Palette to prepare for coloring the creamer. You can then close the Art Materials Palette, if you like.

4. Choose the Waxy Crayon from the Brush Palette. The Controls | Brush Palette will automatically appear. Set the Opacity of the brush to around 33%.

5. From the chapter color set, choose Blue (color #213) and reduce the size of the brush to around 6 with the Brush Size Palette.

6. Draw some designs in the base of the container and around the upper rim. This process is shown in Figure 5.43.

7. Now, choose Rust (color #25). Set the Brush Size to around 3.5 and keep the Opacity at 33%. Add a little more color into the designs. You can see more color added to the areas in Figure 5.44.

Step 5.22—Coloring The Creamer

In an earlier step, you selected a different paper texture to use with the creamer. Notice, when you apply color with the crayon, how different the effect of the crayons looks with another paper texture. This is typical of all brushes that use a Grainy method; paper texture is applied when using brushes that are based in this manner.

To color the creamer, use the following steps:

1. Move the creamer into view using the Magnifier and the Grabber.

2. From the chapter color set, pick Gold (color #63).

3. Select the Default crayon from the Brushes Palette. Adjust the size and opacity of the brush as needed. Notice the nice effect that the Eggscape paper grain gives to the creamer! Leave some area open in the top section of the creamer to color the cream.

Figure 5.43.
Designs are added to
the bowl using the
Waxy Crayon.

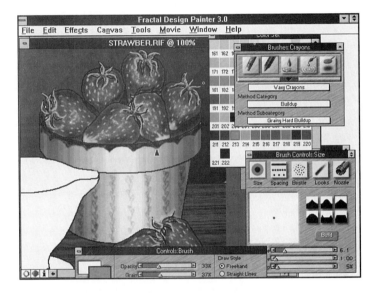

Figure 5.44.
More design is added
to the bowl with a
second color, using the
Waxy Crayon.

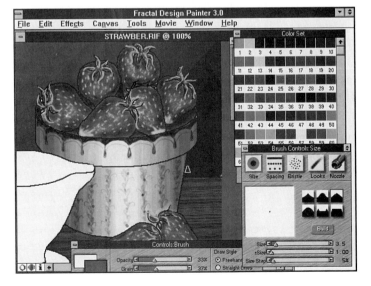

ROTATING THE CANVAS

While you're coloring the creamer, you might find it easier to rotate the canvas while applying your strokes. This is a new feature of Painter 3 that comes in very handy!

The Rotate Page tool lets you rotate the canvas at any angle, similar to the way that you would rotate a piece of paper or canvas when drawing or painting in the real world.

To rotate the canvas, do the following:

1. From the Tools Palette, select the Rotate Page tool.
2. Click inside the document window. The cursor will turn into a hand pointing upward when inside the document. When you click, a rectangle will appear with an arrow pointing toward the top of the document.
3. Rotate the rectangle in the direction you would like to rotate the canvas.
4. Release the mouse or stylus when the rectangle is positioned the way you would like your canvas. The angle of rotation will appear in the Controls | Rotate Page Palette. An example of this is shown in Figure 5.45.

To return the canvas to its normal state, click inside the image once with the Rotate Page tool.

The Controls | Rotate Page Palette displays the current angle of rotation of the page. You also can set the zoom level of the image by clicking inside the zoom level drop-down box.

Figure 5.45.
The canvas can be rotated as you like using the Rotate Page tool from the Tools Palette.

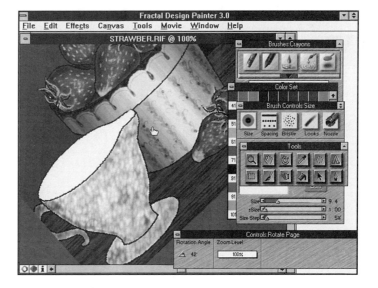

4. Choose the Waxy Crayon and Green (color #201) to add some additional color to the creamer, making it look like it has ceramic glazing. Figure 5.46 shows the progress so far.

CAUTION Take care when approaching the black lines, because the Waxy Crayon smears colors beneath it with the color it applies.

Figure 5.46.
The edges of
the creamer are
colored with the
Waxy Crayons.

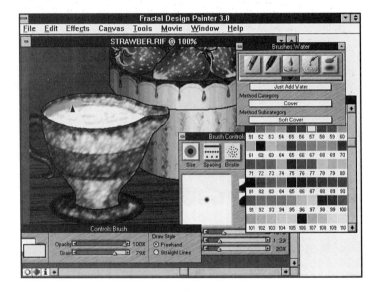

5. Choose the Default crayon again and select Creamy White (color #37). Color some areas in the cream.

6. Select the Water Tools icon from the Brush Palette. From here, select the Just Add Water variant. This brush can be used to blend colors and smooth the strokes a bit. Smooth the edges of the creamer with a narrow-width brush, adjusted in the Brush Size window as needed.

7. To add some highlights around the rim of the creamer, select the Dodge tool. The Dodge brush lightens areas beneath the strokes, eventually turning them to white. Figure 5.47 shows the edges smoothed and the highlights applied.

8. From the chapter color set, choose Brown (color #42). Reselect the Default crayon and apply some color to the edges of the creamer, adding more shape.

9. Center the image on your screen by clicking once with the Grabber tool.

10. Hide all the palettes using the Windows | Hide command or the quick-key combination Ctrl-H in Windows or Cmd-H in Mac.

Figure 5.47.
The rim of the creamer is smoothed using Just Add Water, and highlights are applied with the Dodge brush.

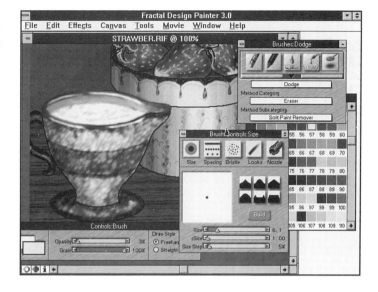

11. To view the image at full screen, shown in Figure 5.48, select the Window | Screen Mode Toggle command or use the quick-key combination of Ctrl-M in Windows or Cmd-M in Mac.

Figure 5.48.
To view the screen in full screen mode, use the Ctrl-M (Windows) or Cmd-M (Mac) key combination or the Window | Screen Mode Toggle command.

Examine your picture to see if there are any other enhancements you should make to the shading. To return to the normal editing window view, click the Up/Down arrow button beneath the program's maximize button at the upper-right corner of your screen.

Finishing the Drawing

To finish the drawing, you'll use a couple of after-the-fact effects that can be applied to an image. You'll apply some texture to the paper and ensure that the image contains printable colors only.

Step 5.23—Adding Paper Grain

As seen, Painter can apply paper grain with grain-sensitive brushes. The areas that were filled with gradients, however, have no texture. You can apply paper texture after the fact to the entire image or to a selected area.

To simplify things, just apply the effect to the entire image. You can turn on the masks from the Objects | Path List Palette and set the Drawing Visibility and Mask Visibility buttons to apply the effect to the wall and table only.

To apply one of Painter's surface textures to the image, do the following:

1. If you want to apply the effect to the entire image, make sure the masks are turned off by choosing the first Drawing Visibility button. There is no need to select an area if you want to apply the effect to the entire image.

2. Choose a paper texture from the Art Materials | Papers Palette.

3. Choose Effects | Surface Control | Apply Surface Texture. The Apply Surface Texture dialog box appears.

4. In the drop-down listbox, choose to apply the surface texture based on Paper Grain. The preview window will adjust to show you what the image will look like when applying the currently selected Eggscape paper grain. If you don't like this choice, you can cancel the command and choose another paper grain from the Art Materials | Papers Palette.

5. There is a Shiny checkbox that will add highlights to the paper grain. The radio buttons adjacent to the Shiny button specify which direction the light source is coming from to determine the light and dark areas of the shininess. For my example, I elected not to use the Shiny feature. If this is your choice, click inside the checkbox to uncheck, or disable, this feature.

6. You can move the image around in the preview window to see how it will be affected. If 100% of the effect is a bit too much, you can adjust the slider to reduce the amount of the effect. For this example, 40% was chosen.

7. Once all the settings have been selected, choose OK or press Enter to apply the effect. Figure 5.49 shows the final result after this step is completed.

After I applied the surface texture to the document, I decided that more shading was necessary. Additional shading was applied to the wall, the strawberry container, and the table Burn brush. This last enhancement can be seen in the final version of the STRAWBER.RIF file, located on the CD furnished with this book.

Figure 5.49.
The Eggscape paper
texture is applied to the
entire image using the
Apply Surface Texture
command.

Step 5.24—Showing Printable Colors Only

In Painter, you can paint with Printable Colors Only by selecting that option in the Art Materials | Colors Palette. Because you have not done so, you can elect to show printable colors after the fact.

This command actually added a nice effect to the paper texture. The color in the wall gradation changed such that it started off solid and then gradually added texture as it approached the shaded areas.

To show the image with printable colors only, choose the Effects | Tonal Control | Printable Colors command. A dialog box appears that enables you to preview the effect in a window. If it looks satisfactory, click OK or press Enter.

Closing Your Document

There are four ways to close the currently active document window:

- Choose File | Close.
- Use the quick-key combination Ctrl-W in Windows or Cmd-W in Mac.
- Double-click the button box at the upper-left corner of the document window.
- Single-click the button box at the upper-left corner of the document window, and then click Close.

Any one of these commands will close a document. If you have made any changes to the document since it was last saved, you will be asked if you want to save the changes before closing it.

Exiting Painter

The Exit command quits the Painter application. After you select this command, Painter will prompt you to save any files that have been edited since you last saved them. After you close all the open files, the application will quit.

Summary

You've learned much more in this chapter than how to color with crayons. You've learned about filling areas, masking areas, working with multiple masks in an image, applying some effects, and setting an image to display printable colors only. You've also learned how to adjust the width and opacity of brush strokes. I'd say this is quite an accomplishment!

In the next chapter, you will work with the Pencil tools to create an image. You'll learn how to apply borders to an image, how to make text look like it's hand-lettered, how to draw straight lines, and more. Continue on!

6

Creating a Label with Pencils

While you can use Painter's Pencil variants for rough sketches and drawing fine-lined sketches, you can use them for colored pictures as well. In this chapter you learn about Painter's Pencil variants, and how to draw and align objects using Painter's grid as a guide. I also cover some basic floater techniques.

Pencil Variants

All the Pencil variants interact with paper texture, so you can achieve many different effects by choosing different paper textures from the Art Materials | Papers Palette. Pencils interact with the paper grain based on the amount of pressure you apply to the stylus. Light pressure penetrates the paper less and allows more of the paper grain to show through. Heavier pressure penetrates the paper more and allows less of the grain to show through. Mouse users can simulate this effect by adjusting the Grain slider on the Controls | Brush Palette.

Because these variants use Buildup methods, your strokes darken as you layer them. You cannot place a lighter stroke over a darker one. To work around this, select a variant that uses a Cover method (such as Chalk or Airbrush) and use it to apply a lighter color over the Pencil strokes. Another way to control results is to change the paper color using the Canvas | Set Paper Color command, and use an eraser to erase part of the image back to the chosen paper color. Chapter 5, "Crayons Project," has a demonstration of this.

To draw with the Pencil variants:

1. Position the mouse or stylus where you want the stroke to begin.
2. Push down on the stylus, or click the mouse, and drag through the stroke.
3. When you finish the stroke, let up on the stylus or release the mouse.

2B Pencil

The 2B Pencil is a soft-leaded pencil that produces antialiased lines. It has a moderately narrow stroke that reacts to paper grain.

Mouse users can adjust the Opacity and Grain sliders on the Controls | Brush Palette. Another way to control results is to set the Opacity and Grain settings in the Advanced Controls | Sliders Palette to respond to Velocity or Direction.

500 lb. Pencil

The 500 lb. Pencil variant produces broad, semi-antialiased strokes that react to paper grain. This variant is good for coloring in large areas with soft, grain-sensitive strokes.

The 500 lb. Pencil varies in opacity and reaction to paper grain based on the pressure you apply with the stylus. Mouse users can adjust the Opacity and Grain sliders on the Controls | Brush Palette. Another way to control results is to set the Opacity and Grain settings in the Advanced Controls | Sliders Palette to respond to Velocity or Direction.

Colored Pencils

The Colored Pencils variant produces semi-antialiased strokes that react to paper grain. The colors build up toward black when layered on top of each other.

You can control the reaction of the Colored Pencils variant to paper grain by the pressure you apply with the stylus. Heavier pressure covers more of the paper grain, and lighter pressure covers less of the paper grain.

Mouse users can adjust the Grain slider on the Controls | Brush Palette. Another way to control results is to set the Grain settings in the Advanced Controls | Sliders Palette to respond to Velocity or Direction.

Sharp Pencil

The Sharp Pencil variant produces thin lines that are semi-antialiased and which respond to paper texture.

The opacity of the stroke, as well as its reaction to paper grain, respond to pressure you apply with the stylus. Lighter pressure allows more paper grain to show through. Heavier pressure covers more of the paper texture.

Mouse users can adjust the Opacity and Grain sliders on the Controls | Brush Palette. Another way to control results is to set the Opacity and Grain settings in the Advanced Controls | Sliders Palette to respond to Velocity or Direction.

Single Pixel Scribbler

The Single Pixel Scribbler is good for sketching out ideas on your canvas. It produces strokes that are antialiased and build up toward black when layered. The opacity of the stroke, as well as its reaction to paper grain, vary with stylus pressure. Light strokes produce lighter lines that allow more paper grain to show through. Heavy strokes produce darker lines that cover more of the paper texture.

Mouse users can adjust the Opacity and Grain sliders on the Controls | Brush Palette. Another way to control results is to set the Opacity and Grain settings in the Advanced Controls | Sliders Palette to respond to Velocity or Direction.

Thick and Thin Pencils

The Thick and Thin Pencils variant produces semi-antialiased strokes that vary in width depending on the direction in which you drag the mouse or stylus. Its effect is similar to that of the Calligraphy Pen, except that the strokes respond to paper grain. Dragging in one direction produces thicker lines, and dragging in the other direction produces thinner lines.

Both the opacity of the stroke and its reaction to paper grain vary with stylus pressure. Light strokes produce lighter lines that allow more paper grain to show through. Heavy strokes produce darker lines that cover more of the paper texture.

Mouse users can adjust the Opacity and Grain sliders on the Controls | Brush Palette. Another way to control results is to set the Opacity and Grain settings in the Advanced Controls | Sliders Palette to respond to Velocity or Direction.

Creating and Merging Documents

This project consists of creating two documents: one for the background design and one for the border design. At the end of the project you merge the two designs to create one document.

Step 6.1. Creating the Background of Your Project

Begin by creating the background image:

1. Create a 640×480 document, setting the resolution at 75 pixels per inch.

2. Click inside the Paper Color square and choose the second color in the top row (off-white) for the paper color, as shown in Figure 6.1.

Figure 6.1.
Create a new 640×480 document, setting the Paper Color to the off-white color square indicated here.

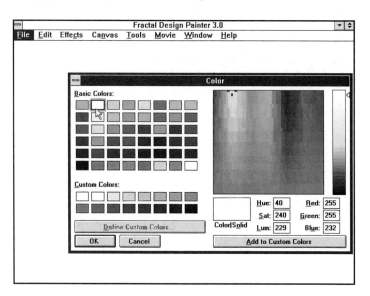

3. Zoom out, if necessary, to view the entire image. You can zoom out with the Magnifier tool, or with the Window | Zoom Out command (Ctrl- - in Windows, Cmd- - in Mac). Figure 6.2 shows the image zoomed out.

Figure 6.2.
Zoom out if you cannot
view the entire
document at once.

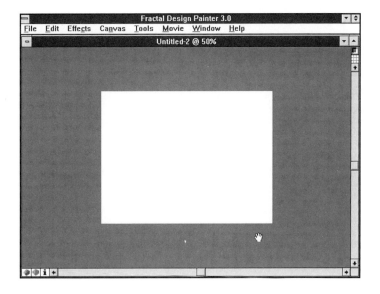

Step 6.2. Adjusting and Displaying the Grid

The label you're designing will have a basic design in the center and will be surrounded by a gradient border. To protect the outside border while you're working on the inside portion, this step creates a rectangular path that masks the inside or outside, as needed, during document editing.

You need some sort of reference to size and place the border accurately when you create the border outline. To draw straight or diagonal lines of a specified length in Painter, use the Grid Options and View Grid commands as a guide.

Use the Canvas | Grid Options command to adjust the grid type, spacing, and color. When you select this command, a dialog box appears in which you can set the following options:

- Grid Format—This determines the type of grid to apply. To select a grid type, click the drop-down box and slide the cursor down to highlight your choice of vertical lines, horizontal lines, rectangular (both horizontal and vertical) lines, or a dot grid.

- Horiz. Spacing—This determines the amount of space between horizontal lines. The units can be in pixels, inches, centimeters, points, picas, columns, or percentages. To select units, click the drop-down box and slide the cursor down to highlight your choice of units.

- Vert. Spacing—This determines the amount of space between vertical lines. The units can be in pixels, inches, centimeters, points, picas, columns, or percentages. To select units, click the drop-down box and slide the cursor down to highlight your choice of units.

- Line Thickness—This sets the width of the gridlines in pixels, inches, centimeters, points, picas, columns or percentages. To select units, click the drop-down box and slide the cursor down to highlight your choice of units.

- Grid Color—This determines the color of the gridlines. To change the color, click the Grid Color box. This opens the Windows color selection dialog box. Choose a color, then click OK to return to the Grid Options dialog box.

- Background—This determines the color of the background of the grid. To change the color, click the Grid Color box. This opens the Windows color-selection dialog box. Choose a color, then click OK to return to the Grid Options dialog box.

- Transparent Background—Check this box to superimpose only the gridlines over your image. The background of the grid will be clear, allowing your image to show through.

You want the outer border of your label to be 40-pixels wide on each side, so you can set your grid spacing at 10, 20, or 40 pixels in both horizontal and vertical spacing. (I chose to set the grid at 20 pixels by 20 pixels.) To adjust grid spacing:

1. Choose the Canvas | Grid Options command. In the Grid Options dialog box, shown in Figure 6.3, choose a Rectangular Grid.

Figure 6.3.
Adjust the grid spacing of the document to 20 pixels wide and 20 pixels high, and turn Transparent Background on.

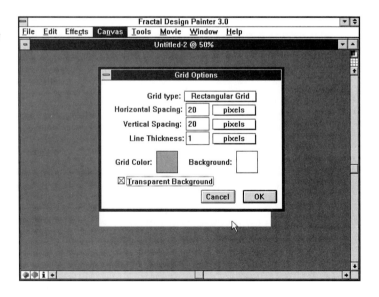

2. Set the horizontal and vertical spacing to 20 pixels.
3. Click the Transparent Background option to enable it.

4. Choose the Canvas | View Grid command, or enter the keyboard combination of Ctrl-G in Windows or Cmd-G in Mac. This turns on the grid display, as shown in Figure 6.4.

Figure 6.4.
Use the Canvas |
View Grid command
to turn the grid display
on and off.

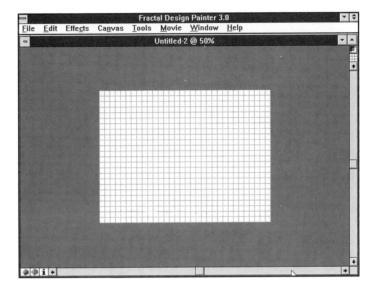

Step 6.3. Creating a Rectangular Path with the Outline Selection Tool

Although there's a Rectangular Selection Tool in the Tools Palette, selections you make with this tool are not placed in the Path List. Therefore, you cannot mask inside or outside that type of rectangular selection. To work around this, you can create a rectangular selection using the Outline Selection Tool and the Straight Line drawing method. When you use the Straight Line option with the Brush or Outline Selection Tool, the tool snaps to the grid whenever the grid is displayed.

1. Open the Tools (Ctrl-1 in Windows, Cmd-1 in Mac), Objects (Ctrl-5 in Windows, Cmd-5 in Mac), and Controls (Ctrl-6 in Windows, Cmd-6 in Mac) Palettes.

2. Use the Grabber to move your image to an area where it's completely visible. Figure 6.5 shows these palettes opened, and the image moved over in view.

3. From the Tools Palette, choose the Outline Selection Tool, the last tool icon in the bottom row. When you do this, the Controls | Outline Selection Palette appears. Notice in the Outline Selection Palette that there are three available drawing mode options: Freehand, Straight Line, and Bézier Curve. The drawing mode that seems most appropriate for this instance is the Straight Line. Select this option, shown in Figure 6.6, from the right section of the Outline Selection Palette.

Figure 6.5.
Arrange the palettes
and document so
everything is visible.

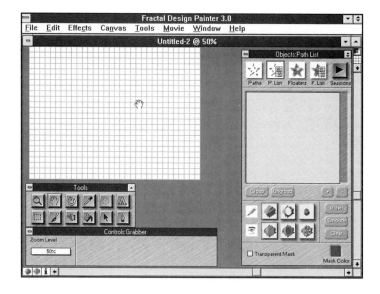

Figure 6.6.
From the Outline
Selection palette,
select the Straight
Line drawing mode.

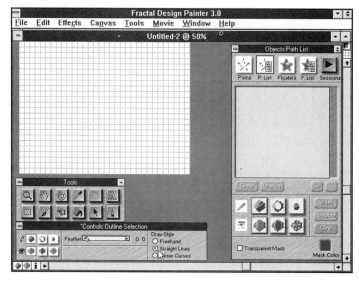

4. Using the Outline Selection Tool, draw a rectangular selection two grid
   squares (40 pixels) from each edge of the document. End the selected area
   at the same point you began: click inside the origin point, displayed as a
   circle with a crosshair in it. After a moment, the outline is replaced with a
   selection marquee, and a path name appears in the Path List. Your screen
   should look similar to the one shown in Figure 6.7.

Figure 6.7.
Draw a rectangle, two
grid spaces away from
each edge.

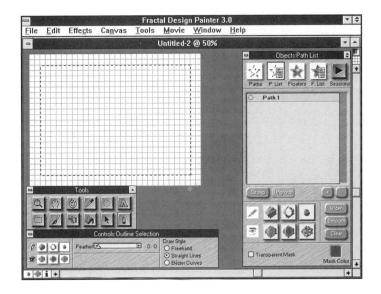

5. Double-click the pathname in the Path List Palette. The Path Attributes dialog box appears.

6. Name the path `Rectangle` and click OK. The name in the Path List Palette changes to reflect the new name, as shown in Figure 6.8.

Figure 6.8.
Rename the selection
using the Path At-
tributes dialog box,
accessed by double-
clicking the path in the
Path List Palette.

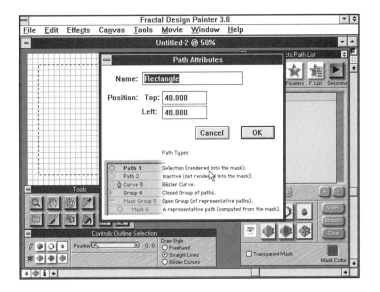

Step 6.4. Setting the Drawing Visibility and Mask Visibility Buttons

At the end of the last step, the third Drawing Visibility and third Mask Visibility buttons are on. You can find the Drawing Visibility and Mask Visibility buttons in three places in Painter:

- In the Controls | Path Adjuster Palette
- In the Path List Palette
- In the lower-left corner of your document window, inside the lower document scrollbar

These buttons work in combinations to determine how a mask affects your image (Drawing Visibility buttons), and how the mask is displayed (Mask Visibility buttons). Table 6.1 shows what effect the Drawing Visibility button and Mask Visibility buttons have in different combinations.

Table 6.1. Functions of the Drawing Visibility and Mask Visibility buttons.

Drawing Visibility Choice			Mask Visibility Choice			Resulting Display
1	2	3	1	2	3	
X			X			Masked areas are hidden from view, and the mask is inactive, letting you draw or edit the entire image.
X				X		The mask is inactive, letting you edit the entire image, but the areas that would be masked, if active, are displayed in red.
X					X	The mask is inactive, letting you edit the entire image, but the areas that would be masked are surrounded by a selection marquee.
	X		X			Areas inside positive paths (selections) are masked, letting you paint outside the path. Areas inside negative paths are unmasked. The masked areas are active, but you can view the entire image while painting.
X			X			Areas inside positive paths (selections) are masked, letting you paint outside the path. Areas inside negative paths are unmasked. The masked areas are displayed in red.

Drawing Visibility Choice	Mask Visibility Choice	Resulting Display
1 2 3	1 2 3	
X	X	Areas inside positive paths (selections) are masked, letting you paint outside the path. Areas inside negative paths are unmasked. The masked areas are surrounded by a selection marquee.
X	X	Areas outside positive paths are masked, letting you paint inside the path. Areas inside negative paths are masked. The masked areas are active, but you can view the entire image while painting.
X	X	Areas outside positive paths are masked, letting you paint inside the path. Areas inside negative paths are masked. The masked areas are displayed in red.
X	X	Areas outside positive paths are masked, letting you paint inside the path. Areas inside negative paths are masked. The masked areas are surrounded by a selection marquee.

With that in mind, follow these steps to adjust the buttons so you can paint inside the rectangular selection and view the masked area in red:

1. By default, the third Drawing Visibility and Mask Visibility buttons are selected when the path appears. To display the mask in red, choose the third Drawing Visibility button and the second Mask Visibility button. Notice that the outside of the rectangle is masked in red.

2. You can close the Path List Palette for the time being. To do so, click the button at the upper-left corner of the palette.

Step 6.5. Coloring the Background Texture

With the border area now masked, you can start coloring in the main background area:

1. Select the Grabber tool from the Tools Palette.

2. Click inside the document once to center the image.

3. Zoom to 100% from within the Controls | Grabber Palette, or with the Magnifier tool.

4. Turn off the Grid Display using the quick-key combination Ctrl-G in Windows or Cmd-G in Mac.

5. Open the Art Materials Palette (Ctrl-3 in Windows, Cmd-3 in Mac).

6. Click the Papers icon.

7. From the default Paper library, choose the Rougher paper texture. Figure 6.9 illustrates this step.

Figure 6.9.
Choose the Rougher
paper texture from the
default Paper library.

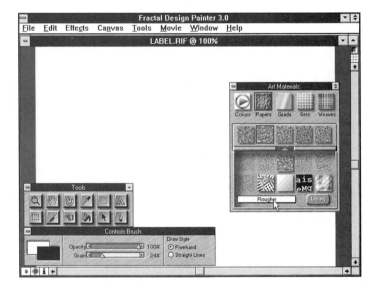

8. Open the Brushes Palette (Ctrl-2 in Windows, Cmd-2 in Mac) and click the Pencils icon.

9. From the list of variants, choose the 500 lb. Pencil variant, shown in Figure 6.10. This Pencil covers a broad area with color. The appearance of the stroke made by this Pencil is somewhat like that of an airbrush, except that it reacts to paper grain.

10. A custom color set has been created for this project and is located on the CD accompanying this book. To load in the color set, click the Sets icon in the Art Materials Palette, which should still be on your screen from the previous step.

11. Click the Library button in the Sets Palette. A dialog box appears, prompting you to select a file.

12. Choose the Chapter 6 directory from the CD accompanying this book, and choose the CHAP06CS.TXT Color Set text file. Click the OK button to load the new color set into Painter. The color set appears on your screen.

13. Select Beige (color BC-47) as shown in Figure 6.11.

Figure 6.10.
Choose the 500 lb.
Pencil from the
Brushes Palette.

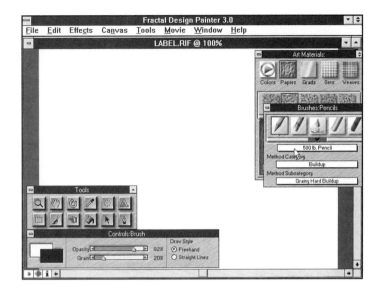

Figure 6.11.
Choose color BC-47
from the Chapter 6
color set.

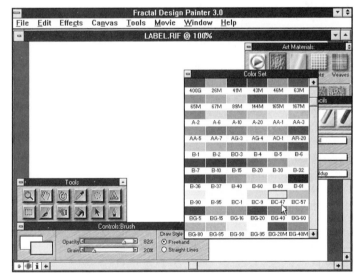

14. Color in the entire area using this brush, paper, and color. Mouse users can adjust the Opacity slider in the Controls | Brush Palette to around 30% for better results. As you apply the strokes, the red masked area is protected. Figure 6.12 shows this step in progress. Cover the edges a little bit more to darken them.

15. Save your image so far as LABEL.RIF, using the File | Save or File | Save As command.

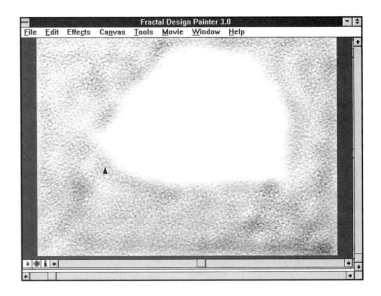

Figure 6.12.
Fill in the entire
background with the
500 lb. Pencil variant.
This figure shows the
area partially filled.

Step 6.6. Adding a Gradient Border

It's time to add a gradient to the outside border. (This should be easy, now that you're a pro at it from the previous chapter!) First, you must adjust the Drawing Visibility buttons and Mask Visibility buttons to protect the area you just painted:

1. Choose the second Drawing Visibility button, which masks the inside of the rectangular area you just painted. Choose the second Mask Visibility if it isn't selected. You should see a big red rectangle surrounded by an off-white border on your screen.

2. Open the Art Materials Palette, if it is not still open, by pressing Ctrl-3 in Windows or Cmd-3 in Mac.

3. Click the Grads icon.

4. From Painter's default Gradient library, select the Sepia Tones gradient, as shown in Figure 6.13.

5. Close the Grads Palette drawer. The gradient adjustment tools appear on your screen.

6. If the Orders selections do not appear at the bottom of the palette, maximize the Grads Palette by clicking the button in the upper-right corner of the palette.

7. Set the red rotation ball at 0 degrees if it needs adjustment.

8. Choose the middle Grads order in the bottom row. This will repeat the gradient in reverse order in the first half and in normal order in the second half.

Figure 6.13.
Mask the inside
rectangle and select
the Sepia Tones
gradient from the
default Gradient
Library.

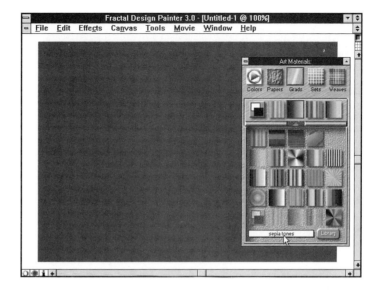

9. Click the Paint Bucket tool in the Tools Palette.

10. On the Controls | Paint Bucket Palette, select to fill with a Gradient (if that is not already selected). The preview window in the Controls | Paint Bucket Palette changes to show your current gradient.

11. Click in the off-white area of your image (the unmasked area). This area is filled with the currently selected gradient. The result is shown in Figure 6.14.

Figure 6.14.
Fill the border with the
Sepia Tones gradient.

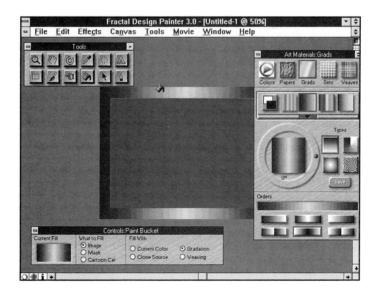

You can save this document now (Ctrl-S in Windows or Cmd-S in Mac), and close it, if you like, or leave it open and minimize it by clicking the minimize button in the upper-right corner of the document window.

Step 6.7. Creating a New Document for the Border Floater

In the following steps, you create a second image with a design that will be incorporated into this background later.

The dimensions of the inside rectangle—the one you colored in with the paper texture—are 560 by 400 pixels (the 640×480 image less 40 pixels on the top, bottom, and sides). You want a design that takes up one-fourth of this size, so follow these steps to create a new 280×200-pixel image using the same paper color as before. You can repeat this design and mirror it around the image to create the entire design.

1. Create a new 280-pixel-wide and 200-pixel-high document, using the same off-white paper color used in the first part of this project. Your screen should look similar to Figure 6.15.

Figure 6.15.
Create a new 280×200 document to begin your border design.

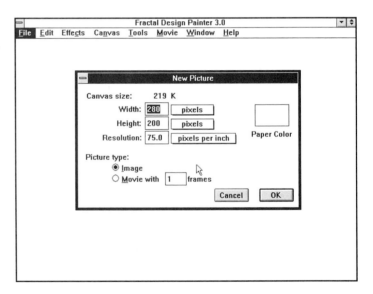

2. With the document open, zoom in to 200% magnification, using the Window | Zoom In command (Ctrl-+ in Windows or Cmd-+ in Mac) or the Magnifier tool, to see the image more clearly. You need to adjust the document window size to see the entire image.

3. From Painter's default Papers Palette, choose the Regular Fine paper texture.

Step 6.8. Importing and Resizing an .EPS Selection

To begin the border design, follow these steps to import an .EPS file as a selection, or *path*. Then you will use the Tools | Selections | Stroke Selection command to draw an outline around the path automatically. This simplifies the process of getting the curves "just right." The .EPS file to import is a design that was created in CorelDRAW. For instructions on how to save a document in the EPS format from CorelDRAW, see Chapter 21, "Integrating with CorelDRAW!"

1. Use the Tools | Selections | Open .EPS as Selection command, as shown in Figure 6.16. The Select EPS File dialog box appears.

Figure 6.16.
Use the Open EPS as Selection command to import the border design.

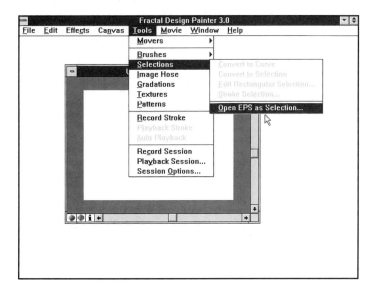

2. In the Select EPS File dialog box, shown in Figure 6.17, choose the Chapter 6 directory or folder on the accompanying CD, where the LABEL2.EPS file resides. Choose that file and click OK, or press Enter, to load the file into the current document.

A group of shapes appears on your screen as Bézier curves. If the selection does not totally appear within the canvas, you can move it into place with your mouse or stylus. Choose the Path Adjuster Tool, and click and drag the Bézier curve path into your canvas.

Normally, you display Bézier curves in a selection when you want to adjust one or more shapes contained in the selection. Examine the selection for a moment to see how the Bézier curves are represented. You can adjust the starting and ending points of a segment in the path by clicking the square symbols in the path. You can adjust the shape of the curve between the start and end points by moving the circular symbols radiating from the square symbol.

Figure 6.17.
Select the LABEL2.EPS
file for the border
design.

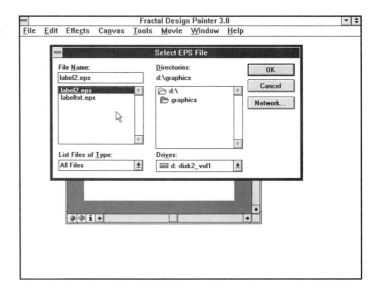

You need not adjust any of the square or circular shaping points at this time, because all of the shaping was done in CorelDRAW. You do, however, have to resize the path so that it completely fills the entire document you now have open.

NOTE If, for some reason, the imported .EPS file is deselected, you can reselect it using the Edit | Select All command.

3. Notice that the .EPS selection is surrounded by an invisible *bounding box*, with square-shaped adjustment points at the center of each side. These adjustment points let you adjust the size, or *scaling*, of the selected area.

   Using these adjustment points, resize the selection by dragging its boundaries until the selection completely fills the document. The cursor will change into arrows when placed over an adjustment point. The arrows designate the direction that the adjustment point can be moved. When done, your screen should look similar to Figure 6.18.

4. To turn the Bézier Curve path into a selection, choose the Tools | Selections | Convert to Selection command. The Bézier curves are replaced by a selection marquee border.

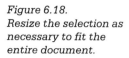

Figure 6.18.
Resize the selection as
necessary to fit the
entire document.

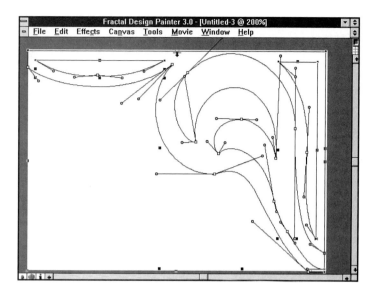

Step 6.9. Coloring the Border

Now start coloring the border design. Save your document often while coloring, especially when trying a new command or feature. This way, if you make a mistake you can revert to the saved image using the File | Revert command.

NOTE Reopening a document, or reverting to the saved document with the File | Revert command, reselects the first Drawing Visibility button and the first Mask Visibility button. This lets you paint over the entire area with the mask display off. Additionally, the paper color reverts to the color chosen when you created the document. Bear this in mind, and reset these features to the state they were in before you reverted the document.

1. Save the design you've made so far as DESIGN.RIF. This lets you periodically update the file while you're working using the File | Save command.
2. From the Brushes Palette, choose the 2B Pencil variant.
3. From the Chapter 6 color set, choose Dark Brown (color C-6).
   Figure 6.19 illustrates these choices.
4. Choose Tools | Selections | Stroke Selection. Figure 6.20 illustrates this command. You will see the selections automatically outlined with the 2B Pencil.

Figure 6.19.
Choose the 2B Pencil
variant and color C-6
from the Color Set.

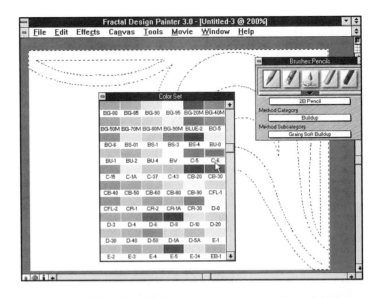

Figure 6.20.
Choose the Tools |
Selections | Stroke
Selection command to
outline the shape with
the 2B Pencil variant.

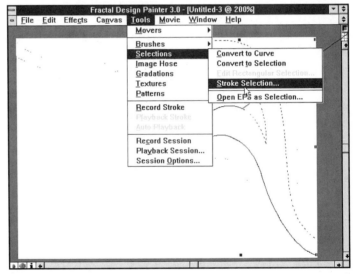

5. When the strokes are complete, your screen should look like Figure 6.21. I used the Ctrl-H command (Cmd-H in Mac) to hide all the palettes for this screen shot.

6. Open the Objects Palette (Ctrl-5 in Windows, Cmd-5 in Mac) and enter the Path List Palette, shown in Figure 6.22. Then choose the Path Adjuster Tool from the Tools Palette.

Figure 6.21.
Outline the strokes
with 2B Pencil lines
using the Stroke
Selection command.

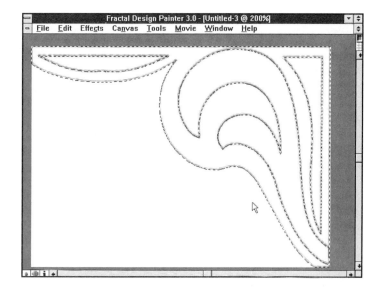

Figure 6.22.
Deactivate the selec-
tions from the Path List
Palette.

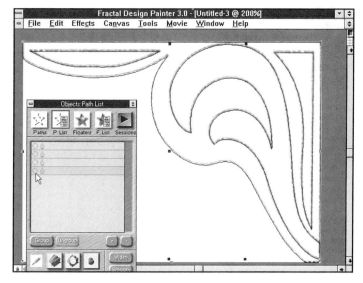

7. If you are using Painter 3.0, four unnamed paths appear in the Path List. Click the dotted circles beside each path (four in all) to deactivate them. Or you can use the following tip to convert the paths into a group.

    If you are using Painter 3.1, the paths you imported will appear as a group named LABEL2.EPS. You can deactivate all four paths contained in the group by clicking the group name to highlight it. Then press the Enter (Windows) or Return (Mac) key to deactivate the paths.

TIP Painter 3.0 users can also convert the four individual paths in this imported .EPS file into a group of four paths. You can use this technique in Painter 3.0 and 3.1 at any time.

Highlight all four paths by Shift-clicking on each name. Then click the Group button beneath the Path List to turn the paths into a group. You can then collapse the group by clicking the arrow symbol next to the group header. At this point, the group is locked and you can activate or deactivate all four paths at once by highlighting the group name and pressing the Enter (Windows) or Return (Mac) key.

8. Choose Edit | Deselect. Then choose the first Drawing Visibility button and Mask Visibility buttons from the Path List Palette.

9. Click the Brush Tool in the Tools Palette. The 2B Pencil and color C-6 should still be active from the last step. If they are not, reselect them. Draw some lines inside the areas shown in Figure 6.23.

TIP You can activate and deactivate one or more of the four paths in the Path List to protect some areas while you color others. Chapter 9, "A Little Glimpse of Heaven," explains how to manipulate paths in the Path List.

Figure 6.23.
Draw some design lines
in the areas as shown
here, using the 2B
Pencil and color C-6.

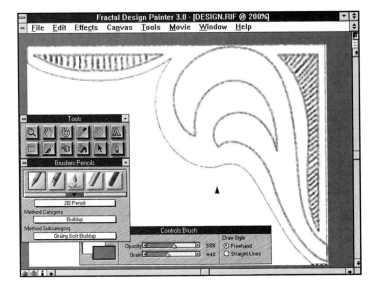

Step 6.10. Selecting a Different Paper Library

In the following steps, you load a library of paper textures that were created using Kai's Power Tools. Instructions for creating the textures appear in Chapter 20, "Integrating with Kai's Power Tools." For now, just observe what you can do with unique paper textures. There are lots of interesting paper textures in the KAIS.PAP library, included on the CD accompanying this book, for you to experiment with. Enjoy!

1. Choose the Art Materials Palette (Ctrl-3 in Windows, Cmd-3 in Mac) if it is not still open.

2. Open the drawer of the Papers Palette to reveal the Library button.

3. Click the Library button, shown in Figure 6.24. The Open Paper Grain File dialog box appears.

Figure 6.24.
Click the Library
button to load in a
new Paper library.

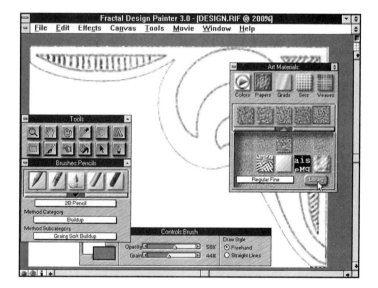

4. Choose the directory or folder where the KAIS.PAP Paper library appears on the CD accompanying this book. Choose the file, as shown in Figure 6.25.

5. Highlight the filename and click OK, or press Enter, to load the new Paper library into Painter.

6. From the drop-down list box inside the Papers Palette drawer, choose texture KPT 16.

7. Close the drawer and maximize the palette, if necessary, to reveal the Scale slider, shown in Figure 6.26.

Figure 6.25.
Select the KAIS.PAP library from the CD.

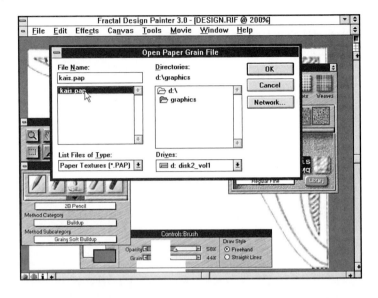

Figure 6.26.
Choose the KPT 16 Texture, and adjust the Scale slider to 50%.

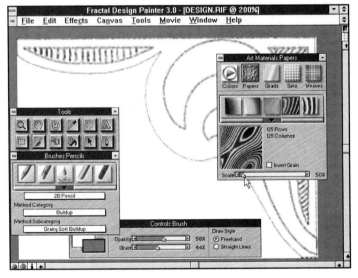

8. Adjust the paper grain scale to 50% to make the pattern smaller.

Step 6.11. Creating a Brush Variant

The 500 lb. Pencil is a nice brush to work with when applying paper textures to an image, as we've already seen. It's a bit too large to fill in the areas you're going to color in here, though. You can create a smaller version of this brush, and save it to the library so you can retrieve it at any time.

1. From the Chapter 6 color set, choose Gold (color PF-1), as shown in Figure 6.27.

Figure 6.27.
Choose color PF-1
from the Color Set.

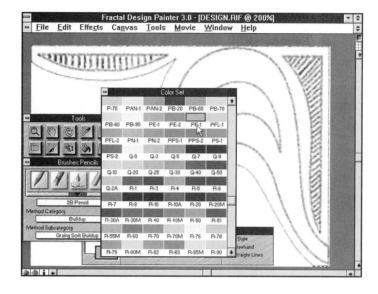

2. From the Brushes Palette, choose the 500 lb. Pencil variant, shown in Figure 6.28.

Figure 6.28.
Choose the 500 lb.
variant of Pencils.

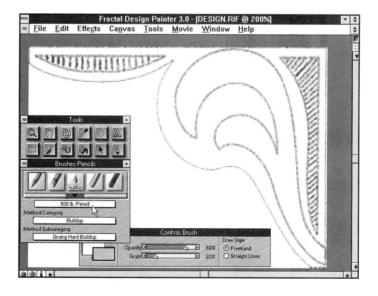

3. Open the Brush Controls Palette, shown in Figure 6.29, and select the Size Palette (if it is not already selected).

4. The Size slider is just beneath the preview window. Move this slider until the brush size is about 10.0. You see the dab (the circular symbol) in the preview window adjust to reflect the new size.

Figure 6.29.
Adjust the Size slider
in the Size Palette
to around 10.

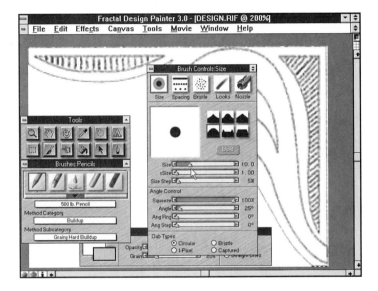

NOTE At this point, users of previous versions of Painter probably will reach for the Build button to build the new brush. However, many of Painter 3's brushes have an auto-build feature now. This makes creating new brushes and variants quicker and easier. The Build button in the Brush Controls | Size Palette will become enabled if the brush needs to be rebuilt. The Build button will be recessed if it does not need rebuilding.

There are two ways to save a variant of a brush:

■ You can use the Save Built Variant command to write over the existing settings of a brush under the same name.

■ You can use the Save Variant command to save the revised brush under a new name, leaving the original brush intact.

In this instance, use the latter method: the 500 lb. Pencil is a nice brush to keep around.

5. Choose the Tools | Brushes | Save Variant command, as shown in Figure 6.30.

Figure 6.30.
Save the revised brush
by choosing the Tools |
Brushes | Save Variant
command.

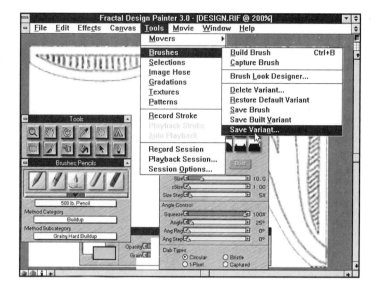

6. A dialog box appears, prompting you to name the new variant of the brush. I called the brush "100 lb. Pencil" because it's about one-fifth the size of the original 500 lb. version. Type in the name and click OK. The new variant is now available as a choice of pencils, permanently!

Step 6.12. More Coloring

Now that you have your paper, color, and brand new brush selected, color in the area surrounding the scroll and the two lined-in areas, as shown in Figure 6.31. Mouse users will achieve better results if the Opacity slider in the Controls | Brush Palette is reduced to around 20%.

1. I chose the Thick and Thin Pencils variant for this step because you can vary its width depending on the direction of the brush stroke. In this manner, it's sort of like a Calligraphy Pen that responds to paper grain. Choose the Thick and Thin Pencils, as shown in Figure 6.32.

2. Choose Smoky Blue (color BU-1) from the color set.

3. Build up some of the color around the outer edges of the scroll, as shown in Figure 6.33. This adds a bit more depth to the image. Start the strokes lightly and then build up some darker areas where you want shadows to appear. Mouse users can reduce the Opacity slider in the Controls | Brush Palette to around 50% for better results.

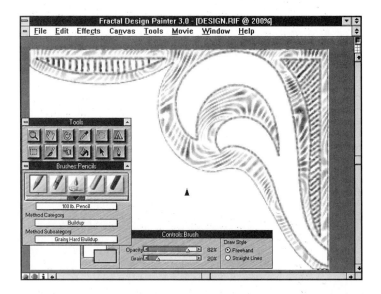

Figure 6.31.
Color in the areas
outside the scroll with
the new 100 lb. Pencil
variant you created.

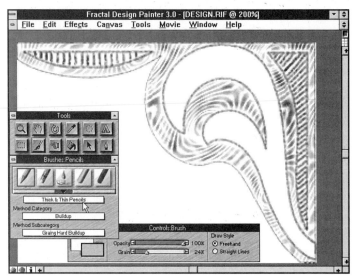

Figure 6.32.
Choose the Thick and
Thin pencil variant
from the Brushes
Palette.

4. Next, choose Burnt Orange (color D-3) (shown in Figure 6.33).

5. Again, using the Thick and Thin Pencils variant, fill in the entire area except for the scroll. The texture starts to show the appearance of wood that has been woodburned and stained. Apply different amounts of coverage so that there are variances in light and dark. Figure 6.34 shows the area completely filled in. Mouse users can adjust the Opacity slider in the Controls | Brush Palette to around 30% for better results.

Figure 6.33.
Build up some blue
shadows around the
scroll with color BU-1.

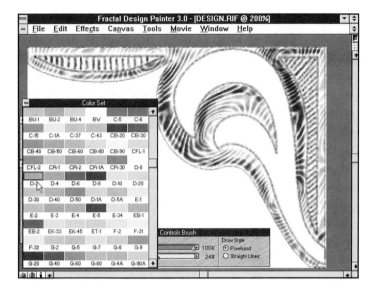

Figure 6.34.
Color over the entire
border using color D-3
and the Thick and Thin
Pencils, with varying
amounts of colors for
shading.

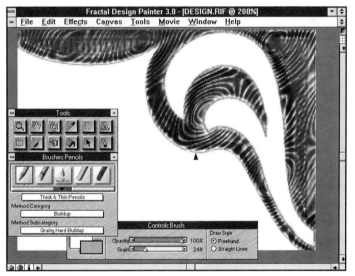

Step 6.13. Reloading the Default Paper Library

The default PAINTER.PAP paper library is found in your Painter directory or folder. Load this library back in now to continue with your project.

1. Click the Library button inside the Papers Palette drawer.
2. Choose the correct directory or folder on your hard drive.
3. Select the PAINTER.PAP file.

4. Choose OK or press Enter (Windows) or Return (Mac).

5. From this library, choose Basic Paper, as shown in Figure 6.35.

Figure 6.35.
Reload the default
Paper Library, and
choose Basic Paper.

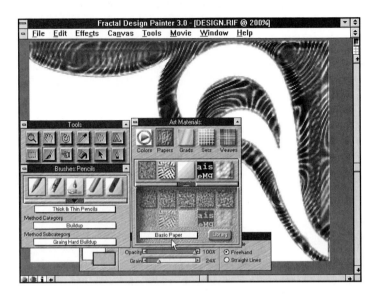

6. From the color set, choose Light Brown (color CR-1A). The location of this color is shown in Figure 6.36.

Figure 6.36.
Choose color CR-1A
from the default color
set.

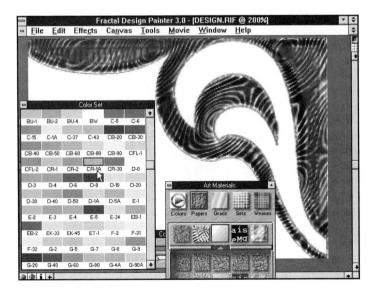

7. Rough in some color in the scroll, using the Thick and Thin pencil. The purpose here isn't to color the area in completely, but just to add some contour to the scroll. Refer to Figure 6.37 for an example.

Figure 6.37.
Rough in some color to shade the scroll. You blend this color with the Just Add Water variant.

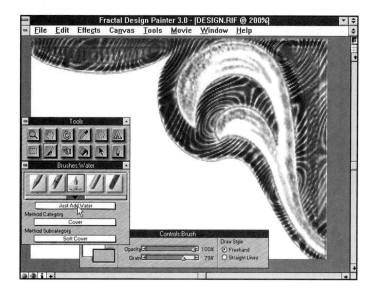

Step 6.14. Blending Color with Just Add Water

Now blend the color in the scroll using the Just Add Water variant of the Water brushes. The Water brushes are represented by a drop of water about to hit a little puddle. This icon is displayed as the currently selected icon in Figure 6.37.

1. From the Brushes Palette, select the Water brushes.

2. Choose the Just Add Water variant. If the brush strokes are too wide, reduce the size to between 8 and 10 in the Brush Controls | Size Palette. This brush needs to be rebuilt if the size is adjusted.

3. Blend the colors of the scroll until it looks smooth. You may decide that the scroll needs more color in the process. If so, revert to the Thick and Thin Pencils variant, add more color, and then return to the Just Add Water variant and blend. Figure 6.38 shows this in progress.

4. Next, add some detail lines, using the same color with the Sharp Pencil variant. This step is shown in Figure 6.39.

Figure 6.38.
Smooth the colors in
the scroll using Just
Add Water.

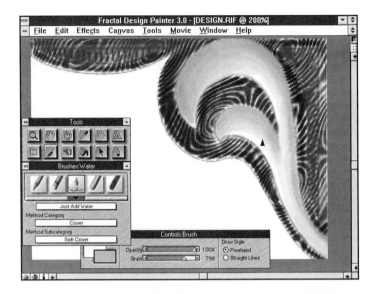

Figure 6.39.
Add some detail lines
to the scroll using the
Sharp Pencil variant.

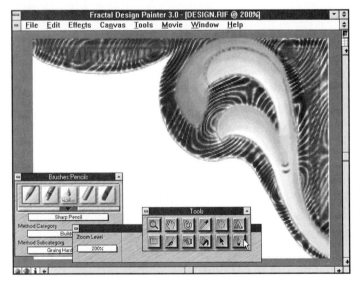

Bringing the Floater into the Background Document

Now that you have your border design colored in, it's time to create a floater and place it into the Floater library. You can then bring the floater into your background image, duplicate it, and add effects to it.

So far you have worked with paths, which basically are outline boundaries that define a specific area to be masked or filled with a color or effect. Paths *do not* contain color or image data—but a floater does.

Floaters can best be defined as an image entity that you can reposition in your document without affecting the background or other floaters in the composition. A floater has its own mask layer, which you can manipulate in the same manner you can the background layer. You can paint on floaters, just like a background image. Additionally, floaters have some special effects of their own, presented as composite methods, discussed later in this chapter.

Step 6.15. Converting the Paths to a Floater

You create floaters from active paths. If you recall, you imported the original design from CorelDRAW as an .EPS selection, so the paths already are created. You must activate the four paths making up the design so you can convert them into a floater.

1. Load in the Objects Palette (Ctrl-5 in Windows, Cmd-5 in Mac) and select the P.List (Path List) icon.

2. If you are using Painter 3.0, there are four unnamed items in the Path List Palette. Click the circles of each item to activate the paths. When a path is active, the circle is represented by a dotted line, and the path in the document is surrounded by a selection marquee. Your screen should look similar to Figure 6.40.

   If you are using Painter 3.1 or if you grouped your paths as outlined in the tip appearing in Step 6.9, make sure that the four paths are collapsed into the group by clicking the arrow beside the group name. Click the group name to highlight it and press the Enter (Windows) or Return (Mac) key to activate the paths. All four paths should be surrounded by a selection marquee.

Figure 6.40.
Reactivate the path borders from the Path List Palette.

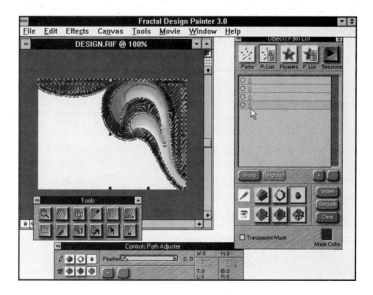

3. Next, click the Floaters icon in the Objects Palette (the third icon). This opens the Floaters Palette, shown in Figure 6.41, from which you can choose floaters or add them to the currently open Floater library. For now, you will place the floater in the default library. You can add floaters to the library with the palette drawer open or closed.

Figure 6.41.
Click the Floaters icon
from the Objects
Palette to open the
Floaters Palette.

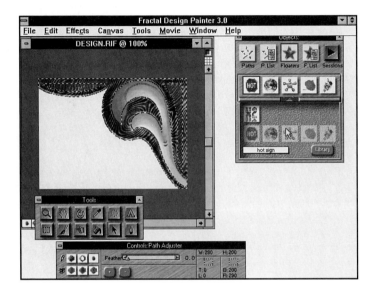

4. From the Tools Palette, select the Floating Selection tool (the third icon in the bottom row).

5. You want to keep the original image intact in the DESIGN.RIF file when you place the floater into the Floater library. To do this, depress and hold the Alt key in Windows, or the Option key in Mac, while you click the Floating Selection tool anywhere on the selected group of paths.

6. Keeping the Alt or Option key and the mouse button (or stylus) depressed, drag the floater out toward the Floaters Palette. You see an outline of the floater attached to the cursor as you drag. When the cursor moves inside the Floaters Palette, the outline changes to an icon-sized square. When this happens, release the Alt or Option key and the mouse button or stylus.

7. When you release the Alt or Option key and the mouse button or stylus, the Save Floater dialog box appears. Figure 6.42 illustrates this dialog box.

8. Name the floater Chap 6 Border, and click the OK button or press the Enter key. The floater icon appears in the Floaters Palette, and you can now use the floater in any document.

9. Save and close the DESIGN.RIF file—you're done with it! Keep the Floaters Palette available for the next step.

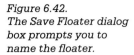

Figure 6.42.
The Save Floater dialog
box prompts you to
name the floater.

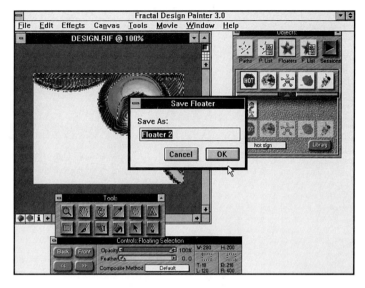

Step 6.16. Placing the First Floater

Now place the first copy of the floater into the first background-image document you created.

1. Reopen or maximize the LABEL.RIF file.

2. Click and drag the Chap 6 Border floater from the Floaters Palette to the LABEL.RIF document, placing the floater in the upper-right corner of the colored rectangle. Don't worry about precise alignment—you take care of that in the next step.

There are two ways to fine tune the placement of floaters:

■ The first method is to place your floater as near to its final position as you can with the mouse or stylus, then use the arrow keys on the keyboard to "nudge" the floater over, one pixel-width at a time, until it appears in the correct spot. The direction of the nudge is pretty self-explanatory: one tap on the up arrow moves the floater up one pixel, one tap on the down arrow moves it down one pixel, and so on.

■ As to the other method of accurately placing a floater: do you recall that you drew the lines of the rectangular selection to snap to Painter's grid, and that you set the grid spacing to 20 by 20? This means you can place your floater to align to a coordinate that is evenly divisible by 20!

To use the latter method:

1. Click the F.List icon in the Objects Palette. The Floater List Palette appears, and the Chap 6 Border floater is on the list.

2. Click the Chap 6 Border name in the Floater List Palette to highlight it. Then press the Enter (Windows) or Return (Mac) key. The Floater Attributes dialog box, shown in Figure 6.43, appears.

Figure 6.43.
The Floater Attributes box lets you name a floater and specify its upper-left coordinate position.

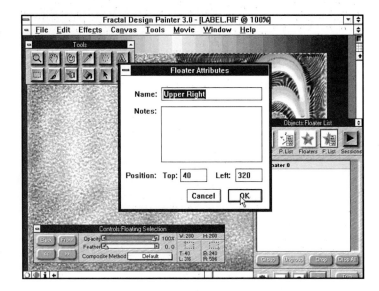

Figure 6.44 clarifies the placement of the inner rectangle and the floaters. When you enter Top and Left coordinate values, the coordinates relate to the point at which the upper-left corner of the floater is aligned. Your overall document is 640-by-480 pixels. From there, you drew a border line 40 pixels in from the outer edges, making the inside rectangle 560×400 pixels, with its upper-left coordinate at 40 Top, 40 Left. Your quarter-size floater border is 280×200 pixels. To align four 280×200 floaters inside the rectangle correctly, use the figures shown in Figure 6.44.

3. Rename the floater Upper Right.

4. To align the floater to its proper grid spot, enter 40 for the Top coordinate and 320 for the Left coordinate. You can use the Tab key to move between the fields in the dialog box.

5. Click the OK button, or press Enter (Windows) or Return (Mac). The floater is realigned to the coordinates you entered in the Floater Attribute dialog box.

Figure 6.44.
The basic layout of your
project, showing the
coordinates of each
item aligned on the grid
squares.

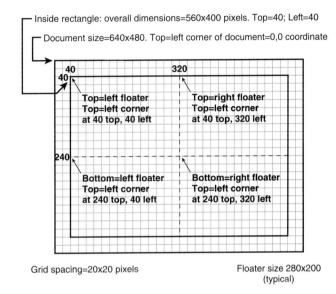

Inside rectangle: overall dimensions=560x400 pixels. Top=40; Left=40

Document size=640x480. Top=left corner of document=0,0 coordinate

40   320

Top=left floater
Top=left corner
at 40 top, 40 left

Top=right floater
Top=left corner
at 40 top, 320 left

240

Bottom=left floater
Top=left corner
at 240 top, 40 left

Bottom=right floater
Top=left corner
at 240 top, 320 left

Grid spacing=20x20 pixels

Floater size 280x200
(typical)

Step 6.17. Duplicating Floaters with the Floating Selection Tool

You can make a copy of this floater by depressing the Alt key in Windows or the Option key in Mac while moving a duplicate to a new location, as follows:

1. Holding down the Alt or Option key, click anywhere on the Upper Right floater and drag the mouse or stylus outward. An outline of the floater follows the cursor.

2. When the cursor is outside the area of the original floater, release the stylus or mouse. Another floater named Upper Right appears in the Floater List Palette. Its name will be highlighted in the Floater List, and the associated floater will be surrounded by a selection marquee in the document window.

Step 6.18. Adjusting the Floater Orientation

This step shows you how to adjust the new floater's orientation. To create the Upper Left floater, you must flip the image horizontally. This command is straightforward:

1. With the duplicate floater still selected, choose Effects | Orientation | Flip Horizontal. Figure 6.45 illustrates this command.

Figure 6.45.
Choose Effects |
Orientation | Flip
Horizontal to reorient
the floater duplicate.

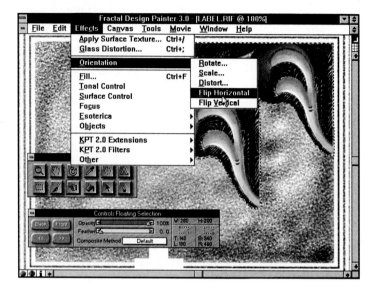

2. When the command is complete, make sure the associated line in the Floater List Palette is highlighted. Press Enter to bring up the Floater Attributes dialog box again.

3. Rename this floater Upper Left.

4. Set the floater's coordinates to 40 Top and 40 Left, and click OK, or press Enter (Windows) or Return (Mac). The new floater is aligned to its proper spot.

5. Continue in the same manner with the remaining two floaters.

   For the Lower Left floater, Alt-click or Option-click the currently active Upper Left floater, flip it vertically with the Effects | Orientation | Flip Vertical command, and set its coordinates to 240 Top, 40 Left.

   For the Lower Right floater, Alt-click or Option-click the Lower Left floater, flip it horizontally, and set its coordinates to 240 Top, 320 Left.

The final result should look similar to Figure 6.46.

Step 6.19. Floater Composite Methods

This is where some of the fun starts. As I mentioned earlier, floaters have some effects that are unique only to floaters. These effects work in conjunction with the floater's mask layer to produce different transparencies. As you experiment with the floater composite methods, accessible on the Controls | Floating

Selection Palette, shown in Figure 6.47, feel free to choose any types you like and adjust the opacity to any degree. Because you didn't feather your selections before creating the floater, the Feather slider is not effective in this instance.

Figure 6.46.
All four floaters have
been oriented and
named.

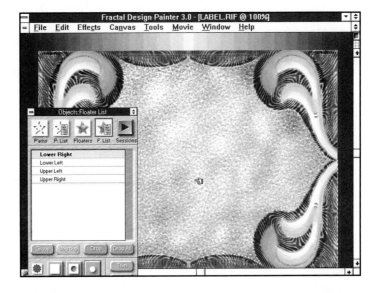

Figure 6.47.
Choose a Floater
Composite method in
the Controls | Floating
Selection Palette.

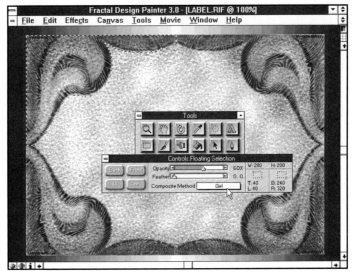

NOTE You could easily have applied the composite method to the first floater before creating the duplicates— that would have saved you the trouble of applying the effect to the four floaters individually. However, I wanted you to experiment a bit with them to see how one effect compared to another in appearance. For example, I had a hard time deciding whether I liked Gel at 60 percent opacity better than Default at 80 percent. The latter ended up winning when I compared the two side by side.

The Floater Composite methods are as follows:

- Default—The Default method of applying floaters covers or hides layers or the background beneath the selected floater.

- Gel—This method tints the underlying floaters or background with the colors in the floater.

- Colorize—This method adjusts the hue and saturation of the image beneath with values from the floater. You can use it to colorize a grayscale image, or turn a colored image into grayscale.

- Reverse Out—This method creates a negative of the area beneath it. Black areas turn white with the floater, and colored images appear like a negative beneath the floater.

- Shadow Map—This method blocks light beneath the floater, letting you create shadowed effects without affecting the image.

- Magic Combine—This method uses luminance values to combine the floater with the underlying image. If an area in the floater is lighter than the area beneath it, the floater appears in the underlying image.

- Pseudocolor—This method translates the luminance of the floater into *hues*: different colors in the spectrum.

When you're done experimenting with the composite methods and the Opacity slider, apply your favorite result to all four floaters, as follows:

1. Click the floater to which you want to apply the effect with the Floating Selection tool.

2. Select the composite method you want to use, and adjust the opacity until you get the results you want. The Feather slider will not work in this case, because you did not apply feathering to the floaters when creating it.

Step 6.20. Adding the Stroked Text

In the following steps, you will import a text outline created in CorelDRAW as an .EPS selection. This text was fitted to a path in the software, as explained in Chapter 21, "Integrating with CorelDRAW!" After you import the text selection, you will use the Stroke Selection command to stroke the text in the same manner as you did the border design.

1. From the Brushes Palette, choose the 2B Pencil.

2. From the Chapter 6 Color Set, choose a *very* dark brown color. Color 43M in the fifth row works well for this.

3. Choose the Tools | Selections | Open EPS as Selection command. Refer to Figure 6.16 for its location.

4. In the resulting dialog box, select and load the LABELTXT.EPS file.

5. Open the Path List Palette. In Painter 3.0, verify that all items in the list are active, except for the Rectangle you created at the beginning of the project. All the circles should be dotted, except the last item, marked Rectangle, which should be a solid gray outline. Figure 6.48 illustrates this step. If you like, group all the active paths (the letters) by clicking the Group button. Then collapse the group by pressing the Enter key.

6. Choose Tools | Selections | Convert to Selection to turn the Bézier curve letters into outline selections. They will become surrounded with selection marquees.

Figure 6.48.
Activate all paths,
except the Rectangle
path created at the
beginning of the project

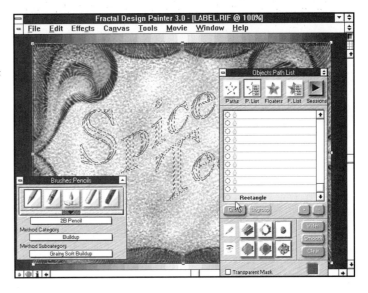

7. Choose Tools | Selections | Stroke Selection. You see the text being outlined with the 2B Pencil, automatically. Figure 6.49 shows the final result. To view the results more easily, turn the marquee selection off by clicking the first Mask Visibility button.

Figure 6.49.
The finished result of the stroked text and floater arrangement.

Summary

In this chapter I explained a bit about using the Pencil variants, and you learned how to create a straight-lined selection that is aligned to a grid. You also learned how to accurately place floaters aligned to the grid. You learned how to import .EPS files as selections, and how to outline them so as to look hand-drawn. Finally, I covered the basics of creating floaters and what their composite methods do. I'd say we covered quite a bit of territory in this project.

Feel free to experiment further with this project using the techniques we've covered. For example, you can create some additional floaters and place them in the centers of the top and sides to make them appear less sparse. You might create some additional text in the center portion, such as adding a fictitious company name to the label, and maybe a marketing slogan. ("Spice up your life" comes to mind as a really bad example—now do you see why I didn't add one?) You could add some additional border lines around the edges, using a brush made out of a Cover method. There's plenty of room for experimentation and creativity left here.

In the next project you create a line-art project using the Pen variants. I also cover the Cartoon Fill method, which you use to fill the image with color. All this prepares you for cartoon animation, which I discuss later in the book!

Pen Project

In this chapter I discuss Painter's Pen variants, which are a common choice for line work and cartooning. I also discuss one of Painter's more advanced fill techniques—the Cartoon Cel Fill method—to prepare you for creating a cartoon animation later in this book. In the process, you learn how to spot and correct leaks in line work.

The Pen Variants

Painter's Pen variants fall into two categories:

- The majority of the Pen variants use Cover methods, which means their strokes cover underlying strokes.

- Two of the variants use Buildup methods, which means their strokes get darker as you layer them.

The Pens produce antialiased strokes, some which vary in width as you apply pressure to the stylus. Although the Pen variants are better suited for line work, you can also use them for colored images as well.

Cover Method Pen Variants

Here are descriptions of the Pen variants that use the Cover method.

Calligraphy Pen

The Calligraphy Pen variant works like its real-life counterpart, complete with variations in stroke width. Though its main purpose is to create calligraphic text, this Pen also produces interesting line work.

This Pen variant produces soft, antialiased strokes that cover underlying strokes. The strokes vary in size based on the pressure of a stylus. Light pressure produces a narrow stroke. Heavy pressure produces a wider stroke.

Mouse users can vary the width of the stroke based on the direction you drag the mouse. You can adjust brush size interactively in the Brush Controls | Size Palette, or by changing the Size category in the Advanced Controls | Sliders Palette to Velocity or Direction.

Flat Color

The Flat Color Pen variant produces broad strokes with a soft, antialiased edge. These strokes cover underlying color. The main purpose for this Pen is to fill large areas with color. This brush should work the same whether you're painting with a mouse or a stylus.

Leaky Pen

The Leaky Pen variant gives the effect of a pen that is dripping ink. The strokes of this Pen are antialiased and vary in size based on the speed at which you drag the mouse or stylus. (This makes the brush work the same whether using the mouse or the stylus.) You can find the setting that gives this Pen that characteristic in the Advanced Controls | Random Palette: the Dab Location Placement slider.

Pen and Ink

The Pen and Ink variant produces soft, antialiased pen strokes that cover underlying color. This tool should work the same whether you're painting with a mouse or a stylus. The width of the stroke varies with the speed at which you drag the mouse or stylus: slower strokes produce heavy lines, and rapid strokes produce thin lines.

You can achieve interesting variations with this Pen when you change speed at various points during a single stroke. For example, start your stroke slowly and end it with a quick pull of the mouse or stylus. You get a stroke that is broader at the beginning and tapers off at the end.

Pixel Dust

The Pixel Dust variant draws a random spray of pixels. The effect is somewhat similar to the effect of an airbrush, but the spray you achieve with the Pixel Dust variant is more opaque and more widely spaced than that of an airbrush. You can reduce the randomness of its spray by adjusting the Dab Location Placement slider in the Advanced Controls | Random Palette.

Scratchboard Rake

The Scratchboard Rake variant is most effective when using white ink on a black background. It produces multilined, antialiased strokes that vary in size and opacity with pressure from the stylus. Light pressure produces a thinner, more transparent stroke. Heavy pressure produces a wider, darker stroke.

You can adjust brush size interactively in the Brush Controls | Size Palette or by changing the Size category in the Sliders Palette to Velocity or Direction. You can adjust opacity interactively on the Controls | Brush Palette.

Scratchboard Tool

Like the Scratchboard Rake, the Scratchboard Tool variant is most effective when using white lines on a black background. It produces soft, antialiased strokes that vary in size with stylus pressure.

Adjust the brush size interactively in the Brush Controls | Size Palette, or by changing the Size category in the Sliders Palette to Velocity or Direction.

Single Pixel

The Single Pixel variant draws pixel-width lines that are antialiased, and that cover underlying colors. Pressure does not affect the width of this pen.

Buildup Method Pens

A couple of Painter's pen variants use build-up methods—that is, they gradually build up colors toward black. These Pen variants would work well for shading colored areas.

Bear in mind that when you use either of these Pen variants you will not be able to apply light ink over darker ink. To accomplish that, select one of the Pen variants that uses a Cover method.

Fine Point

The Fine Point variant produces strokes that cover underlying strokes and that react to the paper texture you choose in the Papers Palette. The strokes have the appearance of those of a ballpoint pen.

The strokes of the Fine Point variant get darker as you layer them, making it suitable for drawing shaded areas. If the strokes turn black too quickly, you can adjust the Opacity slider in the Controls | Brush Palette toward the left to lighten the strokes.

Smooth Ink Pen

The Smooth Ink Pen variant mimics the lines and strokes of a fountain pen. Stroke width varies with the pressure you apply with the stylus: lighter strokes produce thinner lines, and heavier strokes produce wider lines. The strokes build up toward black when you layer them. Move the Opacity slider in the Controls | Brush Palette toward the left to reduce the speed at which the strokes build up toward black.

This Pen is sensitive to paper grain. Heavier strokes penetrate the paper deeper, covering more of the paper grain. Lighter strokes cause more of the paper grain to show through. You can adjust the Grain slider on the Controls | Brush Palette to achieve the same effect.

You can adjust the brush size interactively in the Brush Controls | Size Palette, or by changing the Size category in the Sliders Palette to Velocity or Direction. Adjust grain interactively on the Controls | Brush Palette.

Creating Your Own Color Sets

A premade color set for this project is included on the CD furnished with this book. However, if you prefer to create an identical color set yourself, follow these steps:

1. Open the Art Materials Palette (Ctrl-3 in Windows, Cmd-3 in Mac).
2. Click the Sets icon to open the Sets Palette. Maximize the palette by clicking the button at the upper-right section of the palette so that it appears as shown in Figure 7.1.
3. From the top of the palette, click and drag the Colors icon to place the Art Materials | Colors Palette at the side of the Sets Palette, as shown in Figure 7.2. The Colors Palette will be used to choose colors for the color set.
4. From the Art Materials | Sets Palette, click the New Set button to create a new color set. A small, empty document window will appear on your screen. This document window is shown next to the cursor in Figure 7.3. As you choose colors for your color set, they will be placed into this document window.

Figure 7.1.
From the Art Materials
Palette, click the Sets
icon to open the Sets
Palette.

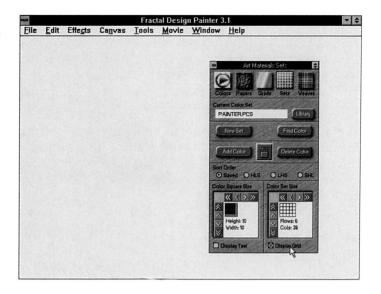

Figure 7.2.
Place the Art
Materials | Colors
Palette next to the
Sets Palette.

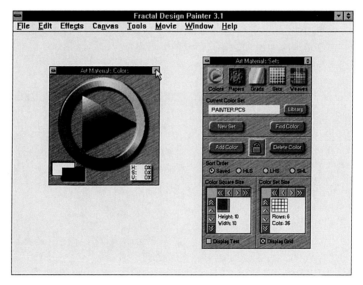

Figure 7.3.
A new empty document window appears on your screen when the New Set button is clicked.

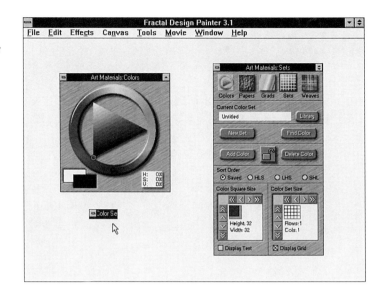

5. The first color added to the color set is black. Choose black (Hue of 0, Saturation of 0, and Value of 0) as your current color. Then click the Add Color button in the Sets Palette to add the color to the color set. Black will appear in the little document window, as shown in Figure 7.4.

Figure 7.4.
Choose black as your current color and click the Add Color button in the Sets Palette to add black to the color set.

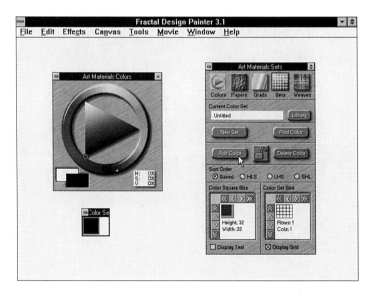

NOTE Hue, Saturation, and Value settings for a given color are displayed in the Art Materials | Colors Palette at the lower-right side of the color wheel.

■ To adjust the Hue (position in the color spectrum) of a color, move the color indicator in the outer color wheel.

■ To adjust the Saturation (purity) of a color, adjust the color indicator in the inner triangle toward the left or right. If you move the Saturation slider completely toward the left, you will have a pure shade of white, black, or gray. If you move the Saturation slider completely to the right point of the inner triangle, the color will be at its purest.

■ To adjust the Value (lightness or darkness) of a color, adjust the color indicator in the inner triangle upward or downward.

6. To add a shade of blue to the color set, verify that the Hue color indicator in the outer circle of the Colors Palette is set to 0. Move the color indicator in the inner triangle until the Saturation figure is around 71% and the Value figure is around 58%, as shown in Figure 7.5. Don't worry about getting these figures exact. If you are within a percentage or two, it will be acceptable for this project.

Figure 7.5.
Adjust the color
indicators to get a blue
shade with Hue at 0%,
Saturation at 71%, and
Value of 58%.

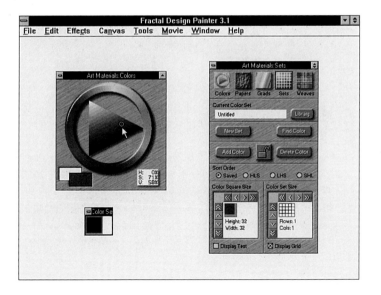

7. Click the Add Color button in the Sets Palette to add this shade of blue to your color set. The new shade appears inside the little document window.

8. Add the remaining colors as shown in Table 7.1. You have already added the first two colors shown in the table. Remember to follow the instructions in the previous note when adjusting the Hue, Saturation, and Value percentages.

Table 7.1. Color Formulas for the Project Color Set

Number	Color	Hue %	Sat %	Val %
1	Black	0	0	0
2	Blue	0	71	58
3	Blue-Violet	6	72	58
4	Violet	11	72	58
5	Violet	14	72	58
6	Red	35	75	56
7	Flesh	35	45	78
8	Green	60	25	42
9	Yellow	44	76	58
10	Dark Green	61	33	20
11	Violet	14	47	78
12	Violet	14	36	71
13	Violet	14	23	59
14	Dark Flesh	34	68	72
15	White	0	0	100

9. To save the color set to your hard drive, click the Library button in the Art Materials | Sets Palette. A warning box appears and asks if you want to save changes to the current color set. Click Yes to continue.

10. The Enter Color Set Name dialog box, shown in Figure 7.6, appears. Windows users will save the color set to a file with a .TXT file extension. Enter the name CHAP07CS for the color set for this project.

Figure 7.6.
Save the color set as
CHAP07CS. It is saved
as a text file.

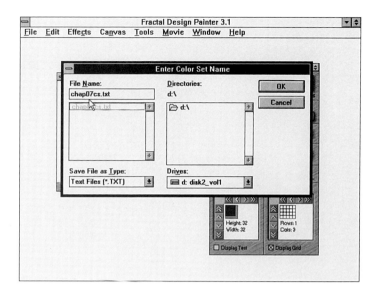

Naming Colors in Color Sets

The color set that I made for this chapter is included on the CD accompanying this book. It does not contain names for the colors. If you want to assign color names for this set, or for the one you created, you can follow the steps outlined below.

1. From the Sets Palette, open the CHAP07CS.TXT located on the CD accompanying this book, or the one you created in the preceding steps.

2. Unlock the color set in order to make changes to it. This includes adding or removing colors, adding text, or displaying text in the color set. To unlock the color set, click the padlock symbol in the Art Materials | Sets Palette so that the padlock is open, as shown in Figure 7.7.

3. To display color labels in a color set, check the Display Text checkbox, as shown in Figure 7.8. Spaces appear beneath the colors to provide room for the text display. If text labels have been assigned, they will appear beneath the appropriate color.

NOTE The color labels you assign are also used to label colors when you apply the Canvas | Annotate and Canvas | View Annotations commands. These commands are discussed in Chapter 29, "Printing in Painter."

When you assign color labels to color sets in Weavings, the colors can only be identified by single letters. For further information on this, see Chapter 13, "Fabrics and Patterns."

Figure 7.7.
Unlock the color set by clicking the padlock symbol in the Sets Palette.

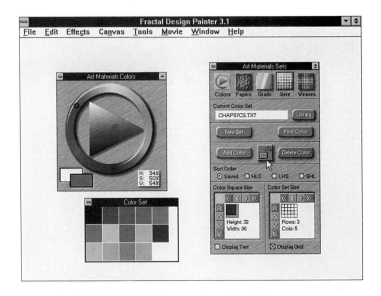

Figure 7.8.
To display color labels, check the Display Text box in the Sets Palette.

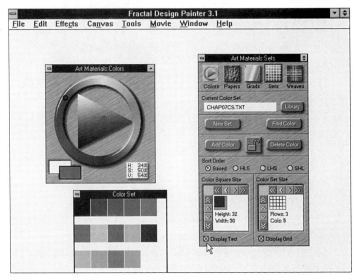

4. To assign a label to the color, go to the color set document. Double-click the color square you want to name. The Color Name dialog box, shown in Figure 7.9, appears.

5. Type in a name for the color. For this example, I used numbers to identify the colors. The completed labeling is shown in Figure 7.10. Color names can be numbers, letters, or a combination of both. It is best to keep the names relatively short so that they can be displayed beneath the color squares.

Figure 7.9.
Double-click the color
you want to name. The
Color Name dialog box
appears.

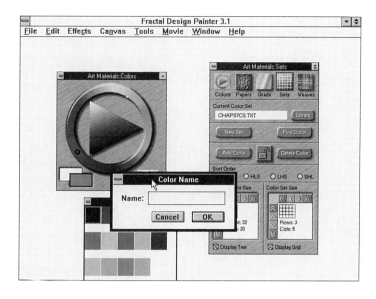

Figure 7.10.
Numbers are assigned
to the colors in this
color set, but you can
assign alphanumeric
labels to your colors.

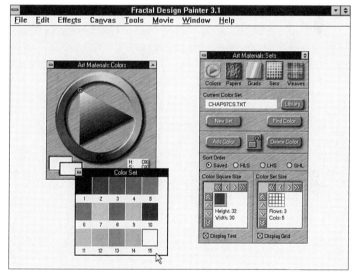

6. You can increase or decrease the width and height of the color squares by
   clicking the arrows beneath the Color Square Size heading in the Sets
   Palette. These arrows are shown in Figure 7.11. The double arrows enlarge
   or reduce the square size by a factor of two. The single arrows enlarge or
   reduce the square size by one pixel at a time.

Figure 7.11.
The Color Square Size
arrows enlarge or
reduce the size of the
color squares in the
color set.

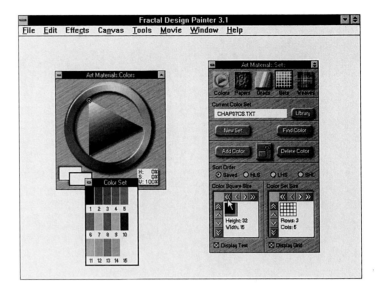

7. You can increase or decrease the number of rows and columns of **squares** in the color set by clicking the arrows beneath the Color Set Size heading in the Sets Palette. These arrows are shown in Figure 7.12. The double arrows enlarge or reduce the rows or columns by a factor of two. The single arrows enlarge or reduce the rows or columns by one **square** at a time.

Figure 7.12.
The Color Set Size
arrows enlarge or
reduce the number
of rows or columns
contained in the
color set.

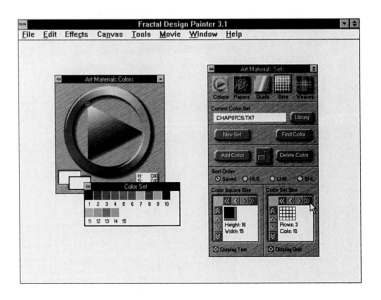

8. When you are finished with your changes, click the Library button in the Sets Palette again to update the changes to your disk. You will be asked for a color set name. Choose the CHAP07CS color set you started with. When you are asked if you want to replace the existing file, choose Yes. The changes will be updated and the color set will be locked again.

The Pen Project

This project is a fairly simple one. You start with some black-and-white line artwork: a drawing of an enchantress. You protect the line work by masking it, and fill the image with color and texture using Painter's Cartoon Cel Fill method. You can then add a little bit more detail using some of Painter's Pen variants.

What is the Cartoon Cel Fill Method?

Painter's Pens draw with antialiased lines. To make the line work appear less pixelly, Painter adds intermediate shades of the line work color and the background color around the basic line to soften the transition from light to dark.

TIP

> If you fill antialiased lines with a solid color, you notice that the intermediate-colored pixels create objectionable spots in the artwork. For example, if black line work on a white background is filled with red, you might see gray pixels between the red fill color and the black lines.
>
> You can use the Cartoon Cel Fill method in Painter to work around this. Start by masking the black line work based on Image Luminance. The mask protects the line work at varying levels of intensity. The black pixels are fully protected, and the intermediate shades of gray are protected at proportionately lower levels. After masking the lines, use Painter's Lock Out Color feature to protect the line color and to identify how much of the mask is protected. Finally, fill the lines by choosing the Cartoon Cel Fill Method from the Controls | Paint Bucket Palette.

This section discusses the steps individually to show you how to use the Cartoon Cel Fill method to eliminate pixelly areas when filling line artwork.

Step 7.1. Creating an Auto Mask Based on Image Luminance

Your first step is to create an Auto Mask based on Image Luminance. This step protects your line work later when you fill your image.

1. From the Painter Unleashed CD, open CHAP07_S.RIF. This is the starting point of your project. Zoom out to view the entire image on the screen, as shown in Figure 7.13.

Figure 7.13.
Open the
CHAP07_S.RIF file
located on the CD.

2. Choose Edit | Mask | Auto Mask, as shown in Figure 7.14. The Auto Mask dialog box appears.

Figure 7.14.
Choose Edit | Mask |
Auto Mask to mask the
lines in the image.

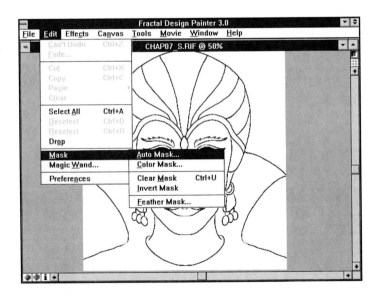

3. Inside the Auto Mask dialog box is a drop-down menu with several options. Choose Image Luminance from this menu, as shown in Figure 7.15. This generates mask transparencies based on the light and dark areas of your image.

4. Click OK, or press Enter (Windows) or Return (Mac), to generate the mask.

Figure 7.15.
Choose to generate the
mask based on Image
Luminance.

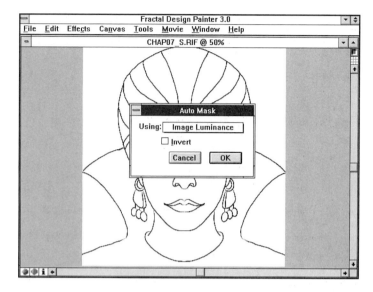

5. Click and hold the second icon at the lower-left corner of your document window. From the three choices that appear, choose the second (or middle) Mask Visibility button. This displays the masked line work in red.

6. Click and hold the first icon at the lower-left corner of your document window. From the three choices that appear, choose the second Drawing Visibility button, which protects the black artwork while you fill the remainder of the document.

7. You can save the document now, if you wish, as ENCHANT.RIF.

Step 7.2. Finding Line Leaks

Next, you learn what happens if the line work isn't properly protected or if there are leaks in the line work.

1. From the Art Materials Palette (Ctrl-3), choose the Sets icon to access the Sets Palette.

2. Click the Library button in the Sets Palette.

3. Choose the CHAP07CS.TXT color set from the CD-ROM accompanying this book. This color set is shown in Figure 7.16.

4. From the color set, choose any color other than black or white. I chose the flesh color (second color located in the second row), as shown in Figure 7.17.

5. Open the Tools Palette (Ctrl-1 in Windows, Cmd-1 in Mac) and select the Paint Bucket.

Figure 7.16.
Load the
CHAP07CS.TXT
Color Set text file
from the CD.

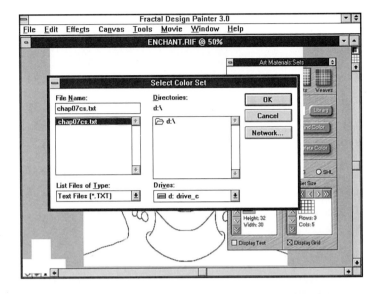

Figure 7.17.
Choose a color other
than black or white
from the color set.

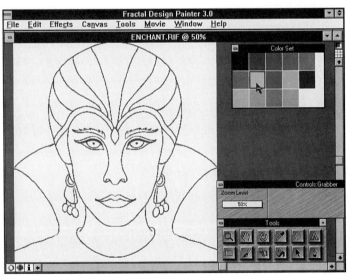

6. Open the Controls Palette (Ctrl-6 in Windows, Cmd-6 in Mac). From the Controls | Paint Bucket Palette, choose to Fill Cartoon Cel with Current Color, as shown in Figure 7.18.

7. Click in the upper portion of the image with the Paint Bucket. A dialog box appears with the message: "Now searching for extent of fill."

Figure 7.18.
Choose to fill a Cartoon
Cel with the current
color.

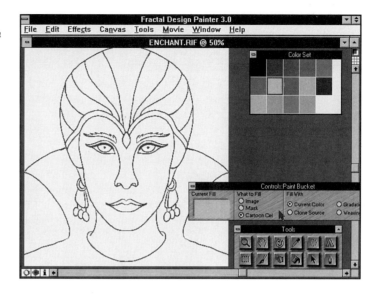

NOTE If the "Now searching for extent of fill" dialog box doesn't go away immediately, it usually means that Painter is getting ready to fill an extremely large area—something that usually indicates a problem if the area you're trying to fill is small.

After a while, you see the image fill with the color you selected, similar to Figure 7.19. The color extends into areas that you don't want to fill. This happens for one or two reasons:

- There is a line leak , which you must close or mask.
- You did not apply the Lock Out color feature before applying the Cartoon Cel Fill.

8. Undo the fill with the Edit | Undo command (Ctrl-Z in Windows, Cmd-Z in Mac), or use the File | Revert command to revert to the version you saved after the line work was masked. This causes your document to revert to its previous state.

NOTE If you revert to the saved document, you must reset the Drawing Visibility and Mask Visibility buttons to protect your line work again.

Figure 7.19.
The fill extends beyond the lines, but you can remedy that.

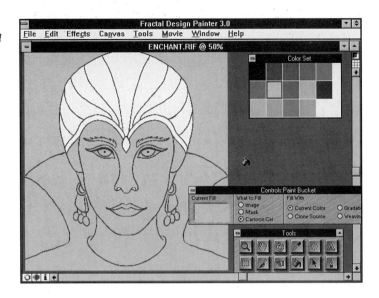

Step 7.3. Enabling the Lock Out Color Feature

You can remedy many of the "leaks" in line work by using Painter's Lock Out Color feature. Implement this through the Paint Bucket tool, as follows:

1. Double-click the Paint Bucket tool in the Tools Palette. The Lock Out Color dialog box, shown in Figure 7.20, appears.

Figure 7.20.
Access the Lock Out Color feature by double-clicking the Paint Bucket.

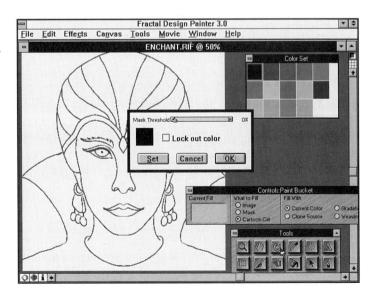

2. Notice a black square at the left of the dialog box. This is the color you want to "lock out" to ensure it remains protected when you apply the fills to your image. For future reference, though, you can change the Lock Out Color to the current primary color when you click the Set button in this dialog box.

3. Check the box adjacent to "Lock out color," as shown in Figure 7.21. This enables the Lock Out Color feature.

Figure 7.21.
Check the Lock Out
Color box to turn on the
Lock Out Color feature.

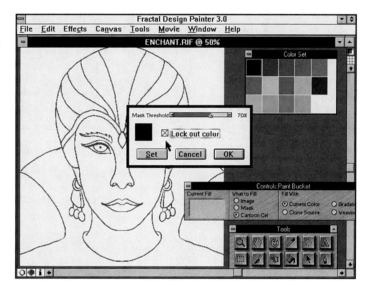

4. Adjust the Mask Threshold slider to around 70%, as shown in the figure.

Here's what the Mask Threshold slider does. As I mentioned, the antialiased lines contain intermediate colors of the line work against the background on which the lines were drawn. You've chosen to protect black with the Lock Out Color feature—but you have yet to tell Painter what we think is "black." There may be very dark shades of gray in the line work that look black to us, but not to Painter. If you think of the line work as a dam, a line leak is a break in the dam. When Painter's Cartoon Cel Fill comes to pixels in the line work that are near-black, but not black, it passes right through them to the other side.

The Mask Threshold slider in the Lock Out Color dialog box is initially set to 0%, meaning that only the color black is protected. Moving the slider further toward the right increases the variance from black that is protected. Setting the slider too low still allows the Cartoon Cel Fill to leak through. Setting it too high makes the Cartoon Cel Fill method behave more like the regular fill, leaving more of the antialiased pixels untouched. With the Mask Threshold slider set at 100 %, the fill behaves identically to the standard fill method.

Step 7.4. Filling in Line Leaks

There are two very obvious line leaks in the image, located at the upper corners of the raised collar. You can fix these leaks in either of two ways:

- Close the line leaks by using black ink and the Fine Point variant.
- Close the line leaks in the masking layer by using black ink and one of the Masking variants, such as the Masking Pen or Single Pixel Masking.

The latter method might be preferable, because it keeps the character of your original artwork while constraining the fill. This section takes you through closing the gaps in the line work using the latter method.

TIP   When using the Masking variants to paint in the masking layer, remember that:
- Black adds to the mask.
- White subtracts from the mask.
- Shades of gray protect the mask at varying intensities.

Because you want to add to the mask in these two areas, start by choosing black as the current color.

1. From the color set, choose black as your current color.
2. Open the Brushes Palette (Ctrl-2 in Windows, Cmd-2 in Mac) and select the Masking icon. These variants are represented by a paintbrush painting over a boy's face.
3. Choose the Single Pixel Masking variant, as shown in Figure 7.22.
4. If the masked areas in your document are not displayed in red, choose the middle Mask Visibility button.
5. Zoom in on one of the corners of the collar using the Magnifier or the quick-key combination of Ctrl-+ in Windows, or Cmd-+ in Mac. Here, in Figure 7.23, you can see the location of the gap.
6. Reselect the Brush tool from the Tools Palette.
7. Using black ink and the Single Pixel Masking variant, close the gap as shown in Figure 7.24. With the mask layer visible, the black color is rendered as red.
8. Do the same on the other side of the collar. When you're done, save the image again with the File | Save command (Ctrl-S in Windows or Cmd-S in Mac). This updates the file on your disk with your line corrections.

Figure 7.22.
Choose the Single Pixel
Masking tool, and black
ink.

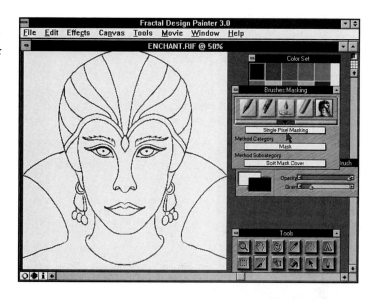

Figure 7.23.
Zoom in on the line leak
with the Magnifier.

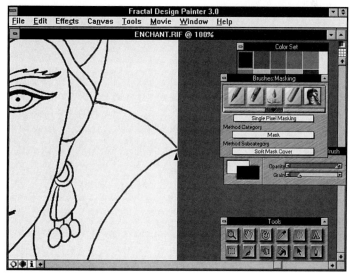

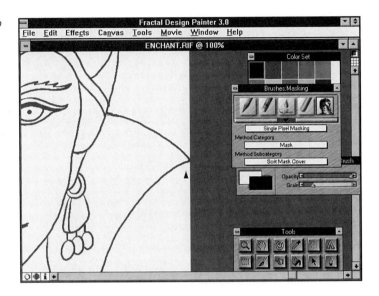

Figure 7.24. Fill the gap in the mask layer with the Single Pixel Masking variant and black ink.

Step 7.5. Filling Areas with the Cartoon Cel Fill Method

The next few pages here go quickly, because it's just a matter of filling the line work with the colors contained in the color set. Step-by-step screen shots clarify where the colors are placed.

1. The Lock Out Color feature should still be enabled from the previous steps. To verify this, double-click the Paint Bucket tool and make sure the current lock out color is black, the Lock Out Color checkbox is checked, and the Mask Threshold slider is set around 70%. Then click OK to exit the dialog box.

2. From the color set, choose Violet 5 (the last color in the first row). Choose the Paint Bucket from the Tools Palette. From the Controls | Paint Bucket Palette, choose to fill Cartoon Cel with Current Color.

3. Fill the band of the hat with this color, as shown in Figure 7.25.

4. Fill the face, neck, and ears with Flesh 7 (the second color in the second row). Refer to Figure 7.26.

5. Next, as shown in Figure 7.27, fill the lips with Red 6 (the first color in the second row).

6. Choose Black. Starting from the center stripe in the hat, fill every other stripe with black. There should be five stripes in all.

7. Fill the eyebrows, the nostrils, the hair, the areas around the earrings, and the collar and dress with black. When complete, your image should look like Figure 7.28.

Figure 7.25.
Fill the band in the hat
with Violet 5 from the
color set.

Figure 7.26.
Fill the face, neck, and
ears with Flesh 7.

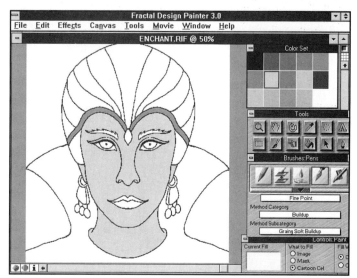

Figure 7.27.
Fill the lips with Red 6.

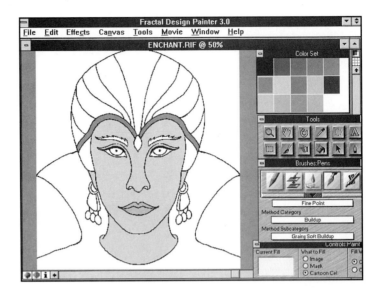

Figure 7.28.
Fill several areas in the
image with black.

8. Using Yellow 9 (the fourth color in the second row), fill in the earrings and the jewel in the center of her forehead, as shown in Figure 7.29.

Figure 7.29.
Fill the jewel of the hat
and the earrings with
Yellow 9.

9. Using Green 8 (the third color in the second row), fill in the irises of the eyes, as shown in Figure 7.30.

Figure 7.30.
Fill the irises of the
eyes with Green 8.

10. Using Blue-Violet 3, fill in the two stripes adjacent to the center stripe in the hat. These are shown in Figure 7.31.

Figure 7.31.
Fill the stripes near the
center black stripe with
Blue-Violet 3.

11. Fill the next two stripes with Violet 4, as shown in Figure 7.32.

Figure 7.32.
Fill the next two
stripes with Violet 4.

12. Finally, fill the remaining two areas in the hat with Violet 5. All areas
should now be filled in, and your screen should look like the one in
Figure 7.33.

Figure 7.33.
Fill the last two stripes
with Violet 5.

Step 7.6. Filling the Background

Now add the background texture to the image. The background was created using Kai's Power Tools Texture Explorer. (You can find instructions for doing this in Chapter 20, "Integrating with Kai's Power Tools.") You first open the background image and set it as the Clone Source. Then, using the Paint Bucket, fill the background areas using the Cartoon Cel Fill method. Here are the steps in more detail:

1. Open the BACKGRND.RIF background image from the Chapter 7 section of the CD accompanying this book.

2. Select it as the clone source using the File | Clone Source command, as shown in Figure 7.34.

3. Now click the ENCHANT.RIF document to make it current. You can select it by dropping down the Window menu and clicking the filename at the bottom of the drop-down menu.

4. From the Controls | Paint Bucket Palette, select to fill a Cartoon Cel with the clone source, as shown in Figure 7.35. A portion of the background image appears in the Current Fill square in the Controls | Paint Bucket Palette.

Figure 7.34.
Select the
BACKGRND.RIF file as
the Clone Source.

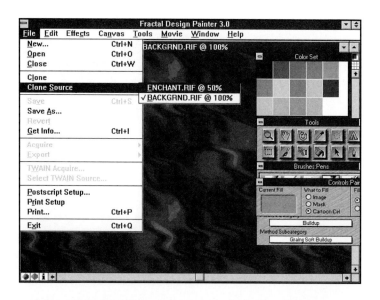

Figure 7.35.
Choose to fill a Cartoon
Cel with the Clone
Source.

5. Fill in the background areas (four in all) with the background clone source image. When complete, your image should look similar to Figure 7.36.

6. When you're done, you can close the BACKGRND.RIF file. (Select it as your current document and then choose File | Close.)

Figure 7.36.
Fill the background
areas with the textured
pattern.

Step 7.7. Enhancing the Image

While you're coloring in some of the enhancements to the drawing, you can edit small mistakes with the Single Pixel Pen variant. Choose a nearby color with the Eyedropper, and zoom into the area to be repaired:

1. Using Dark Green 10 and the Scratchboard Tool (Pen variant), draw a line around the outer edge of the iris. When you're done, the image should look similar to Figure 7.37.

Figure 7.37.
Add some lines in Dark
Green 10 around the
irises with the
Scratchboard tool.

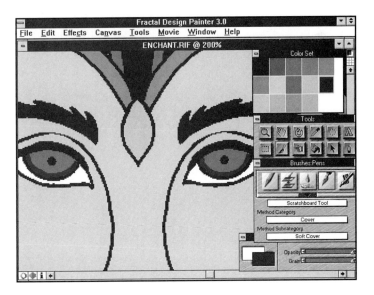

2. Soften the two colors together with Just Add Water (Water variant). Your image should look similar to Figure 7.38.

Figure 7.38.
Blend the Dark Green
10 into the eyes with
Just Add Water.

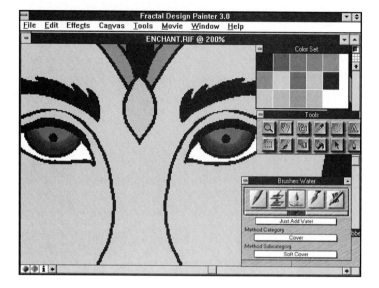

3. Using the Scratchboard Tool variant and flesh color, add some highlights to the lips. Figure 7.39 shows some lines drawn in the lips using this color.

Figure 7.39.
Add some flesh-colored
highlights to the lips.

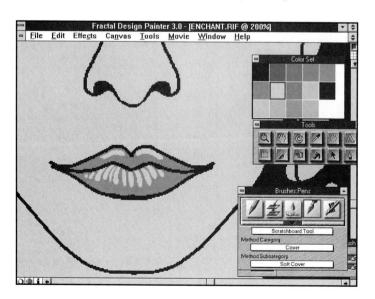

4. Use Just Add Water to soften the highlights and blend them with the shape of the lips. You can use the black line in the center of the lips to create some dark shading near where the lips meet, as shown in Figure 7.40.

NOTE   Be careful when approaching the outer lines of the lips, or you will extend your smoothing into the face color. It might help if you reduce the width of the brush using the Brush Controls | Size Palette.

Figure 7.40.
Blend the highlights on the lips with Just Add Water.

I used three shades of violet for the eyeshadow:

5. Using the Scratchboard Tool (Pen variant), choose Violet 11 and color up to the crease in the lid.

6. Choose Violet 12 and color halfway up toward the eyebrow.

7. Finally, finish up the eyeshadow with Violet 13. When you're done, the eyes should look similar to those shown in Figure 7.41.

Create some eyelashes that start wide at the base but taper off at the end. The Smooth Ink Pen can produce this effect, but it's a little wide for this image—so start by creating a narrower version of that pen.

8. Choose the Smooth Ink Pen variant from the Brushes Palette.

9. Open the Brush Controls | Size Palette and move the Size slider down to 3. If you are using a mouse, a setting of 2 might be a little better for you.

Figure 7.41.
*Add eyeshadow
between the eyes and
eyebrows using three
violet shades.*

10. Build the new brush by clicking the Build button in the Size Palette.

11. Choose the Tools | Brushes | Save Variant command, as shown in Figure 7.42.

12. When prompted to enter a name for the new brush, enter `Small Smooth Ink Pen`.

13. Click OK. Your brush is saved to the current Brush library.

Figure 7.42.
*Create a smaller
version of the Smooth
Ink Pen and save it
using Tools | Brushes |
Save Variant.*

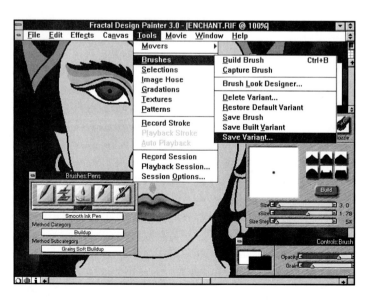

14. Choose black for your current color. Using the new pen, draw in the eyelashes. Vary the pressure, starting off heavier at the base of the eyelash and gradually decreasing pressure toward the end of the lash. Figure 7.43 shows the eyelashes in progress.

Figure 7.43.
Draw in the eyelashes, using heavier pressure at the base and lighter pressure at the end.

15. If you have to, rotate the canvas with the Rotate tool in the Tools Palette. Figure 7.44 shows the canvas rotated.

Figure 7.44.
Rotate the canvas as needed to add the eyelashes.

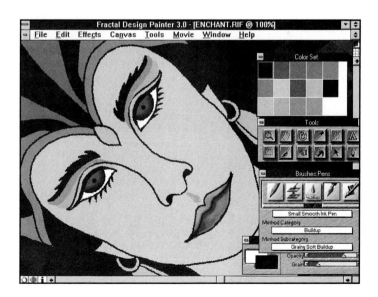

I added a bit of highlighting to the hair using blue. For this step, I created a narrower variant of the Pen and Ink Pen variant and then smoothed blue and black together using Just Add Water (a Water variant):

16. Choose the Pen and Ink Pen from the Brushes Palette.

17. Open the Brush Controls | Size Palette, and adjust the size down to 2.5.

18. Build the new brush by clicking the Build button in the Size Palette.

19. Choose the Tools | Brushes | Save Variant command and save the new brush as `Small Pen and Ink`.

20. Choose Blue 2 from the color set.

21. Draw some lines in the hair areas, as shown in Figure 7.45.

Figure 7.45.
Add some blue lines in the hair area using your new variant of the Pen and Ink Pen.

22. Click the Water icon and choose Just Add Water (Water variant). Smooth the lines into the black base color. Mouse users might want to reduce the Opacity in the Controls | Brush Palette for this step.

23. Next, add some design to the collar area using violet and blue to match colors in the background texture. Choose the Pen and Ink variant and Violet 4. Draw a border line around the collar, a small distance from the edge.

24. Choose the Scratchboard Tool variant and Blue 2. Draw some lacy-looking lines inside the border you just drew. When you're done the image should look similar to Figure 7.46.

Figure 7.46.
Add a border design to
the collar using Violet 4
and Blue 2.

To add more shape to the face, add some cheek color. The Flat Color variant is good for adding large areas of color to an area, but you must reduce its size a bit for this image. Then blend the deeper color in with the base flesh color using Just Add Water.

25. Choose Dark Flesh 14 from the color set.
26. Choose the Flat Color variant, and reduce its size to around 20 in the Brush Controls | Size Palette. You will not have to rebuild this brush.
27. Rough in some color for the cheeks. Don't go to the edge of the face: you want to leave some room in for blending. The coloring should look similar to Figure 7.47.
28. Choose Just Add Water from the Brushes Palette, and blend the cheek color in with the flesh color. When you're done, the image should look similar to Figure 7.48.

TIP This blending takes some time to look just right, so be patient here! Take care in the direction of your blend strokes. If you start in the cheek color, make sure you don't drag out too far into the facial color, because this will increase the size of the cheeks. If the cheeks get too large, you can pull some of the flesh color back in toward the cheek color and blend some more.

Figure 7.47.
Add some Dark Flesh 14 color to the cheek and neck area.

Figure 7.48.
Blend the cheek color carefully into the face and neck using Just Add Water.

The image is done! If you like, you can continue adding detail and color where you feel it is needed. When you're done, save the document again using the File | Save command.

Summary

You now know the basics of coloring line work using the Cartoon Cel Fill method. You've learned how to lock out colors while using cartoon cel fills, and how to fix leaky line work using Painter's Masking variants. You can use these techniques as a good starting point for creating cartoon animation, covered in Chapter 19, "Creating a Cartoon Animation."

In the next chapter, I introduce the Felt Pen tools and discuss how they react with paper and each other.

8

Working with the Felt Pens

Actually, this chapter goes a little bit beyond the Felt Pen variants, because here you create a totally original floater, right from scratch. No starting drawings to load—this time, you're on your own!

The project creates a child's block. The letters of the block are oriented to their proper planes. I show you how to apply some lighting effects to the block, how to make it into a floater, and then how to save it in your own custom Floater Library.

Felt Pen Variants

The Felt Pen variants look and work remarkably like real felt pens. Because they do not use any of the Grainy methods, they cover paper grain rather than interact with it. They create soft, antialiased strokes that build up toward black when applied over each other. Therefore, you can use the Felt Pens to apply shading. Start with light colors and light strokes, which give you a stroke that is closest in value to the currently selected color. Gradually build the strokes up over each other until the color gets darker. Mouse users can reduce the opacity of the brush to achieve the same effect as light pressure applied to a stylus.

Conversely, applying heavy pressure with a stylus turns a stroke black. Mouse users can move the Opacity slider in the Controls | Brush Palette farther toward the right to simulate this. If you find that the strokes turn black too quickly, you can move the Opacity slider toward the left. This causes the strokes to stay lighter longer.

If you build up your colors and then decide they're too dark, and you want to apply a lighter color over an area, you can use one of two methods:

- Select a tool that uses one of the cover methods, such as an Airbrush, Chalk, or Charcoal variant, to paint over the dark area with a lighter color.
- Use the Canvas | Set Paper Color command to select the color you want to lighten to, and then use one of the Eraser variants, such as the Flat Eraser, to erase the dark area to the lighter paper color.

Dirty Marker

The Dirty Marker variant produces strokes that turn black more quickly than those made with the Felt Marker. It also gives the appearance of a marker stroke that has been somewhat smudged. The strokes are soft and antialiased, and vary in opacity based on the pressure you apply with the stylus.

Felt Marker

The Felt Marker variant produces a soft shade of color that builds up toward black when strokes are repeated. You can alter stroke opacity with stylus pressure.

Fine Tip Felt Pens

The Fine Tip Felt Pens variant produces narrow strokes that are similar in appearance to those of felt-tip writing pens. The strokes vary in size based on the speed at which you drag your mouse or stylus. Faster strokes produce thinner lines, and slower strokes produce thicker lines. Repeated strokes build the color up toward black.

You can alter stroke opacity with stylus pressure. The default opacity of this pen is considerably darker than the Dirty Marker and Felt Marker.

Medium Tip Felt Pens

The Medium Tip Felt Pens variant draws strokes that vary in size based on the speed at which you drag your mouse or stylus. Faster strokes produce thinner lines, and slower strokes produce thicker lines. Repeated strokes build the color up toward black. You can alter stroke opacity with stylus pressure. The strokes are slightly broader than those made with the Fine Tip Felt Pens.

Single Pixel Marker

The Single Pixel Marker variant produces a pixel-width stroke that varies in opacity and grain based on the pressure you apply to the stylus. Repeated strokes build up toward black. Usually, you use this Pen for fine touch-up work or rough-sketching an idea.

Step 8.1. Creating the Document

You should know how to do this by heart by now!!!!

1. Create a new, 500-pixel-wide-by-400-pixel-high document using the File | New command, as shown in Figure 8.1. Set the resolution at 75 dpi and the paper color at White.

Figure 8.1.
Create a new 500-pixel-wide-by-400-pixel-high document.

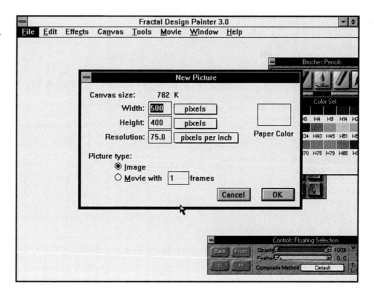

2. Choose the Canvas | Grid Options command.

3. Set the grid spacing to 20-pixels wide and 20-pixels high, as shown in Figure 8.2. Leave the remaining settings at their default values. If yours have been set differently, verify that the other settings agree with the values shown. Choose OK or press Enter (Windows) or Return (Mac) to apply the grid settings.

Figure 8.2.
Set the grid spacing to
20 pixels by 20 pixels.

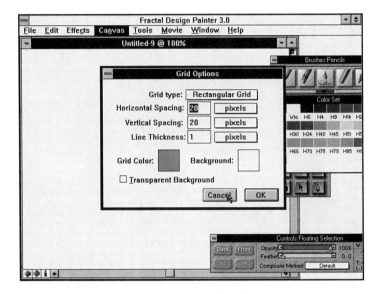

4. To view the grid, choose the Canvas | View Grid command (Ctrl-G in Windows, Cmd-G in Mac).

Step 8.2. Choosing Your Art Materials

You already know you're going to be using the Felt Pens, but you're also going to use another custom chapter color set, located on the CD accompanying this book. There's no need to choose the paper, because the Felt Pens aren't grain-sensitive.

1. From the Brushes Palette (Ctrl-2 in Windows, Cmd-2 in Mac), choose the Fine Tip Felt Pens.

2. Open the Art Materials Palette (Ctrl-3 in Windows, Cmd-3 in Mac) and choose the Sets icon.

3. Click the Library button and open the CH08CS.TXT Color Set text file, located on the CD accompanying this book. The color set appears on your screen.

4. Verify that Black is your current color. It is the default color when a new document is opened.

5. From the Controls | Brush Palette (Ctrl-6 in Windows, Cmd-6 in Mac), click the radio button adjacent to Straight Lines. Your screen should look similar to Figure 8.3.

Figure 8.3.
Choose the Fine Tip Felt Pens and the Straight Line drawing mode.

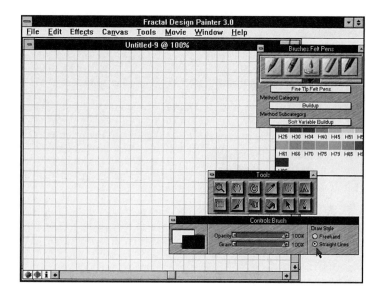

Step 8.3. Drawing the Block Shape

Though your block won't have outlines in its final form, you must draw some reference outlines so you know how to position the letters. Note that you could also create the colored background of the blocks first, and then orient the text accordingly, but I wanted to keep the screen shots clear so that you could easily see what was happening with the selection marquees.

1. Draw the top section of the block as shown in Figure 8.4. Start with the first corner, designated by the arrow in the figure. Then place the second point at three grid spaces up and seven grid spaces to the right. Place the third point six grid spaces to the right and three spaces down from that. The fourth point is placed three grid spaces down and seven grid spaces to the left. Finally, place the fifth point where you started.

2. From the Controls | Brush Palette, click the Freehand radio button, and click again on the Straight Lines radio button. This lets you start a new line in a different place. (Otherwise, the lines would continue from the point you left off.)

245

Figure 8.4.
Draw the first section of the block using black ink.

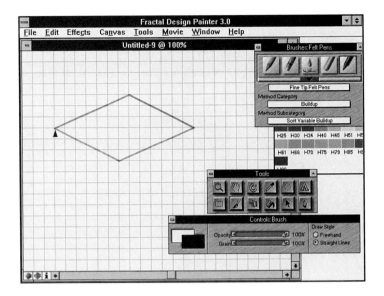

3. Draw the second section of the block as shown in Figure 8.5. This time you need only draw three lines, starting from the extreme left corner of the diamond shape you drew earlier. The block is eight grid spaces high, as shown in the figure.

Figure 8.5.
Draw the second section of the block.

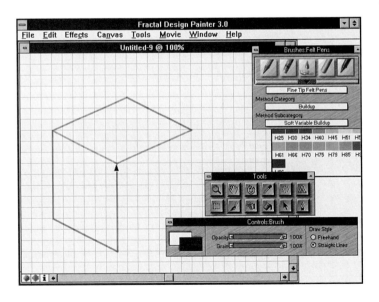

4. Again, reset the straight line mode by clicking Freehand, and then again on Straight Lines. Finish the block with two more lines, as shown in Figure 8.6.

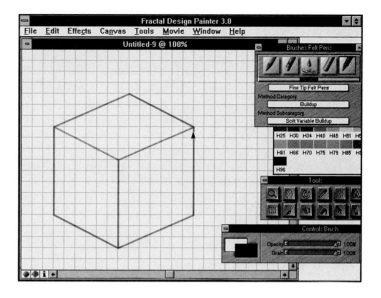

Figure 8.6.
Finish the block with
two more lines.

Step 8.4. Entering and Distorting the Text

I chose a simple, bold font for the block letters and then oriented it to the plane I wanted using the Effects | Orientation | Distort command. This turned the letters into floaters, which I later colored as separate entities and merged with the background block colors. Here's the whole process:

1. Open the Objects Palette (Ctrl-5 in Windows, Cmd-5 in Mac).

2. Click the F.List icon to open the Floater List Palette.

3. Click and drag the P.List icon outside the Objects Palette to open the Path List Palette. I want you to see what happens with paths and floaters as you perform operations on them.

4. From the Tools Palette, choose the Text Selection tool. Choose a font for the block text. (I chose Arial Rounded MT Bold— your font selection may be different). Set the points to 110 in the Controls | Text Selection Palette. If you don't have this font, choose a fairly simple font as a substitute.

5. Click the screen inside the front right section of the block, and type a letter A, as shown in Figure 8.7. Notice that the letter A appears in the Path List Palette. The far-left circle next to the A in the Path List Palette is dotted, indicating that the letter is an active path. The pen-shaped icon adjacent to that indicates that the letter A is an outline selection.

6. Now choose the Path Adjuster tool (the arrow symbol) from the Tools Palette.

7. Click the letter A with the Path Adjuster tool to select it. An invisible bounding box with handles surrounds the letter A.

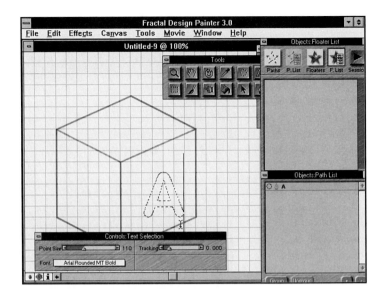

Figure 8.7.
Using the Text Selection tool, type in a large letter A using a simple font.

8. Choose Effects | Orientation | Distort, as shown in Figure 8.8.

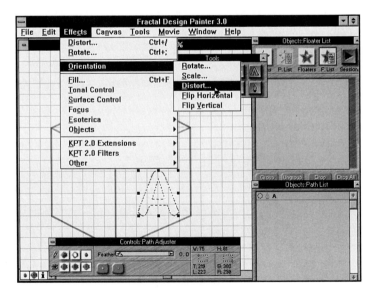

Figure 8.8.
Select the letter with the Path Adjuster tool, and choose the Distort command.

When you choose this command, three things happen:

■ The Distort Selection dialog box appears on screen.

■ The bounding box around the letter A changes slightly, surrounded by a solid outline.

■ A floater appears in the Floater List Palette, as shown in Figure 8.9.

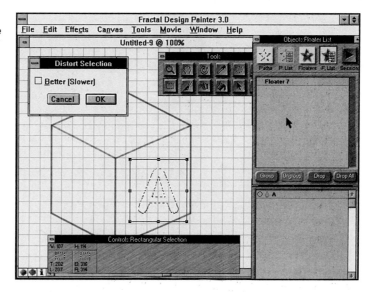

Figure 8.9.
A floater appears in the
Floater List Palette.

When you elected to perform an effect on the letter A path, Painter converted it into a floater. There are some effects, in particular the Orientation commands, that cause this to occur. Changing a path with one of the Orientation commands alters the shape of the original path, in effect moving it from its original location. As you know from Chapter 6, "Creating a Label with Pencils," a path turns into a floater once you click it with the Floating Selection tool and move it. The Orientation commands perform a similar function.

Floaters can be colored, changed with effects, and masked just like a background image. The advantage with floaters, though, is that you can move them around and layer them in any order to form a composition. They also contain their own masking layer; you get to play with those in the next chapter.

Notice that the letter A still also exists in the image as a path. You can eliminate it later (if you like). For now, keep it there in case you make a mistake!

9. Using Figure 8.10 as an example, adjust the corners of the bounding box so the distorted border just fits within the outline of the right side of the box. Match top-left corner to top-left corner, top-right to top-right, and so on.

10. When you're done, click the OK button in the Distort Selection dialog box, shown in the upper-left corner of Figure 8.10. The result should look similar to Figure 8.11.

*Figure 8.10.
Resize the letter's
bounding box just
inside the right front
section of the block.*

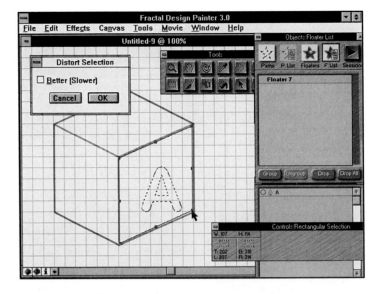

*Figure 8.11.
The letter distorts to fit
the plane of the block
section.*

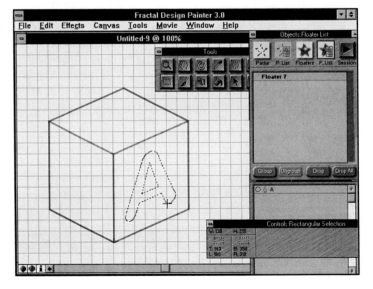

NOTE If your floaters pick up some of the outline of the block during their creation, you can clear the outline from the floater using the Edit | Clear command while the floater is active (surrounded by a selection marquee).

11. Highlight the A floater in the Floater List Palette and press Enter (Windows) or Return (Mac). The Floater Attributes dialog box appears, as shown in Figure 8.12.

Figure 8.12.
Rename the floater in
the Floater List Palette
for identification.

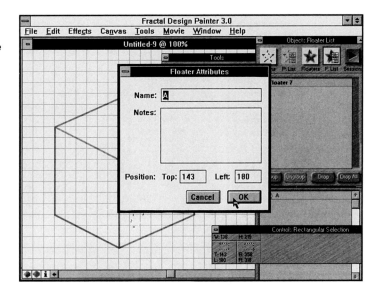

12. Name the floater A.
13. Click OK to exit the Floater Attributes dialog box.
14. Now that you've completed the floater, you don't really need the path version of it anymore. Click the line designating the "A" path in the Path List Palette. The line appears blue.
15. Click the Clear button at the lower-right corner of the Path List Palette, as shown in Figure 8.13.
16. Place the other letters, B and C, using steps 4 through 15 as a guide.

    Apply the B to the top, distorted so the side of the letter is parallel with the upper-left section of the diamond shape. Remember that the upper-right corner of the letter's bounding box goes to the right corner of the diamond shape; the lower-right corner of the letter's bounding box aligns with the lowest corner of the diamond; and the lower-left corner of the letter's bounding box aligns with the left corner of the diamond.

    Add the letter C to the left-front section of the block.

17. When you apply the Distort command to the B, your letter should look like Figure 8.14.

Figure 8.13.
Delete the associated
path from the Path List
Palette.

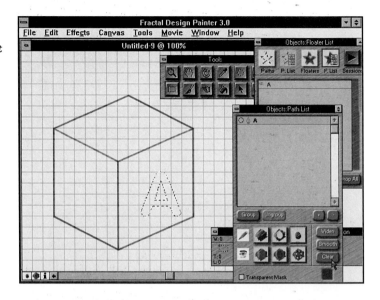

Figure 8.14.
Orient the B as shown
in the top section of the
block.

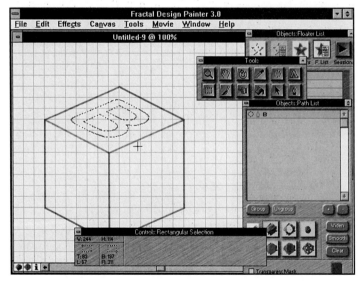

18. When you add the letter C to the final portion of the block, it should be obvious where you drag the bounding box corners. If you pick up some of the box's lines in the process, as shown in Figure 8.15, don't worry—you can clear them out using the Edit | Clear command or erase them with an Eraser tool.

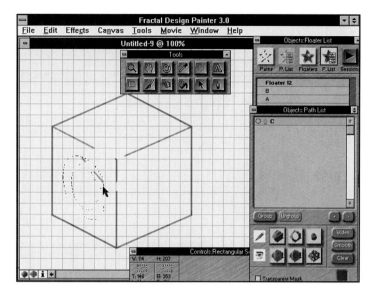

Figure 8.15.
Use the Edit | Clear
command to erase
extra lines you pick up.

19. Delete the other two paths in the Path List Palette by highlighting them and pressing the Clear button in the Path List Palette.

This might be a good time to save your drawing. Save it as BLOCK.RIF, keeping all floater information intact in the saved document.

NOTE   Though you can delete color from a path by selecting it and pressing the Backspace (Windows) or Delete (Mac) key, don't use this method to delete color from a floater. You'll be surprised to see that you won't have a floater anymore! The Backspace or Delete key deletes the currently selected floater from the Floater List Palette, and from your document.

Step 8.5. Creating Paths for the Block

Now you will create paths for the three block faces. Each of these paths will be activated one at a time to color the block sections.

1. From the Tools Palette, choose the Outline Selection tool (the last icon in the bottom row).
2. From the Controls | Outline Selection Palette, choose to create your selections using Straight Lines. Your screen should look similar to Figure 8.16.

Figure 8.16.
Choose the Straight
Line selection mode
from the Controls |
Outline Selection
Palette.

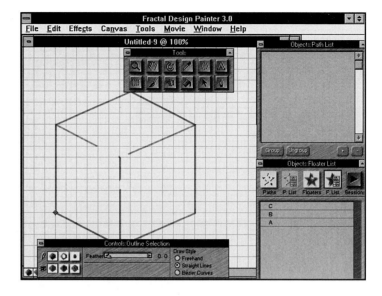

3. Outline one of the sections of the block with the Outline Selection tool. End
your outline at the same point at which you started it. Your screen should
look similar to Figure 8.17.

Figure 8.17.
Draw an outline path
around the first section
of the block.

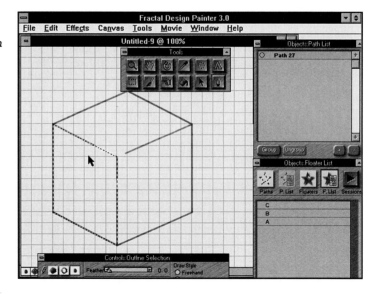

4. Outline the other two sections of the block in the same manner. There
should now be three more paths in your Path List Palette.

5. You need to deactivate the paths in order to assign names that are more descriptive. Deactivate the three paths by clicking the circles at the beginning of their lines. The paths appear in numerical order in the order in which you create them; for example, the first path you created might be Path 3, the second Path 4, and the third Path 5. If you've forgotten which is which, you can activate the path you want to rename. Click its circle in the Path List Palette to see which section it applies to. Then click the circle again to deactivate it before you assign the new name.

6. To rename a path, double-click its name in the Path List Palette. The Path Attributes dialog box appears.

7. Type in a new name for the path and click OK. The new name appears in the Path List Palette. Figure 8.18 shows paths named Top, Right Front, and Left Front.

Figure 8.18.
Rename all three paths
in the Path List Palette.

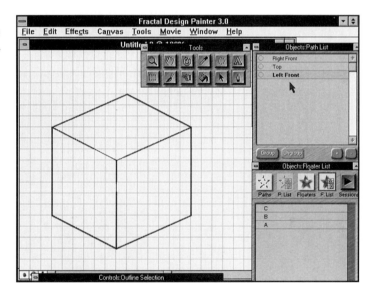

Now combine your paths into a *group*. This prevents accidentally moving one out of location. To group the paths:

8. Shift-click (click while holding the Shift key) on all three pathnames in the Path List Palette. This highlights all three lines in blue. In Painter 3.0, the names are also displayed with bold fonts, as shown in Figure 8.19.

9. Click the Group button located beneath the path list area, as shown in Figure 8.20. The three paths are rearranged beneath a group heading in the Path List Palette.

Figure 8.19.
Select all three paths in the Path List Palette.

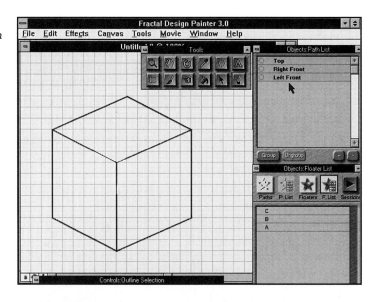

Figure 8.20.
Click the Group button to place the selected paths in a group.

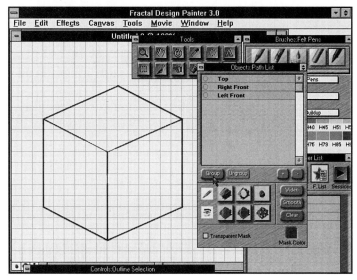

10. With the three paths deactivated, double-click the Group name and re-name the group Block. Choose OK, or press Enter (Windows) or Return (Mac) to exit the dialog box. Your screen should look similar to Figure 8.21.

Figure 8.21.
Rename the group to
something more
identifiable.

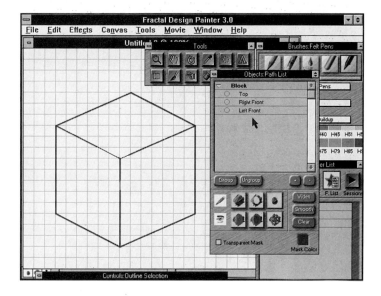

Step 8.6. Coloring the Block

The next step is to color the paths, giving some shape and texture to the block while doing so. Remember that the Felt Pen tools don't interact with paper grain, so you have to add texture by hand. With the Felt Pens, this is easy. You can add texture by varying the amount of pressure or coverage to a particular area, making texture with light and dark areas of color. You can see, as you move your mouse or cursor around, that areas that receive repeat strokes get darker. Use that to your advantage!

Mouse users might want to reduce the opacity of the brushes a bit before use. This causes the colors to build up a little slower, and is equivalent to applying lighter pressure to a stylus.

Before you begin coloring in your block, clear the guidelines from the image:

1. Choose Edit | Select All. This creates a selection marquee box around the entire perimeter of the image.
2. Choose Edit | Clear to clear the initial line work from the background.
3. Choose Edit | Deselect to return to normal editing.
4. From the Path List Palette, click the arrow adjacent to the Block group to drop down the list of parts, if they are not already shown.

5. Click the circle adjacent to the Top portion to activate the path. It appears in your document window, surrounded by a selection marquee.

6. Choose the Medium Tip Felt Pens from the Brushes Palette.

7. From the Chapter 8 color set, choose Orange H45. (The number corresponds to the color's hue value in the Painter color spectrum.)

8. From the Controls | Brush Palette, click the radio button adjacent to Freehand, if it is not already selected. If you are using a mouse, you might also want to reduce the Opacity of the brush to around 50%.

9. Color in the top section of the block with strokes that run somewhat parallel with the straight edge of the letter B. Rotate the canvas with the Rotate Page Tool if it makes your coloring easier.

TIP Don't let your eyes deceive you here—you may think you're not coloring the area beneath the floating letter, but in fact you are! You can use the Floating Selection tool to move the B out of the way if you like, and then reposition it later. This isn't really necessary, because dropping the floaters in place later covers any areas you miss.

I'm showing you this little Painter phenomenon for an important reason: there may be occasions when, working with selections, you don't realize that you've inadvertently created a floater. If you start painting in an image and nothing happens, check your Floater List Palette to see if there are any floaters there that shouldn't be—and delete them. I've had more than a few surprises!

10. As you're coloring the top section of the block, vary the stroke pressure, or vary the opacity and apply some shading to areas with additional strokes. This makes it look a touch like wood. (Remember those blocks you played with as a little child?) When you're done, your block should look similar to Figure 8.22.

11. Choose the Rotate Page tool (third icon in the first row) from the Tools Palette.

12. Rotate the page 90 degrees counterclockwise, so that the letter B is positioned as shown in Figure 8.23.

Figure 8.22.
Color the top section
of the block using the
Medium Tip Felt Pens.

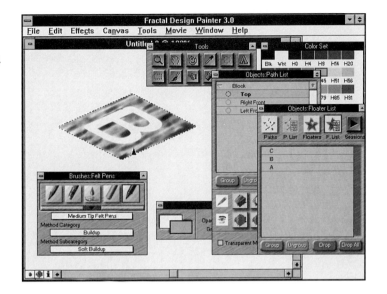

13. From the Path List Palette, deactivate the Top path by clicking its circle.

14. Activate the Right Front path by doing the same.

Figure 8.23.
Rotate the canvas
and color the second
section of the block in
a similar manner.

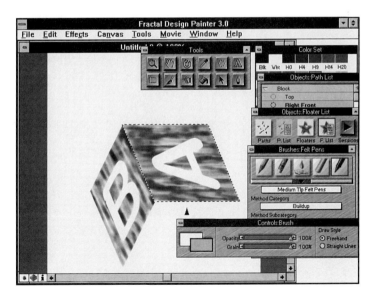

15. Using the same brush and color, and using Figure 8.23 as an example, color in the next section of the block.

16. Deactivate the Right Front path and activate the Left Front path.

17. Color in the final section of the block, shading it a bit darker than the previous two sections, as shown in Figure 8.24.

Figure 8.24.
Shade the third section of the block a bit darker than the previous two.

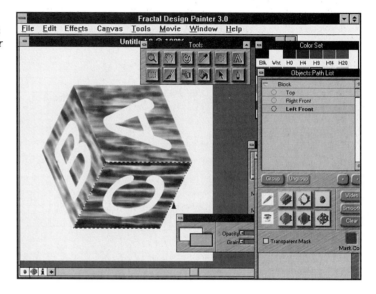

18. Choose the Rotate Page tool again and click inside the image. Your screen returns to normal orientation, as shown in Figure 8.25.

Figure 8.25.
Click the Rotate Page tool to return to normal orientation.

19. Deactivate all the paths in the Path List Palette, making sure all the circles are displayed as light gray solid circles.

Step 8.7. Coloring the Floating Letters

You can move the floating letters anywhere you like while you're coloring them; they don't have to stay in the same spot! When a floater is active and you're coloring it, any strokes that go outside the boundaries of the floater are not drawn into the background.

1. From the Floater List Palette, select floater A. The letter is surrounded by a selection marquee.

2. Choose the Medium Tip Felt Pens from the Brushes Palette, if it is not still selected.

3. Choose Blue H85 from the Chapter 8 color set.

4. Color in the letter with varying strokes, and outline it with slightly darker strokes, as shown in Figure 8.26.

Figure 8.26.
Color the first letter
floater with Blue H85.

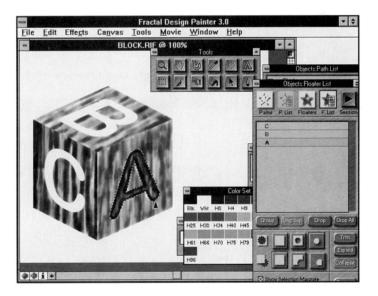

5. You can add some additional detail lines, if you like, using the Single Pixel Marker or the Fine Tip Felt Pens. Remember, though, that the effect of these two brushes is more opaque than the effect of the Medium Tip Felt Pens.

6. Select the B floater from the Floater List Palette, and choose Green H56 from the color set. In a similar manner, color in the letter B as shown in Figure 8.27.

Figure 8.27.
Color the second floater
in a similar manner.

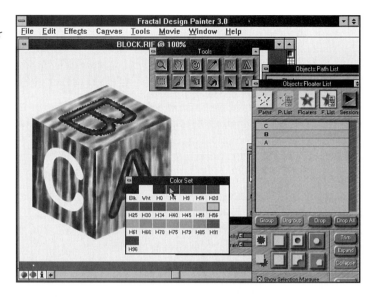

7. Finally, select the C floater from the Floater List Palette and color the floater with Purple H14 from the color set. When you're done, your image should look similar to Figure 8.28.

Figure 8.28.
Select a third color for
the last letter. Now
your floaters are
complete.

Step 8.8. Adding a Drop Shadow to the Letters

You can apply effects to more than one floater at a time by grouping them. With that in mind, add a deep drop shadow to the letters before dropping the floaters to the block background. Start by grouping the floaters to save the trouble of applying the drop shadow to all three floaters individually:

1. In the Floater List Palette, Shift-click to highlight all three floaters: A, B, and C. All three lines are highlighted in blue.

2. Click the Group button, located just beneath the Floater list. A group name appears above the three floaters, as shown in Figure 8.29. A selection marquee also appears around the three floaters in the document window.

Figure 8.29.
Group the selections; a
marquee surrounds all
three.

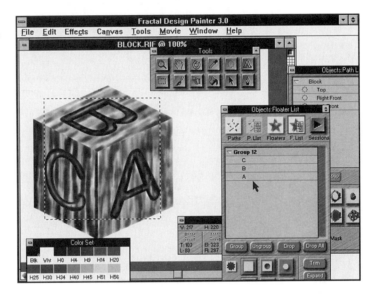

3. Choose Effects | Objects | Create Drop Shadow.

4. In the Drop Shadow dialog box, enter the following figures (shown in Figure 8.30):

   X-Offset: -3 pixels

   Y-Offset: -5 pixels

   Opacity: 80%

   Radius: 5 pixels

   Angle: 114°

   Thinness: 43%

Figure 8.30.
Enter appropriate values in the Drop Shadow dialog box.

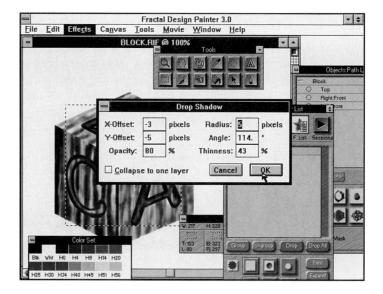

5. Click the OK button in the Drop Shadow dialog box to apply the effect. The letters appear as though they are burnished into the wood, as shown in Figure 8.31.

Figure 8.31.
Apply the drop shadow to all floaters in the chosen group.

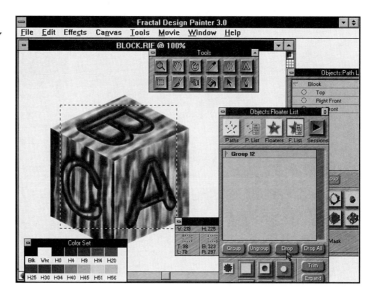

6. To drop the floaters into the background, click the Drop All button in the Floater List Palette. Figure 8.32 shows this button's location. The floaters disappear from the Floater List Palette—because they're no longer floating. Once you drop them, they become a permanent part of the document.

Figure 8.32.
Drop the floaters into
the block background,
and close the Floater
List Palette.

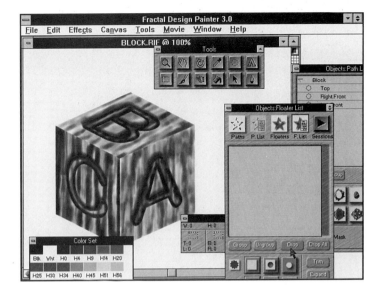

NOTE In Painter 3.0, there is no Undo feature when you drop floaters. Once you have dropped them into the background they become a permanent part of the image. Don't drop the floaters until you're sure you are happy with their appearance and location.

In Painter 3.1, you can apply the Undo command to dropped floaters and restore them to floaters once again!

7. You can close the Floater List Palette for the time being.

Step 8.9. Applying Lighting to the Block

Now apply some lighting to the block to make it appear as though the lighting is directed at its front corner. You apply the lighting a little bit differently to each of the three paths making up the block.

NOTE If there are some additional paths in the Path List Palette (mask group paths) that were inadvertently created, you can safely delete them. The paths that should exist at this point are those in the Block group (Top, Right Front, and Left Front).

1. From the Path List Palette, click the arrow next to the Block group to reveal its contents, if that group is not already expanded.

2. Activate the Top path, and deactivate the other two if they are not already in that state.

265

3. Choose Effects | Surface Control | Apply Lighting. The Apply Lighting dialog box appears.

4. Scroll through the lighting selections, using the right arrow button, until you see the lighting arrangement named Drama.

5. Click the Drama preview icon to select it. Leave the slider settings at their default values.

6. In the preview window at the upper-left corner of the dialog box, notice that the light is identified by two differently sized circles connected by a line. Click the smaller circle and point it toward the bottom corner of the diamond. The light gets brighter in that direction in the preview window.

7. Place the larger circle at about the center of the B. When you have it arranged, it should look similar to Figure 8.33.

Figure 8.33.
Adjust the lighting to point toward the lower corner of the top block section.

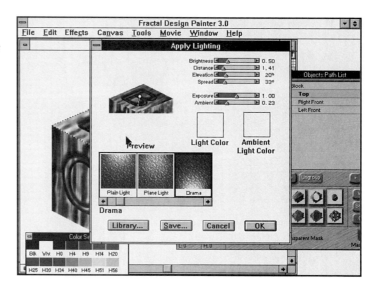

8. Click OK to apply the lighting to the Top section of the block.

9. In the Path List Palette, deactivate the Top section and activate the Right Front section.

10. Again, choose the Apply Lighting command, which you can recall at this point by entering the Ctrl-/ (Windows) or Cmd-/ (Mac) keyboard combination (used in Painter to recall the most recently used effect).

11. Keeping Drama as the selected lighting effect, position the large lighting indicator at the center of the A.

12. Point the smaller indicator toward the upper-left corner of the block section, using Figure 8.34 as a reference.

*Figure 8.34.
The lighting on the
right front section
points toward the
upper-left corner.*

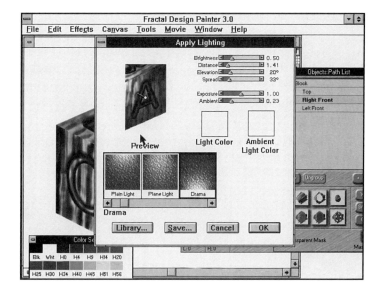

13. Click OK to apply the lighting to the second section of the block.

14. In the Path List Palette, deactivate the Right Front path and activate the Left Front path.

15. Apply lighting again, placing the large circle in the center of the C and pointing the small indicator toward the upper-right corner of the section. When you're done, your final block should look similar to Figure 8.35.

*Figure 8.35.
Point the lighting on
the left front section to
the upper-right corner,
and the lighting is
complete.*

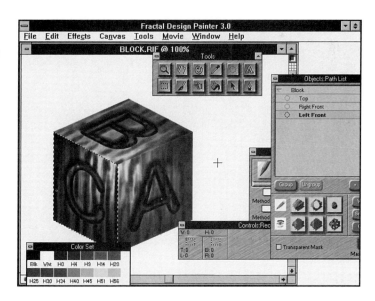

Step 8.10. Placing the Block into a New Floater Library

It's a good idea to save floaters you think you might use at a later time. You can create as many custom Floater libraries as you like! First, make sure all three sections of your block are ready and waiting to be placed into the Floater Palette:

1. Activate all three sections of the block in the Path List Palette, surrounding them with selection marquees, as shown in Figure 8.36.

Figure 8.36.
Activate all three paths in the Path List Palette.

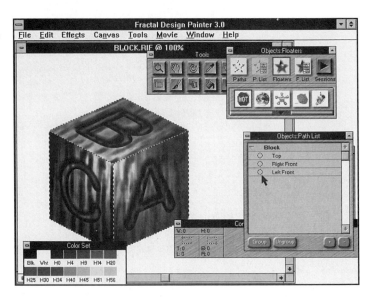

2. Click the arrow beside the Block group name to collapse its contents, as shown in Figure 8.37.

TIP   This is a good habit to get into if you're working with multiple paths and multiple path groups. If you collapse the contents of the paths in a group, you lock the group's contents. This way you won't accidentally activate or deactivate something that's hidden from view!

3. To create a new Floater library, choose Tools | Movers | Floater Mover. The Floater Mover dialog box, shown in Figure 8.38, appears.

Figure 8.37.
Collapse the group so
that the contents are
hidden.

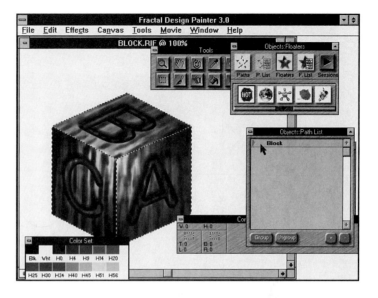

Figure 8.38.
Create a new Floater
library using the
Floater Mover dialog
box.

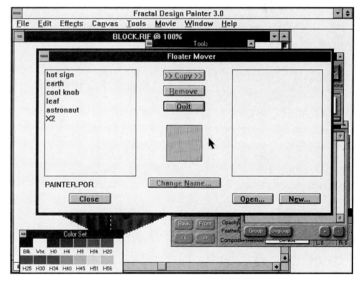

4. At the right side of the Floater Mover dialog box, click the New button. The New Floater Library dialog box appears, prompting you to choose a directory and enter a name for the new floater library. In Figure 8.39, I named the library CHAP08.POR. (Typing the .POR extension is optional; it is automatically assigned when saved.)

Figure 8.39.
Choose the drive and directory, and enter a name for the new library.

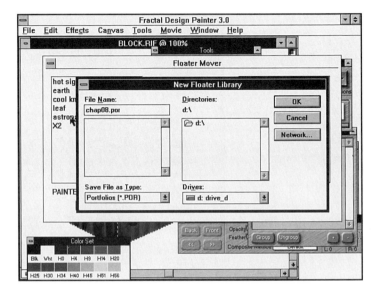

5. You open this library in a moment from the Floater Palette. If you are using Painter 3.1, you can proceed to Step 6.

   If you are using Painter 3.0, you can't open an empty library. You must choose one of the floaters from the list on the left (the currently opened Floater library). In Figure 8.40, I randomly selected the Cool Knob floater and copied it to the new library using the Copy command.

Figure 8.40.
In Painter 3.0, copy one of the floaters from an existing library into the new one. You can delete it later with the Floater Mover.

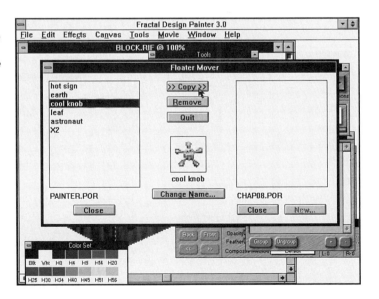

6. Click the Quit button, located in the center of the Floater Mover dialog box, to exit.

7. To open the new Floater library, click the Floaters icon in the Objects Palette. Click the Library button located in the Floaters Palette, as shown in Figure 8.41.

Figure 8.41.
Open the new Floater
Library from the
Floaters Palette.

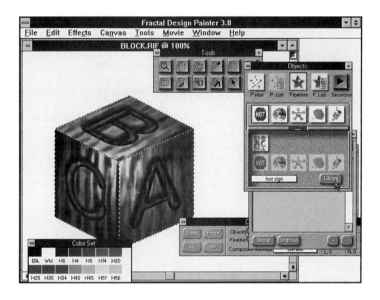

8. From the Open Floater Library dialog box, select the floater library you just saved and click the OK button, as shown in Figure 8.42.

Figure 8.42.
Select the Floater
Library you just
created.

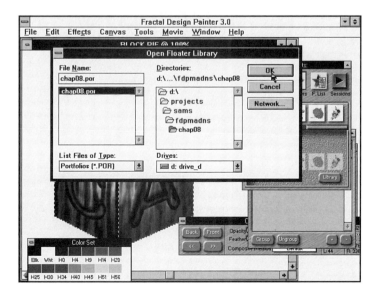

9. From the Tools Palette, select the Floating Selection tool (the third icon in the bottom row, shown as a pointing hand).

10. Click inside the group of three active paths in your document and drag them to the inside of the Floaters Palette while pressing the mouse button. You see an outline of the floater follow the cursor and reduce to icon size once it's inside the Floaters Palette.

11. Once the icon has reduced in size inside the Palette, release the mouse or stylus. The Save Floater dialog box appears, as shown in Figure 8.43.

Figure 8.43.
Enter a name for the
block floater.

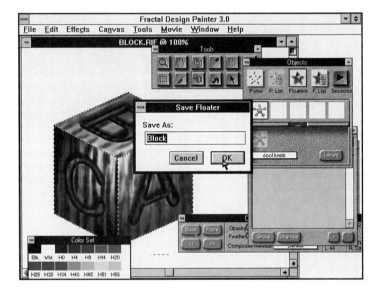

12. Enter a name for the floater, such as `Block`.

13. Click OK, or press Enter (Windows) or Return (Mac). Your floater appears in the Floaters Palette, represented by a little icon of itself.

Figure 8.44 shows three of these floaters placed into a new document. I dragged the first floater from the Floaters Palette using the Floating Selection tool. From the Controls | Floating Selection Palette, I applied the Gel composite method at 16% opacity. I made a copy of the block by Alt-clicking with the Floating Selection Tool (clicking while holding down the Alt key in Windows) and dragged it to a new location. Option-clicking with the Floating Selection tool in the Mac version will accomplish the same thing. I applied the Default composite method at 72% to this second block. I then made a third copy and applied the Default composite method at 100% opacity. You can experiment with any opacities and composite methods you like.

Figure 8.44.
Three blocks I placed
into a document using
different floater effects.

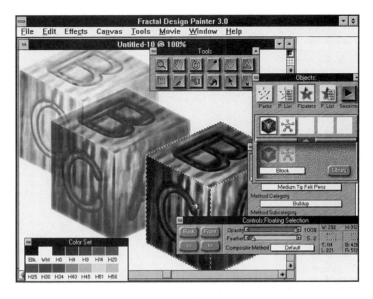

Summary

You've learned a bit more about paths and floaters in this chapter. You know how to create a floater from scratch now, using paths and other floaters in the process. You know how to distort text so that it is oriented on a plane. You also know a little bit about how to apply lighting to selected areas. You saved your totally original floater to a custom library, so you can use it again somewhere else!

The next chapter takes floaters a step further—you learn how masks affect floaters, and how you can arrange them to add to or subtract from each other. Slowly but surely, we're getting to the heart of the Painter program. Keep plugging away!

A Little Glimpse of Heaven

I was originally going to call this chapter the Chalks and Charcoals Project, but it ended up being so much more. As I mentioned in the previous chapter, this project introduces you to working a bit with floater masks. Here you create a heavenly scene, with a little angel who has yet to earn her wings. This picture is meant to form a story in your mind, and no doubt the story will be different for everyone!

The coloring portion of this project is somewhat minimal, and even then it's softened and masked so that there's only a hint of the coloring remaining in the final image. The heart of the project is in working with and arranging multiple floaters while getting a glimpse of one of the neatest capabilities of Painter: its composition powers. Here you see that Painter is far more than a fancy painting program; it's also a composition tool.

This project starts with a photo of a toddler. You mask out the areas you don't want to appear, then create a few selections to help you color in various areas of her garment with the Chalks and Charcoals. Following that, you place the image into a Floater library, along with the other elements that make up the scene. When it's time to place the angel among the clouds, you alter the mask of the floater so it's more opaque at the top and gradually fades toward the bottom. Finally, you place the world in her hands and illuminate it with bright rays from above.

The Chalk and Charcoal variants are somewhat similar; the main difference between the two is that the Charcoals are somewhat softer and a bit less grainy. Both react to paper texture, although this project doesn't rely too much on that ability.

The Chalk Variants

The Chalk variants simulate strokes made with traditional pastels. These tools interact with paper grain, so you can choose different paper textures to achieve some interesting results. When using the chalks, you can vary the size of the stroke with the speed at which you move the mouse or stylus. Dragging the mouse or stylus rapidly produces thinner strokes, while slower speeds produce strokes that are wider. Because the Chalk tools use cover methods, their strokes cover underlying ones.

Chalk strokes also respond to stylus pressure when reacting with paper grain. Heavy pressure on the stylus results in strokes that cover more of the paper grain. Lighter pressure on the stylus allows more of the paper grain to show through. Mouse users can vary the interaction with paper grain by moving the Grain slider in the Controls | Brush Palette. Moving the slider to the left allows more of the paper grain to show through the stroke, and moving the slider toward the right covers more of the paper grain.

Likewise, the opacity of the stroke responds to stylus pressure. Lighter pressure produces more transparent strokes, and increased pressure produces darker strokes. Those using a mouse can achieve the same effect by moving the Opacity slider in the Controls | Brush Palette to the right for darker strokes, and to the left for more transparent strokes.

Artist Pastel Chalk

The Artist Pastel Chalk variant produces strokes that have semi-antialiased edges and react to paper grain. This variant is similar in appearance to those of the Large Chalk, but narrower.

Large Chalk

The Large Chalk variant produces strokes that have semi-antialiased edges and react to paper grain. The strokes are slightly wider than those of the Artist Pastel Chalk, and they cover those beneath. The stroke varies in width with the speed at which you drag the mouse or stylus.

Oil Pastel Chalk

The Oil Pastel Chalk variant has a sharp edge. This Chalk uses Painter's new Captured Dab capabilities, discussed in Chapter 14, "Working with the Brush Tools." The strokes produced by this Chalk variant smear the colors beneath, making this tool a good choice for blending colors. The angle of the stroke varies based on the direction in which you drag it. Stroke opacity and grain respond to stylus pressure.

Sharp Chalk

The Sharp Chalk variant produces strokes that have semi-antialiased edges and react to paper grain. The strokes are slightly narrower than those of the Artist Pastel Chalk, and they also appear slightly more opaque. This chalk would be a good choice for detail work.

Square Chalk

The Square Chalk variant has a chiseled edge, derived from a rectangular captured dab. The angle of the stroke varies based on the direction in which you drag the mouse or stylus. Stroke opacity and grain respond to the pressure you apply to the stylus.

The Charcoal Variants

Painter's Charcoal variants give the appearance of traditional charcoal, including the soft, subtle reaction to paper texture. The width of the strokes produced by these Charcoals varies based on the speed at which you drag the mouse or stylus.

Like Chalk strokes, the opacity (or transparency) of Charcoal strokes varies with pressure you apply to the stylus. Mouse users can vary the opacity of the stroke by moving the Opacity slider in the Controls | Brush Palette.

Because Charcoal is grain-sensitive, choosing different paper textures can produce many different effects in your image. The reaction to paper grain varies based on the amount of pressure you apply to the stylus. For mouse users, moving the Grain slider to the left allows more of the paper texture to show through the stroke; moving the Grain slider to the right causes the stroke to cover more of the paper grain.

Default Charcoal

The Default Charcoal variant produces strokes that have semi-antialiased edges and are extremely sensitive to paper grain. Lighter strokes let more grain show through, and heavier strokes cover more of the paper grain. To achieve the same effect, mouse users can adjust the Opacity and Grain sliders on the Controls | Brush Palette. Another way to control results is to set the Opacity and Grain settings in the Advanced Controls | Sliders Palette to respond to Velocity or Direction.

Gritty Charcoal

The Gritty Charcoal variant produces strokes that have semi-antialiased edges and are sensitive to paper grain. This charcoal produces greater coverage than the other Charcoal variants when reacting with the paper grain, making the strokes appear darker.

Soft Charcoal

The Soft Charcoal variant produces strokes with soft, antialiased edges, and which are sensitive to paper grain. This charcoal is a good choice for blending subtle color transitions together.

Step 9.1. Masking the Background

Start by loading the image and palettes, and masking the background:

1. Open JESSI.TIF, located on the CD accompanying this book.

2. Open the Tools Palette (Ctrl-1 in Windows, Cmd-1 in Mac), Brushes Palette (Ctrl-2 in Windows, Cmd-2 in Mac), Art Materials Palette (Ctrl-3 in Windows, Cmd-3 in Mac) and Controls Palette (Ctrl-6 in Windows, Cmd-6 in Mac).

3. From the Art Materials Palette, click the Sets icon to open the Sets Palette. Click the Library button.

4. Load the CHAP09CS.TXT color set text file located on the CD. Your screen should look similar to Figure 9.1.

5. From the Brushes Palette, click the Masking icon and choose the Big Masking Pen. Using black as your current color, start masking the background area. Start far away from the image of the little girl—this pen is big! Use it to rough in as much mask as you can, as shown in Figure 9.2.

Figure 9.1.
Load the starting
image and palettes.

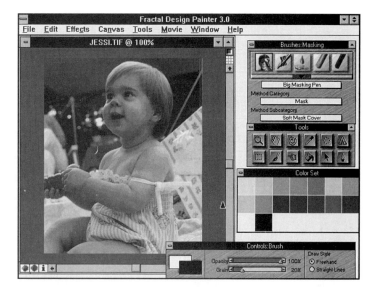

Figure 9.2.
Use the Big Masking
Pen to mask away
large portions of the
background.

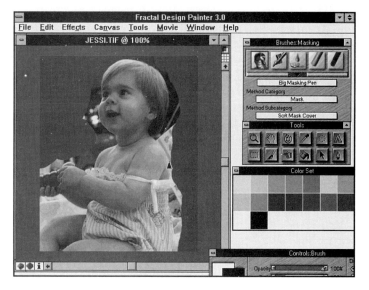

If you make a mistake, you can remove the mask from your image in one of
three ways:

- Use Edit | Clear Mask to completely clear the mask from the area.
- Use Edit | Undo to undo your last stroke.
- Paint with a Masking pen and white as the current color to remove
  the mask from areas you desire.

6. Zoom in on the image to get closer to the background.

7. Select the Masking Pen. You can mask closer to the image with this tool. Continue masking in as close as you can. Figure 9.3 shows this step in progress.

Figure 9.3.
Move in closer with
the Masking Pen.

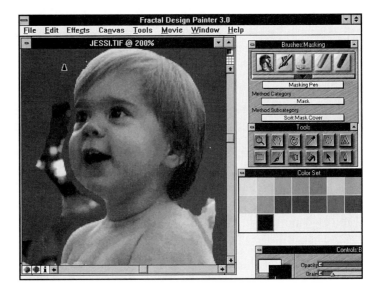

8. To get into really fine areas, such as the little indentations between her fingers, select Single Pixel Masking. This lets you edit the mask one pixel at a time, as shown in Figure 9.4.

Figure 9.4.
The Single Pixel
Masking variant
lets you get into
small areas.

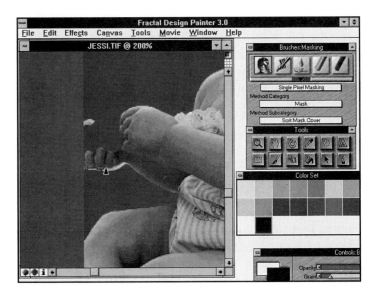

9. Mask out the blue object in her hands entirely, as well as the thumb of the back hand. Refer to Figure 9.5 as an example.

Figure 9.5.
Mask the object from her hand, as well as the thumb of the back hand.

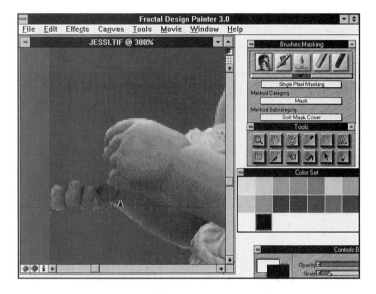

10. When you're done, the image should look similar to Figure 9.6. All areas outside the image of the baby have been masked, and the little ruffle that sticks out from the back side of her sunsuit is also masked away.

Figure 9.6.
All areas of the background have been masked away.

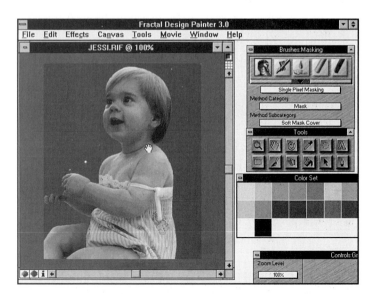

Step 9.2. Turning the Mask into a Selection

You currently have the outside of the image masked. If you turned it into a
selection at this point, you'd have the outside portion of the image selected
rather than the image of the baby. You must invert the mask so the inside of the
baby's image is red, instead of the outside.

1. Choose Edit | Mask | Invert Mask. The baby becomes masked, and the
   outside becomes visible, as shown in Figure 9.7.

Figure 9.7.
*Invert the mask with
the Edit | Mask | Invert
Mask command to
mask the inside of the
baby.*

2. Click the third Mask Visibility button to surround the baby with a selection
   marquee. Your screen should look similar to Figure 9.8.

3. Now open the Objects Palette (Ctrl-5 in Windows, Cmd-5 in Mac) and click
   the P.List icon to open the Path List Palette. You should see a Mask Group
   containing one item in the Path List Palette, as shown in Figure 9.9.

4. Because there's only one item in the Mask Group, you can ungroup it so
   only the masked path is contained in the Path List Palette. To do this,
   click the Mask Group line to highlight it. The Ungroup button becomes
   selectable.

5. Click the Ungroup button.

Figure 9.8.
Convert the mask to a
selection with the third
Mask Visibility button.

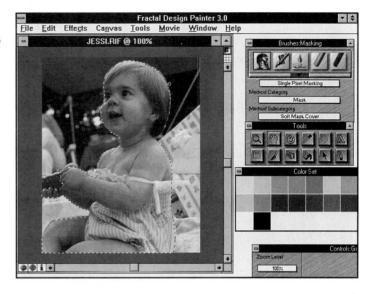

Figure 9.9.
The single masked
image appears in a
masking group in the
Path List Palette.

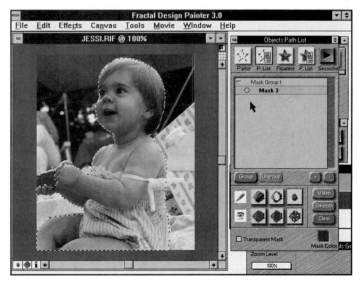

6. The Mask Group line disappears from the Path List, and only one line—the mask for the baby—appears in the Path List. Double-click the name in the Path List and rename it. I named the one in Figure 9.10 Jessi.

Figure 9.10.
Assign a name to the path by double-clicking the name in the Path List.

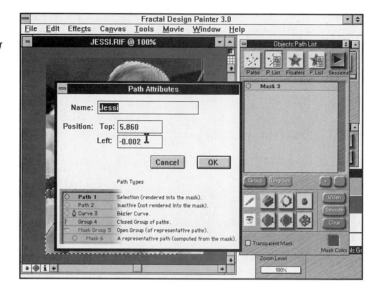

7. If you prefer, you can whiten out the contents of the background so it doesn't distract you when the mask is not displayed. To do this, choose white as your current color and select the Paint Bucket from the Tools Palette. Select the second Drawing Visibility button to color outside the selection, and the third Mask Visibility button to outline the selection with a marquee. Then click outside the selection with the Paint Bucket. The background fills with white, as shown in Figure 9.11.

Figure 9.11.
Clear the background from the image using the Paint Bucket, with the path masked inside.

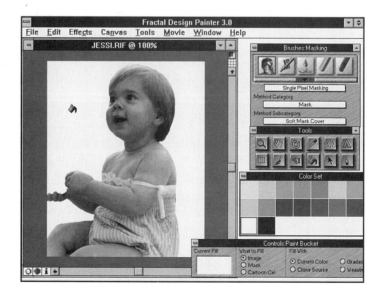

If you haven't already done so, this might be a good time to save your document to .RIF format, using the File | Save or File | Save As command. I gave the document the name JESSI.RIF, but you can name it whatever you like.

Step 9.3. Creating the Outline Selections for the Robe

Now use the Outline Selection Tool to create some selections to protect areas while you color the robe. With the Outline Selection Tool, you can create selections in one of three ways:

- Using the Freehand method, you can create an unrestricted selection, drawing freehand as you would normally. If you've got a *very* steady hand, you might find this the easiest method of creating selections. The disadvantage to this method is that when you release the mouse or stylus the selection completes itself. This means if you want to select an area, and it doesn't entirely fit on screen when you zoom in to get all the detail, your selection will be completed prematurely when you try to move the remaining portion of the image into view.

- You also can use the Straight Lines selection method to select irregularly shaped areas. If you're a person that sometimes can't get the Bézier curves to work just the way you like (I'm one of these!), you can select an area using finely spaced straight lines to surround the selection. This is the method I used to draw the following selections.

- With the Bézier Curve selection method, you can place a starting point for a curve. Then, without releasing the mouse or stylus, drag out a shaping handle in the same direction you want your curve to go. Click again where you want the curve to end. Continue in this manner until you end the selection at the same point it began. After that, you can adjust the control handles to position the curves exactly the way you want them.

Let's create some selections to help us color the robe:

1. From the Path List Palette, click the circle beside the existing path to deactivate it.
2. From the Tools Palette, click the Outline Selection Tool.
3. Choose the method you want to use to create the selection. For our example, I chose the Straight Lines selection mode from the Controls | Outline Selection Palette.
4. Draw a selection around the lower arm, as shown in Figure 9.12.

Figure 9.12.
*Draw a path around the
sleeve of the back arm
using the Outline
Selection Tool.*

5. When the path name appears in the Path List Palette, deactivate the path
   by clicking the circle beside its name.

6. Double-click the path name and rename it `Back Sleeve`, as shown.

7. Similarly, draw an outline path around the bodice of the robe, as shown in
   Figure 9.13.

Figure 9.13.
*Draw another path
where the bodice of the
angel robe is to appear.*

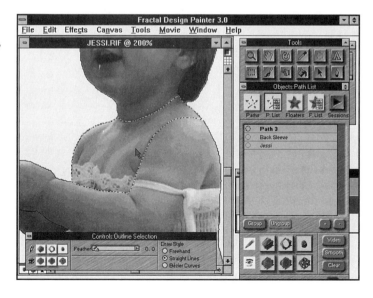

8. Deactivate the new path from the Path List Palette.

9. Double-click the name of the new path and rename it `Bodice`.

10. Finally, draw an outline path for the front sleeve, as shown in Figure 9.14.

Figure 9.14.
Outline the front arm
with another outline
selection path.

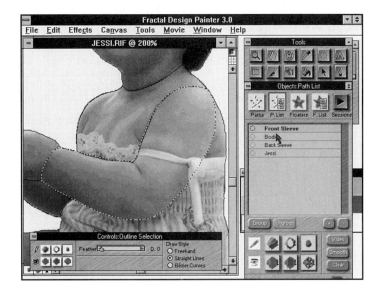

11. Name this path `Front Sleeve`.

Step 9.4. Creating Some New Brush Variants

You might find some of the existing Chalks and Charcoals a bit big for coloring in this image. To help with this, create smaller versions of some of the existing tools, and save them to the existing brush library, or to a custom library of your own, using the Tools | Brushes | Save Variant command. Try some of the following for some new brush variants:

- New Chalk Variants

   Start with the Oil Pastel Chalk and, in the Brush Controls | Size Palette, reduce its size to 7.3. Save the new variant as `Small Oil Pastel`.

   Choose the Artist Pastel Chalk. Reduce its size to 6.1 and save the new variant as `Small Artist Pastel Chalk`.

- New Charcoal Variants

   Start with the Default Charcoal. Reduce its size to 7.8 and save the new variant as `Small Default Charcoal`.

   Choose the Soft Charcoal and reduce its size to 7.3. Save the new variant as `Small Soft Charcoal`.

Step 9.5. Coloring the Selections

You now have four paths in your Path List Palette. It's time to color them in, one by one, using the colors from the CHAP09CS.TXT color set you loaded earlier. If you have since hidden the color set from view, reload it now. Display it on the screen by choosing Ctrl-8 in Windows, or Cmd-8 in Mac. The first five colors in the first row are the main colors to use to shade in the gown.

1. From the Path List Palette, deactivate all paths except for the Back Sleeve path.

2. Choose the third Drawing Visibility button so that all but the inside of the selected path is masked. You can set the Mask Visibility button in any position you prefer.

3. Choose the Small Soft Charcoal brush you created a moment ago.

4. Using the shading of the area underneath the path as a guide, start by applying the darkest shade of blue in the shaded areas of the arm. Gradually work down toward the lighter shades, basing in the color.

5. Switch to the Chalks and select the Small Oil Pastel brush you created. Use this to blend in the colors a bit. Start your stroke in a darker area to drag a bit of that color into the light area. Conversely, start in a light area to drag a bit of that color in toward the dark. Figure 9.15 shows this step.

Figure 9.15.
Color in the sleeve with Chalks and Charcoals, using the shading of the original photo as a guide.

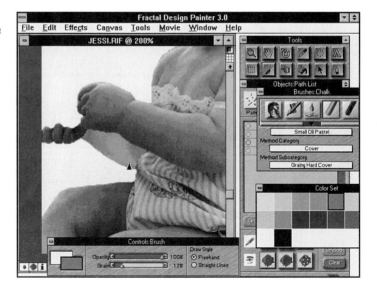

6. Deactivate the Back Sleeve path in the Path List Palette.

7. Activate the Bodice path, as shown in Figure 9.16. Verify that the Drawing Visibility button is set to the third setting, so you color only inside the path.

*Figure 9.16.
Deactivate the Back
Sleeve path and
activate the Bodice
path.*

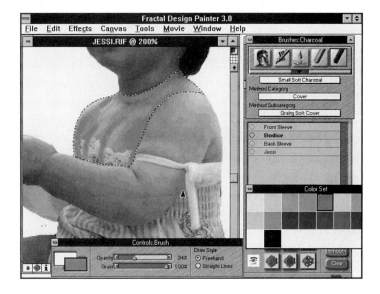

8. Choose the Small Soft Charcoal brush and color in the bodice using the same method as before. Start with the deeper shades and gradually build up color toward the lighter shades. Figure 9.17 shows this step in progress.

*Figure 9.17.
Begin basing in color
using the Small Soft
Charcoal variant you
created earlier.*

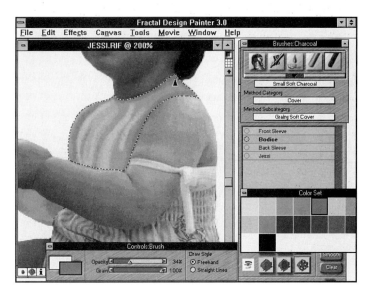

9. Figure 9.18 shows some of the lighter areas added to the bodice. Begin shading back down toward the deeper shades, going over some of the areas with extremely light pressure, or with light Opacity settings in the Controls | Brush Palette. This helps blend the colors a little bit.

Figure 9.18.
Blend colors in using
lighter pressure, or
by reducing the opacity
of the brush in the
Controls | Brush
Palette.

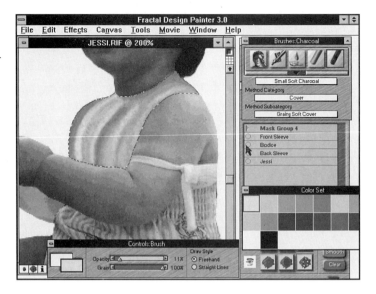

10. To start adding the final touch of softening to the colored area, click the bodice with the Path Adjuster Tool.

11. Choose Effects | Focus | Soften. The Soften dialog box, shown in Figure 9.19, appears. The bodice is shown in the Preview window. Leave the Radius slider set to the default of 3.

12. Click OK. The strokes are softened in the bodice.

Figure 9.19.
Soften the area with
Effects | Focus |
Soften.

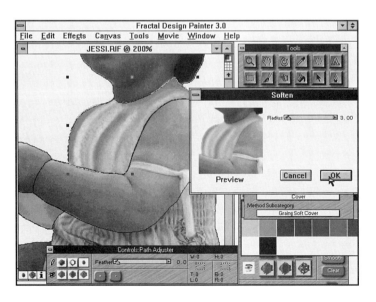

13. From the Path List Palette, deactivate the Bodice path and activate the Front Sleeve path. Verify that the Drawing Visibility button is set to the third choice, masking everything but the inside of the path.

14. Again using the Small Soft Charcoal brush, add the deepest colors at the bottom of the sleeve and work up with lighter shades toward the top, as shown in Figure 9.20. Use the Small Oil Pastel brush to add any shading you feel necessary.

Figure 9.20.
Shade the front sleeve with lighter colors toward the top and deeper shades toward the bottom.

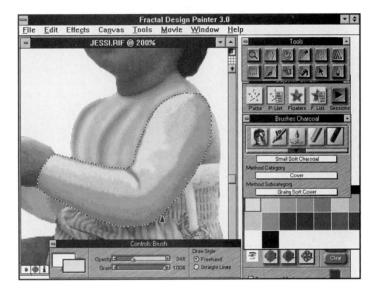

15. Soften the sleeve with the Soften command, again using the default radius of 3.

Step 9.6. Using Negative Paths

What about the rest of the robe? You didn't create a path for it! I did this on purpose. I want to show you the difference between *positive* and *negative* *selections*.

1. Activate all four paths in the Path List Palette by clicking their circles. All four circles are surrounded by dotted lines.

2. Turn on the second Mask Visibility button so the masked areas are displayed in red. Only the background is masked; the image of the baby should be completely visible.

3. Click the Front Sleeve path's name in the Path List Palette to highlight it. Just beneath the Path List are two buttons: one labeled with a plus sign (+), which turns a path into a positive one (the "normal" state), and one labeled with a negative sign (-), which turns a path into a negative path.

4. Click the negative path button (-) for the Front Sleeve. The line in the Path List is displayed with red text, and this path too is surrounded by a red marquee when selection marquees are visible.

5. Repeat this for the Bodice and Back Sleeve paths. When you're done, only the fourth path, Jessi, should be a positive path. Your image should look similar to Figure 9.21 when the red mask is displayed.

Figure 9.21.
Prepare to color the remaining portion of the gown while protecting areas already painted.

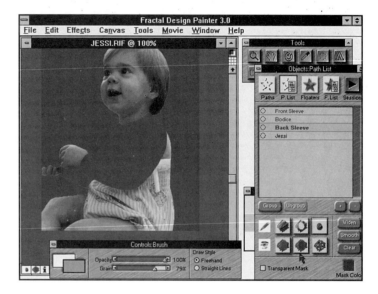

What does a negative path do? Basically, when a path is negative, it reacts the opposite of what it's supposed to:

- The second Drawing Visibility button masks the inside of a positive path, letting you paint outside it. However, if the path is a negative path, the second Drawing Visibility button masks the *outside* of the path.

- The third Drawing Visibility button masks the outside of a positive path, allowing you to paint inside it. However, if the path is a negative path, the third Drawing Visibility button masks the *inside* of the path.

Step 9.7. Painting the Rest of the Robe

I painted the remaining part of the robe with the five blue shades and the Soft Charcoal tool. Use Figure 9.22, the completed robe, as a reference to the following steps.

Figure 9.22.
The angel robe,
complete.

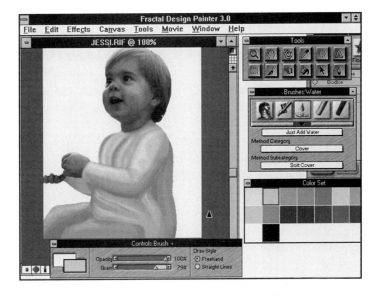

1. Starting with the Soft Charcoal variant, rough in light and dark areas—lighter areas where the sun would hit, deeper shades in the opposite areas.

2. Select the Small Soft Charcoal to add a little more detail to the folds of the robe.

3. Select the Small Oil Pastel to blend in some of the shaded areas.

4. To add the final smoothing, choose the Just Add Water tool and smooth over the rough edges. In this case, you wouldn't use the Effects | Focus | Soften command because that would also soften the face and hands, which are part of the path you're painting.

When you're satisfied with the results, save the image to disk to update it. In the next step you add the angel to the project Floater library.

Step 9.8. Adding the Angel to the Floater Library

Now that all areas are colored in, you can deactivate the three paths that are part of the robe, leaving only the angel as an active path. Then, place it in the project Floater library so you can use the floater any time you like. Here's what you do:

1. From the Path List Palette, deactivate the Front Sleeve, Right Sleeve, and Bodice paths. Leave only the path for Jessi active, surrounded by a selection marquee.

2. From the Objects Palette, click the Floaters icon to open the Floaters Palette.

3. Open the Palette drawer and click the Library button. The Open Floater Library dialog box appears.

4. From the Open Floater Library dialog box, choose the CLOUDS.POR Floater library file from the CD accompanying this book. This is a large file: there are a couple of really big clouds in here!

5. Using the Floating Selection Tool, click the Jessi selection in the document window and drag it into the Floaters Palette. When the outline that follows your cursor reduces to icon size, release the mouse button or stylus inside the Floaters Palette.

6. Name the floater Angel when prompted to do so.

7. You're done with this first document. You can close it if you like, and save the changes to disk.

Now we're getting to the fun part!

Creating Your Own Gradations

There is a gradation library created for this chapter on the CD accompanying this book. If you would rather create your own gradation for the background of the sky, there are some commands in Painter that enable you to do this.

You use the Capture Gradation command to capture a custom-made gradation that appears in the Art Materials | Grads Palette. To create and capture a gradation, follow this procedure:

1. Open or create a Gradation Library to save your gradation to.

2. Draw the colors you want to contain within your gradation in a document window, or capture them from an image that contains smooth changes in color. You can use two or more differently-colored pixels as shown in Figure 9.23. The pixels can be drawn with the Single Pixel Pen.

3. Choose the Rectangular Selection Tool from the Tools Palette. If you are capturing single pixel-width areas, you will find it easier to zoom in at 1200% to the pixels.

4. If the colors in your gradation change from top to bottom (like a sunset, for example), draw a vertical rectangular selection that includes all the colors in your gradation. Painter takes the first column of pixels in the selection area to make its gradation.

   If the colors in your gradation change from right to left, like those shown in Figure 9.24, draw a horizontal rectangular selection that includes all the colors in your gradation. Painter takes the first row of pixels in the selection area to make its gradation.

Figure 9.23.
You can capture a gradient from a row of pixels, as shown, or from an image that contains smooth changes in color.

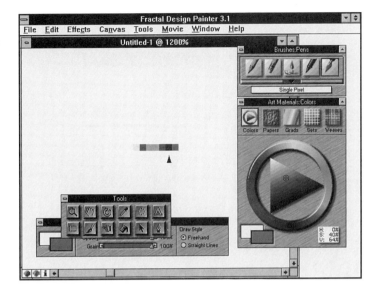

Figure 9.24.
Surround the area you want to capture with the Rectangular Selection Tool.

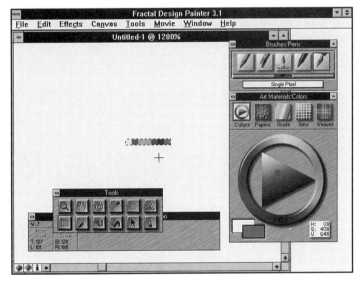

5. Choose Tools | Gradations | Capture Gradation. The Save Color Ramp dialog box appears.

6. Type a name for your gradation, as shown in Figure 9.25, and click OK or press Enter (Windows) or Return (Mac) to capture the gradation. The gradation appears in the currently opened Gradation Library. Figure 9.26 shows an example of a gradient that was created by capturing a few pixels of color. The transitions between the colors are automatically blended.

Figure 9.25.
Assign a name for
the new gradient in
the Save Color Ramp
dialog box.

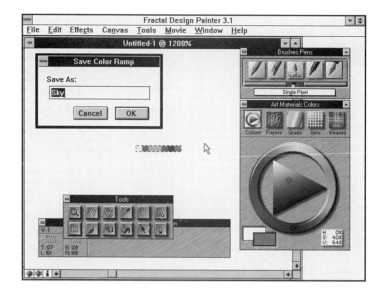

Figure 9.26.
Transitions between
pixel colors are auto-
matically applied to
the gradient.

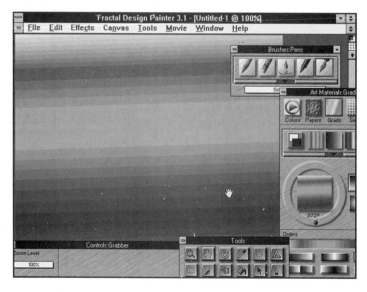

Painter 3.1 allows you to design algorithmic gradations with the Tools | Grada-
tions | Edit Gradation command. This command reveals the Edit Gradation
dialog box.

1. Open the Art Materials | Colors Palette and the Art Materials | Grads
   Palette to edit your gradation. Choose the gradation you want to edit from
   the Grads Palette.

2. Choose the Tools | Gradations | Edit Gradation command. The Edit Gradation dialog box, shown in Figure 9.27, appears. A gradation bar and other controls appear in the Edit Gradation window.

Figure 9.27.
The Edit Gradation dialog box allows you to edit color placement and transitions in the gradation.

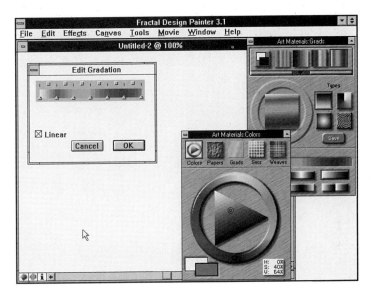

3. Check or uncheck the box beside Linear to identify if you want a linear or non-linear gradation.

   ■ To create a linear gradation, check the Linear box. Linear gradations blend color ramps linearly, using smooth curves.

   ■ To create a non-linear gradation, uncheck the Linear box. With non-linear gradations, you can use the Color Spread slider to adjust the amount of color spread around a selected color control point.

4. Below the gradation bar are two or more arrows, shown near the cursor in Figure 9.28, which identify color control points that can be adjusted or reset to different colors.

   ■ To change a color at a control point, click the color control point to select it. It will appear slightly darker than the other arrows when it is selected. Then, select a new color from the Art Materials | Colors Palette. The gradations in the Edit Gradation dialog box and in the Grads Palette preview square will update to reflect the new color.

   ■ To add a new color control point, click anywhere inside the color bar. A new control point appears without changing the color at the designated location in the bar. You can delete color points by clicking them and pressing Backspace (Windows) or Delete (Mac).

■ To add a new color control point while setting its color to the currently selected color, hold down the Alt key while clicking anywhere inside the color bar. A new color control point appears and the color in the bar changes to the currently selected color.

Figure 9.28.
The arrows in the Edit Gradation dialog box allow you to control color placement in the gradation.

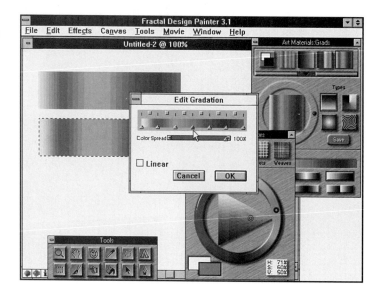

5. Above the gradation bar are square boxes, shown next to the cursor in Figure 9.29. These boxes are located at the midpoint between adjacent color control points. To change the color space for the corresponding color ramp segment, click the corresponding square box.

   ■ The RGB option will blend directly between Red, Green, and Blue components of the two colors.

   ■ The Hue Clockwise and Hue Counterclockwise options will blend between the endpoint colors by rotating around the color wheel.

6. View your changes in the gradation preview bar as they are applied. When you are satisfied with the gradation, click OK or press Enter to create the gradation. If you choose Cancel the changes will not be applied, and the preview in the Grads Palette will return back to the version saved in the library.

7. To save the gradation to the currently open Gradation library, click the Save button in the Art Materials | Grads Palette. The Save Color Ramp dialog box, shown in Figure 9.30, appears. Assign a name to the gradation and click OK. The gradation will be saved.

Figure 9.29.
The square boxes in the Edit Gradation dialog box allow you to adjust the color space for the areas in the gradation.

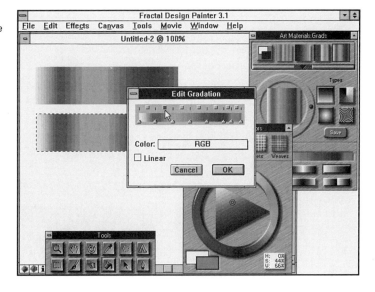

Figure 9.30.
Assign a name for the gradation in the Save Color Ramp dialog box.

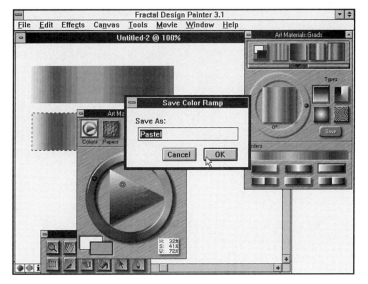

Step 9.9. Creating the Heavens

Your final version of this image can be entirely different from mine. (That's one of the beauties of working with floaters: You can place them anywhere you like, arranged in any front-to-back order you choose.) I started the scene with a new document, filled it with a gradation sky, and then completed it with several floaters from our project floater library. Here are the steps:

1. Open a new 500×400-pixel document.

2. If you don't have the Grads Palette visible on your screen, open the Art Materials Palette (Ctrl-3 in Windows, Cmd-3 in Mac). Click the Grads icon to open the Grads Palette.

3. From the Grads Palette, click the Library button and select the CHAP09.GRD Gradation library from the CD accompanying this book. If you created your own gradation, select the library in which you saved it.

4. Choose the Sky 5 gradation, or the gradient you created, as shown in Figure 9.31.

Figure 9.31.
Open a new image to
create the sky.

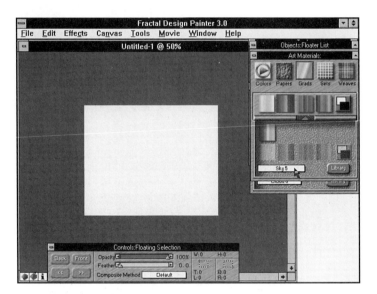

5. Adjust the angle of the gradation so that it is slightly diagonal, to an angle of 273 degrees, as shown in Figure 9.32.

6. Fill the image with the gradation, using the Paint Bucket or the Effects | Fill command (Ctrl-F in Windows, Cmd-F in Mac).

7. To soften the gradation sky, choose Effects | Focus | Soften.

8. In the Soften dialog box, shown in Figure 9.33, adjust the Radius slider to around 10.

9. Click OK or press Enter to apply the effect. The gradation in the sky appears nice and soft now.

Figure 9.32.
Fill the sky with a
slightly angled
gradation.

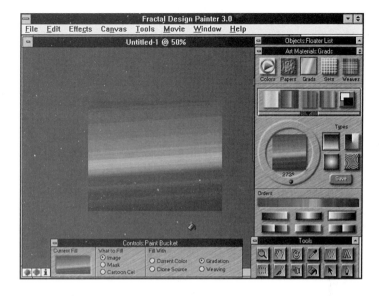

Figure 9.33.
Soften the gradation to
a radius of around 10.

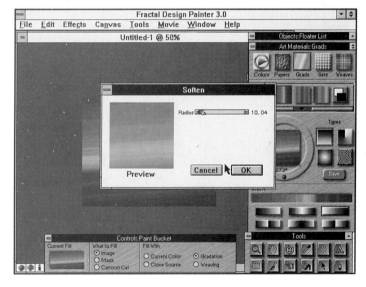

Now for the fun part. Click and drag the F.List icon outside the Objects Palette to place the Floater List Palette out beside the Floaters Palette. You can adjust the layering of the floaters while you're compositing.

Drag one copy of each floater into the document and arrange them any way you choose. As you drag the floaters in, you can alter the layering of the floater by changing the order in which they appear in the Floater List Palette. Items at the top of the Floater List appear in the foremost layers of the image, and items toward the end of the list appear in the back layers.

You may notice that the project Floater library included on the CD contains fewer clouds than the version in the screen shots. After completing the project, I reduced the Floater library to contain only the clouds used in my final version, because the file was considerably larger than the eight-plus megabytes of its present size. You can orient, scale, and combine the five clouds in the present library to create several different clouds of your choosing, though!

The two larger clouds are Cloud 6 and Cloud 9. Cloud 9 is the one I placed in front. (Just had to have our angel sitting on Cloud Nine, didn't I?) Cloud 10 is a nice white, medium-sized cloud, and the smaller clouds are numbered 1 through 3. Now, place all these goodies into your sky.

You may want to arrange your document exactly as shown in the final project file. Table 9.1 gives the order in which the final arrangement appeared in the Floater List Palette, as well as the Top and Left coordinates. You can edit the coordinates of a floater by the coordinates by highlighting the name in the Floater List and pressing Enter (Windows) or Return (Mac). This brings up the Floater Attributes dialog box.

The Composite methods, Opacity settings, and Feathering are those that I set on the Controls | Floating Selection Palette.

Table 9.1. Floater Settings for the Final Image

Floater	Top	Left	Comp. Method	Opacity	Feathering
Cloud 9	272	-209	Default	88%	5.6
Angel	22	140	Gel	82%	0.0
Earth	124	64	Default	80%	2.0
Cloud 6	131	-186	Default	84%	16.0
Cloud 10	71	117	Magic Combine	90%	5.6
Cloud 3	-19	292	Default	80%	5.6
Cloud 2	-9	-12	Default	78%	5.6
Cloud 1	32	100	Default	72%	5.6

If you use these settings, your image now should appear similar to Figure 9.34.

If you have arranged your clouds differently, and the Earth appears in front of the angel's hands, click the Earth line in the Floater list and drag the name so that it appears just underneath Angel in the list. Then position the globe so that it fits in her hands, as shown in Figure 9.35.

Figure 9.34.
Bring floaters in from
the project Floater
library and arrange
them to form the final
composition.

Figure 9.35.
Position the Earth
beneath the Angel in
the Floater list, so it
looks as though the
angel is holding the
Earth in her hands.

Group the angel and the globe so you can move them together, as a group, if you desire. To start, do this:

1. In the Floater List Palette, click the Angel and Shift-click the Earth. Both names are highlighted with blue, as shown in Figure 9.36.

Figure 9.36.
Highlight both the
Earth and Angel lines
in the Floater List
Palette.

2. Click the Group button beneath the Floater List. Both items in the document window are surrounded by a selection marquee, and the names appear beneath a group name in the Floater List, as shown in Figure 9.37.

Note that you still can work on each floater independently by clicking the appropriate floater. To act on them as a group, highlight the group name rather than the individual elements within the group.

Figure 9.37.
Group the Angel and
the Earth. A selection
marquee appears
around both.

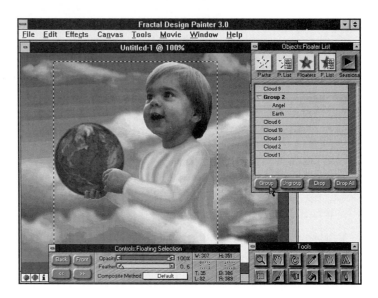

Step 9.10. Altering the Angel's Mask

Floaters have their own masking layers, and you can paint in them or apply effects to them just as you can in the background mask. You should alter the mask of the angel so she appears more opaque toward the top and gradually fades out toward the bottom. To do this, apply a black-to-white gradation in the masking layer. Chapter 12, "Working with the Masking Tools," explains in detail how floater masks interact with background masks. For now, it's enough to know that applying various shades of gray varies the opacity of a floater. Here are the steps:

1. From the Chapter 9 gradation library, select the Two-Point gradation, represented by the black and white overlapping squares. This gradation is shown in Figure 9.38.

Figure 9.38.
Choose the Two-Point gradation from the Grads Palette, with black as your primary color and white as your secondary color.

2. Select black as your primary color and white as your secondary color, if they are not already selected. These colors are in the Chapter 9 color set, or you can choose them from the Art Materials | Colors Palette.

3. Adjust the angle of the gradation so that white is at the upper-left corner of the preview and black is toward the lower-right corner. I positioned the angle in the example at 323 degrees.

4. Click the name Angel in the Floater List Palette, or click the angel image in the document window with the Floating Selection Tool. The angel is surrounded by a selection marquee.

5. From the Floater List Palette, verify that the third Floater Mask Visibility button (top row) and second Floater Interaction button (bottom row) are selected.

6. Choose the Paint Bucket tool.

7. From the Controls | Paint Bucket Palette, choose to fill the Mask with a gradation. Your screen should now look similar to Figure 9.39.

Figure 9.39.
Choose the third Floater Mask Visibility button and second Floater Interaction button to fill the angel's mask with the gradation.

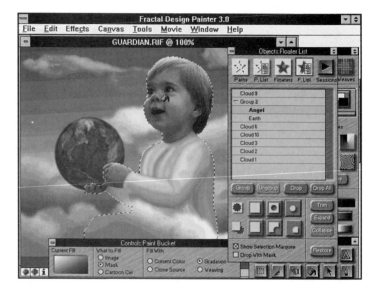

8. Click inside the Angel image with the Paint Bucket tool. The image fills with the chosen gradation in the masking layer: more opaque at the head and less so in the gown.

Step 9.11. Adding Light to the Earth

Now adjust the lighting of the Earth so that it's lit on the upper-left side and shadowed in the opposite direction. (In a moment you add some rays of light to the upper-left corner of the image to complete the effect.)

1. Highlight the Earth floater in the Floater List Palette.

2. Choose Effects | Surface Control | Apply Lighting. The Apply Lighting dialog box appears.

3. The first lighting effect is called Splashy Colors. It contains one blue light and one yellow light. These colors are appropriate for the scene, so go ahead and use them. Point the two light indicators, as shown in Figure 9.40. You see the lighting preview change to reflect the altered positions.

Figure 9.40.
Adjust the lighting
indicators to light the
upper-left area of the
Earth.

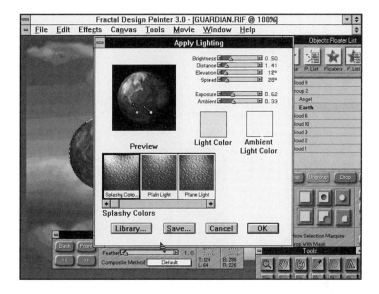

4. When you're satisfied with the results, click OK to apply the effect to the floater.

Step 9.12. Adding the Light Rays

Now add some light rays in the upper-left corner of the document to define the light shining toward the earth. To do this, you create an irregularly shaped path and use the Apply Lighting effect. However, for the lighting to appear over the two cloud floaters in the upper-left corner, you must merge them with the background layer. Otherwise, the lighting effect would be rendered only to the background beneath, and the clouds would appear in front of the lighting effect.

You have three options here:

■ You can highlight each of the two clouds in the Floater List, and click the Drop button to drop one at a time into the background layer. Once you do this, though, they become a permanent part of the background.

■ You can drop all the floaters into the background layer with the Drop All button in the Floater List Palette.

■ If you think you might want to experiment further with the image at a later time, and want to leave all the floaters intact, save it now as a Painter .RIF file. Then save another copy of the image to a different format, or a different file name, before adding the final effect to the corner.

For my example, I chose to save the file as a 24-bit Targa image before applying the final effect. Doing this automatically merges all the floaters into the background, as well as removing any path and masking information contained in the image.

To save the file as a Targa image:

1. Choose the File | Save As command.

2. In the Save File as Type drop-down listbox, choose to save the image in Targa format.

3. A warning appears, shown in Figure 9.41, notifying you that the floaters won't exist as separate objects when you save to this format, and reminding you to also save the document to the .RIF format. Click OK to proceed.

Figure 9.41.
When you save an image to a format other than .RIF, Painter reminds you that the floaters will be merged with the background.

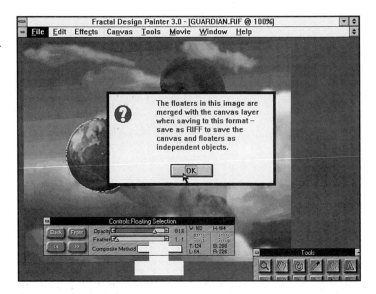

4. Type in a name and choose the drive and directory into which you want to save the file.

5. Click OK, or press Enter, to save the document. You return to the original image, at which point you can save it as a .RIF file if you have not already done so.

   Note that when you are returned to your document window, the floaters are still floating in your image. You have an opportunity to save this image in Painter's .RIF format at this time. To work with the Targa image you just saved, save this current document in .RIF format and close it. Then open the Targa version of the file.

To add the light rays:

1. Open the Targa version of the file.

2. Using the Outline Selection Tool in either Straight Lines or Bézier Curve drawing mode, draw a path that's similar in shape to the one shown in Figure 9.42. When the path is complete, it becomes surrounded by a selection marquee.

Figure 9.42.
Create some ray-shaped lines with the Outline Selection Tool.

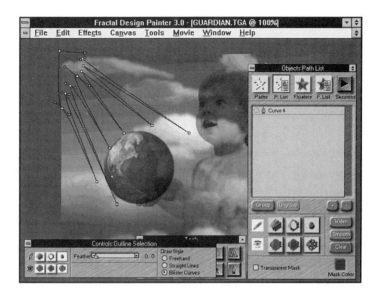

3. In the Controls | Outline Selection Palette, adjust the Feather slider to around 12 or 13.

4. Choose Effects | Surface Control | Apply Lighting. You should be able to recall this command using the quick-key combination of Ctrl-/ in Windows, or Cmd-/ in Mac.

5. Again using the Splashy Color lighting, adjust the lighting indicators so they appear as shown in Figure 9.43. The preview window changes to reflect the new positions.

Figure 9.43.
Position the lights to shine toward the upper-left corner of the image.

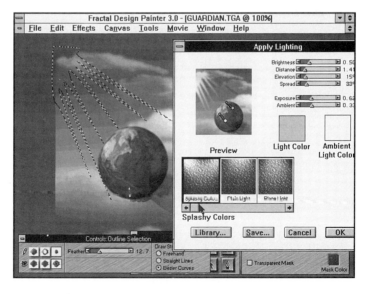

6. Click OK to apply the lighting.

When you apply the final lighting command, your image is complete. If you've followed the directions exactly, it should appear as shown in Figure 9.44. If you've created your own custom version, congratulations! Painter is all about exploration and creativity! It is through exploration that you really begin to learn all the intricacies of layering and masking, and how they combine to produce a final image.

Figure 9.44.
Complete the image by
adding the light rays.

Summary

You've learned a bit about Painter's Chalk and Charcoal composing tools in this chapter, and also a bit more about compositing images with Painter by changing the order in which items appear in the Floater List. You learned about positive and negative paths, and how to use them in combination to protect or unprotect areas. You've seen how varying shades of gray in the masking layers can affect the opacity of a floater. I'd say we've covered a lot of ground here!

In the following chapter you learn about yet another of Painter's layers: the Wet Layer. You use this layer with the Water Color tools to make them react as watercolors do in real life, complete with pooling and color buildup. I also discuss some of Painter's other water-based tools—Liquid tools and Water tools—and the differences between the three types.

Part

III

If You Can Draw This...

10

Painting with Water-Based Tools—The Stained Glass Window

The Stained Glass Window project in this book was created with several of Painter's many brush tools. For this reason, the project is divided among several sections of the book. This project begins with a background created with Water Colors and Liquid variants, as discussed in this chapter. The leaves on the tree were applied with a nozzle file created from water-colored leaves, and the procedure for creating, loading and painting with the nozzle file is discussed in Chapter 15, "Image Hose Project." Finally, the birds in the foreground were painted with the Airbrush variants, and will be discussed in Chapter 11, "Completing the Stained Glass Window."

The Differences Between the Water-Based Variants

Painter has three types of water-based painting mediums: Water Colors, Liquid, and Water. Initially, the differences between the three mediums might not be obvious and might easily be confused with one another. Basically, each medium type serves a slightly different purpose:

- ■ The Water Color variants look and act like traditional water colors, and paint in a separate wet layer above the background. Strokes made with these brushes are not rendered into the background until the canvas is dried with the Canvas | Dry command. This property makes these brushes ideal for tinting existing color and colorizing grayscale images. Of course, watercolor artists will appreciate the realistic strokes, complete with color pooling, that can be achieved with these brushes.

- ■ The Liquid brushes act like thick acrylic paints. Strokes can be applied with or without color. When color is applied with the brush, the strokes blend with and distort the existing color in varying amounts, and with varying effects. You also can move existing color without applying color, using the brush to add effects as though the color were applied with a palette knife rather than a brush.

- ■ The Water brushes do not add color to an image, but can be used to blend colors and to add paper grain effects and stroke work to images created outside Painter, or to photographs.

Water Color Variants

Painter's Water Color variants create paintings remarkably like those of traditional water colors, complete with the subtle effects of pooling (color buildup around the edges of the stroke) and sensitivity to paper grain. With these brushes, moving the Grain slider to the left makes the paint appear flatter, and moving it toward the right will allow more of the paper grain to appear. Also, pressing lightly on the stylus will produce narrower strokes, and pressing heavier will produce wider strokes.

Before painting with the Water Color variants, Painter's wet layer should be activated. The wet layer is a separate layer in Painter that floats above your image layer. The water color strokes you apply with these brushes don't affect your existing image, and stay wet until you set them into the main layer by drying the strokes. If you try to apply strokes using the Water Color brushes without the wet layer turned on, you will be reminded to activate it. The basic procedure for using the Water Color brushes is as follows:

1. Choose a Water Color variant from the Brushes Palette.

2. The wet layer is activated when you choose a Water Color variant. You can toggle the wet layer on and off, if necessary, by choosing the Canvas | Wet Paint command. A checkmark will appear beside the Wet Paint command when it is enabled. If you see the checkmark when you drop down the Canvas Menu command options, there is no need to perform the command.

3. Apply watercolor strokes by positioning the mouse or stylus where you want to begin painting. Drag through the canvas using short or long strokes. Then release the mouse or stylus when the stroke is complete.

4. When you are done making your strokes, choose Canvas | Dry to place them into the background layer.

5. You can apply multiple layers of watercolor strokes if you like, drying the canvas between layers. When you are completely finished using the Water Color paints or if you want to choose another type of brush to paint with, turn the wet layer off by choosing Canvas | Wet Paint again.

TIP Because Water Colors are painted in a separate layer from the background, there are a few things you should be aware of when using these brushes:

- You can undo your most recent stroke using the Edit | Undo command. If you are using Painter 3.1, you can undo multiple strokes. This will erase the stroke from the wet layer.

- Painter's "normal" Eraser variants will not work in the wet layer. To erase Water Color strokes, use the Wet Eraser, which is contained within the Water Color brush variants.

- You can use paths to mask inside or outside areas in the wet layer while painting, just as in the normal layer. However, selections cannot be used to *clear* areas from the wet layer.

- Periodically saving your document will decrease the chances of losing artwork you are happy with! Save the document with the wet layer on— and then resume painting with the wet layer still enabled. If you add some areas you aren't happy with, you should be able to revert back to the saved document and continue again from that point, as long as you don't turn the wet layer off before you resume painting. Note, however, that you have to resume the painting within the same Painter session for this to work correctly.

- All strokes placed in the wet layer can be cleared by first choosing the Canvas | Dry command to place the colors into the background layer and then immediately choosing the Edit | Undo command.

Adjustments for Water Color Brushes

Painter's Advanced Controls Palette contains a subset of controls that are particular to the Water Color variants only. These settings are located in the Advanced Controls | Water Palette and are called Diffusion and Wet Fringe.

The Diffusion setting determines how the watercolors absorb into the canvas. An example of a brush that uses this setting is the Diffuse Water brush. You will notice when painting with this brush that the stroke first appears as a solid line. After a brief wait, the stroke will then diffuse, giving the appearance that the paint is bleeding into the canvas. If you increase the Diffusion setting in the Water Palette, the stroke will bleed even further.

TIP   A quick-key combination applies a Post Diffuse command to your strokes in the wet layer. Both Windows and Mac users use the Shift-D key combination to apply this effect.

The Wet Fringe setting controls the amount of pooling that will occur with the brush, and all of Painter's Water Colors use this setting in varying degrees. As mentioned previously, the watercolor brushes offer the characteristic of having color build-up around the edges of the stroke, just like traditional water colors. This pooling effect can be increased or decreased by adjusting the Wet Fringe setting. Moving the slider toward the left will decrease the pooling amount, and moving the slider toward the right will increase the amount of pooling.

NOTE   It is important to note that the pooling cannot be adjusted once the strokes have been set into the background layer; so if you want to adjust the pooling of a brush, do so while your strokes are still in the wet layer.

Descriptions of Painter's Water Color Brushes follow.

Broad Water Brush

The Broad Water Brush variant is a multiple-bristled rake brush that paints into the wet layer with wide strokes that vary in opacity based on pressure from the stylus. The brush is also sensitive to paper grain. Lighter pressure reveals less paper grain, and heavier strokes show the paper grain more. Besides adjusting the pooling, as mentioned previously, you can further adjust the appearance of this brush with the Contact Angle and Brush Scale settings in the Advanced Controls | Rake Palette.

Diffuse Water

The Diffuse Water variant paints into the wet layer with strokes that build on top of each other and are sensitive to paper grain. Stroke size and opacity vary with the pressure of the stylus. The edges of this brush diffuse after a stroke is made, giving the appearance that they are bleeding into the paper.

You can adjust brush size in the Brush Controls | Size Palette or by changing the Size category in the Advanced Controls | Sliders Palette to Velocity or Direction. You can adjust opacity in the Controls | Brush Palette.

Large Simple Water

The Large Simple Water variant is a larger version of the Simple Water variant. This brush paints into the wet layer with large non-bristly strokes that are sensitive to paper grain. Stroke size and reaction to paper grain are affected by stylus pressure. Mouse users can adjust the brush size in the Brush Controls | Size Palette or by changing the Size category in the Advanced Controls | Sliders Palette to Velocity or Direction. Grain can be adjusted manually on the Controls | Brush Palette.

Large Water

The Large Water variant produces a stroke that is sheer and transparent, making it a good brush to use for smoothing transitions between two colors or for smearing colors a bit in the wet layer. The stroke is sensitive to paper grain, and its size, opacity, and grain sensitivity are affected by the pressure applied to the stylus. Mouse users can adjust the size of the stroke in the Brush Controls | Size Palette or by changing the Size category in the Advanced Controls | Sliders Palette to Velocity or Direction. Opacity and Grain can be adjusted interactively on the Controls | Brush Palette.

Pure Water Brush

The Pure Water Brush variant is a multistroke brush that adds water to the wet layer. The size of the stroke is affected by the pressure applied with the stylus. When you first place a stroke with this brush, a dotted line will appear while the stroke is rendering.

To paint with the Pure Water Brush:

1. Position the mouse or stylus where you want the stroke to begin.
2. Push down on the stylus, or click and hold the mouse button and make a short stroke over an area that has color placed in the wet layer. The stroke will first appear as a dotted line.

3. Let up on the stylus or release the mouse button when the stroke is finished. The stroke will complete its rendering.

The appearance of this brush stroke can be modified by adjusting the Dab Location Placement slider in the Advanced Controls | Random Palette. Mouse users can adjust the size of this stroke in the Brush Controls | Size Palette or by changing the Size category in the Advanced Controls | Sliders Palette to Velocity or Direction.

Simple Water

The Simple Water variant paints into the wet layer with feathery strokes that are sensitive to paper grain. Stroke size, opacity, and reaction to paper grain are affected by stylus pressure. Strokes made with one color with this brush will blend into those made with another color. The appearance of this brush can be altered by making adjustments to the Diffusion and Wet Fringe sliders in the Advanced Controls | Water Palette. Mouse users can adjust the size of the brush in the Brush Controls | Size Palette, and adjust the Opacity and Grain on the Controls | Brush Palette.

Spatter Water

The Spatter Water variant spatters water drops of random size and placement when you drag this brush through the wet layer. You can increase or decrease the randomness of the drops by adjusting the Dab Location Placement slider in the Advanced Controls | Random Palette. The opacity of the drops, as well as their reaction to paper grain, are affected by the pressure applied by the stylus. Mouse users can adjust the Opacity and Grain sliders on the Controls | Brush Palette. Or, the Opacity and Grain settings in the Advanced Controls | Sliders Palette can be set to respond to Velocity or Direction.

Water Brush Stroke

The Water Brush Stroke variant is a multistroke bristle brush. A dotted line appears while Painter computes the stroke.

To paint with the Water Brush Stroke:

1. Place the mouse or stylus where you want to begin the stroke.

2. Push down on the stylus or click the mouse and drag to make a short stroke. A dotted line will appear. Wait until the stroke is rendered before beginning another stroke.

3. Let up on the stylus or release the mouse button when the stroke is completed. Your stroke will appear after it is rendered.

The appearance of the brush can be altered by changing the settings of the Dab Location Placement slider in the Advanced Controls | Random Palette. Mouse users can adjust the size of the stroke in the Brush Controls | Size Palette or by changing the Size category in the Advanced Controls | Sliders Palette to Velocity or Direction.

Wet Eraser

The Wet Eraser variant erases brush strokes made in the wet layer. This brush is pressure-sensitive; lighter pressure will erase less of a color, and heavier pressure will erase more of the color. You can simulate this effect with a mouse by adjusting the Opacity slider in the Controls | Brush Palette.

Liquid Tools

Painter's Liquid Tools look very much like strokes painted with a palette knife when they are used to create oil painting effects. They all use Drip methods, which give them the characteristic of smearing colors rather than painting them on.

With the Liquid variants, you can either apply a new color, selected from the Art Materials | Colors Palette, or smear existing color around. To set up the Liquid variants to push paint around, move the Opacity slider in the Controls | Brush Palette all the way to the left, so that the color is at 0% Opacity (completely shut off). When using a stylus, the amount of pressure you put on the stroke will determine how much of the color gets smeared; pressing heavily will spread more color, and pressing lightly will spread less color.

The pressure of a stylus affects the Drip Method brushes differently than other brush methods. To understand this further, consider how paint reacts when it is applied to a canvas with a palette knife. Using more pressure on a palette knife reveals more of the canvas, and using less pressure applies more paint. This is also true of the Liquid brushes. More paper texture becomes visible when you press heavily, and less paper texture becomes visible when you press lightly. The grain slider behaves as it normally would—moving the slider to the left will cover less of the grain, and moving the slider to the right will cover more of the grain.

To smear color with the Liquid Tools:

1. Place your mouse or stylus where you would like the stroke to begin.
2. Click the mouse or press on the stylus, and drag through the stroke. The more you push the mouse or stylus around, the more the paint will be smeared.
3. Release the mouse or let up on the stylus when you are done painting.

Coarse Distorto

The Coarse Distorto variant smears paint around using semi-antialiased strokes. The size of the stroke varies based on the speed at which you drag your mouse or stylus. Stroke opacity is set at 0%, meaning that no paint will be applied when

you use this brush. The Grain adjustment in the Controls | Brush Palette controls the amount of distortion from the brush. Moving the slider toward tne left will decrease the amount of distortion, and moving it toward the right will increase the amount of distortion.

Coarse Smeary Bristles

Coarse Smeary Bristles smears paint around with semi-antialiased brush strokes that are sensitive to paper grain. The size of the stroke varies with the speed that the mouse or stylus is dragged, and stroke opacity varies with stylus pressure. Mouse users can adjust the Opacity slider on the Controls | Brush Palette to achieve the same effect, or set the Opacity slider in the Advanced Controls | Sliders Palette to respond to a change in Velocity or Direction.

Coarse Smeary Mover

The Coarse Smeary Mover variant smears paint around with semi-antialiased strokes that are sensitive to paper grain. This variant does not apply color. The size of the stroke varies with the speed at which the mouse or stylus is dragged.

Distorto

The Distorto variant smears paint around without adding color. Its strokes vary in size depending on the speed at which the mouse or stylus is dragged. The amount of distortion can be adjusted in the Brush Controls | Size Palette.

Smeary Bristles

The Smeary Bristles variant smears the current color into your image and mixes it with existing color. This brush interacts with paper grain, and the strokes vary in size based on the speed at which the mouse or stylus is dragged. More paper texture will become visible when the stylus is pressed heavily, and less paper texture will appear with light stylus pressure. Moving the Grain slider to the left will reveal more paper texture, and moving it to the right will cover more paper texture.

Smeary Mover

The Smeary Mover variant smears existing paint around in an image without applying color, using strokes that are sensitive to paper grain. The strokes vary in size based on the speed at which the mouse or stylus is dragged.

Thick Oil

The Thick Oil variant is a rake brush that smears the selected color into the image with strokes that are paper-grain sensitive. The size of the stroke varies with the speed at which the mouse or stylus is dragged. Stroke opacity and grain also respond to stylus pressure.

Mouse users can adjust the Opacity and Grain sliders on the Controls | Brush Palette; or the Opacity and Grain settings in the Advanced Controls | Sliders Palette can be set to respond to Velocity or Direction.

Tiny Smudge

The Tiny Smudge variant smears existing paint in very small areas. This brush performs the same whether you use a mouse or a stylus.

Total Oil Brush

The Total Oil Brush variant produces a tight stroke that is sensitive to paper grain and which smears color into the image. Stroke opacity and grain respond to stylus pressure. Mouse users can adjust the Opacity and Grain sliders on the Controls | Brush Palette; or, the Opacity and Grain settings in the Advanced Controls | Sliders Palette can be set to respond to Velocity or Direction.

Water Variants

The Water variants work in the background layer and are used primarily to smudge, blend, and dilute strokes made by Painter's other variants. They also can be used to add or remove paper grain effects from areas of your image without applying additional color.

To smear with Water variants:

1. Position the mouse or stylus where you want the stroke to begin.
2. Push down on the stylus or click the mouse, and drag to make a short stroke or a long stroke.
3. Lift up on the stylus or release the mouse button when you are done painting.

Big Frosty Water

Big Frosty Water is a larger version of Frosty Water. It smears existing strokes with a hard, pixelly edge. Because the strokes are sensitive to paper grain, interesting effects can be achieved by choosing different paper textures from the Art Materials | Papers Palette. Mouse users can adjust the Opacity and Grain sliders on the Controls | Brush Palette. Or, the Opacity and Grain settings in the Advanced Controls | Sliders Palette can be set to respond to Velocity or Direction.

Frosty Water

Frosty Water smears existing strokes with a hard, pixelly edge. Because the strokes are sensitive to paper grain, interesting effects can be achieved by choosing different paper textures from the Art Materials | Papers Palette. Mouse users can adjust the Opacity and Grain sliders on the Controls | Brush Palette; or, the Opacity and Grain settings in the Advanced Controls | Sliders Palette can be set to respond to Velocity or Direction.

Grainy Water

Grainy Water produces hard, pixelly strokes that are sensitive to paper grain. This brush helps maintain the graininess of existing textured strokes, or can be used to add texture to smooth strokes. Stroke opacity and paper grain respond to stylus pressure.

Just Add Water

Just Add Water smears paint with soft, antialiased strokes. This brush smoothly blends colors together while removing paper textures from areas that it paints over. The size of the stroke varies with the speed at which the mouse or stylus is dragged. Stroke opacity and grain respond to stylus pressure.

Single Pixel Water

Single Pixel Water is good for touching up small, zoomed-in areas. The strokes are antialiased and are one pixel wide. This brush performs the same whether you use a mouse or a stylus.

Tiny Frosty Water

Tiny Frosty Water is a smaller version of Frosty Water. It smears existing strokes with a hard, pixelly edge. Because the strokes are sensitive to paper grain, interesting effects can be achieved by choosing different paper textures from the Art Materials | Papers Palette.

Water Rake

The Water Rake is a multiple-bristled brush that has hard, pixelly edges that react to paper grain. Stroke opacity and reaction to paper grain vary based on pressure applied by the stylus.

Mouse users can adjust the Opacity and Grain sliders on the Controls | Brush Palette; or, the Opacity and Grain settings in the Advanced Controls | Sliders Palette can be set to respond to Velocity or Direction.

Water Spray

Water Spray paints water onto an image similar to the way an airbrush does. The width of the stroke varies based on the speed at which the mouse or stylus is dragged. This brush performs the same whether you use a mouse or a stylus.

Step 10.1. Prepare for the Project

As mentioned before, this project is the first of three parts to complete a Tiffany-style, stained-glass image. The background, tree, and leaves will be painted with the Water Colors and Liquid variants. In Chapter 15, "Image Hose Project," you will convert the leaves into an image hose nozzle file and spray them on to the tree. Finally, in Chapter 11, "Completing the Stained Glass Window," you'll use the Airbrush variants to paint the birds and finish the image with some effects.

To start the background, create a document as follows and prepare the tools needed.

1. Create a new 640×820 document. Set the resolution at 75 dpi and the paper color at white.

2. Zoom out, if you like, to see the entire document on your screen. You can use the quick key combination of Ctrl--(Control key plus the minus key) in Windows, or Cmd--(the Command key plus the minus key) in Mac.

3. Open the Tools Palette (Ctrl-1 in Windows, Cmd-1 in Mac), the Brushes Palette (Ctrl-2 in Windows, Cmd-2 in Mac), and the Controls Palette (Ctrl-6 in Windows, Cmd-6 in Mac) and position them out of the way of your image.

4. From the Art Materials Palette (Ctrl-4 in Windows, Cmd-4 in Mac), click the Sets icon. Click the Library button and choose the CHAP10CS.TXT color set, as shown in Figure 10.1. The color set will appear on your screen.

Figure 10.1.
The CHAP10CS.TXT
Color Set will be used
for this project.

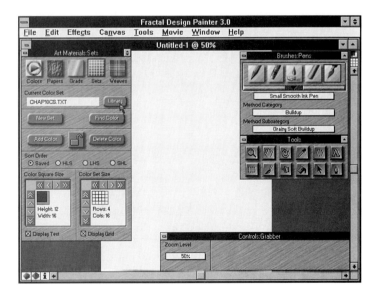

Painting the Background

You are going to start the background by roughing in some colors using the Large Simple Water variant. Later, you can go back and blend colors together using other Water Color variants.

Step 10.2. Basing in the Background Colors

1. From the Brushes Palette, click the Water Color icon and select the Large Simple Water variant. Notice that when you drop down the Canvas menu, as shown in Figure 10.2, the Wet Paint mode is automatically checked and selected for you. This means you will be painting in Painter's wet layer, which floats above the background layer.

Figure 10.2.
The wet layer should be chosen automatically when you select the Water Color variants.

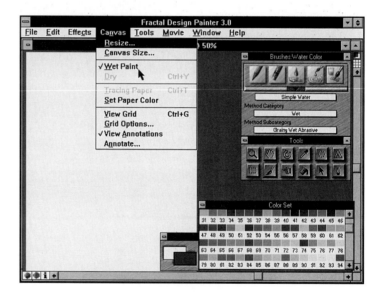

2. From the Art Materials | Papers Palette, choose the Eggscape paper texture, shown in Figure 10.3. This is a nice texture to add to the stained glass background while you're painting.

3. From the Chapter 10 color set, choose Blue #237. Start painting at the top, using broad and long strokes. Then, vary the coverage by applying strokes over one another to get some darker areas. Paper grain will show through as more color and pressure is applied. Fill the upper portion of the screen, as shown in Figure 10.4.

Figure 10.3.
Choose the Eggscape
paper texture from the
Papers Palette.

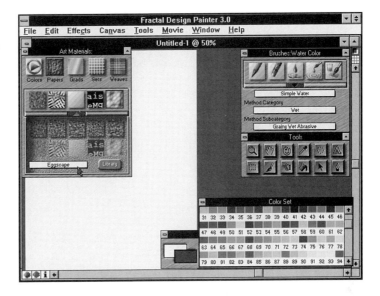

Figure 10.4.
Start painting at the
top of the image with
Blue #237 from the
chapter color palette.

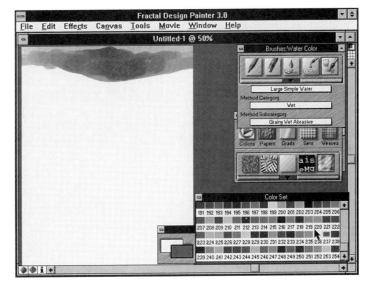

4. Choose Off-White color #236 and add some lighter areas for clouds. This color also can be mixed in with the blue you painted in the previous step to base in areas that are a little more cloudy. You can blend the colors together and reshape the previous areas you applied, if desired, as new strokes are placed. As you're painting this area for the clouds, consider the various layers you're working with as different pieces of glass. For this upper section, I wanted the appearance of marbled glass rather than translucent or transparent glass. You will "marble-ize" the cloudy area with Liquid variants later. Figure 10.5 shows some of this color added.

325

Figure 10.5.
Off-White (color #236)
is added for cloud
areas.

5. Continue down toward the bottom of the background by adding more
colors, again thinking of them as separate sections of glass. For the next
layer, I chose color #228 and painted until about the first 40 percent of the
background was covered, as shown in Figure 10.6.

Figure 10.6.
Color #228 was added
to the next portion of
the image.

6. Next, I added two more layers of color to the sky. I started with color #210
and then added some of color #199 beneath it. Refer to Figure 10.7 for the
progress so far.

Figure 10.7.
*Two more layers of
color are added to the
sky background.*

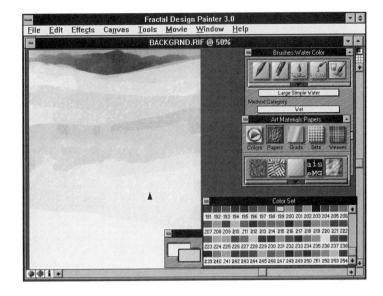

7. A final layer of Color #107 was added to the bottom portion of the image,
as shown in Figure 10.8.

Figure 10.8.
*With Color #107, the
final layer of color is
added to the back-
ground.*

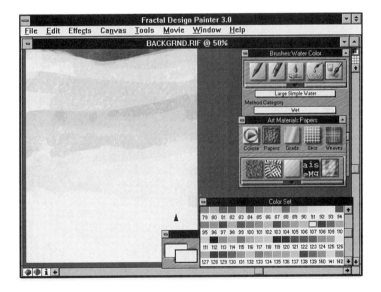

Step 10.3. Enhancing the Sky

Now, all the colors are roughed in for the glass areas and you can add a little
more detail. The Simple Water variant, a smaller version of the Large Simple
Water just used, was chosen to define some more areas for the clouds.

1. Switch to the Simple Water variant in the Water Color tools. Add cloudy highlights to the sky with color #107, which should still be your current color. Highlights were added to the first two "sections" of glass, as shown in Figure 10.9.

Figure 10.9.
Highlights were added
to the first two sections
of glass with color
#107.

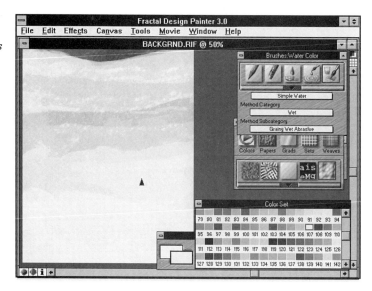

2. Next, some deeper cloud shadows were added with color #232, as shown in Figure 10.10. Vary the pressure of the stylus (or adjust the brush's opacity) to change the amount of coverage applied.

Figure 10.10.
Some shadowed areas
were based in using
color #232.

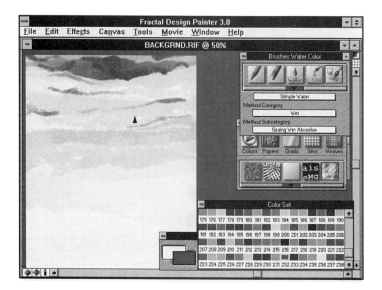

3. When you are satisfied with your sky, dry the canvas using the Canvas | Dry command. This will set the colors in to the background so that you can smear them in using some of the Liquid variants.

Step 10.4. Smearing the Clouds

Now, you'll use some of the Liquid variants to smear the colors of the clouds together. Remember that these colors smear on and interact with paper grain much like paint does when it's applied with a palette knife. Use nice, slow strokes when applying paint with these brushes and vary the opacity to add more or less of your current color.

1. From the Liquid variants, choose Smeary Bristles. Select color #236 from the color set and smear this color into the clouds. You will notice that the existing color drags along with the stroke of the brush. If you start in lighter areas, you can drag the light colors in toward the dark to blend. If you start in the darker areas, you can drag in toward the lighter areas to blend. You also can smear the paint, without applying additional color, by adjusting the Opacity slider in the Controls | Brush Palette to 0% or by switching over to the Smeary Mover, which would accomplish that effect. Try to achieve the look of marbled glass here. (See Figure 10.11.)

2. To add a bit more color interest to the sky, some Light Yellow #107 was added using the Smeary Bristles variant. This color was "scrubbed" in using very short strokes and varying pressure. You also can add more color definition with the Total Oil Brush variant, which would apply the color a bit more transparently. Your image should now start looking a little more cloudy, as shown in Figure 10.12.

Figure 10.11.
The upper portion of the sky is given a marbled glass appearance with Smeary Bristles and Smeary Mover.

Figure 10.12.
Light Yellow #107 and the Smeary Bristles brush or the Total Oil Brush can be used to enhance the clouds.

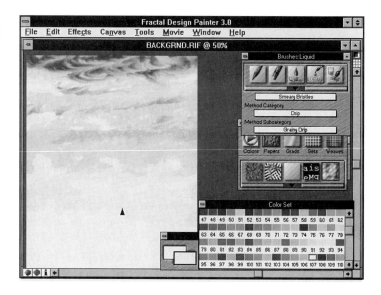

Step 10.5. Adding Some Linework

To make the image look more like a stained-glass image, I added some dark lines to separate some of the areas of the sky. This defined the breaks in the glass sections used to make up the entire piece. Let your design decide where the breaks should go. Don't overdo it, because there will be more "glass pieces" added later that will make it look much more busy.

To define the glass sections, I used one of the Airbrush variants to place my linework, as follows:

1. From the Airbrush variants, select the Feather Tip Airbrush.

2. Choose Dark Gray #1 from the color set.

3. Draw in some linework at suitable breaks in color. Let your scene decide where the lines should go and identify different colors as different pieces of glass placed in the window. When you're done, the image should look somewhat like that shown in Figure 10.13.

Figure 10.13.
The sections of glass
were defined with the
Feather Tip Airbrush
and Dark Gray #1.

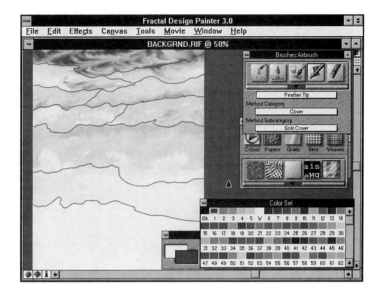

Step 10.6. Adding the Glass Texture

If there are some "glass pieces" in your background image that are nearly solid
in color, these might be good candidates to choose for applying some glass
texture. To do this, you create outline paths just inside the dark gray border
lines of your glass pieces, and then add the glass texture using the Effects |
Focus | Glass Distortion command. Chapter 17, "A Collage of Effects," goes into
detail on creating and editing outline selections.

1. From the Art Materials | Papers Palette, choose the Medium Fine paper
   texture. Adjust the Scale slider in the Papers Palette to read 200%, as
   shown in Figure 10.14.

2. Select an area that you want to apply glass surface texture to. Draw a path
   on the inside edge of the border line with the Outline Selection Tool, as
   shown in Figure 10.15.

3. Choose Effects | Focus | Glass Distortion. The Glass Distortion dialog box,
   shown in Figure 10.16, will appear.

Figure 10.14.
Choose the Medium Fine paper texture and adjust its scale to 200%.

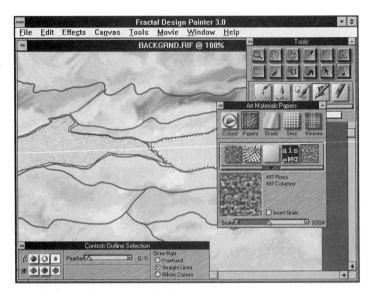

Figure 10.15.
Select the inside of a section of glass with the Outline Selection tool.

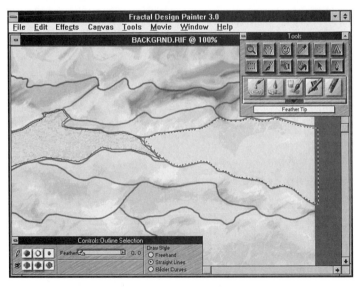

Glass Distortion gives the selection or the entire image the appearance that it is placed behind a pane of glass. There are a couple of adjustment sliders contained in the Glass Distortion dialog box that will alter the appearance of the effect.

Adjusting the amount slider will increase or decrease the amount of the distortion of the effect. Moving the slider to the left will create less distortion, and moving it to the right will increase the distortion. The slider inside the arrow will increase the effect in large amounts. Clicking the arrows at the sides of the slider bar will adjust the effects in small amounts.

Figure 10.16.
Apply Glass Distortion
using Paper Grain, and
adjust the Amount and
Variance sliders as
shown.

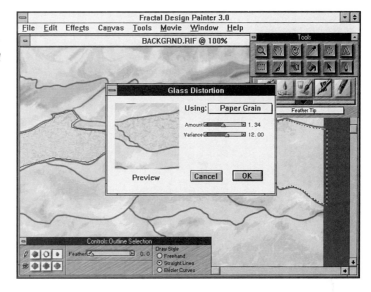

Adjusting the variance slider will increase or decrease the breakup of the glass. Moving the slider to the left will create less breakup, and moving it to the right will increase the breakup. The slider inside the arrow will increase the effect in large amounts. Clicking the arrows at the sides of the slider bar will adjust the effects in small amounts.

You also can apply Glass Distortion based on one of the following methods:

- **Paper Grain** produces an effect similar to textured glass, based on the currently selected Paper Texture from the Art Materials | Papers Palette.

- **Image Luminance** creates texture in the glass based on the light and dark areas of the current image.

- **3D Brush Strokes** is enabled when a clone source and clone document are open, and will produce a three-dimensional texture in the clone document by comparing the differences between the two images.

- **Original Luminance** is enabled when a clone source and clone document are open, and will produce texture based on the light and dark areas of the clone source.

- **Mask** adds texture around a selection.

4. Choose to apply the effect using Paper Grain. Adjust the Amount Slider to about 1.3 and adjust the variance to about 12.00. Click OK to apply the effect. Glass Texture will be applied to the area you chose.

5. Continue in this manner and add glass texture to any additional areas you like. It looks best when applied to areas that are near solid, making those areas look like textured bumpy glass. (See Figure 10.17.)

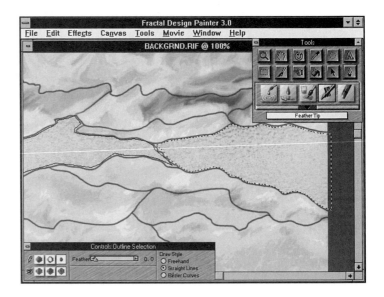

Figure 10.17.
Apply the Glass
Distortion to other
selected areas in the
image, making them
look like bumpy glass.

6. Save the image as BACKGRND.RIF. Keep it open if you want to clone it for the next step.

Step 10.7. Creating the Tree Floater

You will draw the tree in a new document. When drawing the shape of the tree, I used a clone of the sky background (just created) as a guide. This way, I could see the shape of the tree against the background as I drew it.

Step 10.8. Painting the Tree

1. Create a clone of BACKGRND.RIF using the File | Clone command. Keep the original background image open while you draw your tree's outline. The clone document (the copy) should be chosen as your current document.

2. Select the entire clone document using Edit | Select All and clear the selection by using the Backspace key in Windows, or the Delete key in Mac. You can use the Window | Zoom Out command (Ctrl-- in Windows, Cmd--in Mac) with the Screen Mode Toggle (Ctrl-M in Windows, Cmd-M in Mac) to see the entire picture if necessary.

3. Turn on the tracing paper using the Canvas | Tracing Paper command. (You can also click the tracing paper icon in the upper-right document scrollbar). A ghost image of the background will appear, as shown in Figure 10.18.

Figure 10.18.
A clone was created to use as a guide for shaping the tree.

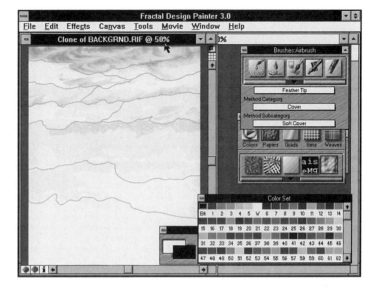

4. Using the Feather Tip Airbrush and Black (the first color in the color set), draw in the shape of the tree as shown in the figure. You may find it easier to first draw the base of the tree and add the branch linework later, as shown in Figure 10.19. When you're done drawing your outline, you can close the original background image or turn off the tracing paper using the Canvas | Tracing Paper command.

Figure 10.19.
Draw the shape of the tree against the background.

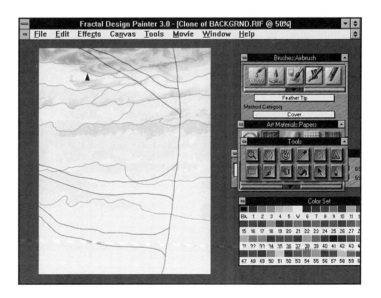

5. Erase any extra lines using the Small Eraser (Eraser variant), as shown in Figure 10.20.

Figure 10.20.
Erase any extra lines
using the Small Eraser.

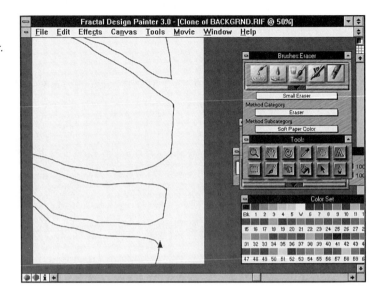

6. Choose Brown #54. Rough in the color of the tree using the Large Simple Water and Simple Water (Water Color) variants. You can then darken some of the areas using the same color with the smaller Simple Water variant. The tree should start taking form, as shown in Figure 10.21.

Figure 10.21.
Large Simple Water
and Simple Water were
used to apply color #54
to start the tree.

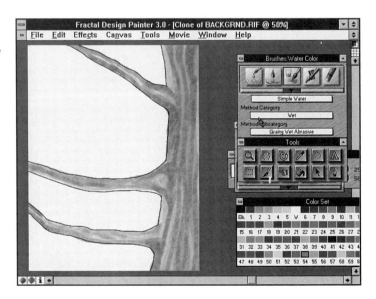

7. To define more light and dark areas, choose the Pure Water Brush variant. This variant can be used to lighten and deepen the colors in the tree. When you first apply strokes with this brush, a dotted line will appear, and then your brush stroke will be rendered in a short time. If you repeat a stroke over a previous one, the colors will deepen. Figure 10.22 shows your progress so far.

Figure 10.22. More definition is added to the tree using the Pure Water Brush.

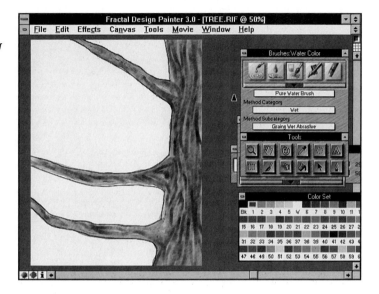

8. Choose Brown #40 and the Diffuse Water variant. This variant is used to add some feathered color to the tree, giving it more texture and substance. When applying strokes with this brush, you will first see a smooth streak of paint applied to the image. After a short time, the stroke will diffuse into other areas of color, giving the appearance of bleeding into the canvas. Figure 10.23 shows texture applied to the tree with the Diffuse Water variant.

9. Dry the canvas again using the Canvas | Dry command. This transfers all your watercolor strokes to the background layer of the image.

10. To add some shading to the left side of the trunk and the underside of the branches, choose Gray #1 and the Simple Water variant. Add some more shading to the tree in areas where you want the bark to appear receded. When you're done, dry the canvas again. The tree is now painted and is shown in Figure 10.24

Figure 10.23.
The bark of the tree is
deepened when you
use Brown #40 and the
Diffuse Water variant.

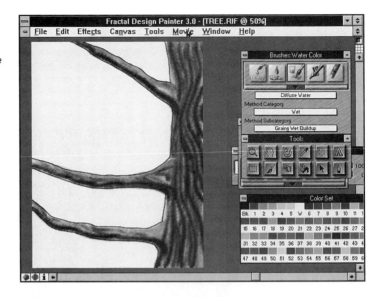

Figure 10.24.
Some final shading
is added with Simple
Water and Dark
Gray #1.

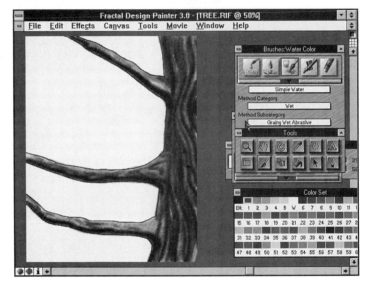

Step 10.9. Floating the Tree

One of the beauties of Painter is that it contains many different ways to achieve
a certain result. There are many ways to create paths and selections in Painter,
and here you have several options. You could create a selection from masks, as
you've done many times already; but if you've colored outside the lines while
drawing your tree, the mask might require a fair amount of touchup. Or, you can
outline only the tree with the Outline selection Tool, which might be a tricky

process because it's large and irregularly shaped. As another alternative, you can outline the smaller blank areas and then invert the selection to select only the tree. Let's give that choice a try here and see how you can change the selections to contain only the tree.

1. Open the Objects Palette (Ctrl-5) and click the P.List icon to open the Path List Palette.

2. Using the Outline Selection Tool, create paths around the white areas of the document. The paths can be created using Straight Lines, Bézier Curve, or Freehand mode, as selected in the Controls | Outline Selection Palette. You can zoom into a specific area by clicking the Magnifier tool and using it to draw a rectangle around the area you want to zoom into. In Figure 10.25, four selections have been created, and their names appear in the Objects | Path List Palette.

Figure 10.25. Outline selections are drawn around the blank areas of the image with the Outline Selection Tool.

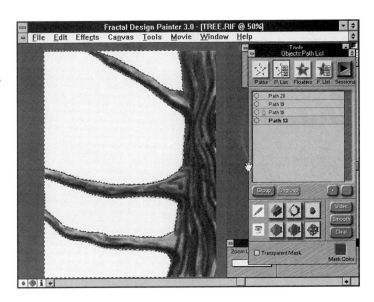

3. Highlight all four names in the Path List Palette (yours may differ from those shown in the figure), and group them by clicking the Group button. A group name will appear above the four path names, as shown in Figure 10.26.

Think about what you've done so far. You've created four separate outline selections that contain everything *but* the area you want to select. If you like, click the second Mask Visibility button at this point. You will see that the four selected areas are shown in red in the masking layer, and the tree is unmasked. Now, revert back to the marquee selection mode by clicking the third Mask Visibility button.

Figure 10.26.
The four paths are
grouped together in the
Path List Palette.

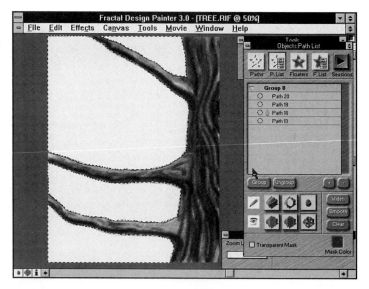

4. To invert the selection to contain only the tree, you can use the Edit |
   Mask | Invert Mask command. This will alter the mask so that the selected
   areas will become unmasked and the tree will become masked. What will
   also happen is that the display in the Path List Palette will change from a
   group of four selections (the four white areas) to a group of one selection
   (the tree). The marquee selection in the image window should also change
   to surround all areas of the tree.

5. Choose the Floating Selection tool from the Tools Palette and click the tree
   to turn it into a floater.

6. From the Objects Palette, click the Floaters icon to open the Floaters
   Palette, shown in Figure 10.27. If you want to place the tree floater into a
   library other than the one you have currently open, choose it at this time
   by clicking the Library button inside the Floaters Palette drawer.

7. Using the Floating Selection tool, click the tree and drag it to the Floaters
   Palette. If you want to keep a copy of the tree in this document, depress
   the Alt (Windows) or Option (Mac) key while dragging the floater. This will
   drag a copy of the floater into the Floaters Palette and keep the original in
   the document. After you release the mouse or stylus to place the tree into
   the floater library, name the floater Tree, as shown in Figure 10.28.

8. If you've dragged a copy of the tree into the Floater Palette and want to
   save your original document, save it as a .RIF file, which will keep the
   selections and floater intact in the document.

Figure 10.27.
Open the Floaters
Palette and choose your
desired Floater Library.

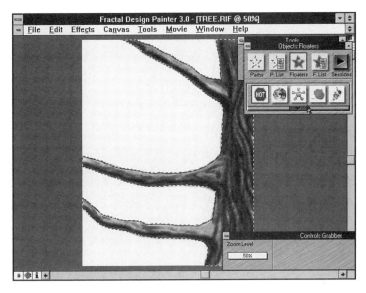

Figure 10.28.
The tree is placed into
the Floater Library and
given a name.

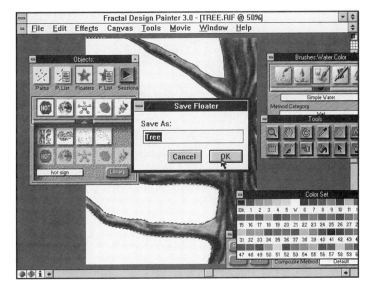

Step 10.10. Placing the Tree in the Background

You won't add any effects to the tree at this time. I just pulled the floater into
the background, positioned it in its proper place, and then dropped it in using
default settings.

1. Open the sky image, BACKGRND.RIF, if it is not still open.

2. Using the Floating Selection tool, drag the floater from the Floaters Palette and place it into the background document. Position the floater in its proper place. If you highlight the Tree in the Floater List Palette and press Enter (Windows) or Return (Mac), the Floater Attributes dialog box will appear. (See Figure 10.29.) The tree floater should be positioned at 0 Top, 0 Left coordinates. Figure 10.30 shows the tree placed in its correct position.

Figure 10.29.
The Floater Attributes
dialog box.

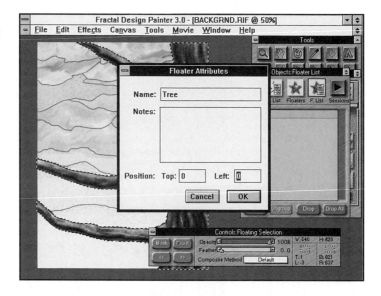

Figure 10.30.
The tree floater is
dragged into the
background image and
positioned in its proper
place.

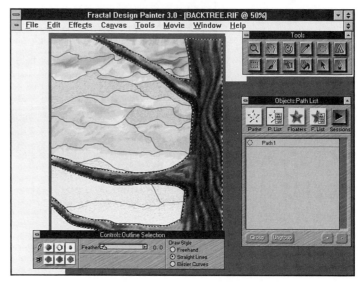

3. Drop the tree floater into the background by choosing the Edit | Drop command or by clicking the Drop or Drop All button in the Floater List Palette. When the image has been dropped, the marquee lines will disappear from the border of the floater.

4. Add Glass Distortion to the tree in a manner similar to the way you did in the background image. Make a selection around the inside border of the tree and choose the Effects | Focus | Glass Distortion command. Adjust the Amount slider to around -.20, and the Variance to around 10, as shown in Figure 10.31. Apply the effect to the tree by clicking the OK button.

5. Save the image as BACKTREE.RIF.

Figure 10.31.
Apply Glass Distortion
to the tree using the
settings in Step 10.10.

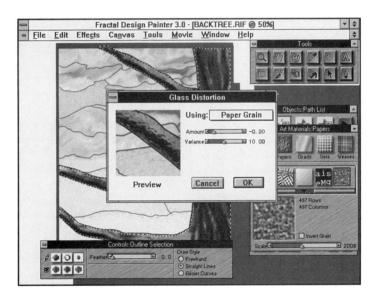

Step 10.11. Creating the Leaves

For the next step, you are going to create some leaves that will be sprayed onto the tree with the Image Hose tools. You can create as many leaves as you like. I chose to create 12 of them, and later positioned and rotated them so that 6 leaves were facing upward and 6 were facing downward.

1. Create a new document. Size it to hold as many leaves as you would like to create.

2. With the Feather Tip Airbrush and black paint, draw some outline shapes for the leaves. You're going to color them in using the Water Color variants. As you create the outlines for the leaves, leave enough space in between them as you draw so that they can be properly selected later on. Size them appropriately for the tree you made earlier and shape them any way you choose. Figure 10.32 shows several leave shapes drawn.

3. Load in the Chapter 10 color set if it is not still selected and displayed. From the color set, choose Green #123. With the Simple Water variant, rough in some color on one side of each leaf, as shown in Figure 10.33.

4. For the lighter side of each leaf, choose Green #85, which is a lighter shade of green. Apply more color using the Simple Water variant. As you are applying the lighter shades, blend the colors together as they merge. Figure 10.34 shows the leaves with both background colors applied.

Figure 10.32.
Draw some leaf shapes using black paint and the Feather Tip Airbrush.

Figure 10.33.
Rough some color in for each leaf with Green #123.

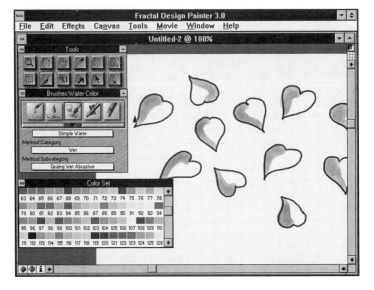

5. To add some deeper shading, the Diffuse Water variant was chosen; it's a bit too big for the tiny leaves, so you're going to reduce its size a little. From the Brush Controls Palette (Ctrl-4 in Windows, Cmd-4 in Mac), choose the Size Palette, shown in Figure 10.35. Adjust the size of the Diffuse Water variant to around 3, and build the brush. If you like, you can save it to the current brush library using the Tools | Brushes | Save Variant command so that you can retrieve it later.

Figure 10.34.
Add Green #85 to the leaves, blending the two colors together where they meet.

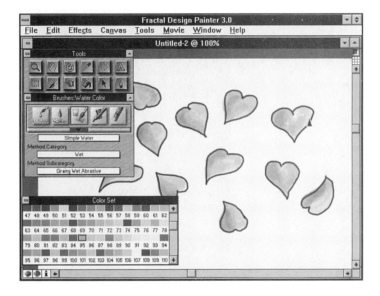

Figure 10.35.
Adjust the size of the Diffuse Water brush to around 3, and save it as a Water Color variant, if you like.

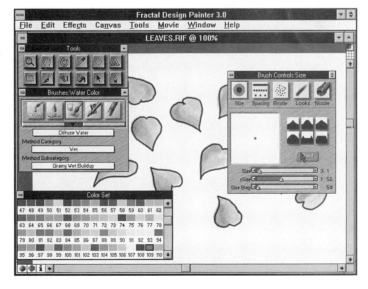

6. Choose Green #101 from the color set. With the smaller Diffuse Water variant, rough in some color for the shading of the leaves. You only need very tiny strokes here—and start them at a slight distance from the edge. If the color goes outside the outline of the leaves, don't worry; you'll be cutting them out as selections later. The shading has been added in Figure 10.36.

Figure 10.36.
Add some feathered
shading with the
smaller Diffuse Water
variant and Green
#101.

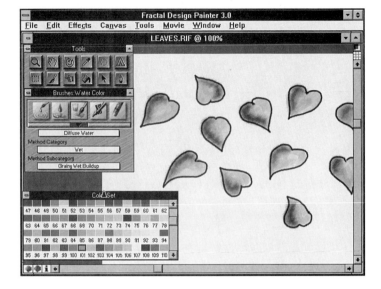

7. To add some vein lines to the leaves, choose the Water Brush Stroke variant. Reduce its size down to around 3.5 in the Brush Controls | Size Palette, and build the brush. Save the new brush to the existing library using the Tools | Brushes | Save Variant command, if you like. Add veins to the leaves using Yellow #93, as shown in Figure 10.37.

8. Dry the canvas to set the colors in the background layer.

9. To add a little bit of blue to the leaves, to coordinate them with the background, choose Blue #228 and the Simple Water variant. With light strokes or a lower opacity setting, add some blue tint to the shadowed side of the leaves.

10. Dry the canvas again. The leaves are now complete.

11. Save your document as LEAVES.RIF, using the File | Save As command.

Figure 10.37.
Veins were added to
the leaves using a
smaller variant of
Water Brush Stroke
and Yellow #93.

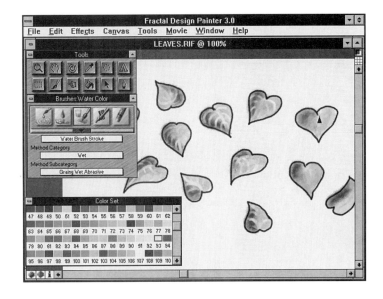

Summary

The background for the stained glass image is all painted, and the leaves are
waiting to be converted into a floater nozzle file. In the process, you've learned
about Painter's Water Color, Liquid, and Water tools. You've also learned about
painting and editing in the wet layer, and about drying the canvas in between
steps of painting.

To complete the background image by adding the leaves to the trees, proceed
to Chapter 15, "Image Hose Project." There, you will learn how to turn the leaves
into a floater nozzle file.

After you make the floater nozzle file in Chapter 15, return to Chapter 11, "Completing the Stained Glass Window." There, you will paint the two birds that are
placed in the foreground of the image. They will be painted using Painter's
Airbrush variants. Following that, you'll combine the birds with the completed
background image and add some effects to round the project off!

Completing the Stained Glass Window

This chapter continues with and completes the Stained Glass Window project you work on in Chapters 10 and 15. If you've been following the project from the beginning, you painted the background and the leaves in Chapter 10, "Painting with Water-Based Tools—The Stained Glass Window." Then, you skipped to Chapter 15, "The Image Hose Project," and turned the leaves into an Image Hose nozzle file and sprayed the leaves on the trees. Now, in this chapter, you're ready to paint the two birds for the front of the image using the Airbrush variants. We'll also apply some lighting effects to the birds using the Apply Lighting command.

Airbrush Variants

Painter's Airbrush variants paint with soft, antialiased sprays of paint that closely resemble the look of traditional airbrushes. The paint covers underlying strokes with varying opacities. In general, all Airbrush variants share some common traits. The size of their strokes vary with the speed at which you drag the mouse or stylus. Quick movement produces thinner strokes, and slower movement increases the width of the stroke.

If you use a pressure-sensitive stylus, you can vary the amount of color applied with the Airbrush by varying stylus pressure. Lighter pressure will spray less paint onto the image, producing lighter strokes. Heavier pressure will achieve more cover power, producing darker strokes. Mouse users can simulate this by adjusting the Opacity slider on the Controls | Brush Palette.

To paint with the Airbrush variants:

1. Place the mouse or stylus where you want to begin the stroke.
2. To apply the paint, click and drag the mouse or press down on the stylus and drag.
3. Lift the stylus or release the mouse button when you are done applying the paint.

Fat Stroke Airbrush

The Fat Stroke Airbrush produces soft, antialiased strokes of paint that cover underlying strokes. The strokes are large and semi-transparent. The maximum density of the stroke is at its center, and it falls off quickly toward the edges. Stroke opacity varies with the pressure applied from the stylus. Opacity can be increased or decreased by making adjustments to the Opacity slider in the Controls | Brush Palette.

Feather Tip Airbrush

The Feather Tip Airbrush produces strokes that are antialiased and which cover underlying strokes. The strokes have maximum density in the center and fall off rapidly toward the edge to light density. The strokes of the Feather Tip Airbrush have more cover power than the Fat Stroke or Thin Stroke Airbrushes. It is best used to add detail lines to an image. The opacity of the stroke varies with stylus pressure. Lighter pressure produces lighter strokes, and heavier pressure produces darker strokes. You can adjust the Opacity of the stroke in the Controls | Brush Palette.

Single Pixel Airbrush

The Single Pixel Airbrush produces a brush stroke that is a single pixel in width, with an antialiased edge. This brush is good for fine touch-up work. The opacity of the stroke can be adjusted in the Controls | Brush Palette.

Spatter Airbrush

The Spatter Airbrush produces very broad strokes that are sensitive to paper grain and that have semi-antialiased edges. It produces coarse, random variations in the size of the droplets of paint. The width of the stroke varies with the speed at which the mouse or stylus is dragged. This effect can be made more pronounced by moving the +/- Size Slider in the Brush Controls | Size Palette toward the right.

Thin Stroke Airbrush

The Thin Stroke Airbrush covers a narrower area than the Fat Stroke Airbrush and is less transparent. It produces soft, antialiased strokes of paint. Opacity of the stroke varies with stylus pressure. Lighter pressure produces lighter strokes, and heavier pressure produces darker strokes. Stroke opacity can also be adjusted in the Controls | Brush Palette.

Step 11.1. Preparing for the Project

There are two uncolored birds located in the Chapter 10 floater library. You can use these birds in your image or make your own. If you want to use these two images, they are contained in the CHAP10.POR floater library located on the CD-ROM furnished with this book. They are quite large, so you might as well create an image that is the same size as the background image you created in Chapter 10.

1. Open a new 640×820 document. Set the resolution at 75 dpi and the paper color at white.

2. Open the Tools (Ctrl-1 in Windows, Cmd-1 in Mac), Brushes (Ctrl-2 in Windows, Cmd-2 in Mac) and Controls (Ctrl-6 in Windows, Cmd-6 in Mac) Palettes.

3. From the Objects Palette (Ctrl-5 in Windows, Cmd-5 in Mac), click the Floaters icon to open the Floaters Palette. Open the palette drawer to find the Library button and load in the CHAP10.POR floater library, located on the CD. This is the same library that you saved the tree into in the previous chapter.

4. From the Art Materials Palette (Ctrl-3), click the Sets icon and load in the CHAP10.TXT color set, located on the CD. This is the same color set used in the previous project.

5. Choose the Airbrush icon from the Brushes Palette and select the Fat Stroke Airbrush from the drop-down list.

Step 11.2. Coloring the Birds

Now you'll start painting with the Airbrushes. I think you'll agree that you can achieve some really beautiful effects and looks with these variants. These are my favorites because of the softness that can be achieved with them.

1. From the Chapter 10 floater library in the Objects | Floaters Palette, choose Bird 1 with the Floating Selection Tool and drag the floater into the new document. Your screen will look similar to Figure 11.1.

Figure 11.1.
The first bird floater is dragged into the document and is ready to be painted.

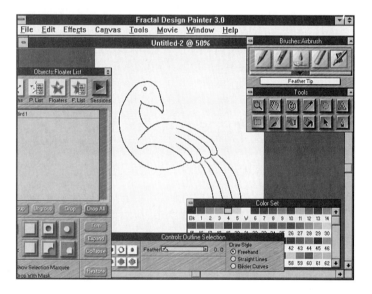

If you look in the Floater List Palette, you will see the floater listed. Also notice that the third Floater Mask Visibility button and first Floater Interaction button are automatically selected. This allows you to view strokes painted on the inside of the floater as you are applying the strokes.

2. Save the document as BIRD1.RIF. This way, you can update your painting periodically with the File | Save command.

3. From the color set, choose Blue #246. With the Fat Stroke Airbrush, color in the neck of the bird as shown in Figure 11.2.

Figure 11.2.
Begin coloring the neck
of the bird with Blue
#246 and the Fat Stroke
Airbrush.

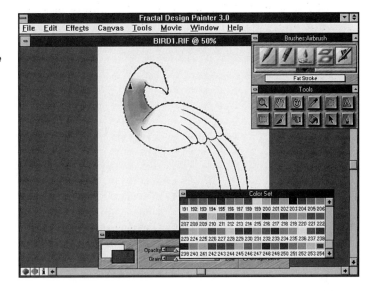

4. To darken the edges of the bird's neck, Blue #254 was chosen. Each side of the neck was deepened in shading, as shown in Figure 11.3.

Figure 11.3.
The sides of the neck
were shaded deeper
with Blue #254.

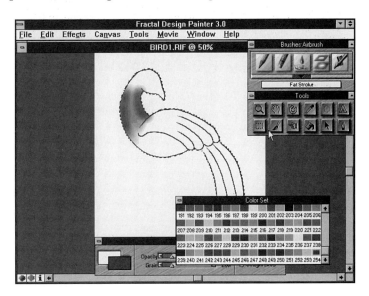

5. Select Purple #54 and add some color within the right half of the neck to add some vividness to the color, as shown in Figure 11.4.

Figure 11.4.
Purple #54 was added
to the right half of the
neck to add some
vividness to the color.

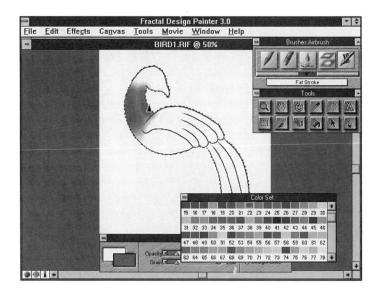

6. Choose the Feather Tip Airbrush from the Brushes Palette and select color #18. Add some feathery strokes to the neck to begin layering some feathers in. Figure 11.5 shows the feathers applied to the entire neck.

Figure 11.5.
Feathery strokes were
added with color #18
and the Feather Tip
Airbrush.

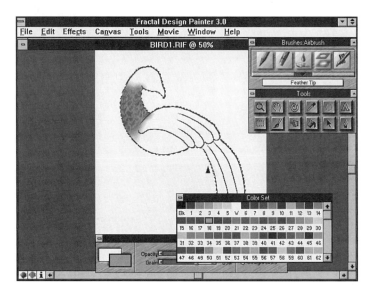

7. To deepen some areas of the neck feathers, choose color #23. Add some shading to the feathers, as shown in the figure. These shadows were primarily applied toward the outside edges of the neck, as shown in Figure 11.6.

Figure 11.6.
*Deepen some of the
feathers with color #23
and the Feather Tip
Airbrush.*

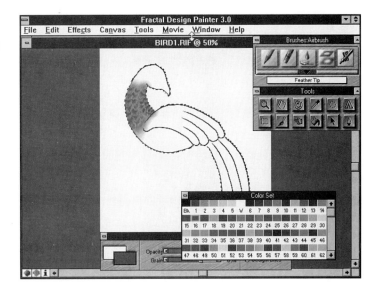

8. Figure 11.7 shows the bird's belly filled with color #231. The color was applied with the Fat Stroke Airbrush.

Figure 11.7.
*The bird's belly was
colored with the Fat
Stroke Airbrush and
color #231.*

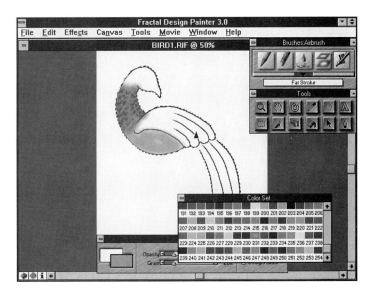

9. Add some shading with color #232 and the Thin Stroke Airbrush. Figure 11.8 shows this additional color applied.

Figure 11.8.
Shading was added
with color #232 and the
Thin Stroke Airbrush.

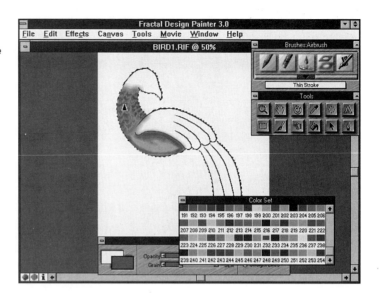

10. Choose the Feather Tip Airbrush and color #244. Add some feathers to the bird's belly as shown in Figure 11.9.

Figure 11.9.
Feathering is added to
the belly with color
#244 and the Feather
Tip Airbrush.

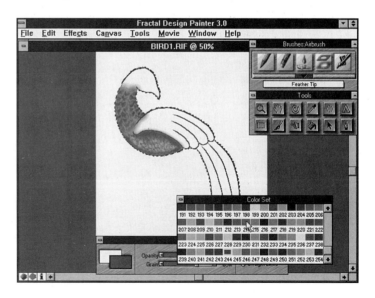

11. To color the wings, the Thin Stroke Airbrush variant was chosen. First, the top of the feathers were colored with color #247, as shown in Figure 11.10.

Figure 11.10.
To start the wings,
color #247 was applied
with the Thin Stroke
Airbrush.

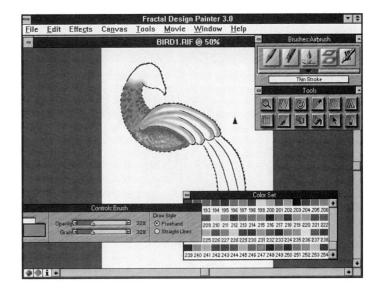

12. Keeping with the Thin Stroke Airbrush, change to Purple #23 and add color to the bottom of the wing feathers, as shown in Figure 11.11.

Figure 11.11.
Purple #23 was added
to the bottom of the
wing feathers with the
Thin Stroke Airbrush.

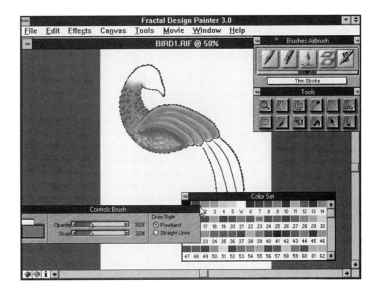

13. The linework in the wing feathers was applied using Purple #20 and the Feather Tip Airbrush. Figure 11.12 shows the linework added.

Figure 11.12.
Linework is added to
the feathers with
Purple #20 and the
Feather Tip Airbrush.

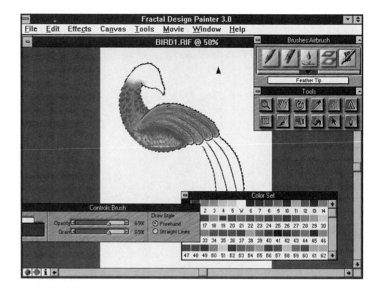

14. Color the tail feathers with color #241 and the Thin Stroke Airbrush at the left half of the tail feather. Add the deeper color #243 to the right side of the tail feathers. When you're done, the tail should look similar to Figure 11.13.

Figure 11.13.
The tail feathers are
colored with the Thin
Stroke Airbrush and
Colors 241 and 243.

15. Add some lines to the tail feathers with color #248. Figure 11.14 shows this step completed.

Figure 11.14.
Linework is added to the tail feathers with color #248.

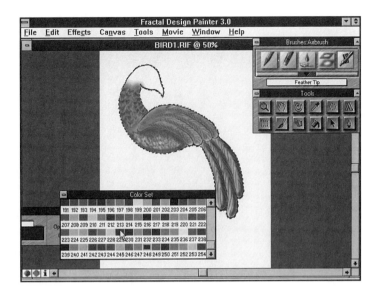

16. The center lines in the wing and tail feathers were added with color #228 and the Feather Tip Airbrush. This color was applied straight through the center of each feather to represent the feather quill.

17. To rough in color for the head, select the Thin Stroke Airbrush and color #237. Fill in color up to where the beak should be, as shown in Figure 11.15.

Figure 11.15.
Color #237 was used for the head, being applied with the Thin Stroke Airbrush.

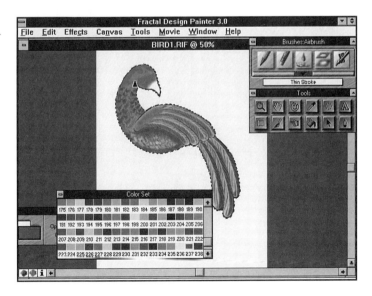

18. Shading was added to the outside edges of the head with color #238 and the Thin Stroke Airbrush, as shown in Figure 11.16.

Figure 11.16.
Color #238 was used to
shade areas of the
head.

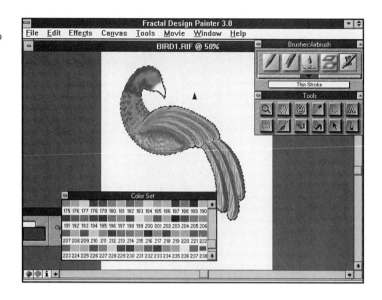

19. For the beak, Gold #55 was selected. The underside of the beak was shaded with Color #53, and some highlight was added with Color #58. Figure 11.17 shows the shading of the beak complete.

Figure 11.17.
The beak was colored
with Gold #55, and
then shaded with #53
and highlighted with
#58.

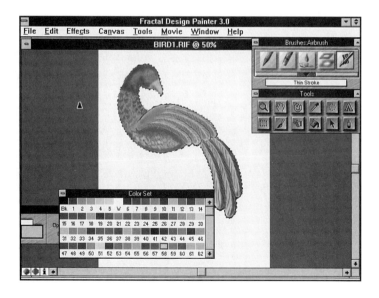

20. The eyes and detail lines were added with Gray #1 and the Feather Tip Airbrush, as shown in Figure 11.18.

Figure 11.18.
Detail lines were added
to the face, beak, and
neck with Gray #1 and
the Feather Tip
Airbrush.

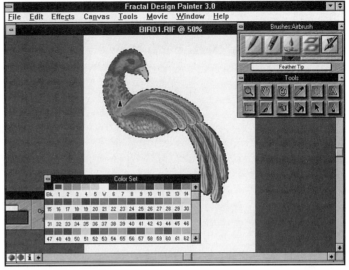

We're done coloring the first bird. The second bird was colored using the same colors and brushes as the first, and is shown in Figure 11.19. Complete the second bird now, to prepare for adding some lighting effects.

Figure 11.19.
The second bird is
colored similarly to the
first.

Let's sidetrack for a moment to learn everything there is to know about the Apply Lighting command—what the settings are for, how you can save your own lighting arrangements, and how to work with the Lighting Mover. Then you can resume your project by trying out some of the lighting techniques on your birds.

All About Lighting

To add some additional highlights and shading to the bird, the Apply Lighting command was used. This command requires a computer that has a Floating Point Unit (also sometimes known as a math coprocessor) in order for it to work.

The Apply Lighting command lets you place white or colored lighting effects in your image, varying them in intensity, angle, and distance. Changing or adding lighting effects to an image will alter its exposure somewhat—adding light and dark areas that may be objectionable in some instances. If you find this to be true, you can correct some of the color change with the Tonal Control commands in the Effects Menu (Adjust Colors or Adjust Selected Colors).

Choosing a Lighting Effect from the Default Lighting Library

To apply one of the lighting effects contained in Painter's default lighting library, use the following procedure:

1. Select part of your image. If no selection is made, Painter will apply the lighting effect to the entire image.

2. Choose Effects | Surface Control | Apply Lighting. The Apply Lighting dialog box appears.

3. A palette of lighting effects is located in the lower-left corner of the dialog box. You can scroll through the effects to find one that looks suitable for your image. Clicking one of the choices will give you a preview of how the lighting effect will affect your image.

4. You can open another lighting library by clicking the Library button. The Open Lighting Library File dialog box appears. Scroll to the directory where your file exists and select the library file you wish to open. It will be saved with an .LIT extension. After selecting the file, choose the OK button and you will be returned to the Apply Lighting dialog box with the selected library.

5. When you find an effect that you like, click OK to apply the lighting effect to your image or selection.

Moving, Adding, and Deleting Lights

The Preview window in the Apply Lighting dialog box contains one or more light indicators that can be moved around and rotated to change the lighting effects in the scene. The small circle in the light indicator points toward the source of the light (use a bulb as an example here), and the larger circle in the symbol points toward the target of the light (the area being lit).

■ To move a light indicator, click its large circle and drag the light to its new location. You will see the effect of the change of location in the preview window.

- To change the direction of the light source (the "bulb"), click the small end and drag it to its new location. The large circle (the target) will remain anchored in its present location.

- To create a new light indicator, click anywhere in the preview window. Its lighting effect can be adjusted with the sliders, as outlined below.

- To delete a light indicator, click once to select it and then press the Backspace (Windows) or Delete (Mac) key. The light will be removed, and the effect of its removal will be seen in the preview window.

Changing the Settings of the Light Indicators

The color, angle, brightness, and elevation of the lights can be adjusted by moving the sliders as follows:

- The Brightness control slider works similarly to a dimmer switch. Moving the slider to the left dims the light, and moving the slider to the right brightens the light.

- The Distance control slider sets the distance between the target (the big circle) and the light source (the small circle). Moving the slider to the left decreases the distance between the two, brightening the effect. Moving the slider to the right increases the distance, softening the effect of the light.

- The Elevation slider adjusts the angle of the light. When the slider is set to 90 degrees, it is shining directly down at the target, giving the lighting effect a more uniform appearance. Reducing the setting to 1 degree makes the effect very shallow, increasing the intensity of the light.

- The Spread slider controls the width of the light beam. Reducing the slider creates a narrow laser-beam type of effect, and increasing the slider fans the beam out more fully.

- The Exposure slider works similarly to exposure in photography. Moving the exposure setting to the left decreases the exposure and makes the effect of the light darker. Moving the slider toward the right increases the exposure and makes the light brighter.

- The Ambient slider controls the surrounding light in the image. Moving the slider to the left reduces the ambient light, creating a wider difference between it and the light source. Moving the slider to the right increases the ambient light, creating a narrower difference between it and the light source.

- To change the color of a light, click the light you want to change. Then, click inside the Light Color square. Select a color for the light, and click OK to return to the Apply Lighting dialog box.

- To change the color of the ambient light, click the light you want to change. Then, click inside the Ambient Light Color square. Select a color for the light and click OK to return to the Apply Lighting dialog box.

When you are done making the changes to the lighting, you can save the revised lighting arrangement by clicking the Save button. This will open up a dialog box that prompts you to enter a name for the new lighting arrangement you have created. The Save feature will save the lights in the currently open scene. You can later move the new lighting arrangement into another library with the Lighting Mover, if desired.

When done making changes in the Apply Lighting dialog box, click OK or press Enter.

Creating a Lighting Library

Lighting Libraries can be created from the Apply Lighting dialog box or from the Lighting Mover. When you create a library from the Apply Lighting dialog box, you can immediately place your new custom-made lighting variants inside. When creating a library from the Lighting Mover, you can move lighting variants from other libraries into the new library.

Creating a New Lighting Library from the Apply Lighting Dialog Box

You can create a new lighting library from the Apply Lighting dialog box. This method lets you immediately place the new lighting arrangement you just created into a library, rather than saving it to the currently open library.

To create a new library from the Apply Lighting dialog box:

1. Create a new lighting scene, using the methods discussed in this chapter.
2. From the Apply Lighting dialog box (opened when creating the variant), click the Library button. The Open Lighting Library File dialog box will open.
3. Scroll to the directory you wish to save your lighting library in and type in a name for the library. The file will be saved with an .LIT file extension in the Windows version.
4. Choose OK to save the library filename. You will then be returned to the Apply Lighting dialog box, where a new blank library file appears in the scrolling window. Your newly created lighting variant can be saved into the new library when you click the Save button.
5. Click OK or press Enter to leave the Apply Lighting dialog box.

Creating a New Lighting Library from the Lighting Mover

You can create a new lighting library from the Lighting Mover. This method enables you to move lighting variants from one library into another library.

To create a new library from the Lighting Mover:

1. Select Tools | Movers | Lighting Mover. A dialog box appears. In the left half of the dialog box, the names of the variants in Painter's default library file appear. The window on the right side of this dialog box will be blank.

2. Underneath the window on the right side of the dialog box, click the New button. This will open the New Lighting Library dialog box.

3. Scroll to the directory where you want to save your lighting library and type in a name for the library. The file will be saved with an .LIT file extension.

4. Choose OK to save the library filename. You will then be returned to the Lighting Mover. At this point, you can move lighting variants from the library opened on the left side of the Library Mover into the newly created library.

5. Click Quit, located in between the two library windows, to exit the Lighting Mover.

Using the Lighting Mover

The Lighting Mover is used to move lighting variants from one library to another. The Lighting Mover is accessed with the Tools | Movers | Lighting Mover command.

To use the Lighting Mover:

1. Choose Tools | Movers | Lighting Mover. The Lighting Mover dialog box appears.

2. The dialog box contains two scrolling windows. When the Lighting Mover is first opened, the names of the lights in Painter's default lighting library are contained in the window on the left side, and the window on the right side is blank.

   ■ To select a different library in the left window, click the Close button. The window will become blank, and the Close button will revert to an Open button. Click the Open button, and choose the directory and lighting library file (.LIT extension) you wish to open. Click OK or press Enter to open the file. The selected library appears in the left window.

   ■ To select a library in the right window, click the Open button and choose the directory and lighting library file (.LIT extension) you wish to open. Click OK or press Enter to open the file. The selected library appears in the right window.

   ■ The preview window in the center of the dialog box shows a thumbnail version of the currently highlighted lighting effect.

- To copy a lighting variant from one library to another, highlight the lighting variant name. Check the preview window to see if this is the effect you want to move. Then, click the Copy button in the top center of the dialog box. The name of the copied variant appears in the opposite window.

- To remove a lighting variant from a library, highlight the lighting variant name. Check the preview window to see if this is the effect you want to remove. Then, click the Remove button in the center of the dialog box. The name of the copied variant will be removed from the window.

- To rename a lighting variant, highlight the lighting variant name. Check the preview window to see if this is the effect you want to rename. Click the Change Name button in the center of the dialog box and enter a new name for the lighting variant. Click OK to return to the Lighting Mover dialog box. The name of the highlighted variant will change to the name you entered.

3. When you are done making changes to the lighting libraries, click Quit, which is located in the center of the Lighting Mover dialog box. The changes are automatically saved to the libraries you worked on.

Step 11.3. Applying Lighting to the Birds

To apply lighting to the first bird, proceed with the following steps:

1. Choose the Floating Selection Tool from the Tools Palette and click the first bird. It will become surrounded by a selection marquee.

2. Choose Effects | Surface Control | Apply Lighting. The Apply Lighting dialog box, shown in Figure 11.20, appears.

3. Experiment with the settings until you get an effect that works well with your bird in the preview window. If you want to create your own lighting arrangement, use the guidelines discussed in the previous section. Try adding a blue light, or a purple light, to bring out the colors of the bird. Or, try changing the color of the ambient light and see what happens to the overall effect. Another idea is to add several medium-brightness lights to the upper side of the bird and some dimly lit lights to its underside.

4. When the preview looks the way you'd like it to appear, you might want to save your lighting arrangement to the library by clicking the Save button located at the bottom of the dialog box.

5. To apply your lighting effect to the bird, click the OK button. The floater will be updated to reflect the lighting arrangement you chose.

6. If some of the linework became washed out when you applied your lighting, you can touch it up using the Feather Tip Airbrush and either Black or Dark Gray #1 from the color set.

Figure 11.20.
Adjust or create a new
lighting arrangement in
the Apply Lighting
dialog box.

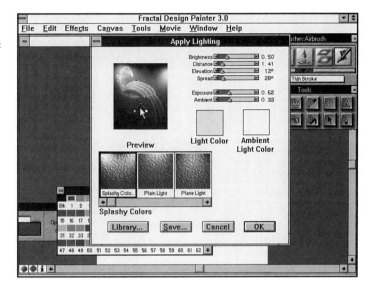

7. When you're done with both birds, use the Floating Selection Tool to place the colored versions of the birds into the floater library.

Step 11.4. Placing the Birds into the Background

Now that you've finished the birds, you can place them into the background that you completed in Chapter 15—that is, the version with the leaves placed with the Image Hose.

NOTE If you have been following this project, you have already jumped to the end of Chapter 15, "Image Hose Project," to create an Image Hose nozzle for your leaves, and applied the leaves to the tree. If you haven't completed that portion of the stained glass window yet, you should complete it before proceeding with the remainder of this project. Or, you can open the BACKTREE.RIF file included on the CD accompanying this book.

1. Open BACKTREE.RIF (the background created in Chapter 15, with leaves placed on the tree). If you haven't completed this step, a version of this image appears on the CD accompanying this book.
2. Drag the two completed bird floaters into the image with the Floating Selection Tool and arrange them to sit on the lower two branches. Bird 1 was placed first, on the upper branch, and Bird 2 was placed second, on the lowest branch, as shown in Figure 11.21.

367

Figure 11.21.
Place the birds on the lower two branches of the tree.

3. Save the image as WINDOW.RIF. This way, you won't overwrite the background version and can use it again for something else, if you like.

4. To add some surface texture to the birds, choose the Eggscape paper texture from the Art Materials | Papers Palette. Then, choose one of the bird floaters with the Floating Selection Tool.

5. Choose Effects | Surface Control | Apply Surface Texture. Apply the surface texture to each bird floater using Paper Grain at 35%, with no shininess, and position the light indicator at the 10:00 position, as shown in Figure 11.22.

   Note that the Apply Surface Texture dialog box provided with Painter 3.1 has additional lighting controls built in. You can apply lighting and surface control to your bird floaters at the same time! The additional features of Painter 3.1's Apply Surface Texture command as discussed in Chapter 17, "A Collage of Effects."

6. After you've applied surface texture to both birds, click the Drop All button in the Floater List Palette to drop both of the birds into the background. This button is shown in Figure 11.23.

Figure 11.22.
Apply surface texture
to each bird floater
using Paper Grain at
35%.

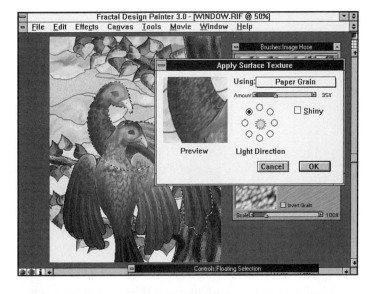

Figure 11.23.
Drop the floaters to the
background layer using
the Drop All button in
the Floater List Palette.

Step 11.5. Adding a Border to the Image

You're going to add a gradient border to the image, to surround it with a frame. First, reduce the size of the window to 75%. Then, you'll apply the border using the Grid display as a guide to its creation. Finally, you'll choose a gradient and rotate it so that you can form a mitered frame around the image.

1. Choose Edit | Select All to select the entire background. Your image will become surrounded by a marquee, as shown in Figure 11.24.

Figure 11.24.
Select the entire image
with the Edit | Select
All command.

2. To scale the drawing, choose Effects | Orientation | Scale. Keep the Constrain Aspect Ratio box checked. This will enable you to scale both horizontal and vertical resolutions simultaneously. Also, keep the Preserve Center box checked to keep the center of the image in the same location.

3. Drag one of the corners of the bounding box, identified by a small square, and position it until the scale dialog box indicates the scale at around 75. The scale percentage will change after you release the mouse or cursor, but you can readjust it as many times as you like until you get to your desired scale. You can also type in the percentage figures in the dialog box. If you are having trouble getting the figures to accept properly, try typing a decimal point after your whole number. Once you get to the desired scale, click OK to apply the command. Figure 11.25 shows this in progress.

4. Note that once the image was rescaled, it was turned into a floater. To send this floater back into the background layer, choose Edit | Drop. The image will then become part of the background again.

5. Turn the Grid Display on with Canvas | View Grid, or click the grid icon in the right document window scrollbar area. The grid display was left at its default settings of 12 pixels horizontally and vertically to create the frame. Figure 11.26 shows the grid display on.

Figure 11.25.
Adjust the scale of the
image to around 75%.

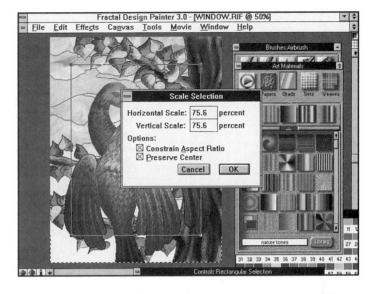

Figure 11.26.
Turn the Grid Display
on with the Canvas |
View Grid command or
by clicking the Grid
icon in the right
document window
scrollbar.

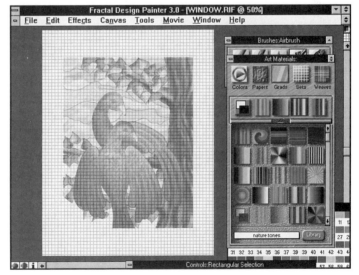

6. Click the Outline Selection Tool. You will see the old paths appear from the original floaters, as shown in Figure 11.27. You can clear them in the Path List Palette by highlighting each one and clicking the Clear button. Or, you can click each path in the image by using the Path Adjuster Tool and pressing the Backspace (Windows) or Delete (Mac) key.

Figure 11.27.
The paths from the
original larger floaters
and image can be
cleared in the Path List
Palette, or by using the
Path Adjuster Tool.

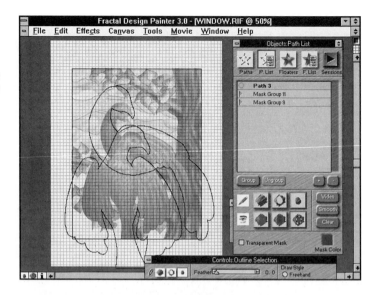

7. Reselect the Outline Selection Tool if you've chosen another tool since the last time you selected it. From the Controls | Outline Selection Palette, select to create paths with the Straight Lines drawing mode. Using the grid to constrain your lines, draw a beveled rectangular path around one of the sides, as shown in Figure 11.28.

Figure 11.28.
Using the Outline
Selection Tool, draw a
beveled rectangle to
form the first section of
the frame.

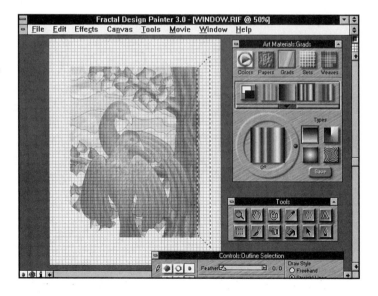

8. From the Art Materials | Grads Palette, choose the Nature Tones gradient. Position the gradient so that the purple color is facing the inside of your

beveled rectangle, as shown in Figure 11.29. The angle should be 0 degrees, 90 degrees, 180 degrees, or 270 degrees, depending on the orientation of the frame side that you are going to fill.

Figure 11.29.
Position the Nature
Tones gradient so that
the purple side is facing
the inside edge of the
frame section you are
going to fill.

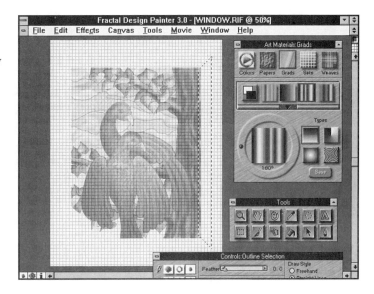

9. Choose the Paint Bucket from the Tools Palette. In the Controls | Paint Bucket Palette, select to fill the image with a gradation. Click the inside of the beveled rectangle with the Paint Bucket. The first side of the frame is formed as shown in Figure 11.30.

Figure 11.30.
Fill the first side of the
frame with the Earth
Tones gradient.

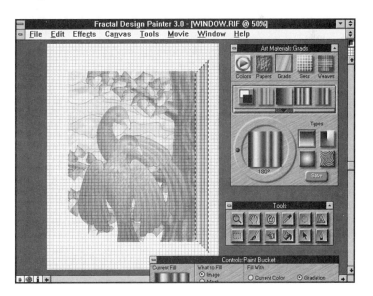

10. Continue with each of the three remaining sides of the frame until it is complete, adjusting the angle of the gradation as appropriate for each section of the frame. Figure 11.31 shows the second side applied to the frame.

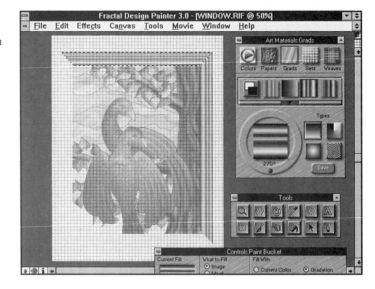

Figure 11.31.
The second through
fourth sides are filled in
a similar manner, with
adjustments made to
the rotation of the
gradation.

11. Figure 11.32 shows all four sides completed. The grid layer has been turned off so that you can view the results better.

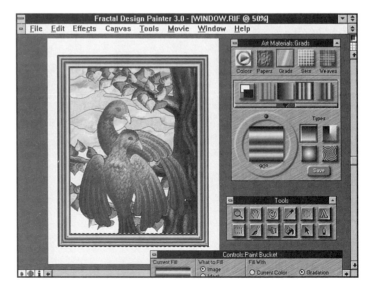

Figure 11.32.
The gradation is
applied to all four sides
of the frame.

12. Again using the Outline Selection Tool with the grid layer turned back on, draw a rectangular selection around the outside of the frame to contain the entire image within a path.

13. Choose Edit | Cut and then Edit | Paste | Into New Image to place the image into a new untitled document. A document window appears with the cropped image inside. You can now save this final document using the File | Save As command.

Summary

Your stained glass image is now complete, spanning techniques and variants from three different chapters. Here, you've learned about the Airbrushes and the soft subtle strokes they can make. You've also learned how to create lighting scenes of your own and how to maintain them in libraries. Lighting and texture were added to floaters for effect. Finally, a gradation was used to create a frame around the entire image. In the next chapter, you'll learn more about painting in the masking layer, and about some of Painter's other masking commands. You'll also work with repeating patterns and learn more about layering and combining floaters.

Working with the Masking Tools

This is a relatively easy project artistically, because I've created the floaters and the background for you. Primarily, this project highlights some points regarding masking. In this chapter I discuss Painter's Masking variants, and how you can apply them to floater masks to put images together. To help you understand this further, I also cover how floater masks work in combination with masks of other floaters, and with the background mask.

You use Painter's Masking variants to modify the masking layers of the background, or of floaters. When you paint in the masking layer, you use shades of gray (including white and black) to define the opacity or transparency of the mask. You can achieve different effects with different settings of the mask visibility options in the Floater List Palette.

To paint with the masking variants in the background layer:

1. Click the third (last) Drawing Visibility button to mask the inside of the selected area.

2. Click the second (center) Mask Visibility button to display the mask in red.

   Both these buttons are accessible at the lower-left corner of your document window, on either the Objects | Path List Palette, the Controls | Path Adjuster Palette, or the Controls | Outline Selection Palette.

3. Choose one of the Masking brushes from the Brushes Palette.

4. Select black as your current color to add to the mask, or white to remove from the mask.

 TIP You can also apply shades of gray to vary the intensity of the mask. The lighter the shade of gray, the more transparent the mask; the darker the shade, the more opaque the mask.

Masking Variants

Painter offers six different Masking variants you can use to modify the masking layers of background or floater images.

Big Masking Pen

The Big Masking Pen variant paints in the masking layer with broad, antialiased lines. This variant is good for masking large areas.

Grainizer

The Grainizer variant produces broad, antialiased strokes that add paper grain effects in the masking layer.

Masking Airbrush

The Masking Airbrush variant produces soft, antialiased strokes in the masking layer.

Masking Chalk

The Masking Chalk variant produces semi-antialiased strokes that interact with paper grain in the masking layer.

Masking Pen

The Masking Pen variant produces smooth, antialiased strokes in the masking layer. The width of the stroke varies with the pressure you apply with the stylus: heavier pressure produces thicker lines, and lighter pressure produces thinner lines.

Single-Pixel Masking Pen

The Single-Pixel Masking Pen variant produces strokes in the masking layer that are one pixel wide and have antialiased edges. This masking variant is good for close, touch up work in the masking layer.

About Floater Masks

To understand how floater masks interact with the background mask, you must look at the masking choices available with floaters. So far, you've used the Drawing Visibility buttons and the Mask Visibility buttons in the background layer, to define or display masked areas in that layer.

Floaters have their own buttons, which work in a slightly different manner. You can find these buttons in the Floater List Palette. The buttons on the top row are the Floater Mask Visibility buttons, and those in the second row are the Floater Interaction buttons. You can achieve different results in how the floaters interact with the background by using these buttons in various combinations.

To illustrate this, consider the following examples. In each of the following images, the document on the left shows the background design as horizontal, black-and-white stripes. The mask is shown as large vertical, red bars. Compare this example document to the image on the right, which includes a floater to demonstrate the function of the buttons.

Figure 12.1 shows the first Floater Mask button (Masking Disabled) selected in the Floater List Palette. This disables the floater's masking information, making the entire floater visible. When you place the first Floater Mask Visibility button in the first position, you cannot paint in the floater with Masking brushes. In the figure, the first Floater Interaction button (Masking Disabled) also is selected. This setting indicates that the floater does not interact with the background mask. The right image in the figure shows that, in this combination, the inside and the outside of the floater are visible above the background layer.

Figure 12.1.
With the first Floater
Mask button and first
Floater Interaction
buttons selected, the
entire floater is visible
above the background
mask.

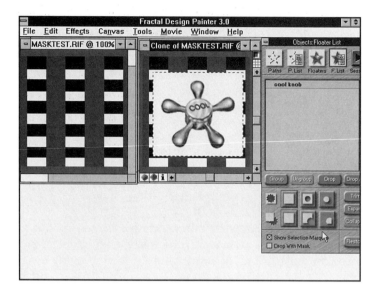

In Figure 12.2, the second Floater Interaction button (Masked Inside) is selected. I still have the Floater Mask disabled, causing the entire floater to be visible and its masking information ignored. Choosing the second Interaction button causes the masked areas of the background to hide the floater. Adding black to the background mask hides more of the floater, and adding white to the background mask reveals more of the floater.

Figure 12.2.
With the first Floater
Mask button and
second Floater Interac-
tion button selected,
the floater's mask is
disabled, and the
masked areas of the
background hide
portions of the floater.

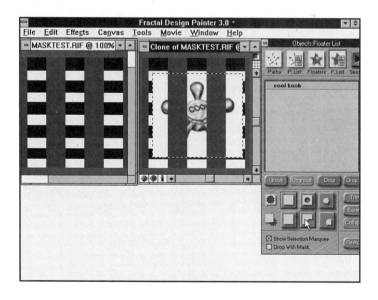

When the third Floater Interaction button (Masked Outside) is selected, as shown in Figure 12.3, the areas that are masked in the background reveal the floater. This works opposite to the previous example: adding black to the background mask reveals more of the floater, and adding white to the background mask hides more of the floater.

Figure 12.3.
With the first Floater
Mask button and third
Floater Interaction
button selected, the
floater's mask is
disabled and the
masked areas of the
background reveal
portions of the floater.

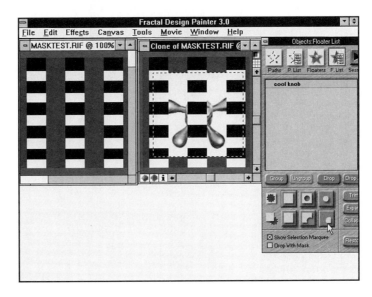

Figure 12.4 shows both the second Floater Mask button (Masked Inside) and the first Floater Interaction button (Masking Disabled) selected. In this mode, the outside of the floater is visible, and the inside of the floater reveals what is underneath. Painting with white in the floater covers more of the background, and painting with black reveals more of the background. Because the first Floater Interaction button is selected, the background mask has no effect here.

Figure 12.5 shows both the second Floater Mask button (Masked Inside) and the second Floater Interaction button (Masked Inside) selected. The outside of the floater is visible, and the inside of the floater reveals what is underneath. Areas masked in the background layer hide the floater. Again, painting with white in the floater covers more of the background, and painting with black reveals more of the background. With the second Floater Interaction button selected, adding white in the background mask layer reveals more of the floater, and adding black hides more of the floater.

Figure 12.4.
With the second
Floater Mask button
and first Floater
Interaction button
selected, the outside of
the floater is visible
above the background
mask.

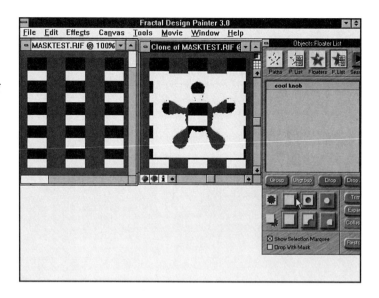

Figure 12.5.
With the second
Floater Mask button
and second Floater
Interaction button
selected, the outside of
the floater is visible,
with portions hidden
by the background
mask.

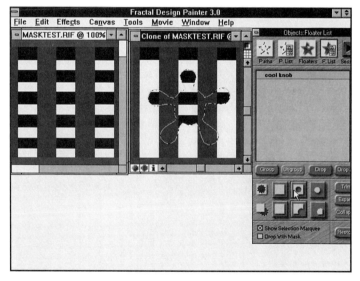

Figure 12.6 shows both the second Floater Mask button (Masked Inside) and the third Floater Interaction button (Masked Outside) selected. The outside of the floater is visible, but unmasked areas in the background hide the floater. Adding white to the floater mask covers more of the background areas, and adding black to the floater mask reveals more of the background areas. Painting with black in the background mask covers more of the background, and painting with white reveals more of the background.

*Figure 12.6.
With the second
Floater Mask button
and third Floater
Interaction button
selected, the outside of
the floater is visible
only in the masked
areas of the back-
ground.*

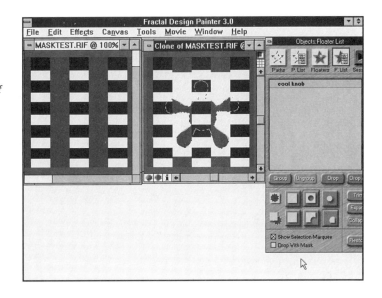

Figure 12.7 shows both the third Floater Mask button (Masked Outside) and the
first Floater Interaction button (Masking Disabled) selected. In this mode, the
inside of the floater is visible, and the outside of the floater reveals what is
underneath. Painting with white in the floater mask reveals more of the background, and painting with black hides more of the background. Because the
first Floater Interaction button is selected, the background mask has no effect
here.

*Figure 12.7.
With the third Floater
Mask button and first
Floater Interaction
button selected, the
inside of the floater is
visible above the
background mask.*

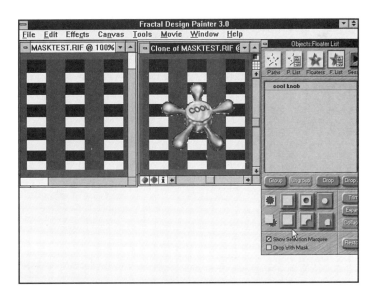

Figure 12.8 shows both the third Floater Mask button (Masked Outside) and the second Floater Interaction button (Masked Inside) selected. The inside of the floater is visible, but areas masked in the background hide the floater. Painting with white in the floater reveals more of the background, and painting with black covers more of the background. With the second Floater Interaction button selected, adding white in the background mask layer reveals more of the floater, and adding black hides more of the floater.

Figure 12.8.
With the third Floater
Mask button and
second Floater Interac-
tion button selected,
the inside of the floater
is visible, but areas
masked in the back-
ground hide the floater.

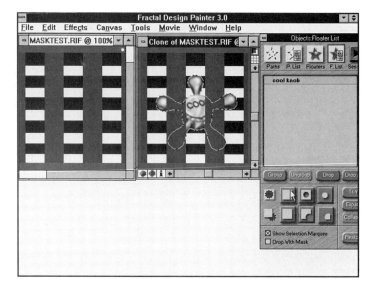

Figure 12.9 shows both the third Floater Mask button (Masked Outside) and the third Floater Interaction button (Masked Outside) selected. In this mode, the inside of the floater is visible, but areas masked in the background reveal the floater. Painting with white reveals more of the background, and painting with black hides more of the background. With the third Floater Interaction button set, adding black in the background mask layer reveals more of the floater, and adding white hides more of the floater.

Figure 12.9.
With the third Floater
Mask button and third
Floater Interaction
button selected, the
inside of the floater is
visible in the masked
areas of the back-
ground.

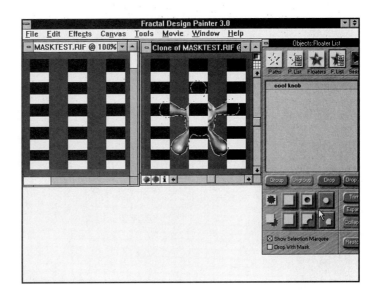

Adding and Masking the Floaters

This Egyptian scene is composed of a background image created in 3D Studio. I used Painter for the texture maps on the pillars, the walls, and the beams on the ceiling of the temple. You also place three floaters into the scene:

- The first floater is an image of ancient Egyptian hieroglyphics. In this project you edit this floater's mask with the Masking Airbrush and, later, place the Floater Interaction buttons so the mask of the hieroglyphics interacts with the mask of the background image.

- You edit the mask of the second floater, a large asp, so that the snake is wrapping itself around one of the columns.

- The third floater, the Egyptian queen, is masked softly around the edges and a little bit on the inside.

Step 12.1. Adding the Hieroglyphics

In this first step, you add the hieroglyphic floater to the scene:

1. Open the TEMPLE.TGA file, located on the CD accompanying this book.

2. Choose the Objects Palette (Ctrl-5 in Windows, Cmd-5 in Mac), and click the Floaters icon.

3. Select the EGYPTIAN.POR Floater Library, located on the CD furnished with this book.

4. From the Floater Library, choose the Hieroglyphics floater.

5. Place it at the top of the image, as shown in Figure 12.10.

Figure 12.10.
Choose the Hieroglyph-
ics floater from the
EGYPTIAN.POR Floater
library.

6. Choose Effects | Orientation | Scale.

7. In the Scale Selection dialog box, shown in Figure 12.11, turn off the checkbox adjacent to Constrain Aspect Ratio. This lets you scale the horizontal and vertical dimensions of the floater independently. In this case, you want to increase the horizontal measurement to 115 percent of its original size.

8. Position the floater to cover the upper portion of the image, as shown in Figure 12.12.

9. In the Objects Palette, click the F.List icon to open the Floater List Palette.

10. Select the third Floater Mask Visibility button (Masked Outside) and the second Floater Interaction button (Masked Inside), so your screen looks similar to Figure 12.13.

*Figure 12.11.
Scale the horizontal
measurement of the
floater to 115%.*

*Figure 12.12.
Place the floater along
the top side of the
image.*

387

Figure 12.13.
Choose the third Floater Mask button and the second Floater Interaction button.

> **NOTE** While you're in this mode, using white with the masking brushes deletes the floater's mask, revealing what is behind it. Painting with black adds to the mask, hiding what is behind it and restoring the floater. Intermediate shades of gray partially reveal what is behind the floater.

Because the Targa file you opened does not currently have a mask, the floater should be completely visible. If you paint the *background's* mask with white in this mode (by deselecting the floater), more of the background is hidden relative to the floater. Painting the background mask with black reveals more of the background against the floater. I illustrate this a bit later. For now, concentrate on the areas of the hieroglyphics that you want to appear transparent, or partially transparent.

11. From the Brushes Palette (Ctrl-2 in Windows, Cmd-2 in Mac), choose the Masking brushes icon, and select the Masking Airbrush.

12. Choose white as your current color, so you can paint portions of the mask away.

13. Using the Masking Airbrush, paint the floater away to blend it into the background. Start with white, and shape the bottom of the hieroglyphics irregularly. If you go in too far, remember that painting with black restores the floater's opacity. You can restore the floater to its original state by clicking the Restore button in the Floater List Palette.

14. Choose a middle shade of gray, and paint some areas of the floater to appear partially transparent.

Step 12.2. Adding the Asp

Now add the asp to the scene, and wrap it around the left-front pillar in the temple. I created the asp by drawing a path shaped like a coiled snake. I then cloned snake skin into the path using a small version of the Straight Cloner variant. (You learn more about this brush in Chapter 16, "Visiting Van Gogh: The Cloner and Artists Brushes.") However, the color is a little off, so part of this step adds some color and texture to the snake with the Effects | Surface Control | Color Overlay command.

1. From the Floaters Palette, drag the asp into the scene. Place it in front of the left pillar.

2. Choose Effects | Orientation | Scale.

3. Reduce the size of the snake to 70 percent of its original size, as shown in Figure 12.14.

Figure 12.14.
Scale the Asp to 70%
of its original size.

4. Using the Dropper Tool, pick a shade of aqua from the pillar. Figure 12.15 shows a good location to pick a color from.

5. From the Art Materials Palette, click the Papers icon to open the Papers Palette.

6. Pick the Hatching paper texture from the default paper library, and reduce its scale to around 25 percent.

7. Choose Effects | Surface Control | Color Overlay, as shown in Figure 12.16. This command lets you place a tint of color at varying transparency on the selected object, and apply paper texture at the same time. When you choose the command, the Color Overlay dialog box appears.

389

Figure 12.15.
Pick a middle shade of
aqua from one of the
pillars.

Figure 12.16.
Add some color and
texture to the asp with
the Color Overlay
command.

8. From the Using menu, choose to apply the effect based on Paper Grain. Set the Opacity slider to 80%, and leave the method at Dye Concentration. These settings are shown in Figure 12.17. Notice in the preview window that an aqua tint appears in the snake skin, and that the paper texture makes the snake appear a little more scaly. Click OK to apply the effect.

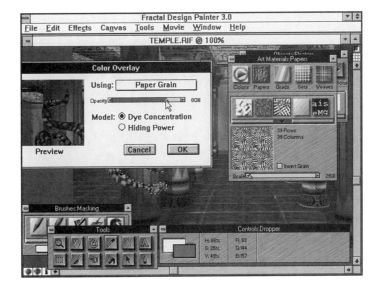

Figure 12.17.
Adjust the Color
Overlay to 80% using
the Dye Concentration
model.

Use the Masking Pen with white paint to paint the floater away in sections. You might find it easier to zoom in a little closer to the snake to edit the floater mask.

9. Choose the Masking Pen from the Brushes Palette, and select white as your current color.

10. Paint the mask of the snake away, starting from the bottom, as shown in Figure 12.18. If necessary, reduce the size of the Masking Pen in the Brush Controls | Size Palette. If you make some errors, remember that painting with black restores any areas you want to correct.

Figure 12.18.
Use the Masking Pen
and white paint to
mask away portions of
the snake, making it
"wrap" around the
pillar.

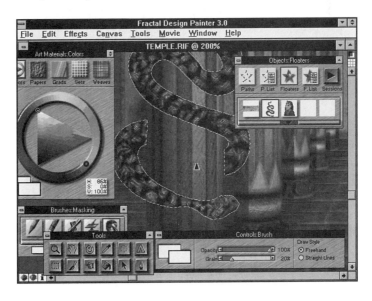

11. Continue masking the other section of the snake that appears at the back of the pillar. When you're done, your image should look similar to Figure 12.19.

Figure 12.19.
All areas of the asp
have been masked.

12. For the final touch, add a drop shadow. Actually, the default shadow values are just perfect for this floater, so all you need do is choose the Effects | Objects | Create Drop Shadow command. Click OK or press Enter to apply the effect to the floater. Figure 12.20 shows the result.

Figure 12.20.
With a drop shadow
added to the asp, this
floater is complete.

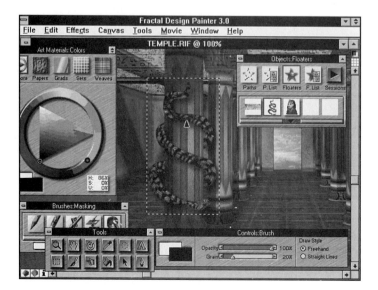

Step 12.3. Adding the Egyptian Queen

The Egyptian Queen floater began with shapes created in CorelDRAW! I created closed curves for the shoulders, headdress, neck, face, and facial features. I imported the artwork into Painter as a set of EPS selections. I then used the selections to protect areas while painting with the Airbrush variants, discussed in Chapter 11, "Completing the Stained Glass Window." With all selections inactive, I touched up final details and shading where needed. Then, I turned the entire group of selections into a floater. If you view the floater with the selection marquee enabled, you can still see the outlines of the paths I used to create it.

I created the queen against a black background, so any areas outside the main portion of the floater will be revealed as black when you soften the edges with the Masking Airbrush. Basically, in this step you soften the edges of this floater into the background, and create a bit of shadow around her in the process. You then create a deeper shadow with the Create Drop Shadow command.

1. From the Floaters Palette, click and drag the Egyptian floater into your document, as shown in Figure 12.21.

Figure 12.21.
Place the Egyptian
floater into the image.

2. Using the Effects | Orientation | Scale command, scale the floater to 75 percent of its original size, leaving the Constrain Aspect Ratio command checked. (If you type in 75, followed by a decimal point, the second figure will automatically change.)
3. After rescaling the floater, position it as shown in Figure 12.22.

Figure 12.22.
Rescale the floater to
75 percent and place it
in position.

4. Choose the Masking Airbrush from the Brushes Palette.

5. From the Art Materials | Colors Palette, choose a middle shade of gray. This partially reveals the black areas outside the floater's boundaries, and partially fades away the inside areas of the floater.

6. Paint around the edges of the floater lightly, blending the areas as you see fit.

7. Choose Effects | Objects | Create Drop Shadow. This time, modify the default settings a little bit to create a shadow that's about three times wider and somewhat deeper than the one you applied to the snake:

   Set the X (Horizontal) Offset at 15 pixels.

   Set the Y (Vertical) Offset at 17 pixels.

   Set the Opacity at 60%.

   Set the Radius at 15.

   Set the Angle at 36.

   Set Thinness at 60%.

Figure 12.23 shows these settings.

After you apply the drop shadow, the shadow at the right side of the floater deepens, as shown in Figure 12.24.

Figure 12.23.
Increase the Drop
Shadow settings for the
Egyptian floater.

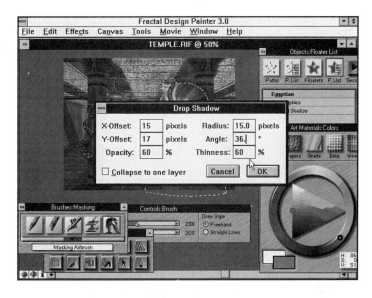

Figure 12.24.
Apply the drop shadow
to the Egyptian floater.

Now you can adjust the background mask to change the effect of the hiero-glyphics.

Step 12.4. Back to the Hieroglyphics

Earlier, I discussed the state of the Floater Interaction button when placing the hieroglyphics. As I mentioned, the Floater Interaction buttons determine how the mask of the floater interacts with the mask of the background. Right now, though, this background doesn't have a mask, so you must generate one.

If you recall, you positioned the Floater Interaction button of the hieroglyphics floater so that adding black to the background's mask would reveal more of the background, and adding white would reveal more of the floater. If you look at the background image, you can see that the tops of the columns appear darker. I wanted the columns to stand out a little more in front of the hieroglyphics, and thought that it would be best to generate the mask based on Image Luminance to accomplish this. Try that now, and see what effect this change of the background mask has on the appearance of the hieroglyphics:

1. Choose Edit | Deselect, or use the quick-key combination Ctrl-D in Windows, or Cmd-D in Mac, to deselect any floaters that may be selected.

2. Choose Edit | Select All to select the background image. The background is surrounded by a selection marquee.

3. Choose Edit | Mask | Auto Mask.

4. In the Using menu, generate the mask based on Image Luminance. The hieroglyphics merge with the background, as shown in Figure 12.25.

Figure 12.25.
Adjust the background mask to create a different effect with the hieroglyphics.

Observe the effect that this mask generation has on the appearance of the hieroglyphics. The areas that are darkest in the background now appear through them. In particular, the columns are now much more obvious. The areas that were lighter in the background show more of the hieroglyphics. The two images now come together in a much more interesting manner. You can blend floaters in this manner as well, and I discuss this more in Chapter 17, "A Collage of Effects."

Summary

Using Masking Brushes or Painter's Masking commands, you can merge floaters with other floaters, or with the background, to create unusual and interesting effects in your Painter documents. Try applying masks based on paper textures, or altering the masks with one of the Grainy method masking tools. Combine multiple floaters, each with their own unique masking layers, to produce a single object. The results are sure to impress!

Fabrics and Patterns

One of the new and truly unique features of Painter 3 gives you the capability to create weave patterns right on your PC. If you examine these patterns closely, you will be amazed by their intricacy. You may become engrossed in the wide range of possibilities that you can create here—from the richly colored plaids of the tartan weaves to the delicate, lace-like qualities of some of the three-dimensional open weave fabric textures.

This chapter is intended more as a study of Painter's Weaves Palette rather than a tutorial or exercise. I've attempted to explain the advanced editing features in the Edit Weaving dialog box so that you can generate your own weave patterns, and I explain the basic skills of changing colors and spacing. Here you go!

The Weaves Palette

The Weaves Palette contains several weave patterns as well as the tools you need to create and save your own weaves. To access this palette, click the Weaves icon from the Art Materials Palette (Ctrl-3 in Windows, Cmd-3 in Mac), as shown in Figure 13.1.

Figure 13.1.
You access the Weaves
Palette by clicking the
Weaves icon in the Art
Materials Palette.

In its smallest state, the Weaves Palette contains space to place five weaves on the drawer front. A preview window in the middle section shows you the current weave and changes applied as you adjust the controls, which are as follows:

Fiber Type: Two fiber types are available. The first, 2-Dimensional, is represented by an icon that looks like a closed weave. Two-dimensional weaves are solid, with no spaces. The second type, 3-Dimensional, enables you to create open-weave fabrics with shadowed areas and spaces between the threads.

Get Color: Located at the right of the Fiber Type selection box, this button enables you to open the color set containing the colors in the weave. After you select this button, you can adjust the colors in the weave using the normal color set editing methods. After you modify the colors, you can apply them to the weave using the Put Color command.

Put Color: Also located at the right of the Fiber Type selection box, this button places the colors that you modified into the currently open weave. You can then save the weave with a different look or apply it to your image.

Edit: Clicking this button opens a dialog box that enables you to adjust the advanced settings of the weaves. You can adjust the warp and weft patterns, create a Tieup pattern, and identify the placement of colors in the patterns. You learn about these capabilities in more detail later in this chapter.

Save: This button saves a weave to the currently open Weaving Library.

Maximize the Weaves Palette by clicking the button at the upper-right corner of the palette, as shown in Figure 13.2. Doing so opens some adjustment sliders.

Figure 13.2.
The button at the upper-right corner maximizes the Weaves Palette, showing the Scale and Thickness adjustment sliders.

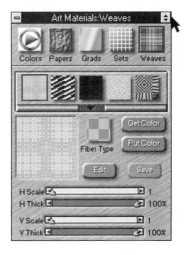

Horizontal Scale: This setting controls the width of the weft (horizontal) fibers. If the weave has 100 threads running horizontally and the horizontal scale is 2, the total width of the weave is 200 pixels before it begins repeating again.

Horizontal Thickness: This setting does not apply to two-dimensional weaves. In the case of three-dimensional weaves, however, this setting determines how much of the horizontal scale the thread takes up. The remaining thickness is an open area, or space, filled with a shadow. If the Horizontal Thickness is set at 60%, for example, the thread takes up 60% of the Horizontal Scale, and the open space and shadow take up the other 40% of the horizontal scale. Reducing this setting makes the weave more open, and increasing the setting closes the weave more.

Vertical Scale: Set at 2. This setting is similar to the Horizontal Scale, mentioned previously, but it controls the width of the warp (vertical) fibers.

Vertical Thickness: Set at 100%. This setting is similar to the Horizontal Thickness, mentioned previously, but it controls the width of the warp (vertical) fibers.

Clicking the Edit button in the Weaves Palette, shown in Figure 13.3, opens the advanced Edit Weaving dialog box. Here, you actually program the weave patterns, colors used in the weave, and the overall size of the weave pattern. You learn about these details later in the chapter. For now, you start with the basics.

Figure 13.3.
The Edit button opens the Edit Weaving dialog box, where you can edit advanced weaving features.

Basic Weave Editing

Basic weave editing consists of adjusting the horizontal and vertical scale and "fiber" thickness and adjusting the colors in the weave to create variations of existing weave patterns. You can save weaves, like other art materials and brushes in Painter, to a library so that you can reuse them at the click of a button or stylus.

Adjusting Horizontal and Vertical Scale for 2-D Weaves

For your first exercise, you adjust horizontal and vertical scaling for two-dimensional weaves. The weaves you use in this exercise are located in the default Painter Weaving Library.

Choosing the Fancy Fabric Weaving

When you open the Weaves Palette drawer, you see icons for the weaves placed in the current library. The weaves that appear on the drawer front are represented by a ghosted image. A click on the Library button opens a dialog box that enables you to choose another Weaving Library.

1. From the Art Materials Palette, choose the Weaves icon to open the Weaves Palette.

2. Open the drawer of the Weaves Palette to reveal the contents inside.

3. From the drop-down list box, choose the Fancy Fabric weave. Your screen should look similar to Figure 13.4.

Figure 13.4.
Choose the Fancy
Fabric weave from the
Weaves Palette.

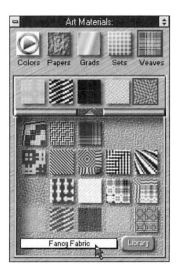

4. The Fancy Fabric weave creates a 90×90 pixel pattern. But to show you how the weave changes when you alter the horizontal and vertical scaling, create a new 180×180 pixel document using the File | New command. (See Figure 13.5)

5. From the Tools Palette (Ctrl-1 in Windows, Cmd-1 in Mac), choose the Paint Bucket. Then from the Controls | Paint Bucket Palette (Ctrl-6 in Windows, Cmd-6 in Mac), choose to fill the image with a Weaving. Your screen should look similar to Figure 13.6.

Figure 13.5.
Create a new 180×180
document using the
File | New command.

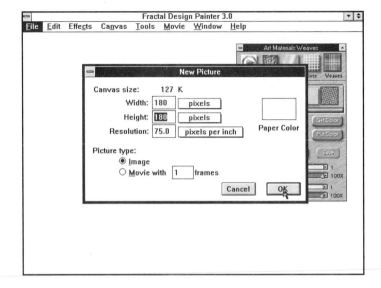

Figure 13.6.
Select to fill the image
with a Weaving in the
Controls | Paint Bucket
Palette.

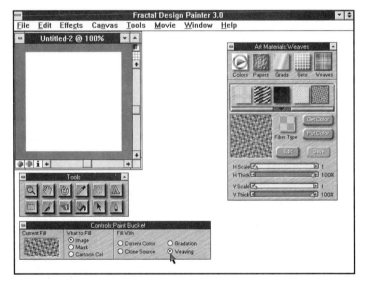

6. Click inside the untitled document to fill it with the default version of
   Fancy Fabric. The image is then filled with the weave pattern, as shown in
   Figure 13.7.

Notice here that the pattern is repeated four times in the document window,
with each quarter of the document containing one complete rendering of the
weave. Now you can adjust the scale of the weave.

Figure 13.7.
Fill the image with the
Fancy Fabric weave.

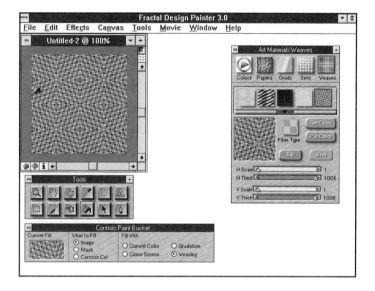

Adjusting the Scale

You adjust the horizontal and vertical scale and thickness of weaves using the horizontal and vertical scale and thickness sliders, contained in the bottom portion of the palette. If the sliders are not visible, you can reveal them by clicking the upper-right button in the palette. This button maximizes and minimizes the Weaves Palette.

Now you're going to create a second 180×180 document and fill it with a double-sized version of the Fancy Fabric weave. To do so, perform the following steps:

1. Create a second 180×180 document using the File | New command.

2. Adjust the H Scale and V Scale sliders of the Fancy Fabric weave until they both read 2. Adjusting the sliders doubles the size of the fibers in the weave and therefore doubles the overall size of the weave. Figure 13.8 shows the settings adjusted.

3. The H Thick and V Thick sliders are ineffective on a two-dimensional weave. For now, you can leave them set at 100%.

4. Using the Paint Bucket, fill the second image with the revised weave. Compare the first version of the weave to the image you just filled. Notice that now the weave has doubled in both horizontal and vertical scale, taking up four times the area that the original weave pattern did. See Figure 13.9 to compare the two versions of the weave.

Figure 13.8.
Adjust the Horizontal
and Vertical Scale
sliders to a value of 2.

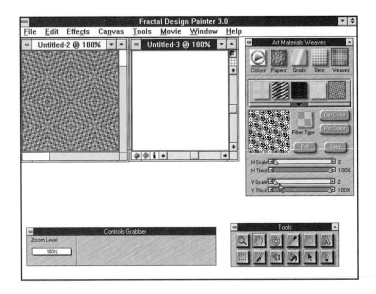

Figure 13.9.
The revised weave is
increased in scale by a
factor of 2.

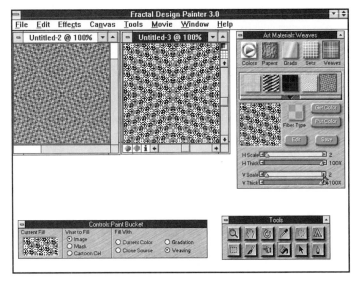

Adjusting Horizontal and Vertical Scale for 3-D Weaves

You adjust three-dimensional weaves in basically the same manner, except that you can increase or decrease the space between the threads by adjusting the Horizontal and Vertical Thickness sliders. A good weave to display this capability is the Wandering Vine weave, located in the default Painter Weaving Library.

Choosing the Wandering Vine Weaving

The Wandering Vine weave has an overall size of 140×140 to display its complete pattern fully. You're going to compare the original 140×140 version of the weave to a version that is triple its size in horizontal and vertical scaling, so create a document that measures 420×420, as follows:

1. From the Art Materials Palette, choose the Weaves icon to open the Weaves Palette if it is not still open.

2. Open the drawer of the Weaves Palette to reveal the contents inside.

3. From the drop-down list box, choose the Wandering Vine weave. Your screen should look similar to Figure 13.10.

Figure 13.10.
Choose the Wandering
vine weave from the
Weaves Palette.

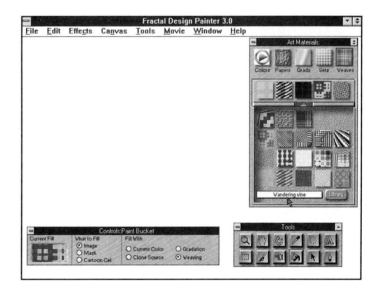

4. Create the 420×420 document using the File | New command, as shown in Figure 13.11.

5. From the Tools Palette (Ctrl-1 in Windows, Cmd-1 in Mac), choose the Paint Bucket. Then, from the Controls | Paint Bucket Palette (Ctrl-6 in Windows, Cmd-6 in Mac), choose to fill the image with a Weaving.

6. Click inside the untitled document to fill it with the default version of Wandering Vine. The weave pattern is repeated three times horizontally and vertically, for a total of nine repetitions. Your screen should look similar to Figure 13.12.

Figure 13.11.
Create a new 420×420 document.

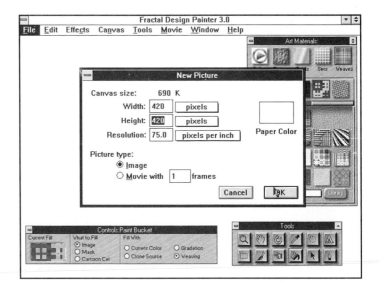

Figure 13.12.
Fill the document with the Wandering Vine weave.

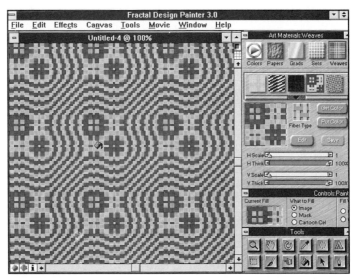

Adjusting the Scale and Thickness

You also adjust the horizontal and vertical scale and thickness of three-dimensional weaves using the horizontal and vertical scale and thickness sliders. With three-dimensional weaves, such as the Wandering Vine, however, you can see adjustments you make to the settings previewed in the window of the Weaves Palette. Explore this feature further, as follows:

1. Create a second 420×420 document using the File | New command.

2. Adjust the H Scale and V Scale sliders of the Wandering Vine weave until they both read 3. Adjusting the sliders triples the size of the "fibers" in the weave, allowing it to fill the new image completely with one rendering of the pattern. Notice that as you adjust the sliders, the image in the preview window changes. Figure 13.13 shows the screen with the size adjusted.

Figure 13.13.
Adjust the scale of the
Wandering Vine weave
to a Horizontal and
Vertical Scale of 3.

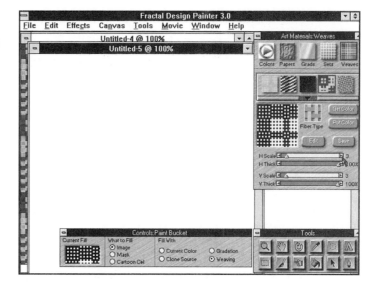

3. The H Thick and V Thick sliders adjust the width of the threads in the weave. Moving the H Thick and V Thick sliders toward the left decreases the thread size and increases the amount of space between the threads. Moving the sliders toward the right makes the thread width larger and eventually closes the gap between the threads entirely. Adjust both sliders so that they read 33%. Doing so creates a single-thread width for the fiber and then creates a double-thread width for the spaces between the fibers. Again, the image in the preview window changes to reflect the changes, as shown in Figure 13.14.

4. Using the Paint Bucket, fill the second image with the revised weave. Compare the first version of the weave to the image you just filled. Notice that now the weave has tripled in both horizontal and vertical scale, taking up nine times the area that the original weave pattern did. Also, if you zoom into the image, as shown in Figure 13.15, you see spaces between the threads and shadowing, which makes the weave appear more three-dimensional.

Figure 13.14.
Adjust the Horizontal
and Vertical Thickness
sliders to a value of
33%.

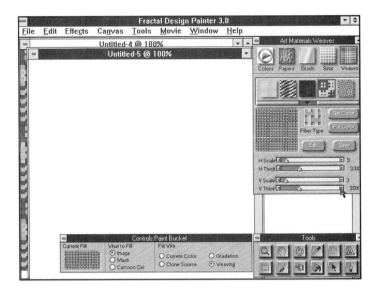

Figure 13.15.
If you zoom in to the
new weave, you see
spaces and shadows
between the fibers.

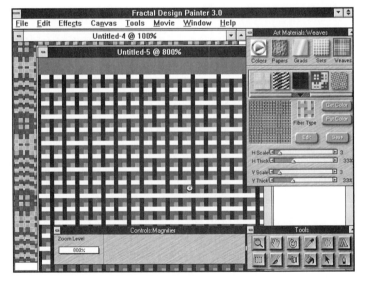

Later in this chapter, you're going to use the three-dimensional view of a weave to compare Tieup patterns to the actual weave patterns generated by Painter. Making this comparison will help you visualize what's going on in the advanced weave settings.

Changing a Weaving's Fiber Type

You can change weave patterns between two- and three-dimensional patterns with the click of a button. In the center of the Weaves Palette, just to the right of the preview window, is an icon that represents the fiber type. Clicking this icon toggles the weave type between the two modes.

Here's how to change the weave type:

1. From the Weaves Palette, select the weave that you want to modify.

2. Select the two-dimensional (checkerboard icon) or three-dimensional (opened weave) fiber type, located to the right of the preview window in the Weaves Palette. The location of this icon is shown in Figure 13.16.

Figure 13.16.
You can choose between a two-dimensional and three-dimensional weave using the Fiber Type icon.

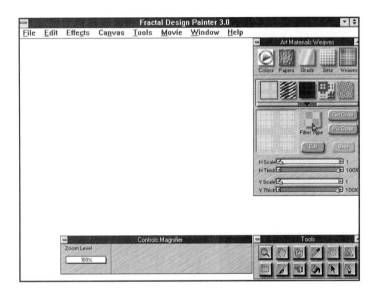

Editing Weaving Colors

Each weave has its own color set, which contains the colors used in the weave. The colors are identified by a single letter only, and the weave program language enables you to use all letters from A to Z. Therefore, a weave can contain up to 26 colors.

To change the colors contained in a weave color set, perform the following steps:

1. Click the Weaves icon in the Art Materials Palette.

2. Select the weave that you want to modify.

3. Click the Get Color button, shown in Figure 13.17. Clicking this button opens the color set associated with the weave.

Figure 13.17.
The Get Color button
opens the color set
associated with the
weave.

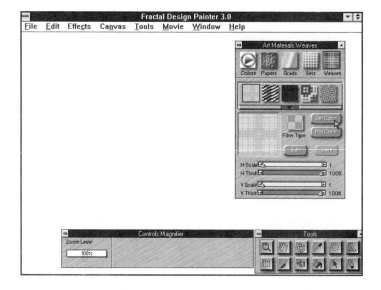

4. If the color designations are not visible in the color set, you can display them by opening up the Art Materials | Sets Palette. With the palette maximized, you see a check box in the lower-left portion of the palette, adjacent to the heading Display Text. Its location is shown in Figure 13.18. If you check this box, the one-letter color designations used in the weave formulas appear.

Figure 13.18.
The Display Text
button in the Sets
Palette displays the
text names of the colors
in the color set.

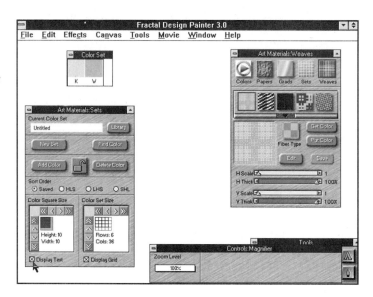

5. Select a new color to place in the weave color set. You can select this color from the Art Materials | Colors Palette or by using the Dropper tool in another image.

6. Press and hold the Alt key in Windows or the Option key in Mac, and click the color in the weave color set that you want to replace. The old color is replaced with the currently selected color. You can replace as many colors in the color set as you like. Figure 13.19 shows the second color changed in the color set.

Figure 13.19.
The second color in the
color set has been
changed.

Second color

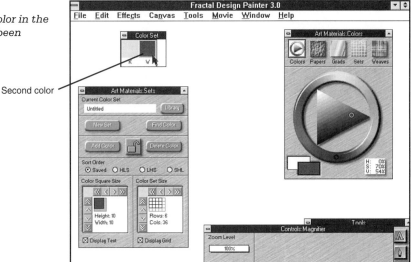

7. Click the Put Color button. The new colors are put into the weave, and the changes show in the Preview box. Figure 13.20 shows the change reflected.

8. To save the changes to a new color set, click its close button at the upper-left corner of the dialog box. You then are asked whether you want to save the changes to the current color set, as shown in Figure 13.21. Click Yes. Name your color set in the Enter Color Set Name dialog box. Then click OK or press Enter. The revised color set is saved with a .TXT file extension, and it is automatically linked with the weave.

Figure 13.20.
Clicking the Put Color
button in the Weaves
Palette updates the
weave with the revised
color.

Put Color button ——————————————

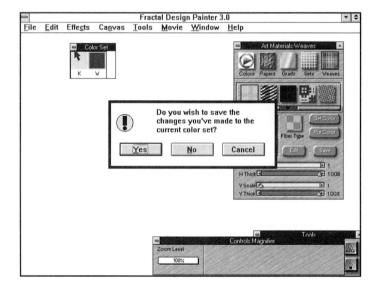

Figure 13.21.
When asked if you
want to save changes
to the color set, click
Yes to continue.

Advanced Weaving Editing—The Heart of the Matter

Clicking the Edit button from the Weaves Palette reveals the Edit Weaving
Dialog box. This dialog box enables you to edit the Tieup patterns, warp and
weft patterns, and colors for the weave. I'll try to explain these procedures in
layman's terms—truthfully, that's the only way I know how to explain them.

> *TIP* If you want to experiment with creating your own weaves, you need to know a bit about Painter's weaving language. The Painter 3 Extras CD, furnished with the registered version of the program, contains a technical note on the Painter weaving language and mentions references that will help you learn more about weaving and weave patterns.

What Are Tieups?

Now take a deep look at the Herring Bone weave found in the BASIC.WEV library. This library is installed in the SUPPLIES subdirectory of Painter when you install the retail version of the program.

Load in the Herring Bone weave as follows:

1. From the Weaves Palette, open the palette drawer. Then click the Library button, as shown in Figure 13.22.

Figure 13.22. Click the Library button in the Weaves Palette.

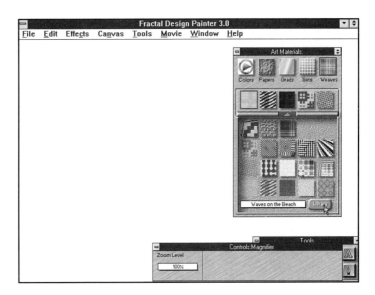

2. Scroll to the Supplies directory of Painter and select the BASIC.WEV library, as shown in Figure 13.23. Then click OK to load the library file.

3. From the drop-down listbox in the library, choose the Herring Bone weave. Figure 13.24 shows this weave selected.

Figure 13.23.
Select the BASIC.WEV
library and click OK to
load the file.

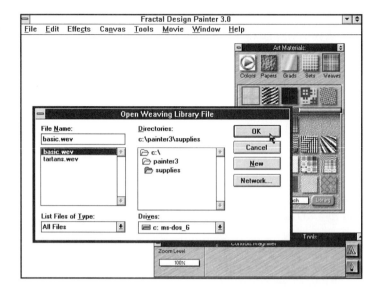

Figure 13.24.
Select the Herring
Bone weave.

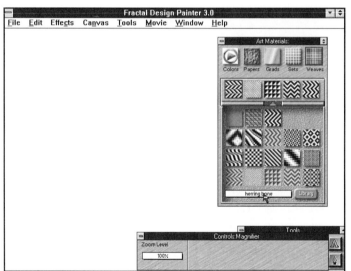

4. With the Herring Bone weave loaded, click the Edit button in the Weaves
   Palette. The Edit Weaving dialog box, shown in Figure 13.25, then appears.

Figure 13.25.
The Edit Weaving
dialog box edits the
advanced features
of a weave.

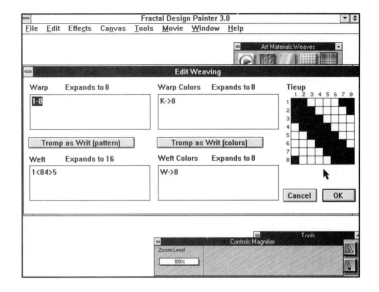

The Edit Weaving dialog box consists of the following items:

- The Warp describes a pattern that is linked to the Tieup, and describes the weaving order of the vertical threads in the weave.

- The Warp Colors describes the arrangement of colors for the vertical threads in the weave. They are linked to a special color set for the weave, as you have already learned.

- The Weft describes the pattern that describes the weaving order of the horizontal threads in the weave. Again, they are linked to the Tieup.

- The Weft Colors describes the arrangement of colors for the horizontal threads in the weave.

- The Tromp as Writ buttons (available for both Patterns and Colors) copy the values from their respective Warp boxes into the corresponding boxes in the Weft. That is, if you enter 1-8 in the Warp, the 1-8 is copied into the Weft when you press the Tromp as Writ button. A good time to use these buttons is when you're creating Tartan Plaids, which use identical thread patterns and colors in the Warp and Weft.

- The Tieup defines which threads are raised and lowered as the weave is created.

The Tieup is located on the right side of the dialog box, as shown in the preceding figure. Notice that it is an 8×8 grid of black and white squares, which, when you click them, revert to the opposite color. The Tieup defines which threads are raised and lowered in the weave, simulating the function of harnesses and pedals in a traditional weaving loom.

If You Can Draw This...

An important point to reiterate here is that weaves are created from horizontal and vertical fibers woven together in a repeating pattern of raised and lowered areas. The threads that run vertically are called the warp fibers, and the threads that run horizontally are called the weft fibers.

Warp Colors

In the Warp Colors section of the Edit Weaving dialog box, you see the entry K->8 for the Herring Bone weave you are examining. This entry designates the color and arrangement of the threads that run vertically in the weave. If you examine the color set for the weave, you see that the letter K designates the color black. The ->8 portion of the entry means that the black is extended across all eight threads in the warp pattern.

Suppose that you had a wooden rod hanging vertically from a stand. On this rod, you tie eight black strands of yarn and let them dangle down vertically toward the floor, as shown in Section A of Figure 13.26. This illustration represents the eight black warp fibers.

Figure 13.26.
In Section A, you see
eight black warp fibers.
Section B shows the
first weft fiber woven
in as it pertains to the
Tieup. Section C shows
the second weft fiber
woven in. Section D
shows the Tieup
pattern compared to
the full woven version.

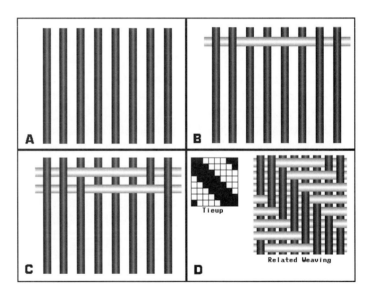

Weft Colors

In the Weft Colors section of the Edit Weaving dialog box, you see the entry W->8. This entry designates the color and arrangement of the threads that run horizontally in the weave. The letter W designates the color white in the color set for this weave. And again, the ->8 portion of the entry means that the white is used for all eight threads in this weave pattern. So, set aside eight strands of white yarn. The Tieup pattern is going to tell you how to weave them in.

What the Tieup Does

Now I'll try to explain the Tieup patterns in the most basic way I can. For the time being, ignore the warp and weft pattern, because in this example, the first eight numbers in each are 1 through 8. Therefore, the Tieup pattern reflects a "What you see is what you get" situation. I get back to the warp and weft later.

Look at the first row of squares in the Tieup pattern. You see two black squares, four white squares, and two black squares again. What does that mean?

Going back to the eight threads dangling on the rod, pull the first thread and the second thread toward you (in your mind). Push the third through sixth threads away from you. And finally, pull the seventh and eighth threads toward you. This arrangement agrees with the black and white squares in the first row of the Tieup.

Now take the first of the eight white threads and pass it vertically between the forward and backward arrangement of black horizontal threads. The white thread should be beneath the first two threads (making black show in the first and second spaces), in front of the next four threads (making white show in the fourth through sixth spaces), and again behind the last two threads (making black show in the seventh and eighth spaces). The first thread is shown woven in Figure 13.26, Section B. Sound familiar? It's identical to the pattern in row one of the Tieup.

In the second row, pull the first three black threads toward you, push the next four away from you, and pull the last toward you. Pass the second white thread through, passing in front of the fourth through seventh threads. Refer to Section C of Figure 13.26 for this example.

Continue on with this logic to repeat the remainder of the pattern. Figure 13.26, Section D, shows all eight strands woven in and compares it to the Tieup.

TIP

The following sums up Tieups easily:

When you see black in the Tieup pattern, the warp thread (the horizontal thread) shows in the weave because it is in front.

Black = Warp

When you see white in the Tieup pattern, the weft thread (the vertical thread) shows in the weave because it is in front.

White = Weft

(Think of Elmer and his kwazy wabbit fwiend to remember this one! It weawwy helped me!)

Warp and Weft Information

Okay, now for the twicky—excuse me, *tricky*—part. What do all these numbers and symbols in the Warp and Weft boxes mean?

The Warp Expands To and Weft Expands To entries in the Edit Weaving dialog box, shown in Figure 13.27, are easy to understand. Figure 13.27 shows the location of one of these entries. The figures at the end of these entries are calculated automatically as you make changes in the formulas contained in the Warp and Weft boxes.

Figure 13.27.
The Expands To
figures are calculated
automatically based
on the warp and weft
patterns.

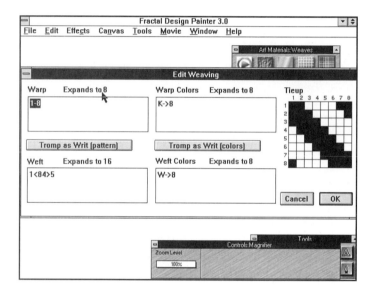

Basically, the Warp Expands To figure indicates how many horizontal fibers it takes to complete the weave. In the example, the warp pattern is indicated as 1-8. This sequence expands to 12345678. Because you have eight numbers in this sequence, you have eight threads. This sequence begins repeating the same pattern at the ninth thread.

Similarly, the Weft Expands To figure represents the number of vertical fibers that it takes to complete the weave pattern and pertains to the height of the weave in threads or pixels. In the example, the pattern is shown as 1<84>5. In Painter's form of weaving shorthand, the first part of the sequence (1<8) means *1 up to 8*. This series starts at 1 and runs in sequence until it gets to 8. That expands to the sequence 12345678. Because you have eight numbers, you have a total of eight threads.

The 4>5 entry *(4 down to 5)* is a little trickier. You start counting down from 4 to 1. To continue with the countdown, the 1 wraps around to 8 (because you have an 8×8 Tieup). So, the 4 down to 5 expands to 43218765. That's eight more threads.

Putting the two portions of the weft sequence together, you have a sequence as follows: 1234567843218765. That's a total of 16 horizontal threads because you have 16 numbers in the sequence. Therefore, the weave Tieup is completed in an 8-wide×16-high grid.

Now you're going to apply the information contained in the Warp and Weft boxes to the Herring Bone weave to determine how it relates to the overall picture. Start by examining Figure 13.28. This figure shows the Herring Bone weave in three states. The top section shows the information displayed in the Edit Weaving dialog box. Here, the Tieup pattern is shown at the top right side, and the warp and weft pattern and colors are also displayed.

Figure 13.28.
The top section shows the Tieup and warp and weft information for the Herring Bone weave. The bottom left shows the Tieup as it relates to the warp and weft entries in the weave. The bottom right shows the patterns as they are woven, which differs slightly from the version on the left.

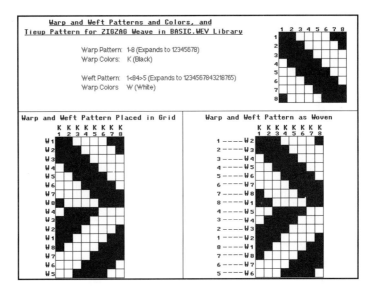

The bottom-left section of Figure 3.28 shows the Tieup as it would appear over the entire weave range. Above the grid are eight Ks. Remember the eight black threads tied on the wooden rod? Here they are again. Below the Ks are the numbers you determined for the warp sequence.

On the side of the 8×16 grid are 16 Ws, indicating 16 white threads. Also along the side is the weft sequence you determined earlier: 1234567843218765.

The first eight rows of the extended grid pattern are basically an exact replication of the Tieup because the warp pattern is 12345678, and the first eight numbers in the weft pattern are 12345678. There isn't too much to show you here. But take a look at the second eight rows of the grid. The ninth weft row has the number 4 adjacent to it. What do you do here? To understand, take a look at Figure 13.29, which highlights the ninth row of the Herring Bone warp/weft pattern adjacent to a picture of the Tieup.

Figure 13.29.
Compare the ninth row
of the Herring Bone
pattern to the original
Tieup pattern.

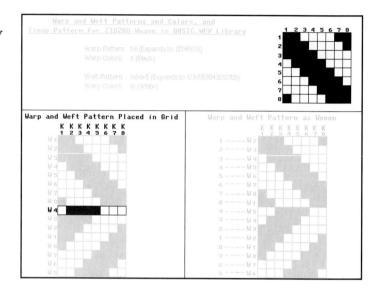

The first warp spot of the Herring Bone pattern (first column heading) corresponds to the number 1. The ninth weft spot, or ninth row, corresponds to the number 4. Therefore, the first column in the ninth row should be colored the same as the first space in the fourth row of the Tieup pattern, as shown in Figure 13.30.

Figure 13.30.
The first column space
in the ninth row of the
Herring Bone weave
agrees with the first
column in the fourth
row of the Tieup.

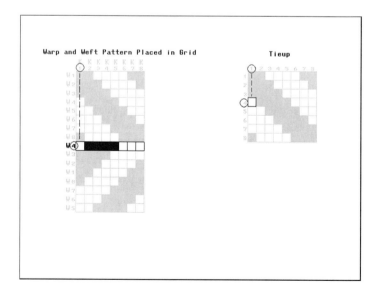

422

Continuing with the remaining seven entries in the ninth row, use Figure 13.30 to see the following:

- The second column should be colored the same as the second column in the fourth row of the Tieup (black).
- The third column should be colored the same as the third column in the fourth row of the Tieup (black).
- The fourth column should be colored the same as the fourth column in the fourth row of the Tieup (black).
- The fifth column should be colored the same as the fifth column in the fourth row of the Tieup (black).
- The sixth column should be colored the same as the sixth column in the fourth row of the Tieup (white).
- The seventh column should be colored the same as the seventh column in the fourth row of the Tieup (white).
- The eighth column should be colored the same as the eighth column in the fourth row of the Tieup (white).

Looking at the Rendered Weaving

Now take a look at what the full pattern looks like when it's woven because there's one more thing to mention. And for this, I can't think of a logical explanation!

Create a 16-pixel wide by 32-pixel high document and fill it with the Herring Bone weave. Your screen should look similar to Figure 13.31.

Figure 13.31.
The Herring Bone pattern is placed into a 16-pixel wide by 32-pixel high document.

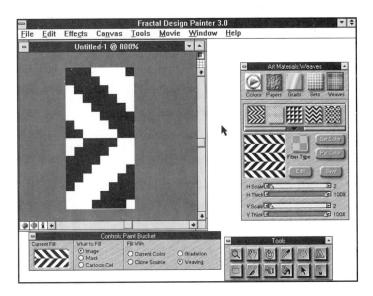

Notice that the actual woven pattern differs slightly from the Tieup you just examined. To understand why, return to Figure 3.28. Here, examine the grid under the Warp and Weft Pattern Placed in Grid heading. This grid pertains to the pattern you just examined when I discussed the warp and weft information.

Now observe the grid placed beneath the Warp and Weft Pattern as Woven, which is identical to the pattern you just filled in the image. At the side of this grid are two sets of numbers. The leftmost set shows the extended version of the weft sequence entered into the Edit Weaving dialog box:

1234567843218765

Compare this to the pattern actually woven. If you examine the black-and-white pattern in this case, you see that what was actually woven was the following weft sequence, shown adjacent to the grid in Figure 13.28:

2345678154321876

If you examine this sequence closer, you see that the weft numbers were each increased by one when the pattern was applied to the weave—where a 1 appeared in the weft sequence, the value in 2 was actually applied to the weave; where a 2 appeared in the sequence, the value in 3 was applied; and so on through 8 in the weft sequence, which was woven as 1. Although this explanation is somewhat confusing, it is consistent with all the weaves I examined.

Adding More Colors to a Weaving

So far, you've examined the warp and weft in black and white only. Now you get to see what happens to the pattern when you add a couple of colors to it. To add colors to a weave, click the Get Color button in the Weaves Palette. Clicking this button opens the color set for the current weave, as discussed earlier.

For this example, add yellow and red to the color set for the Herring Bone weave. Proceed as follows:

1. Click the Get Color button in the Weaves Palette to open the color set for the Herring Bone weave. A color set with black and white then appears on your screen.
2. Drag the Colors icon outside the Art Materials Palette to open a copy of the Colors Palette on the screen.
3. Drag a copy of the Sets icon on your screen to open the Sets Palette. Your screen should look similar to Figure 13.32.
4. From the Colors Palette, choose a bright yellow. Then click the Add Color icon in the Sets Palette, as shown in Figure 13.33.

Figure 13.32.
Drag a copy of the
Colors Palette and Sets
Palettes on your screen.

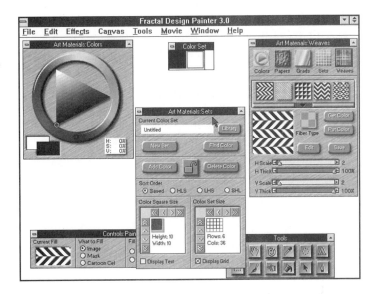

Figure 13.33.
Pick a bright yellow
from the Colors Palette,
and click Add Color in
the Sets Palette.

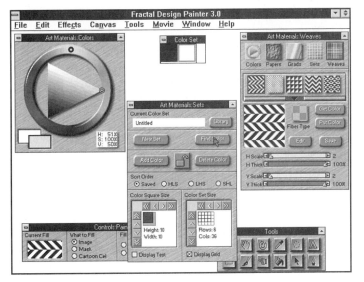

5. To name the color, double-click the yellow square in the weave's color set. A dialog box appears, prompting you to name the color. Because weaves allow only a one-character name, enter Y for yellow; then click OK to return to the Color Set.

6. Now return to the Colors Palette and choose a bright red. Click the Add Color button in the Sets Palette and enter R for red. Now place the yellow and red colors into the Herring Bone weave.

7. With the Herring Bone weave selected in the Weaves Palette, click the Edit button, as shown in Figure 13.34.

Figure 13.34.
Click the Edit button
to access the Edit
Weaving dialog box.

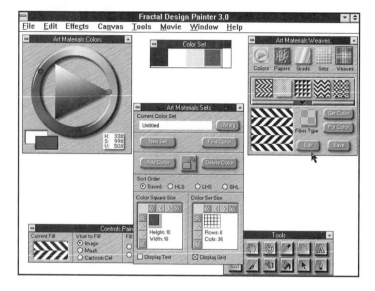

8. In the Warp Colors section of the Edit Weaving dialog box, insert a Y before the K->8 formula. (The screen should look like Figure 13.35.) If you take this step, the vertical warp colors alternate between yellow and black in the new weave.

Figure 13.35.
Edit the Warp Colors to
read YK->8.

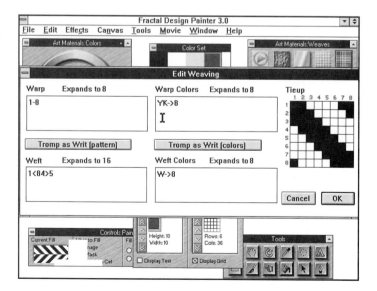

9. Similarly, edit the weft colors to read RW->8. This change alternates the horizontal weft colors between red and white.

10. Click OK to exit the Edit Weaving dialog box.

11. Click the Put Color button in the Weaves Palette to update the weave with the new colors. The weave in the preview window then changes to reflect the new colors you added.

Figure 13.36 shows the Herring Bone weave with the revised color settings. If you compare the black-and-white Pattern as Woven to the version under With Colors Placed, you see the following:

■ The first row of the Pattern as Woven version contains three black squares (warp color in front).

■ The colored version does indeed show the warp threads in front (their color pattern is indicated in the column heading on the grid). You see the three warp colors—yellow, black, and yellow—in the first three spots in the first row.

■ The next four spots in the first row of the Pattern as Woven show white squares, indicating that the weft colors are in front. For this row, the weft color is red. In the color version of the weave, you see red in spaces four through seven.

■ The last spot in the Pattern as Woven version is black, indicating that the warp's black thread should be in the front in the color version—and, indeed it is!

Figure 13.36.
Adding two more
colors to the weave
greatly changes its
appearance.

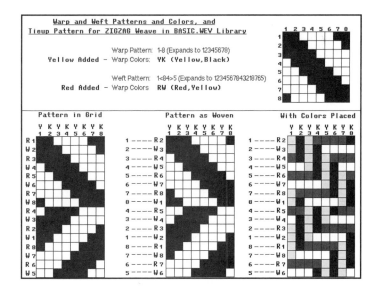

Given what you have learned so far about warp and weft colors and how they relate to the Tieup, add one more revision to the Herring Bone weave. Change the warp pattern to 76758483. The resulting weave is shown in Figure 13.37. See if you can relate everything you've learned to the Pattern as Woven and With Colors Placed versions. This is a test!

Figure 13.37. Now change the warp pattern to 76758483, and compare the results with those shown in this figure.

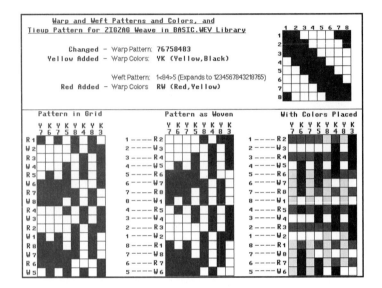

Painter's Weaving Language—Weaving Shorthand

What happens if you want to create a more complex numerical sequence, or create a weave that has hundreds, even thousands, of threads in it? Painter has a set of shorthand commands to serve exactly this purpose. They are explained in detail in the technical note provided on the Painter Extras CD furnished with the program. In brief, the commands are shown in Table 13.1.

Table 13.1. Painter's weave commands.

Function	Symbol	Description and Examples
Upto	< or –	The sequence runs in numerical order from the left operand to the right operand. For example, 1<4 expands to 1234; 1–7 expands to 1234567; and 5>3 expands to 5678123.
Downto	> or –	The sequence runs in reverse numerical order from the left operand to the right operand. For example, 8>1 expands to 87654321; 6–2 expands to 65432; and 1>6 expands to 1876.

Function	Symbol	Description and Examples
Concat	,	The left operand is joined in order with the right operand. For example, 12,34 expands to 1234; and 2(1–4|),(4–1|) expands to 123432,432123 (see Palindrome), which then joined together is 123432432123.
Downup	><	The left operand and right operand are joined together in an alternating down and up sequence. To demonstrate this principle, the numbers in the left operand are shown in italic, and the numbers in the right operand are shown in bold. For example, *1234*><**5678** translates to the following: *1* downto **5** upto *2* downto **6** upto *3* downto **7** upto *4* downto **8**. Expanded (with spaces added for clarification), this is 18765 67812 21876 78123 2187 81234 3218.
Updown	<>	The left operand and right operand are joined together in an alternating up and down sequence. To demonstrate this principle, the numbers in the left operand are shown in italic, and the numbers in the right operand are shown in bold. For example, *1234*<>**5678** translates to the following: *1* upto **5** downto *2* upto **6** downto *3* upto **7** downto *4* upto **8**. Expanded (with spaces added for clarification), this is 12345 432 3456 543 4567 654 5678.
Interleave	~ (or int)	The left operand is interleaved with the right operand. If the right operand is shorter than the left, it is repeated as often as required to complete the interleave process. For demonstration purposes, the numbers in the left operand are shown in italics, and the numbers in the right operand are shown in bold. For example, *12345678*~**1234** expands to *1***1***2***2***3***3***4***4***5***1***6***2***7***3***8***4*.

continues

Table 13.1. continued

Function	Symbol	Description and Examples
Permute	perm	The left operand is permuted based on the pattern of the right operand. The number of figures in the left operand must be equally divisible by the number of figures in the right operand. (For example, if four figures appear in the right operand, the number of figures in the left operand can be 8, 12, 16, and so on.)
		Examine 123456787654321 perm 312. The permute figure, 312, means that the third number in each three-digit section is relocated before the first and second. Therefore, 123 456 787 543 312 perm 312 alters to 312 645 778 354 231 (spaces added for clarification).
		Note: The Pbox function is similar to this, except that the left operand can be any length. For example, 12378 Pbox 312 alters to 31287.
Extend	-> (or ext)	The left operand is extended to fill as many slots as indicated by the right operand. For example, 4367 -> 15 extends to 436743674367436
Block		The right operand determines the number of times a number in the left operand is repeated. For example, if the left operand is 274, the first number on the left is repeated twice, the second number on the left is repeated seven times, and the third number on the left is repeated four times. This continues on as follows: 35682143 [] 274 expands to 33 5555555 6666 88 2222222 1111 44 3333333 (spaces added for clarification).
Template	: (or temp)	The right operand serves as a template for expanding each number in the left operand. For example, if a template is 5654, the second number in the expansion increases by one, then decreases by one, and then decreases by one again. Each number in the left operand is used as a starting point for the template. For example, 12345678 : 5654 expands to 1218 2321 3432 4543 5654 6765 7876 8187.

Function	Symbol	Description and Examples
Repeat	*	The left operand is repeated as many times as the right operand indicates. For example, 3456 * 3 expands to 345634563456.
Palindrome	| (or pal)	Joins a figure to a backward version of itself, with the exception of the first digit. No right operand is required. For example, 1–8| expands to 12345678765432, and 8>2| expands to 876543234567.
Reverse	' (or rev)	Reverses the left operand. For example, 1234' changes to 4321, and 567345' changes to 543765.
Rotate	# (or rot)	Takes the number of figures designated by the right operand (which can be a negative number) and moves them to the opposite side of the remaining figures. For example, 12345678 # 4 takes the first four numbers and moves them after the remaining numbers (changes it to 56781234), and 12345678 # –3 takes the last three numbers and moves them before the remaining numbers. This changes to 67812345.
Block expressions		Used in the Tartan weaves, takes a color and extends it to fill as many spaces as the number following. For example, B 2 G 5 R 7 W 6 K 8 is two blue fibers, followed by five green fibers, followed by seven red fibers, followed by six white fibers, followed by eight black fibers.

When you examine some of the warp and weft patterns in the existing weaves in relation to the guidelines in Table 13.1, bear in mind that, just as in mathematics, sequences surrounded in parentheses are expanded before the other sequences. I could go on for many pages explaining the myriad of combinations that can result from combining one or more of the weaving functions, but I feel that with this basic information and time, you will grow to understand how to make different combinations. It's fun to experiment.

Creating Your Own Weaves

Now you can create your own weaves by changing colors and patterns. After you have modified a weave, you can save it into a library. The process for saving is straightforward.

Saving a Revised Weaving

You can save your revised weaves to your own custom library or to the Painter default library, for later retrieval. Before you save the weave, you should select and make current the library to which you want to save the weave.

To save a revised or new weave, perform the following steps:

1. From the Weaves Palette, open or create a library in which to save a new weave.

2. Choose or create the weave that you want to save.

3. Click the Save button in the Weaves Palette. A dialog box appears, asking you to type in a name for the new weave.

4. After typing the new weave name, click OK or press Enter. The new weave appears in the currently open Weaving Library.

Summary

You've examined the Weaves Palette in great detail. You should now be able to decipher the functions in the advanced editing portion of the Weaves Palette, and can begin to experiment with creating your own colorful and intricate weave patterns.

Part

Advanced Projects

Working with the Brush Tools

I'm going to cover a lot of territory in this chapter. I'll cover Painter's brush variants, as well as their appearances and characteristics. I'll also show how you can create your own brushes and paper textures and save them in libraries.

The Brush Tools

The Brush variants in the Brushes Palette contain oil and acrylic brushes. All the brushes in this group are based on one of the Cover methods, meaning that their strokes cover those beneath them. Moving the Opacity slider in the Controls | Brush Palette toward the left makes the strokes more transparent; moving it to the right makes the strokes more opaque.

Some of the brushes in this category have multiple bristles and give the appearance of true brush strokes, complete with hairline streaks. In Exercises 14.1 through 14.4 in this chapter, I'll discuss how to create a brush that has a bristly appearance and examine the various settings in the Brush Controls and Advanced Controls Palettes.

Big Loaded Oils, Small Loaded Oils, and Loaded Oils

These variants give the appearance of an oil brush that has been dipped in more than one color. The size of their strokes varies with stylus pressure. The only difference between these three brushes is their size—the Big Loaded Oils is basically a larger version of Loaded Oils, and the Small Loaded Oils is the smallest version of the three. With all these brushes, lighter pressure produces lighter strokes, and heavier pressure produces darker strokes. Mouse users can adjust the Opacity slider on the Controls | Brush Palette or set the Opacity setting in the Advanced Controls | Sliders Palette to respond to Velocity or Direction.

Big Rough Out, Huge Rough Out, and Rough Out

The Rough Out variant is a dry brush that is commonly used for roughing out ideas on your canvas. It produces strokes that are thick, with hard, pixelly edges. The strokes cover underlying strokes. The size of the brush varies with the speed at which the mouse or stylus is dragged. The Big Rough Out brush is a larger variant of the Rough Out Brush, and the Huge Rough Out brush is even larger. All brushes share the same characteristics. Mouse users can adjust the Grain slider on the Controls | Brush Palette or set the Grain setting in the Advanced Controls | Sliders Palette to respond to Velocity or Direction.

Big Wet Oils

The Big Wet Oils variant is similar to the Big Loaded Oils variant, except that it mixes its color with the colors underneath. Its strokes vary in size based on the pressure applied by the stylus. Light pressure produces thinner strokes, and heavy pressure produces wider strokes. Mouse users can adjust the Opacity slider on the Controls | Brush Palette, or they can set Opacity setting in the Advanced Controls | Sliders Palette to respond to Velocity or Direction.

Brushy

Brushy is a multiple-bristled variant that varies in stroke width depending on the pressure applied to the stylus. This variant produces very soft, antialiased strokes of paint. The brush quickly runs out of paint, and then drags the colors through which it passes. Strokes produced with this variant have very fine bristle streaks in them. Brush size can be adjusted manually in the Brush Controls | Size Palette, or by changing the Size category in the Advanced Controls | Sliders Palette to Velocity or Direction.

Camel Hair Brush

The Camel Hair Brush variant produces soft, antialiased strokes that cover those beneath them. The size of the stroke varies with the speed at which the mouse or stylus is dragged. The opacity of the stroke varies according to pressure applied to the stylus. Mouse users can adjust the Opacity slider on the Controls | Brush Palette, or the Opacity settings in the Advanced Controls | Sliders Palette can be set to respond to Velocity or Direction.

Coarse Hairs

The Coarse Hairs variant has a small number of coarse hairs that have a softened appearance. The strokes produced by this brush cover those beneath with an antialiased brush stroke. The width and opacity are determined by the pressure applied to the stylus. This brush is created with a captured dab. Brush size can be adjusted manually in the Brush Controls | Size Palette, or by changing the Size category in the Advanced Controls | Sliders Palette to Velocity or Direction. Opacity can be adjusted manually on the Controls | Brush Palette.

Cover Brush

The Cover Brush variant produces strokes with soft, antialiased edges. This brush is not paper-grain sensitive, but its size and opacity vary with stylus pressure. Pressing lightly on the stylus produces narrow, lighter strokes, and pressing heavily on the stylus produces strokes that are wider and darker. Brush size can be adjusted manually in the Brush Controls | Size Palette, or by changing the Size category in the Advanced Controls | Sliders Palette to Velocity or Direction. Opacity can be adjusted manually on the Controls | Brush Palette.

Digital Sumi

The Digital Sumi variant is a multiple-bristled rake brush that looks like several single pixel strokes spaced side by side. There are no expression settings for this brush, so the stroke will appear the same whether you use the mouse or the stylus. You can alter the brush's appearance by making adjustments to the number of bristles in the Brush Controls | Spacing Palette, and the Contact Angle and Brush Scale settings in the Advanced Controls | Rake Palette.

Fine Brush

The Fine Brush variant is created with a captured brush dab. It produces soft, antialiased strokes that cover those beneath, and that change scale very quickly. The size of the stroke, as well as its opacity, varies with stylus pressure. Brush Size can be adjusted manually in the Brush Controls | Size Palette, or by changing the Size category in the Sliders Palette to Velocity or Direction. Opacity can be adjusted manually on the Controls | Brush Palette.

Graduated Brush

The Graduated Brush variant is a multicolored brush that works with one or two colors. Strokes made from this variant cover what is beneath them with a semi-antialiased stroke that reacts to the grain of the paper. By selecting two colors in the Art Materials | Colors Palette, you can specify the color variations in the multicolored stroke of this brush. The Graduated Brush works with both the primary and secondary colors in the overlapping rectangles. Pressing lightly on the stylus will produce strokes of one color, and pressing heavily produces the other color. Brush size can be adjusted manually in the Brush Controls | Size Palette, or by changing the Size category in the Advanced Controls | Sliders Palette to Velocity or Direction. Additionally, the setting for Color in the Advanced Controls | Sliders Palette can be changed to vary with Velocity or Direction.

Hairy Brush

The Hairy Brush variant is a multistroke brush. Strokes made with this variant will appear first as a dotted line before the stroke is rendered. Its strokes are semi-antialiased and cover strokes that are beneath. The strokes look as though they were made with a bristle brush, and include brush-hair lines. The width of the stroke varies with pressure from the stylus. Because the Hairy Brush is paper-grain sensitive, you can choose different paper textures to make the strokes appear differently. Brush size can be adjusted manually in the Brush Controls | Size Palette, or by changing the Size category in the Advanced Controls | Sliders Palette to Velocity or Direction. Opacity and Grain can be adjusted manually on the Controls | Brush Palette.

The Hairy Brush can be modified to give an entirely different appearance. For example:

- To add more bristles to the stroke, adjust the Bristles slider in the Brush Controls | Spacing Palette. Moving the slider toward the right increases the number of bristles in the brush.

- The Hairy brush can paint with multiple colors if you select two colors in the Art Materials | Colors Palette. Dragging the ±HSAV color variability sliders toward the right increases the color variation in the stroke.

Oil Paint

The Oil Paint variant produces strokes that have hard, pixelly edges and that cover strokes beneath them. Stroke size varies with the pressure applied to the stylus. Pressing lightly on the stylus produces narrower strokes, and pressing heavily on the stylus produces thicker strokes. The strokes are sensitive to paper grain, and the amount of penetration into the paper varies with stylus pressure. Applying more pressure to the stylus covers more of the paper grain, and light pressure allows more of the paper grain to show through. You can create additional effects by changing the paper selected in the Art Materials | Papers Palette.

Additionally, the opacity of the Oil Paint variant varies with stylus pressure. Pressing lightly on the stylus produces lighter strokes, and pressing heavily produces strokes that are more opaque.

The Oil Paint variant can be modified by adding more bristles. Do this by adjusting the Bristles Slider in the Brush Controls | Spacing Palette. The Contact Angle, Turn Amount, and Brush Scale sliders in the Advanced Controls | Rake Palette also can be adjusted to make less of the brush touch the paper or to alter its effects when you paint curved strokes.

Brush size can be adjusted manually in the Brush Controls | Size Palette, or by changing the Size category in the Sliders Palette to Velocity or Direction. Opacity and Grain can be adjusted manually on the Controls | Brush Palette.

Penetration Brush

The Penetration Brush variant produces strokes that have hard, aliased edges that cover underlying strokes. The appearance of the brush is similar to acrylic paints when the Effects | Surface Control | Apply Surface Texture command is used to add dimension to the strokes. The size of the stroke changes based on the speed at which the mouse or stylus is dragged.

The Penetration Brush also reacts to paper grain. You can vary the amount of paper grain that appears in the stroke by applying more or less pressure on the stylus, or by moving the Grain Slider in the Controls | Brush Palette. Changing the paper texture while you work adds different effects to the brush.

Mouse users can adjust the Grain slider on the Controls | Brush Palette. Mouse users also can set the Grain setting in the Advanced Controls | Sliders Palette to respond to Velocity or Direction.

Sable Chisel Tip Water

The Sable Chisel Tip Water variant uses a water-like effect to smear the colors in your image. The size of the brush varies with the pressure applied to the stylus. This brush is created with a captured brush dab. Brush size can be

adjusted manually in the Brush Controls | Size Palette, or by changing the Size category in the Advanced Controls | Sliders Palette to Velocity or Direction.

Smaller Wash Brush

This variant has many soft and closely spaced bristles that smear the current color with other colors in an image. Its opacity and grain respond to stylus pressure. Opacity and Grain can be adjusted manually on the Controls | Brush Palette.

Ultrafine Wash Brush

The Ultrafine Wash Brush variant has a large group of fine bristles that smear the current color with the colors in your image. It is created with a bristle dab. Its strokes vary in size based on the pressure applied to the stylus. Light pressure creates narrower strokes, and heavier pressure produces wider strokes. The opacity of the stroke, as well as its reaction to paper grain, varies with stylus pressure. Brush size can be adjusted manually in the Brush Controls | Size Palette, or by changing the Size category in the Advanced Controls | Sliders Palette to Velocity or Direction. Opacity and grain can be adjusted manually on the Controls | Brush Palette.

Creating Your Own Brushes

Throughout this book, there are occasions in which minor modifications have been made to the brushes furnished with Painter. But there are many other ways to modify and create brushes of your own. You also can create your own brush libraries in which to store your modified or newly created brushes.

The commands used to add brushes to or delete brushes from libraries are in the Tools | Brushes menu, shown in Figure 14.1.

Figure 14.1.
The Tools | Brushes
menu contains
commands to create
new brushes and
maintain brush
libraries.

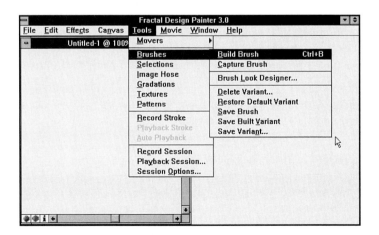

Build Brush (Ctrl-B in Windows, Cmd-B in Mac)

The Build Brush command performs the same function as pressing the Build button in the Brush Controls | Size Palette. It is used to build new brushes and variations of existing brushes. Some brushes have to be rebuilt, or re-rendered, when you make adjustments in size or other brush parameters.

TIP

One way to know whether or not a brush has to be rebuilt is to observe the state of the Build button in the Brush Controls | Size Palette. If the Build button is recessed into the palette and slightly grayed out, the brush does not have to be rebuilt before you use it. However, if the Build button is raised and at full opacity, the brush will have to be rebuilt. Many of Painter's brushes rebuild themselves automatically.

You can build a new brush or brush variant by using one of the following three methods:

■ Choose the Tools | Brushes | Build Brush command.

■ Use the keyboard combination of Ctrl-B in Windows or Cmd-B in Mac.

■ Click the Build button inside the Brush Controls | Size Palette.

Capture Brush Command

The Capture Brush command enables you to capture a brush dab that you created and turn it into a Painter brush. Exercises 14.1 and 14.2 demonstrate how to use this command.

Delete Variant

The Delete Variant command deletes a brush variant from the Brushes Palette. To delete the brush variant, use the following steps:

1. From the Brushes Palette, select the brush variant that you want to delete. For example, if you don't use the brush you create in this chapter after you complete the project, select it as the variant to be deleted.

2. Choose Tools | Brushes | Delete Variant. A dialog box will ask you to confirm that you want to delete the selected brush.

3. Click Yes, to delete the brush. Click No (or press Enter in Windows or Return in Mac) to cancel the operation.

Restore Default Variant

If you have saved over a default brush with the Save Built Variant command, and later decide that you want to restore the original brush, you can use the Restore Default Variant command to restore the default settings of the brush.

441

To use this command:

1. From the Brushes Palette, select the brush variant that you want to restore to its original default settings.
2. Choose Tools | Brushes | Restore Default Variant. The original default settings will be restored to the brush.

Save Brush Command

The Save Brush command allows you to create a new category of brushes in the currently open Brush Library. Exercises 14.1 and 14.2 demonstrate the use of this command.

Save Built Variant

Use the Save Built Variant command when you want to save modifications you have made to an existing brush. This command overwrites the values stored in the previous version of the brush. If you want to save a variant under a different name, choose the Save Variant command, discussed next. You can restore the Built variants to their original default values with the Restore Default Variant command.

To use the Save Built Variant command:

1. Select a brush and modify it with the Brush Controls | Size Palette (most common), or with the other controls contained in the Brush Controls and Advanced Controls Palettes.
2. Select Tools | Brushes | Save Built Variant. The brush is automatically updated with the changes you have made.

Save Variant

Use the Save Variant command when you want to save a new brush variant or when you want to save a variant of an existing brush under a different name.

To save a brush using the Save Variant command:

1. Create or modify a brush in the brush category you want to save it into. (For example, if you are creating a new Airbrush variant, select the Airbrush tools as your current brush category.)
2. Select Tools | Brushes | Save Variant. The Save Variant dialog box will appear.
3. Type a name for your new brush variant.
4. Click OK or press Enter. The new variant name will appear in the list of variants under the category you selected. A brush can have as many as 32 variants.

Changing Properties of a Brush

When you create a new brush, the stroke might not look exactly the way you pictured. If this is the case, there are many brush controls and settings that can make your brush behave exactly as you intended. The CD reference accompanying this book offers a great way to explore ways to fine-tune brushes. For example, if you want to locate the names of all brushes that use the Grainy Soft Buildup method, you can search for them. You also can look at the settings of a particular brush and search for brushes that might have similar characteristics. To fully explore the various controls in the Brush Controls and Advanced Controls Palettes, use the interactive CD reference furnished with this book.

Methods

Methods determine the basic Painter style that defines the brush stroke. For instance, a method containing the word *Cover* in its name indicates that the stroke will cover underlying ones. Examples of these are oil paint strokes. If a method is a Buildup type, the strokes will build on top of each other and eventually turn black. A good example of this type of brush is the crayon. Methods can be soft (antialiased), hard (semi-antialiased), or flat (aliased and pixelly). There are also cloning, masking, and erasing methods.

Methods can be assigned in the Brushes Palette. If you maximize the palette using the arrow at the upper-right corner of the palette, two additional drop-down boxes, shown in Figure 14.2, will appear.

Figure 14.2.
Brush Methods can be
assigned in the Brushes
Palette.

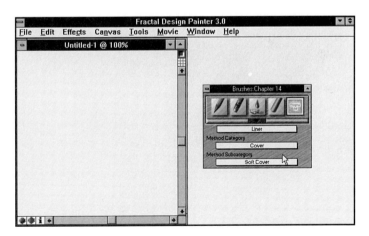

As you've seen so far, there are brushes that interact with paper grain and others that don't. Table 14.1 shows the methods that are used to make brushes that are sensitive to paper grain. This chart can help you narrow your choices, depending on whether or not you would like antialiased, semi-antialiased, or pixelly edged strokes. Other properties are added into the chart so that you can select the right method by cross-referencing the appearance and characteristics you want to obtain. For example, if you want a brush that reacts to paper grain and has antialiased edges, but also will build up strokes toward black, you would use the Grainy Soft Buildup method to define your brush.

Table 14.1. Brush Methods that React with Paper Grain.

Description	Antialiased Edges	Semi-Antialiased Edges	Aliased Edges	Hard Sticky Edges
Covers underlying strokes	Grainy Soft Cover	Grainy Hard Cover	Grainy Flat Cover	Grainy Edge Flat Cover
Builds up underlying strokes toward black	Grainy Soft Buildup	Grainy Hard Buildup		Grainy Edge Flat Buildup
Clones Colors from a Clone Source	Grainy Soft Cover Cloning	Grainy Hard Cover Cloning		
Smears existing paint	Grainy Drip	Grainy Hard Drip		
Paints in Masking Layer	Grainy Soft Mask Cover			Grainy Edge Flat Mask Cover
Paints in Wet Layer	Grainy Wet Buildup; Grainy Wet Abrasive			

Table 14.2 shows more cross-references for brushes that do not react with paper grain. For example, if you want a brush that does not react to paper grain and covers underlying strokes with semi-antialiased edges, you would select the Flat Cover method.

444

Table 14.2. Brush Methods that Do Not React with Paper Grain.

Description	Antialiased Edges	Semi-Antialiased Edges	Antialised Edges
Covers Underlying Strokes	Soft Cover	Flat Cover	
Builds up underlying strokes toward black	Soft Buildup; Soft Variable Buildup		
Clones colors from a clone source	Soft Cover Cloning; Drip Cloning	Hard Cover Cloning	
Smears Existing Paint	Drip; Drip Cloning	Hard Drip	
Paints in Masking Layer	Soft Mask Cover		Flat Mask Cover

In addition to the methods shown in the previous two tables, there are also several Eraser methods.

- **Soft Paper Color** removes brush strokes and restores paper color. The strokes are antialiased. The paper color that is restored with this command can be changed by using the Canvas | Set Paper Color command before using an eraser with this method. This method is typical of the standard erasers (Fat Eraser, Small Eraser, and so on).

- **Soft Paint Remover** removes brush strokes and restores them with white, regardless of the color of the paper. The Bleaching erasers and the Dodge brush are examples using this variant.

- **Soft Paint Thickener** deepens the color of the underlying strokes. The Darkener variants of the erasers and the Burn brush are examples of how to use this method.

- **Soft Mask Colorize** works in the masking layer of a Painter document. Used with the current brush, it replaces the positive areas of the masking layer with the current primary color and the negative areas of the mask with the current secondary color.

The Brush Controls Palette

Open the Brush Controls Palette by using the Windows | Brush Controls command or the quick-key combination of Ctrl-4 in Windows or Cmd-4 in Mac.

This palette is one of two that contain the various settings that make up a brush. The other, the Advanced Controls Palette, is discussed later in "The Advanced Controls Palette." It is here that you can make modifications to a brush or define the settings to create brushes of your own.

Though a bit complex at first, carefully studying the properties of a brush will further your understanding of the results you can expect from a particular brush. With this knowledge, you will soon be customizing and creating your own brushes and brush libraries.

NOTE It is important to note that if you make changes to a brush while painting, the changes are temporary. If you change to another brush and then return to the brush you modified earlier, its settings will have reverted back to its defaults. If you want to keep the changes you've made to a brush, you have to save it using the Save Variant or Save Built Variant commands mentioned previously.

Brush Controls | Size Palette

The Brush Controls | Size Palette, shown in Figure 14.3, is probably the most commonly used member of the Brush Controls palettes. Here, you can adjust the size of the brush stroke and adjust the variance between the narrowest and widest portions of the stroke. Additionally, you can set the profile of the brush to one of six different types of brush dabs.

Figure 14.3.
The Brush Controls |
Size Palette controls the
profile and dab of each
brush.

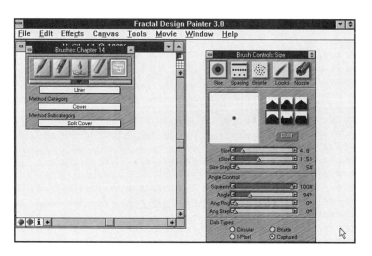

Every brush has a Tip and a Dab type. The Tip is somewhat like a cross-sectional view of the brush hairs. It defines how paint is distributed with each dab from the brush—which areas apply more paint and which areas apply less paint. There are six Tip types, which are listed and described in Table 14.3.

Table 14.3. Settings in the Brush Controls | Size Palette.

Control	Type	Most Common Setting	Setting Range	Function
Tip	Pointed Profile	varies	n/a	More paint is applied toward the center of the stroke, and density falls off rapidly toward the outer edges. Grainy Water is a brush that uses the Pointed profile.
	Medium Profile	varies	n/a	A wide area of dense paint toward the middle, with rapid falloff to light density at the edges. Some cloners, erasers and chalks use this setting, among others.
	Linear Profile	varies	n/a	Maximum paint density at the center with even falloff to lighter density at the edges. Some Crayons, Liquids and Brushes use the Linear Profile.
	Dull Profile	varies	n/a	Maximum paint density at the center with a small amount of falloff toward the edges. Some Pencils, Brushes and Erasers use the Dull Profile.
	Water-color Profile	varies	n/a	Maximum paint density is toward the edge of the stroke, and falls off toward the middle to a medium density. Typical of the Water Color brushes, some Pens also use this setting.
	1-Pixel Edge	varies	n/a	Maximum density throughout the stroke, with the exception of the

continues

Table 14.3. continued

Control	Type	Most Common Setting	Setting Range	Function
				edges, which have a 1-pixel wide antialiased area.
Size		varies	2.0 to 296.8	Determines the overall width of the stroke.
"+/-" Size		varies	1.0 to 2.72	The difference between the narrowest and widest width of the stroke.
Size Step		5%	1 to 100%	Controls how quickly the stroke changes from its narrowest to its widest width. Lower values indicate a smoother transition, and higher values make the transition more rapid.
Dab Type	Circular	X	n/a	Dabs will be circular, or elliptical if angle control is set. The size of the circular dab is controlled in the Brush Controls | Size Palette.
	Bristle		n/a	Bristle dabs will be controlled by the settings in the Brush Controls | Bristle Palette. When this type of brush is selected, a bristle dab will appear in the brush size preview window.
	Captured		n/a	The brush will be made from a captured brush dab, created using the Capture Brush command.
	1-Pixel		n/a	The dab will be 1 pixel in width, and changes in the Brush Controls | Size Palette will have no effect.

Each brush also has a Dab type, which is somewhat like an overhead view of the brush. Each brush stroke is actually composed of a series of dabs placed closely together. The spacing of the dabs can be controlled in the Brush Controls | Spacing Palette, described later in this chapter. Most of Painter's brushes are created with Circular dabs, but there are also three other types of dabs that can be used to make up a brush. Bristle dabs are used to create Bristle brushes, which offer very realistic-looking striations and brush hair lines in your strokes. Captured dabs are created by using the Capture Brush command; I will demonstrate how to create these later in Exercise 14.2, "Creating and Capturing a Brush Dab." Finally, 1-Pixel dabs are one pixel wide and are used most commonly for fine touch-up work.

There is a preview window in the Brush Controls | Size Palette that lets you view changes while building a brush. You also can view the brush dab in one of two different modes by clicking inside the preview window. In the *hard view* of the brush, shown in Figure 14.4, is a pair of circles. The inner black circle shows the minimum stroke width of the brush. The outer gray circle shows the maximum width of the brush. The size of these circles will increase or decrease, depending on the Size and ±Size sliders in the Brush Controls | Size Palette.

Figure 14.4.
The hard view of the brush dab shows the minimum and maximum widths of the brush stroke.

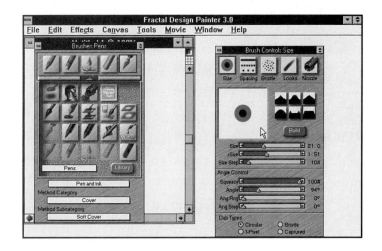

The Size Step slider, shown in Figure 14.5, controls how quickly a brush stroke will change from its narrowest to its widest width during the stroke. If you are using a pressure-sensitive stylus and tablet, changes in width can be controlled by the pressure applied to the stylus. If you're using a mouse, refer to the section later in this chapter that covers the Advanced Controls | Sliders Palette. There, you can learn how to change the size of the stroke based on another property.

Figure 14.5.
The Size Step slider
controls how quickly
the width of the stroke
changes from minimum
to maximum value.

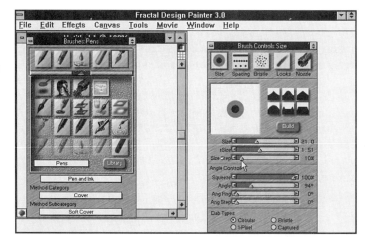

You can change to the brush dab's *soft view,* shown in Figure 14.6, by clicking inside the preview window. In the soft view of the brush, you will see the density distribution of the current brush tip. You will also see the actual appearance of captured brush dabs. The darker areas in this view show where the tip is most dense, and the lighter areas show where the tip of the brush is less dense.

Figure 14.6.
The soft view in the
Brush Controls | Size
Palette show the
density of the brush
stroke.

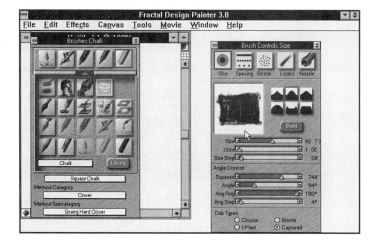

Angled Brush Settings

Table 14.4 shows some additional settings that control properties of an Angled brush. These settings are also found in the Brush Controls | Size Palette.

Table 14.4. Settings in the Brush Controls | Size Palette for Angled Brushes.

Control	Most Common Setting	Setting Range	Function
Angle Squeeze	100%	1 to 100%	Controls the shape of the elliptical dab, or how much a circular dab is "squeezed" to make the ellipse. Lower settings make the dab more round, and higher settings flatten the dab more.
Angle	25	0 to 360 degrees	Sets the angle of the elliptical brush dab. Moving the slider to the left turns the dab clockwise; moving the slider toward the left turns it counterclockwise.
Ang Rng	0	0 to 180 degrees	Controls the range of angles that your brush will contain. If set at 180, your brush will paint every angle from 0 to 180 degrees.
Ang Step	0	0 to 180	If the Ang Rng is degrees set greater than 0, an elliptical brush dab will be placed at every degree increment specified here. Moving this slider toward the left will increase the frequency of dabs in the brush stroke.

Angled brushes are usually created with a Circular brush dab that is flattened using the Angle Squeeze command, and then rotated at an angle defined by the Angle setting. The Ang Rng and Ang Step settings limit the degree orientation and the placement of angles within your brush strokes. If you want to examine some of the brushes that use angle settings, use the Painter Command and

Palette Reference, located on this book's CD, to review settings of the following brushes:

Auto Van Gogh
Calligraphy
Dirty Marker
Driving Rain Cloner
Felt Marker
Flemish Rub
Gritty Charcoal
Impressionist
Impressionist Cloner
Piano Keys
Square Chalk

Brush Controls | Spacing Palette

You might find that after making adjustments to the settings in the Brush Controls | Size Palette, the dabs appear too far apart, making the stroke look like a dotted line. You might also want to change the type of stroke that the brush makes. These types of settings are controlled by the Brush Controls | Spacing Palette, shown in Figure 14.7. Brush Spacing controls the amount of space between the successive dabs that make up a brush stroke. Widening the settings makes the brush appear like a dotted line; narrowing the settings makes the stroke more continuous.

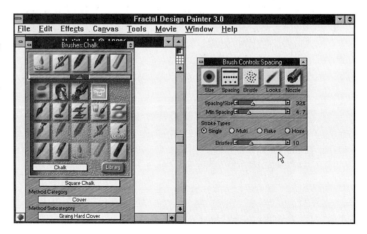

Figure 14.7.
The Brush Controls |
Spacing Palette controls
the amount of space
between the brush
dabs, the type of stroke,
and the number of
bristles in the brush.

Table 14.5 shows the settings available in the Brush Controls | Spacing Palette. Every brush has settings in the Spacing/Size and Min. Spacing sliders; the variations in the settings are too numerous to mention here. The Command and Palette Reference located on this book's CD singles out the various settings so that you can examine them.

Table 14.5. Settings in the Brush Controls | Spacing Palette.

Control	Most Common Setting	Setting Range	Function
Spacing/ Size	50%	1 to 100%	Controls the amount of space between the dabs that make up a stroke. Moving the slider toward the left will decrease the space between the brush dabs, making the stroke appear more dense. Moving the slider toward the right will increase the space between the dabs. Increasing the space too much will produce a stroke that appears like a dotted line, especially noticeable when brushes are increased in size in the Brush Controls	Size Palette. If this occurs, decrease the Spacing/Size slider to reduce the dotted line appearance.
Min. Spacing	1	.1 to 20.0 pixels	Specifies the minimum number of pixels that are spaced between the dabs in the stroke. Moving the slider toward the right will increase the space between the dabs, and will make the stroke appear more like a dotted line.
Stroke Type	Single		A single stroke brush is laid down on a singular path. A single stroke brush can be made to look like a multiple stroked brush by using either the Bristle or the Captured dab types.
	Multi		A Multi (Multiple) stroke brush is made up of several strokes. The Bristles slider controls the number of strokes that make up the brush.

Table 14.5. continued

Control	Most Common Setting	Setting Range	Function
			Multi-stroke brushes can be multicolored, with the color variance set in the Art Materials | Colors Palette.
	Rake		Rake strokes are also made up of several strokes. They can be multicolored as well. The number of bristles in the stroke is set with the Bristles slider at the bottom of the palette. The other settings of a Rake stroke are made in the Advanced Controls | Rake Palette.
	Hose		The Hose stroke is typical of the Image Hose brushes. This stroke is a single stroke, made up of the current Image Hose file which is selected in the Brush Controls | Nozzle Palette.
	Bristles		This slider controls the number of bristles that make up the brush stroke. Brushes can have from 2 to 30 bristles. The most widely used setting for this is 10 bristles.

There are five different stroke types that can make up a brush. The most common stroke type used is the Single stroke, which lays the brush dabs down on your canvas in a single path. The Single stroke type is also used in conjunction with the Bristle or Captured dab types to create brushes that have more of a natural, bristly appearance. You can change the appearance of the brush by revising the stroke type to one of the other three shown here:

■ The Multi stroke type applies several stroke paths together in one single brush stroke. You can set the number of stroke paths by adjusting the Bristles setting in the Brush Controls \| Spacing Palette. You can apply these paths using multiple colors at once. The colors applied can vary based on one of the properties assigned in the Advanced Controls \| Sliders

Palette, described later in this chapter. Examples of multistroke brushes are as follows:

Hairy Brush
Hairy Cloner
Hard Oil Cloner
Oil Brush Cloner
Pure Water Brush
Van Gogh
Van Gogh Cloner
Water Brush Stroke

■ The Rake Stroke is made up of several strokes, which can be multicolored. With the Rake Stroke, you can control the number of bristles in the Brush Controls | Spacing Palette, but additional settings such as contact angle and the spacing between the bristles can be applied in the Advanced Controls | Rake Palette, described later. Examples of strokes using the Rake stroke type are as follows:

Big Loaded Oils
Big Wet Oils
Broad Water Brush
Camel Hair Brush
Cover Brush
Digital Sumi
Loaded Oils
Oil Paint
Penetration Brush
Scratchboard Rake
Small Loaded Oils
Thick Oil
Tiny Smudge
Water Rake

■ The Hose stroke type is used to identify a brush as an Image Hose. Additional Image Hose settings can be identified in the Brush Controls | Nozzle Palette, which is described in Chapter 15.

The Bristles slider in the Brush Controls | Spacing Palette determines the number of bristles in the brush stroke.

Brush Controls | Bristle Palette

When a brush is assigned a Bristle dab type in the Brush Controls | Size Palette, you can use the Brush Controls | Bristle Palette, shown in Figure 14.8, to control the appearance of the bristles in the brush. Bristle settings enable you to create the look of a real brush, complete with hair lines. The diameter of the bristles, random variations in brush marks, density of the bristles, and their variation in size can all be customized in this palette.

455

Figure 14.8.
The Tools | Brushes
Menu contains com-
mands to create new
brushes and maintain
brush libraries.

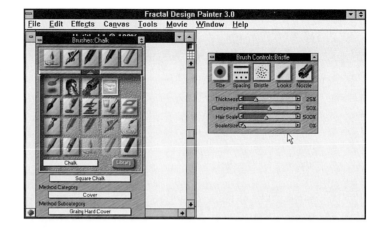

Table 14.6 shows the settings that can be adjusted in the Brush Controls |
Bristle Palette. If you want to see some brushes that work with these settings,
examine the following brushes in the Command and Palette Reference furnished on the CD accompanying this book:

Big Loaded Oils
Big Wet Oils
Loaded Oils
Small Loaded Oils
Smaller Wash Brush
Ultrafine Wash Brush

Table 14.6. Settings in the Brush Controls | Bristle Palette.

Control	Most Common Setting	Setting Range	Function
Thickness	25%	1 to 100%	The Thickness slider controls the diameter of the bristle set of the brush. Moving the slider to the left decreases the diameter of the bristle set. Moving the slider toward the right increases the bristle set diameter.
Clumpi-ness	50%	0 to 100%	The Clumpiness slider produces a random variance across the bristle set. This causes variation in the brush marks. Moving the slider toward the left decreases

Control	Most Common Setting	Setting Range	Function
Hair Scale	500%	100 to 1000%	the amount of randomness. Moving the slider toward the right increases the randomness. The Hair Scale slider controls the density of the bristles in the brush. Moving the slider to the left decreases the bristle density. Moving the slider toward the right increases the bristle density.
Scale/Size	0	0 to 100%	The Scale Size slider controls the amount of size variation in the bristle set. In order for this setting to be effective, the +/- Slider in the Brush Controls | Size Palette must be set to a value other than the minimum value of 1.00. A setting here that is greater than 0% will vary the size of the stroke as it is drawn.

There are two other palettes contained within the Brush Controls Palette. Use the Brush Controls | Nozzle Palette when creating Image Hose brushes. (See Chapter 15, "Image Hose Project.") The Brush Controls | Looks Palette is discussed later in this chapter.

The Advanced Controls Palette

Open the Advanced Controls Palette by using the Window | Advanced Controls command or the quick-key combination of Ctrl-7 in Windows, or Cmd-7 in Mac. This palette contains advanced and specialized settings that make up specialty brushes. It is here that you can make advanced modifications to brushes.

Advanced Controls | Rake Palette

The Advanced Controls | Rake Palette is shown in Figure 14.9. Rake settings are applicable only for those brushes that are specified as Rake Strokes in the Brush Controls | Spacing Palette. Rakes are strokes that are composed of multiple strokes, side by side, giving a somewhat bristly appearance.

Figure 14.9.
*The Advanced Controls
| Rake Palette controls
settings that are
applicable to Rake
strokes only.*

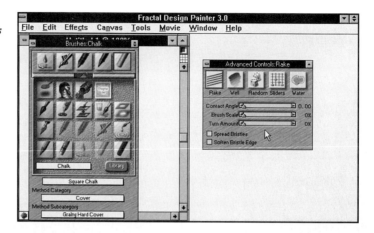

These settings determine the characteristics of a rake stroke—how much of the brush touches the canvas, the spacing between the bristles, how it reacts when you turn the brush, whether the brushes spread farther with pressure, and whether the edges of the brush paint softer than the inner bristles. Table 14.7 shows the settings available in this palette.

Table 14.7. Settings in the Advanced Controls | Rake Palette.

Control	Most Common Setting	Setting Range	Function
Contact Angle	0.00	0.00 to 3.14	If the brush is specified as a Rake type brush in the Brush Controls	Spacing Palette, the contact angle becomes applicable. The Contact Angle slider determines how much of the brush touches the canvas. Decreasing the contact angle setting (moving it toward the left) causes less of the brush to come in contact with the canvas and keeps the width of the bristle dab narrow. This gives the appearance that a small portion of the brush is touching the canvas. Increasing the contact angle setting (moving it toward the right) causes more of the brush to come in contact with the canvas, and will widen the brush to its largest possible

Control	Most Common Setting	Setting Range	Function
			width. This gives the appearance that the entire brush is touching the canvas.
Brush Scale	0%	0 to 2500%	The Brush Scale slider controls the spacing between the individual bristles in the brush. To decrease the space between the bristles, move the slider toward the left. To increase the space between bristles, move the slider toward the right. The size of each bristle is determined by the settings in the Brush Controls | Size Palette.
Turn Amount	0%	0 to 200%	The Turn Amount setting determines how the brush will react when painting a curved line. When painting with a real brush, its bristles widen or narrow depending on their position in the curve. Decreasing the turn amount slider will minimize the amount that the brush changes width. Increasing the turn amount slider will make the variations in the brush more pronounced.
Spread Bristles	Off	On or Off	The Spread Bristles checkbox determines if the bristles of the brush will be spread more when pressure is applied to the brush.
Soften Bristle Edge	Off	On or Off	With the Soften Bristle Edge checkbox on, the outer edged bristles will be transparent.

Advanced Controls | Random Palette

Sometimes you want a stroke to appear as though it is applied randomly—with a jittered, somewhat shaky appearance. You can control the randomness of a brush stroke with the Advanced Controls | Random Palette, shown in Figure 14.10.

459

Figure 14.10.
The Advanced Controls
| Random Palette
controls the amount of
jitter that appears in a
stroke.

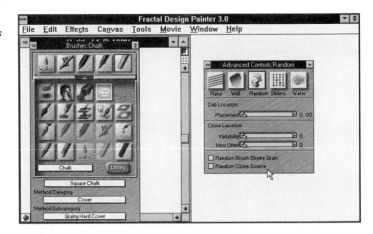

Random settings cause strokes to appear jittered along their edges in a random manner. They also randomize the colors that are picked up from a clone source, as well as placement of paper grain in any image. Table 14.8 shows the settings available in the Advanced Controls | Random Palette.

Table 14.8. Settings in the Advanced Controls | Random Palette.

Control	Most Common Setting	Setting Range	Function
Dab Location Placement	0.00	0.00 to 4.00	The Dab Location Placement Slider introduces a random jitter into the brush stroke dabs, making the stroke appear less smooth. Dabs of paint will appear in a random nature outside the path of the brush stroke. Moving the slider toward the left decreases the amount of randomness in the stroke dabs. Moving the slider toward the right increases the amount of randomness.
Clone Location | Variability	0	0 to 50	The Clone Location | Variability slider controls the randomness of the place at which Painter picks up an image in a

Control	Most Common Setting	Setting Range	Function
			source document for cloning into a destination image. Moving the slider toward the right increases the randomness of the clone location.
Clone Location | How Often	0	0 to 15	The Clone Location | How Often slider determines how often Painter will randomly displace part of an image when it picks up parts from the original source document. Moving the slider to the right increases the time between moves, thereby decreasing the number of times it displaces the image. This makes the clone document smoother in appearance. Moving the slider toward the left decreases the time between moves, thereby increasing the number of times it displaces the image. This makes the clone document rougher in appearance.
Random Brush Stroke Grain	Off	On or Off	With the Random Brush Stroke Grain setting On, a brush will randomize the placement paper grain while making the stroke. This setting will work with any document, not just a clone.
Random Clone Source	Off	On or Off	You can increase the randomness in a clone source by turning on the Random Clone Source option. Pieces will be taken randomly from your source document, causing a lot of distortion in your clone document.

There are a couple of approaches to randomizing the jitter of a stroke. One method is to adjust the setting of the Dab Location Placement in this palette. There are 21 brushes that use this method. The Broad Water Brush, Auto Van Gogh, Flemish Rub, and Impressionist are four that you can examine. The remaining brushes using this approach are listed in the Command and Palette Reference.

Another approach to adding randomness in a stroke is to adjust the Clone Location | Variability and Clone Location | How Often sliders in the Advanced Controls | Random Palette. Five brushes utilize this approach—the Felt Pen Cloner, Chalk Cloner, Melt Cloner, Driving Rain Cloner, and Pencil Sketch Cloner.

You also can randomize how paper grain is applied with the brush. Turning on the Random Brush Stroke Grain will accomplish this function. Brushes using this setting are the Spatter Airbrush, Brushy, Huge Rough Out, Total Oil Brush, and Thick Oil.

Advanced Controls | Sliders Palette

The Advanced Controls | Sliders Palette, shown in Figure 14.11, identifies how the stroke will react to the way you paint it. You can set various parameters set for the stroke's personality—stroke size, jitter, opacity, grain, color, angle, resaturation, and bleed power (which are all user-customizable).

Figure 14.11.
The Advanced Controls | Sliders Palette adds expression to the stroke, based on a number of different types of stroke response.

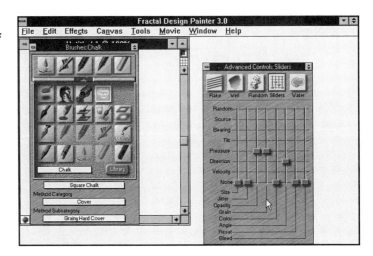

Each of the following parameters can be elected to vary based on *Velocity* (the speed at which you paint the stroke), the *Direction* the stroke is painted, the *Pressure* of the stylus, the *Tilt* of the stylus (not available on some stylus pens), the *Bearing* of the stroke (also not available on some stylus pens), your clone *Source*, or a *Random* change. You can also elect not to assign one of the personality areas by choosing None. If you are using a mouse or a stylus that does not respond to pressure, you will not see any change in expression for those items that have been set to respond to pressure. You can change any of these parameters to respond to Velocity or Direction as an alternative.

SIZE

The Size expression setting determines how the width of the brush stroke will be affected. Most common choices are Pressure, Direction, and Velocity. The minimum and maximum values of brush width are set in the Brush Controls | Size Palette, through the Brush Size and Brush ±Size settings.

JITTER

Stroke Jitter, or the amount of randomness in the edges of the stroke, can also be controlled automatically. The amount of Jitter is set in the Advanced Controls | Random Palette. All brushes furnished with Painter have this setting at None.

OPACITY

You can adjust the Opacity of a stroke in the Controls | Brush Palette. You can have Painter base the stroke opacity automatically on an expression method by adjusting the Opacity slider in the Advanced Controls | Sliders Palette. Users of pressure-sensitive styli would want to set a brush stroke's Opacity to Pressure here, but mouse users might consider changing this setting to Velocity or Direction for some interesting results.

GRAIN

Like the Opacity setting, the Grain of a stroke can be adjusted in the Controls | Brush Palette. The Grain setting determines how much of the paper texture is allowed to show through a brush stroke. You can set this to respond to stylus pressure, but mouse users can also try setting the Grain Slider in the Advanced Controls | Sliders Palette to Velocity or Direction.

COLOR

The Color setting becomes effective with multicolored brushes. You can choose primary and secondary colors from the Art Materials | Colors Palette, where the ±H, S, and V sliders are adjusted to provide color randomness in each stroke. You vary the colors applied with each stroke based on pressure. Mouse users can try to set this at Velocity or Direction.

ANGLE

The Angle setting determines the direction that the brush dab will be painted. This effect is more noticeable with brushes that have elliptical dabs, such as Auto Van Gogh and Flemish Rub.

RESAT

The Resat setting determines how much color is replenished with the stroke. Resaturation amount is determined by the settings in the Advanced Controls | Well Palette.

BLEED

The Bleed setting determines how much the strokes blend or mix together. Bleed amount is determined by the settings in the Advanced Controls | Well Palette.

Advanced Controls | Well Palette

The Advanced Controls | Well Palette, shown in Figure 14.12, provides settings that tell the brush how to interact with the painting medium, how much the paint mixes together, and how quickly or slowly the paint flows from the brush.

Figure 14.12.
The Advanced Controls | Well Palette identifies how colors mix together when strokes are applied.

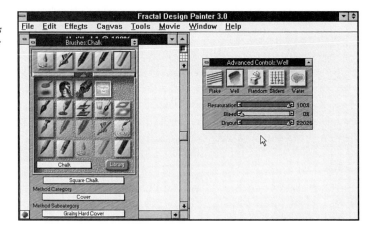

Table 14.9 shows the settings in the Advanced Controls | Well Palette. Many of the Water brushes, brushes with *Wash* in their variant name, and others such as the Waxy Crayon and Oil Pastel use these settings. You can see a complete list in the Command and Palette Reference on the CD accompanying this book.

Table 14.9. Settings in the Advanced Controls | Well Palette.

Control	Most Common Setting	Setting Range	Function
Resaturation	100%	0 to 100%	The Resaturation Slider determines how well a brush replenishes color. In comparison to real world painting, this would most

Control	Most Common Setting	Setting Range	Function
			likely be equivalent to how well a brush loads paint. Moving the slider toward the left decreases the saturation of the brush, making the brushes dry out quicker. Moving the slider toward the right increases the brush's saturation, making the color last longer.
Bleed	0%	0 to 100%	The Bleed setting determines how well colors from the brush mix together. Moving the slider to the left decreases the bleed amount, and makes the color less susceptible to mixing. Moving the slider to the right increases the bleed amount, making the colors mix together more.
Dryout	22026 pixels	1.0 to 22026 pixels	The Dryout setting pertains to how quickly a brush will run out of its paint. Moving the slider toward the left will decrease the number of pixels to which the brush applies paint. Moving the slider toward the right will increase the number of pixels to which the brush applies paint.

Exercise 14.1. Creating a New Brush Type

Use the Save Brush command when you want to create a new brush category in the Brushes Palette. This is a brush folder into which you place brush variants.

Before using the Save Brush command, you might want to create an image to be used as an icon in the Brush Library. You can create the image in any of the drawing formats supported by Painter. Remember that the icon has to be captured as a square.

You're going to make a new brush to be used in our oil painting image. Keep in mind when creating this brush that you want to use it to paint blades of grass in your oil painting. Rather than save this new brush into one of Painter's existing brush types, begin by creating a new brush type of your own. To save a brush category into the Brushes Palette, do the following:

1. Open or create an image to be used as an icon representation of your brush folder. If you don't want to create one now, open the BRSICON.RIF file (located on this book's CD). This image is shown in Figure 14.13. Notice that this image has been created in a square-shaped document.

Figure 14.13.
Create or open an
image to be used as
your Brush Library
icon.

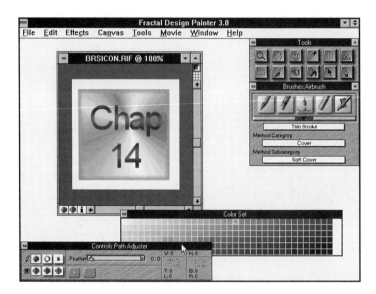

2. If you created your icon image in a square document, such as that shown, you can select the entire image using the Edit | Select All command. If your image is not square, choose the Rectangular Selection Tool from the Tools Palette.

3. To capture a square area, simultaneously press the Ctrl and Shift (Windows) or Control and Option keys (Mac) while using the Rectangular Selection Tool. Then click your mouse or stylus at one of the corners of the area you want to select. You will see the area turn into a square that will follow the cursor as you move it. When the square surrounds the area you want to select, release the mouse or stylus. The selection will turn into a marquee.

4. To place the icon into the currently open Brush Library, choose the Tools | Brushes | Save Brush command, shown in Figure 14.14.

Figure 14.14.
The Save Brush
command places the
icon into the currently
open Brush Library.

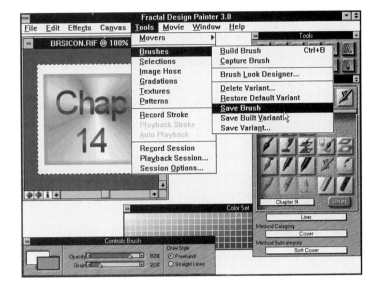

5. After you choose the command, the Save Brush Style dialog box will appear. Name your brush folder. In Figure 14.15, the brush folder has been named Chapter 14. Click OK to place the icon in the Brush Library.

Figure 14.15.
Assign a name to your
brush folder in the Save
Brush Style dialog box.

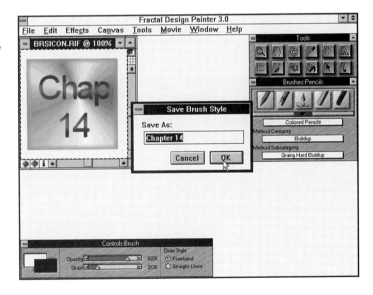

6. Figure 14.16 shows the brush icon placed into the current library. Notice that the box that normally shows the variant names is blank, indicating that no items are in the folder yet.

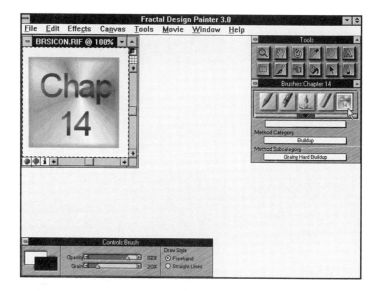

Figure 14.16.
The icon is placed in the Brush Library, ready to accept new brush variants.

Exercise 14.2. Creating and Capturing a Brush Dab

Painter 3 lets you create custom brushes by designing your own brush dabs. These brush dabs, which can be any type of shape, can be captured and placed into the Brush Controls | Size Palette. After that, you can alter settings and save the captured brush into a Brush Library.

Next, you create an image that represents the brush dab:

1. Using the File | New command, create a document with a white paper background. The document can be any size you like.

2. Draw some dots of various sizes and shapes using any of Painter's brushes. In the example shown in Figure 14.17, the Feather Tip airbrush was used. You can use shades of gray to define antialiased or partially transparent areas for the brush stroke. White areas will be fully transparent.

3. One way to add antialiasing around all the dots in your brush dab is to use the Soften command. Choose Edit | Select All to select the entire image. Then, choose Effects | Focus | Soften and set the slider to around 3 pixels. Choose OK to apply the effect to your brush dab.

4. Press Ctrl-Shift in Windows, or Control-Option in Mac while using the Rectangular Selection Tool to draw a square-shaped selection around the dab picture. Your image should look similar to Figure 14.17.

5. Choose Tools | Brushes | Capture Brush, as shown in Figure 14.18.

Figure 14.17.
A square selection is
created with the
Rectangular Selection
tool.

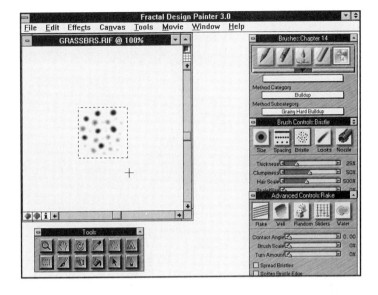

Figure 14.18.
Capture the selected
area as a brush dab
with the Capture Brush
command.

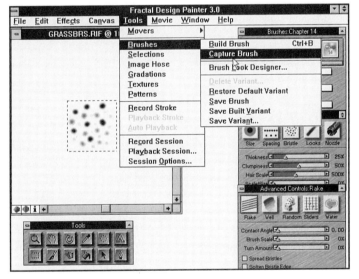

6. You can view your captured brush dab in the Soft View mode within the Brush Controls | Size Palette, as shown in Figure 14.19. Notice that at the bottom of the Brush Controls | Size Palette, the Dab type is identified as Captured.

469

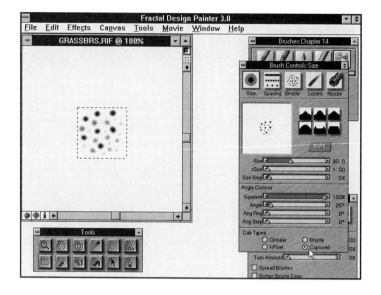

*Figure 14.19.
You can view your
captured brush dab in
the soft view of the
Brush Controls | Size
Palette.*

At this point, you have a brush dab that can be viewed in the Brush Controls |
Size Palette. To view the brush dab, open the Brush Controls Palette (Ctrl-4 in
Windows, Cmd-4 in Mac) and click the Size icon. The dab will appear in the
preview window. The Dab type at the bottom of the Brush Controls | Size
Palette is set to Captured.

Refining Brushes

The next logical step in this process is to make adjustments to the brush settings, in the Brush Controls Palette and Advanced Controls Palette. You can
preview changes in Brush Control settings in one of two ways. One method is to
create a new document. Test strokes you make in the blank document can be
periodically cleared away to make room for new test strokes. In this manner,
you can tell what the strokes will look like in an actual image.

If you want to automatically view changes in the stroke as a brush is revised
and rebuilt, you can use the Brush Look Designer.

The Brush Look Designer

One of the functions of the Brush Look Designer is to let you view changes that
you make to brushes while you are making them. The Brush Look Designer
offers ways to preview what your brush strokes will look like on a light or dark
background, as well as how it will interact with smearing light and dark colors.

You can also save Brush Looks into a library from this window. With Brush
Looks, you can link paper grains or Image Hose Nozzles to a brush and recall

them later from your Brush Look Libraries. This saves you time and allows you to save combinations that work well for you.

To use the Brush Look Designer, use the following procedure:

1. Open the palettes that you will need to design your brush—the Brush Palette (to choose brushes for modification), the Art Materials Palette (to pick sample colors or papers to test your strokes with), and most importantly, the Brush Controls Palette (to modify the characteristics of the brush that you are creating).

2. Choose Tools | Brushes | Brush Look Designer. The Brush Look dialog box will appear.

3. Make changes to your brush in the Brush Controls Palette. As you adjust the settings, click the Build button to build the brush and then watch the changes as a stroke is automatically rendered in the Brush Look Designer preview window.

4. If you want to link a paper texture to a brush, select the paper you want to link and save it along with the brush look.

5. Notice that there are five color windows in the lower portion of the Brush Look dialog box. The first is white. The second is deep brown by default, but you can change the color. The third is black. The fourth is vertical stripes of white and your chosen color. The fifth is horizontal stripes of white and your chosen color.

   - ■ To change the second window and the striped windows to use the current color, click the Set Colors button at the lower end of the dialog box.

   - ■ Clicking the color squares will automatically show you a preview of what your strokes will look like in any given situation. The white area is good for previewing brush strokes on light backgrounds. The current color is good for previewing how your strokes will look on any color, or for testing bleach erasers. The black area is good for testing strokes made with Cover method brushes, and for bleaches. The striped areas are good for testing water colors or brushes that smear existing color.

6. When you are done making changes to your brush, click the Save button. The Name Brush Look dialog box will appear. Type in a name, and click OK or press the Enter key. The Brush Look will then be saved and become available in the currently open Brush Controls | Looks Palette.

Exercise 14.3. Fine-Tuning the Brush

Now that you have a captured brush dab ready to fine-tune, you'll learn about adjusting the Brush Control settings. If you haven't opened the Brush Controls |

Size Palette, do so now. You'll also use the Brush Look Designer to create a new brush.

1. Choose the Tools | Brushes | Brush Look Designer command. The Brush Look dialog box will appear, and an initial stroke will be drawn in its preview window.

2. Make a stroke, from bottom to top, that would be typical of a stroke you would use when painting grass. If you're using a pressure-sensitive stylus, start at the base with heavier pressure and pull quickly toward the top, lightening pressure as you go. You will be able to set the properties of the brush to respond to pressure. If you're using a mouse, start off slowly at the bottom and increase speed toward the top. Here, the brush can be set to respond to Velocity.

3. From the Brush Controls | Size Palette, adjust the Size slider to around 30. In some cases, you may need to build your brush after this step, using Ctrl-B in Windows or Cmd-B in Mac. Your sample stroke will be redrawn in the Brush Look preview window to reflect the increased size of the brush. Your stroke probably looks like a series of dots, as shown in Figure 14.20.

Figure 14.20.
The initial version of
the stroke made with
your captured dab
looks like a series of
dotted lines.

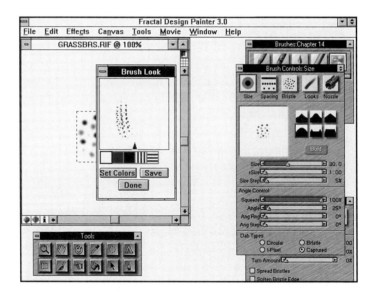

4. Now, adjust the ±Size Slider, shown in Figure 14.21, to around 1.3. Then build the brush using the Ctrl-B (Windows) or Cmd-B (Mac) quick-key combination. This setting represents the amount of variation between the widest and the narrowest part of the brush stroke. Later, in step 13, when you adjust settings in the Advanced Controls | Sliders Palette, you'll be able to see a change in your stroke based on pressure (for stylus users) or Velocity (for mouse users).

Figure 14.21.
Adjust the ±Size Slider
to around 1.3.

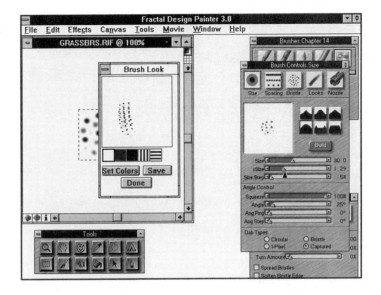

5. I thought it would be nice to have the brush paint blades of grass in with soft, antialiased strokes. Also, I wanted strokes placed in the foreground to cover those previously placed. These characteristics are representative of the Soft Cover method. To assign this Method and Method Subcategory to the brush, go to the Brushes Palette. Change the Method to Cover, and change the Method Subcategory to Soft Cover. Your screen will look like the one shown in Figure 14.22.

Figure 14.22.
The Method and
Method Subcategory
can be selected in the
Brushes Palette.

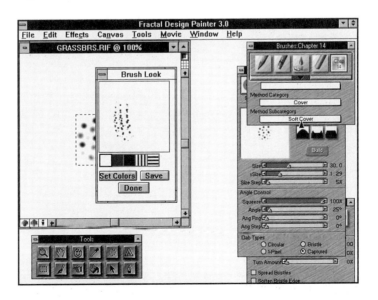

6. Next, go to the Brush Controls | Spacing Palette, which is the icon to the right of the Brush Controls | Size Palette. There are two things to accomplish. First, change the Stroke Type to Rake. This was selected so that you could widen the space between the blades of grass in the Advanced Controls | Rake Palette (discussed later).

7. Now, adjust the Spacing/Size slider until you get the appearance of a solid line, as shown in Figure 14.23. For my brush, I reduced the Spacing/Size slider to 10, which seemed to produce nice, solid lines in the brush stroke. You might find it necessary to use the Ctrl-B (Windows) or Cmd-B (Mac) command to update the stroke in the Brush Look Designer.

Figure 14.23.
Adjust the settings in
the Brush Controls |
Spacing Palette to
make the dots appear
closer.

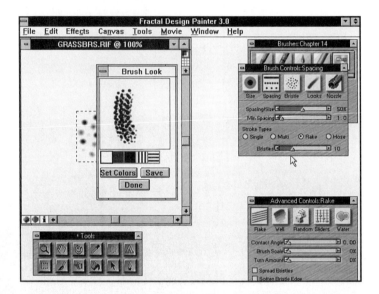

8. Earlier, I defined this brush as one that uses a Rake stroke type. You can refine this type of brush by adjusting settings in the Advanced Controls | Rake Palette, shown in Figure 14.24. Adjust the Brush Scale slider toward the right to widen the space between the brush hairs. This will cause the bristles in the brush to spread out a little, making them look less clumped together and more like individual blades of grass. If you adjust the spacing too far to the right, the brush will begin to look like multiple strokes that have been placed very far apart. For this example, I set the brush scale to 199%.

9. Now, adjust the Contact Angle slider in the Advanced Controls | Rakes Palette. This setting adjusts how much of the brush touches the canvas as you paint. As you move the slider toward the left, less of the brush will touch the canvas, producing narrower strokes. Moving the slider toward the right will have the opposite effect. I used a setting of .43 in my brush.

Figure 14.24.
Adjust the Brush Scale and Contact Angle slider in the Advanced Controls | Rake Palette to spread your brush bristles further apart.

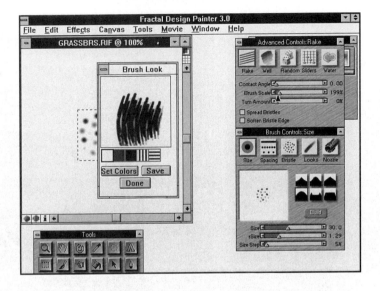

10. Now, let's see what the grass strokes look like in color. Open the Art Materials | Colors Palette (Ctrl-3 in Windows or Cmd-3 in Mac). Maximize it, if necessary, by clicking the button at the top right of the palette. Choose a golden yellow as your secondary color in the back rectangle, and a deep, dark green as your primary color in the front rectangle.

11. Next, go to the Color Variability sliders at the bottom of the Art Materials | Colors Palette. Adjust the ±H, S, and V sliders under the Color Variability heading until you get a nice blend of values in color when you make your strokes. Figure 14.25 shows some adjustments made in the Colors Palette and the resulting strokes in the test image.

Figure 14.25.
Select two colors in the Art Materials | Colors Palette and adjust the Color Variability sliders to apply color variations with the strokes.

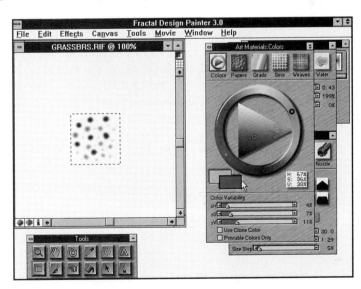

12. Now you'll add some expression settings to your brush stroke. To do this, click the Sliders icon to open the Advanced Controls | Sliders Palette. If you have a pressure-sensitive stylus, set some of the properties of the stroke to respond to the pressure applied by the stylus. If you use a mouse, you might want to try setting some of the properties to Velocity or Direction to achieve similar results. In Figure 14.26, the Size, Opacity, and Color of the stroke are set to respond to stylus pressure, and the reaction to paper grain will respond to the velocity or speed at which the stylus is dragged. Make more test strokes to see how your brush is coming along.

Figure 14.26.
Expression is added
(with Advanced
Controls | Sliders
Palette) to the stroke.

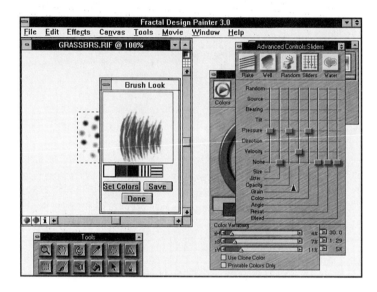

This completes the setting adjustments for this brush. As you can see, creating a brush of your own isn't that difficult! The CD provided with this book contains a Command and Palette Reference that lists in detail what the various brush settings do, and also gives a complete reference of the settings that are pertinent to each brush provided with Painter. An added feature is that you can search for brushes that use a specific brush setting to see how it affects the brush. If you want to get into making more of your own brushes, check it out!

Exercise 14.4. Saving Your Brush

After all that work, you don't want the brush to disappear on you, so you have to save it. You're going to save your brush into the Chapter 14 brush category you created in the previous exercises.

1. Return to the Brushes Palette and verify that the Chapter 14 icon is still the active brush category.

2. Choose Tools | Brushes | Save Variant. The Save Variant dialog box, shown in Figure 14.27, will appear. Type a name, such as *Grassy Brush,* for

your brush. Then click OK to save the brush into the currently selected category.

After this command is applied, you'll be able to select this brush just like any other Painter brush! You should now see the Grassy Brush available as a selection under the Chapter 14 brush category. Each brush category can have up to 32 variants.

Figure 14.27.
The Save Variant
dialog box.

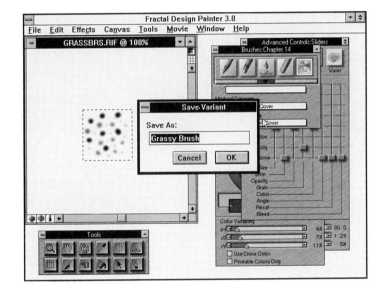

Brush Mover

The Chapter 14 brush category is one of those available in Painter's default Brush Library. You can create a new Brush Library in the Brush Mover and then move your custom brushes into that library. Notice that in most palettes, the number of choices is limited to 25 or less. This keeps the size of the palette somewhat manageable.

NOTE All of the Movers in Painter work in much the same manner. The commands outlined here are fairly representative of the other movers provided with Painter.

Using the Brush Mover

Use the Brush Mover to move brushes from one library to another. You can access the Brush Mover with the Tools | Movers | Brush Mover command.

To use the Brush Mover:

1. Choose Tools | Movers | Brush Mover. The Brush Mover dialog box, shown in Figure 14.28, will appear.

Figure 14.28.
The Brush Mover is
used to create new
brush libraries and
move brushes between
two libraries.

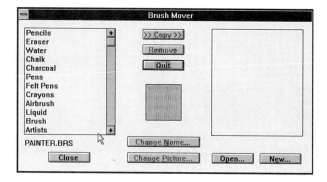

2. The dialog box contains two scrolling windows. When you first open the Brush Mover, the names of the brushes in the currently opened Brush Library are contained in the window on the left side, and the window on the right side is blank.

   ■ To select a different library in the either window, click the Close button beneath the library you want to close. The window will become blank, and the Close button will revert to an Open button. Click the Open button and choose the directory and Brush Library file (.BRS extension) you want to open. Click OK or press Enter to open the file. The items contained in the selected library will appear in the window.

   ■ To open a new library in either window, click the Open button on either side and choose the directory and Brush library file (.BRS extension) you want to open. Click OK or press Enter to open the file. The selected library will appear in the window.

   ■ The preview window in the center of the dialog box shows a thumbnail version of the currently highlighted brush.

   ■ To copy a brush from one library to another, highlight the brush name you want to copy. Check the preview window to see if this is the brush you want to move. Then click the Copy button in the top center of the dialog box. The name of the copied brush will appear in the opposite window.

   ■ To remove a brush from a library, highlight the brush name you want to delete. Check the preview window to see if this is the brush you want to remove. Then click the Remove button in the center of the dialog box. The name of the Brush will be removed from the window.

- To rename a brush, highlight its name. Check the preview window to see if this is the brush you want to rename. Click the Change Name button in the center of the dialog box and enter a new name for the brush. Click OK to return to the Brush Mover dialog box. The name of the highlighted brush will change to the name you entered.

3. When you are done making changes to the brush libraries, click Quit, located in the center of the Brush Mover dialog box. The changes are automatically saved to the libraries you worked on.

Using the Other Movers

Painter comes with a host of other Movers, which work identically to the Brush Mover. With these Movers, you can create and maintain libraries for other Painter elements, using the procedures outlined in the discussion of Brush libraries and the Brush Mover. The movers can be accessed through the Tools | Movers menu, and are as follows:

- The Paper Mover lets you create Paper Libraries and move papers between two libraries. Paper Library files are saved with a .PAP file extension. Painter's default Paper Library is contained in the file PAINTER.PAP, located in your Painter subdirectory.

- The Path Mover enables you to create Path Libraries and move paths between two libraries. Path Library files are saved with a .FRS file extension. Painter's default Path Library is contained in the file PAINTER.FRS, located in your Painter subdirectory.

- The Brush Mover, described earlier, saves its files in the .BRS file extension. Painter's default Brush Library is contained in the file PAINTER.BRS, located in your Painter subdirectory.

- The Brush Looks Mover, described later, saves its files in the .BLK file extension. Painter's default Brush Looks Library is contained in the file PAINTER.SET, located in your Painter subdirectory.

- The Session Mover lets you create session libraries and move sessions between two libraries. Session Library files are saved with a .SSK file extension. Painter's default Session Library is contained in the file PAINTER.SET, located in your Painter subdirectory.

- The Floater Mover enables you to create Floater Libraries and move floaters between two libraries. Floater Library files are saved with a .POR file extension. Painter's default Floater Library is contained in the file PAINTER.POR, located in your Painter subdirectory.

- The Lighting Mover lets you create Lighting Libraries and move lighting scenes between two libraries. Lighting Library files are saved with a .LIT file extension. Painter's default Lighting Library is contained in the file PAINTER.SET, located in your Painter subdirectory.

- The Weaving Mover enables you to create Weaving Libraries and move weavings between two libraries. Weaving Library files are saved with a .WEV file extension. Painter's default Weaving Library is contained in the file PAINTER.SET, located in your Painter subdirectory.

- The Gradation Mover enables you to create Gradation Libraries and move gradations between two libraries. Gradation Library files are saved with a .GRD file extension. Painter's default Gradation Library is contained in the file PAINTER.SET, located in your Painter subdirectory.

Exercise 14.5. Creating a Brush Library

You can use the Brush Mover to create a new Brush Library. Then, you'll move the Chapter 14 brush category into the new library, and delete the category from Painter's default Brush Library.

> **NOTE** You normally create items to place into libraries while you are working on your documents. For example, you drag a floater into the Floaters Palette to place it into a library, and you save a brush to a library using the Tools | Brushes | Save Variant command.
>
> In Painter 3.0, you cannot open an *empty* library (one that contains no elements) to place items inside. You work around this by creating a new library in the appropriate Mover. Then you copy an item from the library at the left side of the Mover into the new library at the right side of the Mover. This creates a library that can be opened, allowing additional items to be placed inside. You can delete the item you initially placed in the library after other items have been added.
>
> Painter 3.1 enables you to open empty libraries and place items inside.

You can create a new Brush library from the Brush Mover. This will enable you to move brushes from one library into another library. The steps to do this follow.

1. Select Tools | Movers | Brush Mover. A Brush Mover dialog box will appear. In the left half of the dialog box, the names of the Brushes in Painter's default library file will appear, with the Chapter 14 brush category listed at the end. The window on the right side of this dialog box will be blank.

2. Underneath the window on the right side of the dialog box, click the New button. This will open the New Brush File dialog box, shown in Figure 14.29. Here, you define the directory and name of your new Brush Library.

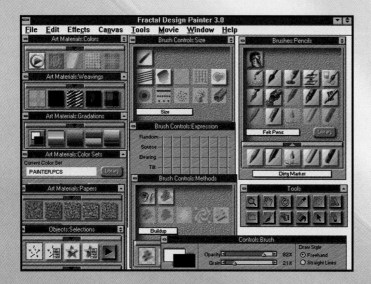

This screen shows just a glimpse of the tools available in Fractal Design Painter.

Here are just some examples of how to use simple colors and textures to create stunning pictures.

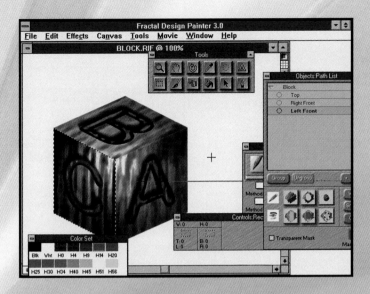

This project in Chapter 8 shows you how to use different lighting effects as well as the different floater effects available.

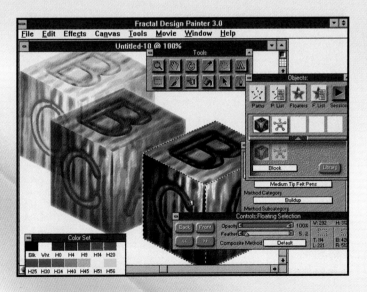

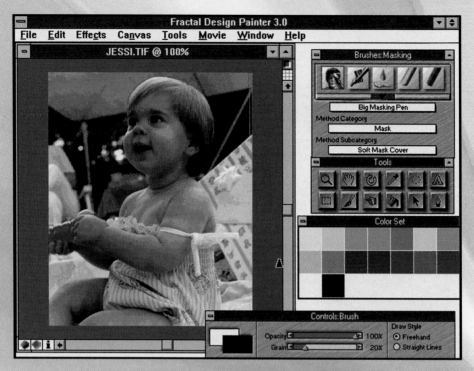

Chapter 9's project demonstrates how to take an existing scanned photo and create an entirely different scene using Painter.

Here, the final touches are added to the Heavenly Kid.

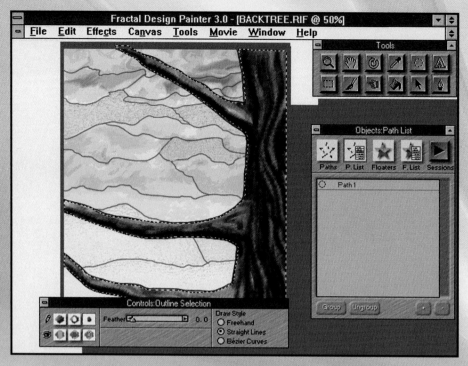

Chapter 10's project of a stained glass window begins with the background, different blues, and an assortment of different brushes provided by Painter.

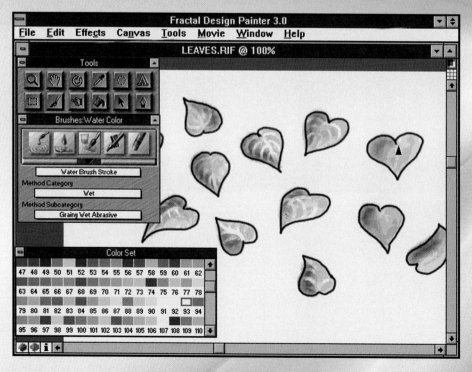

Leaves are drawn and then added to the tree.

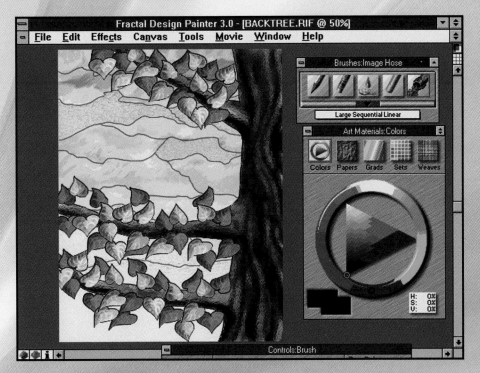

The leaves are placed onto the tree.

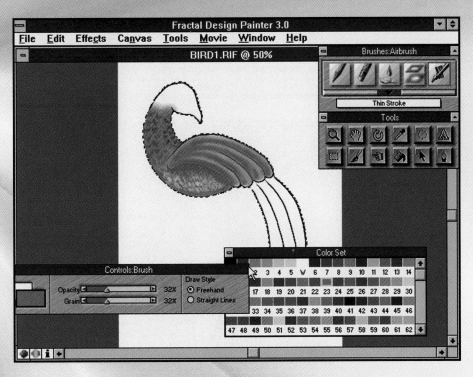

Different stroke techniques are shown for drawing this bird in Chapter 11.

After the birds are created in Chapter 11, they are
added to the stained glass window that was created
in Chapter 10.

A border is added to complete the project.

Another project where a scanned photo is manipulated.

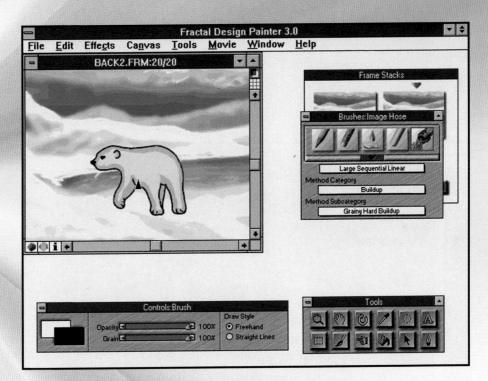

This project in Chapter 19 shows you how to create your own cartoon: first by creating the different poses of your character, next creating the background, and then putting it all together.

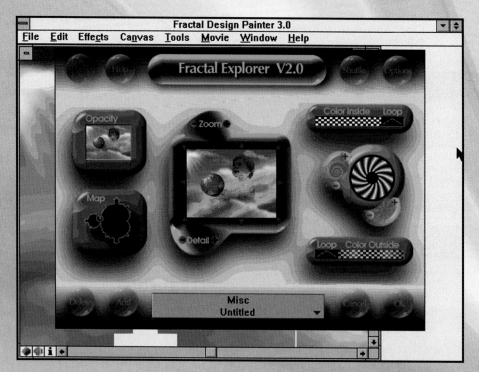

The Fractal Explorer enables you to create fractal effects using variations or hybrids of the Mandelbrot and Julia algorithms in Kai's Power Tools.

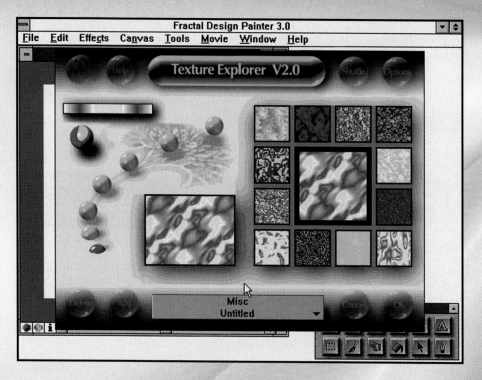

The Kai's Power Tools Texture Explorer window.

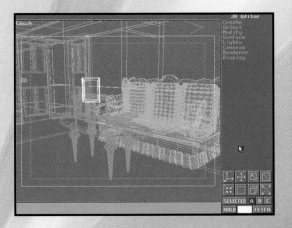
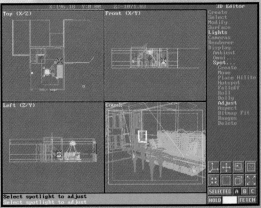

Integrating with 3D Studio.

Two different scenes using the same image.

Strawberries and Cream

You can save either type of combination by clicking the Save button in the Brush Look Designer. After this, the Name Brush Look dialog box, shown in Figure 14.32, prompts you to enter a name for the brush look.

After you save the brush, it appears as a choice in the currently opened library in the Brush Controls | Looks Palette. You open this palette by clicking the Looks icon in the Brush Controls Palette.

Figure 14.32.
You can save a brush/
paper or Image Hose
nozzle file combination
from the Brush Look
Mover.

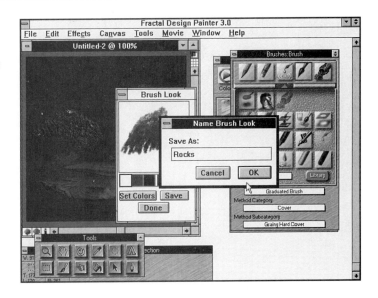

The Brushes Project

The Brushes Project uses techniques such as applying multiple colors with a brush and working with paper grains to achieve three-dimensional brush effects. You'll also use an image hose to paint some plants in the foreground of the image, and you'll have an opportunity to use the grassy brush created in our earlier exercises.

Step 14.1. Painting the Sky with Automatic Strokes

So far in this chapter, you have completed some exercises to help you learn how to create brushes. In the chapter project, which follows, you have the opportunity to use the brush you created.

You begin the image roughing in some sky colors with the Huge Rough Out brush and then applying automatically rendered white strokes using the Brushy brush.

1. Start by opening a 640×480 document. Open the Tools (Ctrl-1 in Windows, Cmd-1 in Mac), Brushes (Ctrl-2 in Windows, Cmd-2 in Mac), and Art Materials (Ctrl-3 in Windows, Cmd-3 in Mac) Palettes.

2. From the Art Materials Palette, choose the Sets icon and then select the CHAP14CS.TXT color set, located on the CD accompanying this book.

3. Using the three blue shades in the color set, rough in some color in the sky with the Huge Rough Out, a Brush variant. Your image will look similar to the one in Figure 14.33.

Figure 14.33.
Rough in some sky
colors with the Huge
Rough Out brush and
the shades of blue in
the color set.

4. Choose Brushy, a Brush variant, and white (the second color in the bottom row) from the color set.

5. Choose Tools | Record Stroke. Draw a short, curved stroke in the sky area. The brush will pick up and move some of the existing color while applying some white at the same time. At the end of the stroke, there will be feathered bristle lines. You can see a hint of this stroke in Figure 14.34.

6. Choose the Rectangular Selection Tool from the Tools Palette and draw a selection around the area of the sky.

7. To render the stroke automatically to the selected area, choose Tools | Auto Playback. The sky will begin to lighten with the white from the brush. You can stop the automatic playback by clicking inside the selected area with your brush or stylus. Your screen will look similar to the one in Figure 14.35.

8. If you want to add more blues back into your automatic brush stroke area, choose one of the shades of blue and then choose the Tools | Auto Playback command again. Click inside the selected area to stop the automatic playback. Figure 14.36 shows some of the color added back in.

Figure 14.34.
*Record a single stroke
of white paint using
the Brushy brush.*

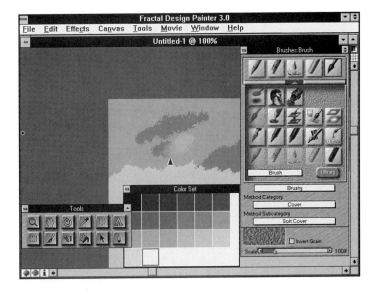

Figure 14.35.
*Select a rectangular
area and use Auto
Playback to apply the
strokes to the selected
area.*

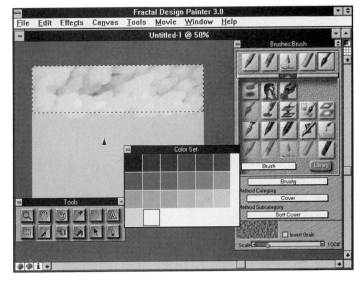

9. To make the clouds and sky look a little more windblown, choose the
   Effects | Focus | Motion Blur command. The Motion Blur dialog box will
   appear. Adjust the radius and angle of the effect until the preview window
   looks suitable, and choose OK to apply the effect. In my example, the
   Radius was set between 7 and 8, and the angle between 25 and 30 degrees.

Figure 14.36.
You can add some blue
back in to the selected
area by reapplying the
Auto Playback
command.

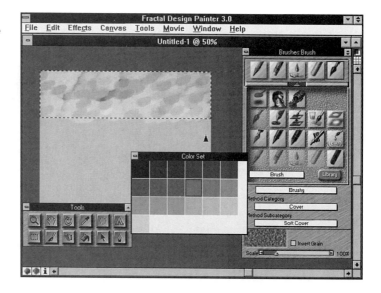

Step 14.2. Coloring the Mountains with Multicolored Strokes

To color the mountains, shades of brown and green were applied using a
multicolored brush. Each time a color was selected, the ±Hue, Saturation, and
Value sliders (±H, S and V) were adjusted to get variations in color as the
strokes were applied.

1. Choose the Outline Selection Tool from the Tools Palette. Using freehand
   drawing mode, draw the outline of mountains beneath the sky, as shown
   in Figure 14.37. You can extend the selection range beyond the image if
   you want; the brush will paint only within the image window.

2. From the Controls | Outline Selection Palette, adjust the feathering of the
   selection to around 3.5.

3. You're going to color the mountains with multicolored, grain-sensitive
   brush strokes. First, choose the Papers icon from the Art Materials Palette.
   From the Papers Palette, select the Rougher paper texture from the drop-
   down listbox.

4. From the Brushes Palette, choose the brush variant called Penetration
   Brush. This brush is sensitive to paper grain.

5. The mountains were colored using the last five colors in the top row,
   starting with dark brown for the most distant mountain at the left side of
   the image, lighter shades of brown for the middle mountain range, and
   green for the hills in the foreground. With each color selected, the Hue,
   Saturation, and Value sliders (±H, S and V sliders) were adjusted in varying
   amounts. An example is shown in Figure 14.38, showing the Hue (±H)
   slider set at 2%, Saturation (±S) at 6%, and Value (±V) at 7%. The strokes
   were randomly *scrubbed* in using varying pressure.

Figure 14.37.
With the Outline
Selection Tool, create a
path to define your
mountain areas.

Figure 14.38.
Paint your mountains
using browns and
greens, with the
Penetration Brush. You
can set the color
variance in the Art
Materials | Colors
Palette.

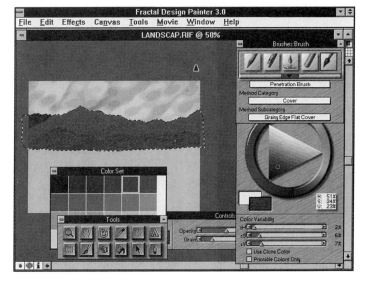

6. After your mountains are done, save the document as LANDSCAP.RIF.

Step 14.3. Applying 3D Brush Strokes to the Mountains

To apply 3D Brush Strokes to the mountains, you have to create a clone source that contains no texture. This will cause the textures applied with your painted strokes to become more three-dimensional (compared to a flat image).

1. Create a new, blank document using the same dimensions as your current image (640×480).

2. Set the new, untitled document as your clone source, using the File | Clone Source command. Then choose the LANDSCAP.RIF project image as your current document.

3. With the mountains path selected and active, choose Effects | Surface Control | Apply Surface Texture. In the Apply Surface Texture dialog box, shown in Figure 14.39, select to apply surface texture using 3D Brush Strokes. Adjust the amount slider, if you want. Click one of the light direction buttons until the 3-D effect in the preview appears to your liking. Check or uncheck the shiny button. Then choose OK to apply the effect to the mountains. Figure 14.40 shows the mountains after the texture has been applied.

Figure 14.39.
Choose to apply surface
texture based on 3D
Brush Strokes.

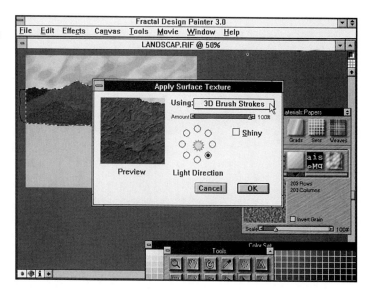

4. Choose Edit | Deselect (Ctrl-D in Windows, Cmd-D in Mac) to deactivate the mountain path.

Figure 14.40.
After surface texture is
applied, the mountains
have more dimension.

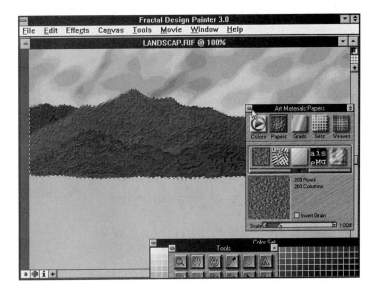

Step 14.4. Coloring the Water

The water was colored using a shade of blue from the chapter color set, with its ±H, S and V sliders adjusted in the Art Materials | Colors Palette. Then, the waves were added in shades of white.

1. From the Brushes Palette, choose the Hairy Brush variant of the Brush tools. Select the fourth color in the second row of the color set as your current color.

2. In the Art Materials | Colors Palette, adjust the ±H, S and V sliders, checking the color variation in the front color rectangle. For this example, I had the sliders set to 10% ±H, 4% ±S, and 9% ±V.

3. Apply a triangular area of varied color in the left portion of your image. Use varying lengths of strokes to add color variation to the water. Figure 14.41 shows the results so far.

4. Choose White from the color set (second color in bottom row) and adjust the sliders to achieve slight variations in the front color rectangle. The settings I used were 4% ±H, 4% ±S, and 9% ±V. Add some choppiness to the water. Mouse users may need to vary the brush size to get similar effects.

5. Using the Rectangular Selection Tool, selected from the Tools Palette, draw a rectangular selection around the water. Try not to extend the selection too far beyond the water area. Choose Effects | Surface Control | Apply Surface Texture. Again, choose to apply the effect using 3D Brush

Strokes. Reduce the Amount slider to around 55-60% and adjust the Light Direction. Shiny is turned off. You will see a preview of the effect in the window, as shown in Figure 14.42. Choose OK to apply the effect.

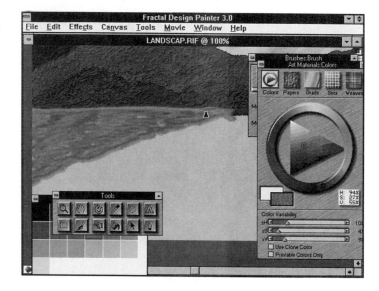

Figure 14.41.
Blue colors are applied to the water using the Hairy Brush.

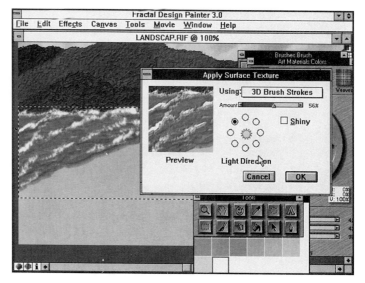

Figure 14.42.
After applying white-caps on the water, apply surface texture again using 3D Brush Strokes.

Step 14.5. Coloring the Grass

Now you have a chance to use the brush you created in a real image! First, you're going to base in a green color in the area for the grass, and apply grass strokes over it.

1. From the Brushes Palette, choose the Big Rough Out variant. Select the fifth color in the first row of the color set and color in the remaining foreground area, as shown in Figure 14.43.

Figure 14.43.
Color the foreground
with green, using the
Big Rough Out variant.

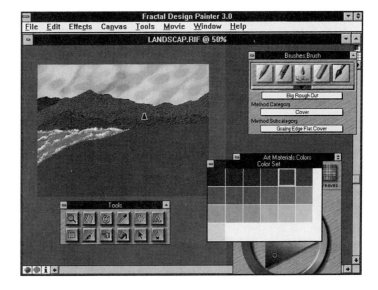

2. Open the drawer of the Brushes Palette and click the Library button. Choose the drive and directory that you saved your Brush Library into, and select the CHAP14.BRS Brush Library, as shown in Figure 14.44. There is also a pre-made version of this Brush Library located on the CD accompanying this book.

Figure 14.44.
Load in the Brush
Library that contains
your Grassy Brush,
created earlier.

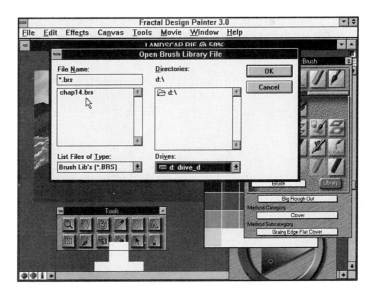

3. From the Art Materials | Colors Palette, click the rear (secondary color) rectangle and choose the golden yellow color in the fifth row of the chapter color set.

4. Click the front (primary color) rectangle in the Art Materials | Colors Palette and choose the fifth color in the top row as the primary color if it is not still selected. Adjust the green color to a slightly darker value in the Art Materials | Colors Palette by dragging the circular indicator inside the triangle downward and slightly toward the left.

5. Adjust the ±H, S and V sliders in the Art Materials | Colors Palette until you get the color mixture you want.

6. Starting from the back portions of the green area, create the grass. Start your strokes at the bottom and stroke upward, releasing pressure while increasing speed slightly toward the end. Figure 14.45 shows the grassy area in progress, and Figure 14.46 shows it completed.

Figure 14.45.
Start applying the
grass from the back,
and work your way
toward the front.

Figure 14.46.
The grassy area is now
complete.

Step 14.6. Coloring the Plant with the Image Hose

The plant in the foreground was painted using one of the Image Hose tools, and some of the nozzle files copied to your hard drive when you installed Painter.

1. To reload the default Painter Brush Library, click the Library button inside the Brushes Palette drawer again. Choose the directory or folder in which Painter was installed on your hard drive. The file PAINTER.BRS (or Painter Brushes) should appear in that directory, as shown in Figure 14.47. Click OK to load the file. Painter's default brushes will be restored in your Brushes Palette.

2. From the Art Materials | Colors Palette, choose Black as your secondary color in the rear rectangle, as shown in Figure 14.48. Then click the front rectangle to reactivate the primary color for later use. Black is going to be mixed with the Image Hose elements to provide darker shading toward the back elements of the plant.

Figure 14.47.
Reload the default
Brush Library from
your Painter directory.

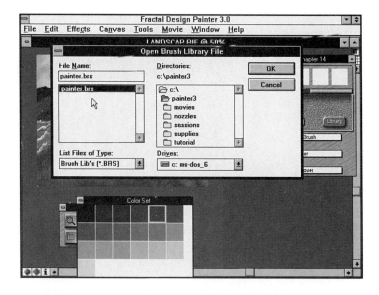

Figure 14.48.
Select black as your
secondary color.

3. Choose Tools | Image Hose | Load Nozzle. In the Select Image dialog box, shown in Figure 14.49, scroll to the directory that Painter was installed to on your hard drive. Then select the NOZZLES subdirectory. You should see several nozzle files. Select PPLANTS.RIF and click OK to load the nozzle.

4. From the Brushes Palette, click the Image Hose icon. You may need to open the palette drawer to gain access to it. Select the Medium Sequential Linear Image Hose.

Figure 14.49.
The PPLANTS.RIF
nozzle file is located in
the NOZZLES
subdirectory of Painter.

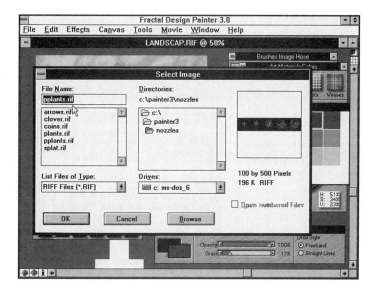

5. Adjust the Grain slider in the Controls | Brush Palette to around 50% to add black to the elements contained in the Image Hose nozzle file. Spray some plants in the foreground of the document, as shown in Figure 14.50.

Figure 14.50.
Mix some black in with
the nozzle file, and
base in an area for your
plant.

6. Next, in the Art Materials | Colors Palette, click the back rectangle to activate the secondary color. Choose the fourth color in the first row of the chapter color set as the current secondary color.

7. In the Controls | Brush Palette, set the Opacity and Grain sliders each to around 70. The elements will now be mixed with green and applied to the background plants at 70% opacity. The foreground elements of the plant will appear lighter than those behind them. Figure 14.51 shows the results so far.

Figure 14.51.
Mix a lesser amount of green with the nozzle file and spray some foreground elements into the plant.

8. Next, choose Tools | Image Hose | Load Nozzle and select the PLANTS.RIF nozzle from the same directory you loaded the previous nozzle file. Figure 14.52 shows this file selected, with its thumbnail in the preview window.

9. From the Brushes Palette, select the Medium Random Spray Image Hose. Leave the Opacity and Grain settings at their default values in the Controls | Brush Palette. Add splashes of little plants scattered here and there in the bigger plant. Your image will look similar to the one in Figure 14.53.

Figure 14.52.
Load the PLANTS.RIF
nozzle file, located in
your Painter
subdirectory.

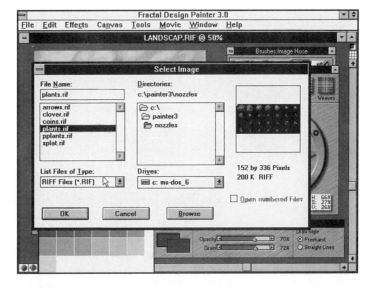

Figure 14.53.
Scatter some elements
into the plant to add
splashes of little plants
here and there.

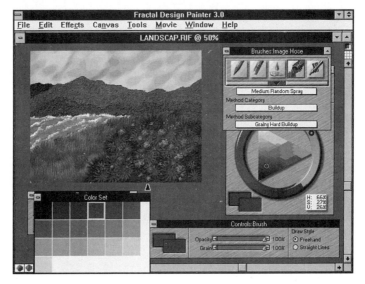

Shading and Highlighting the Mountains

A couple of brushes that fall into their own category are the Burn and Dodge brushes. Burn darkens color beneath it as strokes are applied, with softened strokes similar to that of an airbrush. Dodge creates the opposite effect and lightens colors beneath areas where its strokes are applied. You're going to use these two brushes to add a little more dimension to the mountains.

1. From the Brushes Palette, choose Burn. This brush is shown in Figure 14.54. Adjust its size between 20 and 25.

Figure 14.54.
Choose the Burn brush
from the Brushes
Palette.

2. Add some darkened areas to the mountains at their bases. Figure 14.55 shows some of the areas in the middle mountain range deepened with this brush.

3. Now choose the Dodge brush from the Brushes Palette (shown at the right of the Burn brush in Figure 14.54). Adjust its size to 20–25 and add some highlighted areas to the tops of the mountains. When you're finished, your image will be complete and will look similar to the one in Figure 14.56.

4. Save your document—you're all done!

*Figure 14.55.
Deepen the base of the
mountains with the
Burn brush.*

*Figure 14.56.
Highlight the tops of
the mountains with the
Dodge brush, and
you're done!*

Summary

Now you know how to create brushes from scratch, and you know how each property of a brush affects the look of the brush stroke. If you want to truly customize Painter, you can build brush libraries to hold all your special brushes. You've learned how to paint with multicolored brushes and apply three-dimensional brush stroke effects. Also, you've been introduced to Painter's new Image Hose, which is discussed in more depth in the following chapter. There, you'll learn how to create your own nozzle files.

Image Hose Project

Everyone's talking about them—everyone loves to play with them! The Image Hoses are one of the slickest new features of Painter 3. These brushes paint with images rather than with color, and they're ideal for applying hard-to-paint things such as leaves, flowers, grass, and all those tedious types of items you usually love to avoid.

The concept of Image Hoses is difficult for people to grasp at first, because it is so different from anything that has appeared in graphics software to date. Actually, once you learn what an Image Hose is, its name is quite descriptive. To use an analogy, think of a water hose. It sprays many, many drops of water from its nozzle. An Image Hose is somewhat similar—but instead of spraying many drops of water through its nozzle, it sprays a stream of pictures. The nozzle you attach to the Image Hose contains the pictures that are sprayed.

This chapter discusses how to work with Image Hoses, including how to make your own nozzle files. An Image Hose cannot paint until you load it with a nozzle file. Nozzle files are specially prepared .RIF documents, containing elements that are created from floaters or from Painter movies. The elements in an Image Hose nozzle file are arranged in *ranks*, of which there can be up to three contained in one nozzle file. I will explain the significance of ranks later in this chapter, in the section titled "Loading your Grid-Based Nozzle the First Time."

The Image Hose Variants

The Image Hose variants come in three sizes to handle small-, medium-, and large-sized image sprays. The sizes of the images sprayed through the Image Hose are fixed; that is, if an element takes up a 50×50 pixel area when it is placed into the nozzle file, it will always come out of the Image Hose the same size. If you're spraying small images, use one of the Small Image Hose variants to place the elements closer together. Using a Medium or Large Image Hose variant with small elements spaces the elements farther apart.

You can vary the appearance of the sprayed elements by mixing them with your current *secondary* color—the color that appears in the rear rectangle in the Art Materials | Colors Palette or Controls | Brush Palette. For example, you can mix black with the Image Hose nozzle element to make elements darker in the background and lighter in the foreground. Mix the secondary color with the Image Hose element in varying amounts by adjusting the Grain setting in the Controls | Brush Palette:

- Set the Grain slider at 0 to apply just the secondary color.
- Set the Grain slider at 100 to apply the Image Hose nozzle elements in their true colors.
- Use intermediate settings to mix the two. This is a good way to achieve depth or distance with Image Hose nozzle file elements.

You also can alter the opacity of an Image Hose nozzle file by adjusting the Opacity slider in the Controls | Brush Palette. Move the slider toward the left to decrease opacity, and move the slider toward the right to increase opacity.

This section describes the Painter Image Hoses.

The 3-Rank R-P-D Image Hose

The 3-Rank R-P-D Image Hose is a multiple-rank hose that lets you spray elements into your document based on randomness, pressure, and direction:

- Elements in the first rank are sprayed into your document randomly.
- Elements in the second rank are sprayed into your document based on the pressure you apply to the stylus.
- Elements in the third rank are sprayed into your document based on the direction in which you drag the mouse or stylus.

You must apply special considerations when creating multi-rank image-hose nozzles. These considerations are discussed in the section titled "Loading Your Grid-Based Nozzle the First Time."

The Directional Image Hoses

The Directional Image Hoses deposit images onto the canvas in a linear, not random, fashion. The direction that you drag your mouse or stylus determines which element is sprayed from the nozzle file. The Small Directional Image Hose is designed to spray small images, the Medium Directional Image Hose is designed to spray medium-sized images, and the Large Directional Image Hose is designed to spray large images. You control the spacing of images by adjusting and combining settings in the Brush Controls | Size Palette and the Brush Controls | Spacing Palette.

The Small Luminance Cloner Image Hose

Use the Small Luminance Cloner Image Hose with a cloned image. (You learn more about cloned images in Chapter 16, "Visiting Van Gogh: The Cloner and Artist Brushes.") The light and dark areas of the source image determine how much secondary color is added to the nozzle elements; light areas cause the image-hose nozzle file to be sprayed on darker, and dark areas cause the Image Hose nozzle file to be sprayed on lighter.

The Random Linear Image Hoses

The Random Linear Image Hoses deposit images onto the canvas in a linear fashion, without random placement. The elements are selected at random from the nozzle file. The Small Random Linear Image Hose is designed to spray small images, the Medium Random Linear Image Hose is designed to spray medium-sized images, and the Large Random Linear Image Hose is designed to spray large images. You control image spacing by adjusting and combining settings in the Brush Controls | Size Palette and the Brush Controls | Spacing Palette.

The Random Spray Image Hoses

The Random Spray Image Hoses deposit images onto the canvas randomly; that is, the elements are selected at random from the nozzle file. The Small Random Spray Image Hose is designed to spray small images, the Medium Random

Spray Image Hose is designed to spray medium-sized images, and the Large
Random Spray Image Hose is designed to spray larger images. You control
image spacing by adjusting the Dab Location Placement slider in the Advanced
Controls | Random Palette.

The Sequential Linear Image Hoses

The Sequential Linear Image Hoses deposit images onto the canvas in a linear,
not random, manner. The elements are selected in a sequential order from the
nozzle file. The Small Sequential Linear Image Hose is designed to spray small
images, the Medium Sequential Linear Image Hose is designed to spray
medium-sized images, and the Large Sequential Linear Image Hose is designed
to spray large images. You control image spacing by adjusting and combining
settings in the Brush Controls | Size Palette and Brush Controls | Spacing
Palette.

Using Image Hoses

Here are the basic steps in painting with Image Hoses:

1. Select an Image Hose from the Brushes Palette.
2. Select a nozzle file using the Tools | Image Hose | Load Nozzle command.
3. Position your mouse or stylus where you want to begin painting.
4. Push on the stylus, or click the mouse, and drag the stroke where you
   want to place the elements. You see pictures being sprayed onto your
   document.
5. Release the stylus or mouse button when you're done painting.

The Brush Controls | Nozzle Palette

The Brush Controls | Nozzle Palette settings, used by Image Hose brushes only,
let you select from among Sequential, Random, or Directional sprays from the
hose. You can use these elements separately or combine them. You can elect
whether to spray the images snapped to the Painter's grid, and whether to paint
within the masking layer.

Table 15.1 explains the settings you can adjust in the Brush Controls | Nozzle
Palette.

Table 15.1. Settings in the Brush Controls | Nozzle Palette.

Setting	Option	Function
Ranks	Sequential	The Sequential spray type causes the nozzle to spray elements as you configured

Setting	Option	Function
		them when you saved the nozzle file. Assign this spray type to any of the ranks. The first item in the Floater List is placed in the upper-left position in the nozzle file, and selection continues in a left-to-right sequence in each subsequent row.
	Random	The Random spray type causes the nozzle to select elements from the nozzle file in random order. The Image Hoses that use this spray type are the 3-Rank R-P-D, Small Luminance Cloner, Small Random Linear, Medium Random Linear, Large Random Linear, Small Random Spray, Medium Random Spray, and Large Random Spray.
	Source	The Source spray type causes the nozzle to select elements from the nozzle file based on luminance value. The luminance value in each pixel of the source image is assigned a position in the nozzle file: black (no luminance) is assigned the first position, and white (full luminance) is assigned the last position. You can apply automatic shading using this image-hose type, placing darker nozzle elements toward the back of a stack.
	Bearing	The Bearing spray type causes the nozzle to select elements from the nozzle file based on the bearing of the stylus (if your stylus supports that feature).
	Tilt	The Tilt spray type causes the nozzle to select elements from the nozzle file based on the tilt of the stylus (if your stylus supports that feature).
	Pressure	The Pressure spray type causes the nozzle to select elements from the nozzle file based on the pressure you apply to the stylus. You can achieve an interesting effect when nozzle elements are arranged from smallest to largest in the nozzle file: smaller elements are sprayed with light

continues

Table 15.1. continued

Setting	Option	Function
		pressure, and larger elements are sprayed with heavier pressure.
	Direction	The Direction spray type causes the nozzle to select elements from the nozzle file based on the direction of your stroke. You can achieve interesting effects when nozzle file elements are arranged based on their angle. The Small Directional, Medium Directional, and Large Directional Image Hoses use the Direction spray.
	Velocity	The Velocity spray type causes the nozzle to select elements from the nozzle file based on the speed of your stroke.
	None	When None is assigned as a spray type, only the last element of the nozzle file is painted.
Use Brush Grid		When you check the Use Brush Grid option, the nozzle elements are constrained to the grid set up in the nozzle file. Painting over a grid square paints a new element on top of the previous one.
Add to Mask		The Add to Mask option causes anything painted with the Image Hose to also be applied to the mask. This can help when you're creating more complex nozzle files.

Image Hose Commands

There are three Image Hose commands, available in the Tools | Image Hose menu:

- Use the Load Nozzle command to attach an Image Hose nozzle to the Image Hose variant. You can save loaded nozzle files as Brush Looks to save you reloading them later.

- Use the Make Nozzle From Group command to convert a group of floaters into an Image Hose nozzle file.

- Use the Make Nozzle From Movie command to convert a Painter Movie into an Image Hose nozzle file.

Creating Nozzle Files

In this section you create a file that you can convert to either a floater nozzle file or a grid-based nozzle file. There's a Floater Library named FLOWERS.POR on the CD accompanying this book. This Floater Library contains flowers, a few ferns, and some leaves. You can use this Floater Library to create some little flower arrangements that you can spray into a document with a nozzle file.

When you create a floater nozzle file you don't have to worry about the mathematics of the size of the image. You arrange the floaters in an orderly fashion in the Floater List Palette; group them to create a nozzle file. The dimensions of the nozzle file that is created will be sized appropriately to handle the number of elements in the nozzle file.

However, to prepare for creating a grid-based nozzle file, you must use a bit of mathematics first. You have to look at the dimensions of the largest element in the nozzle file and base your document size on that. For example, if the largest element in your nozzle file measures 100×50 pixels and there are 10 elements, you must create a document that has enough space to place ten 100×50 elements inside it.

The FLOWERS.POR Floater Library has some elements that are quite small, but it also has some that are quite a bit larger. The largest element in this file can be contained within a 70-pixel by 70-pixel space, so you will use that measurement as your grid size.

> ***NOTE*** Grid-based nozzle files can be made up of solid patterns that, when painted using the Brush Grid, form an effect similar to that of a patchwork quilt. The elements in a grid-based nozzle file must be contained within areas that are equal in size, unlike nozzle files made from floaters, which can contain elements of different sizes.

To create a nozzle file:

1. Create a new 490-pixel by 210-pixel image using File | New. This file size will accommodate twenty-one 70×70 grid squares, arranged 7 grid spaces wide and 3 grid spaces high.

2. Choose Canvas | Grid Options, and set up the grid spacing to accommodate the size and quantity of your nozzle elements.

   There are 21 different floaters in this Floater Library. When you're preparing a grid-based nozzle file, you don't want unused grid spaces within the image—so, to contain all the floaters, create an image that is seven grid spaces wide and three grid spaces high. This contains enough spaces to put one floater into each grid square. The width of your document is seven

507

grid squares times the 70-pixel grid width, or 490 pixels. The height of your new document is three grid squares times the 70 pixel grid height, or 210 pixels.

Set the grid at 70 pixels by 70 pixels, as shown in Figure 15.1.

Figure 15.1.
Adjust the grid spacing to 70 pixels wide and 70 pixels high.

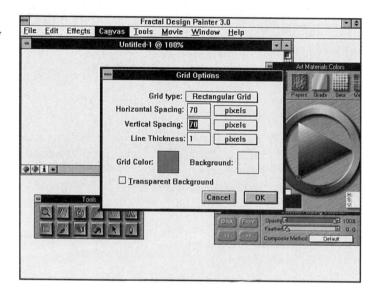

3. Activate the Grid Display by clicking the Grid button inside the scrollbar in the upper-right corner of the document window, or by using the Canvas | View Grid command. You should see seven grid spaces in width and three grid spaces in height in your document window, as shown in Figure 15.2.

Figure 15.2.
Turn on the grid display to view the grid in your image.

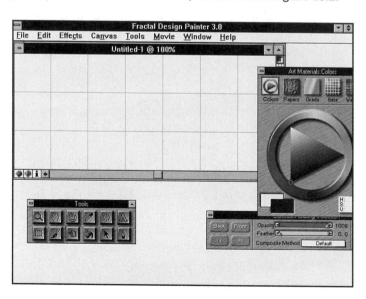

4. Apply some different backgrounds on which to place your floaters. To fill the first grid space, use the Rectangular Selection Tool to draw a 70-pixel square, as shown in Figure 15.3.

Figure 15.3.
Draw a 70-pixel square with the Rectangular Selection Tool.

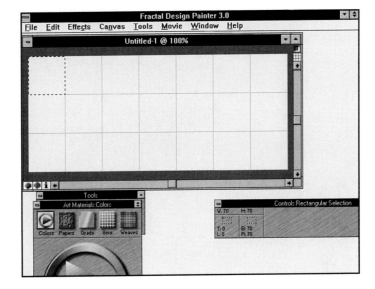

5. To verify the position and size of the selection, choose the Tools | Selections | Edit Rectangular Selection command. The Rectangle Selection dialog box appears. The Top and Left coordinates should each read 0, and the Height and Width measurements should each be 70.

6. Fill the square using the Paint Bucket, selecting a color, a gradation, or a weaving in the Controls | Paint Bucket Palette.

7. To select the areas for the subsequent squares, choose the Tools | Selections | Edit Rectangular Selection command again.

8. For the second square, adjust the left coordinate to read 70, as shown in Figure 15.4. This places the upper-left corner of the rectangle 70 pixels inward from the document.

9. Choose another color or pattern and fill the second square with the Paint Bucket.

*Figure 15.4.
Adjust the coordinates
in the Rectangle
Selection dialog box to
move the selection to
the next square.*

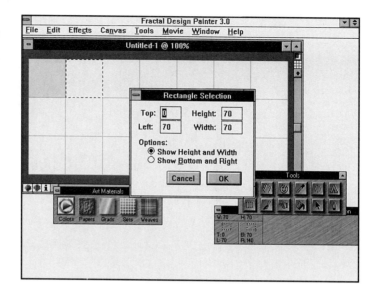

10. Continue with the remaining squares, using the following values for the
    top and left coordinates in the Rectangular Selection dialog box:

    Square #3: Top coordinate = 0; Left coordinate = 140

    Square #4: Top coordinate = 0; Left coordinate = 210

    Square #5: Top coordinate = 0; Left coordinate = 280

    Square #6: Top coordinate = 0; Left coordinate = 350

    Square #7: Top coordinate = 0; Left coordinate = 420

    Square #8: Top coordinate = 70; Left coordinate = 0

    Square #9: Top coordinate = 70; Left coordinate = 70

    Square #10: Top coordinate = 70; Left coordinate = 140

    Square #11: Top coordinate = 70; Left coordinate = 210

    Square #12: Top coordinate = 70; Left coordinate = 280

    Square #13: Top coordinate = 70; Left coordinate = 350

    Square #14: Top coordinate = 70; Left coordinate = 420

    Square #15: Top coordinate = 140; Left coordinate = 0

    Square #16: Top coordinate = 140; Left coordinate = 70

    Square #17: Top coordinate = 140; Left coordinate = 140

    Square #18: Top coordinate = 140; Left coordinate = 210

    Square #19: Top coordinate = 140; Left coordinate = 280

    Square #20: Top coordinate = 140; Left coordinate = 350

    Square #21: Top coordinate = 140; Left coordinate = 420

The finished image looks like a quilt, as shown in Figure 15.5.

Figure 15.5.
With all grid spaces filled, your image looks like a patchwork quilt.

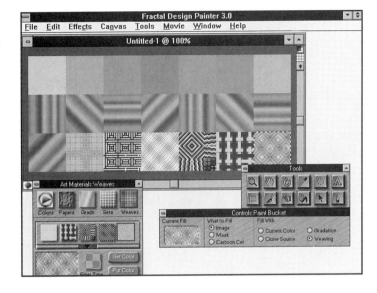

11. From the Objects | Floaters Palette, open the FLOWERS.POR Floater Library located on the CD.

12. Drag each floater out into the document, placing one in each grid square, as shown in Figure 15.6.

Figure 15.6.
Drag the floaters contained in the FLOWERS.POR Floater Library into the document.

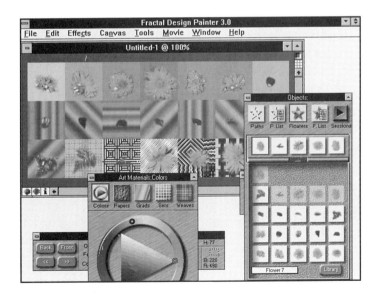

13. Now arrange some of the floaters into a small group. Start by Alt-clicking (Windows) or Option-clicking (Mac) a couple of the leaf floaters and place them near one of the flowers, as shown in Figure 15.7.

Figure 15.7.
Arrange three floaters
in a floater group, and
adjust their location in
the Objects | Floater
List Palette.

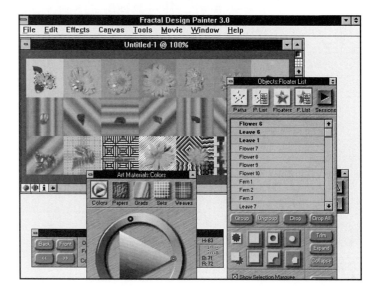

14. For the flower to appear above the leaves, its name has to appear above those of the leaves in the Objects | Floater List Palette. You can identify which floaters are arranged together by clicking the item in the document window to highlight its associated name in the Floater List. You can then drag the highlighted name to a new location in the Floater List to place the names together in a group.

To group the floaters, select the floaters you want to group by Shift-clicking to highlight their names in the Floater List. Next, click the Group button in the Floater List Palette. The group is surrounded by a selection marquee in the document window, and a group heading appears above the three floaters in the Floater List, as shown in Figure 15.8.

15. The Create Drop Shadow command is one of two effects you can apply to a group of floaters. To apply a shadow to this group, choose Effects | Objects | Create Drop Shadow. For the example, I adjusted the floater's opacity to 40% so the shading would be a little more subtle. I left the remaining settings at their default values, as shown in Figure 15.9.

CAUTION You also can apply Effects | Orientation | Scale to a group of floaters—but be careful. You can't scale a group of a group of floaters (a nested group).

Figure 15.8.
Group the floaters with
the Group button,
located in the Floater
List Palette.

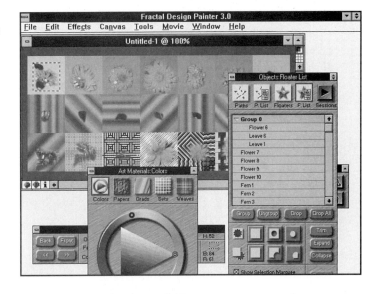

Figure 15.9.
Add a drop shadow to
the floater group using
the Create Drop
Shadow command.

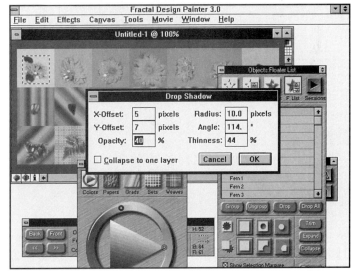

16. Now you must collapse your group of floaters and its drop shadow into one item. This is an important step when creating a floater nozzle file, because each nozzle element has to be a single entity, containing no groups or subgroups. This single entity will consist of the flower, the leaves, and the shadow.

    To collapse the group, click the group's name in the Floater List and then click the Collapse button located at the lower-right of the Floater List Palette. The flowers, leaves, and shadow become one item.

17. You also can apply Drop Shadows to all the floaters in the image simulta-
    neously. To do so, highlight each name in the Floater List by depressing
    the Shift key as you click the names. Click the Group button to group the
    floaters, then choose Effects | Objects | Create Drop Shadow. Figure 15.10
    shows that each floater in the Floater List now has a shadow attached
    to it.

Figure 15.10.
Apply drop shadows
quickly to all floaters in
the Floater List by
grouping them before
applying the command.

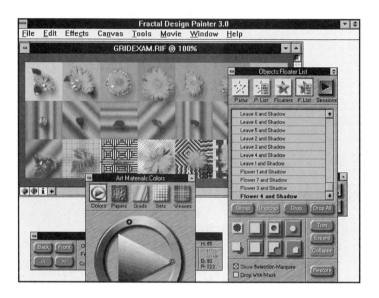

> **TIP**
>
> If you're applying drop shadows to floaters that are destined for nozzle files,
> click the Collapse to One Layer checkbox in the Drop Shadow dialog box. This
> saves you the trouble of individually collapsing the floaters and their shadows to
> one layer before you convert to the nozzle file.

Turning the Image into a Floater Nozzle File

You now have an image that you can use as either a floater nozzle file or a grid-
based nozzle file. When you create a floater nozzle file from this image, the
resulting document will contain only the floaters. When you create a grid-based
nozzle file from this document, you will drop the floaters into the background
layer to add some decoration to the patchwork squares before you create the
nozzle file.

Review what you have done for a moment. You created some little floater
groups, applied shadow to them, and collapsed the groups into one element.

You then grouped all the floaters and applied drop shadows to all floaters at once, indicating while doing so that you want the shadows collapsed into the floater's main layer when applied. All you should have left now is a single group that contains 21 floaters, with no subgroups within the group. Your screen should look similar to Figure 15.11.

Figure 15.11. With all subgroups collapsed, the Floater List Palette should contain only one group of 21 elements.

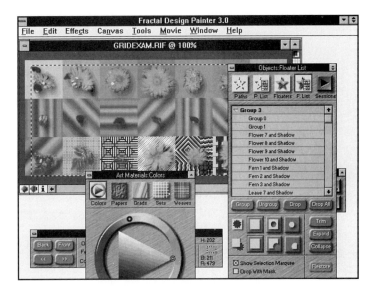

TIP You don't have to include all the floaters in an image in one nozzle file. For example, you can group only the flowers and create a nozzle file from that group. Then you can group all the leaves and create another nozzle file from that group, and group and place the ferns in yet another nozzle file. Having multiple groups in your working document is all right, as long as they are not nested within (a subgroup of) another group.

To turn the floaters contained in this image into a floater nozzle file:

1. If you want your elements sprayed in a predictable order, arrange the items within the Floater List group so the elements you want to spray on first in the stream are placed toward the top, and the elements you want sprayed at the end of the stream are placed toward the end of the group. If you rearrange them, be sure they are all still contained within the floater group you want them part of.

2. Choose the Tools | Image Hose | Make Nozzle from Group command. After a short time, a new document window appears with your floaters arranged in the order in which they appeared in the Floater List. I saved this version of my nozzle file as GRDEX1.RIF.

515

Don't close the original floater document with the background tiles, though; you use it next to create a grid-based nozzle.

Creating the Grid-Based Nozzle

Return to the version of the nozzle creation file that contains the background tiles and floaters. For the grid-based nozzle file, you will use the floaters to decorate the tiles a little bit. To do this, you must drop all the floaters into the background layer to create the grid-based nozzle file. You can do this in one of two ways:

- You can drop all the floaters into the background layer by clicking the Drop All button in the Floater List Palette.
- You can create a clone of the document. This drops all the floaters into the background layer.

When you merge the floaters with the background layer, the names in Floater List Palette disappear, as shown in Figure 15.12.

Figure 15.12.
The floaters disappear
from the Floater List
when you merge them
with the background
layer.

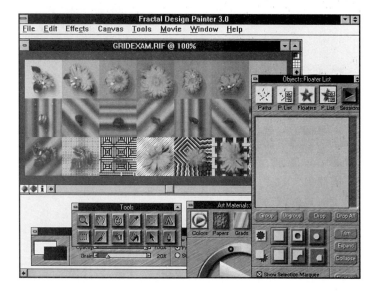

3. In the lower-left corner of the document window, turn on the middle Mask Visibility button to see the mask in red.

4. Turn on the third Drawing Visibility button. You see the mask cover the entire image, as shown in Figure 15.13.

CHAPTER 15

Figure 15.13.
Select the third
Drawing Visibility
button and the second
Mask Visibility button
to display the mask in
red.

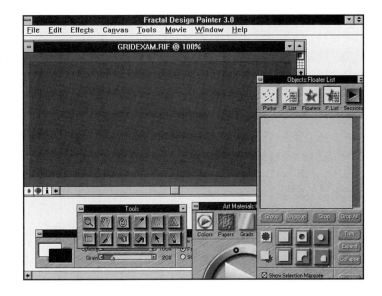

5. For the next step in creating a grid-based nozzle file, you must alter the masking layer by filling it with black paint. You can do this in one of two ways:

   ■ You can use one of the Masking brushes, such as the Masking Pen, with black to paint the mask away.

   ■ An easier method would be to choose the Paint Bucket and black as your current color. In the Controls | Paint Bucket Palette, choose to fill the Mask with the Current Color. Click the red mask, and it is painted away.

NOTE You don't have to paint the entire mask away when making grid-based nozzle files—just paint the mask away in the areas you want to show when you spray your nozzle through the Image Hose!

Using either of these methods, reveal the entire background as shown in Figure 15.14.

6. Save this nozzle file as GRDEX2.RIF.

Figure 15.14.
Paint or fill the entire
mask layer with black
paint, revealing the
background as the
mask layer is painted
away.

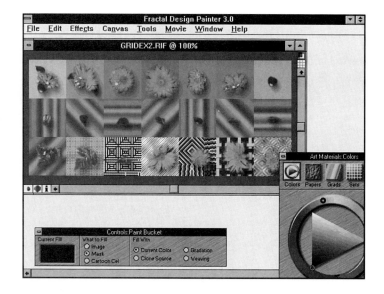

Loading Your Grid-Based Nozzle the First Time

Your nozzle file is now ready to use. There's one additional step when you load the file in for the first time: You have to let Painter know the dimensions of each nozzle element and how many elements are contained within the nozzle file. Right now, Painter can't tell the difference between this nozzle file and a regular Painter document!

Before you open the nozzle file, I need to discuss one more thing about nozzle files—*ranks*. Nozzle files can consist of one to three ranks, each of which can be controlled by a different expression property.

If you use the File | Get Info command when you open a nozzle file, you can see and edit the information that defines the nozzle file. The next few paragraphs explain what 1-Rank, 2-Rank, and 3-Rank image hoses are and what the information in the File | Get Info dialog box should read in the examples given.

First I will explain a 1-Rank nozzle file, because that's what you are creating here. With a 1-Rank nozzle file, all the elements contained in it are controlled by the same expression (for instance, Random, Pressure, or Direction, as identified in the Advanced Controls | Nozzle Palette). Suppose you have an image that contains 10 letters, A through J. Each of these letters is placed in a 30×50 grid space in your document. You load this nozzle file into an Image Hose that has Random control, so that when the 10 letters are sprayed into your document, the letters are picked randomly from the elements. The information that you will see in the File | Get Info dialog box will read as follows in this case:

```
image hose 10 items (height 30, width 50)
```

Now, suppose you want to add another rank to this file to create a 2-Rank nozzle file. Assume that your first group of letters was created with 10-point font size. You create another set of letters, A through J, in 14 points, adding 10 more squares to your document. And you add a third set of A through J in 18 point, again adding 10 more squares to your document. You keep adding more sets of these letters until you have 6 of each letter, or 60 squares in all in your document. You load this nozzle file into an Image Hose that has Random control for Rank 1 and Pressure control for Rank 2. The result is that as you spray your images, you get random letters that increase in size as you increase the pressure on your stylus. Getting interesting, isn't it? The information that you will see in the File | Get Info dialog box will read as follows in this case:

```
image hose 10 by 6 items (height 30, width 50)
```

Now for the third rank. You take those 60 squares you already have created, but now you add the element of direction. The first 60 squares are positioned normally, at a 0-degree rotation. The second 60 squares contain the same letters and same point sizes as the first, but are rotated at 45-degree angles, and so on through 90, 135, 180, 225, 270, and 315 degrees. You now have a total of 480 different elements in your nozzle file (10 letters×6 sizes×8 different angles). You load this nozzle file into the 3-Rank R-P-D Image Hose, which has Random control for the first rank, Pressure control for the second rank, and Direction control for the third rank. The result is that you get random letters that change in size as you apply pressure, and change in angle as you change direction of the stylus. The information that you will see in the File | Get Info dialog box will read as follows in this case:

```
image hose 10 by 6 by 8 items (height 30, width 50)
```

Multi-rank image hoses cannot be created from a floater nozzle file, or a movie nozzle file. To create a multi-rank image hose nozzle, you must create it from a grid-based nozzle file, similar to the one you created in this chapter.

1. Choose one of the Image Hose brushes from the Brushes Palette.
2. To load the grid-based nozzle file you just created, choose Tools | Image Hose | Load Nozzle. The Select Image dialog box, shown in Figure 15.15, appears.

PART IV

Figure 15.15.
Load the GRDEX2.RIF
file into an Image Hose
with the Load Nozzle
command.

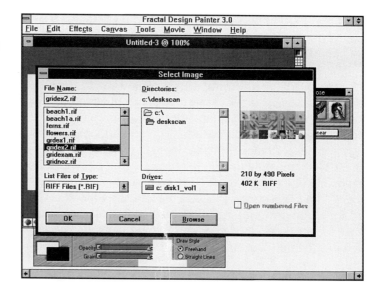

3. Select the GRDEX2.RIF file you just created. Choose OK to load the file.

4. The Nozzle Definition dialog box appears the first time you load the file. Here, you enter the information that defines your grid, the number of elements, and which nozzle rank they appear in. The entries are as follows:

Item Width: Enter the width of your grid spacing (in pixels) in this box. In our example, this figure will be 70.

Item Height: Enter the height of your grid spacing (in pixels) in this box. Again, this will be 70 in our current example.

Index Rank: The number of ranks your nozzle file contains (1 for 1-Rank, 2 for 2-Rank and 3 for 3-Rank nozzles).

Rank 1: The number of elements in the first rank of your nozzle file is entered here. In our case, this should be 21.

Rank 2: The number of elements in the second rank of your nozzle file is entered here. For our example, leave this set at 1.

Rank 3: The number of elements in the third rank of your nozzle file is entered here. For our example, leave this set at 1.

When you have entered the above information, your screen should look similar to Figure 15.16.

5. Click OK to continue loading the file. Your Image Hoses will now paint with the loaded nozzle file. The next time you load in this nozzle file, you will not have to reenter this information.

Figure 15.16.
The Nozzle Defini-
tion dialog box with
information filled in.

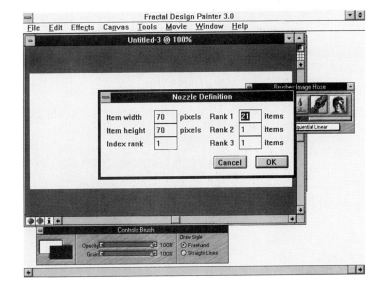

6. Now try to paint with the nozzle file. Notice that the elements are solid squares; this is because the entire mask was painted in with black paint, causing the image to contain no masked areas. But, didn't we want this nozzle file to align to a grid? As you see in Figure 15.17, this isn't happening.

Figure 15.17.
The nozzle file isn't
painting on the grid the
way it's supposed to!

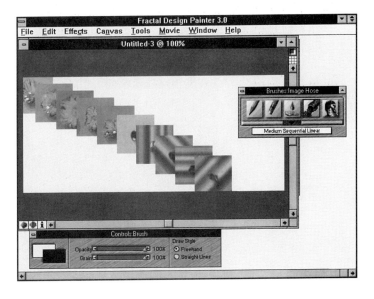

7. To remedy this, open the Brush Controls Palette and click the Nozzle icon. The Nozzle Palette, shown in Figure 15.18 appears.

8. On the right side of the Nozzle Palette, just underneath the Load button, is
   a checkbox labeled Use Brush Grid. If this box is checked, as shown in
   Figure 15.18, any nozzle file will apply its elements, snapping them to
   Painter's brush grid. This pertains to nozzles prepared with floaters and
   with Painter movies as well.

Figure 15.18.
Turn on the Use Brush
Grid button in the
Nozzle Palette.

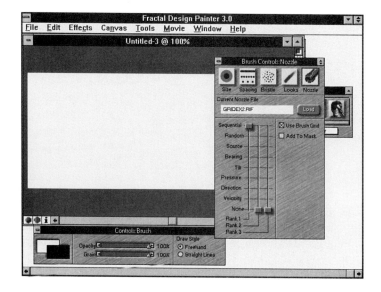

Figure 15.19 shows an image painted after the Use Brush Grid box has been
checked. As you can see, the nozzle elements now align perfectly to the brush
grid you created earlier.

Figure 15.19.
The nozzles adhere
perfectly to the brush
grid with Use Brush
Grid turned on.

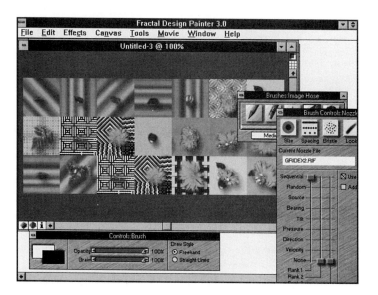

Creating Nozzle Files from Floaters

You can use floaters as elements of a nozzle file, turning them into Image Hose nozzles using the Make Nozzle from Group command on the Tools | Image Hose menu.

There are three points to stress when you prepare floaters:

- Though the nozzle file is created from a group of floaters, it cannot have any subgroups. For example, a floater with a drop shadows actually is a group that consists of the floater and its shadow. You must collapse groups of floaters into one layer before creating the nozzle file. To do so, use the Collapse button in the Floater List Palette.

- Extraneous areas outside the floater should be trimmed, so that the floaters are as compact as possible. To trim a floater, select the floater you want to trim and click the Trim button in the Floater List Palette.

- If you're using a Sequential Image Hose to spray the Image Hose nozzle into your image in a predictable order, you can plan the order in which the nozzle elements are sprayed in the Floater List Palette. Items that appear on the top of the list are sprayed first, and the items on the bottom of the list are sprayed last. When you create the nozzle file, the floaters should appear in their correct order in the nozzle file image. Check it at that time to make sure you have arranged the floaters in their proper order.

Turning Your Painted Leaves into an Image Hose Nozzle File

In Chapter 10, "Painting with the Water-Based Tools—The Stained Glass Window," you created a document that contains some leaves for a tree. To turn these leaves into an Image Hose nozzle, you must first turn them into floaters. You also must properly arrange the floaters in the Floater List Palette so that you can predict which leaves will be applied with the Image Hose as you apply them to the top and bottom of each branch.

For each leaf in the image, perform the following:

1. Using the Outline Selection Tool, draw a path around one leaf.
2. Click the selection with the Floating Selection Tool. It appears in the Floater List Palette. Figure 15.20 shows this in progress.

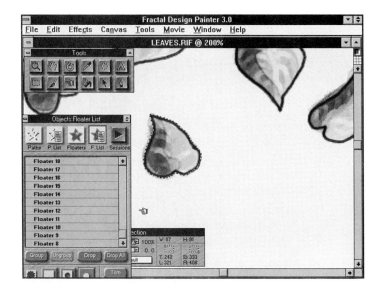

Figure 15.20. Draw an outline selection around each of the leaves you drew for the stained glass project, and click it with the Floating Selection Tool.

Putting Things in Order

1. This step isn't really necessary, but it does help you visualize the order in which you will spray the floaters with a Sequential Image Hose. In the document window, position the floaters in the order you want to spray them. This helps you organize the order in which they should appear in the Floater List Palette.

2. Click the first floater in the image to highlight its associated name in the Floater List Palette. Move this name to the top of the list, because you want to spray it first.

3. Double-click the name of the floater you just relocated. Rename it Leave 1.

4. Proceed in this manner with each leaf in your file. When you're done, rearrange the names in the Floater List to appear in ascending order, as shown in Figure 15.21.

5. Trim any extraneous areas from the outside of each floater by selecting the Trim button, located on the bottom portion of the Floater List Palette. This crops the floater to a rectangular area that contains only the selected area.

6. When you've created all the floaters, you can get rid of the extraneous lines still remaining in the background by choosing the Edit | Select All and Edit | Clear commands.

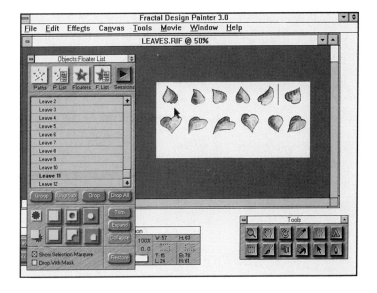

Figure 15.21.
Place the floaters in
order to help you
arrange and name
them properly in the
Floater List Palette.

Turning the Floaters into a Nozzle File

To turn the list of floaters from the previous step into a nozzle file:

1. Shift-click to select and highlight all the leaf floaters in the Floater List Palette. All lines should be highlighted in blue.

2. Click the Group button, shown in Figure 15.22, in the Floater List Palette to group the leaves.

Figure 15.22.
Click the Group button
to group the floaters.

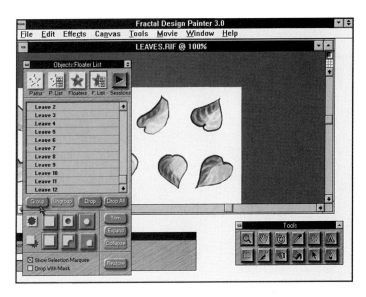

3. The Make Nozzle from Group command turns a group of floaters into a nozzle file. The file is saved in Painter's .RIF format, and requires painting in the masking layer to work properly through the Image Hose tools.

   Choose Tools | Image Hose | Make Nozzle from Group. This command is shown in Figure 15.23.

Figure 15.23.
The Make Nozzle from Group command turns the floaters into a nozzle file.

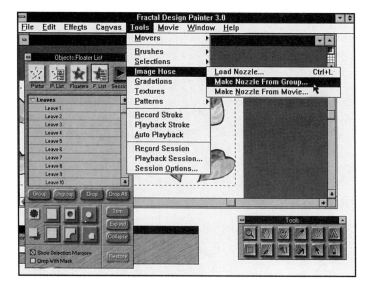

4. A new document appears, with the floaters arranged in the order in which they appeared in the Floater List. Figure 15.24 shows this new document with twelve leaf floaters inside.

Figure 15.24.
A new document appears with the floaters arranged as positioned in the Floater List Palette.

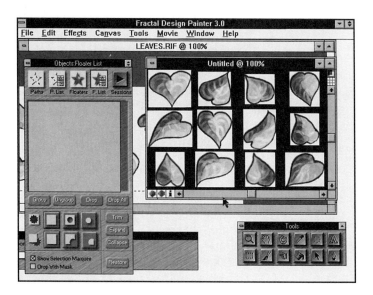

5. Save this file as LEAVENOZ.RIF.

Loading the Leaves into the Image Hose

Now apply the leaf nozzle to the tree you painted in Chapter 10:

1. Open the BACKTREE.RIF image created in Chapter 10. This file should have the sky background, with the tree floater merged into the background.

2. From the Brushes Palette, choose the Large Sequential Linear Image Hose. This Image Hose sprays images in the order in which you saved them. Your screen should now look something like Figure 15.25.

Figure 15.25.
Open the tree you created in Chapter 10, and select the Large Sequential Linear Image Hose.

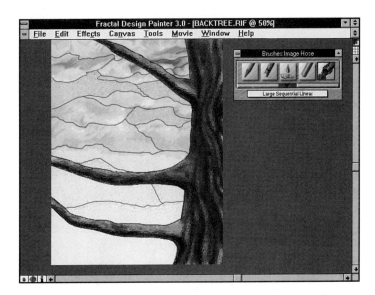

3. Choose the Tools | Image Hose | Load Nozzle command, or use the quick-key combination Ctrl-L in Windows or Cmd-L in Mac.

4. From the dialog box, choose the LEAVENOZ.RIF file you created in the previous step.

Applying the Leaves to the Tree

You can combine the current secondary color with your Image Hose nozzle file to vary the appearance of the images being sprayed. Do this by choosing a secondary color, and adjusting the Grain slider in the Controls | Brush Palette to mix the color and the Image Hose nozzle together. Apply the back layer of leaves as follows:

1. From the Art Materials | Colors Palette, shown in Figure 15.26, click the back rectangle to pick a secondary color.

Figure 15.26.
Click the back rect-
angle in the Colors
Palette to pick a
secondary color.

2. Select black as the secondary color. If you like, you can now click the front rectangle to activate the primary color for further painting later on.

3. In the Controls | Brush Palette, adjust the Grain slider to around 70%, as shown in Figure 15.27. With this setting, the Image Hose will be mixed at 70 percent strength, with a 30 percent strength of the black background color. This makes the leaves slightly darker than they were when created, giving them a shadowed effect.

4. Spray the images one by one, clicking the mouse or stylus at the center point of where you want each leaf placed. If you arranged your nozzle file in order, you should have six leaves facing upward and six leaves facing downward, or something similar. You can place the upward leaves on the top side of each branch, and the downward leaves on the underside of each branch. When you're done, your image should look similar to Figure 15.28.

5. Return the Grain slider to its 100% position, and apply the leaves at their "normal" color in a similar manner. These leaves appear lighter, as if in the foreground. Your image should now look similar to Figure 15.29, and should be complete.

Figure 15.27.
Adjust the Grain slider
in the Controls | Brush
Palette to around 70%.

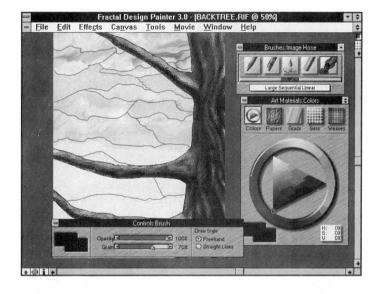

Figure 15.28.
Spray a set of darker
leaves on the tree first,
with the reduced
opacity setting.

6. You now can update the image to your hard disk using the File | Save (Ctrl-S in Windows, Cmd-S in Mac) command. Save the image as BACKTREE.RIF if you want to distinguish it from the version without the leaves placed.

Figure 15.29.
Spray a set of normal colored leaves onto the foreground.

Using Image Hoses with Movies

When you use Image Hoses with a Movie file, one or more nozzle elements is placed on each frame. You can load an animated sequence into the Image Hose, and place the sequence in one or more frames of an animation. You can use Tracing Paper (called Onion Skin in the Movie menu) as a guide to placing the elements and giving them the illusion of movement; see Chapter 16, "Visiting Van Gogh: The Cloner and Artists Brushes," for more about Tracing Paper. Chapter 19, "Creating a Cartoon Animation," gives the procedure of creating and using nozzle files in a Painter movie.

Summary

In this chapter you learned about the Image Hose variants and how to create nozzles in a couple of different ways—grid-based nozzle files and floater nozzle files. You also learned that you can mix nozzle files with the current secondary color to produce different shades of sprayed elements. I also covered how to collapse a group of floaters into one object, as well as creating drop shadows that are automatically collapsed into one layer.

If you're following the stained glass project in order, return now to Chapter 11. In that chapter, you will paint birds and complete the image. Then, some final effects will be added to complete the scene.

Visiting Van Gogh: The Cloner and Artists Brushes

Painter offers several variants you can use to paint like a master. These variants are in two categories: Cloner variants and Artists variants. In this chapter I discuss various ways to clone documents, and describe the variants in these two brush categories.

The Cloner Variants

With the Cloner variants, you can reproduce an image or photograph to make it appear as though it was created in an entirely different medium. There are 13 Cloner variants in all, created from the most commonly used tools.

Chalk Cloner

This variant clones with the look and feel of the Artist Pastel Chalk introduced in Chapter 9, "A Little Glimpse of Heaven." The Chalk Cloner brush produces slightly narrower strokes than its chalk counterpart. The strokes vary in opacity and reaction to paper grain based on the pressure you apply with a stylus. The edges of the stroke are semi-antialiased.

Driving Rain Cloner

The Driving Rain Cloner brush produces narrow diagonal strokes in a clone document. The strokes produced by this brush have soft, antialiased edges and cover underlying strokes. They give the appearance that the image is being viewed through a heavy rain storm.

Felt Pen Cloner

The Felt Pen Cloner variant has characteristics similar to those of the Medium Tip Felt Pen introduced in Chapter 8, "Working with the Felt Pens." The strokes are antialiased, and build up toward black when you apply them over existing strokes. With this cloner you may want to adjust the Opacity slider toward the left so the colors don't build up as quickly. You also can lighten your source document to slow down the buildup.

Hairy Cloner

The Hairy Cloner variant shares the properties of the Hairy Brush, except that the Hairy Cloner variant has the Use Clone Color checkbox in the Art Materials | Colors Palette enabled. (The Hairy Brush variant is introduced in Chapter 14, "Working with the Brush Tools.") Clone documents you create with this variant have the appearance of an image painted with oils. The strokes are semi-antialiased and cover underlying strokes. Stroke size, opacity, and reaction to paper grain respond to the pressure you apply with the stylus. Mouse users can vary the size in the Brush Controls | Size Palette, or vary opacity and grain with those settings in the Controls | Brush Palette.

Hard Oil Cloner

The Hard Oil Cloner variant produces strokes with hard, aliased edges that cover underlying areas. The strokes react to paper grain. Cloning with this brush gives the appearance of an image that was painted with oil paints.

Impressionist Cloner

The Impressionist Cloner variant shares the properties of its Impressionist (Artists Brush) counterpart, except that the Use Clone Color checkbox is enabled in the Art Materials | Colors Palette. This brush smears existing color with short, varicolored dabs of paint. The direction in which you drag the mouse or stylus determines the angle of the dabs.

Melt Cloner

The Melt Cloner variant distorts the colors in a clone document to give the appearance that the image is dripping paint. It can make a clone document look as though you applied paint with a palette knife. Strokes vary in size based on the speed at which you drag the mouse or stylus.

Oil Brush Cloner

The Oil Brush Cloner variant gives the appearance of an image that was painted with oil paints. The strokes cover underlying strokes, and have soft antialiased edges. They vary in size based on the speed at which you drag the mouse or stylus. The Oil Brush Cloner is a multibristled brush, and the stroke appears as a dotted line before Painter renders it.

Pencil Sketch Cloner

The Pencil Sketch Cloner variant clones your image and makes it appear as though it were sketched with pencil. The lines are semi-antialiased, react to paper grain, and cover underlying strokes. Opacity and grain-sensitivity vary with stylus pressure. You also can vary the appearance of the lines by making adjustments to the Clone Location Variability slider in the Advanced Controls | Random Palette.

Soft Cloner

The Soft Cloner variant reproduces an image that looks as though it were painted with an airbrush. The strokes, which are somewhat wide, are soft, antialiased, and cover underlying strokes. They vary in size depending on the speed at which you drag the mouse or stylus.

Straight Cloner

Use the Straight Cloner variant when you want to exactly reproduce part of an image in a clone document. It does not modify or add effects to an image in any way.

Van Gogh Cloner

The Van Gogh Cloner variant applies multicolored brush strokes in the style of Vincent Van Gogh. The strokes are antialiased and cover underlying strokes. This brush works best with very short strokes.

The Artists Variants

With Painter's Artists variants, you can simulate the painting styles of classic artists such as Vincent Van Gogh, Georges Seurat, and the Impressionists. For example, the Auto Van Gogh variant lets you automatically reproduce any image as though it were painted by Vincent Van Gogh. Other variants of the Artists variants let you smear existing colors with circular or elliptical dabs, leaving the impression that many strokes were applied while creating the image. Other variants apply multicolored circular or elliptical dabs of paint in a single stroke.

Auto Van Gogh

The Auto Van Gogh variant works with the Effects | Esoterica | Auto Van Gogh command to quickly and easily add multicolored brush strokes to a clone document. The strokes are soft, antialiased, and cover underlying strokes. You can adjust the size of the automatic strokes with the Brush Controls | Size Palette. Painter automatically determines the direction of the strokes from the light and dark areas in the source document.

Flemish Rub

The Flemish Rub variant smears the colors in the existing image with dabs of paint, creating a look similar to that of the Van Gogh and Impressionist brushes. The angle of the brush dabs vary with the direction in which you drag the mouse or stylus.

Impressionist

The Impressionist variant creates narrow, elliptical dabs of paint. The angle of the dabs varies with the direction in which you drag the mouse or stylus. Reducing the Opacity setting in the Controls | Brush Palette smears paint from the existing image.

Piano Keys

The Piano Keys variant creates multicolored strokes with a ribbon-like appearance. The direction of the ribbons follows the curve of your brush stroke. The stroke is grain-sensitive. The Piano Keys variant uses a captured brush dab.

Seurat

The Seurat variant mimics the painting style of Georges Seurat, applying antialiased clusters of dots. These dot clusters cover underlying strokes. You can increase or decrease the opacity of the stroke by moving the Opacity slider in the Controls | Brush Palette. Moving the slider to the left makes the stroke more transparent, and moving it to the right makes the stroke more opaque.

Van Gogh

The Van Gogh variant creates multicolored strokes painted in the style of Vincent Van Gogh. Unlike the Auto Van Gogh variant, which applies strokes automatically, you use this brush to manually apply Van-Gogh–like brush strokes to your document. The strokes are antialiased, and vary in width based on the speed at which you drag the mouse or stylus. These strokes cover underlying strokes. This brush works best with short strokes. Slower mouse movements produce wider strokes, and faster mouse movements produce narrower strokes.

Creating a Clone Document

In these projects, you explore various ways to clone a document—starting with the choice that is the most automatic. The File | Clone command creates an exact copy of a Painter-compatible document, and also creates a link between the source document and its clone. After creating a clone, you can use cloning commands and brushes to recreate the image with any of the Painter mediums.

Step 16.1. Cloning a Document

To make a clone copy of the project document:

1. Open the FAIR.TGA file, located on the CD accompanying this book. This document is your *source document*.
2. Choose File | Clone. A document window appears containing a copy of the image; this is your *clone document*. The title bar header reads "Clone of (your image name and extension) @ 100%" (or your current zoom factor). When you save this document using its default name, Painter precedes the filename with a C_. For example, if you save your clone document with its default name, Painter calls it C_FAIR.TGA. (The file extension would remain the same.)

Step 16.2. The Quickest Way to Create a Masterpiece

The simplest way to clone an entire document quickly is to use the Auto Van Gogh Artists variant in conjunction with the Effects | Esoterica | Auto Van Gogh command. These two items work together to produce a cloned image painted in the style of Vincent Van Gogh. This command works with photographs, rendered drawings, and any other type of image you can think of.

Painter automatically determines the direction of the strokes by the light and dark areas in your source document. The commands do all the work for you here—you can just sit back and wait for the results. (It's nice to watch someone or something else do all the work for you!)

In the previous steps, you created a clone document of the FAIR.TGA file from the accompanying CD. Now let the virtual Van Gogh do the rest of the work:

1. Select the Clone of FAIR.TGA to make it the current document, as shown in Figure 16.1. One way to do this is to drop down the Windows menu and select the filename from the bottom of the menu box. This way you can change from file to file without minimizing or repositioning open documents.

Figure 16.1.
Choose the clone
document to make it
the current image.

2. Open the Brushes Palette (Ctrl-2 in Windows, Cmd-2 in Mac) and click the Artists icon.
3. From the Artists variants, choose the Auto Van Gogh variant.
4. Choose Effects | Esoterica | Auto Van Gogh, as shown in Figure 16.2.

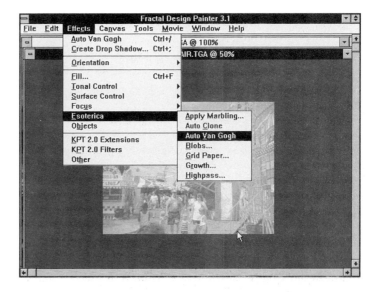

Figure 16.2.
Select the Auto Van
Gogh variant in con-
junction with the Auto
Van Gogh command.

After you apply the command, and before the image appears, two things happen:

- Painter evaluates the light and dark portions of the image to determine where to place the brush strokes.

- Painter then places the brush strokes into the document.

Both these steps are done "behind the scenes," and Painter notifies you of the progress of each step in a dialog box.

When both steps are complete, the image appears on your screen. Figure 16.3 shows the completed result of the transformation.

Figure 16.3.
After a two-step
calculating process,
Painter renders the
image on your screen in
the style of Van Gogh.

You can vary the size of the Auto Van Gogh strokes to suit your document by adjusting the settings in the Brush Controls | Size Palette. Move the Size slider toward the left to produce thinner, smaller Van Gogh brush strokes. Move the Size slider toward the right to produce larger strokes.

You also can enhance the appearance of the brush strokes by applying surface texture with the 3D Brush Strokes option. I describe this technique at the end of the next section.

Painter provides a way to automatically clone a selection or an entire document with any of its brushes. The next few steps tell you how to use the Auto Clone command with a Cloner brush. I then explain how to turn any brush into a cloner.

Step 16.3. Clearing the Clone Document Window

When you use the Auto Clone command, it's easier to monitor the progress of your stroke applications if you start off with a clear clone document. When you clear an image from the clone, a link remains between the clone document and the source document.

> **NOTE** You can clear a selected area, or you can clear the entire document. To clear a selected area, create a selection in the usual manner and activate it, surrounding it with a selection marquee. Then, clear the area by pressing the Backspace key in Windows, or the Delete key in Mac.

To clear the entire document instead:

1. Select the clone of FAIR.TGA as your current document. If you're continuing from Step 16.2, you have the Van Gogh painting in this image. If you're starting from scratch for this step, open the FAIR.TGA image and create a clone document as outlined in Step 16.1.
2. Choose Edit | Select All to surround the entire image by a selection marquee.
3. Press the Backspace key in Windows, or the Delete key in Mac. This clears the image window of the clone image. Don't worry—a link still exists between this document and the source document. Your screen should look similar to the one shown in Figure 16.4.

Figure 16.4.
Clear the clone
document window by
using the Select All
command and then
pressing the Backspace
(Windows) or Delete
(Mac) key.

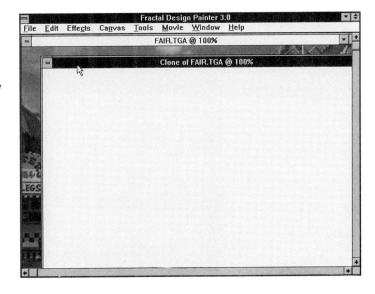

Step 16.4. Using the Auto Clone Command

Now use the Auto Clone command on your fair picture:

1. If you're continuing from Step 16.3, you should have two open documents: the source document FAIR.TGA and a cleared clone document. The clone document should be your active document.

2. For this example, I selected the Hairy Cloner variant from the Cloner variants because it is sensitive to paper grain. Later in this project you use Paper Grain to apply "three-dimensional" brush strokes to the image.

3. From the Art Materials | Papers Palette, choose the Medium paper grain.

4. If you want your cloned colors to appear more random, you can adjust the color variability of the strokes. Do this by adjusting the Color Variability sliders in the Art Materials | Colors Palette, as shown in Figure 16.5. Here, the ±H, ±S, and ±V sliders have been adjusted to 5% each, adding a small amount of randomness to the hue, saturation, and value of the strokes.

5. Choose Effects | Esoterica | Auto Clone, as shown in Figure 16.6. You then see dabs of paint being applied across the entire image. If you're applying the command to a larger image, you may see the strokes being rendered in small square or rectangular areas at a time, but eventually it works its way through the entire image.

Figure 16.5.
Add randomness to
the stroke colors by
adjusting the Color
Variability sliders in
the Art Materials |
Colors Palette.

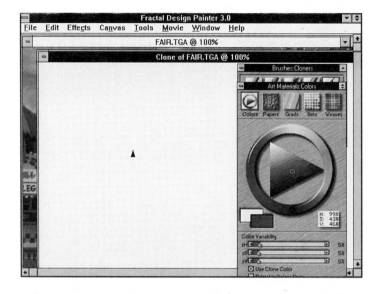

Figure 16.6.
Choose the Auto Clone
command to automati-
cally clone your entire
document, or a selected
area, with the current
brush.

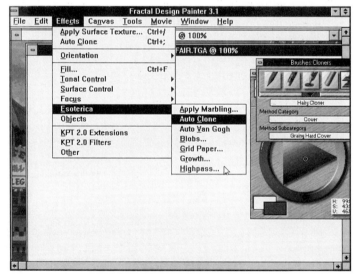

6. When the document appears the way you want it to, click anywhere inside the document to stop the Auto Clone rendering. Figure 16.7 shows the results of this Auto Clone rendering.

Figure 16.7.
The results of Auto
Clone rendering.

Step 16.5. Adding "Three-Dimensional" Brush Strokes

The setting is right to add three-dimensional (3D) Brush Strokes to the image in the current project. To apply this effect, you must have both a source document and a clone document open. For best results, create the clone document using a brush that responds to paper grain.

To add 3D Brush Strokes to your fair painting:

1. Choose Effects | Surface Control | Apply Surface Texture. This command is shown in Figure 16.8.

Figure 16.8.
Add 3D Brush Strokes
with the Apply Surface
Texture command.

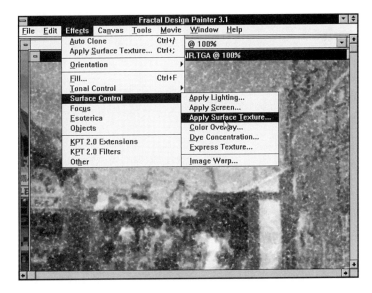

541

2. The Apply Surface Texture dialog box for Painter 3.0 is shown in Figure 16.9. The dialog box that appears for this command in Painter 3.1 is shown in Figure 16.10. On the left side of the dialog boxes are preview windows in which you can move the image around and see how your settings will change the image before you apply them.

3. From the drop-down Using listbox, choose 3D Brush Strokes. (This setting is grayed out if you don't have source and clone documents open.)

4. In Painter 3.0, if you want to add shininess to the canvas, click the Shiny checkbox to activate the Shiny feature. In Painter 3.1, you can adjust the Shine slider to increase or decrease the shininess in the document. You can also adjust the Picture slider to diffuse the amount of reflection of the shine.

5. In Painter 3.0 and 3.1, choose one of the eight Light Direction radio buttons to indicate where the light is to come from. In Painter 3.1, this choice can be a starting point; you can fine-tune the lighting direction by moving the light indicator in the light sphere located beneath the image preview. In addition, you can choose a light color, and adjust the Brightness, Concentration, and Exposure of the light.

6. In Painter 3.0 and 3.1, adjust the Amount slider to increase or decrease the amount, or intensity, of the 3D effect.

Figure 16.9.
In Painter 3.0, choose 3D Brush Strokes from the drop-down Using list, adjust the amount slider as necessary, and apply shininess to the effect, if desired.

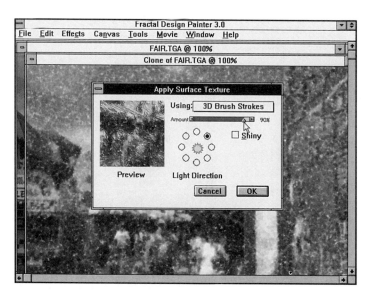

Figure 16.10.
In Painter 3.1, additional controls exist to provide fine lighting adjustments for applying surface texture.

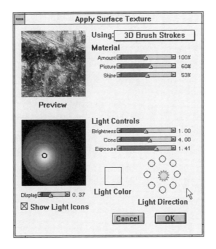

7. After you make your choices, click the OK button to apply the command.

8. You are informed in a dialog box that Painter is applying the surface texture to the image. After a brief time, a new rendering appears in your document window, with the 3D Brush Strokes command applied.

For the example in Figure 16.11, I set the Amount slider to 90% and chose not to use the Shiny feature. These settings applied to Painter 3.0. The settings for Painter 3.1 might differ slightly because of the enhanced lighting controls. Go with what you feel looks right in the preview image.

Figure 16.11.
A sample image with the 3D Brush Strokes command applied.

Step 16.6. Using Tracing Paper

When you're using the cloning brushes, it's sometimes easier to keep track of where you are painting by clearing the clone document window and turning on Painter's Tracing Paper. This lets you view a "ghosted" representation of the source document while you apply strokes with the cloning brushes.

If your source and clone images are the same size, you can use Painter's Tracing Paper command to help you keep track of where you've painted. You can use Tracing Paper between any image and its clone. Toggle Tracing Paper on and off in any of these three ways:

- Choose Canvas | Tracing Paper.
- Use the quick-key combination Ctrl-T in Windows, Cmd-T in Mac.
- Click the Tracing Paper icon, located in the right document window scrollbar. The icon is just beneath the up arrow in the top section of this scrollbar.

When Tracing Paper is on, you see a ghosted image of your source document in the clone document window. The strokes you apply also appear lighter.

NOTE The strokes you apply to an image when Tracing Paper is on appear lighter than normal, so take care not to cover too much when using brushes that use Buildup methods.

Turn Tracing Paper on for your next project:

1. If you are continuing from Step 16.5, make sure the clone of FAIR.TGA is your current image. If you're starting from scratch, open the FAIR.TGA image contained on the CD furnished with this book, and create a clone of it using the File | Clone command. In either case, select the entire document using the Edit | Select All command, and press the Backspace (Windows) or Delete (Mac) key to clear the contents of the document.

2. Turn Tracing Paper on by using the Canvas |Tracing Paper command, the quick-key combination Ctrl-T in Windows, Cmd-T in Mac, or the Tracing Paper icon in the document window scrollbar.

3. Choose the Soft Cloner variant and color the sky area. You might find it easier to outline the basic area with Tracing Paper on, then fill in the remaining area with Tracing Paper off. Use the eraser to clear off any areas that extend into the foreground elements. Figure 16.12 shows the sky colored.

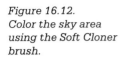

Figure 16.12.
Color the sky area
using the Soft Cloner
brush.

Step 16.7. Making a Clone Document Lighter

If you're cloning with brushes that use a Buildup method, you might find that colors build up too quickly toward black, creating a clone document that is much too dark. If your source document and clone document are the same size, you can clear the contents of the clone document and turn on Tracing Paper. This way, you start off fresh, placing your clone strokes in a clean document. The Tracing Paper serves as a guide to the areas you clone.

On the other hand, you might want to clone between two documents that are different sizes. You can't use Tracing Paper in this case, because that feature becomes enabled only when two images are identical in size. How can you keep track of the areas you clone in this case?

You can do one of two things to remedy these situations:

- In the case of using Buildup brushes, you can reduce the Opacity setting of the brushes in the Controls | Brush Palette to slow down the buildup of the strokes.

- If you plan to create a clone document using many different buildup brush variants, you might find it easier to lighten your source document. This helps reduce the buildup rate for all your strokes, without you having to reduce the opacity of every buildup brush you use.

There are many ways to lighten documents. One method is to use the Effects | Surface Control | Dye Concentration command. When you choose this command, the Dye Concentration dialog box appears with two sliders: a Maximum slider and Minimum slider. Using Uniform Adjustment, which you choose in the drop-down Using listbox, adjust the Maximum slider toward the left to lighten the document. You can preview the changes in the Preview square as you move the slider. When you see the results you want, click the OK button to apply the effect.

Another way to lighten a document is to use the Effects | Tonal Control | Adjust Colors dialog box. This achieves somewhat the same result, but in a slightly different manner. Here, you adjust the value setting of the colors contained in the document.

In this next step you will use the Effects | Tonal Control | Adjust Colors command to create a second, lighter source document to use in cloning the foreground areas of the image:

1. Choose the original photograph, FAIR.TGA, as your current document.

2. Create a second clone document using the File | Clone command. The new clone document appears as your current document.

3. To lighten the clone document, choose Effects | Tonal Control | Adjust Colors. The Adjust Color dialog box, shown in Figure 16.13, appears.

Figure 16.13.
The Adjust Color
command is one of
many ways to lighten a
source document.

4. In the drop-down Using listbox, choose to apply the effect using Uniform Color. This alters all the colors in your image in a uniform manner, without applying additional paper-grain effects.

5. Set the Value slider at 99 to 100%. You can move the image in the preview window to see the changes before applying them.

6. Save the lightened clone as LITCLONE.TGA. This helps you distinguish between it and the other open images. You can delete this image when the project is done.

Step 16.8. Cloning from Multiple Documents

Creating a clone with the File | Clone command automatically creates a link between the source document and the clone document. If you're working with multiple documents, however, and want to change between clone sources, you can create a link between two documents with the File | Clone Source command. The image you select with this command automatically becomes the clone source of any active document.

If you're working with multiple images, you can view the names of the open documents in the drop-down Window menu. Click the Window heading in the menu bar, and the names of the open files appear at the bottom of the menu, as shown in Figure 16.14.

Figure 16.14.
View the names of your open documents in the drop-down Window menu, and select any one to work on.

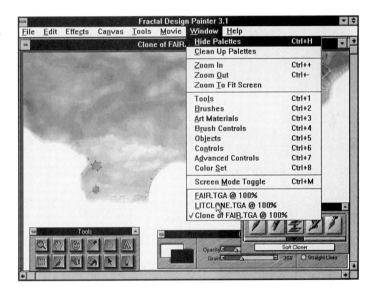

There should now be three documents open. You will clone between two different source documents into the third document to complete the remainder of this project. First, you will start by using the lighter version as the source document.

1. With the list displayed as shown in the figure, click Clone of FAIR.TGA @ 100% to select it as your current document.

2. Using the File | Clone Source command, select the lightened document LITCLONE.TGA as your source document.

3. From the Brushes Palette, choose the Pencil Sketch Cloner brush.

Step 16.9. Cloning with Automatic Strokes

Before using the Pencil Sketch Cloner variant, you might want to read ahead a bit.

You can clone the foreground in this project in two different ways. If you want to try each method now, save your project document as a .RIF file. You can try one method, then revert to your saved document to try the other method.

- The first method is to clone the entire area manually, filling the area with pencil strokes. Using this method, you can control the placement and appearance of the strokes you apply.

- The second method is to clone this large area by recording a brush stroke using the Record Stroke command, and then automatically applying it to the foreground using the Auto Playback command.

NOTE If you do not select an area, Auto Playback is applied to the entire document—rendering over areas you've already colored.

These steps demonstrate how to apply recorded strokes to a selected area of a document with the Auto Playback command:

1. Using the Outline Selection tool, create a selection marquee around the entire foreground of your project document. When you're done, your selection should look similar to that shown in Figure 16.15.

Figure 16.15.
Select an area in your
document in which to
apply automatic brush
strokes.

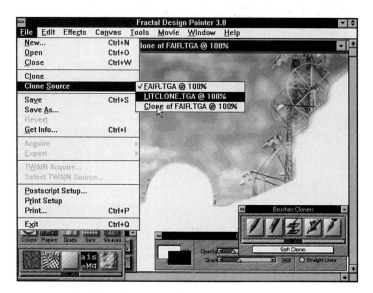

You might want to save your document at this point in case something goes wrong while you're experimenting!

2. From the Brushes Palette, choose the Pencil Sketch Cloner brush as your current brush, if it is not still selected.

3. Choose Tools | Record Stroke, as shown in Figure 16.16. The next stroke you place on your document is recorded and placed in memory. This command records one stroke only.

Figure 16.16.
Record a brush stroke
with the Tools | Record
Stroke command.

4. Draw a stroke onto your document, as shown in Figure 16.17.

Figure 16.17.
Draw a single stroke to
record it for playback.

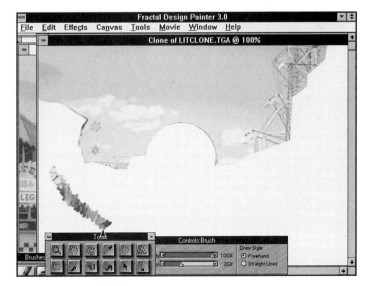

5. If the selection marquee no longer appears around your selected area, you can reactivate the selection by opening the Objects | Path List Palette and clicking the circle beside the pathname in the Path List Palette. The Path List Palette is shown in Figure 16.18, with the selection active.

Figure 16.18. Reactivate a deactivated selection by clicking the circle beside the selection name in the Path List Palette.

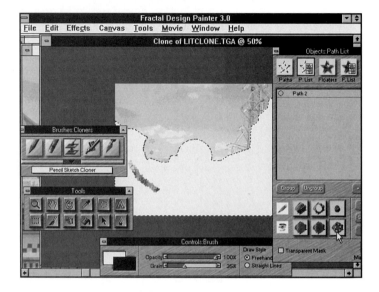

6. In the Path List Palette, or in the lower-left document window scrollbar, verify that the third Drawing Visibility button is activated so that Auto Playback applies strokes to only the inside of the selected area.

7. Choose Tools | Auto Playback, as shown in Figure 16.19. This starts automatic stroke rendering within your selected area.

8. Figure 16.20 shows the automatic rendering in progress. You can stop the process by clicking once inside the selected area, and then resume it until you achieve the desired results.

You also can play a stroke back once each time you click the mouse or stylus in your document. To do this, select the Playback Stroke command and then click in your image at the point at which you want the center of the stroke to appear. You can repeat this playback as many times as you like. To deactivate the Playback Stroke mode, select the Playback Stroke command again.

It may take some time to fill the entire area. You can stop Auto Playback when it's close enough to completion and touch up the uncovered areas manually, if you like. Also, remember that Auto Playback strokes may not look quite as "hand drawn" as if you had done it manually. It can be a real time-saver, though, and one of those things that you can walk away from for a while to get a cup of coffee and relax!

Figure 16.19.
Choose the Auto
Playback command to
automatically repeat
the strokes within your
selected area.

Figure 16.20.
Fill the selected
area with Auto
Playback.

9. When the image is filled to your liking, click inside the image with the mouse or stylus to stop Auto Playback. Figure 16.21 shows the rendering complete.

Figure 16.21.
Click inside the image
with the mouse or
stylus when the stroke
rendering is complete.

If you'd like to experiment with each method, do so now. Then use the result you prefer to continue with the remainder of the project.

Step 16.10. Darkening the Foreground Image

In Step 16.9 you cloned the foreground area with the lightened LITCLONE.TGA image for a reason: so the people in the foreground of the final image could stand out and appear darker—sort of like they were placed into the scene after the fact. Now darken the people in the foreground and return them to the way they appeared in the original image. Begin by switching your source document link to the original source document, FAIR.TGA:

1. Using the File | Clone Source command, select FAIR.TGA (which contains the original photographic image) as your source document, as shown in Figure 16.22.

2. From the Brushes Palette, choose the Straight Cloner variant. This cloner is a bit large for this image, so you might want to adjust the size down to around 6, as shown in Figure 16.23.

3. Use this brush size setting until you get close to the smaller areas of the image, and then reduce the size some more to get closer to the edges.

4. When you have restored the people in the foreground to their original appearance, as shown in Figure 16.24, you can add some extra touches using other brushes. I discuss this in the next step.

Figure 16.22.
Select FAIR.TGA as your source document.

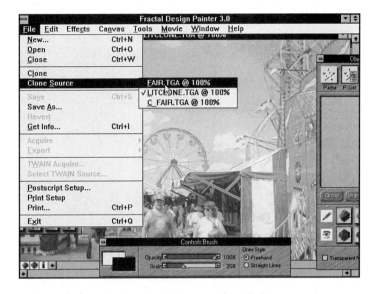

Figure 16.23.
Reduce the size of the Straight Cloner brush in the Brush Controls | Size Palette.

Figure 16.24.
Restore the image of
people in the fore-
ground to its original
state.

Step 16.11. Using Other Brushes as Cloners

You can turn any of Painter's brushes, except the Masking brushes, into cloners by checking the Use Clone Color checkbox in the Art Materials | Colors Palette. Using this method retains the original characteristics of the brush, but the new brush paints with colors from the source document rather than with colors you might select from the Art Materials | Colors Palette.

NOTE The Use Clone Color checkbox resets to its original, unchecked state when you choose another brush.

If you find brush variants you like to use in this manner, remember that you can save variants of brushes as cloners with the Use Clone Color box checked. I discussed saving brush variants in Chapter 6, "Creating a Label with Pencils ."

To illustrate how you can use any of Painter's brushes as cloners:

1. Select the 2B Pencil from the Pencil variants, introduced in Chapter 6, "Creating a Label with Pencils."

2. Open the Art Materials Palette and click the Colors icon. The Colors Palette appears. Maximize the Colors Palette by clicking on the upper-right arrow button.

3. Check the Use Clone Color box at the bottom portion of the palette. Figure 16.25 shows this checkbox. Now the 2B Pencil will use colors from the source document.

Figure 16.25.
Check the Use Clone
Color checkbox in the
Colors Palette to turn
almost any brush into a
cloner.

4. Add some lines to the fun house in the right section of the screen, as shown in Figure 16.26. Notice that instead of using black or your currently selected color, the lines are added in the colors of the source document.

Because the 2B Pencil uses a Buildup method, any linework you produce with it darkens the image and builds it up toward black.

Figure 16.26.
A sample image with
the 3D Brush Strokes
command applied.

Step 16.12. Using Other Cloning Methods

You might also want to experiment with another way of creating cloning brushes. Rather than use the Use Clone Color checkbox in the Art Materials | Colors Palette, you can revise the method the brush uses. There are five cloning methods available for the choosing:

- Hard Cover Cloning clones with strokes that produce semi-antialiased edges. This method works well with brushes that have Hard methods as part of their descriptions.

- Soft Cover Cloning clones with strokes that are soft and antialiased. You can successfully modify brushes using Soft Cover methods, such as the Airbrushes, using this method.

- Grainy Hard Cover Cloning produces semi-antialiased strokes that react to paper grain. This method is suitable for brushes that have Grainy or Hard methods in their descriptions.

- Grainy Soft Cover Cloning produces soft, antialiased strokes that react to paper grain. This method works well with brushes that use methods with Grainy and Soft in their description.

- Drip Cloning produces strokes that melt and spread the colors around. You can use this choice to turn brushes such as the Liquid variant brushes into cloners.

You can change the method of a brush directly in the Brushes Palette. When you maximize the palette, the Method Category and the Method Subcategory appear. In Figure 16.26, shown earlier, these two categories appear in the Brushes Palette.

To change the method to a Cloning method, first click the drop-down Method Category list box. A list of the available method types appears. From this list, choose Cloning.

To select one of the five variants of cloning methods, click the drop-down Method Subcategory box. Here, you can select one of the five methods just described.

When you have made your modifications, you might want to save the brush into your own library using the Tools | Brushes | Save Variant command I introduced in Chapter 6, "Creating a Label with Pencils."

Step 16.13. Adding Paper Texture

If you've experimented with other documents and want to save the results before proceeding with the next few steps, now is a good time. (I like to remind you of this periodically in case you forget!)

You're going to add 3D brush strokes to this image again—this time to see what happens when brushes that are not grain-sensitive are combined with brushes that *are* grain-sensitive. If you remember, in Step 16.5 you cloned the sky using the Soft Cloner. This brush is not sensitive to paper grain. In Step 16.10 you cloned the people image with the Straight Cloner, another brush that's not sensitive to paper grain. However, you cloned the remaining areas with the Pencil Sketch Cloner, a brush that does react to paper grain. When you apply the 3D Brush Strokes command to this image, you see smoothness in areas that were painted with the Soft Cloner and Straight Cloner brushes, and textured areas where you used the Pencil Sketch Cloner brush.

To add 3D brush strokes again:

1. Choose either the FAIR.TGA or the LITCLONE.TGA image as your source document. You want an image in which no strokes have been applied to use this effect. In Figure 16.27, I've selected the FAIR.TGA image as the source document. The other documents are closed.

Figure 16.27.
Select FAIR.TGA (or LITCLONE.TGA) as your source document.

2. Choose Effects | Surface Control | Apply Surface Texture. You want to make the effect a little more subtle than in the previous example.
3. In the drop-down Using listbox, choose 3D Brush Strokes.
4. Turn the Shiny checkbox off if you don't want to add extra shininess to the texture.
5. Adjust the Amount slider to around 50%.

6. Position the Light Direction to achieve the shadowing you want to see in the final image. Figure 16.28 shows these choices made for Painter 3.0. Figure 16.29 shows the dialog box for Painter 3.1, in which your settings may differ.

Figure 16.28. Adjust settings in Painter 3.0 for the 3D Brush Strokes command in the Apply Surface Texture dialog box.

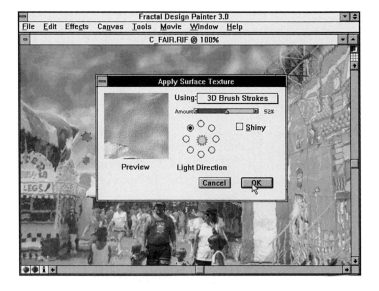

Figure 16.29. Additional adjustments in Painter 3.1 offer enhanced lighting effects, discussed in Step 16.5.

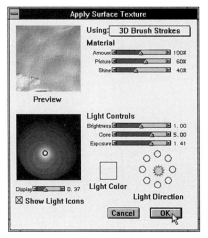

7. When your image appears in the preview window the way you like it, click OK to apply the command.

As you can see in Figure 16.30, the 3D brush strokes are more noticeable in areas where the grain-sensitive brushes were used!

Figure 16.30.
"Three-dimensional"
appearing brush
strokes are more
prominent in areas
painted with Grainy
method brushes.

Step 16.14. Adding Text

Now add some text to the document. You can add text with the Text Selection Tool, adjusting font, point size, and tracking in the Controls | Text Selection Palette:

1. From the Tools Palette, choose the Text Selection Tool. This is the icon with the letter A on it (the last icon in the top row).

2. Use Ctrl-6 in Windows or Cmd-6 in Mac to display the Controls Palette, if it is not already shown on your screen. The Controls | Text Selection Palette appears, as shown in Figure 16.31.

Figure 16.31.
Choose text and font
size in the Controls |
Text Selection Palette.

3. From the Controls | Text Selection Palette, click inside the drop-down Font listbox to select a font you want to use. If the font you wish to select is not shown in the upper portion of the list, you can choose from all the fonts installed on your system by choosing the Other Fonts option. For this example, I chose Braggadocio. If you don't have this font, choose something fairly simple and bold.

4. To change the font size, adjust the Point Size slider toward the right to increase the size of the font. I used a 60-point font in my example, but your font may look better in another size.

5. If you want to adjust the *tracking* of the font (the space between letters), do so with the Tracking slider located on the right side of the palette.

6. Position the cursor where you want the first line of text to be, and type in Come to. *Do not* press the Enter (Windows) or Return (Mac) key. (Multiple lines of text aren't supported—you must enter the text one line at a time.)

7. Open the Objects | Path List Palette, where all the letters in the Path List Palette are be highlighted in blue, as shown in Figure 16.32.

Figure 16.32.
All the letters in the
Path List Palette are
highlighted in blue.

8. Click the Group Button to group the letters.

9. Lock the group by clicking the arrow symbol adjacent to the group heading. All the elements are hidden, except for the group name.

10. You can position the text on the screen in one of two ways. Now that you've linked them all together as a group, you can move the text all at once by using the arrow keys on your keyboard. Alternatively, you can reposition or rescale the text with the Path Adjuster tool and take any of these actions:

Click the Path Adjuster tool on any of the elements inside the group. The Path Adjuster tool changes to an arrow and you can reposition the group.

Click the Path Adjuster tool on one of the outer edges. The Path Adjuster tool changes into an arrow and you can rescale the group.

Click the Path Adjuster tool at a corner of the selected group to rescale the group in both dimensions.

Click the Path Adjuster tool in the middle of the top or bottom to rescale the group in one direction only.

11. Add and position a second line of text—to the Fair!—in the same manner. When you enter the second line of text, the first group in the Path List Palette becomes inactive, and the letters of the second group are highlighted in blue in the Path List Palette, as shown in Figure 16.33.

Figure 16.33.
The second line of text appears in the Path List Palette.

12. Again, choose the Group button.

13. Collapse the second group. You should now have two groups of text showing in the Path List Palette, as shown in Figure 16.34. The first group became hidden when you entered the second line, but not to worry—it's still there!

14. Click both groups in the Path List Palette so they are highlighted in blue.

15. Press the Enter (Windows) or Return (Mac) key. Both lines of text should appear in your document window, surrounded by a selection marquee. Your screen should look similar to Figure 16.35.

*Figure 16.34.
Group both lines of text
in the Path List Palette.*

*Figure 16.35.
Both text lines are
activated and ready for
you to paint them.*

16. In the Path List Palette, or in the bottom-left corner of your document window, verify that the third Drawing Visibility button is selected. This enables you to color only the insides of the letters.

17. Choose the Piano Keys variant from the Artists brushes.

18. Select a shade of red as your current color. The color I used was Hue 35, Saturation 72, Value 46, as shown in Figure 16.36.

Figure 16.36.
Fill the text with the
Piano Keys brush and
a shade of red.

19. You'll get lost using this variant, because it's a fun one! Color in the letters—you'll see that it looks almost like colored strands of crepe paper, or Christmas tree garland.

20. Next, choose a really deep shade of red from the same color triangle.

21. Add some shading to the top and bottom edges of the letters with the Thin Stroke Airbrush.

If you like, you can now add a drop shadow to the text to give it a little more depth. To do this, you have to turn the text into a floater.

NOTE Note that in Painter 3.0 shadows can't be undone! (In Painter 3.1, you can undo drop shadows.) If you make a mistake, you'll have to apply it again from scratch. There are two things you can do in Painter 3.0 to revert back to the version of the floater without the shadow applied:

- One way is to save your document with the letters the way they are now, so you can revert to the saved version if need be.

- An alternative is to place a copy of the letters into the Objects | Floaters Palette by pressing the Alt key in Windows, or the Option key in Mac, while dragging the letters into the Floater library. You can then delete the "wrong" version of the floater from the document, and drag a fresh version from the Floaters Palette into the same location.

22. With the selection marquees still active around the lettering, click the selection with the Floating Selection Tool. When you open the Objects | Floater List Palette, a floater will appear in the Floater list, as shown in Figure 16.37.

Figure 16.37.
Turn the text selection
into a floater so you can
add a drop shadow.

23. To add a drop shadow to the floater, choose Effects | Objects | Create Drop Shadow. In the Drop Shadow dialog box, enter values in the boxes to create a shadow to your liking.

Here's a list of the boxes in the Drop Shadow dialog box:

- X-Offset: the number of pixels the drop shadow is offset on the x-axis (left-to-right)

- Y-Offset: the number of pixels the drop shadow is offset on the y-axis (top-to-bottom)

- Opacity: the transparency of the shadow; 0% creates an invisible shadow, while 100% creates a shadow that is totally black

- Radius: the length of the shadow; the higher this number, the longer the shadow

- Angle: the direction in which the shadow is cast

- Thinness: the amount of fadeout in the shadow; lower numbers produce less fade, and higher numbers produce more fade.

24. After you've made your adjustments in the Create Drop Shadow dialog box, click OK to apply the command. A drop shadow appears behind your letters, as shown in Figure 16.38.

Figure 16.38.
With a drop shadow
added, your image is
complete.

Step 16.15. Cloning Portions of an Image with the Shift-Click (Windows) or Control-Click (Mac) Method

One method of source/clone linking that I haven't yet discussed is the Shift-Click (Windows) or Control-Click (Mac) method. In Windows, if you press the Shift key while clicking in a source document (which in this case can even be your current document), you can identify that area as a link point with your clone document. Likewise, Mac users can press the Control key while clicking in a source document to link it with a clone document.

To explain this further, let's say you have an image that includes an apple, which you want to place in a still-life scene. The apple is positioned in the upper-left of this document, but you want to clone it into the center of a still-life image you're working on.

To do this, make the source document (the picture with the apple in it) your current image. Assuming that you've already selected your cloner brush, press the Shift (Windows) or Control (Mac) key and click some point in the apple (for example, the center).

Now make your clone document (the still-life scene) the current image. Begin cloning in the usual manner where you want the image to appear, starting at the same relative point. That is, if you clicked the center of the apple in the clone source, begin cloning in your clone document where you want the center of the apple to appear.

Continue cloning until the apple appears in full in your clone document. If you haven't modified Painter's general preferences, a crosshair-shaped reference point identifies the place you're cloning from in the source document.

Let's go further. Assume that there's a leaf in your still-life image (the clone document) that you want to reproduce in another area within the scene. Again, use the Shift (Windows) or Control (Mac) key while clicking the leaf's reference point. Then clone the leaf in another area of the same document. You can pick and choose portions of the document in this manner as often as you like, and it's a great way to piece an image together.

Summary

As you've learned, cloning is a great way to create documents quickly. With cloning, you can create a document automatically, or with little effort. You can accomplish cloning with Painter's Cloning brushes or, with minor modifications, any of Painter's other brushes. You can even clone portions of a document into other areas of the same document! Keep experimenting with this feature of Painter; you'll learn more as you go on!

17

A Collage of Effects

Throughout this book, you work with paths, floaters, and effects to create Painter documents. In this chapter, I discuss some additional points about paths and floaters, as well as some effects that haven't been covered in other projects.

Working with Paths and Selections

It may sometimes be a bit confusing to determine the difference between a *path* and a *selection*. But if you remember a few points, it might help clear up the differences between the two.

■ Think of a path as an outline that defines an area to be masked or altered with paint, fills, or effects. The image contained within the path is not actually a part of the path until it is converted to a floater, discussed later.

■ Paths can be active or inactive. When a path is inactive, its outline appears solid in your document window. Masking, effects, and fills cannot be applied to inactive paths.

■ When a path is active, it can be considered a selection. Typically, you activate paths when you want to perform an action on the areas within them. You can activate one or more paths (that is, select multiple areas) concurrently by clicking on the first and then Shift-clicking on remaining paths with the Path Adjuster Tool. Or, you can use the circular icons in the Objects | Path List Palette to activate and deactivate paths.

■ Active paths, or selections, are identified by a moving marquee outline (sometimes known as "marching ants"). The selection marquee is black and white when it represents an active outline selection. A red-and-white marquee represents an active negative outline selection. Finally, a green-and-white marquee represents an active mask selection.

■ One way paths can be created is by using the selection tools in the Tools Palette. These include the Oval Selection Tool, the Text Selection Tool, and the Outline Selection Tool. The Rectangular Selection Tool behaves a bit differently and will be covered next. Paths created using these tools will appear in the Objects | Path List Palette, and they can be activated and deactivated at will during the creation of your document.

TIP If you have a pressure-sensitive stylus, you can also create an outline path that varies in width based on pressure. Select the Outline Selection Tool and place it in Freehand drawing mode. While holding down the Alt (Windows) or Option (Mac) key, draw a line or shape, using varied pressure as you do so. Figure 17.1 shows some of the possible results.

Figure 17.1.
You can create outline
paths that vary with
pressure if you have a
pressure-sensitive
stylus.

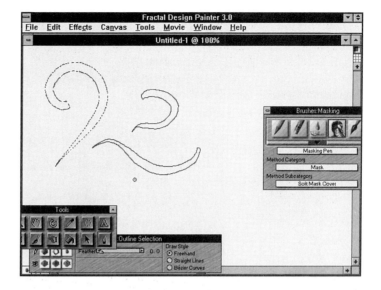

- The Rectangular Selection Tool defines a temporary rectangular or square area on which to perform an action. Areas defined with the Rectangular Selection Tool do not appear in the Objects | Path List Palette. You will notice that outlines created with the Rectangular Selection Tool are always surrounded with marching ants. Therefore, these areas are always selections. The area defined with the Rectangular Selection Tool will remain active until you draw another rectangle or until you select another area to work on.

TIP You can create permanent rectangular paths using the Outline Selection Tool in Straight Line drawing mode.

- You can also create selections using masking commands or masking brushes. Several examples of this technique are given throughout the book. Mask selections also appear in the Objects | Path List Palette, and these can later be activated or deactivated like any other path.
- The Edit | Magic Wand command can be used to select an area or areas based on pixel color.

Creating and Editing Bézier Curve Paths

When you create paths using the Bézier Curve method, you draw outlines around the shape by placing a series of control points around the shape. As you draw the shape, curves begin to form. You can later adjust the curves by moving the handles of the control points. Figure 17.2 shows a Bézier Curve selection being created.

Figure 17.2.
Bézier Curve paths are created by placing and dragging control points and handles.

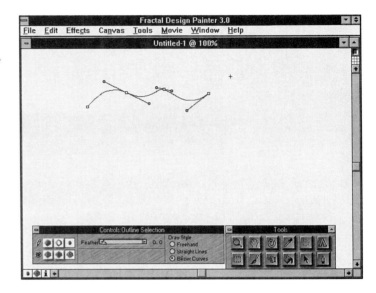

To create a path with Bézier Curves, do as follows:

1. Click the Outline Tool in the Tools Palette. The Controls | Outline Selection Palette will appear if you have the Controls Palette displayed.

2. From the Outline Selection Palette, click the radio button adjacent to Bézier Curves. The cursor will change into a small x when placed inside the document window.

3. Click your mouse or stylus where you want the path to start. Keep the mouse button or stylus depressed as you drag in the direction you want the curve to go. A handle will follow the cursor.

4. When you reach the end of the first curve, click the mouse or stylus again. Then, keep the mouse button or stylus depressed as you drag a second handle to define the shape of the curve.

5. Continue clicking and dragging control points until your selection is completely surrounded. End your path in the same point at which you started. If you don't close the shape off by clicking inside the starting point, new segments will be added to the end of the selection.

- To delete the most recently drawn segment in your selection, press the Backspace key in Windows, or the Delete key in Mac. You can step backwards with the Backspace or Delete key to delete as many segments as you wish.

- To control the length of the curve, increase or decrease the length between the two control points (the point from which the handles radiate). Curves will be narrower if the control points are spaced closer together, and they will be wider if they are farther apart. The control points can also be adjusted after the selection is completely drawn.

- To control the angle of the curve, adjust the length and placement of the handles that control the curve segment. Longer handles will create a larger angle, and shorter handles will create smaller angles. The angle also changes as you drag the handle around in different angles, making the curve sharper or smoother.

TIP You can adjust the Bézier curve to create a sharp point in a curve. Use the Path Adjuster to move one of the handles (indicated by the + symbol) directly above or near its control point (indicated by a square). Figure 17.3 shows a sharp curve created in this manner.

Figure 17.3.
Sharp points can be created in Bézier Curve paths by placing one of the handles at or near its control point.

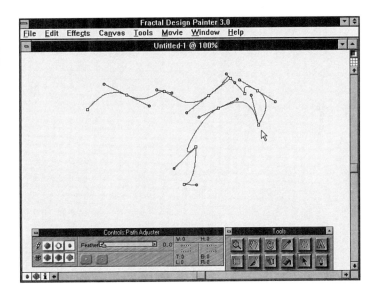

Converting Between Selections and Curves

When you see paths created with Bézier Curve mode displayed showing their control points and handles, the area cannot be acted upon. To use a curved path as a selection, you must convert it into a selection with the Tools | Selections | Convert to Selection command, discussed next.

Convert to Selection

To convert a Bézier Curve path into a selection, choose Tools | Selections | Convert to Selection. A selection marquee replaces the solid lines and nodes of the curves, indicating the conversion is complete.

Convert to Curve

Conversely, the Convert to Curve command, shown in Figure 17.4, is used to convert a selection to editable Bézier Curves. For example, you can convert a text selection to editable curves. Then you can adjust the look of the text by moving nodes and adjusting the Bézier Curves of the text. You can then convert the curves back to a selection with the Convert to Selection command and manipulate it in the usual manners.

Figure 17.4.
Use the Convert to Curve command to convert an outline path into adjustable Bézier curves.

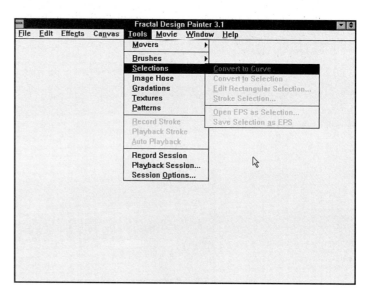

To convert a selection to curves, follow the steps below:

1. Create a selection using any of the selection tools, except the Rectangular Selection Tool.

2. Choose Tools | Selections | Convert to Curve. The selection will turn into a solid outline with white nodes at various points. The solid square-shaped node points can be moved to new locations. The cross-shaped nodes are the control points of the Bézier curves. Moving these nodes will adjust the shapes of the curves that they control. Moving the cursor over one of the nodes will change the cursor display to an arrow when the cursor passes over an editable control point. When the cursor turns into an arrow, click the mouse or stylus, and drag the node to a new location.

3. When the shape of the curves looks acceptable, you can convert it back into a selection with the Convert to Selection command.

TIP   You can also convert between a Bézier Curve path and a Selection by clicking on the icons in the Objects : Path List Palette. Selections are identified by circular icons at the front of each name in the Path list. Curve Paths are identified by a Pen-shaped icon in the Objects : Path List Palette. If a selection can be converted between the two types, both icons will appear beside the name of the path in the Path List Palette, as shown in Figures 17.5 and 17.6.

Figure 17.5.
Both paths in this Path List can be converted between an outline path and a Bézier Curve path from within the Objects : Path List Palette.

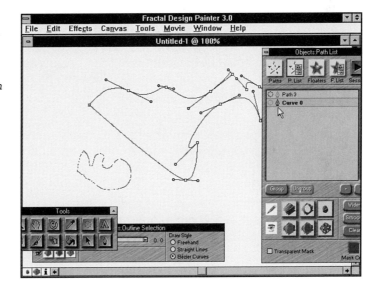

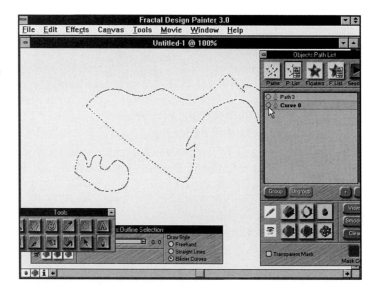

Figure 17.6.
The second path in
the Path List was
converted into an
outline path by clicking
on the circle beside its
name.

Creating and Editing Freehand Selections

In Freehand drawing mode, you can select areas using the Outline Selection Tool. To accomplish this, perform the following steps:

1. Click the Outline Tool in the Tools Palette. The Controls : Outline Selection Palette will be displayed if you have the Controls Palette displayed on your screen.

2. From the Outline Selection Palette, click the radio button adjacent to Freehand.

3. Click where you want your selection to begin, and drag the mouse or stylus around the area you want to select. An outline will appear as you draw the selection, although this line might be difficult to see on dark backgrounds.

4. End the selection at or near the same point you started, and release the mouse or stylus when you're done. A marquee surrounds the selection, indicating that the selected area is active.

You can add to or subtract from a freehand selection to refine your shape. The procedure to edit freehand selections is as follows:

1. Create a selection using the Outline Selection Tool, or activate the path in the Objects : Path List Palette that you wish to edit.

2. Using the Outline Selection Tool, hold down the Shift key and draw a line that shows how you want to revise the shape. Start at a point on the existing outline, and draw your line inward to decrease the size of the existing shape, or outward to increase the size of the shape. End your line at a point on the existing outline.

3. Release the mouse or stylus and the Shift key when you're done. The selection will be redrawn to show the changes you made.

Manipulating Selections

You've learned throughout this book how to manipulate paths and selections in different ways. To summarize, the following sections discuss various ways in which paths can be manipulated.

Manipulating Paths from the Path List Palette

The Objects : Path List Palette contains some other controls that allow you to make changes to paths. These are the Smooth and Widen buttons, shown in Figure 17.7.

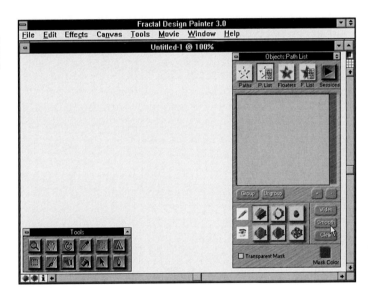

Figure 17.7.
The Smooth and Widen buttons in the Objects | Path List Palette can be used to modify paths.

The Smooth button in the Objects : Path List Palette allows you to smooth lines in a path. For example, you can use this technique to round the edges of a rectangle created with the Outline Selection Tool. Or, it can be used to smooth out paths created in Freehand mode. To smooth a path, use the following procedure:

1. Create a path using the Outline Selection Tool. Or, select a path to be smoothed with the Path Adjuster Tool.

2. From the Objects : Path List Palette, click the Smooth button. The shape of the path will be smoothed.

3. Repeat clicking the Smooth button for additional smoothing, if necessary.

Paths can also be widened from within the Objects : Path List Palette. To widen a path, proceed as follows:

1. Create a path using the Outline Selection Tool. Or select a path to be smoothed with the Path Adjuster Tool.

2. From the Objects : Path List Palette, click the Widen button. The Widen Path dialog box will appear.

3. Enter the number of pixels that you want to widen the path by. Negative numbers will decrease the width of the path.

4. Click OK, or press Enter (Windows) or Return (Mac), to complete the command.

Selecting and Deselecting Paths

We've worked with paths throughout the book, but it doesn't hurt to review some of the important steps. Paths can be selected and deselected by using the following methods:

■ To select a path, simply click it with the Path Adjuster Tool. When you choose it in this manner, handles appear around the selection, indicating that you can adjust the selection with the Path Adjuster Tool. You can also select paths from the Objects : Path List Palette. Click the circle or the pen icon beside its name in the Path List. The icon will be dotted when the associated path is active.

■ To select more than one path, hold down the Shift key as you click the paths you want to select. Each additional click will add a path to the selection. Or you can drag a marquee selection box around the paths you want to select with the Path Adjuster Tool. You can also select multiple paths from the Objects : Path List Palette by using Shift-Click to highlight multiple names.

■ To select all paths, choose the Path Adjuster Tool from the Tools Palette, then choose the Edit | Select All command. Or, you can drag a marquee selection box around all the paths with the Path Adjuster Tool.

■ To deactivate a selection or group of selections while using the Path Adjuster Tool, you can choose the Edit | Deselect command, which will deselect all paths in the image. The path outlines will turn solid, indicating that they are inactive. The deactivated paths can be immediately reselected with the Edit | Reselect command. You can also deactivate paths by clicking anywhere outside the selection.

■ To deselect part of a selection group, hold down the Shift key while clicking on the paths you want to deselect. The other selections will remain active.

> **NOTE** If you use the Edit | Deselect command with any other tool, the selection
> outlines will be invisible and cannot be reselected with the Edit | Reselect
> command.

Maintaining Paths

Use the Path Mover, shown in Figure 17.8, to move paths from one library to
another. You access the Path Mover with the Tools | Movers | Path Mover
command. The steps for using the Path Mover are almost identical to the steps
for the Brush Mover, outlined in Chapter 14, "Working with the Brush Tools."

Figure 17.8.
The Path Mover is used
to move paths between
two libraries, or to
create new Path
Libraries.

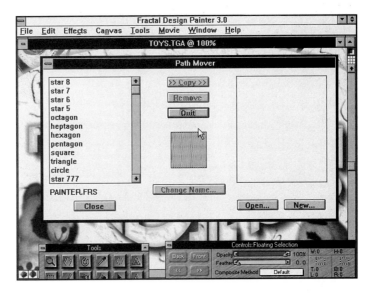

Path Libraries can be created from the Objects : Path List Palette or from the
Path Mover. When you create a library from the Paths Palette, you can immediately place your new custom-made paths inside. When creating a library from
the Path Mover, you can move paths from other libraries into the new library.

Working with Floaters

As mentioned earlier, a floater is, in basic terms, a path or selection that has
image data contained within it. Floaters are typically created by clicking on a
selection with the Floating Selection Tool. Once you create a floater, it can be
moved around within your image. It also has its own mask, which can interact
with the background mask, as I have shown in some projects here in the book.

577

For examples of this, review Chapter 9, "A Little Glimpse of Heaven," and Chapter 12, "Working with the Masking Tools." These chapters provide examples of floater mask and background mask interaction.

> **NOTE** Floaters can be created from a group of selected paths. The outlines of the individual paths can then be seen in the floaters (see the Egyptian floater in Chapter 12 as an example), but you can no longer use them individually once they are contained in a floater. Don't turn multiple paths into a floater until you're done with your editing and painting.

Floaters reside in a separate layer above the background image and contain their own masking layer. You can alter the appearance of floaters without affecting the background image or other floaters. They can be layered above each other and rearranged to suit your composition. Images saved with the .RIF extension, Painter's native format, keep any floaters still floating.

Controls | Floating Selection Palette

The Controls : Floating Selection Palette appears when you select the Floating Selection Tool from the Tools Palette. This palette is shown in Figure 17.9.

Figure 17.9.
The Controls : Floating
Selection Palette allows
you to layer floaters,
adjust their opacity,
and choose composite
methods.

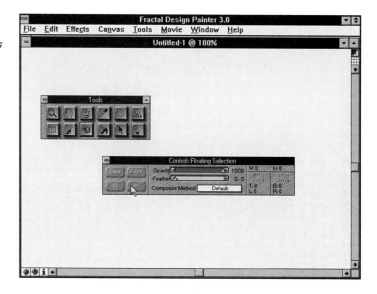

With the Controls : Floating Selection Palette, you can send floaters forward or backward in layers, set their opacity and feathering, and select composite methods. The overall dimensions and X,Y coordinates of the selection are also displayed.

The controls available in the Floating Selection Palette are as follows:

Left Arrow: Sends the currently active floater or floater group back one layer in the stack.

Right Arrow: Sends the currently active floater or floater group forward one layer in the stack.

Back: Sends a floater or group of floaters to the bottom of the stack.

Front: Brings a floater or group of floaters to the top of the stack.

Opacity Slider: Enables you to adjust the opacity or transparency of the floater, from 0% (invisible) to 100% (fully opaque).

Feather Slider: Enables you to adjust the feathering of the floater from 0 pixels (no feathering) to 50 pixels wide. This setting is influenced by the Floating Selection Prefeather setting, set in the Edit | Preferences | General command, which sets the maximum number of pixels allowed for feathering.

Width and Height: The overall width and height of the floating selection is shown in the upper-right corner of the palette

Top Left and Bottom Right Coordinates: The top-left and bottom-right coordinates of the floater are shown beneath the width and height of the floater. The coordinates are calculated from the upper-left corner of your image, with that point being at the 0,0 coordinate. The first number of the coordinate corresponds to the column that the pixel is in (that is, how far left or right into the image it is). The second number of the coordinate corresponds to the row that the pixel is in (that is, how far up or down it is).

Maintaining Floaters

The Floater Mover, shown in Figure 17.10, is used to move floaters from one library to another. You access the Floater Mover with the Tools | Mover | Floater Mover command.

You can create Floater Libraries from the Floater Mover. When creating a library from the Floater Mover, you can move floaters from other libraries into a new library. The procedures for creating and maintaining floater libraries are similar to those outlined for Brush Libraries in Chapter 14, "Working with the Brush Tools."

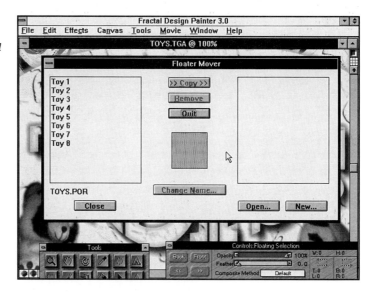

Figure 17.10.
Floater libraries can be
created and maintained
through the Floater
Mover.

Additional Masking Commands

There are some masking commands that have not been mentioned thus far that you might find helpful. The commands are as follows:

Magic Wand

The Magic Wand command allows you to make a selection according to pixel color. You can make adjustments to the selection by moving the Hue, Saturation, and Value sliders to make the selection accept a wider or narrower range of pixels in the color group.

To select a portion of your image with the Magic Wand, do as follows:

1. If you want to select all instances of a particular color or group of colors within your image, use the Edit | Select All command to select your entire image.

2. Choose Edit | Magic Wand. The Magic Wand dialog box (shown in Figure 17.11) appears, and the cursor will change to a magic wand.

3. Click and drag the magic wand in the color or colors you want to select. You can drag the magic wand through a range of colors if you like. Your image will show the selected color or colors masked in red, defining the areas that will be contained in the magic wand selection. If the color is uniform, then the area will be fully selected. The HSV sliders in the Magic Wand window will adjust to reflect the color or colors of the pixels in the area you dragged in.

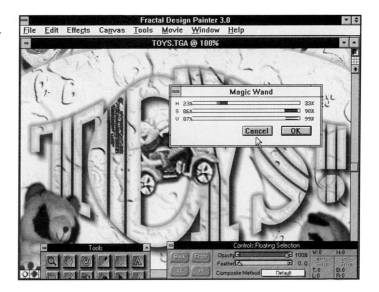

Figure 17.11.
The Magic Wand dialog
box allows you to
select an area based on
color.

4. If the area you want to select is not fully selected, you can add to it. You can increase the HSV levels so more color groups are included. You can do this in one of two ways.

   ■ You can Shift-click and drag around with the Magic Wand, picking up more areas of color in the area you want to select. This method will change the HSV sliders automatically.

   ■ Or, you can adjust the HSV sliders manually by clicking and dragging on them.

4. When your selection appears the way you want, Click OK or press Enter (Windows) or Return (Mac). The area formerly defined by the red mask will now be surrounded with a selection marquee.

Mask | Clear Mask (Ctrl-U in Windows, Cmd-U in Mac)

This command completely clears the mask from the masking layer. To clear the mask:

1. Choose the middle Mask Visibility button in the lower left corner of the document window so that you can see the mask in your image.

2. To clear the mask, choose Edit | Mask | Clear Mask. The mask will be removed from your image.

Mask | Color Mask

Color masks can be generated in Painter by using the following method:

1. Choose Edit | Mask | Color Mask. The Color Mask dialog box will appear. This dialog box is shown in Figure 17.12.

Figure 17.12.
*The color of the mask
can be changed with
the Edit | Mask | Color
Mask command.*

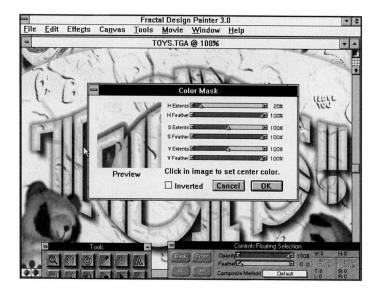

2. The HSV Extents sliders control the amount of variance from the center color that you select to mask. The HSV Feather sliders can be adjusted to feather the edge of the mask based on the hue, saturation, and value of color. Your image can be moved around in the preview window as you adjust the sliders. You can also select a color from the image with the Dropper Tool while the dialog box is open.

3. When the mask appears correct, click OK to apply the mask.

Mask | Feather Mask

This command brings up a dialog box that allows you to adjust the feathering of the masks. To use this command:

1. Choose the middle Mask Visibility button in the lower left side of the document window to view the effect of this command.

2. Choose Edit | Mask | Feather Mask. A dialog box will appear, that prompts you to enter the number of pixels in width that you would like the mask to feather. Painter will allow you to feather the mask up to 50 pixels wide. Type the desired number of pixels in the box.

3. Click OK to complete the command. You will see the adjustment take effect in a short time.

Mask | Invert Mask

This command allows you to invert the mask in the image.

1. Choose the middle Mask Visibility button in the lower-left side of the document window to view the effect of this command.

2. Choose Edit | Mask | Invert Mask. The areas that were masked before the command was applied will become unmasked, and vice-versa.

Painter Effects

Throughout this book, we have worked with a variety of effects, some of which can be applied to your images using several methods. Table 17.1 lists the commands that can be applied to your images in several ways.

Table 17.1. "Using" Option

Command	Uniform Color	Paper Grain	Mask	Image Luminance	Original Luminance	3D Brush Strokes
Tonal Control	Adjust Colors	X	X	X	X	X	
Tonal Control	Adjust Selected Colors	X	X	X	X	X	
Surface Control	Apply Screen		X	X	X	X	
Surface Control	Apply Surface Texture		X	X	X	X	X
Surface Control	Color Overlay	X	X	X	X	X	
Surface Control	Dye Concentration		X	X	X	X	X
Focus	Glass Distortion		X	X	X	X	X

The Using options for the effects listed in Table 17.1 can be described and applied as follows:

If you select Uniform Color as the method to apply the effect, it will be applied across the image or selection in a uniform manner.

If you elect to apply an effect based on Paper Grain, the paper grain currently selected will be used to determine which areas in your image or selection receive more of the effect, and which areas receive less. Areas that are raised in the paper grain will have more of the effect applied, and areas that are recessed in the paper grain will achieve less of the effect. The Art Materials: Papers Palette should be open before choosing the effect. You can select different paper textures from the Art Materials : Papers Palette while the effect's dialog box is open.

If you choose Mask as the method to apply the effect, it will be applied around the selection. This technique is often used to add an embossed effect around a selected area.

With Image Luminance selected as the method to apply the effect, it will be applied to your image based on the light and dark values of your image. Light areas will receive less of the effect, and dark areas will receive more of the effect.

Original Luminance, like Image Luminance, applies the effect based on the light and dark areas of an image. However, Original Luminance will apply the effect on the clone document, based on the light and dark areas of its source document. To use this effect, establish a clone/clone source relationship between two documents, and select your clone document as the current document before choosing the effect command.

3D Brush Strokes also works with a clone and a source document. The effect will be applied to your clone document based on stroke differences between the two documents. This technique is most effective when your image has been painted with grain-sensitive brushes.

TIP If you want to apply 3D Brush Strokes to an image that was created without the use of a clone source, create a blank image the same size as your document. Use the blank document as the clone source. The strokes will show up quite nicely!

Uniform Adjustment, similar to Uniform Color, will apply the effect uniformly over the entire image.

There are a few effects commands that have not yet been covered in this book. We'll use some of them in this chapter's project so that you can get a feel for what they do.

Effects | Esoterica | Growth

The Effects | Esoterica | Growth command creates branch-like designs that resemble the way trees are rendered in drafting. To use the Growth command, follow these steps:

1. Create a new document in which to place your growth patterns.
2. From the Art Materials : Colors Palette, choose the color that you would like for your branches.
3. Choose Effects | Esoterica | Growth. The Growth dialog box, shown in Figure 17.13, appears.

*Figure 17.13.
The Growth command
allows you to create
tree-like shapes in
Painter 3.1.*

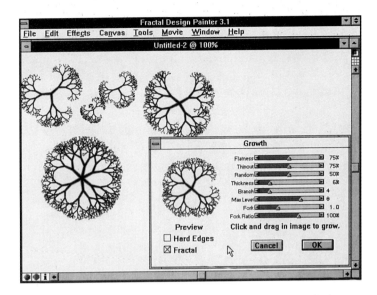

4. Make adjustments to the following settings as necessary while viewing
your growth pattern in the Preview window:

Hard Edges checkbox: Deselecting this check-box will generate growth
patterns with soft edges.

Fractal checkbox: The default growth pattern is closed on the outside by
a ring. Checking this option will generate open-ended growth patterns.

Flatness: This slider reshapes the growth pattern like a lens effect. Move
the slider toward the left for a concave lens effect, and toward the right for
a fish-eye lens effect.

Thinout: This slider affects how the size of the growth pattern is distributed from the center to the outside edges. With the slider set over 100%,
the outside edges will thicken. With the slider set under 100%, the outside
edges will become finer.

Random: This silder affects the symmetry of the growth patterns. Moving
the slider toward the left will generate straighter, more geometric patterns. Moving the slider to the right will generate more distorted and
crooked patterns.

Thickness: This slider adjusts the width of the lines within the pattern.
Move the slider to the left to create thinner lines, and to the right to create
thicker lines. The growth pattern will not get thinner than one pixel.

Branch: This slider determines the number of branches that come from the
center to the outside edge. The setting can be adjusted from 1 to 20, with 3
as the default.

585

Max Level: This slider determines the number of levels or sub-levels of the growth pattern, and sets the way the branches split to the outside edge.

Fork: Applicable to Fractal growth patterns only, this setting adjusts the amount of intricacy in the outermost branches.

Fork Ratio: Applicable to Fractal growth patterns only, this setting affects the tips of the outermost branches.

5. Click and drag your paper to define where you want the growth pattern to appear. You will see an outline of the developing pattern as you drag.

6. To make a different colored growth pattern, choose a different color and repeat the click-and-drag procedure.

7. Click OK or press Enter (Windows) or Return (Mac) to exit the Growth dialog box.

Effects | Esoterica | Highpass

The Effects | Esoterica | Highpass command reduces the number of low-frequency areas in your image and leaves high-frequency areas. Basically, what this command does is remove all the smooth gradations of color in your image and replace them with edges that contain abrupt changes of color.

To apply the Highpass command:

1. Select part of your image. Making no selection will apply the effect to the entire image.

2. Choose Effects | Esoterica | Highpass. The Highpass dialog box, shown in Figure 17.14, will appear.

Figure 17.14.
The Highpass com-
mand reduces the
number of low-
frequency areas in
your image.

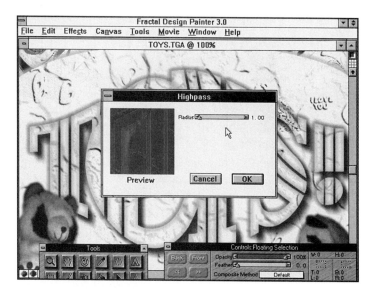

3. Adjust the Radius slider while watching the preview window. This slider signifies the radius (in pixels) around each pixel in the selected area. Moving this slider to the left will suppress larger amounts of low-frequency information, giving the image more edges. Moving the slider to the right will suppress less of the low-frequency information, reducing the effect.

4. Click OK or press Enter (Windows) or Return (Mac) to perform the command.

Effects | Surface Control | Apply Screen

The Effects | Surface Control | Apply Screen command works with three colors chosen in the Apply Screen dialog box and combines them with the light and dark values in the image, and with the currently selected paper texture, to produce a three-color textured effect in your image.

To implement the Apply Screen command, use the following procedure.

1. Select the area you would like to apply the effect to. If you make no selection, Painter will apply the effect to the entire image.

2. If you want to base the effect on a paper texture, select the desired paper texture from the Art Materials : Papers Palette. If you want to base the texture on Original Luminance, open a source document and clone document.

3. Choose Effects | Surface Control | Apply Screen. The Apply Screen dialog box, shown in Figure 17.15, will appear.

Figure 17.15.
The Apply Screen
command reduces a
selected area to three
colors.

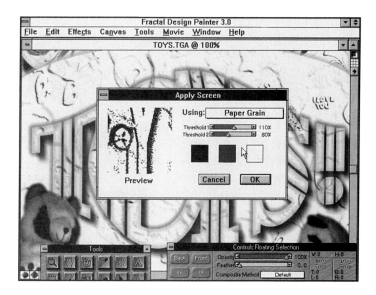

4. Three color squares appear in the dialog box. When choosing colors for these squares, keep the following in mind:

   - Adjusting the Threshold 1 slider will determine how much of the middle and last color will appear in the image. Moving the slider to the left will increase the amount of the last color, and moving it to the right will increase the amount of the middle color.

   - Adjusting the Threshold 2 slider will determine how much of the first and middle color will appear in the image. Moving the slider to the left will increase the amount of the middle color, and moving it to the right will increase the amount of the first color.

5. Choose three colors by clicking in one color square at a time. Each time, the color selection dialog box will appear. Choose a color from the dialog box, then click OK to return to the Apply Screen dialog box.

6. To apply texture to the screen, you can choose one of four methods: Paper Grain, Image Luminance, Original Luminance, or Mask.

7. Once all the adjustments have been made, and the preview window appears correct, click OK or press Enter (Windows) or Return (Mac) to apply the command.

Effects | Surface Control | Dye Concentration

The Effects | Surface Control | Dye Concentration command alters the color intensity of the image while adding surface texture. To use the command:

1. Select the area you would like to apply the effect to. If you make no selection, Painter will apply the effect to the entire image.

2. If you want to base the texture on Original Luminance, open a clone source and clone document.

3. Choose Effects | Surface Control | Dye Concentration. The Adjust Dye Concentration dialog box, shown in Figure 17.16, will appear.

4. The textured appearance can be applied in one of five methods: Uniform Adjustment, Paper Grain, Image Luminance, Original Luminance, or Mask.

5. Adjust the Maximum slider to control the amount of dye applied to the higher areas in the canvas. This slider can be set up to 800%. Adjust the Minimum slider to control the amount of dye applied to the lower areas in the canvas. This slider can be set down to 0%. Lower variations between the two settings will make the canvas appear flatter, and higher variations between the two will add more texture to the canvas.

Figure 17.16.
The Dye Concentration
command alters the
color intensity of a
selected area.

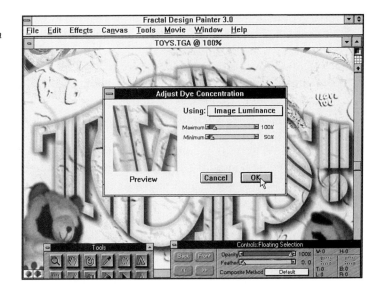

6. Once all the adjustments have been made, and the preview window appears correct, click OK or press Enter (Windows) or Return (Mac) to apply the command.

Effects | Esoterica | Apply Marbling

The Effects | Esoterica | Apply Marbling command creates marbled patterns in your image or selection. This technique is based on the real-world technique of floating pigment on liquid and pulling on the pigment to create marbled color variations.

You can choose to apply paint blobs to your image before using this command, which can enhance the marbled effect. To add blobs of paint, use the Blobs command before following this procedure.

To marble your image:

1. Select part of your image. If you make no selection, the effect will be applied to the entire image.
2. Choose Effects | Esoterica | Apply Marbling. The Apply Marbling dialog box appears.
3. You can see your image in the preview window, along with black lines that will approximate the pulls where the marbling will be applied.
4. While viewing the preview, adjust the sliders in the dialog box. The sliders adjust the following areas:

    Spacing: The Spacing setting represents the amount of space between the teeth of the marbling rake. Moving the slider to the left will narrow the space between the rake teeth, and moving it toward the right will increase the space between the rake teeth. With Left to Right or Right to Left marbling checked, this setting will affect the horizontal spacing of the rake. With Top to Bottom or Bottom to Top marbling checked, this setting will affect the vertical spacing of the rake. The setting is adjustable between 0 and 1.

Offset: The Offset setting controls the amount of space that the rake will shift over the next time it passes over the image. Adjusting the slider to the left will reduce the complexity of the marbling effect. Moving the slider to the right will increase the complexity of the effect. The setting is adjustable between 0 and 1.

Waviness: The Waviness setting determines the depth of the waves in the marbling. Moving the slider to the left will flatten the waves, and moving it to the right will increase the waviness. It is best to make small adjustments to this setting, using the arrows at the right and left sides of the slider bar. The setting is adjustable between 0 and 10.

Wavelength: The Wavelength setting controls the curve of the wave. Moving the slider to the left decreases the overall width of the curve, and moving it to the right increases the curve period. It is best to make small adjustments to this setting, using the arrows at the right and left sides of the slider bar. The setting is adjustable between 0 and 1.

Phase: The Phase setting determines the start point of the wave (that is, whether it starts in the beginning, the end, or some intermediate point of the wave). The settings are adjustable between 0 and 1, with 0 being the beginning of the phase and 1 being the end of the phase.

Pull: The Pull setting controls the amount of ink that is pulled by the rake. Moving the slider to the left decreases the amount of ink that is pulled, and moving the slider to the right increases the amount of ink pulled. This adjustment is not reflected in the preview window. The setting is adjustable between 0 and 10.

Quality: The Quality slider adjusts the amount of antialiasing in the marbling. Increasing the setting improves the quality of the marbling effect, but this also increases the amount of time it takes to calculate. The setting is adjustable between 1 and 4.

5. After making adjustments to the slider, click OK to apply the effect. A dialog box appears, informing you of the progress of the calculations.

Tonal Control Commands

The Tonal Control commands let you alter the Hue, Saturation, and Value settings of the colors in several ways.

- **Hue** is the predominant spectral color. Adjusting the Hue of a color can be likened to dragging the cursor along the outer color wheel in the Art Materials : Colors Palette, or in the color bar in the Art Materials : Small Colors Palette if you choose to use it instead.

- **Saturation** is the amount of brilliance or colorfulness in the color. Compare Saturation adjustment to moving the color indicator in the color triangle of the Art Materials : Colors Palette toward the right or left.

- **Value** is the amount of luminance, or light value, in the color. Adjusting the Value setting in a color can be likened to moving the color indicator in the triangle of the Art Materials : Colors Palette upward and downward.

Effects | Tonal Control | Adjust Colors

The Effects | Tonal Control | Adjust Colors command lets you control the Hue, Saturation, and Value settings of the color individually by adjusting the sliders. (This is similar to the color-adjustment you find on a television set.)

To use Adjust Colors, do as follows:

1. Select the area you would like to apply the effect to. If you make no selection, Painter will apply the effect to the entire image.

2. If you wish to apply color changes based on Original Luminance, open a clone document and its source.

3. Choose Effects | Tonal Control | Adjust Colors. The Adjust Color dialog box, shown in Figure 17.17, will appear.

Figure 17.17.
The Adjust Colors command allows you to adjust all colors in an image using several methods.

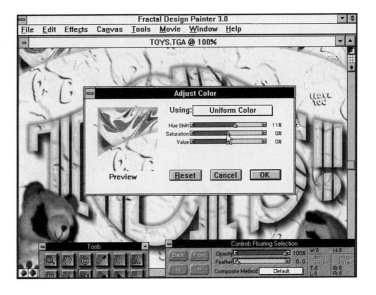

591

4. In the Using drop-down dialog box, select to apply the effect based on Uniform Color, Paper Grain, Image Luminance, Original Luminance, or Mask.

5. While looking in the preview window, adjust the Hue (H), Saturation (S), and Value (V) sliders until the image appears correct in the preview window. Clicking inside the bars will change the color in larger increments, and clicking on the arrows to the sides of the bar will adjust the color in smaller increments.

6. You can click the Reset button to return the preview to its original state.

7. When the preview window looks correct, click OK or press Enter (Windows) or Return (Mac) to apply the command.

Effects | Tonal Control | Adjust Selected Colors

You can use Effects | Tonal Control | Adjust Selected Colors if you want to change the color of an object to a different color. For example, you can change a red sphere to a green sphere, changing its subtle color variations in the process. The changes are applied based on a color's nearness to a selected color.

1. Select the area you would like to apply the effect to. If you make no selection, Painter will apply the effect to the entire image.

2. Choose Effects | Tonal Control | Adjust Selected Colors. The Adjust Selected Colors dialog box, shown in Figure 17.18, will appear.

Figure 17.18.
The Adjust Selected
Colors command lets
you change specified
colors in an image.

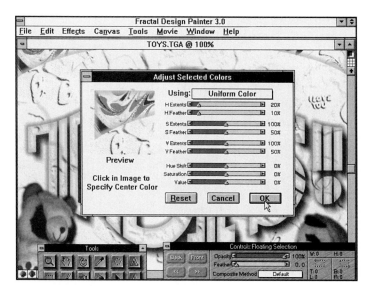

3. From the Using drop-down box, choose to apply the effect based on Uniform Color, Paper Grain, Image Luminance, Original Luminance, or Mask.

4. The prompt underneath the preview window will tell you to select the center color you want to adjust. Click in the image, selecting an intermediate representation of the color you want to change. For example, if you are changing a red sphere to a green sphere, select a color from the middle range rather than from the shadows or the highlights.

5. The lower portion of the dialog box contains sliders for Hue Shift, Saturation, and Value. Moving the Hue Shift slider will adjust the value of the center color to another hue—for example, green. The Saturation slider will change the vividness of the color, and the Value slider will change its luminance.

6. The Extents sliders in the dialog box will adjust the amount of color space affected by the command. Moving the slider to the left will decrease the amount of softness in the color when the command is applied, and moving the slider to the right will increase the amount of softness. The sliders are individually adjustable for Hue, Saturation, and Value extents.

7. The Feather sliders in the dialog box will adjust the number of hues selected for the change. Moving the slider to the left will narrow the range of hues affected by the command, and moving it to the right will increase the range of hues. The sliders are individually adjustable for Hue, Saturation, and Value feathers.

8. When the preview window appears the way you would like, choose OK or press Enter (Windows) or Return (Mac) to apply the effect.

Effects | Tonal Control | Brightness/Contrast

The Effects | Tonal Control | Brightness/Contrast command adjusts the image using an RGB format of adjustment. The brightness and contrast can be adjusted by using the following method:

1. Select the portion of the image that you would like to change. If you make no selection, the effect will be applied to the entire image.

2. Choose Effects | Tonal Control | Brightness/Contrast.

3. In the dialog box, adjust the upper slider to change the contrast of the image. Moving the slider to the left decreases the contrast, and moving the slider to the right increases the contrast. You can click the reset button to return the image to its original levels.

4. Adjust the lower slider to change the brightness of the image. Moving the slider to the left will decrease the brightness, and moving the slider to the right increases the brightness. You can click the reset button to return the image to its original levels.

5. When the preview window appears the way you would like, choose OK or press Enter (Windows) or Return (Mac) to apply the effect.

Effects | Tonal Control | Equalize (Ctrl-E in Windows, Cmd-E in Mac)

The Equalize command adjusts the contrast of the image by adjusting its black-and-white points. The brightness levels are then distributed throughout the entire range of the image. This command generates a color histogram that shows the number of pixels available in each brightness level.

To equalize, do as follows:

1. Select the portion of the image that you would like to change. If you make no selection, the effect will be applied to the entire image.

2. Choose Effects | Tonal Control | Equalize. The Equalize dialog box will appear.

3. There has already been some adjustment made in the image for you. You can, at this point, click OK or press Enter (Windows) or Return (Mac) to apply the effect. If you want to adjust the image further, you can manually adjust the black and white points by following the remaining steps.

4. At the right side of the histogram, drag the white triangle toward the left. Any values in the image that are located to the right of the white triangle will become white. At the left side of the histogram, drag the black triangle toward the right. Any values in the image that are located to the left of the black triangle will become black.

5. To adjust the gamma level in the image, move the Brightness slider to the left to increase gamma (that is, to darken the image) or to the right to decrease gamma (that is, to lighten the image). The gamma adjustment effects only the midtones of the image.

6. Click OK or press Enter (Windows) or Return (Mac) to apply the effect.

Effects | Tonal Control | Negative

The Negative command is pretty straightforward, and it produces exactly what its name implies. Choose Effects | Tonal Control | Negative to turn part or all of your image into a negative image.

The Effects Project

This project is done with floaters and effects. Here we're going to place some floaters into an image and use some effects to create an embossed background. Then, we'll add some lettering using an .EPS selection. Finally, we'll place a few more floaters into the image and enhance them a little.

Creating the Background

To create the background, we start with a blank image. Several floaters are dragged into the image and positioned, resized, reoriented, and then dropped into the background. A clone image is created and cleared, and the embossed effect is created using an effects command.

1. Create a new 640×480 document.

2. Open the Tools Palette (Ctrl-1 in Windows, Cmd-1 in Mac) and the Objects Palette (Ctrl-5 in Windows, Cmd-5 in Mac).

3. From the Objects | Floaters Palette, load in the TOYS.POR floater library, located on the CD accompanying this book. This library is shown in Figure 17.19.

Figure 17.19.
A new image is created, and the TOYS.POR floater library is opened.

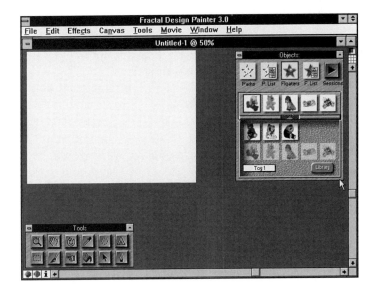

4. Drag one of each floater into your image (there are eight in all), and place them randomly into your document. Figure 17.20 shows one of each floater placed in the document.

Figure 17.20.
One of each floater is dragged into the document.

Now I'll let *you* be the artist. Fill the background completely with copies of these floaters. Rotate them, flip them horizontally, and increase their sizes. Don't apply any effects to them yet, though. Here are some pointers on how to fill the areas quicker:

- To make a copy of a floater, click it with the Floating Selection Tool while holding down the Alt (Windows) or Option (Mac) key on your keyboard. Then drag the floater's outline to a new location in your document and release the mouse or stylus.

- Position the floater in its appropriate layer using the buttons in the Controls | Floating Selection Palette. The left button will move the floater back one layer; the right button will move the floater forward one layer; the Back button will move the floater completely to the back; and the Front button will move the floater completely toward the front.

- To rotate floaters, choose the Effects | Orientation | Rotate command. The Rotate Selection dialog box, shown in Figure 17.21, will appear. You can rotate the floater by dragging one of the corners of its bounding box, or by typing an angle in the dialog box. Positive numbers will rotate the floater counterclockwise. Negative numbers will rotate the floater clockwise.

- You might want to increase the size of some of the floaters so that they take up more room. To resize floaters, choose the Effects | Orientation | Scale command. The Scale Selection dialog box, shown in Figure 17.22, will appear. Floaters can be rescaled visually by making adjustments to the bounding box surrounding the floater, or by entering numbers in the dialog box. To resize to different horizontal and vertical measurements, uncheck the Constrain Aspect Ratio checkbox in the dialog box. The Preserve Center box should be left checked if you want the center point of the floater to remain the same when the floater is rescaled.

Figure 17.21.
Rotate some of the
floaters with the
Effects | Orientation |
Rotate command.

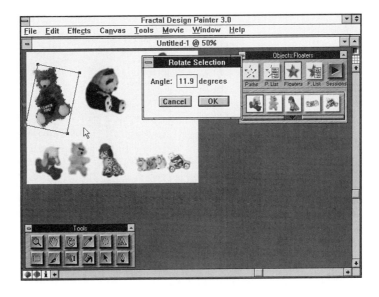

Figure 17.22.
Scale some of the
floaters with the
Effects | Orientation |
Scale command.

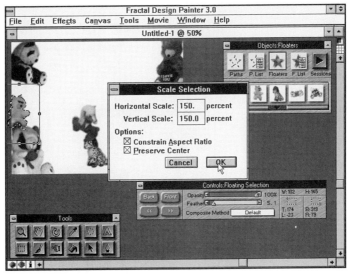

■ To flip floaters so that they face in the opposite direction, use the Effects | Orientation | Flip Horizontal command.

Once your image is filled, it will look something like Figure 17.23. There are some white areas here, but that's fine. Eventually, it will all be filled with pastel colors.

Figure 17.23.
The entire background
has been filled with
floaters.

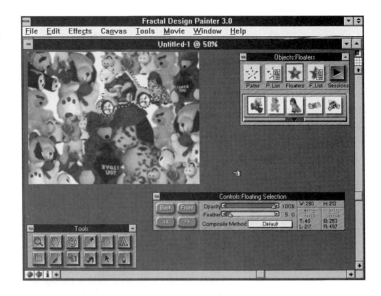

Embossing the Background

To create the embossed effect for our background, you have to drop all the
floaters you just arranged into the background layer. Then, you can create a
clone of the document, from which we can create the embossing.

1. From the Objects Palette, click the F.List icon to open the Floater List
   Palette. You will notice that all the floaters appear in the Floater list.

2. Click the Drop All button, located at the lower-right corner of the Floater
   list. This button is shown in Figure 17.24.

Figure 17.24.
To drop all the floaters
to the background,
click the Drop All
button in the Floater
List Palette.

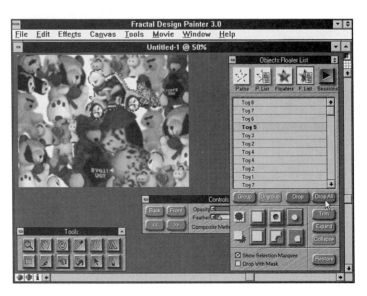

3. Create a clone of your background using the File | Clone command. Clear its contents by using the Edit | Select All command and then pressing the Backspace key on your keyboard. You should now have a blank image on your screen as your current image.

4. Choose Effects | Surface Control | Apply Surface Texture. The Apply Surface Texture dialog box will appear. In the Using drop-down menu, choose to apply the texture based on Original Luminance. You will see a preview of the embossed effect as shown in Figures 17.25 or 17.26. Make any adjustments you like until the preview looks the way you want, and choose OK to apply the command. All the default settings were used in my example, except that the Shiny button was turned off.

Figure 17.25.
The Apply Surface
Texture dialog box for
Painter 3.0.

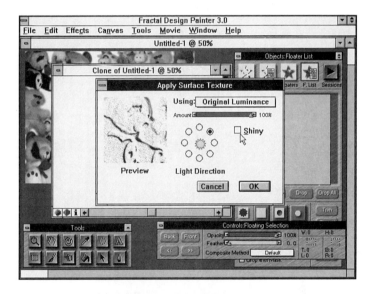

Figure 17.26.
The Apply Surface
Texture dialog box for
Painter 3.0.

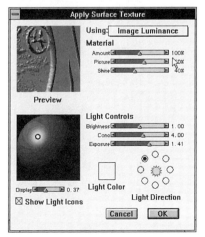

5. After the effect is applied, all floaters should disappear from the Floater List Palette, as shown in Figure 17.27. Additionally, your clone image will now have embossed versions of the floaters you placed in the original document!

Figure 17.27.
Your clone document
becomes an embossed
version of the clone
source.

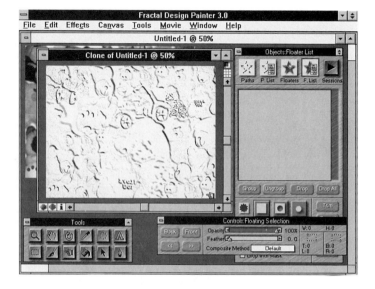

6. To add some color to the embossed effect, first open the Art Materials : Grads Palette. Select the Coppery gradient, shown in Figure 17.28.

Figure 17.28.
Choose the Coppery
gradient from the
default Grads Palette
library.

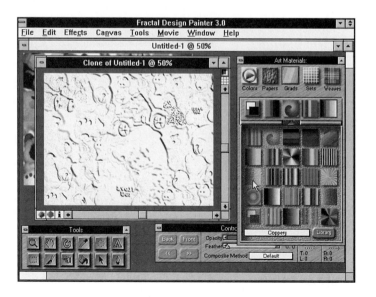

7. Verify that the darkest values of the gradient appear to the left of the gradient in the Orders bar, located in the bottom section of the Art Materials : Grads Palette. If this is not the case, click the third Orders button in the top row, as shown in Figure 17.29. Then, choose the Tools | Gradations | Express In Image command.

Figure 17.29.
Apply the gradient to
the background using
the Express In Image
command.

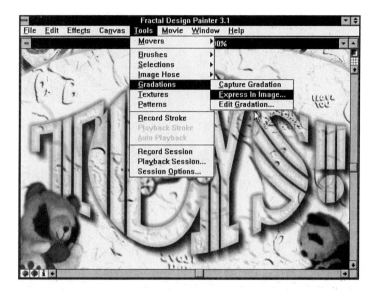

8. Your image should now have some color applied to it. The original darker areas of your embossing were replaced with the colors toward the left of the gradient (its darker values), and lighter areas of the embossing were replaced with the colors toward the right of the gradient (its lighter values).

Adding the Letters

The letters will be added using an .EPS selection. This was created in Corel Draw and is contained in the file named TOYS.EPS, located on the CD accompanying this book.

1. Use the Tools | Selections | Open EPS as Selection command to open the TOYS.EPS file located on the CD accompanying this book. The letters will appear in the center of your document.

2. From the Objects Palette, click the P.List icon to open the Path List Palette. All the paths contained in the EPS Selection file will be highlighted in blue in the Path List.

3. Click the Group button, shown in Figure 17.30, to place all the paths in the letters into a single group.

Figure 17.30.
Group all the paths
contained in the
TOYS.EPS file into a
single group in the Path
List.

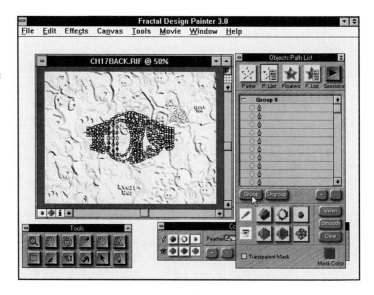

4. Close, or lock, the path group by clicking the arrow key adjacent to the group name. Then use the Enter (Windows) or Return (Mac) key on your keyboard to turn all the paths into selections. All the individual entities in the letters will become surrounded by a marquee, as shown in Figure 17.31.

Figure 17.31.
Close the path group
and activate the paths,
surrounding them with
selection marquees
Path List.

5. You can resize the letters as a group now. Choose the Path Adjuster Tool from the Tools Palette. Then move your cursor over the selections until it turns into a symbol with arrows. At this point, you can click-and-drag with your mouse or stylus to resize the selections visually. Figure 17.32 shows the selections resized.

Figure 17.32.
The second path in
the Path List was
converted into an
outline path by
clicking on the circle
beside its name.

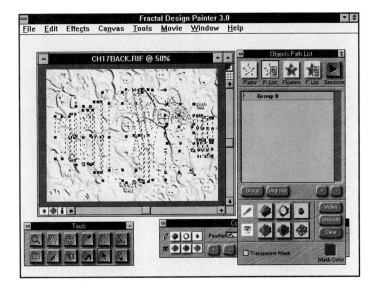

NOTE Another way to resize selections is to choose the Effects | Orientation | Scale command. With this command, a bounding box surrounds the paths, and this can be adjusted as necessary. You can uncheck the Constrain Aspect Ratio checkbox in the Scale Selection dialog box, shown in Figure 17.33, to scale the width and height at different percentages.

Whenever you use Effects | Orientation | Scale, you don't resize the selections only—you resize the image contained within the selections and create a floater in the process.

6. The seventh path in the Path List, shown in Figure 17.34, is that for the inside of the O, which has to be turned into a negative and placed above the outer section of the O (which is now the sixth item in the Path List). Highlight the seventh path in the list, and click the - button underneath the Path List. That path should become surrounded with a red-and-white selection marquee.

Figure 17.33.
The Effects | Orienta-
tion | Scale command
can also be used to
resize selections, but a
floater will be created
in the process.

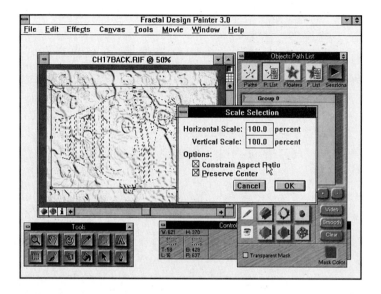

Figure 17.34.
Turn the inside of the O
(the seventh path in
the list) to a negative
path.

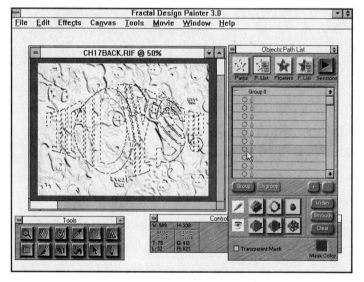

7. Now, position this negative path as the sixth path in the list. The path it is replacing will move to the seventh position in the Path List.

8. When you turn on the red mask display using the second Mask Visibility button, your mask should look as shown in Figure 17.35.

Figure 17.35.
After displaying the
mask in red, the letter
O should be cut out in
the center.

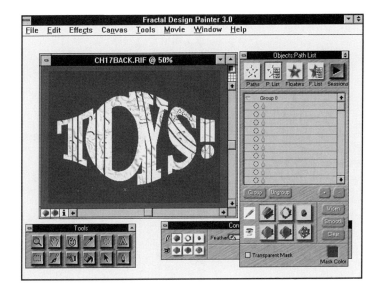

9. Select the second Drawing Visibility button and the third Mask Visibility button from the Objects : Path List Palette. This will protect the inside of the letters and surround the letters with selection marquees.

10. Using the Dropper, choose one of the deepest shades from your background image—either purple or blue.

11. Use the Tools | Selections | Stroke Selection command to outline your letters with a soft outline. When the command is done, your image should look similar to Figure 17.36.

Figure 17.36.
Stroke the outside of
the letters with the
Thin Stroke Airbrush
and deep purple or blue
paint.

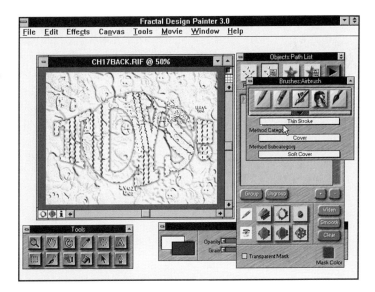

12. Now, using the Dropper, select a lighter shade from your background image—perhaps rose or pink. Choose the second Drawing Visibility button from the Objects : Path List Palette to mask the outside of the letters. Use the Tools | Selections | Stroke Selection command again to stroke the inside of the letters with the lighter color. Your image will look similar to Figure 17.37.

Figure 17.37.
Stroke the inside of the
letters with a lighter
shade from your
background image.

13. Choose the Floating Selection Tool from the Tools Palette, and click once on the selections to turn them into a single floater.

14. From the Objects Palette, click the F.List icon to verify that the floater appears in the Floater list. Then, double-click its name and note the Top and Left positions of the floater, as shown in Figure 17.38. Jot the numbers down for reference in case the floater gets relocated during your future steps (the area behind the floaters is now your paper color, which is white in this case).

15. Use the Effects | Objects | Create Drop Shadow command to apply a drop shadow to the floater. Set the X-Offset to 10 pixels, the Y-Offset to 12 pixels, and check the Collapse To One Layer checkbox, as shown in Figure 17.39.

Figure 17.38.
Note the Top and Left
positions of your floater
in case you have to
move it back to its
original location.

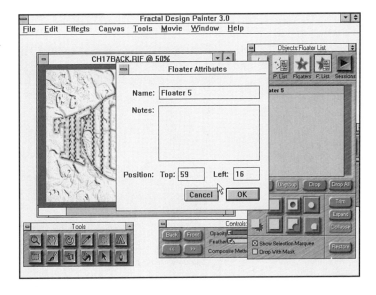

Figure 17.39.
Apply a drop shadow to
the floater, collapsing it
to one layer while
doing so.

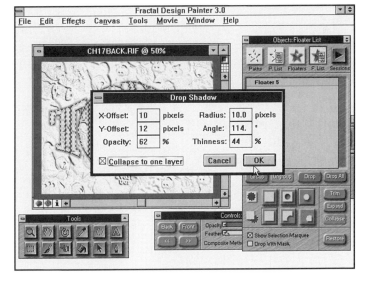

Lightening the Background

We should lighten the background a bit so that the letters stand out a little more. To do this, we will select the background area and then lighten it with the Effects | Surface Control | Dye Concentration command.

1. Choose Edit | Select All. The floater is deselected, and a marquee appears around the background image. Your image should look similar to Figure 17.40.

Figure 17.40.
After the drop shadow
is applied, select the
background using the
Edit | Select All
command.

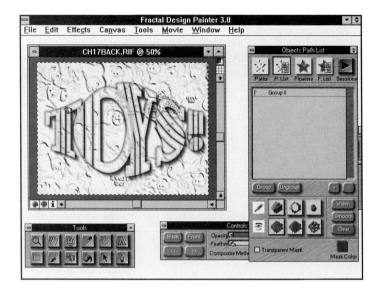

2. Choose Effects | Surface Control | Dye Concentration. The Adjust Dye Concentration dialog box appears, as shown in Figure 17.41. Using Uniform Adjustment, reduce the Maximum slider until your image looks nice and light yet shows enough detail. In my example, I adjusted both the Maximum and Minimum sliders to 39%.

Figure 17.41.
Adjust the Maximum
and Minimum sliders
in the Adjust Dye
Concentration dialog
box to lighten the
background.

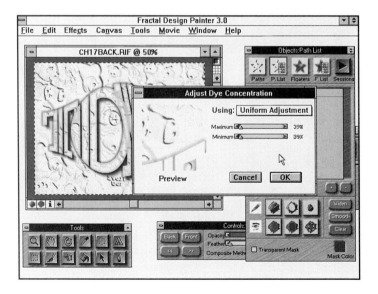

3. If you want to darken the outline around the letters again, go to the Objects | Path List Palette and reactivate the paths for the letters. Then, repeat Steps 10 through 12 from the previous section, "Adding the Letters," to deepen the color. Your image should now look like that shown in Figure 17.42.

Figure 17.42.
With background
lightened and an
optional stroke applied,
the letters stand out
more against the
background.

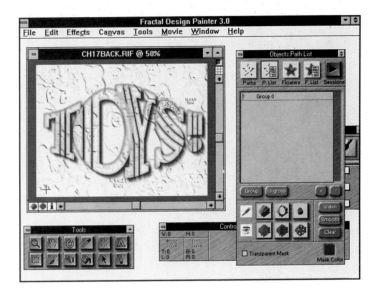

Applying Blobs and Marbling

We're going to create a Bézier Curve selection at the top of the document and apply blobs and marbling to the selected area. Note that these steps require that a floating-point unit (math coprocessor) be present in your computer.

1. From the Tools Palette, choose the Outline Selection Tool. From the Controls : Outline Selection Palette, choose to create a selection using Bézier Curves.

2. Starting from near the upper-left corner of the document, click to place the first point in the selection. Most of the control points remaining in the shape are straight lines between the control points. The only place where a handle is dragged out is the bottom center, which gets dragged out quite far as shown in Figure 17.43.

3. In the Objects : Path List Palette, click the circle beside the curve's name. This converts it to a selection and surrounds it with a marquee.

4. With the Dropper, choose a color from your background image. Pinks, roses, or reds might look nice as colors to add before applying a marble effect to this selection. The color you select will be used to add paint blobs into the selected area.

Figure 17.43.
Use the Outline
Selection Tool in Bézier
Curve mode to create a
shape along the top of
the image.

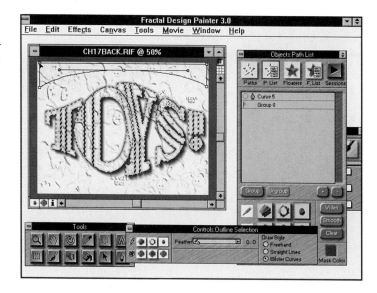

5. Choose Effects | Esoterica | Blobs. The Blobs dialog box appears, as shown in Figure 17.44. Adjust the settings as shown in the figure—15 blobs, a minimum of 15 pixels, and a maximum of 25 pixels. Then, choose OK to apply the effect. Random blobs of paint appear within the selected area after a short time.

Figure 17.44.
Adjust the settings for
the quantity and size of
the blobs in the Blobs
dialog box.

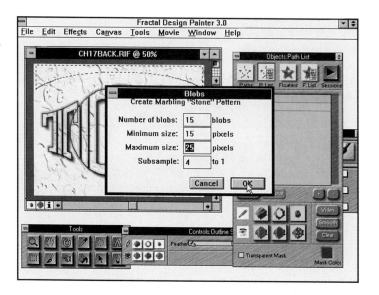

NOTE The Blobs command is very calculation-intensive. The amount of processing time for the Blobs command will increase depending on the quantity and size of the blobs, as well as the size of the area that the effect is applied to.

6. Choose a second color with the Dropper, and repeat the Blobs command using the same settings.

7. To deepen the color of the selected area, choose the Effects | Surface Control | Dye Concentration command. Using Uniform Adjustment, adjust the Maximum slider to a setting over 200%, as shown in Figure 17.45. This will deepen the colors within the selected area.

Figure 17.45.
Deepen the colors in
the selected area with
the Dye Concentration
command.

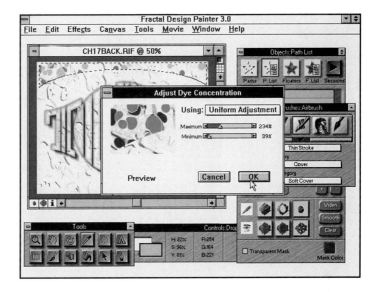

8. Now we apply the marbling. Choose Effects | Esoterica | Apply Marbling. The Apply Marbling dialog box will appear. Adjust the spacing to .30, the Waviness to 1.35, and the Wavelength to .25, as shown in Figure 17.46. The changes appear in the Rake Path preview window as the settings are adjusted. Click OK to apply the effect, and the marble will be rendered similar to the one in Figure 17.47.

Figure 17.46.
Adjust the marbling
settings in the Apply
Marbling dialog box.
Changes in the rake
path can be previewed
in the preview window.

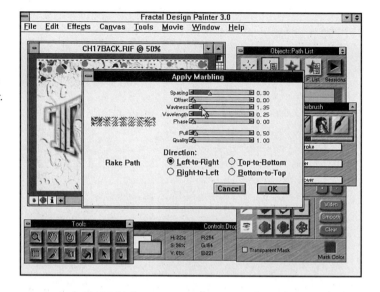

Figure 17.47.
After the marbling is
applied, the selected
area looks more like
marble.

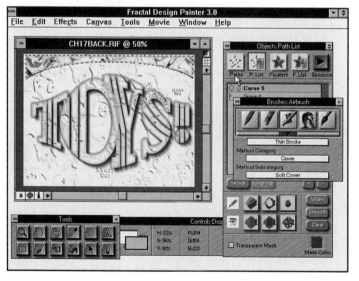

9. You can stroke the outside of the marbled selection using the Tools | Selections | Stroke Selection command, along with the Thin Stroke Airbrush and a soft color. If you perform this step, your image will look like Figure 17.48.

Figure 17.48.
Add a soft border
around the marbled
area with the Tools |
Selections | Stroke
Selection command.

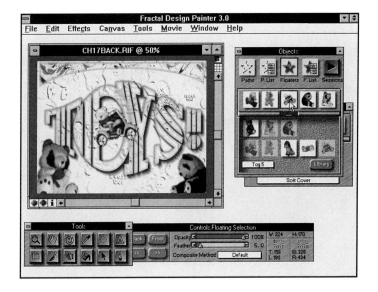

Adding the Final Floaters

Now we're going to place three toys in the foreground of the image. We'll apply different effects to each one.

1. From the Objects | Floaters Palette, drag a copy of Toys 5, 7, and 8 into the image.

2. Click Toy 5 (the one riding the scooter) with the Floating Selection Tool to make it active. Using the Effects | Orientation | Scale command, increase its size to 200 percent. Then position it in the center of the O so it looks like it's riding through it.

3. Choose White as your current color, and select the Masking Pen from the Brushes Palette.

4. From the Objects | Floater List Palette, click the third Floater Mask button and the second Floater Interaction button. Then paint the left side of the floater away so it looks like it's partially behind the O, as shown in Figure 17.49.

5. Using the Effects | Surface Control | Apply Surface Texture command, add surface texture to the toy using Image Luminance.

6. Now, using the Floating Selection Tool, click the white bear with the red ears to make it the active floater.

7. Choose Effects | Tonal Control | Adjust Color. In the Adjust Color dialog box, move the Hue Shift slider toward the left until the red ears turn a shade of purple that works well with the colors in your background. A setting around -12% worked well in my image, as shown in Figure 17.50.

Figure 17.49.
*Edit the mask of
the toy so that it
appears to be
riding through
the "O".*

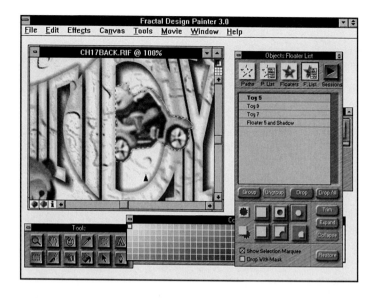

Figure 17.50.
*Adjust the colors in
the second floater to
work with the colors
in the background.*

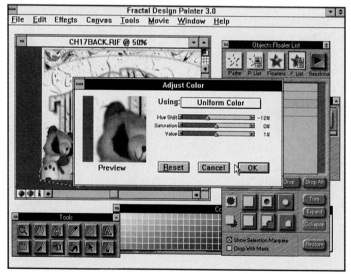

8. For the final floater, the little panda bear, first go to the Art Materials :
   Grads Palette. Verify that the Coppery gradient is still selected as your
   current gradient and that the darkest shades are positioned toward the left
   of the gradient order bar.

9. Choose Tools | Gradations | Express In Image. The colors in the bear will
   be replaced with those contained in the gradient.

10. It's a bit too dark, so we're going to lighten the effect a little bit. Choose Edit | Fade, and keep the Amount slider at the default of 50%. Click OK to apply the command. The gradient colors will partially fade back toward the original colors in the bear. Now that your image is done, it should look similar to Figure 17.51.

Figure 17.51.
With the gradient
applied to the final
floater, our image is
complete.

Summary

Paths, floaters, and effects are a major part of what Painter is all about. It's also an area that begs for further exploration. The more you study how floaters and background interact with each other, the more fascinated you will be about what can be accomplished with Painter. As you explore these areas, you will learn much more than has been covered in this book. Painter is a multi-dimensional program and has many different paths to explore. With that in mind, you are about to explore an area that is totally new to Painter: animation. Get ready for some fun.

Working with Painter Movies

With the release of Painter 3, you have the ability of creating animations in the form of Painter movies (frame stacks), Video for Windows .AVI files (Windows version), QuickTime movies (Mac Version) or a sequence of individually numbered files. In many ways, creating a Painter movie is much the same as creating a single-image Painter document—but effects can be applied to an entire movie, through the use of recorded sessions.

In this chapter, I discuss some of the ways that Painter can be used to composite Painter elements into a movie. I examine how paths can be used in movies, some ways in which floaters can be placed in movies, and how to clone two movies of different resolutions. Before I get on with the project, take a look at some of the key commands used in Painter movies.

Creating a New Movie

If you're starting a movie from scratch, you create it using the File | New command. The procedure for doing this is as follows:

1. From the File menu, select New (or use Ctrl-N in Windows, Cmd-N in Mac). The New Picture dialog box appears.

2. Enter the width and height for your movie if it is to be different from the dimensions shown in the dialog box. Keep in mind that the larger the resolution, the larger your frame stack file will be and the more difficult it will be to play the animation back at an acceptable frame rate.

TIP A common resolution for an .AVI or QuickTime movie file is 320×240 pixels. When an animation of this size is displayed in double size (2× zoom), it will completely fill a 640×480 monitor screen.

3. Painter's default of 75 dots per inch (dpi) corresponds to the resolution of a computer monitor. This resolution should be sufficient for Painter movies that are targeted for computer or video.

4. Set the paper color, if necessary, by clicking the square above Paper Color (at the top right of the dialog box). The standard Windows color dialog box or Mac Color Picker appears. After you have chosen your paper color, click OK. You will be returned to the New Picture box.

5. Click the radio button that specifies you want a Movie picture type, and enter the number of frames that the movie is to contain.

6. A dialog box appears that prompts you to enter a name for the movie. The movies are saved with an .FRM extension (Painter movie frame stacks format) in the Windows version.

7. Next, enter the number of layers of "onion skin" you wish to have in your movie. Onion skin allows you to flip through a series of frames, and you are allowed to have between two and five layers of onion skin.

8. Enter the storage type for your image. You can store it to 8-bit grayscale (256 shades of gray), 8-bit color palette (256 colors), 15-bit color with 1-bit mask, or 24-bit (true) color with an 8-bit mask.

9. Click OK when your selections have been made. Painter then creates the frame stacks, and you are ready to paint your movie.

Frame Stacks Palette

When you create a movie, Painter organizes the frames of the movie in *frame stacks*. Simply put, a frame stack is a series of single images that are placed together in one file. When they are played in order, they give the illusion of movement. This can be compared somewhat to the individual frames of projector-style movies or to individual pictures placed into a flip book.

The Frame Stacks Palette is formed when you create a Painter movie, and it loads when you open a movie or series of numbered files. This palette has controls that resemble those of a VCR and also includes preview images of frames. The Frame Stacks Palette should remain open when you are working on a Painter movie. It will close automatically when you close the movie it represents.

The Frame Stack controls and features are as follows:

Frame Previews: Two to five preview frames appear in the Frame Stacks Palette, depending on the number of onion-skin layers that were specified when creating the file. The frame number appears below the preview, and a red arrow above indicates the currently active frame.

Dotted lines appear before the first frame preview or after the last frame preview.

Frame Information: At the lower-left corner of the palette, you will be told the current frame number and the total number of frames in the movie frame stack. For example, if a movie has 150 frames, and you are currently working on Frame 13, the lower-left corner will display Frame 13 of 150.

"VCR" button 1 (Home): The first button in the Frame Stacks Palette will take you to the first frame in a stack. Depressing the Home key on your keyboard performs the same function.

"VCR" button 2 (Previous Frame): The second button in the Frame Stacks Palette will go to the previous frame in the stack. If you are on Frame 13, clicking this button will take you to Frame 12. The Page Down key on your keyboard will perform the same function.

"VCR" button 3 (Stop Play): The third button in the Frame Stacks Palette will stop playing the movie. If you hold down the Alt (Windows) or Option (Mac) key while you press the Stop Play button, the movie will stop at the frame you were in when you began play.

"VCR" button 4 (Play): The fourth button in the Frame Stacks Palette will play the movie.

"VCR" button 5 (Next Frame): The fifth button in the Frame Stacks Palette will advance you to the next frame. The Page Up key on your keyboard will perform the same function. This button or keyboard equivalent will also add a new frame at the end of the movie each time you press it. The dashed lines that appear in the frame-stack preview area act as placeholders for these added frames.

"VCR" button 6 (End): The last button in the Frame Stacks Palette will take you to the last frame in the movie. The End key on your keyboard will perform the same function.

Painting and Applying Effects to a Single Frame

Painting and applying effects to a single frame of an animation is not much different from painting in any other Painter document. The steps are as follows:

1. Go to the frame you wish to paint or add effects to. This can be done with the Movie | Go To Frame command, with the VCR controls or preview pictures in the Frame Stacks Palette, or by using the Page Up and Page Down keys of your keyboard.

2. Select a brush from the Brushes Palette and a color from the Art Materials | Colors Palette; or, if you are adding effects, choose the effect you wish to apply.

3. Paint on the frame or apply the effect in the usual manner.

4. To paint on the next frame, select it using any of the methods mentioned in Step 1. When you leave the frame you just edited, the changes and strokes will automatically be saved into the current movie file. Once you leave the frame, you will not be able to undo your changes.

Apply a Brush Stroke to a Movie

Painter lets you apply a brush stroke to a movie, such that a portion of the stroke will be rendered into each frame of the movie. This command is ideal for use with the Image Hose brushes.

To try this out, create an animated character or object in a movie file. Then turn this movie into a nozzle file with the Movie | Make Nozzle From Movie command. The procedures for doing this are discussed in Chapter 19, "Creating a Cartoon Animation."

After the nozzle file has been created, you can load the animated nozzle into a Sequential Image Hose brush. Then you can record one stroke of the brush, applying your animated character or object along a determined path in a test image. You can then apply the brush stroke to the movie using the Movie | Apply Brush Stroke To Movie command. (An example of this command is discussed later in Step 18.8, "Applying a Brush Stroke to a Movie.")

To apply a brush stroke to a movie, do as follows:

1. Choose Tools | Record Stroke and record a brush stroke in a test image. You might also find it handy to place a copy of the first frame at the beginning of your frame stack for a scrap image that can later be deleted. In the case of using the command with an Image Hose, create the brush stroke so that the animated portions of the character or object are spaced sufficiently as to indicate movement of the elements. If your first try is not sufficient, choose the Record Stroke command and try again.

2. Choose Movie | Apply Brush Stroke to Movie. The recorded brush stroke will be applied to the movie a portion at a time, spread across the entire range of frames.

Set Grain Position

The Set Grain Position command enables you to set a method of applying paper grain to movies. You can elect to have the paper grain applied in the same manner on all frames, or you can make the paper grain move from one frame to another, which adds interesting effects to your movie. (I show an example of adding paper grain effects to a movie at the end of this chapter.) The basic steps for adding paper grain effects to a movie are as follows:

1. If you want the paper grain in the movie to move randomly, you must first disable (turn off) the Record Initial State checkbox using the Tools | Session Options command.

2. Record a session that applies paper grain to the entire image. The Effects | Surface Control commands are the most obvious choice, but other commands, such as Effects | Surface Control | Dye Concentration, also apply textured effects to an image.

3. Choose Movies | Set Grain Position. The Frame-To-Frame Grain Position dialog box appears.

4. Choose from one of the following methods to apply paper grain:

   - **Grain Stays Still:** No change will be made to the paper grain from one frame to the next

   - **Grain Moves Randomly:** The paper grain will shift randomly from one frame to the next, giving movement to the movie.

   - **Grain Moves Linearly:** The paper grain will shift a specified number of horizontal and vertical pixels (set in the boxes below the command) with each frame in the movie.

5. Once you make your selection, click OK or press Enter (Windows) or Return (Mac) to save the settings.

6. Choose Movie | Apply Session To Movie to apply the paper grain effect to the movie. The paper texture will be applied to each frame in the movie.

621

Video Legal Colors

The colors you see on your computer monitor will look very different when viewed on a composite-video monitor. Because of technical differences between the two video formats, there are notable differences in color display and scan rates. Colors that are pure and crisp on your true-color computer screen may vibrate, wash out, or change to objectionable hues when viewed in the composite-video world. In general, you don't want colors that are destined for video to be pure because they may vibrate when viewed on a composite monitor. The ideal solution to creating images that are destined for video would be to develop your images while viewing the results on a composite-video monitor. Boards manufactured by TrueVision and Matrox, among others, allow you to connect a composite monitor to your computer as a secondary video source. Using special drivers, you can develop your images in Painter while you view them exactly as they will appear on videotape.

If your images are destined for video output, you can apply legal video colors to your Painter documents through the use of the Effects | Tonal Control | Video Legal Colors command. Painter supports both the NTSC (USA) and PAL (European) video formats, which you can select in the command's dialog box.

To display video-legal colors in an image, do as follows:

1. Select the portion of the image that you would like to change. If you make no selection, the effect will be applied to the entire image.

2. Choose Effects | Tonal Control | Video Legal Colors. You can preview the results in the preview window.

3. Select whether you want to apply the command for NTSC (USA) or PAL (European) video format.

4. Click OK or press Enter (Windows) or Return (Mac) to apply the command.

Editing Painter Movies

The Movie Menu commands enable you to edit movies, apply effects to one or more frames through the use of Painter sessions, insert other Painter movies, or define which of multiple opened movies is a movie clone source.

Add Frames

The Movie | Add Frames command enables you to add a specified number of blank frames before a designated frame, after a designated frame, at the start of a movie, or at the end of a movie.

To use the Add Frames command, do as follows:

1. Open or create a movie in the usual manner.
2. Choose Movie | Add Frames. The Add Frames dialog box appears.
3. Enter the number of blank frames you wish to add to your movie.
4. Click the Before or the After radio button. Then enter the number of the frame you want to add the frames before or after.

   To add more frames at the beginning of a movie, click the At Start Of Movie button.

   To add more frames to the end of a movie, click the At End Of Movie button.
5. Click OK, or press Enter (Windows) or Return (Mac), to apply the command.

You can also use the last VCR button in conjunction with the Clear New Frames command to add blank frames to the end of your movie one at a time.

Delete Frames

The Movie | Delete Frames command deletes one or more frames from a movie. To use the Delete Frames command, perform the following steps:

1. Open or create a movie in the usual manner.
2. Choose Movie | Delete Frames. The Delete Frames dialog box appears.
3. Enter the number range of frames you wish to delete from your movie. For example, if you want to delete Frames 10 through 25 from your movie, enter these numbers in the boxes.
4. Click OK, or press Enter (Windows) or Return (Mac), to apply the command.

Erase Frames

The Movie | Erase Frames command erases the contents of one or more specified frames from the movie and leaves the blank frame in the movie. To use the Erase Frames command, do as follows:

1. Open or create a movie in the usual manner.
2. Choose Movie | Erase Frames. The Erase Frames dialog box appears.
3. Enter the number range of frames you wish to erase from your movie. For example, if you want to erase the contents of Frames 10 through 25 from your movie, enter these numbers in the boxes.
4. Click OK, or press Enter (Windows) or Return (Mac), to apply the command.

Go To Frame

The Movie | Go To Frame command jumps to a specific frame in the movie. To use the command, do as follows:

1. Choose Movie | Go To Frame. A dialog box appears.
2. Enter the number of the frame you want to jump to.
3. Click OK, or press Enter (Windows) or Return (Mac), to apply the command.

Clear New Frames

The Movie | Clear New Frames command works in conjunction with the fifth VCR button in the Frame Stacks Palette. Pressing on this button, or pressing the End key on your keyboard, adds one frame to your movie each time the key or button is pressed.

The function of the Clear New Frames command, which is a toggle, is as follows:

- With Clear New Frames enabled, or checked, a blank frame will be inserted at the end of your movie each time the VCR button or End key is depressed.
- With Clear New Frames disabled, or unchecked, the contents of the final frame in your movie will be pasted into a new frame at the end of the movie each time the VCR button or End key is depressed.

Insert Movie

The Insert Movie command inserts the frames of a different Painter movie into the currently open Painter movie. It is similar to the Add Frames command, but instead of inserting frames, it inserts an entire movie. This command only works with Painter .FRM frame stacks; it will not work with a series of numbered files. If you want to insert numbered files, you must convert them to frame stacks first.

To use the Insert Movie command, do as follows:

1. Create or open a Painter movie. This is the movie that you will insert the other movie into.
2. Choose Movie | Insert Movie. The Insert Movie dialog box appears.
3. Click the Before (or the After) radio button. Then enter the number of the frame before which (or after which) you want to insert the movie.

   To insert the movie at the beginning of the current movie, click the At Start Of Movie button.

To insert the movie at the end of the current movie, click the At End Of Movie button.

4. Click OK, or press Enter (Windows) or Return (Mac). The Select Movie dialog box appears.

5. Scroll to the directory or folder where the movie you want to insert resides. Select the movie you want to insert and click Open or press the Enter (Windows) or Return (Mac) key. Painter inserts all the frames of the selected movie at the specified point.

   Note that the movie you insert must have the same pixel-by-pixel dimensions as the movie you are inserting into.

Working with Sessions in Movies

Sessions can be used to apply a series of commands or brush strokes to a Painter movie. In this chapter (and the following one), I'll use sessions to save time in the development of Painter movies. The session commands are described next.

Record Session

The Record Session command begins the recording of a Painter session. This command is the equivalent of clicking the Record button in the Objects | Sessions Palette.

To record a session:

1. Select your session-recording options as outlined under the Session Options command (described in the section titled "Session Options," later in this chapter).

2. Begin the recording session by choosing the Tools | Record Session command or by clicking the record button in the Objects | Sessions Palette.

3. When you complete your session, choose the Stop Recording Session command or click the Stop button in the Objects | Sessions Palette. You will be prompted to enter a name for the session, and it will be saved in the currently open Session Library.

Playback Session

The Tools | Sessions | Playback Session command is used to play back a Painter session in a single document. If you use this command to play back a session into a Painter movie, the session will be applied to only the current frame. To apply a session to all frames in a Painter movie, choose the Movie | Apply Session To Movie command, discussed later in this chapter.

To use the Playback Session command, choose Tools | Playback Session. The Recorded Sessions dialog box appears. Here, the following functions are selectable:

> **Import:** Imports a .TXT script file as a session.
>
> **Export:** Exports a session to a .TXT script file. This file can then be edited, as outlined in the next chapter.
>
> **Get Info:** Displays the session name, the date it was recorded, the name of the artist (obtained from the registration information), and the size of the session file in bytes.
>
> **Playback:** Plays back the selected session.
>
> **Delete:** Deletes the session from the current library.
>
> **Open Library:** Opens a selected .SSK session library.
>
> **Done:** Exits the Recorded Sessions dialog box.

Session Options

The Session Options command opens a dialog box that enables you to set certain parameters before beginning a session recording.

To use the Session Options command, do as follows:

1. Choose Tools | Session Options. The Session Options dialog box appears.

2. If you want to record your session to include the tools and art materials you select (including brushes, color, and paper textures used during the session), check the Record Initial State button.

   If you want to record only a series of brush strokes to be reused with other tools and art materials leave the Record Initial State button unchecked.

3. If you want to record your session as a series of frame captures so that it can be converted to an animation file and played outside of Painter, click the Save Frames on Playback checkbox. Then enter a value, in tenths of seconds, for the frequency at which you want to capture the file. Entering smaller values here will capture the frames more frequently, resulting in a smoother animation but requiring more system resources and processing power to replay. Entering larger values here will capture the frames less frequently.

4. Click OK, or press Enter (Windows) or Return (Mac), when your options are selected. You can then record a session (as outlined in the section on the Record Session command).

Playing Back Sessions at a New Resolution

Sometimes it's beneficial to record a session at a lower resolution so that you can see all your strokes at once. Then you can play back a session at a higher resolution to generate a higher-quality image. You will need to experiment with how much larger your resolution can be when playing back sessions into larger documents. You can't make too big of a jump; for example, four times the size may be too much.

If you want to play back a session at a lower or higher resolution, you must follow some additional steps when you record the session. These steps are as follows:

1. Open a new document in which to record your session.
2. Choose Edit | Select All (Ctrl-A in Windows, Cmd-A in Mac) to create a reference rectangle that will be part of the recorded session. This is a necessary step to play back the session at a higher resolution.
3. Click the Record button (the third button) in the Objects | Sessions Palette or choose the Tools | Record Session command.
4. Proceed with your session in the usual manner, painting strokes inside the selected area.
5. When the session is complete, click the Stop button (the first button) in the Objects | Sessions Palette or choose the Tools | Stop Recording Session command. The Name the Session dialog box appears.
6. Type a name for the session and click OK or press Enter.

A new document has to be created to play the session into. Its dimensions can be larger or smaller than the original recorded session and can also have a different aspect ratio. You can keep the dimensions of the file the same but play back the session into a document with a different pixel-per-inch setting.

To play back a session into a document with a different resolution, follow these steps:

1. Create a new document to play the session into. Set new dimensions or new resolutions as desired.
2. Choose Edit | Select All (Ctrl-A in Windows, Cmd-A in Mac) to create a reference rectangle for the new document. This will create a reference for the rectangle used when recording the session.
3. To play back the session from the Objects | Sessions Palette, click the icon for the session you want to play back. Then click the Play button (the second button) in the Objects | Sessions Palette. The original session will play back into the document, rescaling the strokes, paper textures, and other items appropriately.

Applying Sessions to Movies

With Painter sessions, you can apply effects or any other command to each frame within a Painter movie. First the session must be recorded and saved.

Because the session will be applied to each frame in the movie, you might want to save a single frame from your movie to preview the effect or command before you apply it to the movie. You can do this with the Save As command. Simply move to a frame that you feel is a good representation of your movie, and save it in any one of Painter's supported formats. You can then open this file as a place on which to test the effect or command. You can also make an extra copy of the first frame and place it at the beginning of the movie. This frame can be used when you record your sessions. Later when the movie is complete, you can delete the extra frame with the Movie | Delete Frame command.

To apply sessions to movies, use the following procedure:

1. With a test frame, record a command, a series of commands, brush strokes, or any other Painter procedure that you would like to apply to your entire movie. The session will be saved in the currently opened session library when prompted.

2. Open or select the movie you want to apply the session to.

3. Choose Movies | Apply Session To Movie. From the Recorded Sessions dialog box (described previously under the Playback Session command), choose the session you wish to apply, and click the Playback button. The session will apply itself to each frame of the movie. This can take quite a bit of time with very large movie files (those with many frames or high resolutions).

Session Mover

Use the Session Mover to move sessions from one library to another. The Session Mover is accessed with the Tools | Movers | Session Mover command.

To use the Session Mover, do as follows:

1. Choose Tools | Movers | Session Mover. The Session Mover dialog box appears.

2. The dialog box contains two scrolling windows. When the Session Mover is first opened, the names of the sessions in the currently opened session library are contained in the window on the left side, and the window on the right side is blank.

   ■ To select a different library in either window, first click the Close button to close any opened session library. The window will become blank, and the Close button will revert to an Open button. Click the Open button, and choose the directory and session library file (.SSK extension) you wish to open. Click OK, or press Enter (Windows) or Return (Mac), to open the file. The selected library appears in the left window.

- To open a library, click the Open button, and choose the directory and session library file (.SSK extension) you wish to open. Click OK, or press Enter (Windows) or Return (Mac), to open the file. The selected library appears in the right window.

- To copy a session from one library to another, first highlight the session name you want to copy. Then click the Copy button in the top center of the dialog box. The name of the copied session appears in the opposite window.

- To remove a session from a library, first highlight the session name you want to remove. Then click the Remove button in the center of the dialog box. The name of the session will be removed from the window.

- To rename a session, first highlight the session name. Click the Change Name button in the center of the dialog box and enter a new name for the session. Click OK to return to the Session Mover dialog box. The name of the highlighted session will change to the name you entered.

3. When you are done making changes to the session libraries, click Quit, located in the center of the Session Mover dialog box. The changes are automatically saved to the libraries you worked on.

Creating a Session Library

Session libraries can be created from the Sessions Palette or from the Session Mover. When you create a library from the Sessions Palette, you can place your new custom-made sessions inside it immediately. When you create a library from the Session Mover, you can move sessions from other libraries into the new library.

Creating a New Session Library from the Sessions Palette

You can create a new session library from the Sessions Palette. This method enables you to quickly place a newly created session into a new session library.

To create a new library from the Sessions Palette, do as follows:

1. Open the Objects Palette by using the Window | Objects command, or by the keyboard combination of Ctrl-5 in Windows or Cmd-5 in Mac.

2. Click the Session icon (the fifth icon) to open the Sessions Palette.

3. Click the bar to open the drawer. Inside you will see a Library button.

4. Click the Library button. The Open Session Library dialog box appears.

5. Click the New button in the Open Session Library dialog box. The Create File dialog box appears.

6. Scroll to the directory you wish to locate your new session library in, and type in the name of the library you want to save.

7. Click OK or press Enter (Windows) or Return (Mac) to create the session library. The file will be saved with an .SSK file extension.

Creating a New Session Library from the Sessions Mover

You can create a new session library from the Sessions Mover. This method will allow you to move sessions from one library into another library.

To create a new library from the Sessions Mover:

1. Select Tools | Movers | Sessions Mover. A dialog box appears. In the left half of the dialog box, the names of the sessions in Painter's default library file appear. The window on the right side of this dialog box will be blank.

2. Underneath the window on the right side of the dialog box, click the New button. This will open the New Session Library dialog box.

3. Scroll to the directory you wish to save your session library in, and type in a name for the library. The file will be saved with a .SSK file extension.

4. Choose OK to save the library filename. You will then be returned to the Sessions Mover. At this point, you can move sessions from the library opened on the left side of the Sessions Mover into the newly created library.

5. Click Quit, located in between the two library windows, to exit the Sessions Mover.

Working with Multiple Movies

Just as you can have more than one image file open at once, you can also work with more than one movie file at a time. This enables you to clone movies or composite elements of more than one movie together.

Compositing Movies

To composite movies, perform the following steps:

1. Create a movie that will be the background of the composited movie.

2. Create another movie that consists of the character, or moving object, to be composited into the background movie.

3. Set the middle Mask Visibility button on, so that any mask appears in red.

4. Choose a masking tool, such as the Masking Pen, from the Brushes Palette.

5. Mask the character or moving object in each frame of the animation. If the character or object is part of a movie that already has a background, this

process cannot be performed automatically. Because the object changes shape and position in each frame, the mask needs to be applied manually.

6. Play the movie to preview the mask.

7. If you want to save a backup copy of the masked character, save it to a different filename or directory using the Windows File Manager.

8. Open your background movie, if it is not open, and click to make it active.

9. Choose Movie | Set Movie Clone Source. The background movie will now be the clone source.

10. Select your character movie to make it active.

11. Select the third Drawing Visibility button to paint outside the mask area.

12. Select the Straight Cloner from the Masking variants in the Brushes Palette. Adjusting the brush size so that it is very large will enable you to paint into the character mask one frame at a time very quickly.

13. Paint into each frame of the character movie one frame at a time. You will see the background movie appear beneath the character as you paint. The mask will protect your character as you composite the two movies together.

14. Play the movie, and you will now see an animated character on an animated background.

15. Save a copy of this new movie if you want to composite more to it.

Rotoscoping

Rotoscoping is a process that combines video with computer graphics. You can perform rotoscoping by first digitizing a video movie and converting it to numbered files, to a Video for Windows .AVI file, or to a QuickTime movie file. Then the digitized video can be opened in Painter and converted to a Painter-movie frame stack.

After you import the digitized movie into Painter, you can paint on the frames, or you can add batch effects by applying Painter sessions to the movie file.

Saving Movie Files

Painter automatically saves any changes made to frames when you move to the next or previous frame during the movie edit session. Because of this, it is wise to make a backup copy of any Painter movie before making any changes. This can be done in the Windows File Manager or any other file-management software. Save a copy of the Painter movie under a different name, or in a different directory, before beginning your movie-edit session.

Our First Movie Project

In this movie project, you will first create a small four-frame movie that uses paths to create a halo effect around a crystal ball. This small movie will then be inserted into a new movie six times, to create a larger 24-frame animation. Then an animated sequence will be cloned to the inside of the crystal ball. After that, some floaters will be placed into the movie, both manually and through the use of recorded sessions.

Step 18.1. Starting the Background

To create the halo effect around a crystal ball, let's start by painting a background for the image. You'll paint the background on to the first frame, and paste it into the remaining three frames using a session.

1. Open the Brushes Palette (Ctrl-2) and the Color Set (Ctrl-8).

2. Choose the File | New command, or use the quick-key combination of Ctrl-N in Windows or Cmd-N in Mac. The New Picture dialog box, shown in Figure 18.1, appears. Create a 300×300 movie, with one frame, and set the paper color to black. Click OK to continue.

Figure 18.1.
Create a 300×300 one-frame movie with a black background.

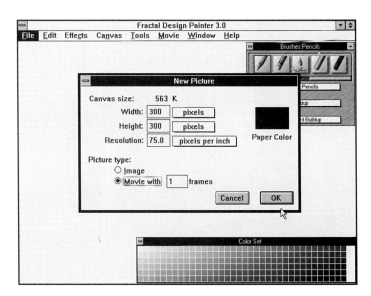

3. When prompted to enter a name for the movie, call it CRYSTAL1.FRM. Choose to create the movie as a 24-bit with color mask. After the movie has been created, your screen will look similar to Figure 18.2. The movie will open on the first frame, as shown in the document-window title bar. The Frame Stacks Palette will also display a red arrow above the current frame.

Figure 18.2.
The new movie and the
Frame Stacks Palette
appear on your screen,
positioned at the first
frame.

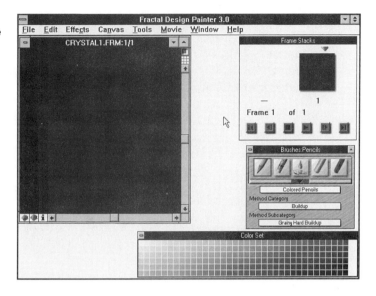

4. From the Brushes Palette, choose the Fat Stroke Airbrush. Then select the first color in the third row of the default Color Set. Spray a misty background onto the first frame. Vary the pressure and the amount of coverage that you apply with the airbrush. Create a cloudy effect, as shown in Figure 18.3.

Figure 18.3.
Paint a cloudy effect on
the first frame with the
Fat Stroke Airbrush.

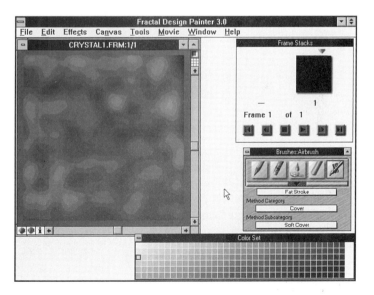

5. Drop down the Movie menu box by clicking the Movie heading in the menu bar. Verify that the Clear New Frames command is unchecked, as shown in Figure 18.4. If this is unchecked, you can copy the contents of the first frame (which is also the last in the current animation) into three additional frames using the Page Up key.

Figure 18.4.
Verify that the Clear New Frames command is unchecked in the Movie menu.

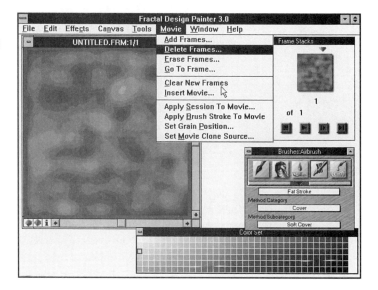

6. Press the Page Up key three times to add three copies of Frame 1 into your animation. You should now have a movie with four identical frames contained in it.

7. Press the Home key on your keyboard to return to the first frame of the animation.

Step 18.2. Adding the Crystal Ball and Halos

Now that you have your background in all four frames, the next step is to add the crystal ball and the halo. You're going to use paths to create these items. When you create paths in a movie, they will be available to all frames within that movie. You can activate or deactivate different paths on each frame to apply colors or effects. This part of the project will illustrate how you can select and use different paths on each frame.

1. Open the Tools Palette (Ctrl-1) and the Controls Palette (Ctrl-6).

2. Choose the Oval Selection Tool from the Tools Palette. Press the Ctrl and Shift keys simultaneously, and draw a circular selection measuring around 180 pixels. Place it toward the bottom-right section of the background. The dimensions of the circle will be shown in the Controls | Oval Selection Palette.

3. In the Controls | Path Adjuster Palette, adjust the feathering of the path to around 2. This will increase the size of the path slightly. Your screen should look similar to Figure 18.5.

Figure 18.5.
Create a circular path,
measuring 180 pixels,
and feather it to
around 2.

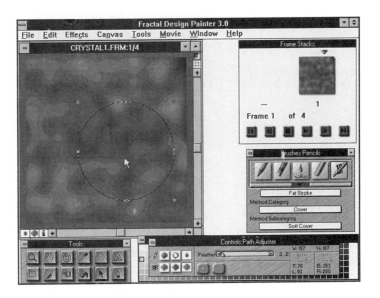

4. If your path is not located as shown in Figure 18.5, you can use the Path Adjuster Tool to move it. Select the Path Adjuster from the Tools Palette, and click inside the circle. Keeping the mouse button or stylus depressed, you will see the cursor change to four directional arrows. Move the path into place and release the mouse button or stylus when you have it positioned correctly.

5. From the Objects Palette (Ctrl-5), choose the P.List icon to open the Path List Palette. You will see the first path, the circle, in the Path List, as shown in Figure 18.6.

6. Choose the Outline Selection Tool from the Tools Palette. Using Freehand drawing mode, draw an irregularly shaped border around the circle, similar to that shown in Figure 18.7. This will be used as the first frame of the halo effect around the crystal ball. This second path appears in the Path List when the path is complete.

7. In the Controls | Outline Selection Palette, adjust the feathering of the first halo to somewhere between 20 and 25 pixels.

8. Repeat Steps 6 and 7 to draw three more paths in a similar manner, each one shaped slightly different than those previous. Your Path List should now contain five paths in all, and your screen should look similar to Figure 18.8. The circle path should be feathered around 2, and the halo paths feathered between 20 and 25.

635

Figure 18.6.
The first path will be
shown in the Path List
Palette.

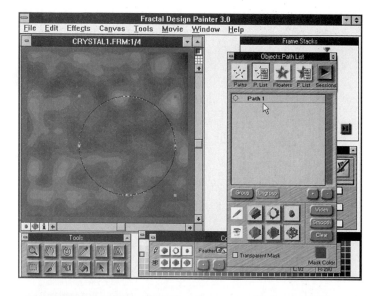

Figure 18.7.
Draw an irregularly
shaped border around
the circle using the
Outline Selection Tool.
A new path appears in
the Path List.

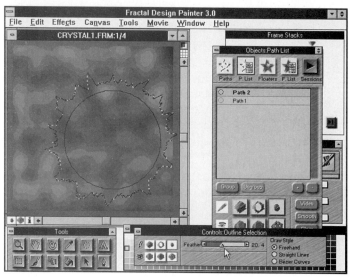

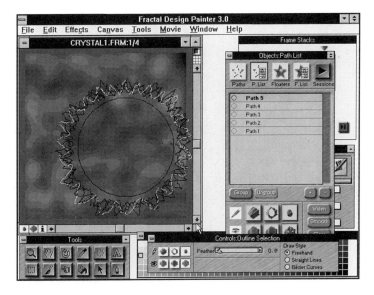

Figure 18.8.
Five paths have been created and appear in the Path List.

Each path you have created identifies an area of the background that can be masked, colored, or edited with effects. If you deactivate all paths except one of the halos, and then fill the active path with a color, the halo will fill completely as a solid entity.

However, you want to fill only the portion of the halo that appears outside the circle. To do this, you have to activate two paths: the circle, and one of the four halo paths you have created. You have to use the circle to "cut out" the area of the halo you don't want to fill. In order to accomplish this, the circle has to appear above the halo in the path list.

There is one additional step. If both paths are positive and the third Drawing Visibility button is set to mask the outside of the paths, you can color or fill the inside of both paths. That isn't what you want to do. You will have to identify the circle as a negative path, so that it will be masked differently than the halo. Turning the circular path into a negative path would mask the *inside* of this path, while the halo remains masked outside. This achieves the results you want.

9. If you are not on the first frame of the frame stack, enter that frame by clicking the first VCR button in the Frame Stacks Palette, or by pressing the Home key on your keyboard.

10. In the Objects | Path List Palette, click the path representing the circle to highlight it. This path is shown as Path 1 in our example, but your numbers may vary. It should be at the bottom of your path list, and it should be the lowest numbered path of your list. Drag this path to the top of the list and turn it into a negative path by clicking the - button, as shown in Figure 18.9.

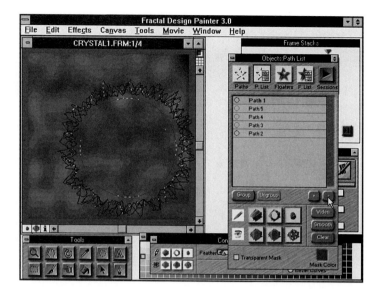

Figure 18.9.
Move the circular path
to the top of the Path
List and click the -
button to make it a
negative path.

11. Click in the circle beside the name of the circular path to activate it. The circle in the Path List will be shown as a dotted line when the path is active. Additionally, the circular path in the image is surrounded by a red circle, indicating that it is an active negative path.

12. Also activate the path for the first halo you drew. This is shown as Path 2 in our example. There should now be two active paths in the Path List and in your document.

13. From the Color Set, choose the third color (yellow-green) in the second row. Choose the Paint Bucket from the Tools Palette, and verify in the Controls | Paint Bucket Palette that you are filling the image with the current color. Click inside an area between the circle and the halo to fill the area with the current color. Your screen should look similar to Figure 18.10.

14. Use the Page Up key to advance to the next frame. In the Path List, activate the path for the circle and for the next halo path you created. Figure 18.11 shows Path 1 (the circle) and Path 3 (the second halo) activated. Fill this path using the same color with the Paint Bucket.

15. Repeat Step 14 for the two remaining frames, using Path 1 and Path 4 in the third frame, and Path 1 and Path 5 in the fourth frame.

16. Play the sequence using the fourth VCR button in the Path List Palette. You should see the glow changing from frame to frame. The animated halo should be nice and soft.

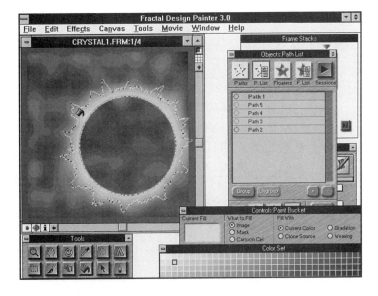

Figure 18.10.
Fill the area between
the two paths with
yellow-green, chosen
from the default Color
Set.

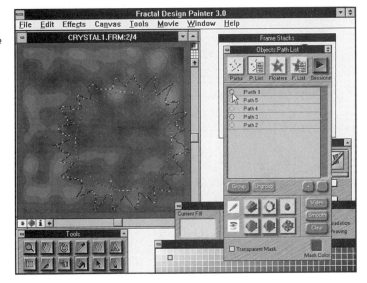

Figure 18.11.
In the second frame,
the second halo and the
circle are activated
before filling the area.

17. If all went well, you can delete the paths associated with the halos from the Path List. To do this, press the Shift key and activate each of the names in the Path List associated with the halos. All four paths should be highlighted in blue, and their status circles should be displayed as dotted lines as shown in Figure 18.12. Then click the Clear button located at the bottom of the Path List Palette. You should then have one path remaining: the circular path for the crystal ball.

Figure 18.12.
You can delete the halo
paths by activating all
four and choosing the
Clear button in the
Path List Palette.

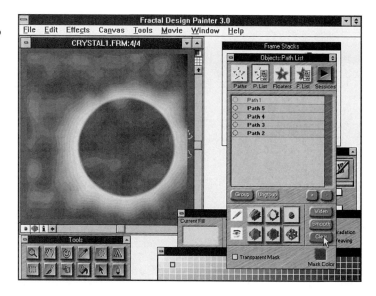

Step 18.3. Coloring the Crystal Ball

Now that our halos have been added, you can add the crystal ball to the foreground. You'll color the circular path in the first frame, and then turn it into a floater that can be pasted into the remaining three frames.

1. Return to the first frame in the frame stack if you are not already there. Do this by pressing the Home key on your keyboard or by using the first VCR button in the Frame Stacks Palette, as shown in Figure 18.13.

Figure 18.13.
Return to the first
frame of the movie
stack.

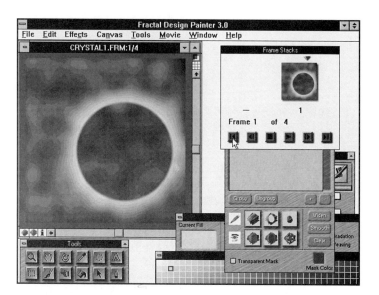

2. Activate the Crystal Ball path, and turn it back into a positive path by highlighting it in the Path List and clicking the "+" key, as shown in Figure 18.14.

Figure 18.14.
Change the circular
path back to positive
with the "+" button in
the Path List Palette.

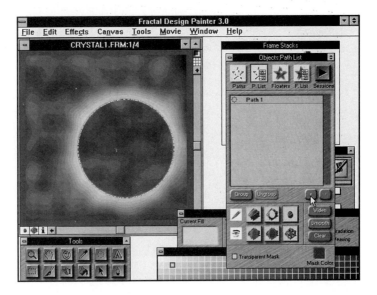

3. Choose black as your current color (the last color in the default Color Set), and fill the inside of the circle with the Paint Bucket.

4. The Fat Stroke Airbrush should still be selected from when you painted the background. To add some shape to the crystal ball, choose white (the first color in the color set) as your current color. Spray around the edges of the circle to define the outline of the crystal ball. Add some shape to the crystal ball by applying more highlights on one side. If you add too much, you can change the color back to black and spray some of the white away. When you're done, the first frame should look similar to that shown in Figure 18.15.

5. With the Crystal Ball Path still active, choose the Floating Selection Tool, and click the path. It will turn into a floater. You will be able to see the floater in the Floater List Palette, as shown in Figure 18.16.

6. Advance to the next frame using the Page Up key. The floater appears on the second frame, in the same location it appeared in the previous frame. If you perform some kind of action on the floater before you leave this frame, a copy of the floater will be dropped into the background. You want the floater to be dropped into the same location here. What you can do is press the up-arrow key on your keyboard once to shift the floater up one pixel, and then press the down-arrow key once to return it to its original position. Then press the Page Up key to advance to Frame 3. You should see a copy of the floater appear on the second frame in the Frame Stacks Palette.

Figure 18.15.
Add some shape to the
crystal ball with white
paint and the Fat
Stroke Airbrush.

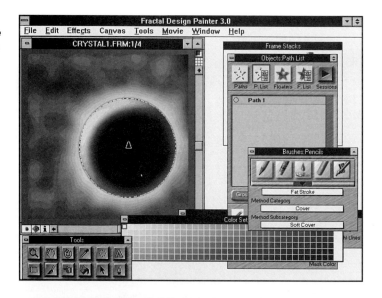

Figure 18.16.
Turn the crystal ball
into a floater. A floater
appears in the Floater
List Palette.

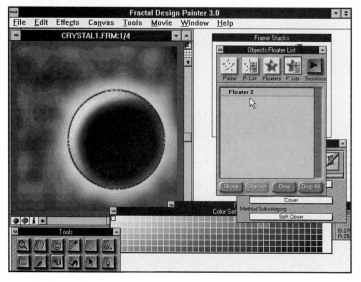

7. In Frame 3, perform the same actions: Use the up arrow to shift up one pixel, use the down arrow to shift back to the original location, and use Page Up to advance to Frame 4. You should see the crystal ball pasted into Frame 3 in the Frame Stacks Palette.

8. In Frame 4, the last frame, choose the Edit | Drop command to drop the floater into the last frame. The floater should disappear from the Floater List Palette. All four frames should now have the crystal ball in place.

9. You can close this movie file now, using the File | Close command.

Step 18.4. Inserting the Movie into Another

You're going to take the small four-frame animation you just created and paste it into a new movie six times to create a 24-frame background. Later, some additional effects will be added.

1. Create a new one-frame 300×300 pixel animation (the same size as the crystal ball you just created). Make the background white. Your screen will look similar to Figure 18.17.

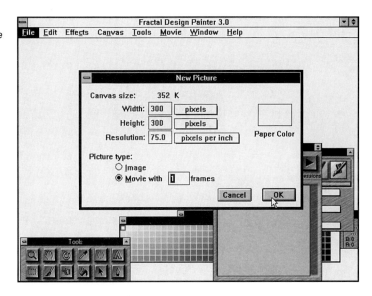

Figure 18.17.
Create a new one-frame animation, using the same resolution as the first.

2. When prompted for a name in the Enter Movie dialog box, call it CRYSTAL2.FRM, as shown in Figure 18.18.

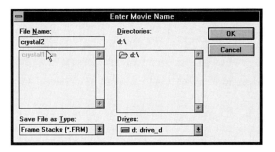

Figure 18.18.
Name the movie CRYSTAL2.FRM, to distinguish it from the earlier version.

3. Choose the Movie | Insert Movie command. The Insert Movie dialog box appears, as shown in Figure 18.19. Choose to insert the new movie at the start of this movie, as shown. Click the OK button to continue.

Figure 18.19.
Choose to insert the
movie at the start of
the current movie.

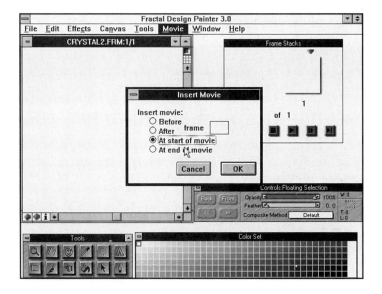

4. In the Select Movie dialog box, shown in Figure 18.20, choose the
   CRYSTAL1.FRM movie you created earlier.

Figure 18.20.
Choose to insert the
CRYSTAL1.FRM movie
into this movie.

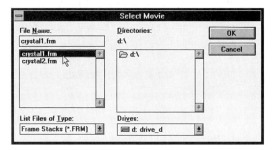

5. Repeat the Insert Movie command five more times, after which you should
   have a total of 25 frames in the movie. The 25th frame will be the single
   blank frame that was created when the new file was made. You'll delete
   this last frame when you're done.

Step 18.5. Cloning a Movie of a Different Size

Movies can be cloned much like single-image Painter documents. Two movies
can be opened at once, and then a link can be created between them using the
Movie | Set Movie Clone Source command. With the link created, advancing to
the next frame in the clone movie will automatically advance the clone-source

movie to the next frame. There are some exceptions that cause the automatic advancing to not work, though, as you'll demonstrate in the following section of the project.

You can clone between movies of different sizes, but remember that they normally align with each other at the upper-left corners. You can use the Shift-click method of cloning to clone a specific area of a clone-source movie into another movie. This is how you'll clone some images into our crystal ball.

1. Choose the File | Open command (Ctrl-O in Windows, Cmd-O in Mac). In the Select Image dialog box, shown in Figure 18.21, check the Open Numbered Files checkbox in the lower-right corner. Then double-click the TEMP0001.TGA file, located on the CD, to identify it as the first file in the sequence. Next, double-click the TEMP0024.TGA file to identify it as the last file in the sequence.

Figure 18.21.
Open TEMP0001.TGA
through
TEMP0024.TGA,
located on the CD
accompanying this
book.

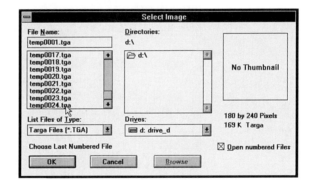

2. When prompted to enter a name for the new movie, name it TEMPLE.FRM. Choose to make the movie 24-bit with an 8-bit mask.

3. With the TEMPLE.FRM as the active document, choose the Movie | Set Movie Clone Source command, shown in Figure 18.22.

4. From the Brushes Palette, choose the Cloner brushes, and select the Soft Cloner as your current brush.

5. With the Soft Cloner selected, hold down the Shift key, and click inside the center of the doorway in the first frame of the TEMPLE.FRM animation. The arrow in Figure 18.23 shows the location where you should click. This identifies the starting point of the cloning area for the image. After you perform this function, though, the automatic advance link between the two movies becomes disabled. You'll have to advance between each movie independently, as you'll demonstrate later.

Figure 18.22.
*Make the new movie
the clone source with
the Set Movie Clone
Source command.*

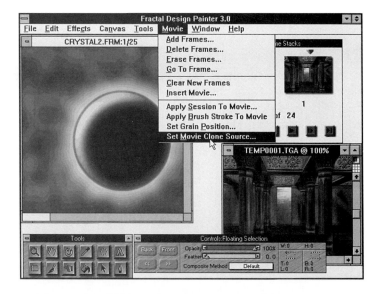

Figure 18.23.
*Shift-click with the
cloner brush inside the
clone-source movie to
identify the starting
point of the cloned
area.*

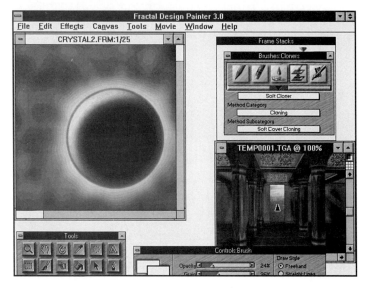

6. Click the CRYSTAL2.FRM movie to make it current. Verify that you are on
    the first frame (or the same frame number as the clone-source movie).
    Starting in the middle of the crystal ball, paint a clone of the temple anima-
    tion. Your image should look similar to Figure 18.24.

7. For each of the remaining 23 frames, repeat the following sequence:
   - Activate the TEMPLE.FRM movie to make it current.
   - Use the Page Up key to advance to the next frame.
   - Activate the CRYSTAL2.FRM movie to make it current.
   - Use the Page Up key to advance to its next frame. Verify that you are on the same frame number in the two animations.
   - Clone the inside of the crystal ball with the Soft Cloner.

8. When you are done with the 24th frame, do not press the Page Up key. This will add an additional frame to the end. You can delete the blank 25th frame, and any additional frames you may have added, by choosing the Movie | Delete Frames command. In the resulting dialog box, shown in Figure 18.25, enter the number(s) of the frames you want to delete.

9. Close the TEMPLE.FRM movie file. Now, if you play the movie, you will see a moving image inside the crystal ball. When the movie is done playing, return to the first frame.

Figure 18.24.
Starting at the center
of the crystal ball, clone
the temple inside using
the Soft Cloner.

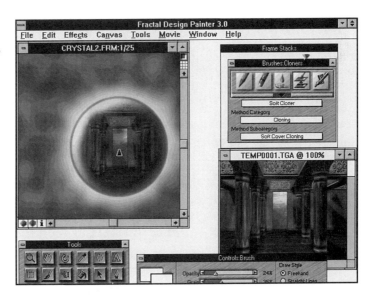

Figure 18.25.
Delete frame 25, and
any other extra frames
you may have added,
using the Movie |
Delete Frames com-
mand.

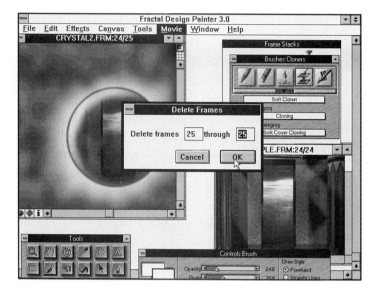

Step 18.6. Adding Floaters to Movies

There are several ways to add floaters to movies; you can position them manually or with the use of sessions. You've already seen that floaters are dropped automatically into a frame when advancing to the next.

When adding floaters to movie files, you can work with background masks and floater masks in the same manner as with single images. To illustrate this, let's apply an Image Luminance mask to all the frames in the movie with a recorded session.

1. Choose Tools | Record Session. The following step will be recorded into the session file.

2. Choose Edit | Mask | Auto Mask. In the Using menu, it should default to the Image Luminance method. Click OK to apply the effect.

3. Choose Tools | Stop Recording Session. When prompted to enter a name for the session, call it Mask Image Luminance.

4. To apply the mask to all the frames in the movie, choose Movie | Apply Session To Movie. The Recorded Session dialog box, shown in Figure 18.26, appears. Choose the Mask Image Luminance session just recorded.

5. Click the Playback button to apply the session to the movie. Each frame will be masked based on Image Luminance. Now you'll pull a floater in from the Floaters Palette and mask it also.

6. From the Objects Palette, click the Floaters icon to open the Floaters Palette. From Painter's default floater library, choose the Earth floater. Drag it into the first frame of the CRYSTAL2.FRM movie. Position it as shown in Figure 18.27.

Figure 18.26.
The Recorded Session dialog box enables you to choose a session to be applied to the movie.

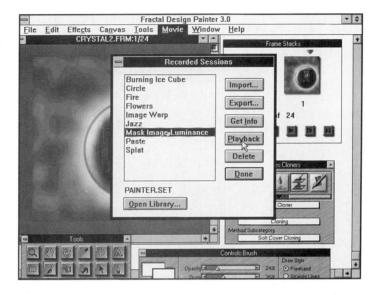

Figure 18.27.
Pull the Earth Floater, from Painter's default Floater Library, into the first frame of the movie.

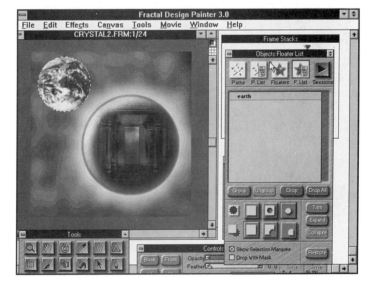

7. In the Objects Palette, click the F.List icon to open the Floater List Palette. At the bottom of the palette, click the third Floater Mask Visibility button (the third button in the top row), and the second Floater Interaction button (the middle button in the bottom row).

8. Choose Edit | Mask | Auto Mask, and apply a mask to the floater using Image Luminance. After this command is applied, there will be a thin line that appears at the right side of the floater, as shown in Figure 18.28. This line can be painted away using the Masking Pen and white paint.

Figure 18.28.
After masking the
floater based on Image
Luminance, edit the
line from the floater
using white paint and
the Masking Pen.

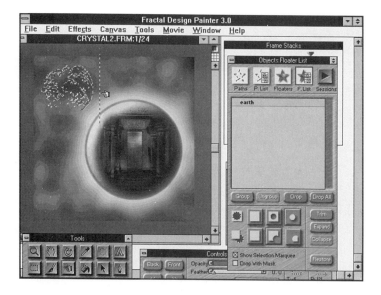

9. Position the Earth floater where you want it to appear in the first frame. In the example shown in Figure 18.29, the floater is in the upper-left corner of the image.

Figure 18.29.
Move the floater into
position in the first
frame.

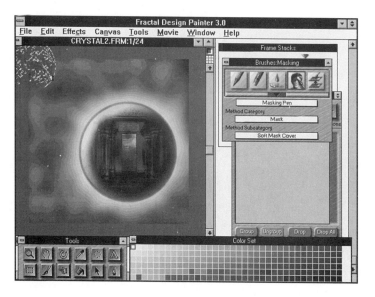

10. Use Page Up to advance to the next frame. When you leave the first frame, its floater will be dropped into place automatically. The floater will then appear in the same location on the second frame. Using the Floating

Selection Tool, or the arrow keys on your keyboard, position the floater to a new location on the second frame.

11. Repeat Step 10 for all frames in the Painter movie, moving the floater around the perimeter of the animation.

12. When you reach the last frame of the animation, choose Edit | Drop to drop the floater into the final frame. Figure 18.30 shows the final frame with the floater dropped into place.

Figure 18.30.
In the last frame,
position the floater and
then choose the Edit |
Drop command to drop
it into place.

Step 18.7. Using Sessions to Move Floaters Automatically

You can also use recorded sessions to move a floater in an animation, as the following steps will show. You'll add a couple of clouds into the animation, starting one from the left side and another from the right. The clouds will move at different rates across the front of the crystal ball.

1. Return to the first frame of the animation, using the Home key on your keyboard.

2. Open the CLOUDS.POR floater library, which was used in Chapter 9. Choose Cloud 1, and drag it into the first frame of the movie, placing it toward the bottom left of the document window as shown in Figure 18.31. In the Controls | Floating Selection Palette, set the Opacity of the floater to 65%.

3. Now you'll record a session that will move the floater toward the right by 20 pixels. Choose Tools | Record Session to begin.

651

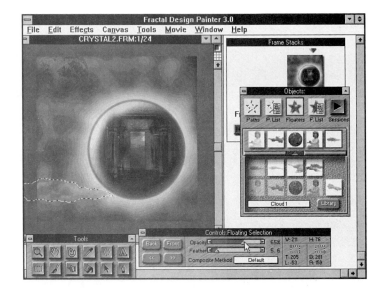

Figure 18.31.
Place the Cloud 1
floater into the docu-
ment and set its
Opacity to 65%.

4. Using the right-arrow key, move the cloud floater toward the right by 20 spaces. Lower numbers will move the floater more slowly, and higher numbers will move it more rapidly.

5. Choose Tools | Stop Recording Session. When the Name The Session dialog box shown in Figure 18.32 appears, call it `Move Right 20 pixels` or something similarly descriptive.

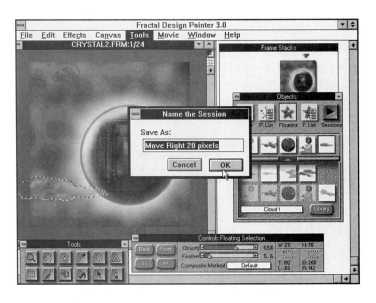

Figure 18.32.
Assign a descriptive
name for your session
in the Name The
Session dialog box.

6. Choose Movie | Apply Session To Movie. In the Recorded Sessions dialog box, highlight the session you just recorded, and click the Playback button. The cloud will be dropped into each frame of the movie, offset by 20 pixels. Eventually, it will move completely off the image window.

7. When the session stops, use the backspace key to delete the floater from the first frame.

8. To add a second cloud to the animation, choose the Cloud 2 floater from the floater library. Increase the size of the cloud to 200 percent of its original size, using the Effects | Orientation | Scale command. Then, click the floater with the Floating Selection Tool and move it toward the bottom right of the image.

9. In the Controls | Floating Selection Palette, adjust the Opacity of the second cloud to 55%. If you'd like to try one of the other compositing methods besides default, experiment to see which effect is to your liking before you record your session.

10. Again, choose Tools | Record Session. This time, move the cloud toward the left by eight pixels, using the left-arrow key on your keyboard.

11. Choose Tools | Stop Recording Session. Name the new session Move Left 8 Pixels, as shown in Figure 18.33.

*Figure 18.33.
Create a session to move another cloud eight pixels to the left, and assign it a descriptive name.*

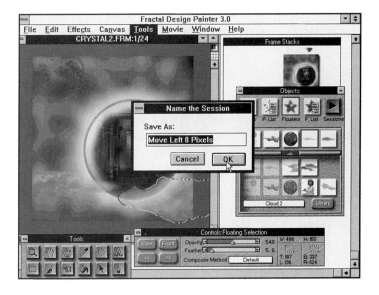

12. Apply this new session to the movie using the Movie | Apply Session To Movie command. Don't forget to clear the floater from the first frame, with the backspace key, after the session has completed. When you play the

movie back, the larger cloud will move slower than the first cloud you added. Figure 18.34 shows our second cloud placed into the animation. After you're done placing the clouds, close the Objects Palette.

Figure 18.34.
The second cloud is
added to the animation
and moves in the
opposite direction.

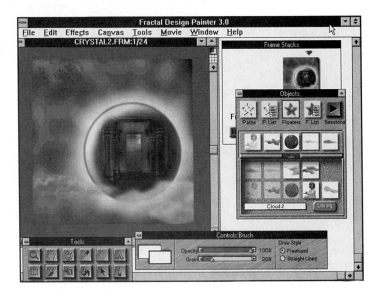

Step 18.8. Applying a Brush Stroke to a Movie

Animated effects can also be applied to a movie by using the Movie | Apply Brush Stroke To Movie command. This command is ideal for spraying a character into an animation using an Image Hose because it places a portion of a brush stroke into each frame of the animation. Though you're not going to use an Image Hose when applying a stroke to this movie, this example clearly illustrates how the command works. A curved brush stroke will be recorded and then applied to the movie. When it is rendered into the movie, it will give the appearance of a falling star.

1. Return to the first frame if necessary, using the Home key. From the Brushes Palette, choose the Thin Stroke Airbrush.

2. Using the Dropper, pick a yellow color from the halo area of the image, as shown in Figure 18.35.

3. Choose Tools | Record Stroke. Draw a curved line in your image, starting from the top, as shown in Figure 18.36.

4. Choose Edit | Undo to erase the stroke from the image. The stroke will still be retained in memory.

5. Choose Movie | Apply Brush Stroke To Movie. A small section of the stroke will be placed into each frame of the movie.

Figure 18.35.
Choose yellow from the
halo area of the image
with the Dropper.

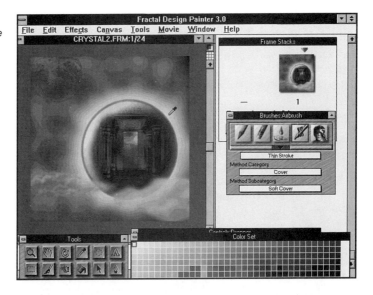

Figure 18.36.
Draw a curved stroke in
the first frame, starting
from the top.

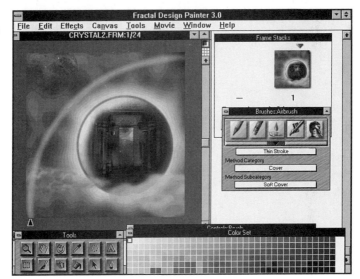

Step 18.9: Saving to a Compressed .AVI File

One way to save a Painter movie into another format would be to save it as a
Video for Windows .AVI file. There are several compression options, but the one
you'll discuss here is the Cinepak compression method, which is one of the most
widely used.

Compression reduces the amount of data in each frame of the animation file. This is done so that your computer's processor can play the animation back more efficiently. However, compression can reduce the quality of an image. Experimentation with the various settings will help you learn the right balance between processor speed and quality.

As a rule, you don't want to add compression to an .AVI file until it is in its final version. Therefore, if you want to later add sound to your Painter movie, you should use a method that does not compress the images, such as Full Frames Uncompressed.

1. Choose File | Save As. The Save Movie dialog box, shown in Figure 18.37, appears. Select to save the movie as an .AVI file, at 15 frames per second. This frame rate is about half that of videotape, but it will be easier for your computer to process and keep up with. Slower computers may need to have the FPS rate reduced even further, depending on the resolution of the animation. Click OK to continue.

Figure 18.37.
Choose to save the
movie as an .AVI file, at
15 frames per second,
in the Save Movie
dialog box.

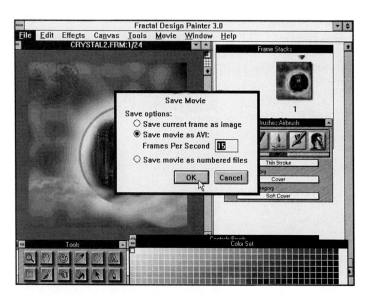

2. The Enter Movie Name dialog box, shown in Figure 18.38, appears next. Here, choose the directory you wish to save the file into, and type in a name for the file. Click OK to continue.

3. The Video Compression dialog box appears next. Click the arrow at the right of the Compressor drop-down box, and choose Cinepak Codek by Supermatch as the compressor type.

4. By default, the Compression Quality defaults to 75. Increasing this setting makes the file size larger, but it does improve the quality of the image.

Adjust this setting to 85 to see if you prefer its results over those of the default setting.

Figure 18.38.
Select the directory you
wish to save the file
into, and type in a
name for the file.

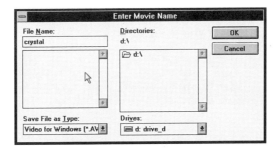

5. You can also adjust the Data Rate when using the Cinepak compression method. The data rate should be set no greater than that of the storage device it will be played from. For example, some CD-ROM drives have a data transfer rate of around 150 KB, and faster double and triple-speed CD-ROM drives can transfer data at 300 KB or greater. Hard drives can transfer data as slowly as 80 KB but also as fast as 300 KB. If you have targeted your animation for mass distribution, 150 KB might be a good compromise.

6. The key-frame setting identifies how often a key frame should be placed in the .AVI file. Key frames help keep video and audio tracks in sync with each other. This setting can be left at its default value for our example.

7. Click OK after all settings are as shown in Figure 18.39. The file will be saved into an .AVI file, which can then be viewed in the Windows Media Player or other multimedia software.

Figure 18.39.
Select your video
compression method
and set other compres-
sion settings in the
Video Compression
dialog box.

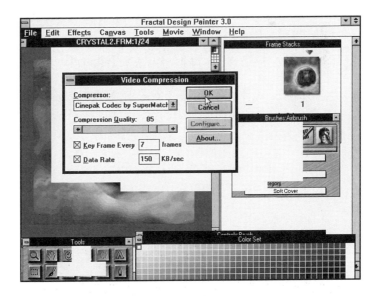

Saving to a QuickTime Movie

Mac users have the option of saving Painter movies as QuickTime movies. The procedure is similar to saving as a Video for Windows .AVI file, except that you don't have to worry about compression options.

1. Choose File | Save As. The Save Movie dialog box, shown in Figure 18.37, appears. Save the movie as a QuickTime movie and click OK to continue.

2. The Enter Movie Name dialog box appears next. Here, choose the folder you wish to save the file into, and type in a name for the file and click OK to continue.

3. The file is saved as a QuickTime movie, which can then be viewed in any multimedia software.

Animating Paper Texture

The following steps are optional for this project. If you're not sure that you will like animated paper-grain texture on your animation, you should make a copy of your Painter movie first. This is because changes are automatically saved into Painter movies as they are updated into the frames. You can make a backup copy of a Painter movie in one of two ways. The first method would be to close the file and make a copy of it using the Windows File Manager or other file-management software. You can also keep the document open and save it as a series of numbered files that can later be reloaded and saved as a Painter movie. Using this method, you won't have to exit the Painter program. (Instructions for saving the file to a series of numbered files are given in Chapter 23, "Converting to Other Animation Formats.")

To apply animated paper grain to the Painter movie, proceed as follows:

1. From the Art Materials | Papers Palette, choose a paper texture that you would like to animate in your movie. For our example, the Hatch paper texture in the default Painter library was chosen. This texture is shown in Figure 18.40.

2. Choose Tools | Session Options. In the Session Options dialog box, shown in Figure 18.41, uncheck the Record Initial State radio button.

Figure 18.40.
Choose a paper texture
to apply to the Painter
movie.

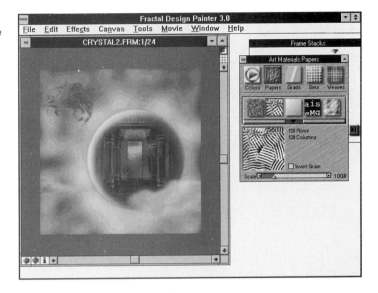

Figure 18.41.
Uncheck the box beside
Record Initial State in
the Session Options
dialog box.

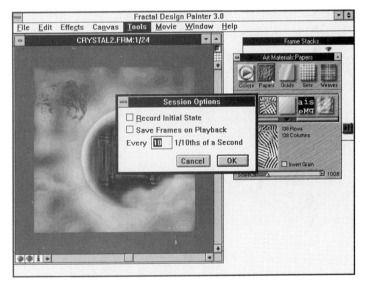

3. Choose Movie | Set Grain Position. The Frame-to-Frame Grain Position
   dialog box appears, giving you three choices for applying the paper
   grain to the movie. Select to change the grain randomly, as shown in
   Figure 18.42.

Figure 18.42.
Choose one of three
methods to apply paper
grain to the movie.

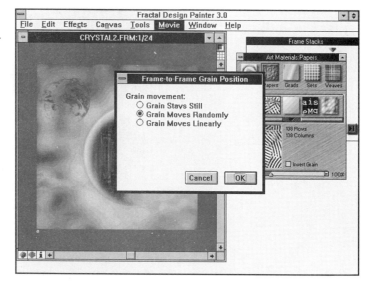

4. Choose Tools | Record Session to begin recording a session that applies paper grain.

5. Choose Effects | Surface Control | Apply Surface Texture. In the Apply Surface Texture dialog box, select to generate the texture using Paper Grain. Adjust the lighting orientation, the amount of the effect, and whether or not you want the shiny effect added to the grain. Your screen will look similar to Figure 18.43 or Figure 18.44. Click OK when your choices are made.

Figure 18.43.
Choose to apply surface
texture based on Paper
Grain in the Apply
Surface Texture dialog
box.

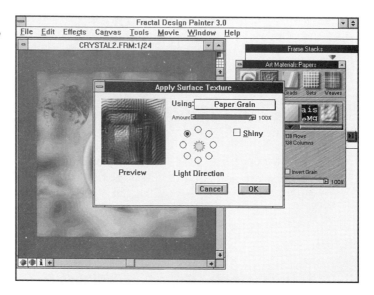

*Figure 18.44.
In Painter 3.1, the
Apply Surface Texture
dialog box offers
additional lighting
choices.*

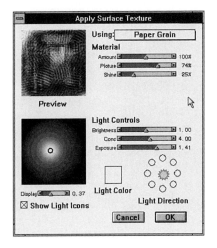

6. Choose Tools | Stop Recording Session. Assign an appropriate name to the session when prompted to do so.

7. Choose Edit | Undo to remove the effect from the first frame. Otherwise, it will be doubled on that frame after the effect is applied to the movie.

8. Choose Movie | Apply Session To Movie. Select the session you just recorded, and click the Playback button. After you complete the session, the grain will move randomly from frame to frame.

Summary

You've learned quite a bit about working with paths and floaters in animations and some of the basic techniques in applying sessions to movies. These ideas are just the beginning—the rest is up to you. In the next chapter, you'll learn more about Painter movies by creating a cartoon animation. You'll also learn about some advanced and powerful ways to use Painter sessions.

Creating a Cartoon Animation

In this chapter, you create an animated character running across a scrolling background. In the process, you learn how to clone a movie and how to use and apply sessions to make your animation tasks easier.

You trace an animated polar bear from 10 digitized images of a running polar bear. You can find these 10 images on the CD accompanying this book.

The background starts out as a still image, but I show you how to automate the process of turning it into an animated background. I think you'll agree, after seeing what recorded sessions can do in regard to movie-making, that Painter is a powerful animation tool.

Step 19.1. Loading Numbered Files

Start by loading in the 10 digitized images of the polar bear. You can find them on the CD accompanying this book; they are named BEAR0001.TGA to BEAR0010.TGA. By now, you're probably quite familiar with the File | Open command.

1. From the File menu, choose the File | Open command (Ctrl-O in Windows, Cmd-O in Mac).

2. From the Select Image dialog box, choose the drive and directory from which you want to load the files.

3. Click inside the Open Numbered Files checkbox, located at the bottom-right side of the dialog box, as shown in Figure 19.1.

Figure 19.1.
Click the Open num-
bered Files checkbox in
the Select Image dialog
box.

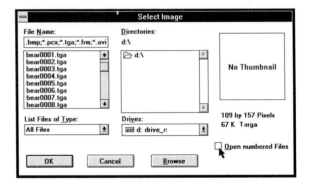

4. Choose First Numbered File appears just above the OK button on the lower-left corner of the dialog box. Here, select the BEAR0001.TGA file, shown in Figure 19.2, by double-clicking it.

5. The phrase Choose Last Numbered File then appears just above the OK button. At this point, select the BEAR0010.TGA file, shown in Figure 19.3, by double-clicking it.

6. The Enter Movie Name dialog box, shown in Figure 19.4, appears. The .FRM extension should automatically appear in the Save File as Type dropdown box. Scroll to the drive and directory into which you want to save the file. Then enter BEAR in the File Name box. Click OK to continue creating the movie.

   Entering the .FRM extension at the end of the filename is optional because the extension chosen in the Save File as Type drop-down box is automatically assigned.

Figure 19.2.
Choose
BEAR0001.TGA as the
first frame for the
movie.

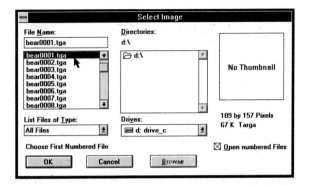

Figure 19.3.
Choose
BEAR0010.TGA as the
last frame of the movie.

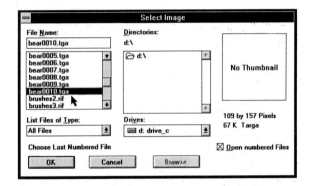

7. The New Frame Stack dialog box, shown in Figure 19.5, appears. Here, you define the number of layers of onion skin that you want the frame stack to have. The number of layers defines how many frames you see in the Frame Stacks Palette, and superimposed one above the other when you're using the Tracing Paper feature while editing a movie. Also, here you select the Storage Type for the movie, which basically defines its color depth.

8. For this example, choose two layers of onion skin and 24-bit color with 8-bit mask, the default values. After you make these choices, click the OK button. Painter reads in the numbered files, and a frame stack with 10 frames is created.

Figure 19.4.
In the Enter Movie
Name dialog box, enter
BEAR for the movie
name.

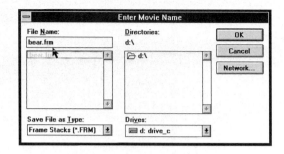

Figure 19.5.
Choose two layers of
onion skin and 24-bit
color with 8-bit mask as
the movie storage type.

Step 19.2. Creating a New Document to Use as the Clone

As I mentioned earlier, you're going to use this polar bear as a guide to creating an animated polar bear. To create the animation, you need to create a second movie that contains 10 blank frames (the same number of frames as in the original image). You use this new movie as the clone movie, and you use the digitized bear as the clone source.

Your task is to create a new frame stack that is the same size as the original movie. To find out the size of the digitized movie, you can click the Information button (the I button) in the lower-left corner of the BEAR.FRM document window. You then see that the digitized frames are 157 pixels wide and 109 pixels high.

You are going to create a new movie with blank frames and of the same dimensions as the original BEAR.FRM movie so that you can trace the bear. To create the new movie, perform the following steps:

1. Choose the File | New command. In the New Picture dialog box, shown in Figure 19.6, enter 157 for the width and 109 for the height (the same dimensions as the original BEAR.FRM file).

Figure 19.6.
Create a second
157×109 frame stack
for the clone document.

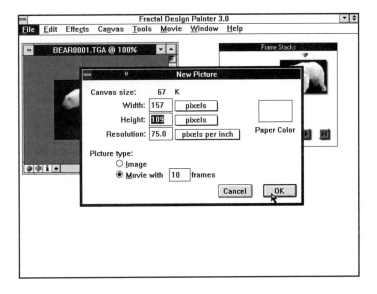

2. Under Picture Type, click the radio button adjacent to Movie, and enter 10 as the number of frames. Set the paper color to white, if not already selected, by double-clicking the box beneath the Paper Color label. After you enter the settings, click OK to proceed.

3. In the Enter Movie Name dialog box that appears, choose the drive and directory to which you want to save the file, and enter BEAR2 as the second movie name, as shown in Figure 19.7. Choose OK to continue.

Figure 19.7.
Name the second movie
stack BEAR2.FRM.

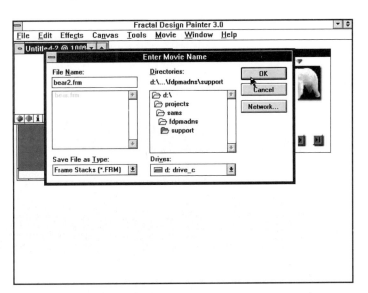

4. In the New Frame dialog box that appears, as shown in Figure 19.8, again choose two layers of onion skin and 24-bit color with 8-bit mask. Click OK to accept these settings, and the second frame stack is created.

Figure 19.8.
Again, create two
layers of onion skin
and a 24-bit movie.

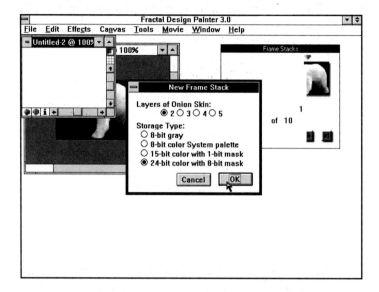

Figure 19.9 shows both movies displayed on the screen. The Frame Stacks Palette reflects the contents of the current movie, which in this case is the blank movie you just created. In the Frame Stacks Palette, a red arrow appears above frame 1. This arrow indicates that frame 1 is the current frame you are editing.

Figure 19.9.
The new movie
document appears
on the screen.

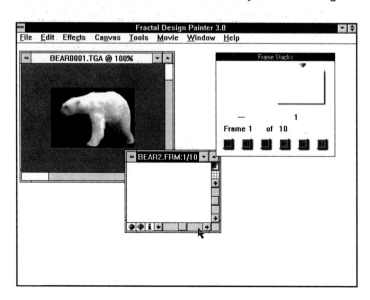

Tracing the Movie

Now that you've created the original movie and the blank frames, you can trace the bear. To accomplish this, you first have to create a link between the original bear and the blank frames. Then you can trace the bear using one of Painter's Pen variants. Now proceed with setting the clone source.

Step 19.3. Setting the Movie Clone Source

To be able to trace the bear from the digitized video into the new animation, you need to set the original digitized frame stack as the movie clone source, as follows:

1. Click the BEAR.FRM frame stack to make it current. The title bar is highlighted, indicating that it is currently selected. Your screen should look similar to Figure 19.10.

2. From the Movie menu, select the Set Movie Clone Source command, as shown in Figure 19.11. Choosing this command creates a link between the two movies on your screen, with the BEAR.FRM as the clone source and the blank movie as the clone movie.

Figure 19.10.
Select the original
digitized bear frame
stack as the current
movie.

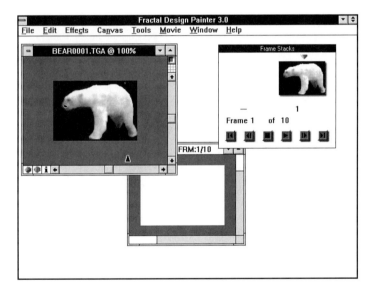

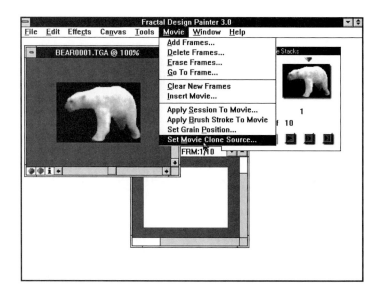

Figure 19.11.
*Choose Movie | Set
Movie Clone Source to
make the BEAR.FRM
frame stack the movie
clone source.*

Step 19.4. Using Tracing Paper in Movie Files

Now you need to display the digitized bear inside the blank frames so that you can trace it. As you learned previously, using the Canvas | Tracing Paper command enables you to do this.

You also can implement Tracing Paper in movies in one of two ways. When you're working in a single movie, Tracing Paper superimposes frames one above the other, with the number of layers determined by the layers of onion skin in the movie. Then you can use the ghosted images of frames before or after the current frame as a guide for drawing the current frame.

When you're using the Tracing Paper command between a movie and its clone source, the Tracing Paper displays the clone source as a ghosted image in the current frame. The clone source movie and clone document movie are linked together in such a way that when you advance or move back to a given frame in the clone movie, the corresponding frame of the clone source is ghosted in the clone movie window.

To turn on the Tracing Paper, proceed as follows:

1. Click the BEAR2.FRM frame stack to make it current, as shown in Figure 19.12.

2. Choose the Canvas | Tracing Paper command. You then see a ghosted image of the digitized bear appear in the BEAR2.FRM frame stack, as shown in Figure 19.13.

Figure 19.12.
Select the BEAR2.FRM
frame stack to make it
current.

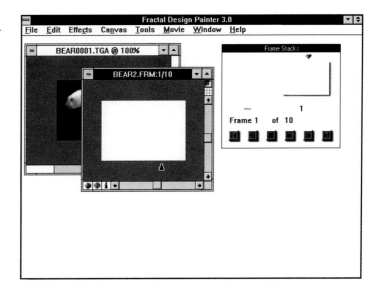

Figure 19.13.
Turn on Canvas |
Tracing Paper to see a
ghosted image of the
clone source in the
frame stack.

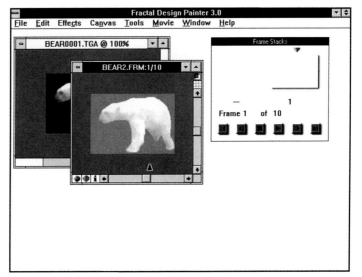

Notice that if you advance to subsequent frames using the fifth VCR button in the Frame Stacks Palette, or the Page Up key on your keyboard, the frames of the BEAR2.FRM frame stack (the clone document) are automatically linked with the corresponding frames in the BEAR.FRM, or original clone source document. Clicking the first VCR button in the Frame Stacks Palette or the Home key on your keyboard returns you to the first frame.

Step 19.5. Tracing the First Frame

Now you're going to begin tracing the first frame. If you like, you can enlarge the window size and zoom in closer for tracing by using the Window | Zoom In command, or by using the quick-key combination of Ctrl-+ (the Control key plus the + key) in Windows, the Cmd-+ (the command key plus the + key) in Mac, or by using the Magnifier in the Tools Palette. Zooming in helps you see the areas to be traced better. Now select the Fine Point Pen to trace the bear, as follows:

1. Open the Brushes Palette using Ctrl-2 in Windows or Cmd-2 in Mac or the Window | Brushes command.

2. Click the Pen icon, and choose the Fine Point Pen from the dropdown list box in the Brushes Palette. Your screen should look similar to Figure 19.14.

Figure 19.14.
From the Brushes
Palette, choose the
Fine Point Pen.

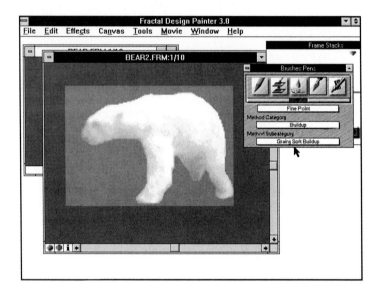

3. Select Black as your current color if it is not already selected.

4. With the Fine Point Pen, outline the shape of the polar bear in the first frame of the Painter movie. Basically, you are just outlining the shape of the bear here. You can add as much or as little detail to the tracing as you like. The only details I added were a little curve for the ear and black areas for the eyes and nose. If you like, you can also draw lines to define the toes. Figure 19.15 shows an example of the tracing in progress.

You can use the Edit | Undo command immediately after drawing a line if you don't like the way it looks. (Remember, in Painter 3.1, you can undo multiple steps.) Or you can use one of the Eraser variants to remove line work you aren't happy with. Erasing using either the Eraser variants or the Bleach variants works well in this case because the background color is white.

Figure 19.15.
You trace the first
frame using the Fine
Point Pen and black
ink.

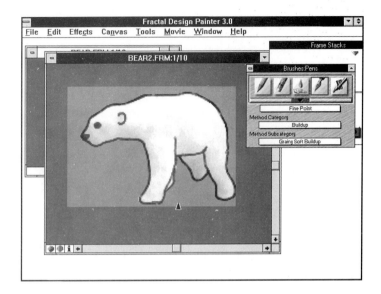

Remember also that you can use the Rotate Page tool from the Tools Palette to position the canvas as necessary to draw your line work.

Step 19.6. Tracing the Remaining Frames

After you trace the first frame, you can trace the remaining frames in a similar manner. Advance to the next frame, trace it, and continue this process until you've traced all 10 frames.

TIP
When you advance to the next frame, the changes made to the frame you are moving from are automatically updated into the Painter frame stack. Sometimes you may find that you've made an error that might be difficult to change later in the process of the movie.

You cannot save a backup copy of a movie using the File | Save As command. Although you can save the movie to an AVI file, which saves it in an animated format, this method does not retain the masking, selection, and floater information contained in the movie.

To work around this problem, you can periodically save your movie as a series of numbered .RIF files, which retain all the Painter particulars. You might want to use this approach before you experiment with a new procedure or before you apply a session. Then, if you aren't satisfied with the results, you can restore the movie to its previous state by loading the numbered .RIF files in as a new movie.

To trace the remaining frames in the frame stack, proceed as follows:

1. To advance to the next frame, click the fifth VCR button in the Frame Stacks Palette, as shown in Figure 19.16. The second frame appears inside the movie document window.

Figure 19.16.
Click the Advance button in the Frame Stacks Palette to advance to frame 2.

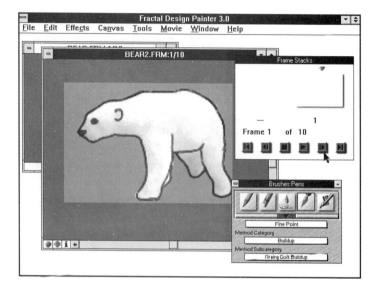

2. Notice that the image you traced in the first frame now appears on Frame 1 in the Frame Stacks Palette, as shown in Figure 19.17. A red arrow appears above blank frame number 2, indicating it as the current frame.

Figure 19.17.
The first traced frame is shown in the Frame Stacks Palette, with the red arrow indicating frame 2 as the current frame.

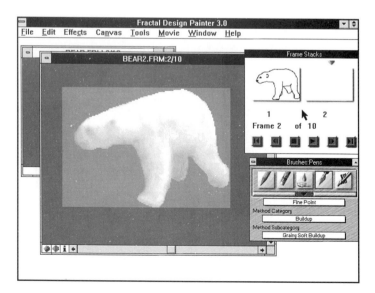

3. Now resume tracing. Using the same method as before, trace the second frame. Figure 19.18 shows the second frame in progress.

Figure 19.18.
You trace the second
frame in the same
manner as the first.

4. Continue in the same manner with the remaining frames until you have traced all 10.

Step 19.7. Deleting Extra Frames

If you mistakenly add frames by clicking the fifth VCR button beyond the tenth frame, as shown in Figure 19.19, you can delete the extra frames by using the Movie | Delete Frames command, as follows.

1. If you try to delete the frame you are currently on, you are notified by a beep that you can't do that. If, for example, you want to delete Frame 11, move to any one of Frames 1 through 10.
2. Choose the Movie | Delete Frames command, as shown in Figure 19.20.
3. When the Delete Frames dialog box appears, enter the starting and ending numbers of the frames you want to delete. In the example, you want to delete Frames 11 through 11, as shown in Figure 19.21.

Figure 19.19.
*You can inadvertently
add Extra frames if you
click the Advance
button beyond the last
frame of the movie.*

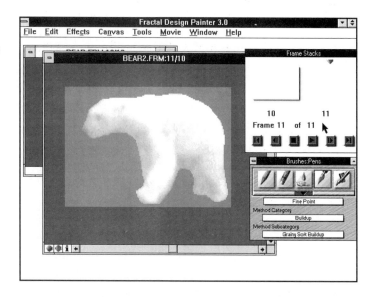

Figure 19.20.
*Choose Movie | Delete
Frames to delete
frames from the movie.*

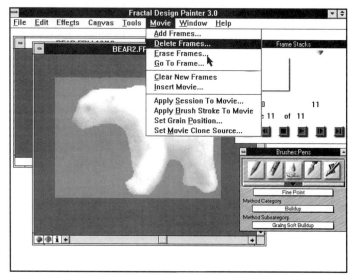

Figure 19.21.
Enter the frame
numbers you want to
delete.

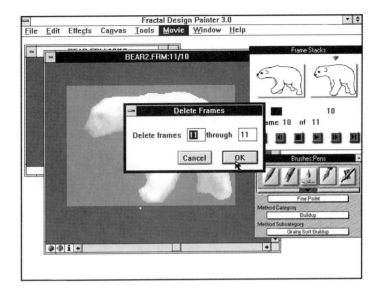

Step 19.8. Playing the Animation

Now that you have traced all 10 frames of the polar bear, as shown in Figure 19.22, you probably want to see what your movie looks like. When you play the movie, the clone source disappears from the movie you play, and you can view only the tracing. Seeing the tracing in motion enables you to see whether you need to fix any areas to provide smoother motion.

Figure 19.22.
All the frames in the
movie have been
traced.

You can play the animation by clicking the fourth VCR button, as shown in Figure 19.23. You may need to zoom back to 100 percent zoom factor before playing the animation, however. Remember that you are working on a 24-bit file here, which means that a great deal of image data has to be pushed through your computer for processing. Enlarging the window only increases the number of pixel changes that the processor has to calculate to play the animation. You may see "tearing" in the playback when it is displayed at a larger zoom factor. To help remedy this situation, zoom out to make the animation smaller.

Figure 19.23.
You can play the
animation by clicking
the fourth VCR button.

Step 19.9. Closing the Clone Source Movie

Now that you have traced the bear, you might want to compare one frame to the next. You don't need the BEAR.FRM clone source anymore, so you can close it now, as follows:

1. Click the BEAR.FRM frame stack to make it current, as shown in Figure 19.24.

2. To close the document, you can use the quick-key combination Ctrl-W in Windows or Cmd-Win in Mac, or you can click the button in the upper-left corner of the document, shown in Figure 19.25, and select Close.

3. To remove the digitized image of the bear from the Tracing Paper, choose the Canvas | Tracing Paper command twice—the first time to remove the image and the second to restore the Tracing Paper.

Figure 19.24.
To close the clone
source animation, click
it to make it current.

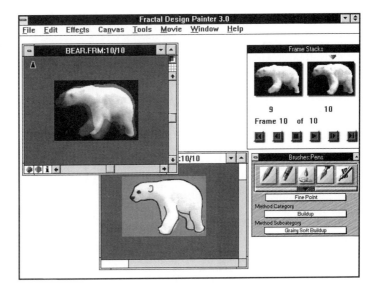

Figure 19.25.
Close the movie using
the quick-key combina-
tion Ctrl-W in Windows
or Cmd-W in Mac, or by
selecting Close from
the dropdown menu at
the upper-left side of
the document.

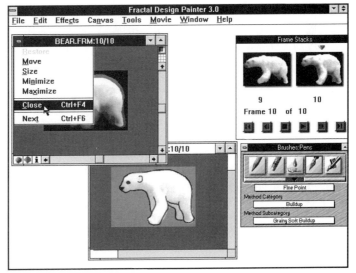

4. Now two frames are superimposed one atop the other, as shown in Figure
   19.26. Two frames appear because that was the number of layers of onion
   skin you defined when creating the frame stack. You can use the Tracing
   Paper to compare the current frame with the previous frame and add any
   detail you want to enhance the tracing.

Figure 19.26.
*Choose Canvas |
Tracing Paper once to
clear the Clone Source
image, and a second
time if you want to turn
it back on to see two
traced images.*

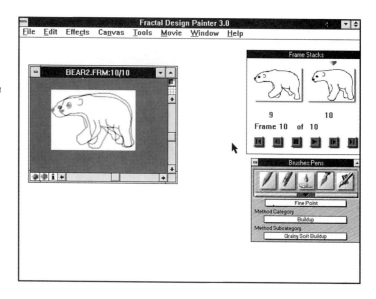

Coloring the Frames

Now you're going to color the frames. Typically, you do this manually, and you can use the Tracing Paper and the small images in the Frame Stacks Palette as a guide to where colors were placed in the preceding frame. First, though, you want to protect your line work from any ink or paint that might pass over them.

You have a small 10-frame animation here. It really wouldn't be too bad to mask each frame manually, would it? But compare this to the task of creating a one-minute animation—that would be 1800 frames at 30 frames per second. You would be entering commands and pushing buttons for hours. You therefore can automate the task by recording a session that masks each frame automatically, based on Image Luminance. You can then apply this session to each frame in the movie using the Apply Session to Movie command.

Now you're ready to start by creating the session.

Step 19.10. Recording an Auto Mask Session

Next, you create a session that masks each frame based on Image Luminance so that you can use the Cartoon Fill on each frame. Proceed as follows:

1. Return to the first frame by clicking the first VCR button in the Frame Stacks Palette.

2. Choose Tools | Record Session, as shown in Figure 19.27.

Figure 19.27.
Choose Tools | Record
Session to record a
command or series of
commands that can be
played into each frame.

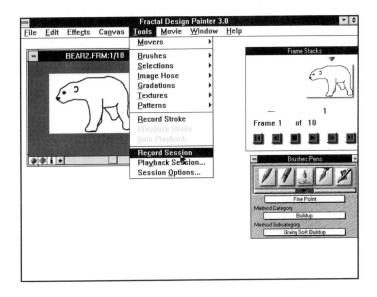

3. At this point, you are in the record session mode, and any keystrokes you
   make are recorded. Be sure to enter only commands and strokes that you
   want to record. Follow the next few steps carefully.

4. Choose Edit | Mask | Auto Mask. The Auto Mask dialog box appears.

5. Image Luminance should be the default mask type. If not, choose this
   method from the drop-down list box, as shown in Figure 19.28, and click
   OK to generate the mask in the first frame.

Figure 19.28.
Choose the Edit | Mask
| Auto Mask command,
and generate the mask
based on Image
Luminance.

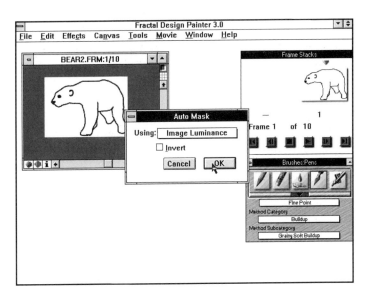

6. Now stop recording. Choose Tools | Stop Recording Session, as shown in Figure 19.29.

Figure 19.29.
Choose Tools | Stop
Recording Session to
complete the session
recording.

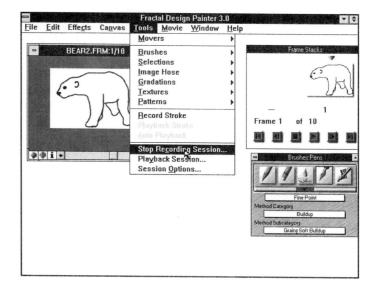

7. The Name the Session dialog box, shown in Figure 19.30, prompts you for a name for the session. Name the session Image Luminance Mask, as shown in Figure 19.30, and click OK.

Figure 19.30.
Save the recorded
session as Image
Luminance Mask.

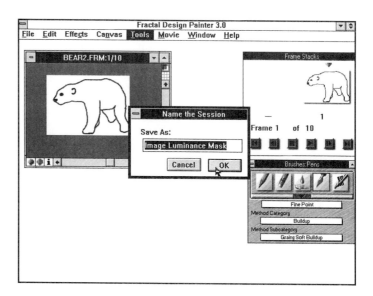

Step 19.11. Playing Back the Session in the Movie

Now you can apply the mask to all frames in the movie. For this procedure, you can sit back and watch the computer do all the work. Remember: If you're working on an animation with many frames, playing back sessions can take a long time. Your tiny animation takes no time at all, so you don't have a long break.

To apply the session to the movie, proceed as follows:

1. Choose the Movie | Apply Session to Movie command, as shown in Figure 19.31.

Figure 19.31.
To generate the mask in all frames of the movie, choose the Movie | Apply Session to Movie command.

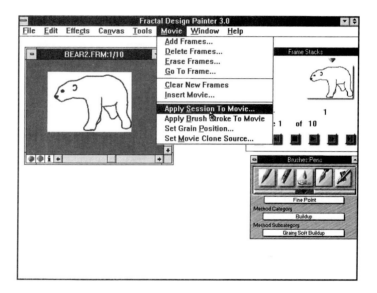

2. When the Recorded Sessions dialog box appears, click the Image Luminance Mask session you just recorded.

3. Click the Playback button in the Recorded Sessions dialog box. This button renders the session into each frame of the movie.

A status box appears, indicating that Painter is applying the session to the movie. The command is then repeated across all 10 frames of the animation. The images in the Frame Stacks Palette move in accordance with the changes being made to each frame as they are applied.

You can view the mask in each frame by choosing the second Mask Visibility button from the lower-left corner of the Frame Stacks Document window. Then you can advance one frame at a time or play the animation using the fourth VCR button to see that the mask has been applied to each frame. Neat, huh? Wait— there's more on sessions later that will really get you thinking!

Coloring the Bear

Now you're going to fill in the bear with an off-white (light gray) color using the Cartoon Fill method. I discussed this method fully in Chapter 7, "Pen Project," so I just highlight the steps here for your reference.

Step 19.12. Setting the Lock Out Color

For the first step in the Cartoon Fill method, implement the Lock Out Color feature and set the lock out color to black to protect your line work. Proceed as follows:

1. Choose black as your current color if it is not already selected.

2. Double-click the Paint Bucket tool to reveal the Lock out color dialog box, as shown in Figure 19.32.

Figure 19.32. Double-click the Paint Bucket tool to enable the Lock Out color, and set the slider as necessary to protect your line work.

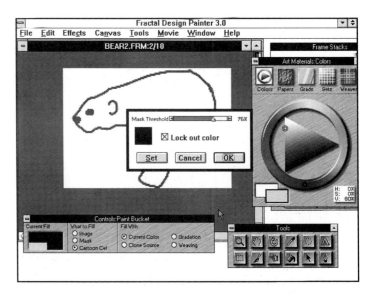

3. If the color is indicated in the box adjacent to the Lock out color checkbox, click the Set button, which changes the lock out color to your currently selected primary color (which is black).

4. Verify that the Lock out color checkbox has an x in it.

5. Adjust the Mask Threshold slider as necessary to protect your line work sufficiently. Too low a setting causes the fill color to bleed through the lines. Too high a setting causes some of the antialiased lines to be filled improperly, creating objectionable white spaces in the fill. You have to experiment with which setting works best for your image. In the example, a setting of 76% works well.

6. Click OK to return to the document window.

Step 19.13. Filling the Bear

In this step, you fill the bear with a light gray. The Paint Bucket tool should still be selected from the previous step. Fill the bear using the following steps:

1. From the Art Materials | Colors Palette, choose a light gray. You select pure grays by dragging the color indicator as far to the left in the color triangle as possible. You can, of course, select a color that is not quite pure gray—after all, this is your bear!

2. From the Controls | Paint Bucket Palette, set to fill a Cartoon Cel with the Current Color.

3. Starting from the first frame, fill the bear by clicking inside the body. Then fill other areas, such as the legs, to complete the coloring on the first frame. Your screen should look similar to Figure 19.33.

Figure 19.33.
Fill the polar bear with
a light gray in all
frames using the
Cartoon Fill method.

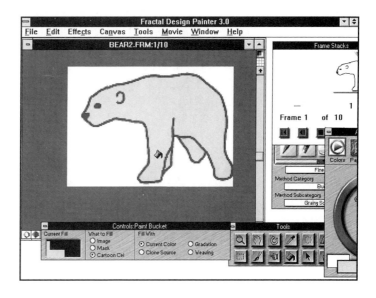

4. Advance to the next frame using the Page Up key. This way, you can advance to the frames using one hand and fill the areas with the other. The process goes a lot faster that way.

5. Continue filling the remaining frames in this manner.

Step 19.14. Shading the Bear

Now that you have the base color in the bear, you can add some shading using a slightly deeper shade of gray. Here's how:

1. Drag the color indicator in the Art Materials | Colors Palette downward vertically from the present color. View the change of color in the Primary Color rectangle until the color changes to one that you like.

Figure 19.34.
Choose a slightly
deeper shade of gray to
add shadows to the
bear.

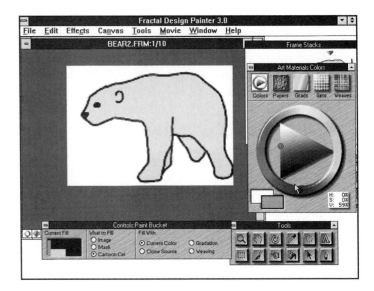

2. From the lower-left corner of the BEAR2.FRM movie window, verify that your line work is protected. Choose the second Drawing Visibility button. You can also view the mask in red by choosing the second Mask Visibility button.

3. From the Brushes Palette, choose the Pen and Ink pen variant. Shade the first frame, as shown in Figure 19.35.

4. Continue with the remaining frames. Remember that you can use the Tracing Paper as a guide to your shading. Or, if viewing two images at once is confusing, you can also use the thumbnail image in the Frame Stacks Palette as a guide to how you applied the shading in the previous frame.

5. After you shade all 10 frames, play back the animation to see how it flows together. Make any changes you feel are necessary until the animation flows smoothly.

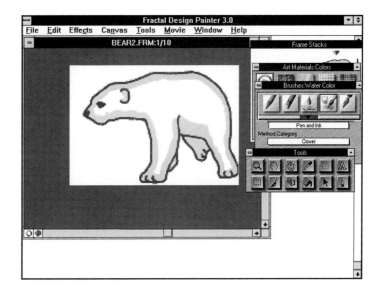

Figure 19.35.
Turn on the mask to
protect the black line
work, and shade the
bear with the Pen and
Ink pen variant.

Step 19.15. Masking Outside the Bear

Now you want to generate a mask outside the bear. Later, you invert this mask so that you can generate a nozzle file from this little animation.

Although you can automatically mask a color using the Edit | Magic Wand command, this command masks only contiguous areas of a color. Generating a session using this command isn't appropriate for your animation because, in some cases, multiple areas of the color you want to mask are contained in one frame. The Magic Wand leaves some of the areas unmasked.

So, you generate a mask based on current color instead, which masks all instances of a current color. To start this process, fill the areas outside the bear with a color other than black or white using the Cartoon Fill method. Choosing a different color ensures that the colors contained in your colored bear are left unmasked. In my case, I chose a light tan. Proceed as follows:

1. Select your color from the Art Materials | Colors Palette.
2. Choose the Paint Bucket tool from the Tools Palette.
3. From the Controls | Paint Bucket Palette, choose to fill the Cartoon Cel with the Current Color.
4. Fill the areas outside the bear in each frame with the current color. Figure 19.36 shows one of the frames filled outside the bear.

*Figure 19.36.
Choose a color other
than black or white,
and fill the areas
outside the bear in
each frame.*

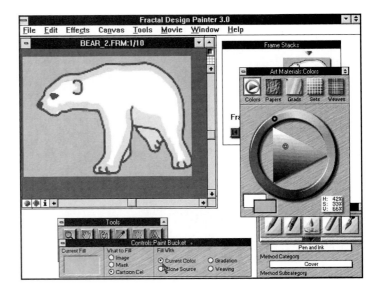

NOTE Before you proceed to the next step, you might want to save the files as individually numbered .RIF files, using the File | Save As command. When you generate the mask for the current color, the line work becomes unprotected as the mask you generate replaces the line work mask. For this reason, double-check your bear animation to make sure it's done the way you want it before you generate this other mask.

Without changing your current color, proceed to the next step to record a session that masks the current color in each frame. If you're not sure where the commands are located, remember that the steps are similar to the previous Image Luminance Mask session you recorded, and you can use those screen shots as references.

5. Choose Tools | Record Session. You are now in record session mode, and any strokes and commands you make are recorded.

6. Choose Edit | Mask | Auto Mask. This time, choose to mask the image using Current Color, as shown in Figure 19.37. Click OK to generate the mask.

7. Choose Tools | Stop Recording Session to end the recording. Save it as Mask Current Color, and proceed directly to the next step.

8. Choose Tools | Playback Session. From the Recorded Session dialog box, choose the Mask Current Color session just recorded, and click the Playback button. The Color Mask is generated in all 10 frames.

9. Play back the animation with the second Mask Visibility button on to verify that the mask has been applied correctly in each frame. You should see the areas outside the bear displayed in red.

Figure 19.37.
Without changing the current color, generate an Auto Mask in each frame, based on Current Color.

Step 19.16. Turning the Movie into a Nozzle File

Now you're going to turn your bear into a nozzle file so that you can place him (or her, if that's your preference) into the background image later using one of Painter's Image Hoses. This process is easy:

1. Choose Tools | Image Hose | Make Nozzle from Movie, as shown in Figure 19.38.

2. After a brief pause, a new image opens on your screen, containing all 10 frames of the bear placed in two rows of five images, as shown in Figure 19.39.

Before you save the image as a .RIF nozzle file, you have to perform one more step. If you examine all the nozzle files furnished with Painter, you notice that the area that is painted with the Image Hose is actually what is masked, not the background as you have here. Fixing this problem is easy:

1. Choose Edit | Mask | Invert Mask. If you have the second Mask Visibility button on, you see the inside of the bear and the line work turn red, and the outside of the bear appears in the color you filled the background with. Your screen should look similar to Figure 19.40.

2. Save the file as BEARHOSE.RIF in the directory of your choice. You also can find a version of this file on the CD accompanying this book.

Figure 19.38.
Choose the Make
Nozzle from Movie
command to turn the
movie into an Image
Hose nozzle file.

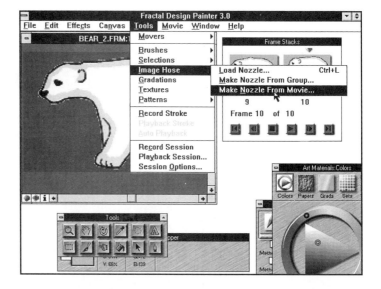

Figure 19.39.
A file with each of the
10 frames contained in
the image opens.

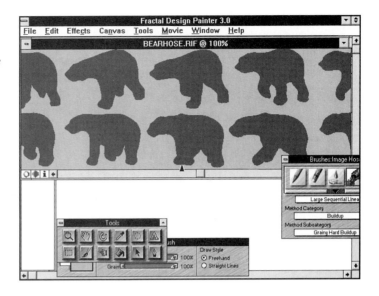

Figure 19.40.
Invert the mask so that
the inside of the bear is
red, and save the file as
BEARHOSE.RIF.

Creating the Background Image

I'm always looking for shortcuts when I create animations. When it came to the background, I thought it would be easier to draw the background in one contiguous image and then use Painter's Sessions capabilities to do the rest of the work in making the background move. I knew this approach would be easier than drawing and coloring each frame by hand. Remember, I told you that something that would really get you thinking was in store? Well, here it comes.

The end result of your animation is a movie that is 320 pixels wide and 240 pixels high. I wanted to place the animated bear in a stationary location and move the background while he was running.

If you create a background image that is 320×240, the scrolling would repeat too often, and it wouldn't look very good. So I created a background that was twice the width—640 pixels wide and 240 pixels high—to paint the background scene. To do the same, proceed as follows:

1. From the File menu, choose the New command. Or use the quick-key combination Ctrl-N in Windows or Cmd-N in Mac. The New Picture dialog box appears.

2. Create a single image with a white background that is 640 pixels wide× 240 pixels high. Your screen should look similar to Figure 19.41. Then click OK to create the image.

Figure 19.41.
Create a new 640×240
document for the
background image.

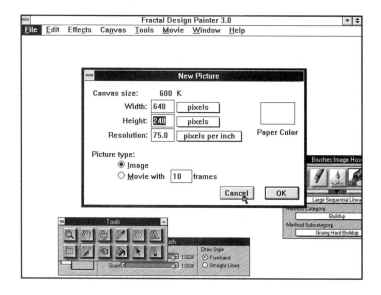

Step 19.17. Filling the Background with a Gradient

To start with the background, I selected the Night Sky gradient from Painter's default gradient library. Then I built the snowy mountains and water above that.

To fill your background with the gradient, proceed as follows:

1. From the Art Materials Palette (Ctrl-3 in Windows, Cmd-3 in Mac), click the Grads icon.

2. Choose the Night Sky gradient from the drop-down listbox inside the palette drawer. Your screen should look similar to Figure 19.42.

3. Close the palette drawer and adjust the angle of the Night Sky gradient by moving the red ball to the bottom of the circle until it reads 270 degrees. This way, you apply the gradient in a perfect horizontal line (you want this image to be seamless), with black toward the bottom, as shown in Figure 19.43.

4. Select the Paint Bucket from the Tools Palette.

Figure 19.42.
Fill the document with
the Night Sky gradient
from the Grads Palette.

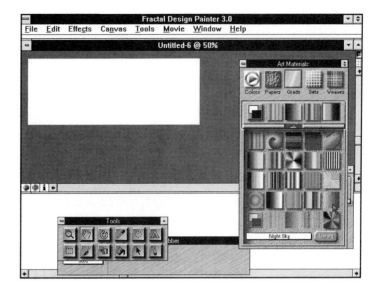

Figure 19.43.
Adjust the angle of the
gradient to 270 degrees
(black is on the
bottom).

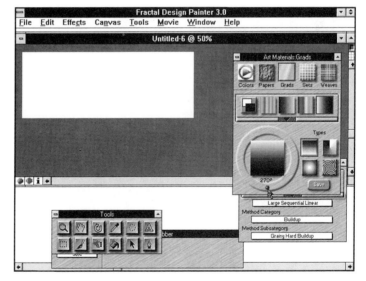

5. In the Controls | Paint Bucket Palette (Ctrl-6 in Windows, Cmd-6 in Mac), choose to fill the image with a gradient. Your screen should look similar to Figure 19.44.

6. Click anywhere inside the background image to fill the area with the Night Sky gradient. Figure 19.45 shows this step completed.

Figure 19.44.
From the Tools | Paint Bucket Palette, choose to fill the image with a gradient.

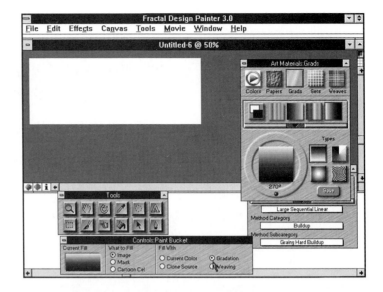

Figure 19.45.
The background is filled with the gradient. Now you can apply the foreground art.

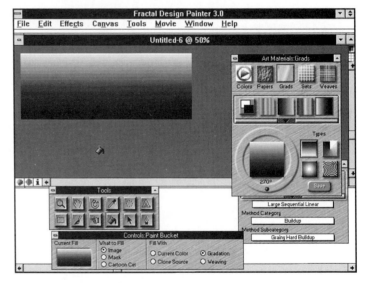

Step 19.18. Using Wraparound Color

As I hinted earlier, you want your background image to be seamless. That is, when you place one end of the background against the other end of a copy of itself, you don't want any seams or breaks in color continuity. A Painter feature, Wraparound Color, enables you to create a seamless image almost effortlessly.

You implement the Wraparound Color feature by turning an image into a captured pattern. Start by selecting the entire image, as follows:

1. Choose the Edit | Select All command, as shown in Figure 19.46. The entire image is surrounded by a bounding box.

Figure 19.46.
To use Painter's Wraparound Color feature to create a seamless image, start by selecting the entire image.

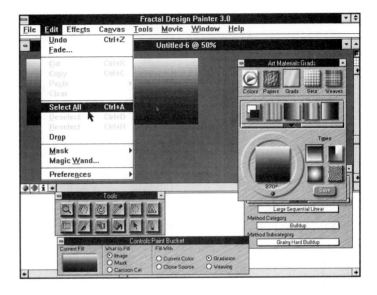

2. Choose Tools | Patterns | Capture Pattern, as shown in Figure 19.47. A new untitled document window with the background gradient placed inside appears. This document has the Wraparound Color feature now implemented.

Figure 19.47.
Choose Tools | Patterns | Capture Pattern to enable the Wraparound Color feature.

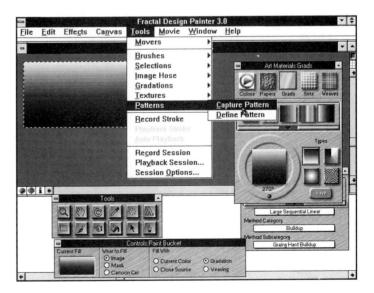

While you're painting your background scene, notice that if you extend your cursor beyond any of the edges, some color appears at the opposite end of the image at approximately the same point. That is, if you are drawing a horizontal line and extend it over one of the sides, you see a line started at the same height on the opposite side of the drawing. If you draw a vertical line and extend it over the top or bottom, you see it begin at the same width point on the opposite side. You can see this easier if you zoom out so that the entire image is in view. Use the hints of color at the opposite ends as guides to where the color has to line up.

Coloring the Scene

Now it's your chance to play, and freeform is the rule here. Visualize what it looks like at the North Pole where these polar bears live—nice clear blue sky with a scattering of clouds here and there, and snowy mountains and snow-drifts all over the place. Perhaps, here and there, some areas of water where thin ice cover has begun to melt from the rays of the sun. Got the picture?

To create the background, I used the Airbrush variants. The main colors I used were whites and grays, with perhaps a touch of light brown to add color to shaded areas.

1. If you want to use my version of the file as a guide or to use the eyedropper to pick up the colors used, you can find the file on the CD accompanying this book. Look in the section for this chapter and choose the file BACKGRND.RIF, which is the final version of the background image.

2. Choose the Thin Stroke Airbrush and an off-white/light gray to fill in the base of the background shape of the mountains. Notice as you draw that the wraparound color lets you know where the color has to end on the other side.

3. Add some shadowed areas in the foreground, using deeper shades of gray or light brown. Your image may look similar to Figure 19.48.

4. Add some clouds in the upper portion of the image using the same shades. You can vary the opacity of the stroke, if you like, by moving the Opacity slider in the Controls | Brush Palette. Moving the slider toward the left makes the strokes more transparent, which would be nice for the clouds and sky. Moving it toward the right makes the strokes more opaque.

5. Choose pure white and the Feather Tip Airbrush and draw some stark highlights on the snow, defining the ridges of snow drifts. Also add some highlights into the clouds, but do them with light pressure or reduce the opacity a bit if you're using the mouse. Figure 19.49 shows what is done so far.

6. The gradient area is too dark to show as a water pool, so lighten it a little. With the eyedropper, select a lighter blue from the sky above, and then choose the Fat Stroke Airbrush, which has a nice transparency. Reduce the size if you want by opening the Brush Controls | Size Palette. Lighten some of the gradient where your water will be. Just a touch here and there will do it. Then choose pure white again and lighten some more.

*Figure 19.48.
You paint snowy mountains using the Thin Stroke Airbrush and various shades of white, gray, and light brown.*

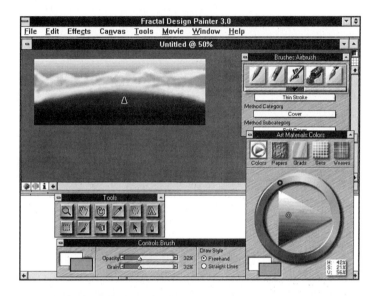

*Figure 19.49.
Add pure white highlights to the snow using the Feather Tip Airbrush. You can add clouds using whites and grays and the Thin Stroke Airbrush.*

7. After you have filled in the base of the color for the water, continue with the snow in the foreground, using the same colors and methods you used for the background hills. After you add shaded areas and highlights, your image should start looking like Figure 19.50.

Figure 19.50.
Lighten the area where
you want the water by
using the Fat Stroke
Airbrush and white
paint. Then add snow
to the foreground using
the same shades used
previously.

8. Complete the document by choosing the Feather Tip Airbrush and white again, as shown in Figure 19.51. Add highlights wherever you feel they are necessary. I added highlights to define a border around the water. I also reduced the transparency of the Feather Tip Airbrush and added some streaks in the water area and in the clouds. Remember, you're the artist here—do whatever you like.

Figure 19.51.
Add more defining
highlights to the snow
using pure white and
the Feather Tip
Airbrush.

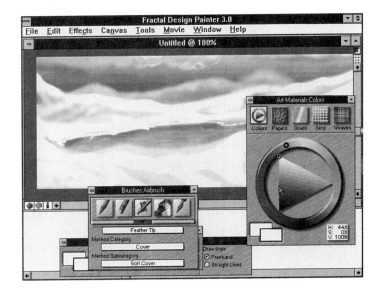

Repeating the Background

To create the scrolling background, you're going to crop 320×240 sections from this background image and, using a nifty recorded and edited session, generate 20 frames of animation automatically. But before you begin cropping, consider the following for a moment. You have a 640×240 image that you've created for your background. You want to generate a number of frames that is evenly divisible by the number of frames in your polar bear animation (which is 10).

If you divide the 640 width figure by 10, you come out with 64 pixels. If you have each of the frames changing by 64 pixels each time, that might be too much of a change to look realistic. In other words, that bear will really be trucking along because the background will be moving extremely fast. If you divide the 640 width figure by a factor of 20 (which is also evenly divisible by the number of frames in the polar bear animation), you have to move the cropping rectangle 32 pixels for each subsequent frame. That might be a little more acceptable. So far, so good.

But when the rightmost point of the cropping rectangle moves as far right as it can, the leftmost side of the rectangle still has a ways to go before it can complete cropping all 20 frames. So that you can crop the remaining portion of the animation, you have to place a copy of your background adjacent to the original one. This procedure offers the added benefit of verifying that your image is indeed seamless.

Before you increase the size of the document, capture your background as a pattern again. Proceed as follows:

1. Choose Edit | Select All to select the entire image.

2. Choose Tools | Patterns | Capture Pattern again, as shown in Figure 19.52. Your background then opens into a new, untitled document.

Figure 19.52.
Select the image, and
choose the Tools |
Patterns | Capture
Pattern again.

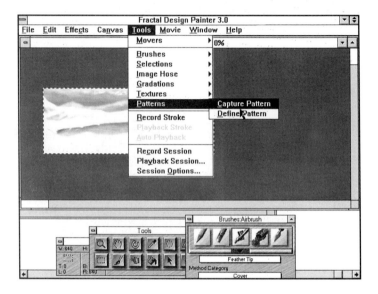

Increasing the Size of the Document

To increase the document size, you use the Canvas Size command located in the Canvas menu. You're going to add 640 pixels to the right side of the document to accommodate the second copy of the background, as follows:

1. Choose Canvas | Canvas Size. The Canvas Size dialog box appears.

2. From the Canvas Size menu, enter 640 to add 640 pixels to the right of the document, as shown in Figure 19.53.

3. Click OK or press Enter in Windows or Return in Mac to continue.

4. Choose the Paint Bucket from the Tools Palette (Ctrl-1 in Windows, Cmd-1 in Mac).

5. From the Controls | Paint Bucket Palette (Ctrl-6 in Windows, Cmd-6 in Mac), select to fill the image with the Clone Source. The Clone Source, in this case the background image you captured as a pattern, is displayed in the Controls Palette preview window.

6. Click to fill the second half of the document with a copy of the background image. Your screen should look similar to Figure 19.54.

Figure 19.53.
Add 640 pixels to the right side of the image using the Canvas | Canvas Size command.

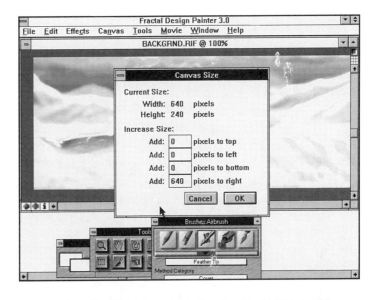

Figure 19.54.
Fill the second half of the document with the Clone Source using the Paint Bucket.

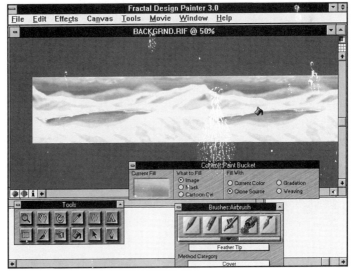

Step 19.19. Creating the Scrolling Background

Now you're ready for the exciting stuff. As I mentioned earlier, you want to crop out 20 320×240 rectangles from your background and create a scrolling animation from them. You have also already determined that each rectangle is offset by 32 pixels from the previous and next rectangle.

So, isn't it pointless to create a session that crops out 20 rectangles and saves them into individual files because you would be doing it all manually anyway? The answer is yes—and no. The fact is, you have to create a session that crops and saves areas from the first two files only. You can then export the session to a text file, examine what changed between the first and the second, and copy and edit the text file to complete the rest of the task. That is a real time-saver. Now it's time to record the session of the first two frames.

Recording a Session to Create the Frames

Because your bear is facing toward the left side of the screen while he's running, meaning that he would be running from right to left, you have to start the first frame of the scrolling background from the right side of the screen. Follow the next few steps carefully so that you record your session properly. Of course, now that you know you can edit session files, you can always take out the commands that don't belong there.

1. Hide all palettes except the Tools Palette (Ctrl-1 in Windows, Cmd-1 in Mac) and the Controls Palette (Ctrl-6 in Windows, Cmd-6 in Mac). This way, you have more room to see things.

2. Bring the right side of the double background image into view so that the last 400 pixels or so are in view. Figure 19.55 gives a good view of the image.

Figure 19.55.
Display the background
image so that at least
the rightmost 400
pixels or more are
shown.

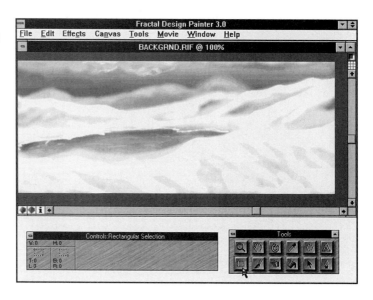

3. Choose Tools | Record Session. You are now in recording mode (aren't you nervous?). You might want to read the following recording steps thoroughly first before you press any keys. That way, you'll have an idea of where I'm heading here.

4. Select the Rectangular Selection tool from the Tools Palette.

5. Using the figures displayed in the upper-left corner of the Controls | Rectangular Selection Palette as a guide, click at or outside the upper-right corner of the document, and drag your mouse or cursor until the dimensions of the rectangular selection read 320 pixels wide and 240 pixels high. Figure 19.56 shows this step completed.

Figure 19.56. Create a 320×240 rectangular selection at the far right of the document.

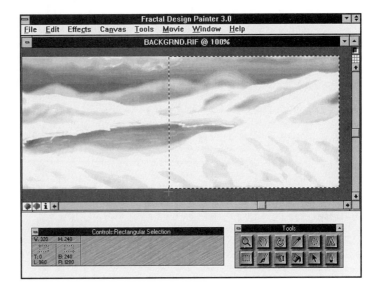

6. Choose Edit | Copy to copy the selection into the Clipboard.

7. Choose Edit | Paste Into New Image to copy the contents of the Clipboard into a new document window. The document appears, as shown in Figure 19.57, and is indexed as the current document.

8. Choose File | Save As. Scroll to the drive and directory you want to save the file into, and choose to save to the .RIF file extension if not already shown in the Save File as Type dropdown box.

9. Type in the name BACK01 as the name of the first frame, as shown in Figure 19.58, and click OK or press Enter (Windows) or Return (Mac) to save the frame.

10. Choose File | Close to close the BACK01.RIF file.

11. Choose Edit | Deselect to deselect the rectangular area. This step is important.

12. To start the image for the second frame, choose the Rectangular Selection tool again, and start a rectangular selection about 32 pixels inward from the top-right corner of the document. If you don't get the first coordinate exact, don't worry—you are going to edit the coordinates in the text file anyway.

Figure 19.57.
Copy the selection
into the Windows
Clipboard, and then
paste it into a new
document.

Figure 19.58.
Save the first frame
as BACK01.RIF.

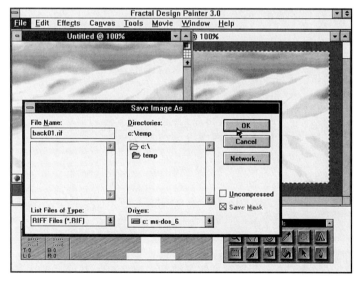

13. Drag the Rectangular Selection tool until the dimensions of the selection again read 320 pixels wide by 240 pixels high. Figure 19.59 shows the second area selected.

Figure 19.59.
*Select the second area
with the Rectangular
Selection tool.*

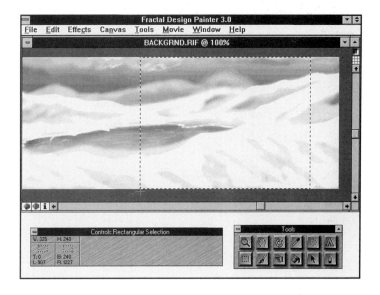

14. Again, choose Edit | Copy.

15. Again, choose Edit | Paste | Into New Image.

16. Save the second image as BACK02.RIF, in the same directory as the first.
    This step is shown in Figure 19.60.

Figure 19.60.
*Save the selection for
the second frame as
BACK02.RIF.*

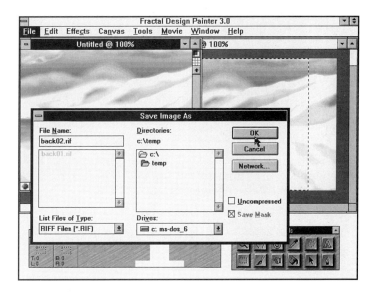

17. Close the BACK02.RIF file using the File | Close command.

18. Choose Tools | Stop Recording. Now you can relax.

19. In the Name the Session dialog box, save the session as Scrolling Background. See Figure 19.61.

Figure 19.61.
Save the session as
Scrolling Background.

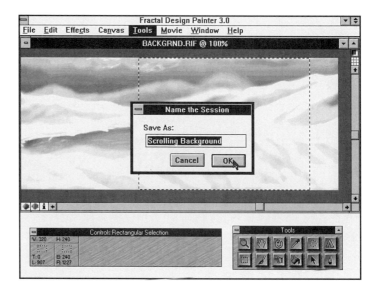

Step 19.20. Editing the Session File

To examine and edit the session, you have to export it to a text file. You can accomplish this by accessing the Recorded Sessions dialog box using the Tools | Playback Session command. Then the session is exported to a text file from within that dialog box. Proceed as follows:

1. Choose Tools | Playback Session. The Recorded Sessions dialog box appears.

2. Highlight the Scrolling Background session you just recorded, as shown in Figure 19.62. Then click the Export button.

3. In the Enter Script Name dialog box that appears, save the text file as 20FRAMES.TXT, as shown in Figure 19.63, in the directory of your choice.

4. From the Windows Program Manager, load in Notepad. If Windows was installed with the default options, you can access Notepad by clicking the Notepad icon in the Accessories program group. If you're using a Mac, load in any program or utility that enables you to save in ASCII text format.

5. Open the 20FRAMES.TXT file, as shown in Figure 19.64.

Figure 19.62.
Export the recorded
session to a text file
through the Recorded
Sessions dialog box,
accessed with the
Tools | Playback
Session command.

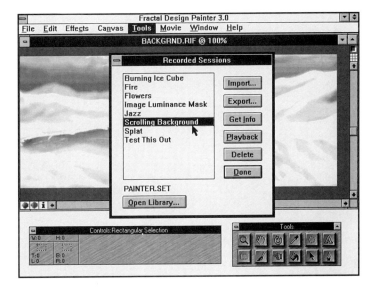

Figure 19.63.
Save the text file as
20FRAMES.TXT.

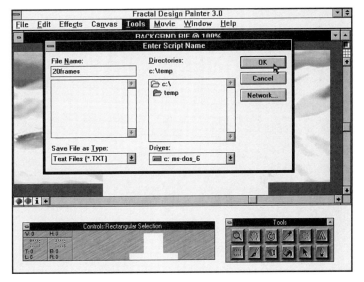

Figure 19.64.
Load the
20FRAMES.TXT file
into Windows Notepad.

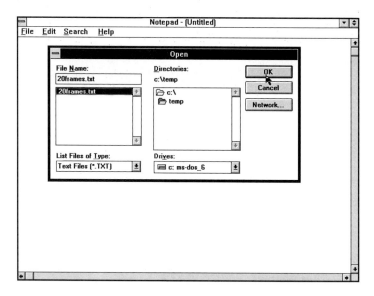

The following code listing shows the contents of the 20FRAMES.TXT file as recorded. Your version of the file may differ slightly but will contain the key areas that you're looking for.

```
is_painter_3
artist_name "Denise M. Tyler"
start_time date Sun. Mar 12, 1995 time 12:41 AM
start_random 1710743633
variant "Painter Brushes" "Image Hose" "Large Sequential Linear"
texture "PAINTER.PAP" "Basic Paper"
grain_inverted unchecked
scale_slider    1.00000
portfolio_change "Painter Portfolio"
gradation "PAINTER.SET" "Night Sky"
weaving "PAINTER.SET" "Waves on the Beach"
use_brush_grid unchecked
add_to_mask unchecked
color red 0 green 0 blue 0
background_color red 255 green 255 blue 255
rectangle_selection top 0 left 960 bottom 240 right 1280
copy
frisket_draw_mode 0
frisket_display_mode 0
paste_into_new_picture
save_as "C:\TEMP\BACK01.RIF" type 1 flags 1
close
deselect
rectangle_selection top 0 left 907 bottom 240 right 1227
copy
frisket_draw_mode 0
frisket_display_mode 0
paste_into_new_picture
save_as "C:\TEMP\BACK02.RIF" type 1 flags 1
close
end_time date Sun. Mar 12, 1995 time 12:41 AM
```

If you examine the file, recall that you started the capture of the second frame by deselecting the rectangle from the first frame. You ended by closing the saved version of the file. So, you can repeat Frames 2 through 20 by copying the lines starting at deselect and ending at close. Then all you have to do is edit the coordinates of the rectangles and change the filename to reflect the proper frames.

Highlight the lines shown in Figure 19.65 (yours may differ slightly based on the dimensions of your second selection and the directory you chose to save the file to). Then create 18 more copies of this selection before the last line of the session (the end time statement). When I created my extra copies, I inserted an extra space to identify the start and end point of each frame. Spaces are okay in a session script file.

Figure 19.65.
Copy these lines into the Clipboard, and paste them into the script file 18 more times.

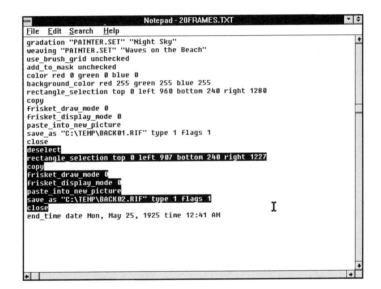

Edit the following items in your script file:

■ Make sure that all filenames run in order from BACK01 through BACK20.RIF.

■ Edit the right and left coordinates of all 20 frames (including the first and second that you recorded while in Painter). The coordinates that you should enter are shown in Table 19.1.

Table 19.1. Left coordinates and filenames for the BACK2.FRM animation.

Left Coordinate	Right Coordinate	Save File As
608	928	BACK01.RIF
576	876	BACK02.RIF
544	864	BACK03.RIF
512	832	BACK04.RIF
480	800	BACK05.RIF
448	768	BACK06.RIF
416	736	BACK07.RIF
384	704	BACK08.RIF
352	672	BACK09.RIF
320	640	BACK10.RIF
288	608	BACK11.RIF
256	576	BACK12.RIF
224	544	BACK13.RIF
192	512	BACK14.RIF
160	480	BACK15.RIF
128	448	BACK16.RIF
96	416	BACK17.RIF
64	384	BACK18.RIF
32	352	BACK19.RIF
0	320	BACK20.RIF

After you have edited your session script file, it should appear something like
the following. The finished version of my script file is included on the CD accompanying this book. You may need to change the directory that the files are
saved to, however.

```
is_painter_3
artist_name "Denise M. Tyler"
start_time date Sun. Mar 12, 1995 time 2:59 PM
start_random 1710743633
variant "Painter Brushes" "Image Hose" "Large Sequential Linear"
size_slider    5.00008
plus_or_minus_size_slider    0.00002
build
texture "PAINTER.PAP" "Basic Paper"
grain_inverted unchecked
scale_slider    1.00000
portfolio_change "Painter Portfolio"
gradation "PAINTER.SET" "Night Sky"
```

```
weaving "PAINTER.SET" "Waves on the Beach"
use_brush_grid unchecked
add_to_mask unchecked
color red 0 green 0 blue 0
background_color red 255 green 255 blue 255
new_tool 6
rectangle_selection top 0 left 608 bottom 240 right 928
copy
frisket_draw_mode 0
frisket_display_mode 0
paste_into_new_picture
save_as "C:\TEMP\BACK01.RIF" type 1 flags 1
close

deselect
rectangle_selection top 0 left 576 bottom 240 right 896
copy
frisket_draw_mode 0
frisket_display_mode 0
paste_into_new_picture
save_as "C:\TEMP\BACK02.RIF" type 1 flags 1
close

deselect
rectangle_selection top 0 left 544 bottom 240 right 864
copy
frisket_draw_mode 0
frisket_display_mode 0
paste_into_new_picture
save_as "C:\TEMP\BACK03.RIF" type 1 flags 1
close

deselect
rectangle_selection top 0 left 512 bottom 240 right 832
copy
frisket_draw_mode 0
frisket_display_mode 0
paste_into_new_picture
save_as "C:\TEMP\BACK04.RIF" type 1 flags 1
close

deselect
rectangle_selection top 0 left 480 bottom 240 right 800
copy
frisket_draw_mode 0
frisket_display_mode 0
paste_into_new_picture
save_as "C:\TEMP\BACK05.RIF" type 1 flags 1
close

deselect
rectangle_selection top 0 left 448 bottom 240 right 768
copy
frisket_draw_mode 0
frisket_display_mode 0
paste_into_new_picture
save_as "C:\TEMP\BACK06.RIF" type 1 flags 1
close
```

```
deselect
rectangle_selection top 0 left 416 bottom 240 right 736
copy
frisket_draw_mode 0
frisket_display_mode 0
paste_into_new_picture
save_as "C:\TEMP\BACK07.RIF" type 1 flags 1
close

deselect
rectangle_selection top 0 left 384 bottom 240 right 704
copy
frisket_draw_mode 0
frisket_display_mode 0
paste_into_new_picture
save_as "C:\TEMP\BACK08.RIF" type 1 flags 1
close

deselect
rectangle_selection top 0 left 352 bottom 240 right 672
copy
frisket_draw_mode 0
frisket_display_mode 0
paste_into_new_picture
save_as "C:\TEMP\BACK09.RIF" type 1 flags 1
close

deselect
rectangle_selection top 0 left 320 bottom 240 right 640
copy
frisket_draw_mode 0
frisket_display_mode 0
paste_into_new_picture
save_as "C:\TEMP\BACK10.RIF" type 1 flags 1
close

deselect
rectangle_selection top 0 left 288 bottom 240 right 608
copy
frisket_draw_mode 0
frisket_display_mode 0
paste_into_new_picture
save_as "C:\TEMP\BACK11.RIF" type 1 flags 1
close

deselect
rectangle_selection top 0 left 256 bottom 240 right 576
copy
frisket_draw_mode 0
frisket_display_mode 0
paste_into_new_picture
save_as "C:\TEMP\BACK12.RIF" type 1 flags 1
close

deselect
rectangle_selection top 0 left 224 bottom 240 right 544
copy
frisket_draw_mode 0
frisket_display_mode 0
```

```
paste_into_new_picture
save_as "C:\TEMP\BACK13.RIF" type 1 flags 1
close

deselect
rectangle_selection top 0 left 192 bottom 240 right 512
copy
frisket_draw_mode 0
frisket_display_mode 0
paste_into_new_picture
save_as "C:\TEMP\BACK14.RIF" type 1 flags 1
close

deselect
rectangle_selection top 0 left 160 bottom 240 right 480
copy
frisket_draw_mode 0
frisket_display_mode 0
paste_into_new_picture
save_as "C:\TEMP\BACK15.RIF" type 1 flags 1
close

deselect
rectangle_selection top 0 left 128 bottom 240 right 448
copy
frisket_draw_mode 0
frisket_display_mode 0
paste_into_new_picture
save_as "C:\TEMP\BACK16.RIF" type 1 flags 1
close

deselect
rectangle_selection top 0 left 96 bottom 240 right 416
copy
frisket_draw_mode 0
frisket_display_mode 0
paste_into_new_picture
save_as "C:\TEMP\BACK17.RIF" type 1 flags 1
close

deselect
rectangle_selection top 0 left 64 bottom 240 right 384
copy
frisket_draw_mode 0
frisket_display_mode 0
paste_into_new_picture
save_as "C:\TEMP\BACK18.RIF" type 1 flags 1
close

deselect
rectangle_selection top 0 left 32 bottom 240 right 352
copy
frisket_draw_mode 0
frisket_display_mode 0
paste_into_new_picture
save_as "C:\TEMP\BACK19.RIF" type 1 flags 1
close

deselect
```

713

```
rectangle_selection top 0 left 0 bottom 240 right 320
copy
frisket_draw_mode 0
frisket_display_mode 0
paste_into_new_picture
save_as "C:\TEMP\BACK20.RIF" type 1 flags 1
close

end_time date Sun. Mar 12, 1995 time 2:59 PM
```

Step 19.21. Applying the Session to the Document

Now you have to update the session you recorded with the new values in the 20FRAMES.TXT file, as follows:

1. Choose Tools | Playback Session.
2. Click the Import button.
3. From the dialog box, choose the 20FRAMES.TXT session script file from the directory you saved it to.
4. When you're asked for a name to save the script file as, enter Scrolling Background. When Painter informs you that a session of that name already exists, as shown in Figure 19.66, answer Yes when it asks whether you want to replace the existing version.

Figure 19.66.
Answer Yes to replace the old version of the recorded session with the edited version of the script file.

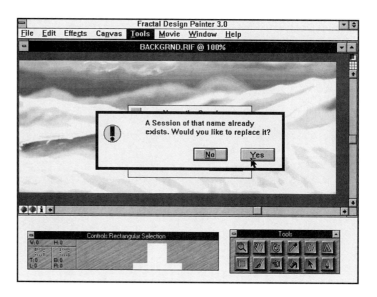

5. Click the Playback button to play the session into the document. If all goes well, you should have 20 frames, named BACK01.RIF through BACK20.RIF in your chosen directory when it's complete.

Step 19.22. Opening the Numbered Files as a Movie

You're probably quite familiar now with the procedure of opening numbered files, but here you are doing it again:

1. Using the File | Open command, open the BACK01.RIF through BACK20.RIF files, as numbered files, to create a 20-frame Painter movie. Figure 19.67 shows the first frame selected.

Figure 19.67.
Open the RIF files
created with the
session script file as
numbered files.

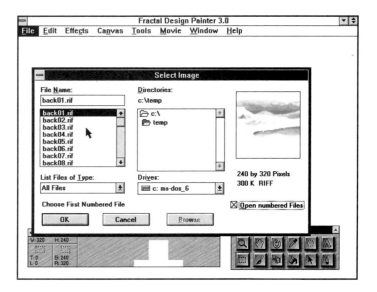

2. When prompted to enter a name for the movie, name it BACK2.FRM, as shown in Figure 19.68. In Chapter 23, "Converting to Other Animation Formats," this file is used to illustrate different ways of converting to other animation formats.

3. From the Brushes Palette, choose the Image Hoses. Select the Large Sequential Linear Image Hose, which sprays images in sequential order. See Figure 19.69.

Figure 19.68.
Enter the name
BACK2.FRM for the
new movie.

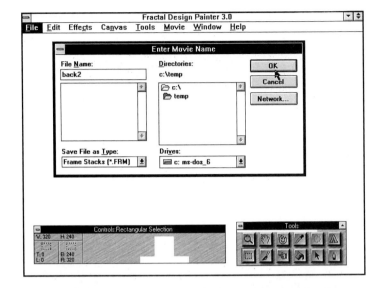

Figure 19.69.
From the Brushes
Palette, choose the
Large Sequential Image
Hose.

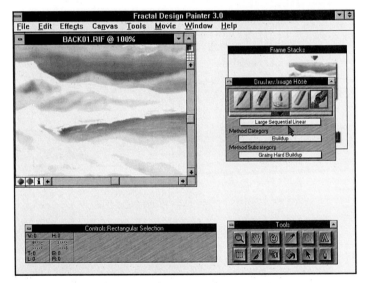

4. Choose the Tools | Image Hose | Load Nozzle command, as shown in
   Figure 19.70. When the Select Image dialog box appears, load in the
   BEARHOSE.RIF file you created earlier in this chapter. (Remember him?)

*Figure 19.70.
Load the
BEARHOSE.RIF nozzle
file into the Image Hose
nozzle using the Load
Nozzle command.*

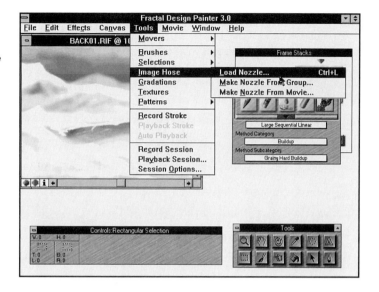

5. Starting at Frame 1, click just below mid-point to place the first frame of
   the bear on the first frame of the background. Figure 19.71 shows a good
   location to place the first bear.

*Figure 19.71.
Click the first bear into
the background image
at the lower center of
the image.*

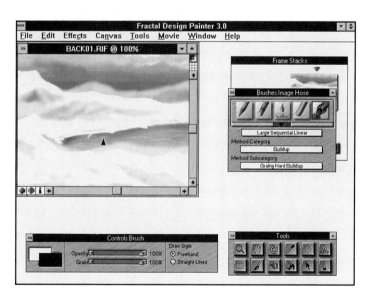

6. Try to keep your mouse or cursor hand stationary while clicking the Image Hose through the remaining frames. Leave your cursor hand where it is, and advance to the next frame with the other hand using the Page Up key.

7. Continue until you've placed the bear in all 20 frames of the background, as shown in Figure 19.72. Then play the animation. Look at him go!

Figure 19.72.
Paste the bear into
all 20 frames of the
animation.

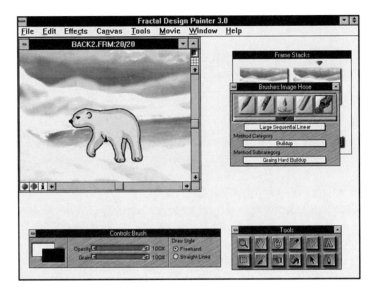

You can now convert the finished animation to an .AVI file using the File | Save As command, which is discussed in Chapter 23, "Converting to Other Animation Formats." In addition to .AVI files, I discuss how to convert to Autodesk animation and Quick Time for Windows formats using commercial and shareware utilities.

Summary

You've covered quite a bit of ground here. Now that you know how to create a cartoon animation and work with Painter's scripting utilities, the sky's the limit.

The next few chapters discuss integrating Painter with some popular graphics and animation software programs. First, I discuss Kai's Power Tools, which offer some of the neatest third-party, plug-ins imaginable.

Integrating with Other Applications

Integrating with Kai's Power Tools

More and more of today's graphics software packages, including Painter, offer compatibility with third-party, plug-in filters—extensions to your software package that allow effects developed by other software manufacturers to be applied to your images, without leaving the program. Without a doubt, one of the leading choices for plug-ins is HSC Corporation's Kai's Power Tools. Version 2.0 of these extensions is discussed in this chapter.

Installing Kai's Power Tools

Like other Windows and Mac programs, Kai's Power Tools installation is pretty straightforward, and enables you to select a plug-in directory other than its own if it senses that you have software with plug-in capability. Kai's Power Tools requires about 12 MB of hard disk storage.

Although not required, it's recommended that you use Painter and Kai's Power Tools in true-color mode to fully appreciate the subtle color variances that the gradations and effects provide. Kai's unique interface is also appreciated more when viewed in true-color mode.

Configuring Painter to use Kai's Power Tools

To configure Painter to use Kai's Power Tools, or any other third-party plug-in filters, use the Edit | Preferences | Plug-Ins command. This command enables you to specify a third-party plug-in to use with Painter.

To specify a third-party plug-in, do the following:

1. Choose Edit | Preferences | Plug-Ins. A dialog box appears.
2. Scroll through the list of available drives and directories until you find the one you want. If you have installed Kai's Power Tools using the default settings under Windows, its plug-ins are found in the C:\KPT directory.
3. Click one of the filters to indicate that this is the directory you are choosing to use in Painter.
4. Click OK to make your selection. The next time you start Painter, the plug-ins become available in Painter's Effects menu, toward the bottom of the drop-down menu box.

NOTE It is important to note that the use of some of the filters provided with Kai's Power Tools will increase your memory requirements. Memory-intensive plug-ins such as the Fractal Explorer may not function well when used in conjunction with Painter on slower machines, or those with less than 16 MB of memory.

What is Kai's Power Tools?

Kai's Power Tools 2.0 is a suite of special effects filters that can be used with Painter and other popular software programs. When installed for use within Painter, you can access its effects through Painter's Effects | KPT 2.0 Extensions and Effects | KPT 2.0 Filters menu choices. Its highly artistic interface, most appreciated when viewed in true-color mode, is an indication of the creativity that abounds in and from the software package. Available in both Windows and Mac versions, it is a sensational addition to Painter. Once you start playing with it, you just can't stop; the Explorer Guide manual furnished with the program even warns you of this, explaining that this was Kai's whole intent!

The plug-ins furnished with Kai's Power Tools 2.0 fall into two categories.

One-Step Filters

The one-step filters are selected from Painter's Effects | KPT 2.0 Filters menu choice and perform the effect automatically with no user interaction. You simply choose the effect you want to apply, and then get the results. There are 27 filters in all. (See Figure 20.1.) My personal favorites are the Glass Lens filters, which give the appearance that you are looking at your image through a glass lens; Page Curl, which turns and rolls a corner of your document as though a page is starting to turn; and Vortex Tiling, which creates a kaleidoscopic effect on an image. Other filters smudge, diffuse, and add pixel noise to selected areas.

Figure 20.1.
Kai's Power Tools
comes with many one-
step filters that are
compatible with many
graphics software
packages.

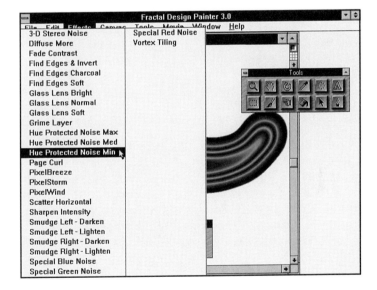

User Interface Filters

The User Interface Filters are clearly the heart of KPT's software plug-ins. These filters, shown in the menu of Figure 20.2, require user interaction before they are rendered. With these filters come endless possibilities in creating fractal textures, gradients, and patterns that can be applied to your image as effects or used as texture maps. Take my word for it, you can get pleasantly lost for hours in the explorers. Once you start playing with them and moving the interface buttons around, it's hard to leave.

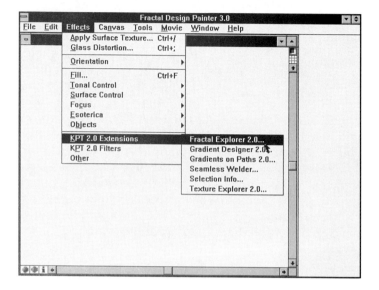

Figure 20.2.
The User Interface
Filters provide a
limitless choice of
effects and textures
that can be used in
your Painter docu-
ments.

The Fractal Explorer creates fractals in conjunction with colors from hundreds of provided gradients, or those you create yourself. (See Figure 20.3.) The fractals are created with variants of the Mandelbrot and Julia algorithms, or hybrids of both. You can apply the fractals to your images in a number of different merging techniques. A preview window shows you in advance how the fractal will appear when merged with your image.

The Gradient Designer is the heart of the User Interface Filters, because all of the effects are derived from the colors contained in the currently selected gradient. (See Figure 20.4.) The Gradient Designer helps you to create stunning gradients in a variety of shapes and methods. The colors contained in the gradient are chosen by moving and sizing a bracket above the gradient preview window, and then picking colors from a color bar that appears when needed. Again, the preview window shows how the gradient will affect your image.

With Gradients on a Path, you first draw and feather an outline path in Painter, as shown in Figure 20.5. The amount of feathering applied to the selection controls the width of the gradational effect.

Figure 20.3.
The Fractal Explorer
enables you to create
fractal effects using
variations or hybrids of
the Mandelbrot and
Julia algorithms.

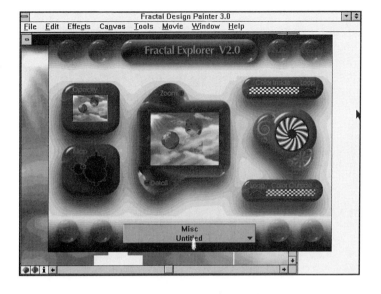

Figure 20.4.
The Gradient Designer
defines the colors that
will be used in the
other Explorer mod-
ules.

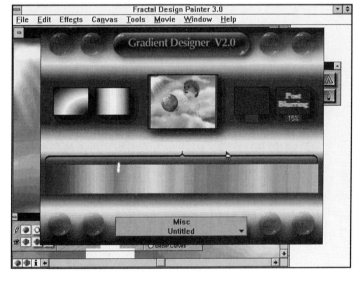

Next, a gradient is selected from within the Gradients on Paths module (see
Figure 20.6). When you're satisfied with the chosen colors, you click the OK
button to apply the effect to the selected area.

Figure 20.5.
To apply a gradient to a
path, a path is created
and feathered in
Painter.

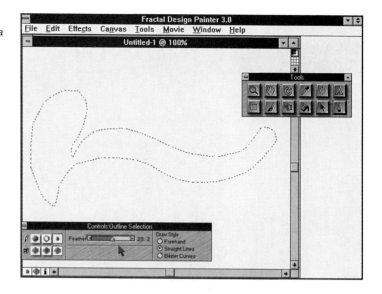

Figure 20.6.
A gradient is chosen
from within the
Gradients on Paths
module.

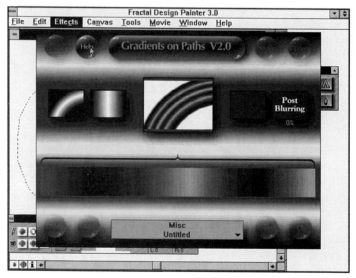

The results are similar in appearance to the folds of a draped piece of satin cloth, with the direction of the folds controlled by you. Figure 20.7 shows one example of a gradient that was created from a path.

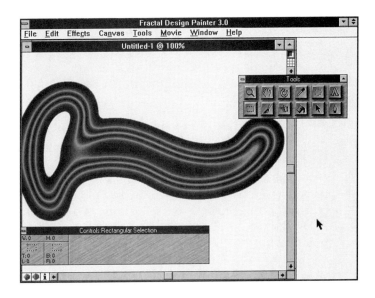

Figure 20.7.
The final result of the
gradient placed on the
Painter path.

The Texture Explorer creates an endless supply of textures that can be used as effects to apply to your images, as repeated patterns or texture maps in 3-D rendering programs, or as paper textures in Painter. I'll discuss in a moment how to create some of the most creative paper textures you'll ever come across!

The Seamless Welder is another handy tool. It turns any texture map into a seamless tile by comparing the colors on the edges of the selections and blending them, which is very handy for the final step toward creating a paper texture or tile from images that aren't quite seamless.

In one chapter, it's virtually impossible to explain in detail everything that Kai's Power Tools can do. But, I can show you a couple of ways that Kai's Power Tools can enhance your use of Painter. First, I'll discuss creating those unique paper textures that I mentioned earlier.

Creating Paper Textures with Kai's Power Tools and Painter

As mentioned earlier, Kai's Power Tools works from within Painter as an extension. To create a paper texture, you're going to open up a square-shaped document in Painter, apply a texture to it using Kai's Texture Explorer, capture the paper texture, and save it to a paper library in Painter. Then, I'll show you how that paper texture works.

The Steps in Kai's Power Tools

Due to the fact that Kai's Power Tools generates paper textures randomly, your screen may not appear exactly as the screen shots shown here. The main thing here is to have fun, and pick something you think would make a great paper texture to work with!

Let's start by opening a new image:

1. From the File menu, choose New, or use the quick key combination of Ctrl-N in Windows or Cmd-N in Mac. The New Picture dialog box appears. (See Figure 20.8.) For our example, a 256×256 pixel document was created, and its resolution was set at the default 75 pixels per inch. Kai's Power Tools creates textures that repeat in any one of the following five resolutions: 96×96, 128×128, 256×256, 512×512, and 1024×1024. Higher resolutions create more detail in the paper texture, but also cause less repititions in the image.

Figure 20.8.
Create a square-shaped document in Painter as the first step to making a paper texture with Kai's Power Tools.

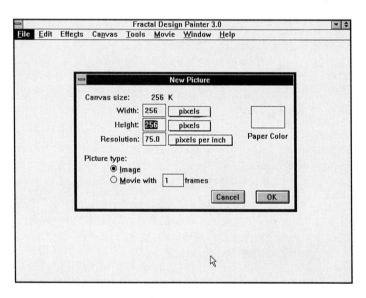

2. Choose Effects | KPT 2.0 Extensions | Texture Explorer 2.0. The location of this command is shown in Figure 20.9.

3. The Texture Explorer window appears. This window is shown in Figure 20.10. Let's take a moment to explore this a bit.

4. I've already mentioned the area that shows the current texture surrounded by its 12 cousins. This is located at the right side of the screen. If you place your mouse inside the preview square of the current texture, your cursor changes to show that a drop-down list is available. Click this point to reveal a drop-down menu from which you can select the resolution of the texture you want. Because you've created a 256×256 document, choose the 256×256 resolution.

Figure 20.9.
Choose the command to launch Kai's Power Tools Texture Explorer.

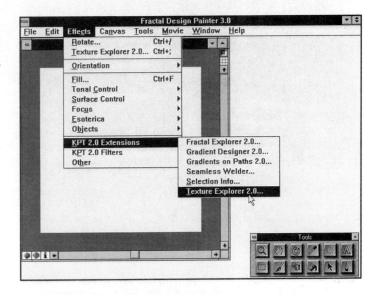

Figure 20.10.
The Kai's Power Tools Texture Explorer window appears.

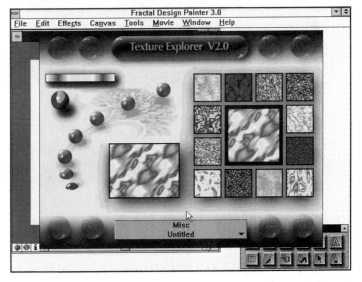

It's readily apparent that Kai's Power Tools is not your standard graphics program. The Texture Explorer is void of the standard Windows buttons and gray, white, and blue interface. On the upper portion of the screen are four buttons, two each to the right and left of the title bar. The first button is the Minimize button. The second button summons help for the Texture Explorer. The third button is the Shuffle button, which sets different processes from which the textures are generated. The fourth button is the Options button, from which a process can be selected manually from a list.

The left side of the screen contains three areas: the Gradient Preview Bar, the Color Mutation Ball, and the Color Mutation Tree. Clicking the Gradient Preview Bar allows access to a gradient preset menu, as well as to the Gradient Designer in which you can design your own gradients. Selecting a gradient places its colors in the Preview Bar, and applies it to the current texture.

Just beneath the Gradient Preview Bar is the Color Mutation Ball. Clicking this button re-renders the current gradient (shown as the largest box on the right side of the screen) in a variety of colors as 12 cousins that surround the current gradient. You can select any one of these cousins as the current gradient if one of them is more appealing to you.

In the area beneath the Color Mutation Ball is the Texture Mutation Tree. Clicking on one of the Texture Mutation Tree balls regenerates the cousins using varying levels of mutation. This changes the appearance of the random-ness of the cousins' textures. Clicking the first button, toward the bottom, regenerates the cousins while using the least amount of mutation. Clicking the last, or highest, button regenerates with the greatest amount of mutation.

TIP   You can fit the texture map to a rectangular or square area of any size by selecting the Tile Size of Selection choice when using the texture size selection box.

5. From the upper-right corner of the screen, click the Options button and select Choose Normal Apply. This applies the texture you create at 100-percent opacity to the entire image or selected area.

6. Basically, just play in the texture explorer until you get a texture you like. Figure 20.11 shows a good candidate placed in the current texture box.

7. If you find a texture you like and want to hang on to it while you explore some more, lock it in place by pressing the Alt key in Windows or the Option Key in Mac while clicking it with the mouse. It will be surrounded by a red border, indicating that it has been locked. Performing the Alt-Click (Windows) or Option-Click (Mac) procedure again unlocks it. You can lock in as many textures as you like while you're exploring, and only the un-locked squares are replaced with new textures to choose from. Figure 20.12 shows a couple of choices that have been locked in place in this manner.

Figure 20.11.
*A likely choice is found
and selected for the
current paper texture.*

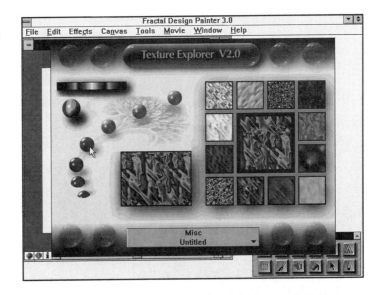

Figure 20.12.
*Textures can be held in
place while you search
for more by clicking a
square while holding
down the Alt key.*

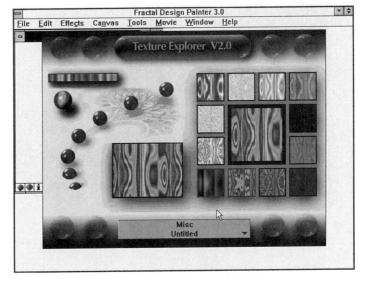

8. You can take a look at the complete texture by clicking inside the current
texture box. This enlarges the texture to its full size. This is shown in
Figure 20.13.

Figure 20.13.
*To see the full texture,
click inside the current
texture box.*

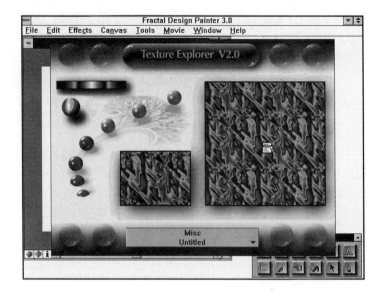

9. Once you have a texture you like in the current texture window, click the
   OK button to apply it to your image. (See Figure 20.14.) The OK button is
   located in the lower-right corner of the Texture Explorer.

Figure 20.14.
*Click the OK button to
apply the texture to the
image.*

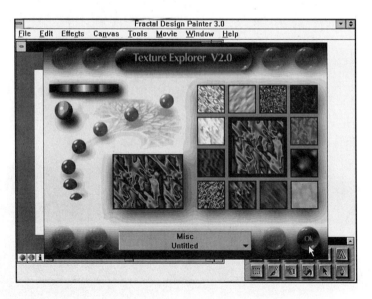

Your image should now be filled with the texture you created in Kai's Power
Tools, as shown in Figure 20.15. The next step is to change this image into a
paper texture.

Figure 20.15.
The texture created in
Kai's Power Tools is
applied to the image in
Painter.

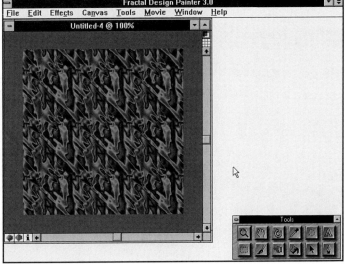

The Steps in Painter

The texture you selected from the Kai's Power Tools Texture Explorer might be in color, but when it is saved as a paper texture it is converted to shades of gray. Colors will be applied to the texture as you draw in your image with a grainy-based brush, discussed later.

To convert the image into a paper texture, perform the following steps:

1. Choose Edit | Select All. The entire image is surrounded with a selection marquee.

2. From the Art Materials Palette, choose the Papers icon. If the library to which you want to save the new texture tool is not currently selected, click the Library Button and select another.

3. Choose Tools | Textures | Capture Texture, as shown in Figure 20.16.

4. A dialog box appears. (See Figure 20.17.) Type a name for the texture in the dialog box and choose OK. The new texture is now available for use in the Paper Library. You can adjust the Crossfade slider, if you want, to add some softened effects to the edges. But because this texture is already seamless, you can keep the Crossfade slider all the way to the left, or at a very low value.

Figure 20.16.
*After selecting the
entire area, choose
Tools | Textures |
Capture Texture to
create a texture in the
current paper library.*

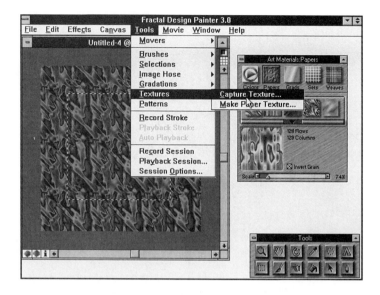

Figure 20.17.
*Click the OK button to
name the texture and
place it in the current
Paper Library.*

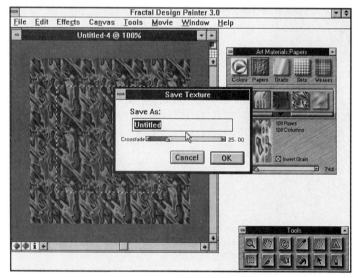

What About Colored Patterns?

What if you want to use the texture as it is, colors and all, in your Painter document at a later time? You can now easily save it as a Painter document, or other compatible format, to retrieve later. But you can also make a repeated pattern that can be applied to your image with the Paint Bucket, repeating the texture automatically while doing so.

To convert the image into a repeating pattern, perform the following steps:

1. Choose Edit | Select All. The entire image is surrounded with a selection marquee.

2. Choose Tools | Patterns | Capture Pattern, as shown in Figure 20.18.

Figure 20.18.
The Capture Pattern
command turns the
texture into a repeating
pattern.

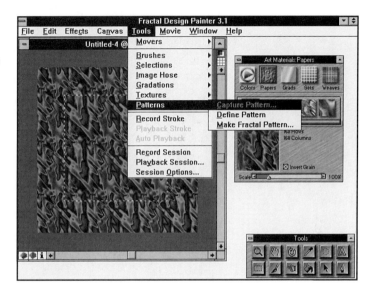

3. A new untitled document window opens with the texture inside.

4. At this time, you can open a new document or select a different document, and apply the captured pattern as a repeating texture by clicking inside an area or making a selection with the Paint Bucket. On the Controls | Paint Bucket Palette, you must choose to fill the area with the Clone Source, and you then see your texture in the preview window.

Using Your New Paper Texture

If you don't have access to Kai's Power Tools but would like to experiment with the types of paper textures it can produce, I've provided a library on the CD called, appropriately, KAIS.PAP. There are 25 different textures in this library, all of them created in Kai's Power Tools. When you see what can be done, I'm sure you'll want to run out and get Kai's Power Tools for yourself!

To check out the great paper textures, complete the following steps:

1. Open a new image. It can be any size you want. Figure 20.19 shows a new image window created.

Figure 20.19.
Open a new document to try out your Kai's paper textures.

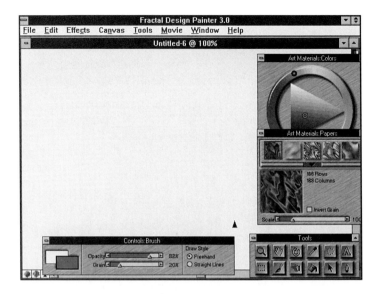

2. Choose a brush that uses a grainy method. For the examples in the screenshots, I used the 500-lb. Pencil because it gave a somewhat airbrushed look, and was nice and soft in appearance.

3. Select one of the paper textures from the KAIS.PAP library. For this example, I selected the KPT 15 texture and set the Paper Scale to 80 % in the Art Materials | Papers Palette.

4. Choose a color from the Art Materials | Colors Palette, or from a color set. Color with your image using this color. This step is shown in Figure 20.20. Watch as your brush fills the image with intricate shapes!

5. Choose a second color, if you like, and apply more color to the image. You can also click in the Invert Grain checkbox to invert the paper grain. This checkbox is shown when you maximize the Art Materials | Papers Palette. This switches the paper textures so that the high areas become low and the low areas become high.

Figure 20.21 shows a variety of effects that were achieved using the textures found in the KAIS.PAP library furnished with on CD. I'm sure that about experiment with these textures, you'll gain all sorts of inspiration about what can be done by combining the power of Kai's Power Tools with Painter.

Figure 20.20.
Place some color onto your document using a grainy brush, such as the 500-lb. Pencil.

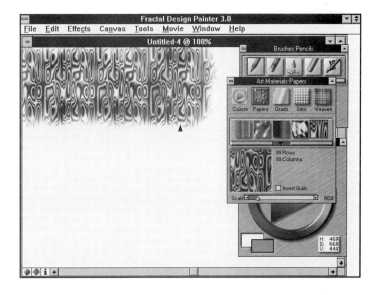

Figure 20.21.
Some examples of paper textures created with Kai's Power Tools and colored in Painter.

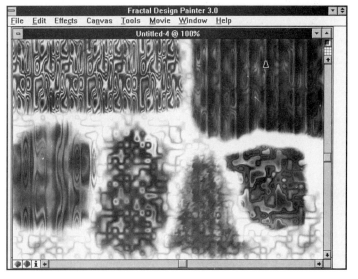

Summary

This is by no means a complete overview of Kai's Power Tools, but it does offer you a glimpse of the many ways that these plug-in filters can enhance your use of Painter. Create stunning fractal gradients and textures and merge them into your image. Capture magnificent paper textures and repeated patterns. Apply gradients to controlled shapes and paths that are drawn in Painter. Kai's Power Tools, like Painter, is a program that begs for exploration. And, the combination of these two programs together is astounding!

Integrating with CorelDRAW!

One of the most popular graphic programs available today is Corel Corporation's CorelDRAW!. Now in version 5.0, this package gives you great bang for the buck, with draw, paint, animation, desktop publishing, presentation, and other features all bundled into one package. There are so many ways to integrate CorelDRAW! with Painter that it would take many, many pages to go into depth. However, I can highlight some ways in which CorelDRAW! can enhance your use of Painter.

The CorelDRAW! 5.0 Package

CorelDRAW! comes with several self-contained modules, each serving a different function. You can use elements from one module in another module—for example, you can bring a Corel PHOTO-PAINT document into the CorelDRAW! module for further enhancement and modification. The programs of interest to Painter users are primarily the CorelDRAW!, Corel PHOTO-PAINT, and CorelMOVE applications, although some of the other applications, such as CorelTRACE, CorelMOSAIC, and CorelSHOW, can also assist you in graphic creation, cataloging, and presentation. If you want to import some of your Painter documents into a newsletter or publication, Corel VENTURA can assist you in layout and composition.

CorelDRAW!

The CorelDRAW! program is a vector-based draw program. The advantage of draw programs is that you can rescale or resize artwork without losing detail. You create documents using Bézier shapes and curves.

Creating Objects

Although Painter offers similar means of creating shapes by using Bézier curves to create selections, CorelDRAW! offers several features that make shape creation easier. You can draw shapes in freehand or in Bézier-curve mode, after which you can adjust the curves either by moving the control points or by reshaping the curve itself—a nice feature! You can add or delete nodes (the starting and ending points of curves) as necessary to fine-tune the shape of your object.

Figure 21.1 shows some of the ways in which CorelDRAW!'s tools can assist you in creating shapes. You can combine two shapes by welding, intersecting, or trimming, and then combine the modified shape with yet other shapes (one at a time). With *welding*, you join two shapes into one, with the overlapping linework removed. *Intersection* is just the opposite: the overlapping portions of objects become a new entity. *Trimming* cuts one overlapping shape away from another.

You also can *blend* two shapes in such a way that the first shape gradually changes into the second shape in a specified number of steps.

Figure 21.1 shows entities made with these four methods.

In Figure 21.2, I've got five shapes grouped as one object for the starting shape of a blend, and a single square as the ending shape of the blend.

Figure 21.1.
CorelDRAW!'s editing
tools help you create
complex shapes easily.

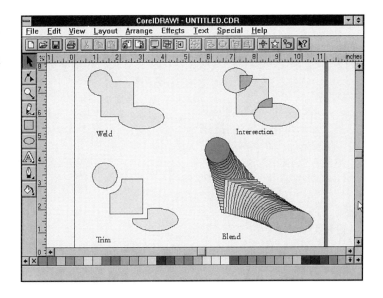

Figure 21.2.
Select a group of
shapes for the start-
ing point of the blend,
and a single shape as
the ending point.

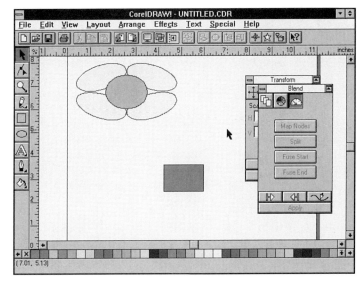

Figure 21.3 shows the results after I applied a 20-step blend to the group of
shapes. I left the linework on in this case so you could see the transitions of the
shapes. Blends also follow along a path, such as a curved line.

741

Figure 21.3.
The Blend command
blends the shapes and
colors of two images.

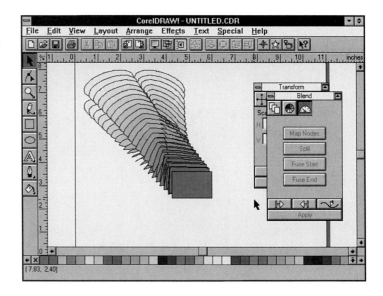

You can blend objects in both color and in shape. One of the main uses for blends in CorelDRAW! art is to provide irregularly shaped gradation fills. When you use blends in this manner, you generally turn the outline colors off so that only the fill color blends between your starting and ending color choices.

Text Manipulation

Some of the nicest features of CorelDRAW! lie in its ability to perform special effects on text, and the program offers no shortage of fonts for you to manipulate. If the thousands of fonts aren't enough for you, you can even create your own fonts and symbols, exporting them to either True Type or Adobe Type Manager formats. You can fit text to a path or within a shape to create interesting emphases.

For some of the commands to work properly, you first must convert the text to curves. Figure 21.4 shows some text fit within a shape, or *envelope*.

At the click of a button, you can cause text and other Corel artwork to extrude into other elements for a three-dimensional look. There are several preset extrusions, which include extrusion type, fill type, and lighting arrangements. You also can create your own extrusions and save them. Figure 21.5 shows the text from the previous figure extruded into a three-dimensional type object.

Figure 21.4.
*You can fit text within
a shape, or envelope,
as shown here.*

Figure 21.5.
*You can cause text
(and other objects)
to extrude into objects
to appear three-
dimensional.*

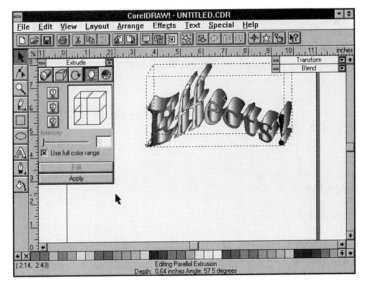

Clip Art

If you're not into making your own shapes, have no fear. The three CDs that
accompany the program contain thousands of clip-art images from several
different manufacturers, waiting for you to modify and group them in any way
you see fit.

You can use CorelDRAW!'s clip art in Painter in one of two ways:

■ Use the File | Export command to export the CorelDRAW! clip art as a bitmap image. You can export CorelDRAW! clip art to all formats supported by Painter except the .RIF format. Use the clip art as is, or add enhancements using Painter's brushes and tools.

■ The other way to use Corel art is to import it into Painter as an .EPS selection, after which you can use it as you would any other path or selection in Painter.

In the next section I discuss this second use.

Exporting Corel Art as an .EPS Selection for Painter

If you want to use a piece of CorelDRAW! art as a selection, there are a couple of checks to make first to save yourself some work within Painter.

First, CorelDRAW! supports the use of open shapes—but Painter automatically closes these open shapes when it creates the selections. For example, if your exported CorelDRAW! document contains a curved line indicating a closed smile on a face, Painter closes the selection by drawing a straight line between the end points of the smile, making it semicircular. Check the CorelDRAW! artwork to see if any open shapes exist, and remove them if necessary.

Also, take care with areas in the CorelDRAW! art that were blended. Figure 21.6 shows an example of a CorelDRAW! image that contains blended areas. Figure 21.7 is the same image, except that I turned all the fill colors off and changed all outlines to black. This reveals all the shapes in the art. As you can see, some areas contain so many shapes placed together they appear almost solid black. These are the areas where I used blends to create gradations.

Figure 21.6.
This CorelDRAW!
image contains many
nice gradation fills,
created with blends.

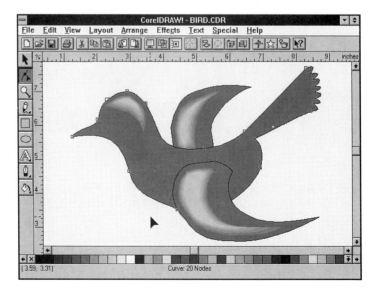

Figure 21.7.
Turn off the clip art's
fill and turn on all
outlines to see areas
that might be objec-
tionable when used
as paths.

In Figure 21.8, I modified the CorelDRAW! art by removing the shapes that represented the gradation fills. Now, only the basic shape of the artwork remains—which would be a little more manageable when you use them as paths in Painter.

Figure 21.8.
Clean up crowded
areas before exporting
clip art to an .EPS file.

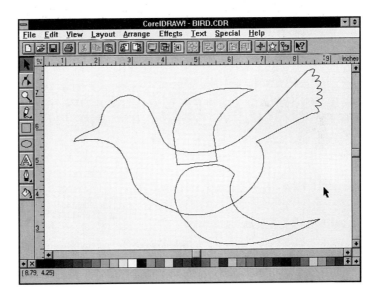

You can export the shapes to an Adobe Illustrator EPS file to bring them into Painter for use as paths and selections. The Adobe Illustrator 3.0 format works quite flawlessly in Painter. After you choose the File | Export command and select Adobe Illustrator AI/EPS as your chosen file format, the Export Adobe Illustrator dialog box appears, as shown in Figure 21.9. If you have text in your CorelDRAW! art, choose to export the text as curves, as shown in the Export Adobe Illustrator dialog box.

Figure 21.9.
Export the cleaned-up
clip-art image as an
Adobe Illustrator
.AI.EPS file in Adobe
Illustrator 3.0 format.

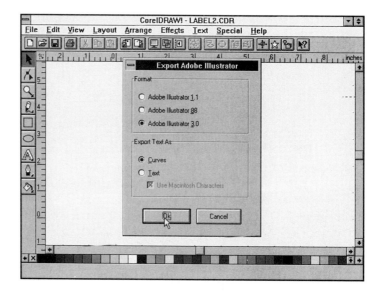

When you use the Adobe Illustrator export option, you can write the file using an .AI or an .EPS extension. When you specify a name for the file you're exporting, include the .EPS extension with the name you type. If you don't include the extension, the file will be saved with an .AI extension.

To bring the .EPS file into Painter, use the Tools | Selections | Open EPS as Selection command. This brings the file into Painter as a Bézier-curve path. You then can change the Bézier curves into selections by using the Tools | Selections | Convert to Selection command.

Gradient Creation

You also can use CorelDRAW! to assist in gradation creation. In Painter, one way to create a gradation is to arrange a series of single pixels of different colors in a line and then select the line with the Rectangular Selection Tool. You then convert the line of pixels to a gradation with the Tools | Gradations | Capture Gradation command. Painter 3.1 also provides the Tools | Gradations | Edit Gradation command that enables you to edit color placement and blending in the gradient.

It's sometimes difficult, though, to visualize what the gradation will look like when you're placing the pixels together. If you use CorelDRAW! to create gradations, you can view the color blends and control the color placements precisely. To access the gradation creation routines, choose the Fountain Fill button from the toolbar's Fill flyout. The Fountain Fill dialog box, shown in Figure 21.10, appears. If you choose the Custom gradation type, you can insert and blend between many colors, as shown in the figure. You can adjust the angle and number of steps contained in the gradation in the Options section, at the top of the dialog box and to the left of the gradation preview box.

Figure 21.10.
Create custom grada-
tions in CorelDRAW!'s
Fountain Fill dialog
box.

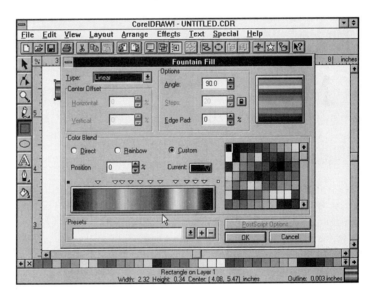

You can fill several areas with different gradations, as shown in Figure 21.11, and then export the file to a bitmap format recognized by Painter (.TGA, .TIF, .BMP, and so on). In Painter, capture the gradation using the Tools | Gradation | Capture Gradation command, and place it in a gradation library of your choice.

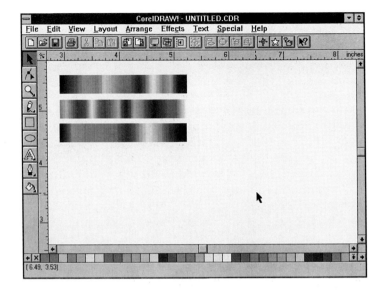

Figure 21.11.
Arrange several
gradations in a
CorelDRAW! docu-
ment before exporting
them to a bitmap
format compatible
with Painter.

CorelMOVE

CorelMOVE, the animation module of the CorelDRAW! package, offers some features that might be of interest to Painter animators. In Chapter 23, "Converting to Other Animation Formats," you see how to use CorelMOVE to convert a Painter movie to the QuickTime for Windows format. You also can use CorelMOVE to compose animations based on a timeline sequence.

In CorelMOVE, you create animations by identifying backgrounds, props, and actors. *Props* basically are items in the animation that don't move, but that you can place in layers in order to move your *actors* (the moving objects in the animation) in front of or behind them. When you're importing images as actors from other programs, you can use white or black as a transparent color. This means that any pixels in your Painter artwork that are either pure black or pure white are ignored by CorelMOVE, if you so specify. This lets you import characters as animation cels. You can export images from Painter as individual Targa, .PCX, or .TIF files.

NOTE True-color files are dithered when brought into CorelMOVE, which alters the appearance of the true color file somewhat.

If you have a moving background, such as the one you created in Chapter 19, "Creating a Cartoon Animation," the easiest way to import the file would be as a CorelMOVE actor. In Figure 21.12, I chose CorelMOVE's File | Import | Actor from Bitmap Files command. The figure shows the resulting dialog box. Here, I've chosen the range of frames comprising the background.

Figure 21.12.
Create an animated
background in
CorelMOVE by
importing the
numbered files
as actors.

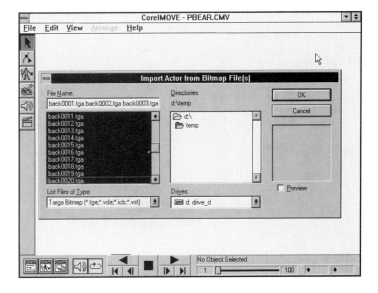

Next, select the import imaging options, as shown in Figure 21.13. I chose high-quality dithering so the images could be best represented in color in the CorelMOVE program. Because this is a background, I don't need or want to identify a transparent color, so I didn't select one. After I applied these commands, the images appeared in the document editing window.

Figure 21.13.
Don't use a trans-
parent color for
the background.

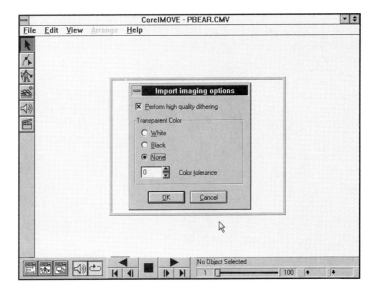

749

The same approach applies to importing actors you've developed in Painter. In Painter, fill any areas you want to be "invisible" with white or black pixels. Then export the frames to numbered Targa files. In CorelDRAW!, import the Targa files as an actor. Figure 21.14 shows the 10 frames of the polar bear you created in Chapter 19 selected for import as a CorelMOVE actor.

Figure 21.14.
Select all numerical
files you want to import
as an actor into
CorelMOVE.

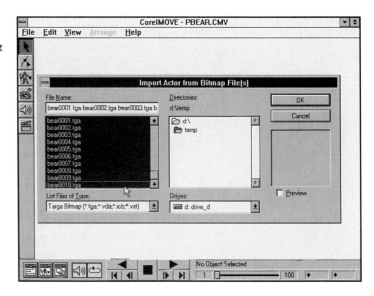

When choosing the imaging options for the polar bear, I selected white as the transparent color, as shown in Figure 21.15. I left color tolerance at 0 to prevent having the light-gray areas in the bear identified as transparent.

Figure 21.15.
Identify transparent
colors with either
white or black when
you import actors into
CorelMOVE.

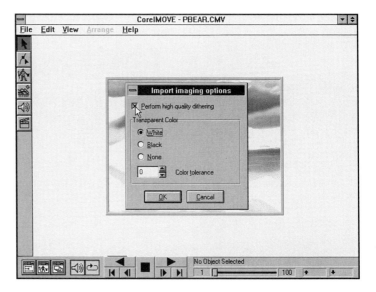

One feature that definitely will spark your interest is that in CorelMOVE you can add sound to your animation, using the Timeline feature to add and layer sound effects. For the most part, you must record your sounds in another program. (Alternatively, you can use sounds from existing sound libraries—providing you obtain permission to do so.) CorelMOVE supports a wide variety of sound formats, some of which are shown in Figure 21.16.

Figure 21.16.
CorelMOVE supports
several different sound
formats.

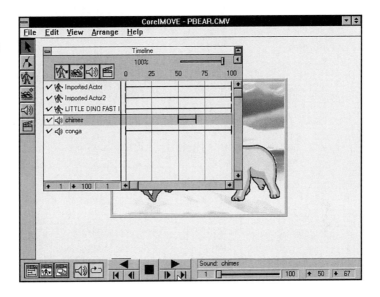

You can place a prop, actor, or sound so that it appears within certain frames of the animation using CorelMOVE's Timeline. Layering and positioning objects in Timeline is similar to moving items in Painter's Path List or Floater List. In Figure 21.17, three actors are shown placed in all frames of the animation. A background sound—the Conga—plays throughout the entire animation. In addition, some chimes play during frames 50 through 67.

With CorelMOVE's Wave Editor, illustrated in Figure 21.18, you can modify your sounds by reversing them, echoing them, and making them louder, softer, longer, or shorter. Additionally, you can save the sound in another frequency or depth—for example, you can convert a 44 KHz 16-bit sound file to an 11 KHz 8-bit sound file.

Figure 21.17.
You can layer and
sequence the elements
of the animation in
CorelMOVE's Timeline.

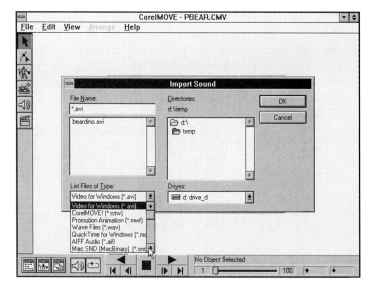

Figure 21.18.
You can edit sounds
and convert them from
within the Wave Editor
included in the
CorelMOVE program.

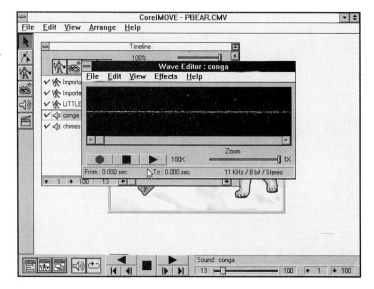

Corel PHOTO-PAINT

Corel PHOTO-PAINT is a paint- and image-editing program similar to Painter in many ways, yet different enough to be worthy of a look. Although there's some overlap in features between the two programs, each of them excels in different areas, making the combination of the two programs a good match.

One of the nice features of Corel PHOTO-PAINT is that you can open a wide variety of bitmap and vector formats and save to many types of bitmap formats. Figure 21.19 shows just some of the formats supported by Corel PHOTO-PAINT when you're opening files.

Figure 21.19.
Corel PHOTO-PAINT
can open a wide variety
of images in both
bitmap and vector
formats.

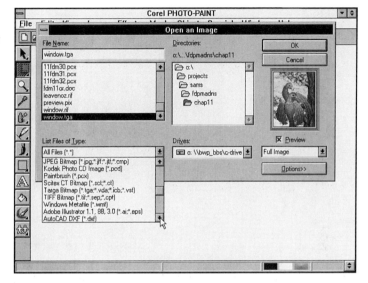

As shown in Figure 21.20, exporting to vector formats from bitmap files is not supported—but you can save documents to a wide range of bitmap formats. If you want to save to vector formats such as .DXF, you can use Corel Trace to trace the bitmap, import the traced image into CorelDRAW!, and save to a vector format from there. You can save bitmap files from Corel PHOTO-PAINT in color depths ranging from black and white to true color, making Corel PHOTO-PAINT a good choice for converting to 256-color image formats.

One feature that might be of interest to Painter users is the color management and calibration procedures available in Corel PHOTO-PAINT. You can achieve color calibration by generating a profile based on the scanner, monitor, and printer you have, so that color is consistent from start to end of a project. Access the Color Management commands from Corel PHOTO-PAINT's file menu. The System Color Profile dialog box appears, as shown in Figure 21.21. Several presets are available, and if your equipment is not listed you can manually generate your own profiles.

Figure 21.20.
Corel PHOTO-PAINT
can save to bitmap
formats; saving to
vector formats is not
supported.

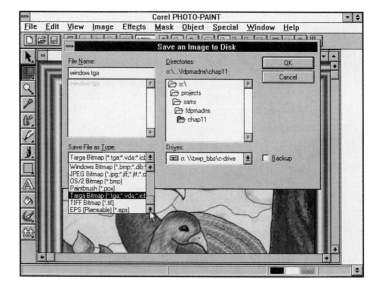

Figure 21.21.
Corel PHOTO-PAINT's
Color Management
features let you
calibrate to your
monitor, printer, and
scanner for color
consistency throughout
a project.

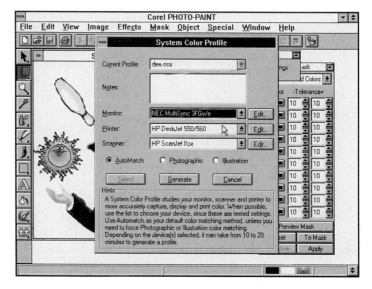

If you want to manually adjust the color calibration settings for your monitor,
use the image window shown in Figure 21.22. Using a true-color picture provided with the CorelDRAW! package, you can adjust the settings and sliders
until the colors on your monitor agree with the colors in the printed image.

Figure 21.22.
Calibrate monitor
colors visually in Corel
PHOTO-PAINT's
Interactive Monitor
Calibration screen.

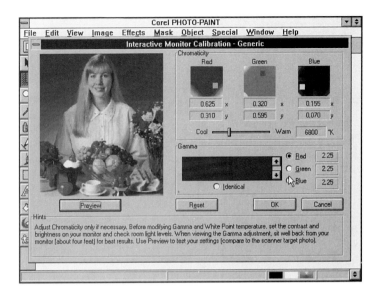

You also can calibrate to your printer, or verify and adjust the calibration settings against an actual printout from your printer. You can print a calibration image from the Printer Characterization dialog box shown in Figure 21.23, and then adjust the colors on your screen to match those of the printout. (Do this after you have calibrated to your monitor.)

Figure 21.23.
Calibrate your printer
so your screen colors
agree with the printer's
colors.

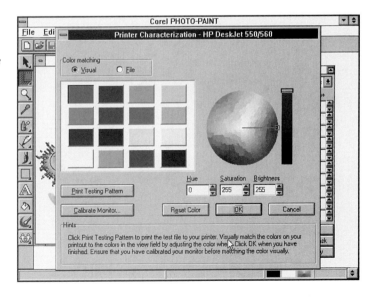

Summary

If you're looking for a vector-based drawing program, CorelDRAW! is definitely worthy of your attention. Because of the great combination of drawing, painting, animation, and desktop publishing tools, it's a package that can fill many needs. The highlights mentioned above are only a small fraction of the ways in which you can use CorelDRAW! and Painter together to produce interesting and creative artwork. There's no doubt that you will discover many more!

Using Painter for Texture Maps

Computer artists involved in creating graphics with 3-D modeling and rendering software often turn to Painter to create texture maps and background images. Painter's combination of true-color graphics handling and its capability to add texture to images make it an ideal choice for texture map creation. And, with Painter's wrap-around feature, seamless tiles can be created easily. This chapter discusses tips and tricks for creating texture maps for 3-D rendering programs.

Patterns Commands

As discussed in Chapter 19, patterns can be captured using the Tools | Patterns | Capture Pattern command, and the resulting captured area is converted into a new, untitled image. This image then has Painter's Wrap Around Color feature enabled, which automatically wraps color applied over the edge of one side onto the opposing side of the image. Tiles created using this feature can be placed adjacent to each other, and no visible seams will appear.

To implement this feature, perform the following steps:

1. Open or create an image on which to base the pattern. You can start with a blank image if you are creating your seamless tile from scratch.

2. Select an area with the Rectangular Selection Tool. If no selection is made, the entire image will be clipped.

3. Choose Tools | Patterns | Capture Pattern. The selected area will be clipped into a new untitled document. Figure 22.1 shows a blank image captured as a pattern in this manner.

   If you have an area defined as a pattern, you can use the Shift key with the Grabber Tool to move the top, bottom, left and right sides of the image into the center of the image. Press the Shift key while using the Grabber Tool and move the image to position the seams toward the inside. This enables you to see exactly how the image will look when it's used as a repeating pattern!

Figure 22.1.
Seamless texture maps
can be started with a
blank image as a
pattern.

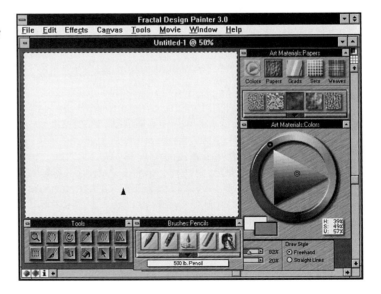

4. Draw your image in the usual manner. Notice that as the mouse or stylus is dragged over one edge of the image, color appears in the appropriate location at the opposite side of the document. This is shown in Figure 22.2.

Figure 22.2.
As you color over edges in the captured pattern, the color wraps around to the opposite side, creating a seamless image.

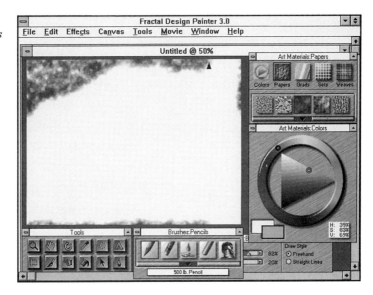

5. Continue building up color in your scene until it is complete. The colors will continue to wrap around to the opposite sides during the creation of the texture map. Figure 22.3 shows a texture map completed in this manner.

If you want to turn the entire area of an image into a pattern, you can use the Tools | Patterns | Define Pattern command. There is no visible verification after you perform this command.

After you apply this command to an image, use the Effects | Fill command or the Paint Bucket Tool to fill the image with a Clone Source. The pattern defined with the Define Pattern command will be used as the fill.

You can also apply the Tools | Patterns | Define Pattern command to a blank image, which will turn on the Wrap Around Color feature of Painter. This feature is discussed in Chapter 19, "Creating a Cartoon Animation."

Figure 22.3.
The seamless tile is
completed, and its
edges will blend
together when placed
in a tiled sequence
against itself.

Scaling Texture Maps Appropriately

When you create scenes in 3-D modeling programs, many different texture maps are used to compose a scene. Using different maps helps reduce the amount of memory required to render the scene if your bitmaps are sized as small as possible. For example, if you are applying a wallpaper texture to walls and the camera in your scene is positioned so that the walls remain fairly distant in your scene, you can keep the wallpaper pattern relatively small in size. If you intend to zoom in close to the wall at some point in your animated scene, however, you might want to make the wallpaper texture map a bit larger so that the detail will be shown in the close-up shots.

One way to accomplish this might be to create a large version of your texture map and add in all the detail you feel would be necessary if your camera were placed close to the image in the scene. Then, you can rescale this texture map and save it into different resolutions, providing different versions of the map for various camera requirements.

In Painter, texture maps can be scaled down by selecting the texture map and then using the Effects | Orientation | Scale command. When you chose this command, the Scale Selection dialog box, shown in Figure 22.4, will appear.

Figure 22.4.
Images can be scaled down using the Effects | Orientation | Scale command.

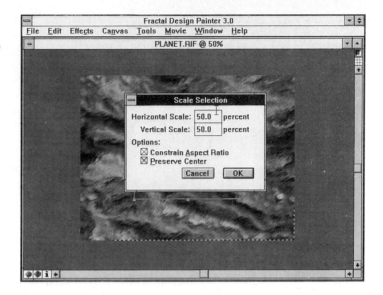

At this point, you can scale the texture map in one of two ways:

- Enter numerical input in the boxes provided. For example, if you want to reduce the scale of the image to 50% of its original size, make sure that the Constrain Aspect Ratio checkbox is checked. Then, enter 50 in either the Horizontal or Vertical scale box. The other figure will automatically change to 50%.

NOTE   If you are using Painter 3.0, you may need to follow with a decimal point the percentage figure you enter in the Horizontal or Vertical Scale box.

- Scale the selected area by dragging one of the corners of the selected area until the image reaches the visual size you would like it to be. When the selection is scaled in this manner, the decimal readouts in the Scale Selection dialog box will revert to the new percentage values when you release the mouse or stylus.

New Painter 3.1 Texture and Pattern Commands

Painter 3.1 offers two new commands that are good for texture maps. The Effects | Tonal Control | Express Texture command and the Tools | Patterns | Make Fractal Pattern command offer a couple of new and interesting ways to create textures.

Effects | Tonal Control | Express Texture

The Effects | Tonal Control | Express Texture command generates a light contrast version of an image in grayscale format. It is similar to the Effects | Surface Control | Apply Screen command but has antialiasing built in. You can use this effect to achieve results similar to printing on high-contrast paper.

1. Select the area you would like to apply the effect to. If you make no selection, Painter applies the effect to the entire image.

2. Choose Effects | Tonal Control | Express Texture. The Express Texture dialog box appears.

3. From the Using drop-down box, choose a method of determining the amount of color to adjust in the image:

   - Paper Grain: Painter applies the effect based on the high and low areas of the paper texture.

   - Image Luminance: Painter applies the effect based on the light and dark areas of the image.

   - Original Luminance: Painter applies the effect based on the light and dark areas of the clone source.

   - Mask: Painter applies the effect around a selection.

4. Adjust the sliders in the dialog box while observing the changes in the Preview window. The slider controls are as follows:

   - Gray Threshold: Use this slider to determine where the threshold is. Moving the slider to the left produces low-contrast settings that generate pure gray. Setting the slider near the center generates medium contrast, producing several levels of grayscale. Moving the slider to the right generates high-contrast images with mostly blacks and whites.

   - Grain: Use this slider to determine how deep the effect penetrates the grain of the paper. Moving the slider to the left penetrates less of the paper, and moving the slider to the right penetrates more of the paper.

   - Contrast: Use this slider to adjust the contrast of the effect. Moving the slider to the left decreases contrast, and moving it toward the right increases contrast.

5. Click OK or press Enter to apply the effect.

Tools | Patterns | Make Fractal Pattern

The Tools | Patterns | Make Fractal Pattern command is new to Painter 3.1 also. This command enables you to generate fractal pattern designs within Painter. A preview window helps you design your pattern.

To generate a fractal pattern from within Painter, follow these steps:

1. Choose Tools | Patterns | Make Fractal Pattern. The Make Fractal Pattern dialog box appears.

2. Adjust the Power slider to control the amount at which you zoom in to or out from the fractal pattern. Moving the slider to the right zooms out from the pattern, enabling you to see many smaller patterns. Moving the slider to the left zooms in closer to the pattern, enabling you to see fewer larger patterns.

3. Adjust the Feature Size slider to define the number of prominent features within the fractal pattern. Moving the slider toward the right will increase the number of times that the features repeat within the tile.

4. Adjust the Softness slider to vary the amount of softness at the edges of the pattern.

5. Click the appropriate Size radio button to define the size of your pattern. The choices represent the width and height of the square tile that you want to generate and you can choose from 128-, 256-, 512-, 1024-, and 2048-pixel-wide and high square patterns. Depending on the amount of memory you have, some choices may be grayed because larger files require much more memory to calculate.

6. When all adjustments are made, click OK or press Enter to generate the fractal pattern. After calculating, Painter will display your pattern in a new document window.

After generating the fractal pattern, you can capture it as a paper texture using the Tools | Textures | Capture Texture command to place the paper into the current paper texture library.

 TIP You can also generate nice cloudy backgrounds for your images using the Tools | Patterns | Make Fractal Pattern command. After you create the fractal pattern as indicated here, select a suitable sky-colored gradation from a Gradation Library. Then use the Tools | Gradations | Express in Image command to create a cloudy sky.

Fitting Bitmaps to Models

Sometimes, detailed texture maps can give the illusion that the modeling of an object is actually more complex than it really is. If your cameras remain at a suitable distance from the object, a detailed texture map can trick the eye into believing that a simple box is actually a stereo receiver, or that the back of a rocking chair is intricately carved. Texture maps also can be animated in some rendering programs; a flat texture map can become a fish tank complete with swimming fish and bubbling water.

One trick that sometimes comes in handy when creating texture maps is to render a straight-on view of the object that the material will be mapped onto. Depending on the complexity and shape of the object, the sample image can be rendered in wireframe or as a solid representation of the mesh if the linework in the image is more complex. Figure 22.5 shows a column that was modeled in a 3-D rendering program. This column was rendered using a wireframe material and saved to a Targa file for input to Painter.

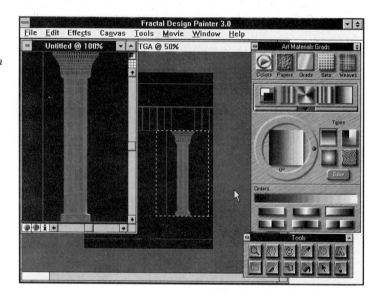

Figure 22.5.
You can use a simple rendering of an object as a guide to creating a properly sized texture map.

In Painter, the image was cropped so that the height of the texture map was equal to the height of the column. Allowances were made in the width of the crop so that the bitmap could be wrapped around the column in cylindrical fashion, without distorting the appearance of the texture map too much. The cropped area was then cut and pasted into a new image.

Because the columns are going to be placed into a scene in which a camera will move between two rows of columns, the texture will have to be created in a higher resolution. If this is not done, the texture map will not have enough detail when the camera gets closer to the column. The sample image was resized to twice its size in pixels, using Painter's Canvas | Resize command.

Figure 22.6 shows the Resize Image dialog box. The units of measure were changed to pixels, the Constrain File Size checkbox was unchecked to enable the creation of a larger file, and the width and height increased by a factor of 2 to double the size of the bitmap. This larger image provides a sufficient amount of detail as the camera passes by the columns.

Figure 22.6.
Images can be scaled
to larger sizes using
the Canvas | Resize
command.

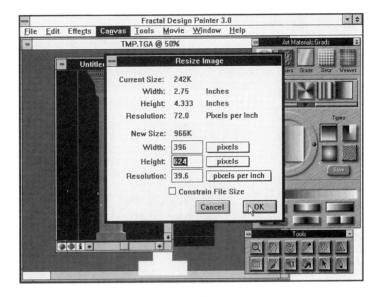

Using the shape of the rendered column as a guide, a texture map was created. The top and bottom sections of the texture map were filled with a pattern that gave the appearance of carved wood, and the center section was filled with a marbled texture pattern. Gold bands were also added to the areas just below and above the carved wood. When mapped on to the column, the changes in materials appeared in locations appropriate to the shape of the 3-D mesh file. Figure 22.7 shows the result placed adjacent to the original sample mesh rendering.

Figure 22.7.
Changes in texture are
placed in appropriate
places using the
original sample image
as a guide.

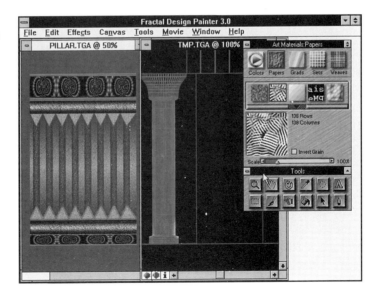

Figure 22.8 shows the column as it is rendered onto the 3-D object. The carved material on the beams and the wall textures were also created in Painter. The raised and recessed areas in the beams were achieved by using the same bitmap as both a texture map and a bump map.

Figure 22.8.
The column is shown
rendered into a 3-D
scene.

TIP

It is rare for real-world objects to be perfectly flawless. One technique for improving the appearance of texture maps in 3-D rendered art is to age or *dirty up* the appearance of your texture maps. Adding little touches of dirt, smears, or scratches make an image look less like it is generated by a computer.

You can apply aging to texture maps either by hand, or by applying different paper textures to your images. The latter method can be done during creation of the texture maps, or after the fact by using the Effects | Surface Control | Apply Surface Texture command or some of the Effects | Tonal Control commands.

Other Types of Maps

3-D modeling software frequently supports other types of maps as well; for example, bump maps can be used to raise or lower areas in an otherwise flat texture map. Opacity maps can vary the transparencies in a material or object when it is rendered to the scene. Reflection maps, sometimes known as environment maps, can be used to provide highlights and reflections in metallic and polished surfaces.

I'm sure you can see similarities between a couple of these map types and the functions contained within Painter. For instance, a bump map can be compared to the raised and lowered areas in Painter's paper grains, the effects achieved after 3-D Brush strokes, or other surface textures applied to an image. Bump maps in 3-D modeling and rendering programs work in a similar manner: Areas with lower luminance values in the bump map recede from view, and areas with higher luminance values in the bump map are raised. It might be easier, even necessary, to create bump maps in grayscale format. Or, you can convert colored bitmaps to grayscale in a number of ways in Painter. Let's look at another way that a bump map can be created.

To begin, a 320×240 image was created. The Grid Display settings were left at their default settings of 12 × 12 pixels, and the grid display was turned on. A rectangular area, 8 × 4 grid squares, was created with the Outline Selection Tool in Straight Lines mode, as shown in Figure 22.9.

Figure 22.9.
A rectangular area is selected using the Grid Display as a guide.

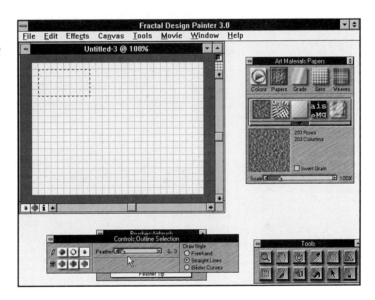

Surface texture was applied to the selected area in two steps. First, a suitable paper texture was chosen—one that would make the rectangle look like concrete. This paper texture was used to apply surface texture based on paper grain. The effect was applied at 100%, with Shiny off, and with the light direction at the 7 o'clock position.

Next, the Effects | Surface Control | Apply Surface Texture command was chosen again. This time, embossing was added to give the rectangle a three-dimensional appearance. This was done by using Mask as the method of applying the texture. The light direction was positioned at the 5 o'clock position so that the shadows would appear at the right and lower sides of the brick. Figure 22.10 shows the result in the Preview window.

Figure 22.10.
Surface texture is
applied to the rectan-
gular selection in two
steps.

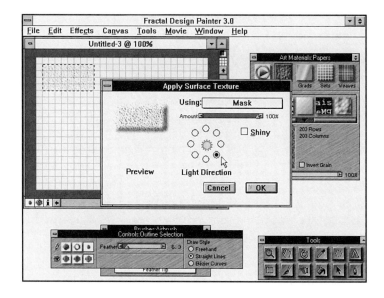

The single block was copied into the clipboard and pasted several times to create a brick pattern. The bricks were also aligned to the grid spacing. All the floaters were dropped to the background layer, and a rectangular selection was created to include two rows of bricks, as shown in Figure 22.11.

Figure 22.11.
A rectangular selection
containing two rows of
bricks was created.

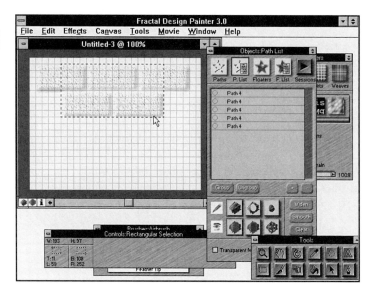

This rectangular selection was captured as a pattern, using the Tools | Patterns | Capture Pattern command. Then, a larger image was created, and the pattern was applied to the image by using the Paint Bucket and filling the image with Clone Source. The result is shown in Figure 22.12.

Figure 22.12.
A larger image was
filled with the captured
pattern, creating a
brick wall bump map.

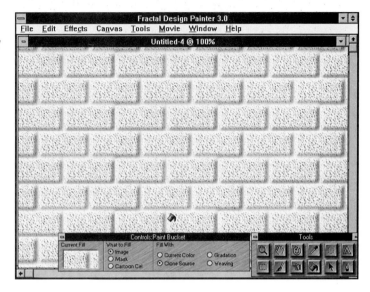

This pattern also can be used as a paper texture by selecting a square area with the Rectangular Selection Tool. The Tools | Selections | Edit Rectangular Selection command was used to verify that the dimensions of the selection were equally divisible by the measurements entered in the Grid Spacing command (in this case, by 12).

The selection can be converted to a paper texture using the Tools | Textures | Capture Texture command. The Crossfade slider in the Save Texture dialog box was reduced to 0, because no smoothing was needed to make the texture appear seamless. The texture was assigned a name, as shown in Figure 22.13. After choosing the OK button, the paper texture appears in the currently opened Paper Library.

Opacity maps are used in some 3-D rendering programs to vary the transparencies of an object. An opacity map can be likened to Painter's masking layer. Opacity maps are typically created in shades of gray. As with Painter's masking layer, the shades of black, white, or gray vary the amount that the texture is mapped on to the object, making some areas appear fully or partially transparent.

Figure 22.13.
*The Crossfade slider is
reduced to zero in the
Save Texture dialog
box before saving the
paper texture.*

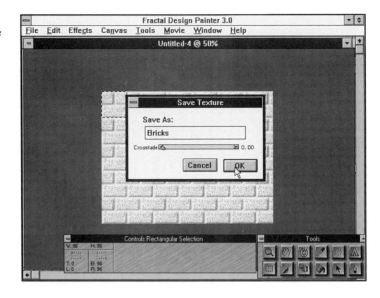

You can convert images into grayscale in a number of ways in Painter. One
method of achieving grayscale images is to use the Effects | Tonal Control |
Adjust Colors command. When you chose this command, the Adjust Colors
dialog box, shown in Figure 22.14, will appear.

Figure 22.14.
*Images can be con-
verted to grayscale
using the Adjust Colors
command.*

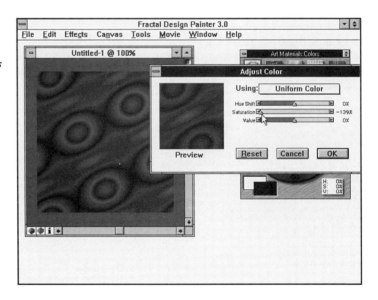

In the Adjust Colors dialog box, choose to apply the effect based on Uniform Color. Then, adjust the Saturation slider (the middle slider) all the way to the left. Notice as you do this that the image in the preview window changes to gray shades. Figure 22.15 shows the image converted to grayscale shades.

Figure 22.15.
The image is now
converted to shades
of gray.

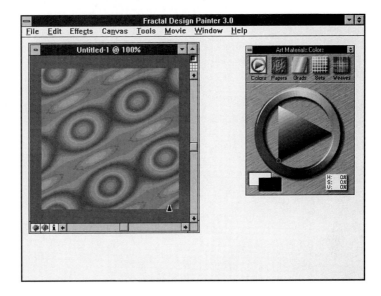

There is another method of converting to shades of gray, which I feel provides slightly better results. This method seems to retain the detail in the image, providing more subtle variations in the shades of gray. This method uses a two-point, black-to-white gradient.

From the Art Materials Palette, click the Grads icon to open up the Grads Palette. Using black as your primary color and white as your secondary color (the default settings), click the Two Point gradient, shown in Figure 22.16.

NOTE You can also use the Tools | Gradations | Express in Image command to generate a negative grayscale image. Choose white as your primary color and black as your secondary color in this instance.

Click the first Order button in the top row in the Grads Palette. This will position the gradient so that black appears on the left side of the gradation preview bar, located just above the order selections. Your screen should look similar to the one in Figure 22.17.

Figure 22.16.
Select the Two-Point
gradient from the
Grads Palette.

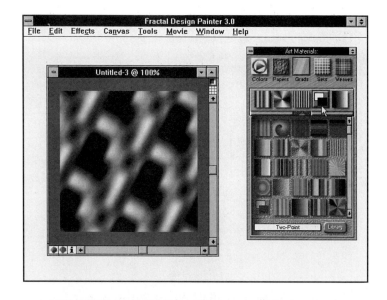

Figure 22.17.
Position the gradient
so that black appears
at the left side of the
gradient preview bar.

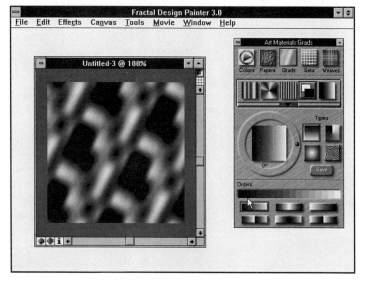

Next, choose the Tools | Gradations | Express In Image command, shown in Figure 22.18. This command will replace the colors in the image with suitable gray shades—and does an excellent job at providing detail that I feel is more true to the original image.

Figure 22.19 shows the results achieved after the effect is applied. Try these methods on two copies of the same image to see which you prefer.

Figure 22.18.
Apply the colors in the gradient to your image with the Express In Image command.

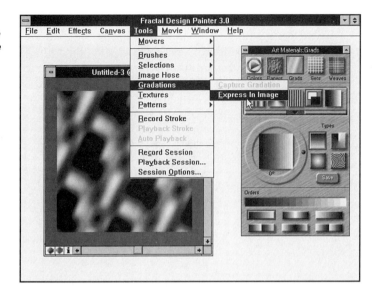

Figure 22.19.
This image has been changed to gray shades with the Express In Image command.

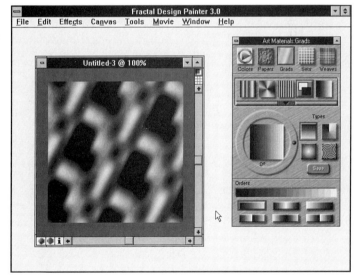

Try It Yourself!

If you don't have a 3-D rendering program, the CD furnished with this book has some demo versions of 3-D software that you can use to experiment. On the Windows side is a demo version of Caligari trueSpace. This software program is rapidly becoming the most popular Windows-based 3D rendering and animation program. It enables you to model and render 3-D stills and animations. The demo version included with this book is fully functional except for saving and printing files. The demo provided is Version 1.3, but a new version of trueSpace will probably be available by the time this book reaches the shelves. trueSpace 2.0 promises many exciting new features, including a real-time 3-D renderer! If you are interested in this product and want to learn more, you can find support on CompuServe, in the GUGRPA (Graphics Users Group A) Forum, section 8 (trueSpace UG). You can also contact Caligari as directed in the demo software to obtain dealer information.

The trueSpace interface consists of various icons, arranged in groups, that perform specific functions. These icons are located at the bottom of the screen. If you left-click and hold on the icons that have small green triangles in the left corner, additional icon choices become available in a pop-up. If you right-click on the icons that have small red triangles in their right corners, a property panel becomes available for the icon's function settings. I describe the functions of the icons briefly so that you can explore the features of trueSpace with a little more insight.

Figure 22.20 shows the Render icons. The first icon in this group enables you to choose ways to examine or apply materials to the objects in your scene. The second icon enables you to specify the UV Projection (how texture maps will be applied to objects). The third icon is the Material Rectangle, which enables you to create and apply Material rectangles to an object. The fourth icon provides four ways to add lights to your scene.

Figure 22.20.
Four render icons
provide ways to ren-
der, apply and create
materials, and add
lighting to your scenes.

Inspect, Paint Face,
Paint Over Existing
Material, Paint Object

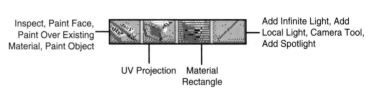

Add Infinite Light, Add
Local Light, Camera Tool,
Add Spotlight

UV Projection   Material
Rectangle

Figure 22.21 shows the Edit Icon group. The first icon offers undo and redo functions. The second icon erases (deletes) the currently selected object. The third icon makes an identical copy of the currently selected object. Finally, the fourth icon enables you to glue objects together in hierarchical sequences or unglue them to create more complex objects.

Figure 22.22 shows the Animation Icon group. The first icon brings up the Animation Tool, which contains VCR-like controls to play, record, and edit animations. The second icon is the Path Tool, which you can use to define motion paths for the objects in your scene. The third icon is the Constraint Tool, which offers two choices for constraining an object's rotation. The fourth icon calls up the Animation Project Window, which graphically displays animation actions and events.

Figure 22.21.
*Four edit icons offer
ways to undo actions,
copy or erase objects,
and glue or unglue
objects.*

Undo, Redo

Glue as Child, Glue as Sibling, Unglue

Erase   Copy

Figure 22.22.
*The Animation icons
provide tools to create
and edit animation
sequences.*

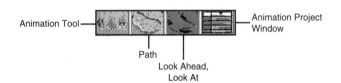

Animation Tool

Animation Project Window

Path

Look Ahead, Look At

Figure 22.23 shows the Library icons. The first icon calls the Material Library so that you can load or save materials which have been created with the Material Rectangle previously mentioned. The second icon brings up the Path Library, which you use to save paths that you have defined in your animations. The third icon enables you to create primitive shapes, such as cylinders, spheres, and toruses, at the click of a button. These primitive shapes serve as starting points for your modeling projects.

Figure 22.23.
*The Library icons
enable you to create
primitive shapes and
load and save materials
and paths.*

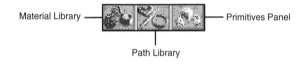

Material Library

Primitives Panel

Path Library

The Utility icons are shown in Figure 22.24. These icons provide ways to modify the primitive shapes by adding more faces, scaling, rotating, and normalizing their positions. The first icon brings up five ways to modify the geometry of a shape. The second icon provides three choices to normalize scale, rotation, and location of an object. The third icon displays the X, Y, and Z coordinates, relative to the currently selected object. The fourth icon toggles the Grid on and off, which enables you to create arrays of objects easily.

The Object Navigation icons, shown in Figure 22.25, provide ways to position and link objects. The first icon is the Object Tool, with which you can select a current object or action. The second icon is the Object Move tool, which you can use to reposition an object in a scene or animation. The third icon is for the Object Rotate Tool, which enables you to rotate an object in a scene or animation. The fourth icon is the Object Scale icon, which you can use to enlarge or reduce an object in a scene or animation.

Figure 22.24.
The Utility icons provide ways to modify the geometry of the objects in your scene.

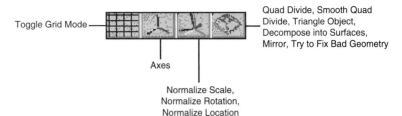

Toggle Grid Mode

Quad Divide, Smooth Quad Divide, Triangle Object, Decompose into Surfaces, Mirror, Try to Fix Bad Geometry

Axes

Normalize Scale, Normalize Rotation, Normalize Location

The fifth icon shown in Figure 22.25 is not actually part of the Object Navigation group. This is the Hierarchy Navigation icon, which offers two choices for navigating through hierarchical objects (those that are glued together as discussed previously in Figure 22.21.

Figure 22.25.
The Object Navigation Icons enable you to select objects and move, rotate, and scale them. The Hierarchy Navigation icon enables you to navigate through a hierarchical chain of objects.

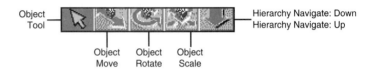

Object Tool

Hierarchy Navigate: Down
Hierarchy Navigate: Up

Object Move   Object Rotate   Object Scale

Figure 22.26 shows the Model Icon group. The first icon is the Point Edit group, where you can select and manipulate individual points, edges, or groups of edges in an object. The second icon offers ways to bevel, sweep, lathe, and tip objects or groups. The third icon offers ways to deform objects, as if they were bits of clay. The fourth icon adds text to your scene, enabling you to create animated logos. The fifth and sixth icons provide ways to create polygons and spline shapes in your scene.

Figure 22.26.
The Model Icon group provides additional ways to modify and shape objects.

Point Edit: Context, Point Edit: Faces, Point Edit: Edges, Point Edit: Vertices

Bevel, Macro/Sweep, Lathe, Tip, Sweep

Text: Horizontal
Text:Vertical

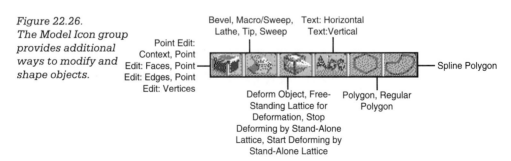

Spline Polygon

Deform Object, Free-Standing Lattice for Deformation, Stop Deforming by Stand-Alone Lattice, Start Deforming by Stand-Alone Lattice

Polygon, Regular Polygon

Lastly, Figure 22.27 shows the Window Group icons. The first icon in this group provides four ways to render the scene: wireframe display, current object, rendering the scene to the screen, and rendering the scene to a file. The second icon changes your view of the scene: to perspective, front view, left view, top view, or view from the object. The third icon enables you to move the scene along an axis so that you can change the view on your screen. The fourth icon changes the rotation of the scene on your screen. The fifth icon zooms into or away from the scene. The sixth icon creates a new perspective view of the scene so that you can work with more than one view at a time. The seventh icon enables you to close or dock all the setting panels on your screen, to look at the currently selected object, or to reset the view to its default settings. The last icon, the Settings Panel icon, enables you to set program operation parameters.

Figure 22.27.
The Image Group icons affect how the scene is displayed on your screen and also enable you to set some program operation parameters.

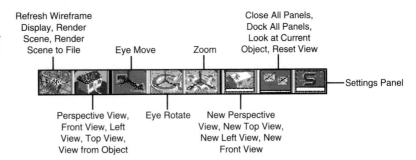

Refresh Wireframe Display, Render Scene, Render Scene to File

Eye Move

Zoom

Close All Panels, Dock All Panels, Look at Current Object, Reset View

Settings Panel

Perspective View, Front View, Left View, Top View, View from Object

Eye Rotate

New Perspective View, New Top View, New Left View, New Front View

When you first start the trueSpace demo, a sample mesh file appears on your screen, consisting of several different objects. Figure 22.28 shows an example of the default trueSpace screen. To pick an object, choose the Object Tool (the first icon shown previously in Figure 22.25) and click an object to select it. It is displayed with white wireframe lines, as shown in Figure 22.28.

Figure 22.28.
Select an object with the Object Tool to make it the current object. Selected objects are highlighted with white lines.

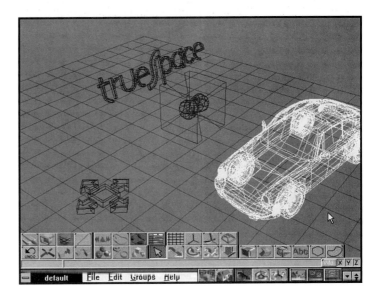

You can render a single object or render the entire scene. To render the entire scene, refer back to Figure 22.27 to locate the Window Group icons. The first icon in this group offers five rendering options. Click and hold the left mouse button and drag the mouse over the icons until the help bar (located above the menu selections) reads "Render Scene," as shown in Figure 22.29. Release the mouse button to render the scene. After the scene is rendered, all objects appear solid and are represented with different materials.

Figure 22.29.
After you render the scene, the objects appear solid, with different materials applied to them.

NOTE If the help bar does not appear above the main Menu bar, click on the Help menu title to select Help Bar from the menu choices. When the option is checked, as shown in Figure 22.30, the help bar offers a description of the icon functions as you pass the cursor over them.

Refer back to Figure 22.20 to locate the Render icons. The first icon in this group contains four icons that relate to an object's material. Left-click and drag to find the Inspect icon, and release the mouse button. Four material panels, shown in Figure 22.31 appear on your screen. Click the Inspect icon to select it. It will look as though it is pressed inward when it is active. Your cursor changes into a magnifying glass. Click the magnifying glass on an object to inspect its material. The four material boxes change to display the material of the selected object.

Figure 22.30.
If the help bar does not appear on your screen, choose Help | Help Bar. A check appears beside the command when the help bar is activated.

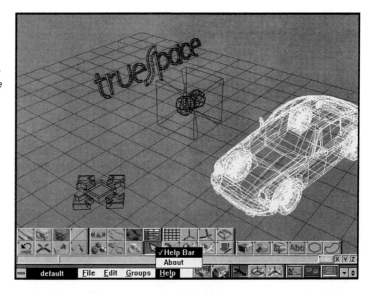

Figure 22.31.
Four material panels enable you to define and create materials for your objects.

The first material panel indicates the basic color of the material. To change it, click within the hexagon to select the hue and then drag the indicator in the bar on the right side to choose lightness or darkness. The second material panel shows a rendered representation of the material.

The third material panel is that which you will be interested in if you want to use a texture map for a material. To choose a texture map for your material, right-click the first icon in the third column (shown beneath the cursor in Figure 22.32). The Texture Map dialog box appears. Click the icon again with your left mouse button to use a texture map in the material you are editing.

Figure 22.32.
You can select a
texture map from the
Texture Map dialog
box.

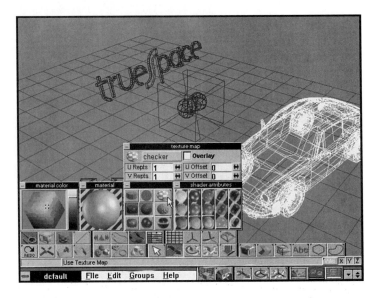

NOTE You can choose a bump map in a similar manner, using the Use Bump Map icon located just beneath the Texture Map icon. Bump maps make a texture appear more three-dimensional, and use light and dark values to create raised and lowered surfaces in the material.

Beneath the Use Bump Map icon is the Use Environment Map icon, which adds reflection properties to a material. Environment Maps are great to use on metallic and shiny surfaces.

From the Texture Map dialog box, click inside the material name square. In Figure 22.32, the material name is shown as "checker." When you click the material name, the Get Texture Map dialog box appears. This dialog box is shown in Figure 22.33. Choose Targa Files from the List Files of Type dialog box to load a 24-bit Targa file you created and saved from Painter. After you load a file, the material will be re-rendered with the texture map applied. After you experiment with other settings in the material panels, save your material into a library by clicking the first icon shown in Figure 22.23. The procedures to save a material are fairly intuitive.

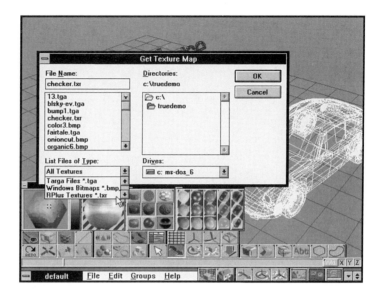

Summary

Painter can be used in many ways to create texture maps and background images for 3-D modeling and rendering programs—texture maps that range from realistic to totally imaginary. Now, with Painter's animation techniques, you also can use frame stacks to create animated texture maps for programs supporting this type of material. Great materials start with great graphics software; and for many, Painter is the program of choice.

Converting to Other Animation Formats

Painter can save animation files in several ways: in Painter's frame stacks format (.FRM), as a Video for Windows file (.AVI Windows version only), as a QuickTime movie file (Mac version only), or as a series of numbered files in the image formats supported by Painter. Although most Windows-based multimedia software supports the .AVI animation and QuickTime formats in their native platforms, there may be occasions when you need to convert to other animation formats that are compatible with other multimedia software programs. For example, some PC multimedia authoring tools also support the Autodesk animation formats (.FLI and .FLC extensions), as well as QuickTime for Windows (.MOV extension). As another example, you might require an animation that can be run in the DOS environment—here, the Autodesk animation formats might be your choice.

This chapter will show you several methods of converting to other animation formats, with both commercial and shareware applications. I'll discuss using the following software programs to convert animations:

- Dave's Targa Animator (shareware)
- Video for DOS (shareware)
- CorelDRAW! 5.0 (CorelMOVE module)
- Autodesk Animator Pro

Mac users might want to check out the CD that accompanies this book for a demo of Debabelizer, which does conversions of many graphics types including cross-platform formats.

Saving a Painter Movie as an .AVI File

In 1992, Microsoft introduced digitized video to the Windows PC with the release of Video for Windows. Initially released as a retail package and also bundled with video capture boards, the Video for Windows .AVI file format offered a way to compress video and audio information into one interleaved file so that both could be played concurrently on a PC. Because of the amount of information that has to be processed to display video and audio data concurrently, the size of the captured video was initially quite small by today's standards (160×120 pixels). The compression methods used in the initial release also resulted in graphics with a blocky appearance. Nevertheless, the excitement of the technology caught on and offered us an early glimpse of what was to come in the multimedia world.

Since Video for Windows initial release, computer hardware has advanced to the point that larger-sized video files can be captured and displayed. Additionally, more efficient compression methods have been developed, which offer better image quality and enhanced performance. Though you are still not quite at the level of playing a full-screen video with sound on a PC at 30 frames per second without special hardware assistance, Video for Windows can now give us at least quarter-screen (320×240 resolution) video with respectable frame rates on 486 and Pentium computers.

Painter's movie stack files can be saved to the .AVI format. To begin, load in a Painter frame stacks file (.FRM extension), using the File | Open command. For this example, I have used the BACK2.FRM frame stack file that was created in Chapter 19, "Creating a Cartoon Animation." Figure 23.1 shows this movie file loaded in Painter. You can use any frame stacks file to perform the following steps.

Figure 23.1.
A Painter frame stacks
file is loaded or created
in Painter.

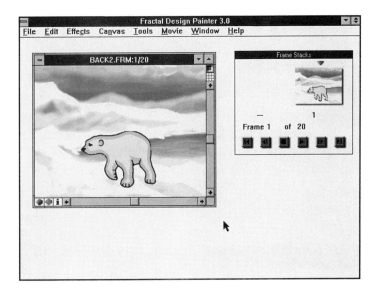

To save the file to .AVI format, choose File | Save As. The Save Movie dialog box appears. (See Figure 23.2.)

Figure 23.2.
When you choose the
File | Save As com-
mand, the Save Movie
dialog box appears.

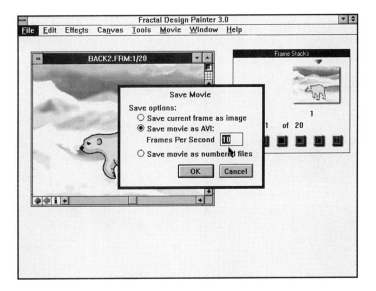

From the Save Movie dialog box, click the radio button adjacent to *Save movie as AVI*. Then, enter the number of frames per second that you want to save the file as. My animation example was chosen to run at 10 frames per second, so this number was entered in the Frames Per Second entry box, visible in Figure 23.2.

AVI TIP

Regular videotape is recorded at approximately 30 frames per second. However, your target PC may not be able to play an .AVI file at that frame rate. If you have developed an animation that is 640×480 pixels and contains a lot of motion and pixel change from one frame to the next, you may need to reduce the frame rate of the animation to 10 frames per second (perhaps even lower) to play back correctly. Smaller animations with less pixel movement can be set at higher frame rates. As you gain experience with pixel changes and how they perform on various hardware configurations, you'll be able to better gauge what frame rates are acceptable to you and your hardware.

Entering larger frame rates will provide smoother animation, but it may be hard for slower computers to play the frames back sufficiently. Lower frame rates may result in choppier animation, but will be easier for slower computers to play. Lower values also reduce the size of the file, which may be beneficial if storage space is at a premium.

When you have entered your desired frames per second, click the OK button in the Save Movie dialog box to continue the saving process. The Enter Movie Name dialog box appears. (See Figure 23.3.) Here, scroll to the directory to which you want to save your file and enter a name for the animation. In this example, I named the file POLBEAR.AVI. Then click OK to continue the save process.

Figure 23.3.
Name the animation in
the Enter Movie Name
dialog box.

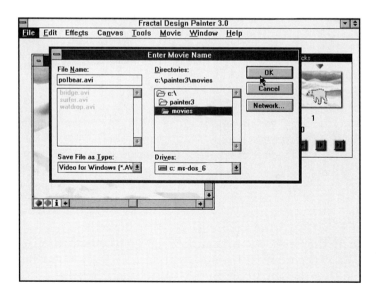

During the next step of the .AVI file save, you are prompted to choose a compression format in the Video Compression dialog box. Some of the available choices for frame compression methods are shown in Figure 23.4. My POLBEAR.AVI file is provided on the CD for you to view.

Figure 23.4.
Choose a compression
mode from the Video
Compression dialog
box.

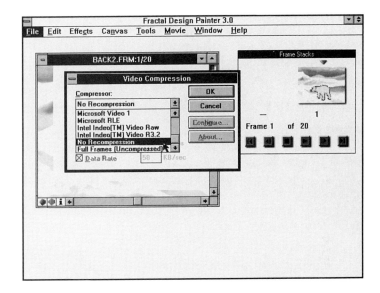

From the Video Compression dialog box, click OK after selecting the compression method. A status bar informs you of the compression progress, and then you are returned to the movie edit window. The .AVI file can then be viewed in the Windows Media Player, or any multimedia software program that supports .AVI files.

As mentioned earlier, a video file is compressed to reduce the amount of data that is processed by your computer. Compressing the video reduces image quality a bit, and you will notice a difference in its appearance after it is compressed. You will also notice differences in video quality from one compression format to another. If you intend to add sound to the .AVI file, which requires that it be recompressed, your best option might be to initially save it as Full Frames (Uncompressed), the last option shown in Figure 23.4. This option saves all the frames as an .AVI file, but does not degrade the image quality, as the file data is left intact. If you try to play an .AVI file saved in this method, playback speed will be very slow.

The following files, provided on the *Fractal Design Painter 3.1 Unleashed* CD, were saved in the various .AVI file formats supported by Painter. They were saved with the default settings provided with each compression format. Increasing the Compression Quality and Data Rate settings can improve the appearance of an .AVI file. You can experiment with compression settings to

787

improve image appearance. Compare the size of these files to their playback quality to see the results of each compression method:

FULLFRAM.AVI	Saved in Full Frame (Uncompressed)
INDEO32.AVI	Saved in Intel Indeo (TM) Video R3.2
INDEORAW.AVI	Saved in Intel Indeo (TM) Video Raw
MSVID1.AVI	Saved in Microsoft Video 1
NORECOMP.AVI	Saved in No Recompression
CINEPAK.AVI	Saved in Cinepak Codec by Supermatch

Saving a Painter Movie as Numbered Files

If your intent is to convert a Painter movie to another animation file format through third-party software, it is best to save the movie as a series of numbered Targa files. This is the choice for two reasons. First, all the software programs mentioned here support importing numbered files saved in this format. Second, if an animation is saved as an AVI file that uses one of the compression methods, such as Cinepak compression, the image suffers some reduction in quality. It's best to start with the cleanest, truest images possible.

To save a Painter movie to individually numbered files, choose the File | Save As command. The Save Movie dialog box appears. (See Figure 23.5.) This time, select the radio button adjacent to the *Save movie as numbered files* option, and click OK to accept the choice.

Figure 23.5.
Choose the Save movie
as numbered files
option to save the
Painter movie as
individually numbered
files.

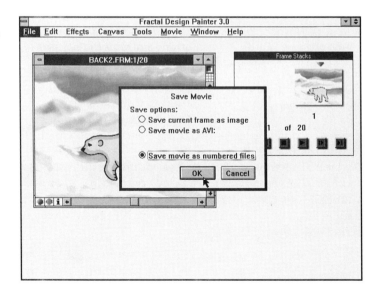

After clicking the OK button, the Save Image As dialog box appears. (See Figure 23.6.) From the drop-down box, you can select any one of Painter's supported file formats. As mentioned before, the Targa format is accepted by all of the third-party programs I will be discussing, so you should choose to save in the Targa format.

Figure 23.6.
Select to save the files
in the Targa file format.

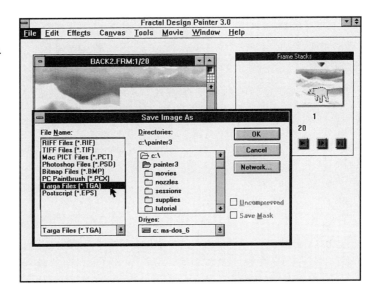

Next, choose the directory you want to save your file to and name your file in the File Name box, as shown in Figure 23.7. When naming the file, you must reserve at least as many placeholders as there are frames in the animation. For example, the animation has 20 frames, which means that there must be at least two number placeholders in the filename. The first frame can be named PBEAR01, and the resulting frames, saved in sequential order as PBEAR02 through PBEAR20, are automatically given the .TGA file extension. Numbered files named PBEAR001.TGA through PBEAR020.TGA have been furnished on the CD for you to experiment with.

Click OK after you have named your first file and selected the directory you want to save the numbered files to. You will be informed of the progress as the numbered files are saved.

Figure 23.7.
Choose the directory
you want to save the
file to, and type in a
name for the file. Then,
choose OK or press
enter to begin saving
the sequence.

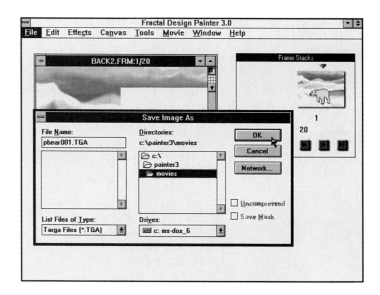

Converting Numbered Files to Animations

Now that you've saved your animation into a series of numbered Targa files, I'll look at several ways you can convert them to other animation formats. I'll start with shareware programs first. There are two shareware programs available that do an excellent job of converting numbered files to Autodesk animations: Dave's Targa Animator, by David K. Mason, and Video for DOS, by Bob Williamson.

Using Dave's Targa Animator to Convert to Autodesk Formats

Dave's Targa Animator is available on many computer bulletin boards across the country because it is a very popular animation conversion program. It can be obtained on CompuServe by logging into the Computer Animation Forum (Go COMANIM), and downloaded from Library 3, Animation Sources. The full registered version of the program can be ordered directly from the author. At press time, the beta of Version 2.2 was newly released, and this is the version discussed here.

Dave's Targa Animator, or DTA, accepts a wide variety of file formats (as shown in Table 23.1) and converts them to Autodesk .FLI or .FLC file format, as well as other optional methods. The Autodesk animation format differs from .AVI in that it is a graphics-only format; in other words, no sound is interleaved in the animation file. Additionally, the files are limited at the present time to 256 colors. However, the Autodesk format offers the advantage that it can be played in both DOS and Windows environments. This file format is a common choice for game developers.

Table 23.1. Dave's Targa Animator Input Formats

Extension	Description
.ANI	Presidio PC Animate Plus Animation Files
.BMP	Windows Bitmap Format
.DIB	Windows .DIB Files
.FLC	Autodesk Animator Pro Animation Format, any resolution, 8-bit
.FLI	Autodesk Animator Animation Format, 320×200 resolution, 8-bit
.GIF	CompuServe Graphic Format, Version 87a or 89a
.IFF	Amiga IFF/ILBM Pictures
.ILB	Amiga IFF/ILBM Pictures
.IMG	Vivid Ray Tracer 24-bit .RLE image files
.LBM	Amiga IFF/ILBM Pictures
.PCX	Z-Soft PC Paintbrush Format, 256-color or 24-bit
.RLE	MindImage 2 SIRDS Run-Length Encoded depth files
.TGA	Truevision Targa Files; 8-, 16-, 24-, or 32-bit; compressed and uncompressed
.VAN	VistaPro VRLI 256-color Animation Files

Converting to FLC with Dave's Targa Animator

Although Dave's Targa Animator has several other features, which I will highlight later, the focus here is to discuss how to convert Targa files to an Autodesk animation format. Because Dave's Targa Animator is a DOS command-line conversion program, no screen shots are available here, but the commands used for the conversions are featured in monospaced typeface.

To show an example of the command-line syntax, assume the following:

- The Dave's Targa Animator program is located on your C: hard drive, under a directory called DTA.
- The Targa files that you want to convert are located in your C:\GRAPHICS directory, and are called PICT0001.TGA through PICT0100.TGA (100 files in all).
- You want to save the animation to your C:\FLICS directory, under a filename called MOVIE.FLC. The output file directory and name is specified using the /O command switch discussed next.

To generate an Autodesk animation using the above scenario, enter the following command line from the DOS prompt:

```
C:\DTA\DTA C:\GRAPHICS\PICT*.TGA /OC:\FLICS\MOVIE.FLC
```

After you type the preceding command, a palette is created by examining all the frames in the series. The program then reads each individual Targa file and maps the palette to each frame. The entire process is quite fast—a 100-frame, 200-pixel by 200-pixel animation was generated in one minute on a 486DX2/66 with 16 MB of RAM.

By default, the size of the animation will be the same size as your original Targa files. So, if the original Targa files were created in 320×240 resolution, the animation is also rendered to that resolution. The animation is also, by default, converted to 256 colors. Although you can specify a 16-bit .FLX animation file generation with a special command switch, there is only one DOS program available that will play these files (the Tempra software series originally published by Mathematica). Also, by default, the speed of the animation is set at zero. You can specify a different speed, to slow the play of the animation, by entering the /S command line switch followed by a number, as follows:

```
C:\DTA\DTA C:\GRAPHICS\PICT*.TGA /OC:\FLICS\MOVIE.FLC /S25
```

This command renders the animation with a speed of 25.

Other Features of Dave's Targa Animator

As mentioned, Dave's Targa Animator does not just do animations. There are a host of other features available with this shareware utility.

- It can create a single optimized 256-color palette from a series of true-color pictures, and then create an Autodesk Animation out of them.

- It can save the palette as an Autodesk Animator .COL color file, or as a MAP palette file for the PICLAB and FRACTINT shareware graphic programs.

- It can convert pictures to several still image formats, including .TGA, .GIF, .PCX, .BMP, and .DIB.

- It can generate animations in any of the following resolutions: 320×200, 320×240, 320×400, 320×480, 360×480, 640×480, 640×400, 800×600, 1024×768, 1280×1024, or user-specified. Animations can be 8-bit FLI or FLC (Autodesk) or 16-bit .FLX (Tempra) format.

- It can read in Autodesk .COL palette files, or PICLAB or FRACTINT.MAP Palette files, and render an animation to that palette.

- It can do multi-layer compositing, in which animations can be layered one atop another with command-line processing, or by script file. Chroma-key colors can be specified to define transparent areas of the animations when compositing.

■ It can average images together for a variety of effects, including simulated motion blur and red/blue 3-D images and animations.

Using Video for DOS to Convert to Autodesk Formats

Video for DOS, written by Bob Williamson, is another shareware animation generator that does a great job of converting a series of still images to several animation formats. These include Autodesk's .FLI and .FLC, the Video for Windows .AVI format (without sound), and MPEG format (.MPG). Release 1.6a is dated December 5, 1994. The shareware version is available on CompuServe in the COMANIM Forum Library 3, Animation Sources, under the filename VFD.ZIP. This shareware program can be ordered directly from the author or through Public Software Library (PsL) in Houston, Texas. The Video for DOS input formats are as follows:

Extension	Description
.DIB	Windows DIB Files (all .BMP and .RLE)
.BMP	Windows Bitmap Format (1-, 4-, 8-, 16-, and 24-bit)
.RLE	Windows Run Length Encoded Bitmaps (4- and 8-bit)
.BMP	OS/2 Bitmap Files (1-, 4-, 8-, and 24-bit)
.TGA	Truevision Targa Files (8-, 16-, 24-, and 32-bit)
.GIF	(Registered version only), PC and Mac, Version 87a and 89a
.PCX	(Registered version only), 8 and 24-bit
.FLC	Autodesk Animation Format, any resolution, 8-bit
.FLI	Autodesk Animation Format, 320×200 resolution, 8-bit
.AVI	.RLE and 8-, 16-, and 24-bit Full Frame
.RAW	MPEG Files, produced with DMPEG.EXE Version 1.1, 8- and 24-bit (shareware)

Like Dave's Targa Animator, Video for DOS is a command-line program. Its syntax is similar to that used by the previous program, so I will repeat the example used previously.

For this example, assume the following:

■ The Video for DOS program is located on your C: hard drive, under a directory called VFD.

■ The Targa files that you want to convert are located in your C:\GRAPHICS directory, and are called PICT0001.TGA through PICT0100.TGA (100 files in all).

■ You want to save the animation to your C:\FLICS directory, under a filename called MOVIE.FLC. The output directory and filename is specified by using the -O switch, shown next.

To generate an Autodesk animation using the preceding scenario, the following command line can be entered from the DOS prompt:

```
C:\VFD\VFD C:\GRAPHICS\PICT*.TGA -OC:\FLICS\MOVIE.FLC
```

After you type the preceding command, the program creates a histogram of all the Targa files and determines the total number of colors in all. Then, it promotes the colors to a 256-color palette, and maps the palette to each Targa file. The entire process took about 2 or 3 minutes for a 100-frame, 200-pixel by 200-pixel animation on a 486DX2/66 with 16MB of RAM.

One advantage that Video for DOS has over Dave's Targa Animator is that you can specify, by a switch setting, to map the animation to a Windows Identity Palette. If you intend to display the animation in Windows under 256-color-graphics modes, you should be aware that Windows reserves 20 colors for its system display. These colors are placed in the first 10 and last 10 slots of a 256-color palette. If animations or graphics are created without these 20 system colors in their proper locations in the palette, you will notice your Windows interface colors become messed up whenever the graphic or animation is displayed on the screen.

Video for DOS makes creating Windows-compatible animation very easy. When you use either the -W1 or -W2 switch in the command line, VFD places the 20 standard Windows colors in the first and last 10 slots, and uses the remaining 236 color slots for the colors contained in the animation. You can elect to include the 20 system colors in the animation (using the -W1 switch), or elect not to include any of the 20 system colors in the animation (using the -W2 switch).

To generate a Windows Identity Palette that maps the 20 Windows colors in with the animation file, use the following command option:

```
C:\VFD\VFD C:\GRAPHICS\PICT*.TGA -OC:\FLICS\MOVIE.FLC -W1
```

To generate a Windows Identity Palette that does not map the 20 colors in with the animation file (the better option), use the following command option:

```
C:\VFD\VFD C:\GRAPHICS\PICT*.TGA -OC:\FLICS\MOVIE.FLC -W2
```

When you examine the palettes generated by either of the previous methods, you notice that the first 10 and last 10 slots of the palette contain all twenty Windows system colors.

Using CorelDRAW! to Convert to QuickTime for Windows

CorelDRAW! Version 4.0 introduced an animation module called CorelMOVE, which added animation capabilities to an already popular graphics software program. With Version 5.0 of CorelDRAW!, the CorelMOVE module can save to several animation formats, including Video for Windows .AVI format, and a Windows-compatible version of the Mac QuickTime animation format, called QuickTime for Windows.

To convert Targa files to either of these formats using CorelMOVE, open the Corel Program Group by clicking its icon, as shown in Figure 23.8.

Figure 23.8.
To convert to anima-
tion formats using
CorelMOVE, click its
icon in the Corel
Program Group.

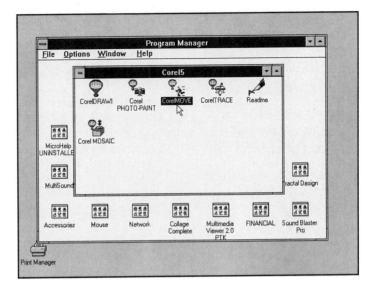

When the CorelMOVE program is started, create a new file using the File | New command. You don't need to enter a name for the CorelMOVE file, because you're using it only as a conversion method at this point. Then, choose the File | Import command, shown in Figure 23.9, and select to Import an Actor from Bitmap Files to load the Targa file sequences into the program.

Figure 23.9.
Create a new Corel
movie file, and then
Import the Targa
sequences using the
Import Actor from
Bitmap Files option as
shown.

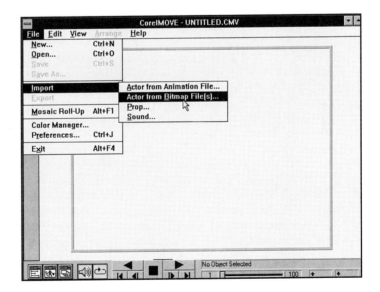

The Import Actor from Bitmap Files dialog box appears. (See Figure 23.10.) Choose the directory in which your files appear. Then, in the Filename listbox, click the first file in the series. Use the scrollbar in the dialog box to scroll down to the last file in the series, and shift-click the last file in the sequence (click the last file while holding down the shift key). You should see all of the files in the sequence become highlighted, as shown in Figure 23.10. When all the files are highlighted, choose OK or press Enter to import them to the Corel animation.

Figure 23.10.
Choose the directory you want to save the file to, and type a name for the file. Then, choose OK or press Enter to begin saving the sequence.

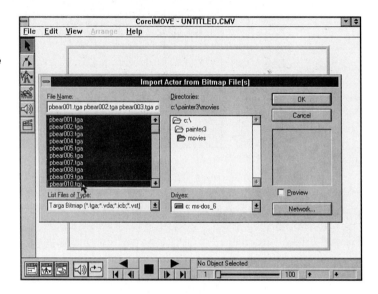

You may notice now that the animation window appears larger than the Targa files you just imported into it. To make the animation window the same size as the Targa files (320×240 pixels in the case of the PBEAR001-PBEAR020.TGA files in your screen examples), choose the Edit | Animation Info command, or use the quick-key combination of Ctrl+A. This command is shown in Figure 23.11.

The Animation Information box appears. (See Figure 23.12.) In this box, you can adjust the animation window size by entering the appropriate dimensions in the Window Width and Height box. For this example, 320 was entered as the Width, and 240 was entered as the height. These dimensions agree with the resolution of the original Targa files loaded in. Click OK to apply the new size to the animation window, and you see the window resize.

Figure 23.11.
Adjust the animation
size with the Edit |
Animation Info
command.

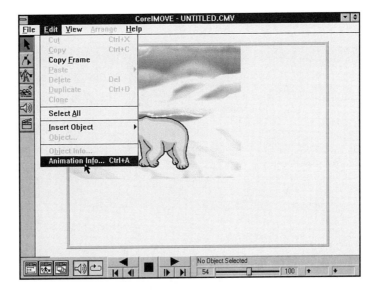

Figure 23.12.
The new height and
width dimensions are
typed in the Window
Height and Width
boxes.

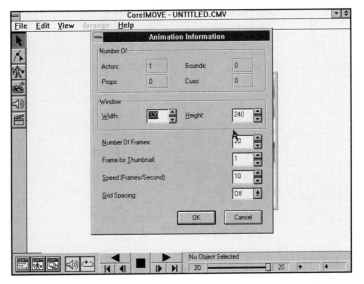

Now that the Targa Files have been imported into CorelMOVE and the animation window is set to the correct size, you need to export it to one of the formats supported by CorelMOVE. To export the file, choose the File | Export | to Movie command, located as shown in Figure 23.13.

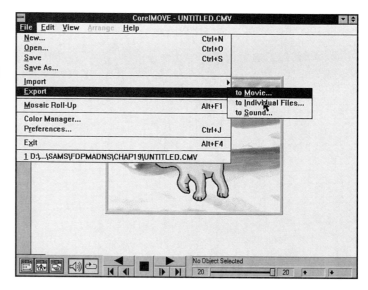

Figure 23.13.
To export the Targa
Files to another
animation format,
choose the File | Export
| to Movie command.

When the Export to Movie dialog box appears, click the List Files of Type drop-down box to choose the format into which you want to save the Targa files. (See Figure 23.14.) Notice that besides Video for Windows and QuickTime for Windows, you can also save to MPEG movies and two other Mac animation formats: PICS animation and Mac Pict Images. For this example, I selected the QuickTime for Windows (*.mov) format. There are no compression options available when selecting QuickTime format. After you type a name in the File Name box and choose the directory you would like to save the QuickTime animation to, you click OK or press the Enter key and the file is saved to the chosen directory. Though the file size is roughly twice that of the Video for Windows .AVI file generated from the same source, the quality is excellent and the playback is very fast and smooth.

You can also use CorelMOVE to convert many types of animations into individually numbered files. The types of animation files that CorelMOVE imports are as follows: Video for Windows .AVI, Autodesk .FLI and .FLC, CorelMOVE .CMV, Promotion animation MWF, MPEG Movie .MPG, QuickTime for Windows .MOV, Mac PICS Animation .PCS, and Mac Pict Images with .PCT extension. This means that animations created in any of the previous formats can be saved as individually numbered Targa files, and then imported into Painter for editing.

For informational purposes, Figure 23.15 shows the file formats that CorelMOVE can save individually numbered files into. These formats are Windows Bitmaps (.BMP, .DIB, and .RLE), CompuServe Bitmaps (.GIF), JPEG Bitmaps (.JPG, .JFF, .JFT, and .CMP), OS/2 Bitmaps (.BMP), PC Paintbrush (.PCX), Targa Bitmap (.TGA, .VDA, .ICB, and .VST), and TIFF Bitmap (.TIF).

Figure 23.14.
Choose a drive,
directory, and file
format, and name the
animation in the Export
to Movie dialog box.

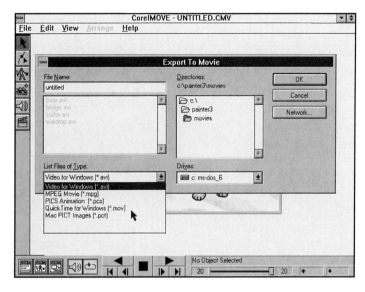

Figure 23.15.
CorelMOVE can also
save to individually
numbered files in a
number of different file
formats.

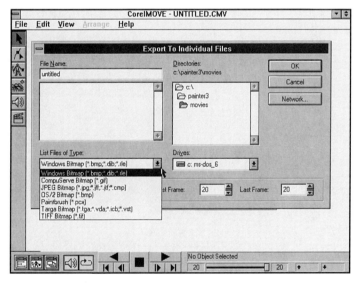

Chapter 21, "Integrating with CorelDRAW!," discusses other ways in which
CorelDRAW! and Fractal Design Painter can complement each other.

Using Autodesk Animator Pro to Convert to FLC Animations

The Autodesk family of multimedia animation products are well known for their
quality and production value, and have since become a standard Windows
animation format supported by many multimedia authoring and development

programs. Animator Pro is a DOS-based, two-dimensional animation program that enables you to generate 256-color animation files in any resolution supported by your VESA-compatible VGA card. VESA drivers are provided with the software package.

One of Animator Pro's strengths lies in its proprietary scripting language called POCO, which is somewhat a subset of the C programming language. With POCO routines, Animator Pro can be programmed to do advanced tasks automatically. One of the POCO routines furnished with the software is called NUMPIC. This routine enables you to import and export numbered files to and from the Autodesk animation format.

To convert a series of Targa files using Animator Pro's NUMPIC routine, choose the Poco | Numpic command, as shown in Figure 23.16.

Figure 23.16.
The POCO | Numpic command enables you to convert numbered files into an animation.

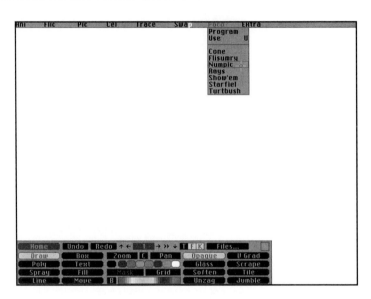

After choosing this command, the Convert Between Flic and Pictures dialog box appears. (See Figure 23.17.) From this dialog box, choose Option 2, Load Pics as Flic.

Figure 23.17.
Choose to Load Pics as Flic.

A dialog box appears, prompting you to choose the base name of the numbered pictures (see Figure 23.18). Locate the directory in which your numbered files appear by either typing the directory in the Dir: box, or by clicking the drive letter boxes to the right of the file list window. Then click the first filename in the sequence from the file list box. The POCO routine then scans for all subsequently numbered files and determines how many files are in the sequence.

Figure 23.18.
Choose the first file
in the numbered
sequence from the file
list box.

The POCO routine informs you of the number of pictures it has found in the sequence. You then choose one of four loading options, as shown in Figure 23.19.

Figure 23.19.
You can choose one of
four loading options for
the numbered files.

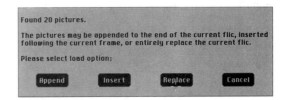

Append: Inserts the numbered files at the end of the currently loaded animation. Because you currently have a one-frame animation created (the blank frame on your screen counts as the first frame), the numbered files will begin loading at frame 2 of the animation.

Insert: Inserts the numbered files after the current frame of the animation. Again in the example, the numbered files will start loading on frame 2 if this option is selected.

Replace: Replaces all frames of the current animation with the imported numbered files. This is the option you should select at this time.

Cancel: Leaves the dialog box and aborts the POCO routine.

Click Replace to load the numbered files in as an animation. You then see another dialog box that asks whether you want to force the flic size to the picture size, as shown in Figure 23.20. You would answer No to this question if all the Targa files were different sizes. Because all of the Targa files in the sequence are the same size, and you want to create an animation that is the same size as the files, choose Yes in response to this dialog box.

Figure 23.20.
Choose to force the
animation size to the
size of the incoming
pictures.

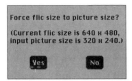

The Targa files created in Painter are in 24-bit true color resolution. Autodesk
animations can be a maximum of 256-colors. To achieve the best color palette
possible for the animation, choose Option 4 from the Color Handling Options for
RGB Pictures dialog box, which appears next and is shown in Figure 23.21. You
can experiment with the other options if you would like to compare the results.

Figure 23.21.
Choose to load the
Targa Images with the
256-color handling
option.

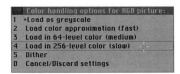

After this final option is selected, the POCO routine loads each file individually.
When the POCO routine is finished, all of the files will be contained in one
animation file. You can click the Exit menu option at this time to leave the
POCO routine. (See Figure 23.22.)

Figure 23.22.
Exit the POCO routine
after all files have been
loaded into the
animation.

You can examine the file size of the animation by clicking the Extra | Info
command, shown in Figure 23.23.

Figure 23.24 shows the information obtained with the Extra | Info command.
The first line shows your available free memory and the size of the largest
available block of memory. The second line shows how much RAM is required
to update the information in the current frame. The third line shows how much
additional RAM is required to process the changes in the next frame of the
animation. The fourth line shows how much RAM is required to process the
changes in all frames of the animation. This figure is relatively close to the total

size of the animation. In addition, the fourth line shows the average amount of RAM required to process each frame, which is obtained by dividing the total updates by the number of frames in the animation. Finally, the last line tells you the resolution of the animation.

Figure 23.23.
Information about the
animation is displayed
when you click the
Extra | Info command.

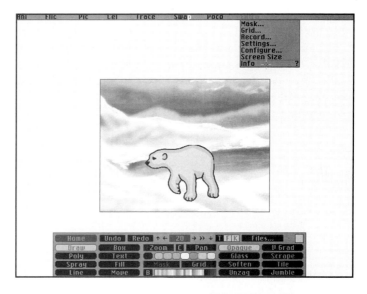

Figure 23.24.
The Extra | Info
command informs
you of the memory
requirements for the
animation.

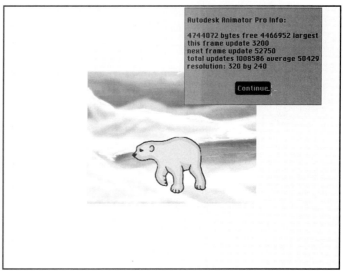

You can reduce the memory size of the animation by performing one additional step. Animator Pro contains some powerful palette manipulation tools in its Palette menu. Here, colors can be cut and pasted between palettes, rearranged into gradients of several types, and other powerful features. But one of the strongest features is the capability to generate a single optimum palette from a series of images.

> **NOTE** When the Targa files were imported, each frame was given its own 256-color palette. As a result, each frame of the animation has a slightly different palette, which adds to the overall size of the animation. The size of the animation can be reduced by determining the best single palette for all the frames, and then pasting that optimum palette into each frame of the animation. This can be done by accessing the Palette menu with the Ani | Palette command, shown in Figure 23.25.

Figure 23.25.
You can create a single palette to be pasted into every frame of the animation by accessing the Palette menu.

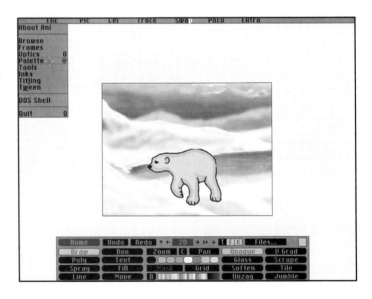

To generate a single palette, choose the Palette | One Palette command, as shown in Figure 23.26.

After you choose the command, Animator Pro confirms whether you want to proceed with creating a single palette. This confirmation is shown in Figure 23.27. Answer Yes here to generate the single palette.

Figure 23.26.
One palette can be created by choosing the Palette | One Palette command as shown here.

Figure 23.27.
Answer Yes to confirm that you want to generate a single palette for the animation.

Animator Pro examines each frame of the animation and counts the total number of colors contained in the animation. Then, it determines the best 256 colors to place in the palette, after which it pastes the new palette into each individual frame. The cursor is returned to the screen when the process is done.

You can exit the Palette Menu by right-clicking the mouse. Now, if you reexamine the total updates figure with the Extra | Info command, you see that the size of the animation is reduced from the previous example, as shown in Figure 23.28.

Figure 23.28.
The size of the animation is now reduced after creating a single palette.

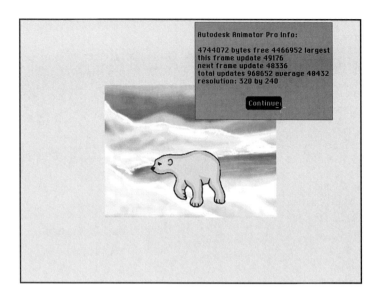

Finally, save the animation to your hard disk with the Flic | Files command, shown in Figure 23.29.

Figure 23.29.
The Flic | Files command lets you save the animation to your hard disk.

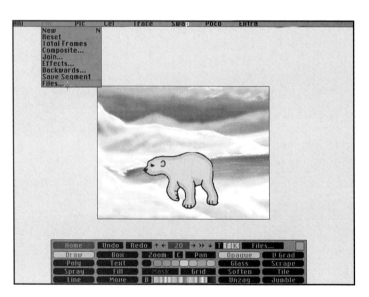

Another dialog box appears. (See Figure 23.30.) Here, make sure the Flic button is highlighted on the right half of the dialog box, and click the Save button.

Figure 23.30.
Verify that the Flic
button is highlighted
on the right and click
Save to save the
animation.

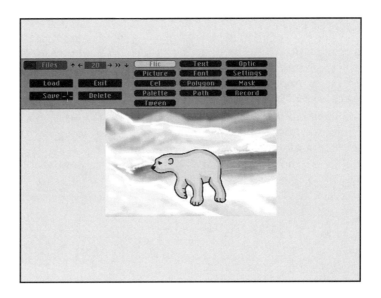

Choose the directory you want to save the animation to and type a name in the File: box at the upper-right corner of the screen. Then click the Save button to save the animation to disk, as shown in Figure 23.31. Your file is then saved to your hard drive. In this example, I named the file POLBEAR.FLC. This animation can be found on the CD accompanying this book.

Figure 23.31.
Enter a name for the
animation and click the
Save button.

Summary

In this chapter, you learned a bit more about some of the other animation formats available for the PC, and how to convert Painter movies to two other formats supported by Windows multimedia. The next few chapters discuss several programs that will enhance your exploration into computer animation. You'll learn about using morphing programs for special effects, how to integrate sound into your animation with Video for Windows and other similar tools, and how animation programs such as Animator Pro, Caligari trueSpace, and 3D Studio can make animation easier. Enjoy your venture into the world of animation!

24

Using Morphing Programs for Special Effects

Morphing—the process of transforming an image or a series of images over a range of frames—is one of several popular special effects used in computer animation today. Without a doubt, the king of the hill in regards to morphing and special effect software is Elastic Reality, by Elastic Reality, Inc. (formerly ASDG). This software program is available in Windows, Windows NT, Macintosh, and SGI platforms. You've seen the effects of Elastic Reality in major motion pictures, television shows, videos, and commercials. The combination of conventional graphics tools, slick rendering options, and fast rendering speed make this program a tool of choice for many animation professionals. This chapter gives you an overview of some of the key capabilities of the Elastic Reality (ER) package.

What Is Elastic Reality?

Elastic Reality is a professional special-effects program that enables you to create warps, morphs, mattes, composite images or animations, and transitional effects. Unlike many morphing programs that use grids to define warping areas, Elastic Reality uses shapes drawn in freehand or Bézier curve mode to identify areas. Starting and ending shapes are then joined together and linked with correspondence points so that the shapes *tween* smoothly from the starting and ending images in shape, position, and color. These shapes can even be warped and moved in separate layers, allowing you to overlap areas during the morphing process. Morphs can be applied to a single image (called a *warp* in this instance), two different images, or two different series of images, allowing you to apply these special effects to moving objects as well.

The TransJammer application furnished with the Elastic Reality package provides many transitional wipes and effects to add to your animation projects. This application also can be used to link several smaller warps and morphs together as one animation. TransJammer was bundled with earlier versions of Elastic Reality, but at time of publication it had been released as a separate product with additional transitional effects.

Before going further into the heart of the program, I'll define some of the terminology. Basically, Elastic Reality can help you with the following types of effects:

- **Warps** stretch, distort, and reshape a single image, making it appear animated. This effect works with a single image. You create shapes that identify how the image is to be distorted. For example, you can turn a smile into a frown, make a nose grow, or make eyes open wider.

- **Morphs** work with two images or two image sequences. They typically transform one object into another completely different object. You've probably seen many examples of this in motion pictures—humans changing into animals, faces changing into monstrous distortions, or balloons changing into machine guns. These are all examples of morphs.

- **Animation** can be added to single images, or to help create the in-betweens for a starting and ending image.

- **Composites** are images that are made of pieces from other images. Painter is a fine compositing tool, but Elastic Reality might help you composite animations more quickly.

- **Mattes** define which areas of an image or series of images will be opaque or transparent when you combine them, similar to the function of Painter's masking layers.

- **Transitions** perform wipes, dissolves, fades, and other fancy transitional effects between one image and another. Transitional effects are performed under the TransJammer application provided with Elastic Reality.

How Are They Done?

You may be familiar with some morphing programs already. Many morphing programs work with a grid-based approach to identify how an image is to be stretched and reshaped. This sometimes provides unpredictable results, and can be difficult to master.

Single Image Warps

To begin a warp in Elastic Reality, load an image into the A Image Roll, as shown in Figure 24.1.

Figure 24.1.
To begin a warp, load
an image into Elastic
Reality's A-Roll.

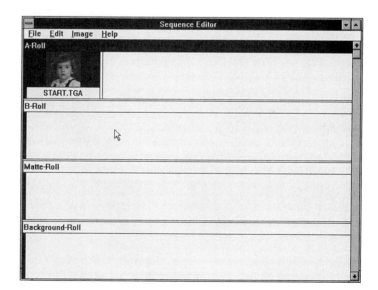

The next step is to identify the starting and ending shapes of the warp. Figure 24.2 shows some shapes created and a preview of the ending result. Notice that two shapes—the starting shape and the ending shape—are defined for each eye. The same is true for the mouth. The lines around the face and the nose act as barriers so that these areas won't be distorted during the warping process.

Figure 24.2.
Starting and ending shapes, as well as barrier shapes, are created with Elastic Reality's drawing tools.

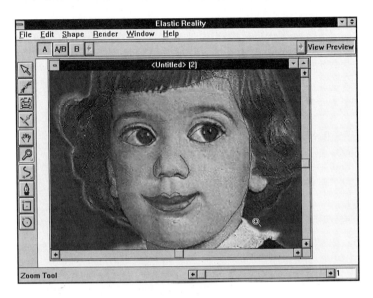

With Elastic Reality, these areas are identified when you draw outline shapes around them. This can be compared to creating paths in Painter. (If you know how to do that, you already know how to create the starting and ending shapes in Elastic Reality!) These shapes can be drawn using ER's freehand Pen tool, or with the Bézier curve tool. Closed shapes are necessary for defining areas to be masked, or to control transparency levels as the images are processed. Open shapes can be used to define items like expression lines in a face (frown lines, wrinkles, and dimples) and other areas that would be difficult to identify with closed shapes. Besides identifying areas to be warped or morphed, shapes also act as barriers to prevent warping or morphing from extending into certain areas in your projects. Additionally, shapes can be grouped so that different parameters can be applied. Some shapes can warp or morph more quickly or slowly than others, for example.

Once the shapes have been created, you must create links between the shapes. The program needs this information in order to calculate the transitions. With warps, shapes are joined together in the same image roll. The process for joining shapes is discussed in more detail in the morphing steps, which follow.

When a shape is created in Elastic Reality, it is initially given four *correspondence points*. These points identify key areas that, when connected with those of another shape, control the behavior of the tweens. The location of correspondence points can be moved to appear in appropriate locations within each shape. For example, if you are morphing a smiling mouth into a frowning mouth, correspondence points would be placed at the corners of each mouth (among other locations). This keeps the corners of the mouth in track during the tween. Complex shapes will undoubtedly require more than four of these points, and they can be added easily.

Once shapes are linked and their correspondence points are defined and adjusted, the next step is to render the sequence. There are a range of options available: The animation can be rendered to a series of individual frames, to various animation formats.

Morphing Still Images

You can use morphing to gradually change one image into another image and save the results as an animation file. Morphing is what Elastic Reality is all about. Figure 24.3 shows two images that have been prepared in Painter to be used for a morphing sequence.

Figure 24.3.
Two images chosen for a morphing sequence were prepared in Painter.

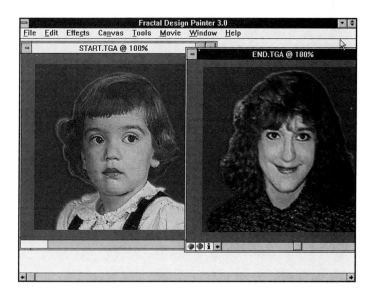

The morphing process is similar to that of warping, except that a starting image or series of frames is loaded into the A-Roll, and the ending image or series of frames is loaded into the B-Roll, as shown in Figure 24.4. If you want to add a matte or a background image to the project, you can load them into their respective rolls.

Figure 24.4.
A starting image is
loaded into the A-Roll,
and an ending image is
loaded into the B-Roll.

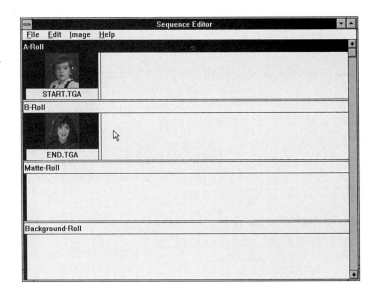

When working with morphs, starting shapes are identified in the A-Roll as red outlines. Figure 24.5 shows an A-Roll image with shapes defined for the hair, facial features, and neck areas.

Figure 24.5.
The A-Roll shapes are
defined and are
indicated by red lines
in the A-Roll image.

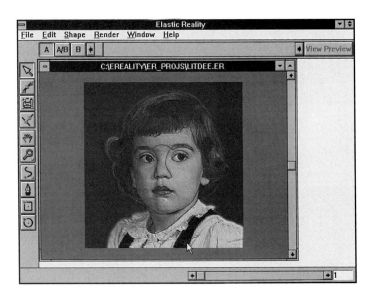

Ending shapes are created in the B-Roll image and are identified with blue lines. In Figure 24.6, the same areas (hair, facial features, and neck) have been defined for the ending image.

Figure 24.6.
The ending shapes
have been defined in
the B-Roll image and
are indicated by blue
lines.

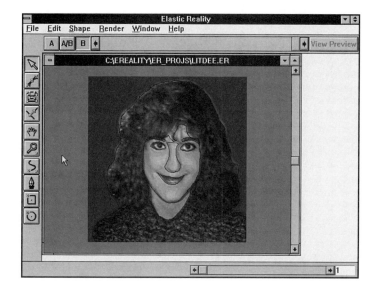

To link objects from one image into the other, you enter into the A/B Roll view mode. Then, two shapes are selected with the Pick tool—with the starting shape selected first and the ending shape selected second. These shapes are joined together with the Shape | Join command.

To adjust the correspondence points, click a joined pair of shapes and then click the Correspondence tool. A preview of how the transition will be rendered appears on-screen, as shown in Figure 24.7. The dotted lines indicate the paths of the links, and the larger squares indicate the correspondence points of the shapes. For the eyes, four correspondence points (the default value) appear for each eye. Notice that correspondence points are located in the corners of each eye, because this is a very important key point to maintain proper shaping of the eyes during their transitions.

More complex shapes require more than four correspondence points. For example, the nose has more than 10 correspondence points that were added to ensure that the areas of the nose stayed aligned properly during the morph. This can be seen in Figure 24.8.

You also can define areas that are to remain unchanged in both images. These shapes can be placed in the A/B Roll; in other words, they will appear in both images. These shapes will appear within purple outlines. One important point to remember when creating shapes is that the edges of shapes cannot cross or overlap each other in a roll.

Figure 24.7.
For morphs, shapes are
joined and their
correspondence points
set in the A/B Roll
viewing mode.

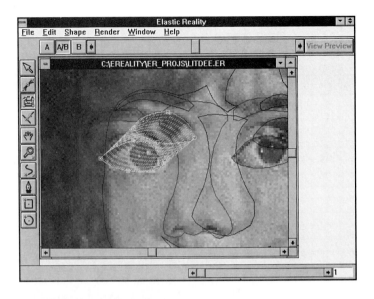

Figure 24.8.
More complex objects
require the insertion of
additional correspon-
dence points.

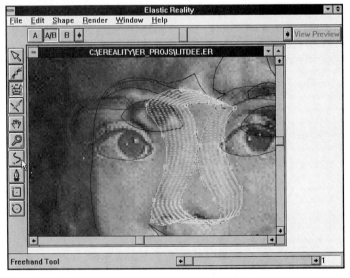

NOTE Most commonly, an A-Roll shape is joined to a B-Roll shape during morphing. But if you also want to add warps to the final animation, you can join an A-Roll shape to an A-Roll shape, or a B-Roll shape to a B-roll shape. A/B Roll shapes can be joined only to other A/B Roll shapes.

You can preview the movement of your shape transitions by choosing the Wireframe Preview command, shown in Figure 24.9. Here, you can see a wireframe image of your shapes rendered in real time. The preview can be ping-ponged so that you see your shapes change from start-to-end-to-start, repeatedly. This helps you preview your morph before it is actually rendered.

Figure 24.9.
The Wireframe Preview lets you preview the changes in your shapes before the effect is rendered.

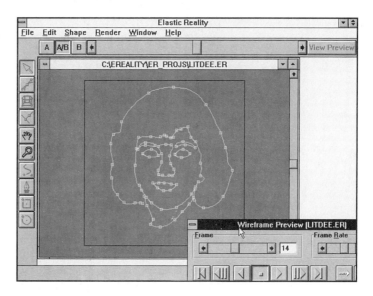

Morphing Animations

If you want to morph one animation sequence into another, such as a walking man into a walking tiger, you can employ the use of the Key Frame Control, shown in Figure 24.10. This controls the shapes over time. Here, key frames specify frames in which shape information changes. This saves you from creating shapes and their correspondence points in each frame of the animation. As mentioned, you can arrange shapes into groups, and the morphs can be applied in varying rates of speed. Groups also can be assigned to Group Depths, which places the groups into layers.

Rendering the Effect

Elastic Reality offers four types of warp styles, which are used in warping and morphing projects. You can access these styles in the Render Options dialog box, shown in Figure 24.11.

Figure 24.10.
The Key Frame Control can be used to streamline key shape definitions for morphing of animated sequences.

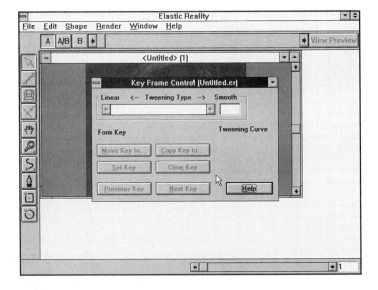

Figure 24.11.
Four different types of rendering are selectable from the Render Options dialog box.

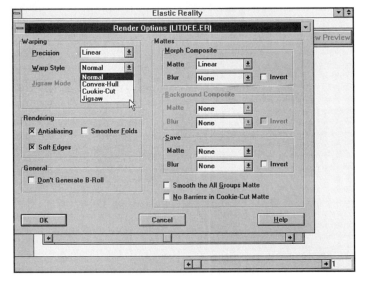

Each warp style has a slightly different purpose. The Normal style is chosen if you want to include areas near the borders of the image in your warps and morphs. Another warp style is the Convex Hull style, where the defined shapes are rubber-banded. Only the shapes defined are contained within the rubber band, and all other image data is ignored and turned to black. The Cookie Cut style warps only the closed shapes in the project; all open shapes are ignored.

This warp style can be used to remove areas from the image and turn the remaining areas to black. The Jigsaw style works similar to the Cookie Cut style, except that open shapes can be included as well. This is the style typically used when layering warps and morphs atop each other, and it can produce some very interesting results. Options also can be set for controlling matte types and transparencies.

Images can be rendered to individual bitmap files or several different animation formats. These are available in the Output Options dialog box, shown in Figure 24.12.

Figure 24.12.
You can select to
render to individual
bitmap files or to
several animation
formats in the Output
Options dialog box.

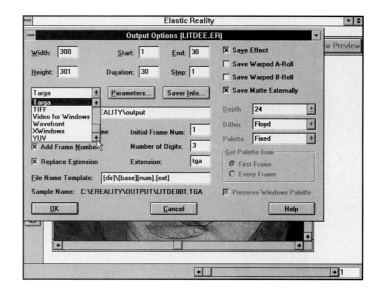

Transitions

Earlier versions of Elastic Reality include an application called TransJammer, where transitional effects can be added to your animation files. Transitional effects are typically used to change from one animation sequence or still frame to another. Rather than use the traditional fade-to-black/fade-from-black approach, TransJammer offers dynamic ways of transitioning between two portions of an animation sequence. There are crossfades, shape transitions, wipes, blends, and some truly unusual transitions, such as Balloon Pop (shown in Figure 24.13). Each effect is described in the main screen, and you are informed if the effects require A-Roll, B-Roll, and background images—or a combination. These effects will help save you a considerable amount of time when compared to other methods. At press time, TransJammer was available as a separate application and included many more transitional effects.

Figure 24.13.
TransJammer provides
several fancy transi-
tional effects that will
save you lots of time
and provide quality
results.

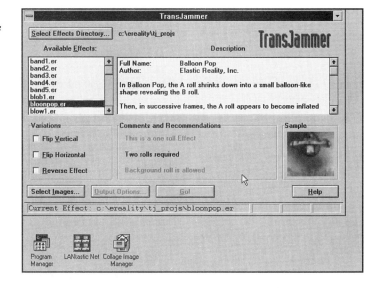

TransJammer can be used to chain several morphing or warping sequences together. One of the TransJammer effects is a pass-through, which allows you to arrange multiple AVI files in order and save them as a single AVI file. If you want to morph a cat into a dog, a dog into a whale, and then change the whale back into a cat, each morph can be prepared individually and then chained together using the pass-through effect.

Summary

This only skims the surface of what Elastic Reality can do for you. You've seen the results of this program in Hollywood productions; now you can achieve the same results on your desktop. The quality of the results are bound to amaze you!

Integrating with Video for Windows

One of the most exciting technologies available today involving animation and video editing is the capability to capture digitized video sequences and integrate the video with animation sequences. This technique, known as *rotoscoping,* can be accomplished in a number of ways. One method is to capture video on a frame-by-frame basis, using prosumer or professional-grade, frame-accurate video decks. This method provides excellent results, but can be time-consuming and expensive. Another method is to capture video in real time using a video capture board. Using this method, video is captured more quickly, but different results are to be expected depending on the capabilities of your video capture board and the speed of your computer's microprocessor. Lower-priced video capture boards might provide 15–20 frames per second of digitized video in a 320×240 window. Higher-end boards can achieve better results, even capturing full-screen video at a full 30 frames per second. Shop wisely for a video capture board; again, you get what you pay for. But be warned—you'd better have a very large hard disk with lots of free space to use this technology. Capturing video can eat up precious hard disk space very quickly!

If you have a video capture board, chances are that Microsoft Video for Windows was bundled with it. This is currently the only way that this software program is distributed. Updates to the program are available directly from Microsoft. Video for Windows is a software application that enables you to capture and edit video frames from video camera or videotape. The two main applets in the Video for Windows package are VidCap, which captures live video, and VidEdit, which enables you to cut, paste, insert, and delete movie frames or sounds into the video sequences. This chapter discusses video capture and editing using the Video for Windows tools.

The VidCap Program

The VidCap program enables you to capture video sequences from a video camera or videotape recorder/player connected to your video capture board. In order for VidCap to work, a Video for Windows-compatible video capture board must be properly installed and configured in your system. The capture driver should also be installed and set up in Windows. Instructions for configuring your video capture board's IRQ and memory base requirements should be included in your board's documentation.

If you want to capture sound along with the video but your video capture board does not include sound capture capabilities, a sound card should also be properly installed and set up to operate as a Windows sound capturing device. A sound board is not necessary to capture video, but a sound card capable of recording 16-bit, 44 kHz sound files ("CD quality") is strongly recommended.

Figure 25.1 shows the entry screen of the VidCap program. Video can be previewed in a window, the size of which is selectable in one of the Video for Windows configuration screens.

Figure 25.1.
The VidCap program is
used to capture video
sequences to your hard
disk.

Setting the VidCap Window Preferences

The VidCap Preferences dialog box, shown in Figure 25.2, is used to set some of the display preferences of the video capture window. Here, you select whether or not you want the status bar and toolbar to be displayed while capturing, and whether you want the image to be centered in the VidCap dialog box preview window. You also can select the background color of the preview window and the maximum number of frames you want to capture. This way, if you walk away from your computer, your hard drive won't be overfilled with video data. The choices here are 32,000 frames (enough for 15 minutes of captured video at 30 frames per second) or a whopping 324,000 frames (3 hours at 30 frames per second).

NOTE Most users will want to select 32,000 frames as the maximum number to capture; the latter choice is not for the faint at heart. Consider the following example, which uses the minimum options to determine the disk space required. Capturing one minute (1,800 frames) of 160×120 pixel, 8-bit (256 color) video sequence with 8-bit mono 11.25 kHz sound consumes around 23 MB of disk space. As the capture size, capture depth, and sound quality increase, the size of the capture file goes up drastically. It's a good thing that hard drive prices are going down, isn't it?

Figure 25.2.
The VidCap Preference
dialog box enables
you to select display
options for the capture
window, as well as the
maximum number of
frames you want to
capture.

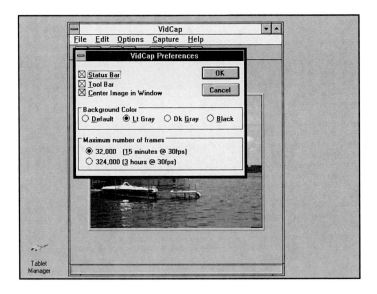

Setting the Capture Resolution

You can select the resolution of the captured video in the Video Format dialog box, shown in Figure 25.3. Here, you can select the width and height of the digitized sequence. The options might vary with different capture boards. You also can select the image format. Again, the space available on your hard disk should be considered here. Eight-bit video captures don't look as good as 24-bit captures, but they consume much less disk space.

Figure 25.3.
Video format prefer-
ences are chosen in
the Video Format
dialog box.

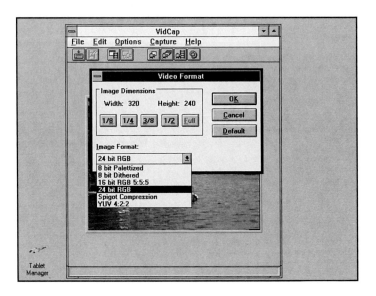

Setting the Video Source

In the Video Source dialog box, shown in Figure 25.4, you select whether your video capture source is Composite (used for most consumer-grade videotape recorder/players) or S-VHS (used for higher-end consumer or pro-sumer video sources). The Video Standard is also selected here; as the choices show, NTSC is the standard for U.S. video formats, and PAL is the standard for European formats except France, where SECAM format is the standard.

Figure 25.4.
Set the Video Source options to agree with the format of the video source from which you are capturing.

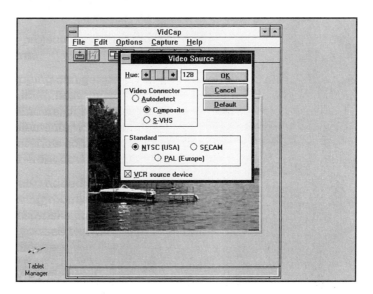

Setting the Audio Source

The Audio Source is selected in the Audio Format dialog box, shown in Figure 25.5. Here you choose between 8-bit and 16-bit sound capture, whether you want to capture the sound in mono or stereo mode, and whether you want 11 kHz, 22 kHz, or 44 kHz frequency. Naturally, the higher the numbers, the higher the quality of the sound you capture. If you have the space, select the highest option supported by your sound card. It can always be converted to a lower number during the editing process.

Figure 25.5.
Select your sound
options in the Audio
Format dialog box.

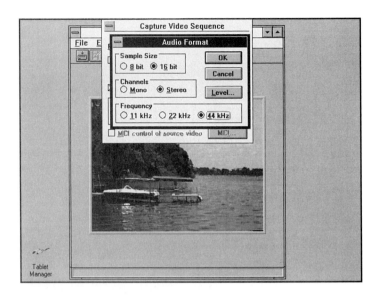

Setting a Capture File

The last step in the preparation for capturing a video sequence is to set a capture file, as shown in Figure 25.6. This capture file acts as a placeholder on your hard drive where the video data is streamed into, and should be sized sufficiently to contain the entire sequence you are attempting to capture. Before setting the capture file, you should defragment your hard drive using a hard disk defragmenting program. If you have DOS 6.0 or above, a disk defragmenting program is included as a utility. Other popular disk defragmenting programs are contained in Norton Utilities and PC Tools.

Figure 25.6.
A capture file is set up
on your hard disk to act
as a placeholder for the
video capture file.

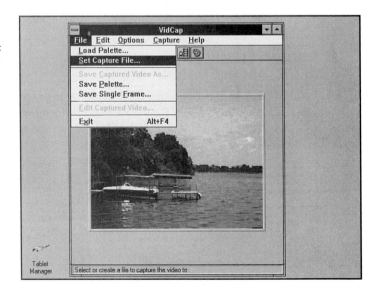

NOTE If you are using disk compression software such as Doublespace or Stacker, the video capture file should be located on an uncompressed portion of your hard drive. Capturing a video sequence to a compressed drive results in frame loss because the data is compressed as it is captured. This produces undesirable results and incomplete video captures.

After all the options are set and the video capture file is in place, all that's left to do is capture the video. The video capture process is started with the Capture Video command, shown in Figure 25.7. You can stop the capture by pressing the Esc key, after which the captured sequence appears in the VidCap window. Then you can use VidEdit to fine-tune the capture.

Figure 25.7.
The video capture
is initialized with
the Capture Video
command.

The VidEdit Program

The VidEdit program is used to edit your captured video sequences. Here, movies can be combined, rearranged, enhanced with sound, and converted to a series of still images.

The File menu, shown in Figure 25.8, allows you to open an .AVI file for editing.

Figure 25.8.
The File menu is used
to open or save files in a
variety of formats.

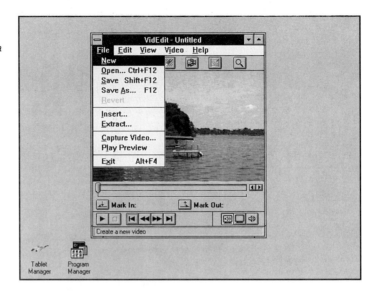

You also can import files into other animation formats, or select a sound file to be incorporated into the animation with the Insert command. After this command is chosen, the Insert File dialog box, shown in Figure 25.9, appears. Notice that a variety of file types are available here—animation formats, .DIB (bitmap) sequences for importing numbered files, and a variety of sound file formats. To insert a sound at a particular location, you can advance to the frame at which you want the sound effect to start and then insert a sound file starting from that point.

Figure 25.9.
A variety of animation,
bitmap, and sound files
can be brought into the
movie with the Insert
File command.

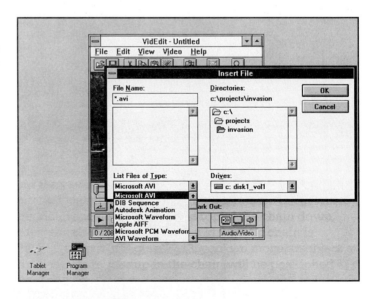

Frames can be cut and deleted from the video sequence as well. To select a range of frames, position the slider at the starting point of the area you want to cut. Then click the Mark In button, located at the bottom of the VidEdit window. Position the slider so that the last frame you want to select appears in the VidEdit window, and press the Mark Out button. This identifies a range of frames that you can cut or copy into the Clipboard, extract to another file, or delete from the video sequence completely. Sequences placed in the Clipboard can then be pasted into another area of the same sequence.

The Video menu, shown in Figure 25.10, is where compression options can be selected. As mentioned in previous chapters, compression methods vary in quality. If you intend to add further enhancements to the video in Painter, it is best to choose the Full Frames - Uncompressed method of saving to an .AVI file. You also can save the video capture to individual bitmap files using the File | Extract command.

Figure 25.10.
File compression
options are selected in
the Video menu before
compressing the
captured video.

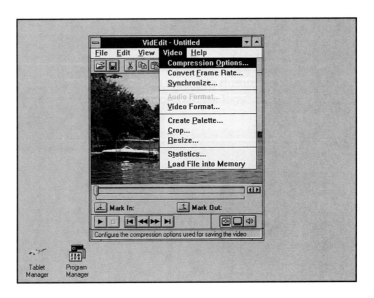

The Video menu provides other features as well. The frame rate can be converted so that the compressed video sequence plays better on slower computers. You also can generate a 256-color palette that can be pasted back into the .AVI sequence if your movie is destined for games or multimedia applications. A 236-color option also exists, which includes the 20 standard Windows system colors in the .AVI file, leaving 236 optimum colors for the movie file itself. This prevents conflicts with the Windows interface colors and maintains the integrity of the interface displays.

Summary

Video for Windows offers you a good introduction to the world of digitized video. More and more video capture programs are available that allow for more sophisticated video capture and editing techniques. If you are new to this area, I heartily recommend *PC Video Madness* by Ron Wodaski, also published by Sams Publishing. This book goes into the hows and whys of video capture from start to finish, and also gives a great overview of many capture boards available. This book also compares the various video compression formats, allowing you to view the comparisons and test their performance on your system.

26

Integrating with Animator Pro

Autodesk Animator Pro is a DOS-based, two-dimensional, 256-color animation program that packs a lot of punch. Its wealth of animation tools and effects, along with its strong palette manipulation tools, have established the program as a strong leader in the animation market. The animations are resolution-independent; that is, you can create an animation that is limited in size only by the video board in your computer. If your video board supports 1280×1024 in 256 colors, your animation can be developed in that resolution. VESA drivers, provided with the software, or VESA-compatible cards are required for resolutions higher than 320×200.

There are some advantages to creating 256-color animations, especially if they are destined for games or multimedia. Many multimedia programs require the use of 256-color graphics. Additionally, currently 256-color games are the norm. When developing multimedia or game applications, one has to consider the types of systems that will run the applications. Power users might think it common to have 486 and higher computers with 16 MB or more of memory and true-color video boards; but the architecture of the average home computer is more like a 386-based computer with 4 to 8 MB of memory and a maximum of 256 colors.

Animations in this resolution also require far less hard drive space during development. The final size of the animation discussed in this chapter is 2,954,464 bytes. This is due to the fact that Animator Pro stores only the pixel changes, or pixel updates, from one frame to the next when creating the animation. Compare this to nearly 40 MB when the animation was converted to individual 256-color .PCX files, and exceeding 200 MB when converted to 200 24-bit Targa files or to a Painter movie.

The disadvantage, of course, is the color limitation. It takes some fancy color shuffling to create an ideal 256-color palette. This is especially true for animation, where features such as motion blur and varying shadows increase the requirement for subtle color differences. It may be your preference to initially create a true-color animation in Painter and then convert it to 256 colors using methods similar to those discussed in Chapter 23. However, you can still take advantage of Animator Pro's tweening and optic features for developing outline work that can be imported into Painter as numbered files.

An Overview of Some of Animator Pro's Features

To give you an idea of some of the capabilities of Animator Pro, I'll give you an overview of the steps used to create a simple 200-frame animation using some of the program's key features.

The animation depicts an abstract fractal-type tree growing in a hilly landscape. After the tree grows from the ground, flowers and more branches bloom. An animated shadow grows along with the tree on the grass. Then a couple of cartoon birds fly from the left to the right side of the screen. Using Animator Pro, this 200-frame animation was created in about an hour and a half, including the note taking! Figure 26.1 shows one of the frames from this animation.

Figure 26.1.
This 200-frame animation was created in no time using Animator Pro's animation features.

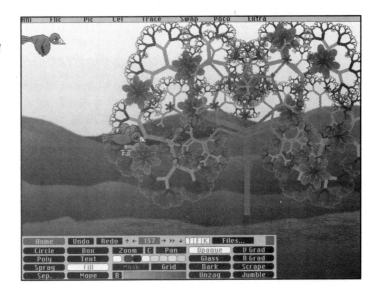

Creating the Flower

I began by creating an animated cel for the growing flower buds. The first frame was filled with white, and then the total length of the animation was increased to 25 frames. By using this method, the contents of the first frame were copied into the remaining 24 frames in a matter of seconds.

Next, I entered Animator Pro's Tween menu. Tweening is a feature that is a definite plus in an animation program. With this feature, starting and ending shapes are drawn. If necessary, key points are linked between the two shapes. Then the number of frames to be rendered are specified. Animator Pro then renders the in-between shapes automatically.

Animator Pro comes with several shapes that are tweenable, but you can also create your own and save them to disk. For our example, I chose one of the built-in shapes—the petal—as shown in Figure 26.2.

To begin, I clicked the screen at the center point of the petal and dragged the mouse out a slight distance to create a very small petal. This is shown in Figure 26.3.

Figure 26.2.
*I chose the Petal shape
as the tween shape.*

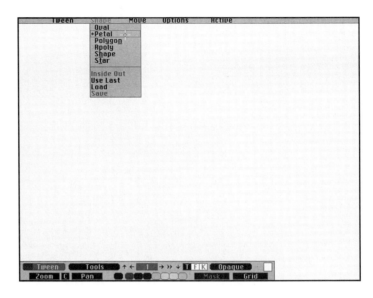

Figure 26.3.
*I drew a small petal for
the start shape.*

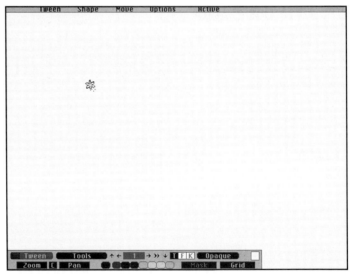

Next, I drew a larger petal for the ending tween shape, as shown in Figure 26.4. Note that unlike shapes are also used as tweens; for example, a square polygon can be tweened into a circle, a petal into a rectangle, or a star into a flower.

Figure 26.4.
I drew a larger petal for
the end shape.

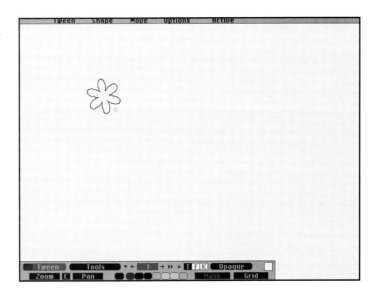

I selected a red gradient from the palette, the darkest shade first in the color series, and the lightest shade toward the end. Then I chose the center of the petal as the origin point for the gradient. The end point of the radial gradient reached just outside the outside of the large end petal shape, as shown in Figure 26.5.

Figure 26.5.
A radial gradient,
centered in the petal
and ending just outside
the end shape's
borders.

I rendered the radial gradient to each of the 25 frames, with Fill turned on. This created a solid petal with darker shades toward the center and lighter shades toward the outside. To outline the petal, I chose a light shade of red and turned the Fill off. I re-rendered the tween to the same frames, outlining the gradient petal with light red.

To create the smaller inside section of the petal, I clipped the completed petal as a cel. I chose the white background color as the Key color, making any white pixels on the screen invisible. Before applying the Cel | Clip command, I turned on the Time button on so that all non-white pixels would be clipped from each of the 25 frames, creating an animated cel.

I increased the length of the animation to 35 frames, using the Flic | Total Frames command. This copied the contents of frame 25 (the end petal shape) into frames 26 through 35. The animated cel was then rotated so that the petals of the superimposed frame covered the gaps left by the first frame. Figure 26.6 shows the first frame of the animated petal cel turned.

Figure 26.6.
The animated cel was rotated over the first so that the new petals would fill in the gaps of the first petals.

I wanted to start growing the second set of petals just before the first set was at its full size. I also wanted the second set of petals to be smaller in diameter than the first set. To accomplish this, I created a 15-frame segment in the Time Select dialog box, located in Figure 26.7, and positioned the slider such that the cel would be pasted to the last 15 frames of the animation. The first 15 frames of the original petal were superimposed over the petal already rendered on the screen.

*Figure 26.7.
The rotated cel was
rendered to a 15-frame
segment of the
animation.*

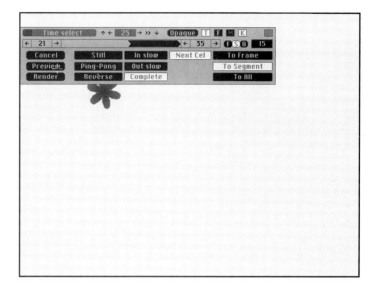

Creating the Fractal Tree

I created the fractal tree using TURTBUSH, which is one of the POCO routines furnished with Animator Pro. As mentioned in Chapter 23, POCO is Animator Pro's proprietary scripting language. Because it is a C interpreter, Animator Pro can be programmed to perform complex animation functions automatically.

I created a new animation and filled the first frame with white. I increased the length of the frame to 50 frames, copying the contents of the first white frame into the remaining 49. I applied TURTBUSH by selecting the routine from the POCO menu, as shown in Figure 26.8. The routine was rendered over all 50 frames of the animation, creating a growing fractal tree.

Using the last frame of the tree as a guide for placement, I added several of the animated flower bud cels to the tree. Recall that the final length of the animated flower bud was 35 frames. To apply the first flower, I increased the length of the tree animation by 35 frames, to 85 frames. This copied the final frame of the tree to the last 35 frames of the animation.

Then I loaded the animated flower cel into memory. I moved it to a suitable location using the Cel | Move command. Then I turned the time button on and chose the Cel | Paste command. I adjusted the segment slider so that the flower would be applied to the last 35 frames of the tree animation.

Figure 26.9 shows the first petal placed, and the process of adding the second. To offset the growth of the second flower, I increased the animation by another five frames, copying the contents of the last frame into five more frames. Then I moved the segment slider in the Frames dialog box to contain the last 35 frames in the animation. I moved the cel to a new location with the Cel | Move command. Finally, I rendered the next petal to the last 35 frames using the Cel | Paste command. The second petal started and ended its growth five frames after the growth sequence of the first petal.

Figure 26.8.
The TURTBUSH POCO routine was applied to a 50-frame animation.

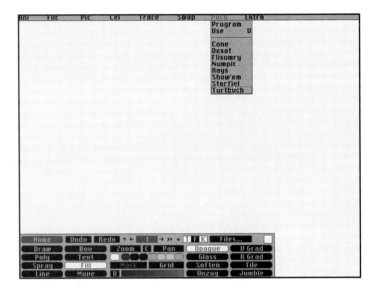

Figure 26.9.
Each petal was rendered to a 35-frame segment, following increasing the total frames of the animation by 5 to offset their growth.

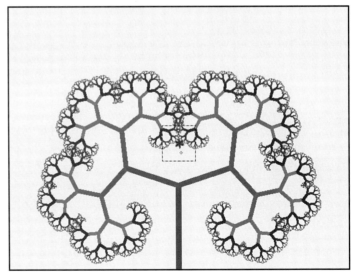

After I added 10 petals, offsetting the growth of each by 5 frames, the total length of the animation increased to 130 frames. In the Time Select dialog box, shown in Figure 26.10, I chose to clip the cel from all frames, rather than from the indicated segment. After the cel was clipped, I saved it to disk. This new animated cel was going to be used to create some smaller animated branches in the tree.

To add the branches, I increased the flic to 200 frames. This copied the contents of the final tree in bloom to 70 more frames. The segment size was increased to 130 frames in the Frames dialog box, shown in Figure 26.10, to agree with the length of the cel clipped in the previous step.

Figure 26.10.
The segment was adjusted to include all 130 frames of the animated tree cel.

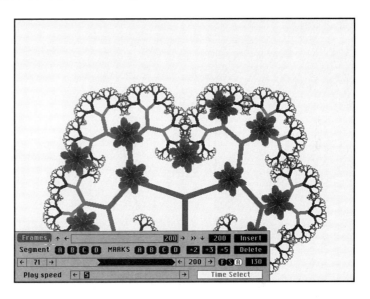

Using the Cel | Stretch command, I reduced the tree cel in size by 50% in each direction, creating a smaller version of the tree to be used as the branches. Figure 26.11 shows the outline of the reduced cel size.

Using the Cel | Turn command, I rotated the cel so that it would grow diagonally outward from the base of the tree. I moved the start point of the tree branch to the center joint of the existing tree, as shown in Figure 26.12.

Figure 26.11.
The cel was reduced in
size by 50% in each
direction.

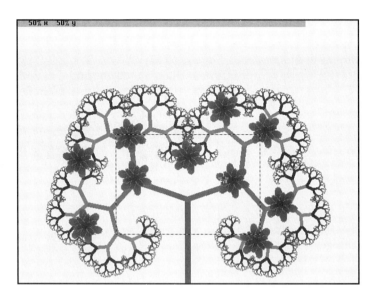

Figure 26.12.
The reduced branch
was then turned and
moved to its location.

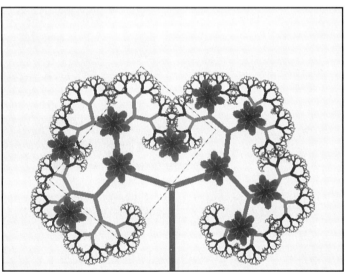

With the Time button turned on, I chose the Cel | Paste command. I adjusted the settings to render the 130-frame branch to a segment ranging from frame 71 to frame 200, as shown in Figure 26.13.

Keeping the segment settings the same, I turned the branch so that it faced the opposite side of the tree, as shown in Figure 26.14. I rendered another branch to the same range of frames as the first branch placed.

*Figure 26.13.
The animated branch
was rendered to the
last 130 frames in the
animation.*

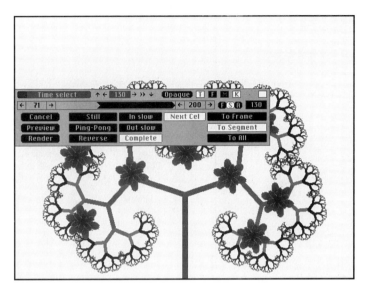

*Figure 26.14.
A second branch was
added to the same
segment.*

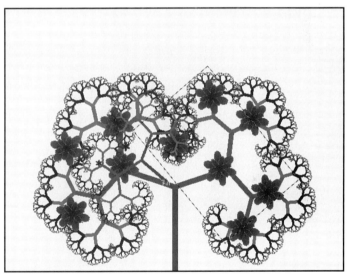

Finally, I turned the cel to a horizontal position and moved it down slightly so that some of the void in the center would be filled with another branch, as shown in Figure 26.15. Again, this was rendered to the same segment. Finally, I clipped the final tree and saved it as a 200-frame animated cel.

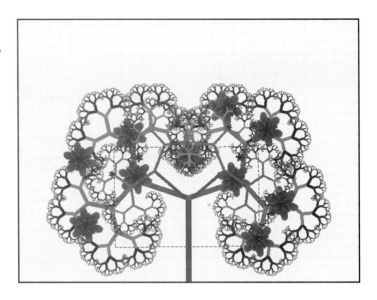

Figure 26.15.
A third branch was added to fill some of the void in the center.

Pasting the Tree Animation to a Background

I created a background image using the same palette as the tree cel. This prevented any color replacement from occurring when the cel was pasted into the background. You can go the other way as well. If, for example, you create your background image in Painter and reduce it to 256 colors, you can arrange the palette from that background into gradients with Animator Pro's palette commands. Then you can save the color palette to disk and create your petals and tree animation from that same palette. This prevents objectionable color substitutions when you merge the two together into a single animation. Later, I'll show you how to composite the tree into a background that has a different palette.

I created a new animation and loaded the background image into a single frame. Then I increased the animation to 200 frames to agree with the length of the animated tree. I loaded the cel of the completed tree into memory. I moved it off-center and pasted it into all frames, using the Cel | Paste command with the Time button turned on. This rendered the tree over the background image in all frames.

I added the shadow with 25%-strength Dark ink. First, however, I stretched the 200-frame animated cel until the X coordinate read -15. This created a narrow, mirrored version of the tree. I adjusted the position of the cel so that the base of mirrored shadow lined up with the base of the tree. I then pasted it into each frame using the Cel | Paste command. The final frame is shown in Figure 26.16.

Figure 26.16.
The animated tree cel
was pasted into a 200-
frame background
image.

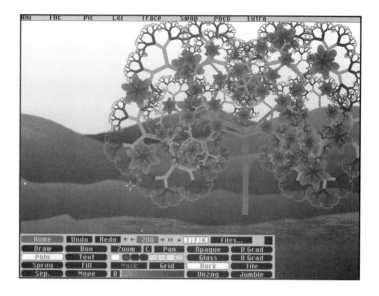

Pasting the Bird into the Animation

To create the flying bird, I used an existing cel as a guide. I drew the first frame
and repeated its contents in the second frame. The contents of the second
frame were inserted into the next frame as a Blue Frame, and then I traced the
new frame using the previous frame as a guide. After all frames were completed, I colored the frames using Animator Pro's inks and tools. After I drew
and colored the bird, I captured it as an animated cel and saved it to disk.

I loaded the bird cel into memory and, using the Cel | Move command, moved it
to its start point at the left side of the screen, as shown in Figure 26.17.

Figure 26.17.
The animated bird cel is
moved to its starting
location using the Cel |
Move command.

To create the illusion of flight, I opened Animator's Optics menu. This dialog box, shown in Figure 26.18, allows you to move objects along straight or spline paths, increase or decrease the size of objects over time, rotate, spin, and turn items, and perform combinations of any or all of the above. After accessing the menu, I clicked the screen and an outline of the bird's starting position appeared on the screen. I dragged this to the opposite side of the screen to identify its ending position, which was totally off-screen on the other side. I rendered this motion path to the last 48 frames of the animation for the first bird.

Figure 26.18.
The Optics menu allows you to move objects over time in a variety of combinations.

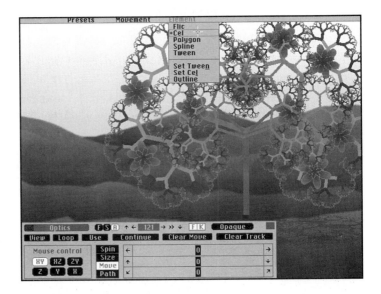

To animate the second bird, I cleared the values from the Optics menu from the first path and placed the second bird into start and end positions in a similar manner. I rendered the second bird to a 48-frame segment that started several frames before the first, making the two birds appear on screen at different times and following each other.

There are two versions of this animation on the accompanying CD. The first is the 640×480 version of the completed animation. This larger version will consume more than 200 MB of disk space if you try your hand at editing it as a 24-bit Painter movie, so I've also provided a smaller 320×240 version if you want to experiment. It can be converted to single images using any of the methods discussed in Chapter 23, "Converting to Other Animation Formats," or directly from Animator Pro, using the NUMPIC POCO routine.

Compositing Animations with Different 256-Color Palettes

Animator Pro offers a way to composite two animations that contain different palettes, using the Flic | Composite command. For this example, I composited a background created in Painter with the animated fractal tree.

To prepare for this process, I saved the animated tree as a flic. I saved it with the key color (the "invisible" color) set to the white background color. The key color is represented by the first color slot beneath the Zoom button in the center of the Animator Pro menu bar, and can be set to any color contained in the 256-color palette. Saving the animation with the proper key color is an important step when compositing flics. If I hadn't taken this step, the incoming tree would be composited over the background as a solid rectangle, filled with the white color as the background.

To start, I created a background image in Painter and converted it to 256 colors using Animator Pro's AniConvert program, furnished with the program. Then I loaded it into Animator Pro and copied it to a 200-frame animation—the same length as the animated tree. I selected Opaque ink, highlighted in Figure 26.19, before using the Flic | Composite command. Note that flics can be composited using any of Animator Pro's ink types—glass, three types of gradients, dark, and a host of others.

Figure 26.19.
Opaque ink is selected before choosing the Flic | Composite command.

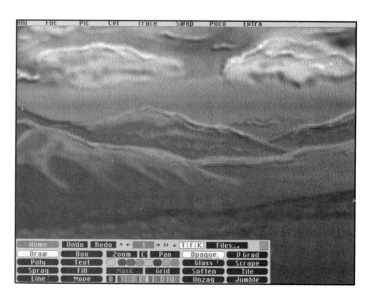

Before I composited the flic, I made Frame 1 the current frame so that the compositing would begin with that frame. Then I chose the Composite command, shown in Figure 26.20.

Figure 26.20.
The Flic | Composite command was chosen to merge the two animations together.

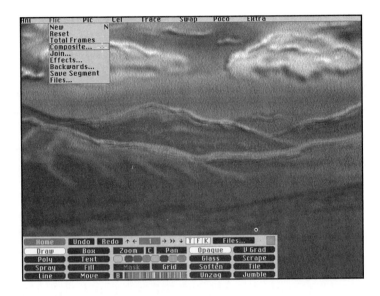

When you composite flics, you have three choices—Overlay, which composites the incoming flic over the existing one; Underlay, which composites the incoming flic beneath the existing one; and Cross-fade, which blends the two flics together. These choices are shown in Figure 26.21. For this example, I chose to overlay the tree on the background.

Figure 26.21.
Overlay was chosen as the composite method.

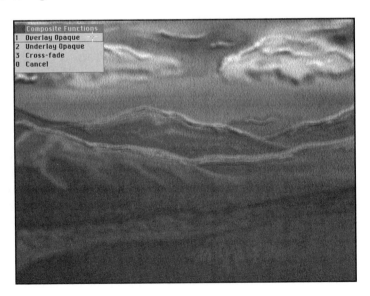

When asked how to handle the color maps, I chose to combine the two color palettes. After I verified that the compositing was to start with the current frame, the two animations were joined together. Figure 26.22 shows the result of one of the frames. If you examine the palette, you can see that it contains colors from both flics.

Figure 26.22.
The two animations are composited, and a palette containing colors from both is created in the process.

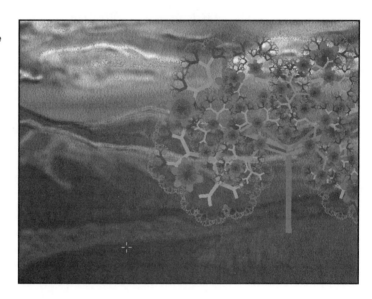

Animator Pro's Palette Tools

One of the nicest features of these tools is the capability to arrange the palette in a variety of gradients. This feature can be applied to the entire palette or to a selected range of colors from within the palette. Figure 26.23 shows the entire palette selected, and the gradient sort methods shown. Luma Sort sorts the palette by luminance, spectrum sorts the palette by hue, and gradients sorts the palette by color saturation.

You also can reduce the number of colors in an image or animation by choosing the Value | Squeeze command, shown in Figure 26.24. The palette for the image or animation can be reduced to a user-specified number of colors. This is especially handy when you composite elements or images together to create an optimum 256-color palette. You can cut and paste the values from other palettes into the free slots generated by reducing the colors.

Figure 26.23.
Animator Pro's palettes can be sorted in one of three ways.

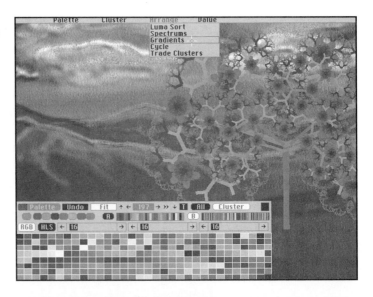

Figure 26.24.
The Value | Squeeze command allows you to reduce the number of colors contained in the palette, creating free space to combine colors from another image.

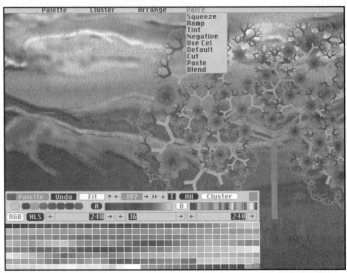

An excellent way for using this feature is to revise the palette of an animation to contain the 20 standard Windows system colors. To do this, fill an image with a gradient that contains all the colors included in the animation's 256-color palette. Then squeeze the palette for that image to 236 colors; those values are cut and pasted into a new palette in slots 10 through 245. (The first slot of the palette is considered to be slot 0.) Slots 0 through 9 would contain the first 10 Windows system colors, and slots 246 through 255 would contain the remaining

10 Windows system colors. You can cut and paste this revised palette to every frame of the animation over time, creating an animation that does not conflict with Windows system colors when played.

NOTE At press time, Autodesk began shipping Animator Studio, a 24-bit Windows 2-D animation program. In addition to offering a true-color solution to a majority of Animator Pro's capabilities, Animator Studio offers sound editing tools that allow you to synchronize animation and a soundtrack. Animation and sound files can be stretched or compressed to fit each other. Animator Studio supports masking and alpha channels, plug-in filters, and much, much more. It's a worthy successor to the very popular Animator Pro.

Summary

This is by no means a thorough overview of the features of Animator Pro, but I hope that you have an idea of some of the time-saving features it has to offer. The next chapter highlights some of the capabilities of another popular Autodesk animation package—3D Studio, a professional-grade 3-D modeling, rendering, and animation program.

Integrating with Autodesk 3D Studio

Many computer graphics artists turn to Painter to create texture maps for use in 3-D modeling and animation software. With Painter's new animation capabilities, the compatibility goes beyond texture map creation—now, Painter can be used for post-production and animation editing as well. In this chapter, I'll give you an overview of a strong leader in the world of PC-based 3-D animation programs—Autodesk 3D Studio. If you are not familiar with 3-D modeling and rendering programs, this chapter will help you visualize the basics of object creation, how materials are applied, and how to create materials for your objects.

If you're looking for a great 3-D modeling and animation program, consider Autodesk 3D Studio. This software package has been established as the leader in PC-based animation software, with good reason. The combination of features, rendering quality, and rendering speed have made 3D Studio the platform of choice for many professional animation studios and multimedia/game developers. Its capability to render animation files over a network of up to 9,999 workstations also helps cut down on production time.

Currently in its fourth release, 3D Studio is a DOS-based modeling and rendering package. A recent announcement from Autodesk has indicated that the next release will move to the Windows NT platform, which will open up enormous possibilities for program expansion and capability. If you're not familiar with 3D Studio, this chapter will give you a general overview of what the program is all about.

The 3D Studio Suite

The 3D Studio package is made up of five main modules: the 2D Shaper, the 3D Lofter, the 3D Editor, the Keyframer, and the Materials Editor. All modules work together to build and create three-dimensional scenes and objects that can be animated. Plug-in modules, called IPAS routines, are available with the software package and as third-party packages to enhance the use of the program. IPAS routines typically perform functions that automate or streamline tasks, or that add special effects or advanced modeling and animation techniques to a project. One of the most exciting IPAS routines that has been furnished with Release 4 of 3D Studio is the addition of the Inverse Kinematics Plug-in.

The 2D Shaper

The 2D Shaper is shown in Figure 27.1. This module is used to create two-dimensional views of objects. Basic shapes such as quadrilaterals, circles, ellipses, and equal-sided polygons can be created quickly and easily. More complex shapes can be created by performing Boolean operations between two shapes, by moving and adjusting vertices in the shapes already drawn, or by using the Line or Freehand tools to create linework. The 2D shaper also can use PostScript fonts as text objects. Shapes can also be imported into the 2D shaper in either .DXF or .AI (Adobe Illustrator) format.

The basic function of the 2D Shaper is to create shapes that will represent one or more views of an object, or a portion of an object. These shapes are brought into the 3D Lofter, where they are transformed into three-dimensional objects.

Figure 27.1.
The 2D Shaper is
used to create two-
dimensional shapes
that can be lofted into
3-D mesh files.

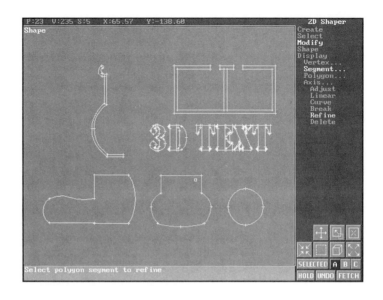

The 3D Lofter

With the 3D Lofter, two-dimensional shapes are given a third dimension. Shapes
are imported from the 2D Shaper and are lofted over a path that defines the
third dimension.

In the most basic lofting procedure, an object such as the top view of walls is
drawn in the 2D Shaper. This polygon is loaded into the 3D Lofter, as shown in
Figure 27.2.

Figure 27.2.
The two-dimensional
shape is brought into
the 3D Lofter, where
the height of the shape
is added.

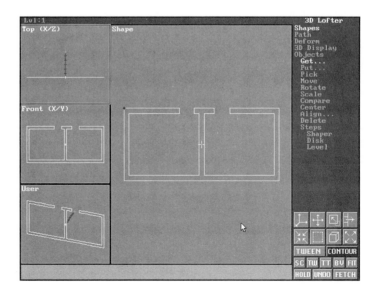

In the Lofter, the height of the walls is defined by length of the path, shown in the Top (X/Z) view in Figure 27.3. When you loft the object you add the third dimension to the walls—a finished result is shown in Figure 27.6. Before lofting, you also can assign mapping parameters to the object. These mapping parameters define how a bitmap image is wrapped onto or around the object you create. Mapping will be further discussed in the section titled "The 3D Editor".

Figure 27.3.
Mapping parameters
can be applied during
the lofting process.

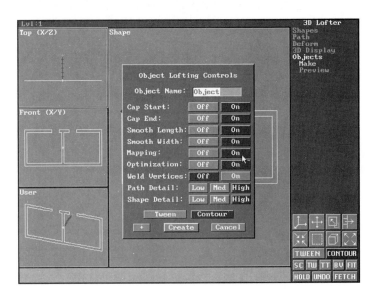

You can also modify the shape of the path to loft an object. As an example, the path can be changed to a circular shape to create a glass, a column, or a wheel. In Figure 27.4 you see a cross section of one half of a vase that was created in the 2D Shaper. That shape is imported into the Lofter and placed so that the inner edge of the shape is aligned with the center of the circular path, as shown in the Top viewport of Figure 27.4. Then, the outer edge is revolved around the path, producing an object that appears as though it was turned on a lathe. Again, you can see the finished result in Figure 27.6.

Three-dimensional paths also can be used for modeling. Paths can be created in three-dimensional CAD programs, such as AutoCAD, and imported into 3D Studio in .DXF drawing format. A good example for use of a three-dimensional path is the track of a roller coaster, where the path not only moves in direction but also moves in height. A cross-section of the roller coaster track can be modeled and centered on this three-dimensional path. After lofting, the track appears in three dimensions.

Another way to create three-dimensional shapes with the Lofter is to use the most powerful feature of this module—deforming. By using Deform, you can specify different views of an object and loft them into a three-dimensional shape. When using Deform to create 3-D meshes, one view is selected as the shape to be applied to the path. Then, either one or two additional shapes are created and assigned to the X and Y views of the object. Using Figure 27.5 as an example, a circle is defined as the shape that will be deformed to fit the other two views. The Fit Y shape is the side view of a cartoon-style foot, and the Fit X shape is the view of the foot as seen from the front. When the Deform command is applied, the circle is deformed to fit within the boundaries of the other two shapes. The result is shown in Figure 27.6.

Figure 27.4.
The SurfRev Path can
be used to create
objects that look as
though they were
lathed.

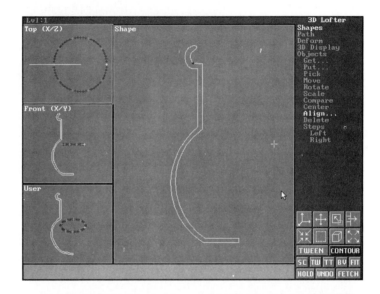

Figure 27.5.
More complex shapes
can be created using
the Deform tools in the
3D Lofter.

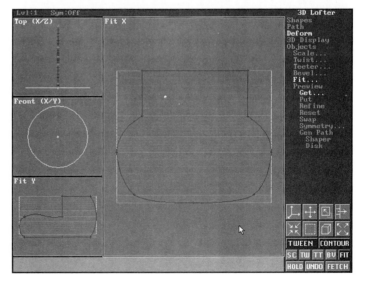

Figure 27.6.
The previous examples
after they have been
lofted.

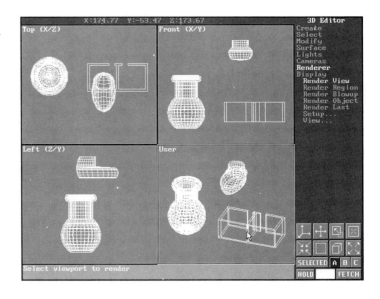

The 3D Editor

After shapes are lofted, you move to the 3D Editor to see them as three-dimensional wireframes. The 3D Editor is also where materials and mapping parameters are applied to the objects. You also can create primitive shapes such as spheres, cylinders, tubes, and boxes in this area of 3D Studio. Objects can also be joined or subtracted from one another by using the Boolean sculpting techniques provided in this module. Figure 27.7 shows some objects that have been created with more detail. All objects were created using the 2D Shaper and 3D Lofter.

Figure 27.7.
This living room scene
was created using the
2D Shaper and 3D
Lofter, and is now
ready for materials to
be applied.

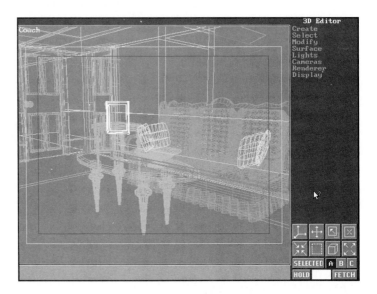

In the 3D Editor, the main focus is to assign materials and mapping parameters to objects. Here is where you build your scenes. Lights and cameras are placed in the scene to prepare it for rendering. Materials can be chosen from material libraries furnished with the program, or from libraries of materials you create yourself in the Material Editor.

If there are objects in your scene that do not have mapping applied to them (you will be notified when rendering if this is the case), you can apply mapping in one of three types in the 3D editor.

- Planar mapping applies a bitmap image to an object as a flat surface. Compare this to placing a label on a flat envelope. This flat plane is projected through the three-dimensional object until it reaches the opposite side.

- Cylindrical mapping wraps a bitmap around an object, sort of like a label on a tin can.

- Spherical mapping projects the bitmap out in all directions from the center of the mapping point.

The technicalities of mapping can get pretty involved, so I won't go into the details here. As you can imagine, things can get a little tricky if your objects aren't perfect planes, cylinders, or spheres. Mapping can be adjusted and rotated, and applied to elements within an object as necessary. It's generally a good idea to loft your materials so that mapping parameters are applied automatically—saving a lot of work down the road.

Lights and cameras are also added to the scene in the 3D Editor. These are shown placed into the living room scene in Figure 27.8. In the Top (X/Z) view, the lights are shown as asterisks. In the Camera view in the lower-right portion of the 3D Studio screen, you see two diagonal lines that indicate directions that two of the lights are shining.

There are three types of lights. Ambient light is the minimum amount of light shining in the scene. This is generally set to a low value. If it is set too high, your images will appear flat and washed out. Omni light shines in all directions and can be used in areas where spotlight placement is difficult. Spotlights cast shadow-mapped or ray-traced shadows, and also can project bitmap images much like a movie projector. The projected bitmaps can be still images or a series of moving images. Lights can be white or colored, or dim or bright. There are a lot of choices here, and lighting can be used to achieve wonderfully dramatic effects in a 3-D scene. This is one of the key areas that make a good three-dimensional image a great three-dimensional image.

One or more cameras can be placed into your scene, each providing a different view. Cameras can be rolled and dollied, and can have their fields of view and perspective adjusted. New to Release 4 is the Camera Control and Match Perspective feature, where a camera's view can be aligned with a photographic image used for a background.

Figure 27.8.
*Lights and cameras
have been placed in the
living room scene, and
materials have been
applied.*

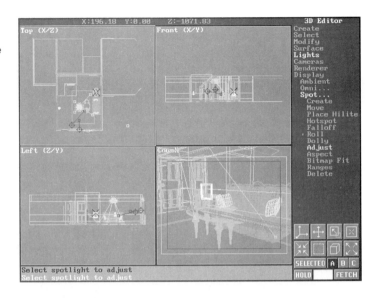

After all the materials are assigned and cameras and lights placed, you can render the scene. You can render still images from the 3D Editor, either in 256-color or true-color formats. These formats are shown in Figure 27.9. If you want to preview your scene before it is rendered, you can use the Fast Preview Plug-in that can be used from any camera viewport. This is another new feature of Release 4.

Figure 27.9.
*3D Studio can render
still images in 256-color
or true-color formats.*

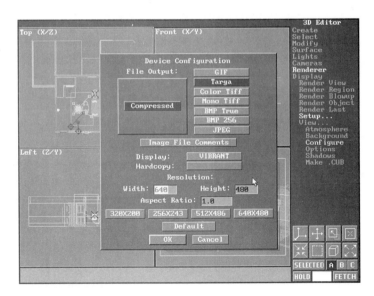

The Keyframer

The Keyframer is where motion is applied to cameras, lights, and objects in your scene. The illusion of motion can be achieved in different ways. You can move a camera within a scene, as shown in Figure 27.10, change positions of objects, or change shapes of objects with the use of morphing techniques. 3D Studio's method of morphing differs from methods used by morphing programs such as Elastic Reality, discussed in Chapter 24. Two objects containing exactly the same number of vertices must be selected to perform the morph.

Figure 27.10.
One way to animate a scene is to link a camera so that it moves along a path.

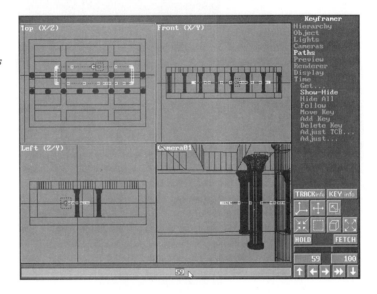

Objects in 3D Studio are frequently composed of many parts and pieces that together make up a single object. Figure 27.11 shows a human figure composed of many different parts. When applying motion to the pieces, apply hierarchical linking to define and constrain movement of objects to certain motion ranges, angles, and axes, or to move one object based on the movement of an object it is linked to.

Another feature added to Release 4 is the addition of Inverse Kinematics, which can be accessed from the Program menu, as shown in Figure 27.12.

Figure 27.11.
More complex objects are composed of many different parts that can be linked together for animation purposes.

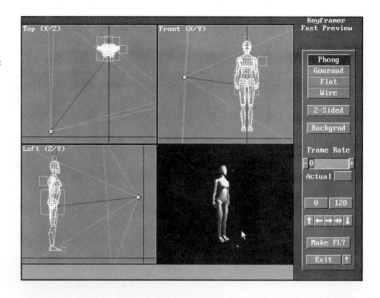

Figure 27.12.
The Inverse Kinematics IPAS, a major new feature of 3D Studio, is accessed through the Program menu.

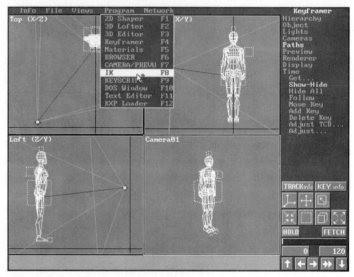

The IK Plug-in takes hierarchical linking one step further—in fact, it gives it a totally new approach. This feature is especially useful in character animation, which was formerly a very tedious process. Before implementation of this IPAS routine, objects were individually positioned from the top of the chain down. With the new Inverse Kinematics IPAS routine, once a kinematic chain is defined through the IK Plug-in, shown in Figure 27.13, you can move an object at the end of the chain, and all objects higher up in the chain will be positioned accordingly.

Figure 27.13.
Kinematic chains are
defined using the
Inverse Kinematics
dialog box.

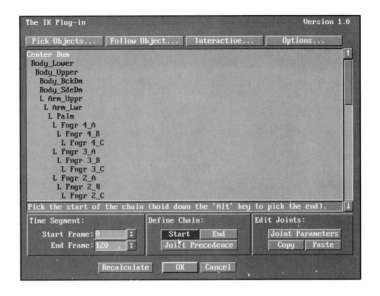

Figure 27.14 shows a preview frame of a bird that has been animated using the
Inverse Kinematics Plug-in. Its feet are linked to invisible dummy objects, and
told to follow paths. Notice that the upper portions of the legs follow automatically.

Figure 27.14.
This bird's feet are
instructed to move
along a path, and the
rest of the leg follows
appropriately.

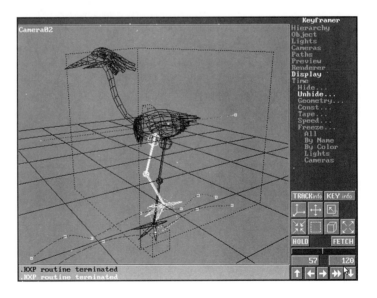

It is also through the Keyframer that the Video Post dialog box is accessed. The
Video Post dialog box, shown in Figure 27.15, is used to composite images and
objects in the keyframe scene together into a single animation.

861

Figure 27.15.
The Video Post dialog
box is used to compos-
ite images or anima-
tions.

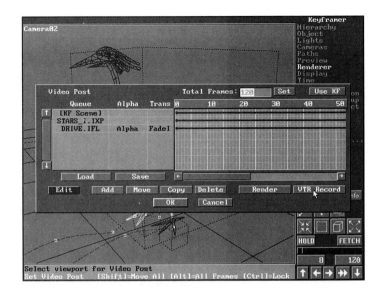

Now that you know a little bit about how scenes are built and how animations
are created, I'll explain a couple of ways that Painter images and movies can be
applied to 3D Studio.

Using the Video Post dialog box, you can easily composite your Painter animations together and render them to videotape in the process. To do this, save
your Painter animations as individually numbered Targa files and then generate
an image file list (.IFL file) in 3D Studio for each animation you want to composite. A utility, called MAKEIFL.EXE, provided with recent releases of 3D Studio
aids in creation of the .IFL files, saving you the trouble of typing in the paths
and file names of each image contained in the list. The .IFL filenames are then
entered into the Video Post dialog box in the order you want them to be
composited. Images appearing in the back layers of the composite are entered
at the top of the list, and images to be composited into the foreground are
entered below.

The Material Editor

You can select materials from the material library provided with 3D Studio, or
you can create your own material library. 3D Studio comes with a CD-ROM that
is packed with great texture maps—backgrounds, marbles, woods, wallpaper
patterns, architectural materials, animated texture maps, and more.

Chapter 22, "Using Painter for Texture Maps," discussed some ways in which
Painter could be used to create materials for 3-D rendering programs. It is in 3D
Studio's Material Editor that you turn the Painter images into materials that can
be mapped onto your 3-D objects.

There are several settings in the Material Editor, which is shown in Figure 27.16. The most basic materials consist of assigning three values of a color, labelled Ambient, Diffuse, and Specular. Generally, the Ambient color is the darkest shade of an object—that which appears in the shadows. The Diffuse color is the color of the lit portion of the object (its "real" color). The Specular color defines the color of the highlights of the object. Other properties, such as shininess, transparency, reflection blur, and amount of self-illumination (if any) can be adjusted with sliders.

Figure 27.16.
The Material Editor can be used to create textures of many types, ranging from simple to extremely complex.

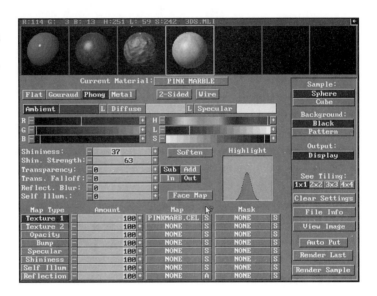

Materials can be rendered in one of four methods. Flat, the lowest level, maps material on to each face of the mesh object and performs no smoothing. This results in an object with a faceted appearance. Gouraud, the next highest level, produces a smoothly shaped object by hiding the edges of the faces that compose the geometry. Phong shading improves the smooth look of Gouraud shading by providing more detail in regards to the specular highlights of images. And finally, Metal shading, the highest level, produces a metallic effect on an object by mixing the ambient and diffuse colors of the material a bit differently. You can create wireframe materials by clicking the Wire button located at the upper center of the Material Editor window.

Using Painter Images for Texture Maps

You can assign your Painter texture maps in the bottom portion of the Material Editor screen. To assign a bitmap file to a material, click on one of the rectangles that appear beneath the Map heading at the lower portion of the screen. A dialog box appears from which you can choose a bitmap file from your hard drive. 3D Studio Release 4 will accept .TGA, .TIF, .BMP, .PCX, and .JPG images as texture maps. You can define one or two texture maps to produce a material. If two texture maps are used, the one assigned as Texture 2 takes precedence over the first.

Using Painter Movies for Texture Maps

3D Studio texture maps can be animated as well. For example, let's say that you create an animation in Painter that depicts fish swimming in a fish tank, showing the water, the fish, some plants and some bubbles. In 3D Studio, this animation can be turned into a material and mapped onto a rectangular box. You can create a Painter movie and save it as individually numbered files. Then, you generate an Image File List and assign the .IFL file as the texture map for the material.

Using Painter for Other Types of Maps

There are many other types of maps that can be used in 3D Studio as well. These materials also can be still images or animations.

- Opacity maps generate opaque and transparent areas in a material, similar to the way Painter's masking layer works. In 3D Studio, if you use an opacity map in conjunction with a texture map, you can create materials that have "holes" in them. Opacity maps should be generated in grayscale, with black identifying transparent areas and white identifying fully opaque areas. In Painter, you can generate grayscale images by choosing colors from the left side of the color triangle in the Art Materials | Colors Palette. You can also convert a color image to grayscale as discussed in Chapter 22, "Using Painter for Texture Maps."

- Bump maps add bumpiness to a material, using black or darker shades to identify receded areas and white or lighter shades to identify raised areas. Bump maps do not have to be created in grayscale, although doing so will help you visualize how the bump map will affect your material.

- Specular maps work in Phong shading mode to apply the colors of the assigned bitmap to only the specular highlights of an object. Nice colorful texture maps would work well here.

- A Shininess map varies the intensity of the specular highlights of a material based on the light intensity of the bitmap. Grayscale or color images should work for these types of maps.

- Self Illumination maps identify areas in a material that appear as though they are producing their own light.
- Reflection maps create the effect of a reflected image in an object.

Each of these map types can be applied at varying levels by adjusting the sliders in the Material Editor. Each of these map types can also be assigned its own masking images as well. There are also advanced settings for many of the material types that allow you to fine-tune the appearance of 3D Studio materials. It's a real science, and the Material Editor provides infinite possibilities in material creation.

Summary

3D Studio is a program that takes a while to master because of its bountiful supply of features. An excellent place for learning techniques from the authors and masters of this program is on CompuServe in the AMMEDIA forum. There, you can learn how to use the software from some real heavy-hitters in the animation industry. You'll also find that many 3D artists use Painter to enhance their 3D projects because of its respectable and bountiful list of features. Now, with the addition of Painter's animation capabilities, the two programs mesh together even better than before!

VI

Hardware Input and Output

28

Scanning in Painter

You might be an artist who prefers to sketch your ideas on paper first and scan them into your computer. Or, you may have taken some photos long ago that you now want to enhance with Painter. You can scan images directly from Painter using a special set of commands available in the File menu: Select TWAIN Source and TWAIN Acquire.

TWAIN is an industry-standard protocol that enables you to exchange information between scanning devices and software programs. TWAIN-compliant software, such as Painter, provides a direct link to your TWAIN-compliant scanner's interface through a special dynamic link library (DLL) located in your Windows system directory. This file, called TWAIN.DLL, is usually furnished with newer scanners. If you have a scanner but do not have TWAIN.DLL, contact your scanner manufacturer for compatibility questions and ask to obtain a copy of the appropriate driver. If you do not have a TWAIN-compliant scanner installed in your system, the scanning commands will be unavailable (grayed out) in the File menu.

Choosing Your Scanner

Scanning from within Painter is a relatively simple process. The first step is to select the scanner you want to access with the File | Select TWAIN Source command.

To select a scanner, do the following:

1. Choose File | Select TWAIN Source. This command is shown in Figure 28.1.

2. The Select Source dialog box, shown in Figure 28.2, will appear. This dialog box gives you a list of the available TWAIN-compliant scanners installed on your system. In this example, the dialog box shows the software used with the Hewlett-Packard ScanJet IIcx, which uses DeskScan II software. Highlight the scanner you want to use, and click the Select button.

Figure 28.1.
Choose the scanner you want to use with the File | Select TWAIN Source command.

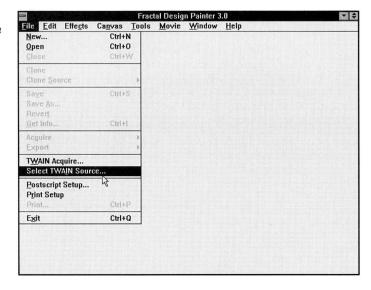

Figure 28.2.
Highlight the scanner
you want to use and
click the Select button.

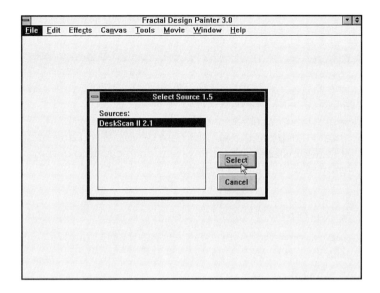

Scanning the Document

Use the File | TWAIN Acquire command to scan the document. This command will initialize your scanner interface software. After the scanning is complete, an untitled document containing the scanned image will be opened in Painter. The following example shows a document scanned with the ScanJet IIcx.

1. Choose the File | TWAIN Acquire command, as shown in Figure 28.3.
2. Your scanner interface software will be opened within Painter. With the ScanJet IIcx, the DeskScan II software appears in a dialog box within Painter, as shown in Figure 28.4.

In this case, a color photo was placed in the scanner's document area. The photo was previewed in the software when the user clicked the Preview button located at the bottom-left side of the scanner software window.

After previewing, DeskScan II determined that the best scanning option would be Sharp Millions of Colors (which can be overridden by choosing another scanning type in the Type drop-down listbox). For this example, the computer screen was selected as the Path, but other devices, such as printers and typesetting machines, can be designated as paths as well. Basically, the path chosen determines the dots per inch (dpi) resolution of the scan.

To define the area to scan, zoom in on the image with the Zoom button, shown in Figure 28.5.

Figure 28.3.
The scanning process
begins with the File |
TWAIN Acquire
command.

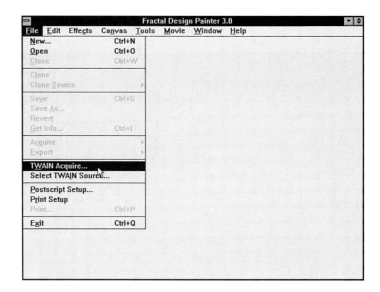

Figure 28.4.
The scanner's software
interface will appear in
a dialog box within
Painter.

The area to be scanned is defined by an adjustable rectangle. Alternatively, irregularly shaped areas can be defined with a lasso tool in the scanning software. Once the area to be scanned is defined, you can make further adjustments to the image before it is scanned. Settings such as brightness and contrast can be adjusted before scanning, with changes reflected in the preview window. In addition, you can increase or decrease the scale of the image before scanning. The final size of the document, in inches and in disk space, is displayed in the left portion of the screen. Once all settings are complete, the Final button, shown in Figure 28.6, is pressed. The document will then be scanned.

After the scan is complete, the scanner interface software dialog box will automatically close. An untitled document containing the scanned image will appear in Painter, as shown in Figure 28.7.

Figure 28.5.
Zoom in closer to better
determine the area to
be scanned.

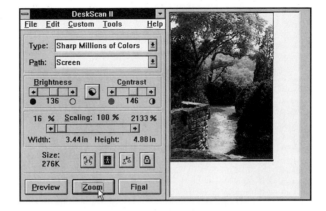

Figure 28.6.
Choose the Final
button to scan in the
document after all
settings are chosen.

Figure 28.7.
The scanned image will
appear in an untitled
document window in
Painter.

Scanning Tips

To achieve the best results when scanning images, you should consider a couple of factors. What is your final target destination—computer screen or printer? What resolution should the document be scanned at?

Scanning Resolution

Although it is true that scanning at higher resolutions produces higher-quality scans, there are cases in which scanning at higher resolutions will be a bit of overkill. For example, if your target device is a computer screen, it doesn't pay to scan an image at 300 dpi unless the original image is very small. Here's why.

If your image is destined for computer screen output—for example, a multimedia presentation or a game—the most common size of the final image is 640×480 pixels. The most common resolution to scan a document at for this target source is 75 dpi, which would display an image in its appropriate dimensions on a 14-inch computer monitor. At 75 dpi, your original image can be up to 8.53 inches wide and 6.4 inches high to properly fit within the 640×480 pixel resolution. If you increase the scanning resolution to 100 dpi, your original can be no larger than 6.4 inches wide and 4.8 inches high in order to fit on the screen. Increasing the scanning resolution to 300 dpi would mean that your original could be no larger than 2.13 inches wide and 1.6 inches high. It's hard to draw in an area that size, but larger resolutions would be more appropriate if you are scanning something small, such as a 35mm slide.

However, if your target device is a printer, your scanning resolution should be set to agree as closely as possible to the output of the printer. Here, scanning at lower resolutions will decrease the size of the printed image. For example, many printers used in home offices are designed to output 300×300 dpi. Many newer printers can go as high as 600×300 or 600×600 dpi. If images are scanned at 75 dpi for these devices, the final printout will be considerably smaller than the original.

If you are using a service bureau to do your printing for you, you should check with them to see what resolution your documents should be scanned and saved into.

Color Accuracy

To maintain color consistency between your scanner, your computer monitor, and your color printer, you can use color calibration software. This software helps minimize the differences between each step of the process. Colors scanned with a calibrated scanner will more closely match those of the original image. The image will be displayed correctly on your computer monitor if your monitor is calibrated. Also, color printouts from desktop color printers, such as those used in a home office, will be enhanced and more true to the original.

If you are using a professional printing service, you might want to check with them to see if color calibration software should be used. It's generally not a good idea to use color calibration with traditional offset printing.

Summary

Scanning images can prove to be a real time-saver for those who find it more natural to create ideas on paper first, and then color them in Painter. Having this capability also can increase your ability to use original photos and artwork as a starting point for image editing and creation. You've learned that scanning images from within Painter is very easy! Now that I've discussed inputting an image from an external device, I'll discuss how to output a Painter document to a printer. You'll find it just as easy as scanning!

29

Printing in Painter

In this chapter, I discuss printing from Painter and show some related commands that can be used during and after you create your images. I'll cover using the Printable Colors Only option while painting, and changing a document to contain only printable colors after the fact. Also, I demonstrate how to force an image to a color set that contains specific colors, such as Pantone colors, and show how to annotate the image to show the location of some of the Pantone colors.

Creating a Document for Print

If you know what size your final document has to be when printed and know the resolution in lpi (lines per inch) of the printer it will be printed on, you can create a document of the proper size using the File | New command. For example, assume you are creating an image that, when printed, will take up a rectangular area that is 4-inches wide and 2.5-inches high on the printed page. The destination printer prints at 150 lpi. As a rule, the pixels per inch resolution of your document should be twice the amount of the lpi (lines per inch) of the destination printer. In the new picture dialog box, the entries would look like those in Figure 29.1.

TIP The rule of thumb for determining your document resolution is as follows:
Printer lpi * 2 = image pixels per inch.

Figure 29.1.
Width, Height, and
Resolution information
are entered in the New
Picture dialog box.

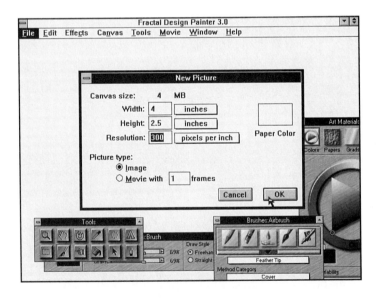

Notice that when you enter this information, the width and height entries agree with the desired image size. The units of measure, normally shown in pixels, were changed to inches from the drop-down listbox. Additionally, the Resolution figure was changed from the default of 75 to 300 pixels per inch. This is equal to twice the lpi of the destination printer.

TIP When determining file resolution, you need to consider what your final output will be. If you are sending your image to an offset printer, you should check with your printing service bureau to see what the suggested lpi will be. Use the previously stated rule of thumb to double the recommended lpi for the pixels-per-inch setting of your document.

If you're using a service bureau to print to a high-end color printer, such as an Iris print, consult with them as to the recommended pixel-per-inch setting. Iris prints can use settings of 200 to 300 pixels per inch. Note that many high-end, continuous tone color printers do not use lpi settings. Their resolutions may be given in pixels per inch; therefore, you should not double the recommended figure.

For laser and inkjet printers such as those typical for home use, a resolution setting of 150 pixels per inch is acceptable.

For Line Art, a 300-pixels-per-inch resolution is generally recommended. If you click the Information (i) button in the lower-left corner of the document window after creating the document, you will see a preview of how the image will be printed on your target printer. Also displayed will be the size of the document in pixels. In the preceding example, the document created was 1200×750 pixels. This agrees with the width (4 inches) and height (2.5 inches) multiplied by 300 pixels per inch.

TIP If you learn, after you've created your image, that it was created too small to be printed correctly, you can increase the size of the document with the Canvas | Resize command.

Painting with Printable Colors

As you create your image, there are a couple of ways that you can ensure that the image is being created with printable colors. The first method is used when selecting colors from one of Painter's color palettes.

If you maximize the Art Materials | Colors Palette, you will see the color variability sliders in the bottom section. Beneath the sliders are two checkboxes, one with the label Printable Colors Only. If you paint with this checkbox filled, as shown in Figure 29.2, the color displayed in the primary color rectangle will appear solid if the color you chose is printable, and dithered, or varying in color, if the chosen color is not printable. This dithered color display reflects how your chosen color will actually be printed. And, during this mode, your brushes will apply only printable colors to your image.

Figure 29.2.
Checking the Printable
Colors Only checkbox
in the Art Materials |
Colors Palette enables
you to paint with only
printable colors and
view how the colors
will be printed.

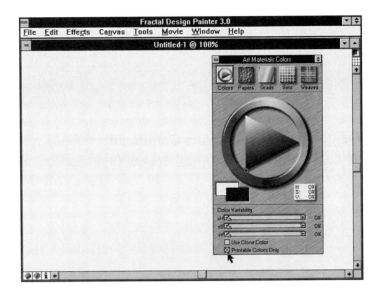

A second method of choosing only printable colors for painting is to choose colors from a color set known to contain only printable colors. For example, the PANTONE.PCS color set, furnished with Painter, is a good choice. This color set can be found in the SUPPLIES subdirectory of Painter when the program is installed. Figure 29.3 shows this color set loaded in.

Figure 29.3.
The PANTONE.PCS
color set is a good
choice for selecting and
painting with printable
colors.

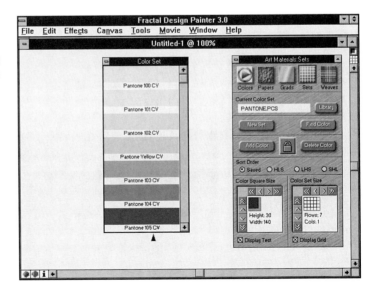

Changing an Image to Printable Colors

If you did not create your image using Printable Colors Only or want to convert an image, such as a photograph, to contain only printable colors, there are a couple of ways you can convert images. The first way is to use the Printable Colors command, located in the Effects | Tonal Control menu. The second method is to posterize your image using a color set that contains only printable colors.

Using the Printable Colors Command

You can use the Effects | Tonal Control | Printable Colors command to force the image into printable colors. This method is the preferred method for photographic, quality artwork, or art that contains very subtle transitions of color. The procedure to do this is as follows:

1. Select the portion of the image that you would like to change. If no selection is made, the effect will be applied to the entire image.

2. Choose Effects | Tonal Control | Printable Colors. You can adjust the view in the preview window by using the grabber to view the changes before the effect is applied.

3. Click OK or press Enter (Windows) or Return (Mac) to apply the command.

Figure 29.4 shows the image created in Chapter 7 with half of the image selected for the Printable Colors command. After the command was applied, there was a noticeable difference in the blue-violet and violet shades, which were more subdued in the Printable Colors version. If you want to compare the results, this file is included on the CD accompanying this book, and was saved as ENCHANT2.RIF.

Figure 29.4.
All or part of an image
can be forced to contain
only printable colors
with the Effects | Tonal
Control | Printable
Colors command.

Posterizing an Image to the Pantone Color Set

Another way to change your image to printable colors is to posterize the image using a color set that contains only printable colors. Again, the PANTONE.PCS color set is a good candidate for this. This method works best for colored line art work or areas that have stark transitions from one color to another. This procedure is accomplished as follows:

1. Open the document that you want to posterize.

2. Select an area to apply the effect. If no selection is made, the effect will be applied to the entire image.

3. Open the PANTONE.PCS Color Set. Alternatively, you can create your own color set that contains only printable colors.

4. Choose the Effects | Tonal Control | Posterize Using Color Set command, shown in Figure 29.5. After the command is applied, an information dialog box will inform you of the progress of the conversion. If your image contains many colors, this could take a while. When completed, your image will contain only colors that are included in the Pantone Color Set.

Figure 29.5.
The Posterize Using
Color Set command fits
an image to a specific
palette.

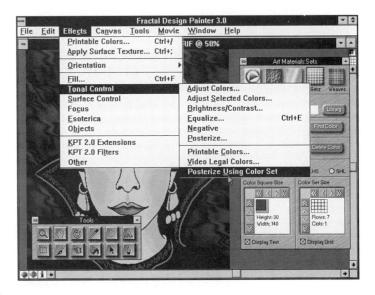

Annotating an Image

If you want to place identification labels on your image or floaters to reference the colors within, you can use the Painter's Annotate feature. This feature uses the color names assigned in the color set used to create the image to apply color labels. Because the annotations appear in a separate layer on top of the Painter document, the labels can be displayed or hidden from view by using the Canvas

View Annotations command, shown in Figure 29.6. Note that when you apply annotations to a floater, the annotations will move along with the floater if it is relocated in your image.

Figure 29.6.
The Canvas | View
Annotations command
is used to turn the
display of annotated
colors on and off.

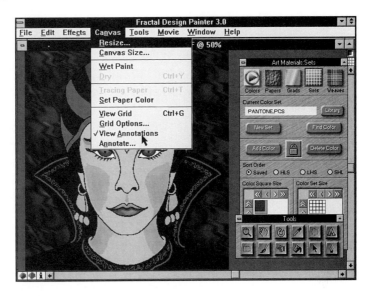

To show you an example of this, open the ENCHANT3.RIF file located in the Chapter 29 directory of the accompanying CD. This image has been posterized to the Pantone color set and already has some annotations applied. You can add more annotations by following this procedure:

1. Turn on the display of the existing annotations using the Canvas | View Annotations command.

2. Choose Canvas | Annotate, as shown in Figure 29.7. A small dialog box, containing a Done button, will appear in your screen. This button is clicked after your canvas is annotated.

3. Click the color in the image that you want to annotate. Drag the cursor to an area outside the color. When you release the mouse, the name of the color (assigned in the Color Set) will appear with a line pointing toward the annotated section. If Painter does not find an exact match, an approximation of the color will be found and an asterisk will appear beside the name, indicating that it is a replacement color.

4. Repeat Step 3 for each of the colors you want to annotate. After you apply the annotations, your screen will look similar to Figure 29.8.

5. After creating all annotations, click the Done button or press Enter (Windows) or Return (Mac).

Figure 29.7.
The Canvas | Annotate command is used to add or delete a document's annotations.

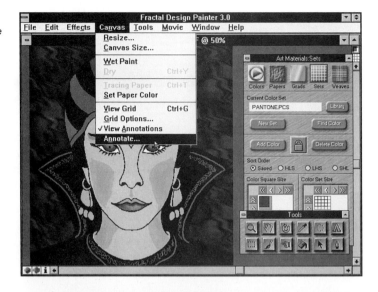

Figure 29.8.
Add as many annotations as are necessary to identify your color areas.

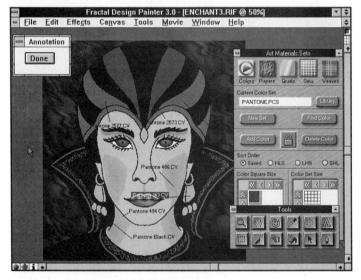

Deleting Annotations

If you've created an annotation that was placed inadvertently or decide later that you want to remove annotations from an area or floater, you can delete some or all of the annotations with the following procedure.

1. Choose Canvas | Annotate. The Annotate dialog box containing a Done button will appear.

2. Using the mouse or stylus, click the annotation tag that you want to delete.

3. Press Backspace (Windows) or Delete (Mac). The annotation will be removed from the image.

4. Continue deleting annotations as necessary. When completed, click the Done button in the Annotate dialog box.

Finding Colors

As mentioned, Annotate defines an approximation of a color with an asterisk beside it. This gives you an indication that the color that was approximated will be reproduced as closely as possible when printed with the color name beside the asterisk.

You also can do a manual search through the color set to find the closest match to a particular color; or, you can search for a color by name.

To search by color, proceed as follows:

1. Choose a color from your image, using the Dropper tool, as shown in Figure 29.9.

2. Open the color set that contains the colors that you want to compare to by clicking the Library button in the Art Materials | Sets Palette.

3. From the Sets Palette, click the Find Color button, as shown in Figure 29.10.

4. When the Find Color dialog box, shown in Figure 29.11, appears, choose to select the color closest to the current color. Then, click the Search button to search through the color set.

Figure 29.9.
With the Dropper tool,
click a color in your
image to select it.

Figure 29.10.
Click the Find Color
button in the Sets
palette to find the color
in the set that is
nearest to the currently
selected color.

Figure 29.11.
The Find Color dialog
box lets you search
through the color set by
name or by closest
match to the currently
selected primary color.

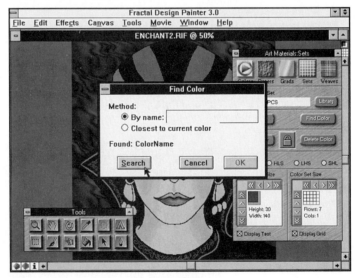

If the search is successful, the color name of the nearest color in the color set
will be returned and displayed above the Search button, as shown in Figure
29.12. The returned color will also be chosen as your current color and will be
displayed in the Colors Palette or in the proper color set. You can then replace
the color in your image with this color using normal fill or painting techniques.

Figure 29.12.
The name of the closest color in the color set will appear above the Search button.

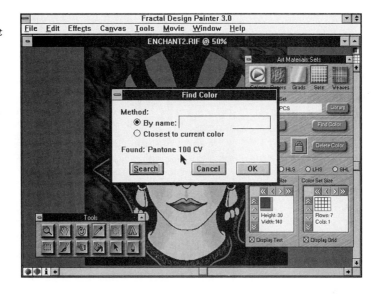

Adjusting Document Size

The Canvas | Resize command can be used to make changes in the size and resolution of your document. For example, the ENCHANT.RIF file was created at 75 dpi for display on a computer monitor. At this resolution, the document would be measured at 10.133-inches wide and 10.667-inches high, as shown in the upper portion of the Resize Image dialog box in Figure 29.13.

Figure 29.13.
At 75 dpi, the image would measure 10.133 inches by 10.667 inches.

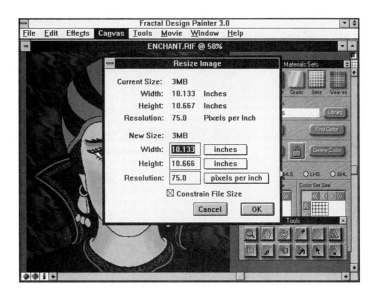

If this image were printed to a 300-dpi printer at four times the resolution of the original image, the resulting printout would measure 2.533 by 2.666 inches. You don't want this to happen, so you have to resize the image to agree with the resolution of the printer.

To increase the size of the document, first turn off the Constrain File Size checkbox, located in the Resize Image dialog box. This checkbox is on when you want to freeze the amount of space that the file occupies. Because you want to increase the file, you have to disable this feature. Then, the Resolution figure is increased to 300. These changes are shown in Figure 29.14. Note that these changes would increase the file size to 38 MB, as shown in the New Size area of the dialog box.

Figure 29.14.
The Constrain File Size
checkbox is unchecked,
and the resolution of
the image is increased
to 300 dpi.

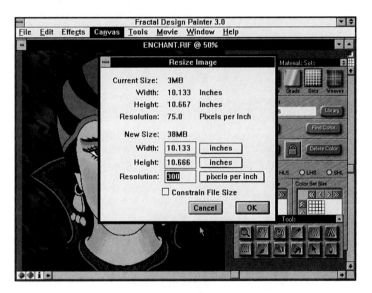

Now, decrease the overall size of the image, because the 10.133 inches by 10.667 inches will not fit within the printed page. To do this, enter the desired width or height in the appropriate New Size box. The other value will change automatically in proportion with the figure entered. In Figure 29.15, the Height figure was changed to 6 inches, and the Width figure was adjusted automatically to 5.7 inches. Note also that the resulting file size reduced to 12 MB.

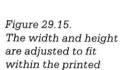

Figure 29.15.
The width and height
are adjusted to fit
within the printed
page.

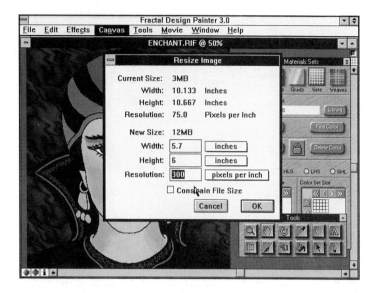

Setting Up Your Printer

In Painter 3 for Windows, the Print Setup and PostScript Setup commands are used to set up printing options for your specific printer. In Painter 3 for Mac, the Page Setup Command accomplishes the same basic functions. The differences between the two are as follows:

Print Setup (Windows Version)

The File | Print Setup command brings up the Print Setup dialog box, shown in Figure 29.16. This dialog box enables you to choose from the printers installed on your computer or network. You also can select print orientation of the paper (portrait or landscape), paper size, and paper source. Clicking the Options button located at the right side of the dialog box opens up a dialog box that contains options specific to the chosen printer.

PostScript Setup (Windows Version)

The File | PostScript Setup command brings up the PostScript Settings dialog box, shown in Figure 29.17. This dialog box provides additional settings that are applicable to PostScript printers only. Here, settings such as dot gain, monitor gamma, spot type, and halftone screen frequency and angle are entered. Many of the settings are recommended in your printer manual, or you can contact your printing service bureau.

Figure 29.16.
The Print Setup
command identifies the
target printer, the
paper size, orientation,
and other options
specific to the printer
chosen.

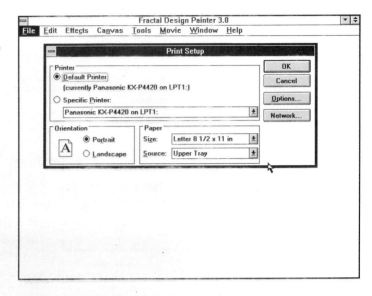

Figure 29.17.
The PostScript Setup
command opens the
PostScript Settings
dialog box, where dot
and halftone screen
settings can be
entered.

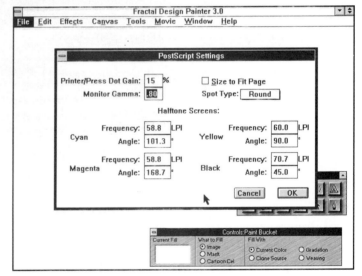

Page Setup (Mac Version)

In Painter 3 for Mac, the Page Setup command enables you to select paper type, paper orientation, and printer settings. The PostScript settings, mentioned previously under the File | PostScript Setup command for Windows, also apply to this command in the Mac.

Print (Ctrl-P)

When you are ready to print your file, the File | Print command is chosen. The Print dialog box, shown in Figure 29.18, appears, and more options can be selected. Usually, the only setting that is changed here is the number of copies you want to print. There are a few other items that are applicable to PostScript printing. Unless stated otherwise, the following items pertain to both Windows and Mac.

Figure 29.18.
The Print dialog box
appears when the
File | Print command
is chosen.

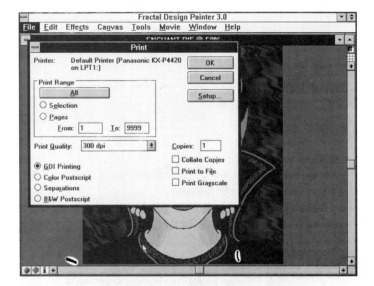

- **GDI Printing (Windows version)** is usually selected when printing to a printer that uses Windows Graphic Device Interface. Printers of this nature are laser and desk-jet printers without PostScript capability.

- **Color Quickdraw (Mac version)** is selected when printing to a printer that uses Mac Quickdraw interface. Printers of this nature are also laser and ink-jet printers without PostScript capability.

- **Color PostScript** can be selected if you are printing to such printers as the Tektronix color thermal printer or QMS ColorScript printer. Other options for PostScript printers can be found in the PostScript Setup dialog box, mentioned previously.

- **Separations** can be selected if you are printing to a PostScript printer. A separate plate will be printed for each of four colors (cyan, magenta, yellow, and black) and will also include registration marks, a color bar, and the color name printed on the sheet.

- **Black and White Postscript** should be selected if you are printing to a black-and-white PostScript laser printer.
- **Black and White (Mac version)** can be selected if you are printing to black-and-white laser printers.
- The **Print Grayscale** box (Windows version) should be checked if you want to print a grayscale copy of your color image.

Summary

This chapter showed ways to prepare your Painter documents for printing, as well as getting the images out to hardcopy. With this final chapter, you now know Painter from beginning to end! I had a lot of fun sharing ideas with you! Now that my job is over, I'm going back to paint some more; it's your turn to get to work!

Enjoy many, many happy hours of painting and animating with Painter!

Index

Index

Did You Know...

Add to Your Sams Library Today with the Best Books for Programming, Operating Systems, and New Technologies

The easiest way to order is to pick up the phone and call

1-800-428-5331

between 9:00 a.m. and 5:00 p.m. EST.

For faster service please have your credit card available.

ISBN	Quantity	Description of Item	Unit Cost	Total Cost
0-672-30517-8		CorelDraw! 5 Unleashed (Book/CD)	$49.99	
0-672-30570-4		PC Graphics Unleashed (Book/CD)	$49.99	
0-672-30516-x		Corel Photo-Paint Unleashed (Book/CD)	$45.00	
0-672-30612-3		The Magic of Computer Graphics (Book/CD)	$45.00	
0-672-30492-9		Cyberlife! (Book/CD)	$39.99	
0-672-30320-5		Morphing Magic (Book/Disk)	$29.95	
0-672-30524-0		Absolute Beginner's Guide to Multimedia (Book/CD-ROMs)	$29.99	
0-672-30413-9		Multimedia Madness, Deluxe Edition! (Book/Disk/CD-ROMs)	$55.00	
0-672-30638-7		Super CD-ROM Madness (Book/CD-ROMs)	$39.99	
0-672-30590-9		The Magic of Interactive Entertainment, 2nd Edition (Book/CD-ROMs)	$44.95	
❏ 3 ½" Disk		Shipping and Handling: See information below.		
❏ 5 ¼" Disk		TOTAL		

Shipping and Handling: $4.00 for the first book, and $1.75 for each additional book. Floppy disk: add $1.75 for shipping and handling. If you need to have it NOW, we can ship product to you in 24 hours for an additional charge of approximately $18.00, and you will receive your item overnight or in two days. Overseas shipping and handling adds $2.00 per book and $8.00 for up to three disks. Prices subject to change. Call for availability and pricing information on latest editions.

201 W. 103rd Street, Indianapolis, Indiana 46290

1-800-428-5331 — Orders   1-800-835-3202 — FAX   1-800-858-7674 — Customer Service

Book ISBN 0-672-30707-3

PLUG YOURSELF INTO...

THE MACMILLAN INFORMATION SUPERLIBRARY™

Free information and vast computer resources from the world's leading computer book publisher—online!

FIND THE BOOKS THAT ARE RIGHT FOR YOU!

A complete online catalog, plus sample chapters and tables of contents give you an in-depth look at *all* of our books, including hard-to-find titles. It's the best way to find the books you need!

● STAY INFORMED with the latest computer industry news through our online newsletter, press releases, and customized Information SuperLibrary Reports.

● GET FAST ANSWERS to your questions about MCP books and software.

● VISIT our online bookstore for the latest information and editions!

● COMMUNICATE with our expert authors through e-mail and conferences.

● DOWNLOAD SOFTWARE from the immense MCP library:
  - Source code and files from MCP books
  - The best shareware, freeware, and demos

● DISCOVER HOT SPOTS on other parts of the Internet.

● WIN BOOKS in ongoing contests and giveaways!

TO PLUG INTO MCP: →

GOPHER: gopher.mcp.com
FTP: ftp.mcp.com

WORLD WIDE WEB: **http://www.mcp.com**

Home Page What's New Bookstore Reference Desk Software Library Macmillan Overview Talk to Us

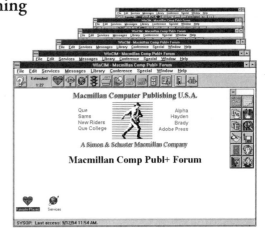

What's on the CD

The companion CD contains the author's online reference to Fractal Design Painter 3.1, all images discussed in the book, demos of commercial applications, and much more!

PC Installation Instructions:

1. Insert the CD-ROM into your CD-ROM drive.
2. From File Manager or Program Manager, choose Run from the File menu.
3. Type <*drive*>INSTALL and press Enter, where <*drive*> corresponds to the drive letter of your CD-ROM. For example, if your CD-ROM is drive D:, type D:INSTALL and press enter.
4. Follow the on-screen instructions in the installation program. Files will be installed to a directory named \FDPUNL, unless you choose a different directory during installation.

INSTALL creates a Windows Program Manager group called "FDP 3.1 Unleashed." This group contains icons for exploring the CD-ROM.

Macintosh Installation Instructions:

1. Insert the CD-ROM disc into your CD-ROM drive.
2. When an icon for the CD appears on your desktop, open the disc by double-clicking its icon.
3. Double-click the icon named Guide to the CD-ROM, and follow the directions.